THE
INTERNET
DIRECTORY

THE
INTERNET
DIRECTORY

ERIC BRAUN

Fawcett Columbine • New York

A Fawcett Columbine Book
Published by Ballantine Books

Copyright © 1994 by Eric Braun

All rights reserved under International and Pan-American Copyright Conventions. Published in the United States of America by Ballantine Books, a division of Random House, Inc., New York, and simultaneously in Canada by Random House of Canada Limited, Toronto.

Library of Congress Catalog Card Number: 93-90457

ISBN: 0-449-90898-4

Cover design by David Stevenson
Text design by Alexander J. Klapwald

Manufactured in the United States of America

First Edition: January 1994

10 9 8 7 6 5 4 3 2 1

This book is dedicated to
Citizenship
because every freedom
has responsibilities attached,
without which it would be
meaningless.

TABLE OF CONTENTS

ACKNOWLEDGMENTS

This book would not exist were it not for Owen Lock. Not only was it his idea, but he edited it, contributed greatly to its contents, and cajoled me enough so that it actually became a reality. The other person without whom this book wouldn't exist is Ellen Key Harris, about whom I can't say anything that wouldn't sound incredibly sappy so I'll just say "thanks for doing the dishes."

Many thanks to Alex Klapwald for cheerfully designing a beautiful book, and to Mark Leger, Eric Rochow, Walter Pienciak, and Steven Bookman for all their hard work processing mountains of raw data.

There are also many people from the Internet community to whom I am indebted for helping me in my information gathering, and for allowing me to use information they collected. Thanks to Stephanie da Silva, Phil Eschallier, Michael Gleason, Scott Hoppe, Peter Kaminski, Lawrence Landweber, David Lawrence, Ann Okerson, Peter Scott, Michael Strangelove, and Scott Yanoff.

I am also greatly indebted to Alexis Rosen and Panix (my Internet access provider), first, for running an excellent service, and second, for understanding when my disk quota was often a little bit over...

And finally, I must thank Adam King for not complaining while I wasn't working on Snap Mail.

INTRODUCTION

Welcome to *The Internet Directory*, version 1.0, the most complete hardcopy guide to the resources from around the world that are available via the Internet.

HOW TO BECOME A NET CITIZEN

First, you need to learn what the Internet is—what services it provides and what tools you need to access those services. "An Internet Refresher" provides a brief overview for those who have a nodding acquaintance with the information services that the Internet provides. If terms like *telnet*, *FTP*, and *gopher* are new to you, then you need a how-to guide like Ed Krol's *The Whole Internet Guide & Catalog*, Tracy LaQuey's *The Internet Companion*, or Mark Gibbs's and Richard Smith's *Navigating the Internet* (see the bibliography at the end of this volume).

    Second, you need to learn the conventions of proper behavior on the Internet. This is called netiquette, and observing it is extremely important if you want to be successful and productive in your use of the Internet. Unless you have been using the Internet for a long time, make sure you read "Netiquette And Internet Culture," an introduction to proper behavior on the Internet and to issues of net citizenship. There are no Internet police as yet, and none are needed because the proper observation of netiquette by most Internet visitors makes the Internet a nice "small town" place to be, despite the fact that millions of people "live" in it. Let's keep it this way.

    Third, you need to learn where to go! This book is full of lists that direct you to the thousands of places to go and things to see on the Internet. Use the table of contents to browse the lists by type (e.g., Usenet newsgroups; mail lists; FTP archives, etc.); use the index to find things by topic. If you're not yet on the Internet, see Chapter 12 to find a local access provider.

A FEW WORDS ABOUT CHANGE

By its nature the Internet is ephemeral. It changes and grows by the second. From the time I stop adding information to the manuscript of *The Internet Directory* to the earliest opportunity for the finished book to reach your hands (approximately one month), thousands of new people will have joined the Internet, new gopher servers will have come online, mailing lists will have changed addresses, and so on. This book is clearly not the final word—you have to get online for that. But even when you *are* online, remember that even the most up-to-date resources contain errors. Much of the information for this book was derived from the most up-to-date lists of resources available and then verified for accuracy. A full 10 percent of the resources listed online don't appear in this directory because I couldn't access them as they were listed. And of the remaining resources, more than a third had nontrivial mistakes! Because of the phenomenal growth of the Internet, it was also impossible for me to include every resource I know about. Verifications and new information arrive in my mailbox all the time, so I had to set a cutoff date after which any new information would appear in the next edition. This book most certainly has some errors in it and just as certainly doesn't list a few important resources. If you find a mistake or if you are the owner of a resource that you would like to see listed, drop me a note. The e-mail address for updates and corrections is `anansi@jungle.com`.

HOW THIS BOOK IS ORGANIZED

Each of the chapters in the directory covers a particular information service or resource type. Entries in each chapter are in alphabetical order. If you are looking for information on a particular topic, you should use the index. Each chapter begins with a short explanation of the information service or resource it covers, followed by these sections:

Entry Format: A description of how the entries in the chapter are formatted

Where to Find It: A description of how I got the information in the chapter

Comments: Any extra important facts about the information in the chapter

Netiquette: Important pointers on how the resources listed in the chapter should be used

Entries: The entries themselves

HOW THIS BOOK WAS COMPILED

The guiding philosophy behind the directory is to list as much information of absolutely any sort as can be located, so long as I can verify, with the resource owner or maintainer, the address, accessibility, and procedures for using it. The "Where to Find It" section at the beginning of each chapter explains how I compiled the information for that chapter. It should give you a good idea of where to find the latest information as well as how to go about doing research on the Internet.

AN INTERNET REFRESHER

WHAT IS THE INTERNET?

This is a much-discussed question to which there is no one answer. Nor is there a single answer to the more sticky question of what it means to be on the Internet. This question is typically answered in terms of what kind of data transport protocol a computer uses to communicate with other computers, the one called "TCP/IP" being what definitely puts you on the Internet. But I offer a different definition of the Internet:

The Internet is the collection of information services available on the interconnected computer networks that span the globe.

From my point of view, the more access you have to the different services the Internet provides, the more on the Internet you are. I emphasize the services, not the data transport protocol used. True, many of the services to which this book is a directory are currently available only to those computers that communicate via the TCP/IP data transport protocol. But others, like e-mail, are available on practically all networks. Thus I would say that any computer that can take advantage of inter-network e-mail is at least partially on the Internet.

Most of this book is a directory to what is accessible via the the Internet's information services: data, computers, interest groups, and more. These services can be grouped into three categories: communication services, connection services, and data-access services. We'll look at each separately.

COMMUNICATION SERVICES

Communication services allow people to send messages to each other. The Internet provides two main communication services: electronic mail (e-mail) and newsgroups (the so-called Usenet). E-mail is much like regular mail, but with a few added conveniences and much faster delivery. In fact, Internet users have come to refer to the regular postal service as "snail mail" (commonly abbreviated s-mail). Newsgroups, on the other hand, don't have much to do with news as we know it—a one-way communication service from reporter to audience. On the Internet, newsgroups are a true two-way, interactive communication service, perhaps best thought of as discussion groups in which anybody can "publish" articles relevant to the interests of the particular newsgroup.

E-mail

A sample e-mail message:

```
From: anansi@jungle.com (Anansi T. Spider)          ← The header starts here
To: brother.tiger@forest.com
```

```
Subject: Where can I find fly databases?
Date: Wed, 15 Sep 93 11:29:59 PDT
Reply-To: anansi@jungle.com
Content-Type: TEXT/PLAIN; charset=US-ASCII
X-Mailer: uAccess - Macintosh Release: 1.6v2
```
                                              ← the body starts here
```
Brother Tiger,
>                                  ← ">" indicates a quote from earlier e-mail
> I've got some info but I'm swamped.
> Can I get it to you later this month?
>
That's fine ... I'm in no major hurry at the moment.
cheers ... -Anansi

Anansi T. Spider     Trickster Supreme    anansi@jungle.com  ← signature
```

The header: The e-mail header contains `From:` and `To:` addresses and the subject and date of the message as well as other, sometimes cryptic information. This information is in a standardized format because it needs to be interpreted by the software responsible for routing the e-mail to its destination. You can read more about these standards in the Request For Comment (RFC) documents 822, 1049, and 1341 (see Chapter 15).

The body: The body of a piece of e-mail is usually just the message typed in by the sender. Sometimes the body will contain a few other things. For example, if the e-mail has been forwarded or returned, the beginning of the body will be the header of the forwarded or returned piece of mail. Also, the body will sometimes contain an attachment. With the advent of MIME, the Multipurpose Internet Mail Extensions standard (see RFC 1341), the body of an e-mail message can even contain encoded pictures and audio.

People often append a "signature" to the body of their e-mail. This makes it easy for the recipient to find information on the sender, such as a return e-mail address. A signature can be very useful because the `From:` address in the header may be garbled by some mail-forwarding software. This is especially true for people who send e-mail to the Internet via some other connected network or UUCP.

E-mail Addressing

Addressing on the Internet can get quite complicated if you delve into its depths, and there are whole books devoted to the topic. But basically, what you need to know is that an Internet e-mail address is of the form *user@host*, where *user* is the login name of the person you are sending mail to, and *host* is either the domain name or IP number (more about these below) of the computer where that person has an account. Addressing e-mail to people on non-TCP/IP networks is often just the same as addressing e-mail to someone directly on the Internet because "alias" domain names have been set up. In such cases your e-mail sending software may be able to translate the e-mail address for you. Sometimes, however, this does not work. See

Chapter 13 for more details on sending e-mail to people on other networks.

IP Numbers and Domain Names

Any computer directly on the TCP/IP portion of the Internet has a numerical address assigned to it. You can always use that number to reference the host. For example, if you wanted to send e-mail to `tiger@forest.com` and `forest.com` had the IP number `[198.7.1.7]`, you could send your e-mail to `tiger@[198.7.1.7]`. Notice that in an e-mail address the IP number must be put in brackets.

Using a domain name is a much more convenient way of referring to a host, since words are more easily remembered than numbers. Domain names are translated to IP addresses by special computers called domain-name servers. The software of the originating computer substitutes the IP address to send its e-mail. (For more details on this process, see RFCs 1034 & 1035.)

Another thing to keep in mind about domain names is that, as previously noted, many hosts that are on other networks and are never directly connected to the TCP/IP portion of the Internet are still assigned domain names. Mail sent to those domains gets translated into an address that the gateway computer to the given network can understand. For example, if Mr. Anansi T. Spider had an account on the Bitnet node JUNGL, you could send him e-mail to `anansi@jungl.bitnet`. This address gets translated by the name servers to `anansi%jungl.bitnet@cunyvm.cuny.edu`. The new domain name `cunyvm.cuny.edu` is a gateway computer that is on both the Internet and Bitnet and will forward the mail to the proper Bitnet node and user by examining the user portion of the e-mail address, `anansi%jungl.bitnet`.

It is often the case, especially for larger institutions, that you don't need to specify the full domain name of a host when addressing e-mail. This is because people often have accounts on many hosts, and hosts appear and disappear as people and computers move around. For example, you could send mail for the computer science professor Anansi Spider at Yale University to the address `anansi@cs.yale.edu`. Even though there is no single host `cs.yale.edu` the name server will translate the `cs.yale.edu` domain name to the host that Yale's Computer Science Department has registered as being responsible for forwarding mail to the proper destination.

Bounced Mail

A piece of e-mail will undoubtedly be returned to you at some point or another. Examining a piece of returned mail to figure out what happened can be tricky. Below are some examples of session transcripts for e-mail that has been returned for some of the more common reasons, as well as explanations of what happened and what you can do about it, if anything.

Host Unknown

```
--- Transcript of session follows ---
554 pipkins@vicstoy.oua.org... 550 Host unknown (Authoritative
```

```
answer from name server)
```

The domain name `vicstoy.oua.org` does not exist.

User Unknown

```
   --- Transcript of session follows ---
While connected to gps1 [129.11.128.109] (ether):
>>> RCPT To:<TEX5HAD%cms1.ucs.leeds.ac.uk@leeds.ac.uk>
<<< 550 <TEX5HAD%cms1.ucs.leeds.ac.uk@leeds.ac.uk>... User unknown
550 <TEX5HAD@cms1.ucs.leeds.ac.uk>... User unknown
```

TEX5HAD is not a person who has an account on this system.

Connection Timed Out

```
   --- Transcript of session follows ---
421 csd-reserved2.Stanford.EDU (TCP)... Deferred: Connection timed
out during user open with csd-reserved2.Stanford.EDU
```

Though the host name is known, a connection could not be established with it after several retries. Usually the `Subject:` heading will tell you for how many days delivery was attempted.

Service Unavailable

```
   --- Transcript of session follows ---
Connected to mailhost:
>>> DATA
<<< 554 sendall: too many hops 27 (25 max): from , to (null)
554 <salim@mesis.esrin.esa.it>... Service unavailable
```

This error can occur for a number of reasons, and it will usually be explained in the transcript. In this particular case, the problem is that the mail was forwarded too many times. Each time it gets forwarded to a different computer, a "hop count" gets increased by one. If the hop count gets too big, mail will be sent back to you. This prevents mail from bouncing around the Internet forever trying to get to its destination. Another frequent reason for the `Service unavailable` message is that though the message was delivered to the proper address, it couldn't actually be added to the user's mailbox for one reason or another—for example, the user's disk quota had been exceeded.

In all cases you can try to send the mail again and see if it gets through. It's a good idea to wait a day or two for the problem to get cleared up.

Unknown Error

```
   --- Transcript of session follows ---
554 <aidsnews@aol.com>... unknown mailer error 1
```

This type of error usually occurs when the destination computer crashes or has a problem during transmission. Try sending the mail again.

Mailing Lists

Mailing lists are a very important extension of the communication services provided by e-mail. This directory lists thousands of interest groups that use mailing lists to carry out their discussions. A mailing list is just a group of e-mail addresses maintained either manually, by some person who takes on the responsibility of forwarding mail to all the people on the list, or automatically, by a computer program. Such a computer program is called a mail reflector. Mail reflectors usually have two addresses: the address to which all mail is sent that is to be distributed to everybody on the list, and the address to which changes to the mailing list are sent. Please see Chapter 1 for more information on specific mail reflectors and how to use them, and for crucial netiquette tips on using mailing lists.

Usenet Newsgroups

Usenet newsgroups are, after e-mail and mailing lists, the Internet's most widely used communication service. Theoretically, Usenet provides the same type of service as is provided by e-mail mailing lists—discussion groups. In practice, however, Usenet is a much more robust service because, unlike e-mail, it was specifically designed to provide discussion-group services. Just imagine what would happen if all newspaper reporters worked freelance and mailed you a copy of their stories every day instead of having them published in a newspaper. Pretty soon your mailbox would be impossibly full. Usenet is the Internet's mechanism for organizing the thousands of messages on hundreds of topics that are sent every day. Perhaps for the first time in history, freedom of the press is not contingent on owning a press. You can simply publish your ideas on Usenet.

Chapter 2 contains a recent listing of all the newsgroups that are distributed worldwide. Many of these newsgroups are not available to everyone, since it is up to the system administrator of each host computer to determine which newsgroups that computer will process. This is usually determined by how much extra processing power and disk space is available, since some of the "optional" groups take up large amounts of space. Also, you will probably find a number of local-area interest groups available on your system that are not published in the directory.

Other Communication Services

The Internet also provides some direct communication services that allow people to communicate in real time, as if over a telephone. The two main services of this type are Talk and Internet Relay Chat (IRC).

Talk

Talk is a two-person communication service. When you run Talk, you specify the Internet address of the person to whom you wish to speak. A message is sent to that person indicating your talk request. Once your request is acknowledged, you can "talk" simply by typing. The software splits your screen into two portions: in one you see what you type and in the other you see what the other person types. Talk is an interesting mode of communication in that you see each character as it is being typed. Because people generally type more slowly than they talk, multiple lines of conversation take place at the same time. Try it—it's a strange experience!

Internet Relay Chat

Internet Relay Chat (IRC) is the citizens band radio of the Internet. This communication service is different from Talk in the same way Usenet is different from e-mail: it is designed for group discussions. When you log on to an IRC server, you will be presented with a large number of channels on which people are chatting. A channel's name usually describes the general thrust of the conversation, or at least the language being used (remember that the Internet is a worldwide entity). When you join a channel, you immediately begin receiving messages sent by others on that channel. IRC differs from Talk in that you compose an entire line of text before sending it off.

CONNECTION SERVICES

The Internet's connection services provide access to its destinations, the millions of computers interconnected by it. Using a connection service, you can log on to practically any computer on the Internet and use it just as if you were sitting at a terminal right next to it (provided, of course, that you have an account and know the password to the computer!)

Telnet

Telnet is the most widely used connection service on the Internet. You can think of telnet simply as a "virtual" terminal. You provide telnet with the host name of the computer you want to connect to (see the section on e-mail addressing above), and it sets up a connection, sends to the computer the keystrokes you type, and displays on your screen the characters the computer sends back. That's all there is to it. Telnet is used most often along with a resource provided by some institution, such as the computerized card catalog of a library. On the Internet, online library catalogs are called OPACs (for Online Public Access Catalogs), and Chapter 3 is a directory to most of the OPACs in the world that are accessible via telnet.

DATA-ACCESS SERVICES

Data-access services are a bit more complicated and more varied than the communication services, simply because accessing data is a much less well-structured activity. Also, like most everything else on the Internet, databases and the tools to access them have been added continually to the Internet throughout its evolution.

The Client-Server Model

To understand the Internet's major data-access services, you need to understand what is known as the client-server model of software design. Client-server software was developed to solve the efficiency problems of providing network information services. It does this by separating a service's software into two parts: the user-interface software (the client) and the data-handling software (the server).

The problems of efficiently providing information services between computers connected by networks are clearly shown by examining what happens when you log into a library catalog using a connection service like telnet (see above). Every aspect of that service, from doing actual searches in the card catalog to displaying characters on your screen, is being controlled by the library's computer. Telnet is acting only as a dumb terminal. This is inefficient for two reasons: (1) the library's computer is wasting its processing time by sending to your computer commands that draw the screen and by processing each keystroke that you type; (2) sending these commands across a network adds unnecessary traffic. If telnet could be made smarter—that is, if it could take on some of the tasks, such as displaying entire menus or interpreting your keystrokes—then the library's computer could spend more of its time answering search requests (i.e., providing its service), and network traffic would be decreased. Such an enhanced telnet would become the *client* of a library-service *server*.

Client-server software is usually designed so that many clients can be connected to one server. Telnet itself is actually based on the client-server model, but only for the relatively simple connection service. The data-access services described below provide more extensive client-server interactions.

FTP and Archie

Perhaps the most frequently used data-access service on the Internet is the File Transfer Protocol (FTP), a network-wide client-server standard for sending files from one computer to another. Software that implements both the client and the server portions of FTP exists for virtually every kind of computer that can communicate using TCP/IP. FTP allows users to connect to any other computer (given, of course, that they have an account and know the password) and transfer files.

Many computers on the Internet have been set up as file archives with special "anonymous" accounts so that, by means of FTP, users who have no routine access to such computers can still make use of the huge number of interesting and useful files that they contain. FTP archives store a huge range of files, from computer programs that you can run on your home computer to text files containing all the recent decisions of the Supreme Court. Chapter 5 provides a directory of many of the anonymous-FTP archives that are available on the Internet.

Using FTP

When using an FTP client, you first establish a connection with a computer running an FTP server by specifying a valid account and password. When accessing an anonymous-FTP archive, you simply type `anonymous` at the computer's request for a user name, and type your e-mail address when prompted for a password. Once you are connected, you can issue various commands to list files or transfer them to or from the computer you have connected to. Since these commands are from the Unix command set, the novice Internet visitor should read the relevant section in the Internet manuals by Krol or LaQuey before using anonymous FTP. At a minimum, you should understand how to list files (`ls`), change directories (`cd`), set the data type to binary (`bin`, used, e.g., for "zipped" files), and retrieve files (`get`). For more information on FTP archives, see the introduction to Chapter 5.

Archie

Although FTP programs provide you with access to the data archives at anonymous-FTP sites, there remains the problem of finding the data you want in the mountains of files stored in those archives, and across the many archives that exist. Archie is a program that solves this problem by providing indexing of FTP archives. This is how it works: periodically, anonymous-FTP sites send information on the contents of their archives to a few computers on the Internet. These computers run the Archie-server software. If your host computer has Archie-client software, you can use it to send queries to the server software about files in the participating archives. The server software searches its database and sends back descriptions and locations of materials that match your query. For people who don't have Archie-client software on their host computers, there are a few computers on the Internet whose public Archie clients are accessible via telnet (see Chapter 4).

FTP by mail

For computers that don't have access to the FTP data service but do have e-mail, a special computer has been set up by DEC (Digital Equipment Corporation) to which you can send e-mail requesting a particular file on a particular computer. The DEC computer will make an FTP connection for you and then e-mail the file to you. (If the file is large, it may be sent to you in convenient segments—you are responsible for putting it back together.) For further information, send e-mail to `FTPmail@decwrl.dec.com`. The body of your mail should contain only the word `help`. Use this resource sparingly or it will disappear! Remember, it is only one computer for thousands of users across the entire Internet.

Gopher and Veronica

Gopher is a relatively new addition to the Internet, but the data available via this service is growing at an amazing rate. The idea behind gopher was to provide an organized, user-friendly way of getting access to information on the Internet. What makes gopher unique is the fact that it is menu driven. Gopher servers send clients a list of menu items to display to the user. These menu items can include things from data resources (e.g., text files or sounds) to the names of other menus to links to other gopher servers. This last item is the conceptual breakthrough provided by the gopher data service because it allows for a decentralized database system that looks well organized to the user. The whole conglomerate of all gopher menus is called "gopherspace," and it is indeed a kind of space that you will wander through as you look for information on the Internet.

Veronica

Veronica is to gopher as Archie is to FTP. It provides an indexing service for the many menus of gopherspace. As the number of gopher servers grows, finding the particular gopher server with the information you want becomes a big problem—though not impossible, since you could just "tunnel" around from gopher to gopher looking for it. However, a solution similar to Archie was created for gophers, and not surprisingly it was called Veronica. But Veronica is a bit more sophisticated than Archie, and is also directly available from within gopher. It works like this: Periodically, gopher servers send information on what is in their gopher databases to the Veronica database. The Veronica database has an entry for almost every word of every menu item in every gopher database. Thus it is extremely useful for performing broad searches. The problem is usually to make the searches specific enough to yield a reasonable number of matches.

The beauty of the gopher concept is that Veronica forms links to the actual menu items you want—not just displays their locations (as does Archie). The gopher-client software can thus build a custom menu of all of these items. You then scan the menu for entries that look particularly interesting, and, when you select one, your gopher client will reach out to the gopher server where that information is stored. One problem with this, however, is that sometimes the Veronica database is out of date and lists an entry that has been removed from its gopher server. When you attempt to access that little gem, you find out it is no longer there. But such is the nature of a changing universe.

WAIS

WAIS stands for Wide Area Information Server. It is a particular implementation of the Z39.50 protocol which provides yet another data-access service over the Internet. Unlike both FTP and gopher (which require the use of Archie and Veronica for doing searches), this protocol directly addresses the problem of searching for the information you want. It works like this: If you have data—let's say it's text files containing Supreme Court decisions—to which you want to provide access, you use special indexing software to create an index of the files. Then you set up a WAIS server to provide the access to this resource (see Chapter 7 for a list of WAIS resources). A user can then search for all the Supreme Court decisions that have anything to do with abortion by utilizing a WAIS client to query your resource. The client will return a "hit list" of all the files that match the query, and from that list the user can request the actual files.

WAIS clients and servers for many computer platforms are available free on various FTP archives (see Chapter 7).

WWW

WWW stands for World Wide Web. Though this data service is quite new, it is perhaps the most interesting of all the information services available since it conceptually encompasses all the others. Like gopher, it links servers transparently, yet the interface is not a menu of items to choose from, but a hypertext page of text or graphics with "live" cross-links that you can select. The links can be to anything: other hypertext pages, indexes of the information on a particular WWW server, text files, sounds, etc. The possibilities are staggering. Chapter 8 provides a list of public WWW clients that you can access via telnet. Check it out!

NETIQUETTE AND INTERNET CULTURE

All technology requires wisdom in its wielding. The Internet requires it doubly since it is a social technology, not an instrumental one. What follows are some of the dos & don'ts and ways of looking at the Internet that I have picked up over the years that I have been a part of it. They are the sorts of conventions that any social group might develop, so think of this section as an orientation to a different culture.

CITIZENSHIP VERSUS CONSUMERISM

Don't look at your relationship to the Internet as that of a consumer. Though this book is a directory to the resources on the Internet, it must not be viewed simply as a catalog that you can use for your shopping. A much better analogy is that of a phone book that can put you in touch with your fellow net citizens. Consider yourself a citizen of the Internet, and remember that most of the resources listed in this book were created by people in their spare time purely because they had some special interest. This, too, is how you should approach the Internet: What can you do to add richness and depth to this community?

The Internet is not a commercial service. Even though you may be paying an Internet access provider, what you are paying for is the use of the provider's hardware and software, just as you might pay Ford for a car that makes your access to the highways of the nation possible. And while everyone with a car has the right to use the highways, everyone also has responsibilities and a set of rules to follow. It's the same with the Internet. So when you are out there on the network's roads, think of yourself as a citizen.

CORRECT MANNERS WHEN USING RESOURCES (JUST PLAIN UNCOMMON SENSE)

Each of the Internet's information services has different requirements for the proper approach to take when using it, so I have put netiquette pointers at the beginning of each chapter to guide you through the particulars of good manners for each resource. But there are a few things that generally apply across the board.

The Categorical Imperative

Always remember that the person on the other end of the line is exactly that, a person. There is a great temptation to begin to think of people as resources, especially because, on the many newsgroups and mailing lists, it is so easy just to ask a question and get an answer from someone very knowledgeable. But don't treat people as means to your ends. A good way to make sure you don't do this is to give as much as you receive. There is probably a newsgroup or mailing list where you can provide answers to other people's questions. Subscribe.

The Tragedy of the Commons

Always keep in mind the ethical principle called the tragedy of the commons, which is illustrated by the following story: There was once a village with a beautiful commons. There came a time of drought, and all the villagers' local pasturelands dried up, so they had to take their cows far and wide to provide them with enough pasture. No cows were allowed to graze on the commons, but one day a villager who was generally a hard worker was just a bit too tired take his cow to the distant pastures. So he thought to himself that if he let his cow graze on the commons, well, it wouldn't hurt the commons at all—after all, it was just one cow. So "just this once" he let his cow graze on the commons, and then called it back in the evening. The only problem was that the next day all the other villagers had the same thought, and in a week or so the commons was ruined. If only the one villager had broken the rules "just this once" no harm would have been done. But all the villagers kept telling themselves "just this once" and their commons was destroyed.

Like our natural environment, the Internet is a delicately balanced system that can only take so much abuse before it shuts down. So remember that the computers you connect to are finite resources—they have only a certain amount of processing power and disk space. Many provide specific instructions on how and when you should connect to them. Follow those rules. Also, in many cases resources have been mirrored around the world. If a local version of the resource is busy, wait for it to be freed up. *Don't* use the one on a different continent unless you absolutely must, especially if what you want to do is download large files. The transcontinental links are limited resources. Sure, you could do it "just this once," but don't.

The Signal-to-Noise Ratio

It's very easy to blabber on the Internet. In e-mail this is fine—after all, e-mail is (or should be) private communication. But when it comes to newsgroups and mailing lists, the so-called signal-to-noise ratio becomes very important. Messages you send to these forums can get propagated to hundreds of thousands of people (and in a few years this may be millions). Thus, it is very important that all of what you say be meaningful. Add quality, not quantity, to any discussion. Don't be tempted by how easy it is to join into a conversation. Adding your two cents' worth is probably a bad idea—wait till it's at least a buck's worth!

Another source of noise in communication is excessively long signatures. Keep your signature to a minimum. A large cutesy signature is cute only the first time someone sees it. After that it gets annoying. And it takes up bandwidth.

The Flame

It is very easy to rant and rave on the Internet. This is called "flaming." People on the Internet say what sound like odd things, but before you fire off a response, try to remember that the Internet is by far the most diverse human environment you can take part in. People's "crazy" ideas are usually just ideas that are different from your own. So if you must respond to something you strongly disagree with, be civil. And remember that keeping an open mind is a crucial part of being a good net citizen.

One of the major sources of flaming on the Internet is misunderstood irony or sarcasm. In speech we rely on our tone of voice, facial expression, and body language to convey the message that we are being ironic. On the Internet, we often can't do this; we must write what we think explicitly or mark what we write as ironic. The convention for doing this is to add a "smiley" after the ironic part of a message. The smiley is sideways and it shows up as :-) or :) —a colon followed by a close parenthesis, with the hyphen optional. So, for example, in a recent piece of mail I wrote: `That sounds like a dodge if I ever heard one! :-)` I included the smiley to make sure that the tone of my message was not accusatory. Remember also that to many people on the Internet, English is a foreign language. Detecting irony is even more difficult for people writing and reading in a language not their own.

INTERNET HOAXES

There are a few Internet hoaxes of which you should be aware. One particularly nasty one, since it is very wasteful of bandwidth, is the chain letter. Some chain letters have seemingly good intentions, like e-mail to a terminally ill boy who wants to break the world record for get-well messages. Ignore them all! Chain letters on the Internet are just as illegal as they are on the regular postal system. Most commercial Internet access providers have rules to the effect that anybody caught participating in a chain letter will be kicked off the system. This is a good rule.

Some of the more devious hoaxes involve hackers who are trying to learn passwords to break into computer systems. It is not too difficult on the Internet to send e-mail that impersonates someone else. Occasionally e-mail is sent that purports to be from your system manager asking you for your password for some seemingly innocuous reason. Don't e-mail your password to anyone for any reason. If you have to give someone your password, do it over the phone, or in person.

So, after all that, welcome to the Internet. It's an exciting place to be.

THE
INTERNET
DIRECTORY

1. MAILING LISTS

Mailing lists have usually been divided into two classes, Internet and Bitnet, but since this distinction is becoming less and less important, I have merged the two into one large list. There are a few things you should be aware of regarding the differences between the two kinds of list, however. Bitnet mailing lists are almost all handled by a program called Listserv. For more information on how to use a Bitnet listserv, simply send e-mail with `help` in the body of the message to any Bitnet listserv, `listserv@bitnic.educom.com`, for example. Mailing lists on the Internet, however, are handled in a variety of ways. Many of them are processed by people who keep track of all the addresses of subscribers and forward all submissions manually. There are also a number of different programs that handle mailing lists as well—Majordomo, Unix listserv, listproc, and Mail-serv, to name a few. Each of these works slightly differently, but you can find out about all of them by sending them e-mail with the single word `help` in the body of the message. Please note that ± addresses listed below in the form "list-name-request@host.domain" are sometimes aliases for people and sometimes aliases for one of the programs listed above. If the list is being run by a computer, the entry will include exact directions on what to send in a subscription request. Otherwise there are no instructions; send a personal request, as it will be read by a person.

Entry Format:

Item
Number

1-n   **List Name:** Description of what the list is about and any special information (access limitations, topic restrictions, special etiquette , etc.). *Moderated*

       i `contact address` for more info (usually a person, though sometimes a machine)

       ± `e-mail address` for subscription requests

       Archive: indicates if list is archived and gives address and methods of access (FTP, gopher, etc.)

       Language: indicates if a language other than English is used on the list

       Gated: indicates if list is gatewayed with a newsgroup and if bi/unidirectionally ($\Leftrightarrow \Leftarrow \Rightarrow$).

       Other: anything else about the list, for example, if it is available as a digest

Where To Find It: There are a number of "lists of lists" that contain information on mailing lists. Many of the entries in this chapter were found in those lists, but the majority were found by querying listservs directly about the lists they carry. You can do this by sending the word `list global` to `listserv@bitnic.educom.edu` in the body of your message. Of course, this will only give you a list of Bitnet mailing lists. My main source of Internet mailing lists was the Publicly Available Mailing Lists (PAML) list that is posted to the Usenet newsgroups `news.newusers` and `news.groups`. Many thanks are due to Stephanie daSilva for maintaining this list and giving me permission to publish her descriptions.

There is also a mailing list (NEW-LIST) that serves as a clearinghouse for all new mailing lists that are created. Its archives are a good source of information on what is available (FTP `vml.nodak.edu`). Whatever the source, all entries in this chapter were verified and are published here by permission of the owner or moderator of the list. Please check Chapter 11 (Online Resource Lists) for more sources of information on mailing lists.

Netiquette: Many mailing lists are a completely public forum and are gated with newsgroups, so be sure to read the netiquette section in Chapter 2. Here is a list of things to keep in mind when submitting articles to a mailing list:

- Remember, the net is made up of *people*. Don't say anything you wouldn't in a face-to-face setting. If you disagree with someone, be civil, and when someone is rude and doesn't follow common netiquette (which does happen, unfortunately) *don't* respond in kind.
- Familiarize yourself with a mailing list before you submit e-mail to it. Each list has its own rules of order and limits as to what is appropriate to discuss. Follow these rules.
- Follow up via personal e-mail, not by submitting to the list—unless you are absolutely sure that the follow-up is relevant to all (or at least most) members of the list.
- Keep the signal-to-noise ratio low:
  - When quoting, only quote relevant portions, not the whole message, and especially not the header or signature of a message. You have an editor; use it!
  - Single-line submissions of the "Me, too" and "Yes" variety are usually inappropriate. You should be adding substance to a discussion, not body.
  - All administrative requests should go to the *i* or ± address. When you subscribe you will receive the submissions address. You should *never* post any subscription, unsubscribe or other administrative messages to that address. If you do so, everyone in the list will needlessly have to read your request and you will look like a fool.
- Remember that mailing lists are extremely varied. Some are purely for entertainment; others are places where real work gets done. What may be appropriate on one list won't be on another.

Comments: Some sites may have trouble accessing Bitnet addresses. Where possible I have given the equivalent Internet addresses for Bitnet hosts. In cases where they are not available, you should translate the addresses as described in Chapter 13.

Entries:

1-1 **9NOV89-L:** On the fall of the Berlin Wall.
    i `axel@avalanche.cs.tu-berlin.de` (Axel Mahler) or
        `gschwind@db0tui11.bitnet` (Bitnet: `GSCHWIND@DB0TUI11`) (Gerard
        Gschwind)
    ± `listserv@db0tui11.bitnet` (Bitnet: `LISTSERV@DB0TUI11`) [body =
        `SUBSCRIBE 9NOV89-L` first-name last-name]
    Archive: `listserv@db0tui11.bitnet`

1-2 **12step:** Discussions and questions on 12-step programs such as Alcoholics Anonymous,
    Overeaters Anonymous, Alanon, ACA, etc.
    i ± `suhre@trwrb.dsd.trw.com` (Maurice Suhre)

1-3 **30something:** About actors, episodes, plots, characters of the "thirtysomething" TV show.
    i ± `30something-request@virginia.edu`

1-4 **AARPUB-L:** AAR Electronic Publication list.
    i `kawazoe@jpnimrtu.bitnet` (Bitnet: `KAWAZOE@JPNIMRTU`) (Yoshiyuki Kawazoe)
    ± `listserv@jpnimrtu.bitnet` (Bitnet: `LISTSERV@JPNIMRTU`) [body =
        `SUBSCRIBE AARPUB-L` first-name last-name]
    Archive: `listserv@jpnimrtu.bitnet` (Bitnet: `LISTSERV@JPNIMRTU`) [body =
        `INDEX AARPUB-L`]

1-5 **AASCU-L:** For the members of the American Association of State Colleges and Universities.
    i `gerland@ubvms.cc.buffalo.edu` (Jim Gerland)
    ± `listserv@ubvm.cc.buffalo.edu` (Bitnet: `LISTSERV@UBVM`) [body =
        `SUBSCRIBE AASCU-L` first-name last-name]

1-6 **AATG:** For members of the American Association of Teachers of German.
    i `itae100@indycms.bitnet` (Bitnet: `ITAE100@INDYCMS`) (Harry Reichelt)
    ± `listserv@indycms.iupui.edu` (Bitnet: `LISTSERV@INDYCMS`) [body =
        `SUBSCRIBE AATG` first-name last-name]
    Archive: `listserv@indycms.iupui.edu`

1-7 **AAUA-L:** For members of the American Association of University Administrators.
    i `neuner@canisius.bitnet` (Bitnet: `NEUNER@CANISIUS`) (Jerry Neuner)
    ± `listserv@ubvm.cc.buffalo.edu` (Bitnet: `LISTSERV@UBVM`) [body =
        `SUBSCRIBE AAUA-L` first-name last-name]
    Archive: `listserv@ubvm.cc.buffalo.edu`
    Gated: ⇔ `bit.listserv.aaua-l`

1-8 **ABC:** About the ABC Programming Language.
    i ± `abc-list-request@cwi.nl` (Steven Pemberton)
    Archive: FTP `mcsun.eu.net` in `/programming/languages/abc/`; mail-serv
        `info-server@hp4nl.nluug.nl` [body = `two lines: request`
        `programming/languages/abc topic abc.intro`]

1-9 **ABE-L:** For members of the Brazilian Statistical Association.
    i `rklein@brlncc.bitnet` (Bitnet: `RKLEIN@BRLNCC`)
    ± `listserv@brlncc.bitnet` (Bitnet: `LISTSERV@BRLNCC`) [body = SUBSCRIBE

ABE-L first-name last-name]

1-10 **ABEP-L:** For discussion of matters of interest to Brazilian postgraduates, coordinated from the UK.

   i `msbaas@central1.lancaster.ac.uk` (Antonio Artur De Souza) or `dst4wrk@brufsc.bitnet` (Bitnet: `DST4WRK@BRUFSC`) (Vilton Wronsky Ricardo)

   ± `listserv@ibm.ufsc.br` (Bitnet: `LISTSERV@BRUFSC`) [body = `SUBSCRIBE ABEP-L` first-name last-name]

   Language: Portuguese

   Other: Subscription is limited. Requests will be sent to list owner for approval.

1-11 **ABILITY:** On the study and advancement of the academically, artistically, and athletically able.
Moderated

   i `atsjc@asuacad.bitnet` (Bitnet: `ATSJC@ASUACAD`) (Sanford J. Cohn)

   ± `listserv@asuvm.inre.asu.edu` (Bitnet: `LISTSERV@ASUACAD`) [body = `SUBSCRIBE ABILITY` first-name last-name]

   Other: Subscription is limited. Requests will be sent to list owner for approval.

1-12 **ABLE-L:** For discussion and submission to the Ability Journal.

   i `atsjc@asuacad.bitnet` (Bitnet: `ATSJC@ASUACAD`) (Sanford J. Cohn)

   ± `listserv@asuvm.inre.asu.edu` (Bitnet: `LISTSERV@ASUACAD`) [body = `SUBSCRIBE ABLE-L` first-name last-name]

   Archive: `listserv@asuvm.inre.asu.edu`

1-13 **ABSLST-L:** For members of the Association of Black Sociologists and other interested scholars.

   i `3zasib3@cmuvm.bitnet` (Bitnet: `3ZASIB3@CMUVM`) (Robert G. Newby)

   ± `listserv@cmuvm.csv.cmich.edu` (Bitnet: `LISTSERV@CMUVM`) [body = `SUBSCRIBE ABSLST-L` first-name last-name]

   Archive: Available to subscribers only.

   Other: Subscription is limited. Requests will be sent to list owner for approval.

1-14 **ACADEMIC:** On computational science in Brazil.

   i `roberto@brufmg.bitnet` (Bitnet: `ROBERTO@BRUFMG`) (Roberto Alves Nogueira)

   ± `listserv@vm1.lcc.ufmg.br` (Bitnet: `LISTSERV@BRUFMG`) [body = `SUBSCRIBE ACADEMIC` first-name last-name]

   Archive: Available to subscribers only.

   Language: Portuguese

1-15 **ACADV:** For the ACADV Network, on academic advising in higher education. *Moderated*

   i `00hlcaldwell@bsuvc.bsu.edu` (Harold L. Caldwell)

   ± `listserv@vm1.nodak.edu` (Bitnet: `LISTSERV@NDSUVM1`) [body = `SUBSCRIBE ACADV` first-name last-name]

   Archive: Available to subscribers only.

   Other: Subscription is limited. Requests will be sent to list owner for approval. Subscribers will be asked to indicate their employment in academic advising.

1-16   **ACC-L:** On products for amateur radio service manufactured by Advanced Computer Controls.

i ccoprfm@gitvm1.bitnet (Bitnet: CCOPRFM@GITVM1) (Monte Freeman)

± listserv@gitvm1.gatech.edu (Bitnet: LISTSERV@GITVM1) [body = SUBSCRIBE ACC-L first-name last-name]

Archive: listserv@gitvm1.gatech.edu

1-17   **ACCES-L:** For the organizers of engineering competitions held in Canada.

i cfes@jupiter.sun.csd.unb.ca (Canadian Federation of Engineering Students)

± listserv@unb.ca (Bitnet: LISTSERV@UNBVM1) [body = SUBSCRIBE ACCES-L first-name last-name]

1-18   **ACCESS-L:** For users of Microsoft Access database software.

i rimg@unb.ca (List Management)

± listserv@unb.ca (Bitnet: LISTSERV@UNBVM1) [body = SUBSCRIBE ACCESS-L first-name last-name]

Archive: listserv@unb.ca

1-19   **ACDGIS-L:** On Geographical Information Systems (GIS) and related technologies with focus on Middle Europe.

i wigeoarn@awiwuw11.bitnet (Bitnet: WIGEOARN@AWIWUW11) (Zoltan Daroczi)

± listserv@vm.akh-wien.ac.at (Bitnet: LISTSERV@AWIIMC12) [body = SUBSCRIBE ACDGIS-L first-name last-name]

Language: German

1-20   **ACES-L:** For members of the Atlantic Congress of Engineering Students (ACES)—topics relating to engineering students in the Atlantic region of Canada.

i cfes@jupiter.sun.csd.unb.ca (Canadian Federation of Engineering Students)

± listserv@unb.ca (Bitnet: LISTSERV@UNBVM1) [body = SUBSCRIBE ACES-L first-name last-name]

1-21   **ACM-L:** For members of the Association for Computer Machinery, a computer science organization that includes computer engineers, MIS, programmers.

i ross@ucf1vm.bitnet (Bitnet: ROSS@UCF1VM) (Brian Ross)

± listserv@kentvm.kent.edu (Bitnet: LISTSERV@KENTVM) [body = SUBSCRIBE ACM-L first-name last-name]

Archive: listserv@kentvm.kent.edu

1-22   **ACMR-L:** For members of the Association for Chinese Music Research.

i tedk@uhunix.uhcc.hawaii.edu (Bitnet: TEDK@UHUNIX)

± listserv@uhccvm.uhcc.hawaii.edu (Bitnet: LISTSERV@UHCCVM) [body = SUBSCRIBE ACMR-L first-name last-name]

Archive: Available to subscribers only.

1-23   **ACRA-L:** On resource sharing, telecommunications, and technology among libraries in south central New York.

i mraish@bingvmb.bitnet (Bitnet: MRAISH@BINGVMB) (Martin Raish)

± listserv@bingvmb.cc.binghamton.edu (Bitnet: LISTSERV@BINGVMB) [body = SUBSCRIBE ACRA-L first-name last-name]

Other: Subscription is limited. Requests will be sent to list owner for approval.

1-24 **ACTIV-L:** Information for activists involved in peace, empowerment, human rights, and justice.
Moderated

i `mathrich@mizzou1.missouri.edu`

± `listserv@mizzou1.missouri.edu` (Bitnet: `LISTSERV@MIZZOU1`) [body = SUBSCRIBE ACTIV-L first-name last-name]

Archive: `listserv@mizzou1.missouri.edu`

1-25 **ACTNOW-L:** On college and organizational activism and related topics.

i `el406006@brownvm.bitnet` (Bitnet: `EL406006@BROWNVM`) (David B. O'Donnell)

± `listserv@brownvm.brown.edu` (Bitnet: `LISTSERV@BROWNVM`) [body = SUBSCRIBE ACTNOW-L first-name last-name]

Archive: Available to subscribers only.

1-26 **ACTOR-L:** For users of Actor, an object oriented programming language for MS Windows. Mostly about Actor, but also object oriented program design, implementation, maintenance, and differences between versions.

i `vrdp3plu@hmar15.bitnet` (Bitnet: `VRDP3PLU@HMARL5`)

± `listserv@hearn.nic.surfnet.nl` (Bitnet: `LISTSERV@HEARN`) [body = SUBSCRIBE ACTOR-L first-name last-name]

1-27 **ACUA-L:** On internal auditing within higher education, including federal regulations, job openings in internal audit, "how to's." *Moderated*

i `intaudir@uvmadmin.bitnet` (Bitnet: `INTAUDIR@UVMADMIN`) (Chuck Jefferis)

± `listserv@uvmvm.uvm.edu` (Bitnet: `LISTSERV@UVMVM`) [body = SUBSCRIBE ACUA-L first-name last-name]

Archive: `listserv@uvmvm.uvm.edu`

Other: Subscription is limited. Requests will be sent to list owner for approval.

1-28 **ACUHOI-L:** For college and university housing officers. *Moderated*

i `acuho@sru.bitnet` (Bitnet: `ACUHO@SRU`) (Paula Olivero)

± `listserv@psuvm.psu.edu` (Bitnet: `LISTSERV@PSUVM`) [body = SUBSCRIBE ACUHOI-L first-name last-name]

1-29 **ADAPT-L:** On library adaptive technology.

i `clewis@american.edu` (Chris Lewis)

± `listserv@american.edu` (Bitnet: `LISTSERV@AUVM`) [body = SUBSCRIBE ADAPT-L first-name last-name]

Archive: `listserv@american.edu`

1-30 **ADDICT-L:** For scholarly discussion of addiction-related topics other than alcohol or drug addiction, including co-addiction, sexual addiction, recovery.

i `ddelmoni@kentvm.bitnet` (Bitnet: `DDELMONI@KENTVM`)

± `listserv@kentvm.kent.edu` (Bitnet: `LISTSERV@KENTVM`) [body = SUBSCRIBE ADDICT-L first-name last-name]

Archive: `listserv@kentvm.kent.edu`

1-31 **ADLTED-L:** For communication among Canadian adult educators.

    i `l_davie@utoroise.bitnet` (Bitnet: `L_DAVIE@UTOROISE`) (Dr. Lynn Davie) or `lihein@uregina1.bitnet` (Bitnet: `LIHEIN@UREGINA1`) (Dr. Larry Hein)

    ± `listserv@max.cc.uregina.ca` (Bitnet: `LISTSERV@UREGINA1`) [body = SUBSCRIBE ADLTED-L first-name last-name]

    Archive: `listserv@max.cc.uregina.ca`

    Other: Subscription is limited. Requests will be sent to list owner for approval.

1-32 **ADND-L:** For players of the Advanced Dungeons and Dragons Role-Playing Game.

    i `c014bds@utarlvm1.bitnet` (Bitnet: `C014BDS@UTARLVM1`) (Brad Samek)

    ± `listserv@pucc.princeton.edu` (Bitnet: `LISTSERV@PUCC`) [body = SUBSCRIBE ADND-L first-name last-name] or `listserv@utarlvm1.uta.edu` (Bitnet: `LISTSERV@UTARLVM1`) [body = SUBSCRIBE ADND-L first-name last-name]

    Archive: `listserv@utarlvm1.uta.edu`

1-33 **adolph-a-carrot:** Severed Heads/Ralph Records.

    i ± `adolph-a-carrot-request@andrew.cmu.edu`

1-34 **adoption:** About anything and everything connected with adoption. Please join the list and listen in for a while before submitting.

    i ± `adoption-request@think.com`

1-35 **ADS-L:** On the American Dialect Society.

    i `maynor@ra.msstate.edu` (Natalie Maynor)

    ± `listserv@uga.cc.uga.edu` (Bitnet: `LISTSERV@UGA`) [body = SUBSCRIBE ADS-L first-name last-name]

1-36 **ADVANC-L:** For users of GEAC Advance, a library computer system.

    i `alileste@idbsu.bitnet` (Bitnet: `ALILESTE@IDBSU`) (Dan Lester)

    ± `listserv@idbsu.idbsu.edu` (Bitnet: `LISTSERV@IDBSU`) [body = SUBSCRIBE ADVANC-L first-name last-name]

    Archive: `listserv@idbsu.idbsu.edu`

1-37 **ADVISE-L:** For advisors, consultants, and other User Services staff at the various institutions on the net to exchange ideas and information.

    i `harold@uga.bitnet` (Bitnet: `HAROLD@UGA`) (Harold Pritchett) or `serveman@ebcesca1.bitnet` (Bitnet: `SERVEMAN@EBCESCA1`) (Christina Blanxer) or `info@ndsuvm1.bitnet` (Bitnet: `INFO@NDSUVM1`) (Marty Hoag) or `gerland@ubvms.cc.buffalo.edu` (Jim Gerland)

    ± `listserv@uga.cc.uga.edu` (Bitnet: `LISTSERV@UGA`) [body = SUBSCRIBE ADVISE-L first-name last-name] or `listserv@ebcesca1.bitnet` (Bitnet: `LISTSERV@EBCESCA1`) [body = SUBSCRIBE ADVISE-L first-name last-name] or `listserv@ubvm.cc.buffalo.edu` (Bitnet: `LISTSERV@UBVM`) [body = SUBSCRIBE ADVISE-L first-name last-name] or `listserv@vm1.nodak.edu` (Bitnet: `LISTSERV@NDSUVM1`) [body = SUBSCRIBE ADVISE-L first-name last-name]

    Archive: `listserv@uga.cc.uga.edu` or `listserv@ebcesca1.bitnet` or `listserv@vm1.nodak.edu`

1-38 **AEICNR:** For academic exchanges between professionals, scholars, and students in China and their counterparts in North America and the rest of the world. *Moderated*

i `ghuang@carson.u.washington.edu` (Guyang Matthew Huang)

± `listserv@uwavm.u.washington.edu` (Bitnet: `LISTSERV@UWAVM`) [body = SUBSCRIBE AEICNR first-name last-name]

1-39 **AERAMC-L:** American Education Research Association (AERA)—media, culture, curriculum.

i `jswartz@uafsysb.bitnet` (Bitnet: `JSWARTZ@UAFSYSB`) (Jim Swartz)

± `listserv@uafsysb.uark.edu` (Bitnet: `LISTSERV@UAFSYSB`) [body = SUBSCRIBE AERAMC-L first-name last-name]

Archive: `listserv@uafsysb.uark.edu`

1-40 **aeronautics:** One-way feed from `sci.aeronautics` newsgroup. On various technical aspects of aviation, such as aerodynamics, structures, and propulsion.

i `aeronautics-request@rascal.ics.utexas.edu`

± `majordomo@rascal.ics.utexas.edu` [body = `subscribe aeronautics`]

Gated: ⇐ `sci.aeronautics`

1-41 **AETS-L:** On improving the education of science teachers.

i `jpeters@uwf.bitnet` (Bitnet: `JPETERS@UWF`) (Joe Peters)

± `listserv@uwf.cc.uwf.edu` (Bitnet: `LISTSERV@UWF`) [body = SUBSCRIBE AETS-L first-name last-name]

Archive: Available to subscribers only.

Other: Subscription is limited. Requests will be sent to list owner for approval.

1-42 **AFAM-L:** On African-American research.

i `elspaula@mizzou1.bitnet` (Bitnet: `ELSPAULA@MIZZOU1`) (Paula Roper)

± `listserv@mizzou1.missouri.edu` (Bitnet: `LISTSERV@MIZZOU1`) [body = SUBSCRIBE AFAM-L first-name last-name]

Archive: `listserv@mizzou1.missouri.edu`

1-43 **AFRICANA:** On information technology and Africa.

i `pbwelb@wmvm1.bitnet` (Bitnet: `PBWELB@WMVM1`) (Paa-Bekoe Welbeck)

± `listserv@wmvm1.cc.wm.edu` (Bitnet: `LISTSERV@WMVM1`) [body = SUBSCRIBE AFRICANA first-name last-name]

Archive: `listserv@wmvm1.cc.wm.edu`

1-44 **AGEN-KS:** On ASAE knowledge systems.

i `ling@pisces.bitnet` (Bitnet: `LING@PISCES`)

± `listserv@rutvm1.rutgers.edu` (Bitnet: `LISTSERV@RUTVM1`) [body = SUBSCRIBE AGEN-KS first-name last-name]

Archive: `listserv@rutvm1.rutgers.edu`

1-45 **agenda-users:** About the Microwriter Agenda handheld computer.

i ± `agenda-users-request@newcastle.ac.uk`

1-46 **AGENG-L:** On agricultural engineering and intelligent control.

    i `jbeilag@gwdg.de` (Johannes grosse Beilage)

    ± `listserv@ibm.gwdg.de` (Bitnet: `LISTSERV@DGOGWDG1`) [body = SUBSCRIBE AGENG-L first-name last-name]

    Archive: `listserv@ibm.gwdg.de`

1-47 **AGRIS-L:** The Food and Agriculture Organization of the U.N. AGRIS/CARIS Coordinating Centre.

    i `gilsn2@irmfao01.bitnet` (Bitnet: `GILSN2@IRMFAO01`) (Lebowitz A. I.)

    ± `listserv@irmfao01.bitnet` (Bitnet: `LISTSERV@IRMFAO01`) [body = SUBSCRIBE AGRIS-L first-name last-name]

    Archive: `listserv@irmfao01.bitnet`

1-48 **AIB-CUR:** On libraries in Italy.

    i `pierre@iuavbc.unive.it` (Pierre Picotti)

    ± `listserv@icineca.cineca.it` (Bitnet: `LISTSERV@ICINECA`) [body = SUBSCRIBE AIB-CUR first-name last-name]

    Archive: Available to subscribers only.

1-49 **AICS-L:** On architectures for intelligent control systems.

    i `meystma@duvm.bitnet` (Bitnet: `MEYSTMA@DUVM`) (Michael Meystel)

    ± `listserv@ubvm.cc.buffalo.edu` (Bitnet: `LISTSERV@UBVM`) [body = SUBSCRIBE AICS-L first-name last-name]

    Other: Subscription is limited. Requests will be sent to list owner for approval.

1-50 **aids:** Two-way feed from the Usenet newsgroup `sci.med.aids`. Mostly about medical issues of AIDS with some discussion of political and social issues, as well as the postings to AIDS NEWS and Health InfoCom News mailing lists. NOTE: Unlike info-aids, postings to this list are NON-confidential. *Long Posts*

    i ± `listserv@vm.usc.edu` (Bitnet: `LISTSERV@USCVM`) [body = SUBSCRIBE AIDS first-name last-name] or `aids-request@cs.ucla.edu` (Daniel R. Greening)

1-51 **AIDSBKRV:** For reviews of materials on AIDS, safer sex, and sexually transmitted diseases. *Moderated*

    i `u50095@uicvm.bitnet` (Bitnet: `U50095@UICVM`) (H. Robert Malinowsky)

    ± `listserv@uicvm.bitnet` (Bitnet: `LISTSERV@UICVM`) [body = SUBSCRIBE AIDSBKRV first-name last-name]

    Archive: Available to subscribers only.

1-52 **AIKIDO-L:** On aikido, a Korean martial art.

    i `gms@psuvm.bitnet` (Bitnet: `GMS@PSUVM`) (Gerry Santoro)

    ± `listserv@psuvm.psu.edu` (Bitnet: `LISTSERV@PSUVM`) [body = SUBSCRIBE AIKIDO-L first-name last-name]

1-53 **AIR-L:** For institutional researchers/university planners. *Moderated*

    i `nelson_l@plu.bitnet` (Bitnet: `NELSON_L@PLU`) (Larry Nelson)

    ± `listserv@vtvm1.cc.vt.edu` (Bitnet: `LISTSERV@VTVM1`) [body = SUBSCRIBE AIR-L first-name last-name]

Other: Subscription is limited. Requests will be sent to list owner for approval.

1-54 **AIRCRAFT:** On fixed-wing and rotary-wing aircraft, modern, classic, and antique, including listings of airshows and similar events.

i fragakis@indiana.edu (Stelios Fragakis) or sheehan@indiana.edu (Mark C. Sheehan)

± listserv@grearn.bitnet (Bitnet: LISTSERV@GREARN) [body = SUBSCRIBE AIRCRAFT first-name last-name]

Archive: listserv@grearn.bitnet

1-55 **AIX-L:** On AIX, IBM's Unix operating system.

i gettes@pucc.princeton.edu (Michael Gettes, Coordinator)

± listserv@pucc.princeton.edu (Bitnet: LISTSERV@PUCC) [body = SUBSCRIBE AIX-L first-name last-name]

Archive: listserv@pucc.princeton.edu

Gated: ⇔ bit.listserv.aix-l

1-56 **AIXNEWS:** This list is a redistribution via mail of the comp.unix.aix newsgroup.
Moderated

i gettes@pucc.princeton.edu (Michael Gettes, Coordinator)

± listserv@pucc.princeton.edu (Bitnet: LISTSERV@PUCC) [body = SUBSCRIBE AIXNEWS first-name last-name]

Gated: ⇔ comp.unix.aix

1-57 **al-stewart:** On the musician Al Stewart.

i zen@sun.com (Dan Farmer)

± al-stewart-request@death.corp.sun.com

1-58 **ALACRO-L:** For those involved in the leadership of state and regional library associations.

i u59936@uicvm.bitnet (Bitnet: U59936@UICVM)

± listserv@uicvm.bitnet (Bitnet: LISTSERV@UICVM) [body = SUBSCRIBE ALACRO-L first-name last-name]

1-59 **ALF-L:** For exploring the working conditions of academic librarians.

i tkodar@yorkvm2.bitnet (Bitnet: TKODAR@YORKVM2) (Tiit Kodar)

± listserv@yorkvm1.bitnet (Bitnet: LISTSERV@YORKVM1) [body = SUBSCRIBE ALF-L first-name last-name]

Archive: Available to subscribers only.

1-60 **allman:** On the Allman Brothers, players of rock, blues, jazz, and southern rock.

i ± allman-request@world.std.com

1-61 **ALLMUSIC:** For discussions about all forms and aspects of music.

i eduardo@ufrj.bitnet (Bitnet: EDUARDO@UFRJ) (Eduardo)

± listserv@ufrj.bitnet (Bitnet: LISTSERV@UFRJ) [body = SUBSCRIBE ALLMUSIC first-name last-name]

1-62 **alpha-osf-managers:** Fast-turnaround troubleshooting tool for managers of DEC Alpha AXP systems running OSF/1.

i alpha-osf-managers-request@ornl.gov [body = help]

± `majordomo@ornl.gov` [body = `subscribe alpha-osf-managers`]

1-63 **ALTLEARN:** On alternative approaches to learning.

i `drz@sjuvm.bitnet` (Bitnet: `DRZ@SJUVM`)

± `listserv@stjohns.edu` (Bitnet: `LISTSERV@SJUVM`) [body = `SUBSCRIBE ALTLEARN` first-name last-name]

Archive: `listserv@stjohns.edu`

1-64 **ALUMNET:** Newsletter for alumni of Trinity University, including campus and alumni news, campus newspaper headlines, messages from the alumni, job searches, and continuing education. *Moderated*

i `rblysone@trinity.edu` (Dr. Robert Blysone) or `scurry@trinity.edu` (Stephen Curry)

± `listserv@vm1.tucc.trinity.edu` (Bitnet: `LISTSERV@TRINITY`) [body = `SUBSCRIBE ALUMNET` first-name last-name]

Archive: Available to subscribers only.

Other: Weekly digest. Subscription is limited. Requests will be sent to list owner for approval.

1-65 **AMALGAM:** On dental amalgam and mercury poisoning.

i `uj21@dkauni2.bitnet` (Bitnet: `UJ21@DKAUNI2`) (Siegfried Schmitt) or `ry52@dkauni2.bitnet` (Bitnet: `RY52@DKAUNI2`) (Thorsten Alteholz)

± `listserv@vm.gmd.de` (Bitnet: `LISTSERV@DEARN`) [body = `SUBSCRIBE AMALGAM` first-name last-name]

Archive: `listserv@vm.gmd.de`

1-66 **AMATH-IL:** On applied math in Israel. *Moderated*

i `schuss@math.tau.ac.il` (Zeev Schuss)

± `listserv@taunivm.tau.ac.il` (Bitnet: `LISTSERV@TAUNIVM`) [body = `SUBSCRIBE AMATH-IL` first-name last-name]

1-67 **Amazons International:** A newsletter digest dedicated to the image of the female hero in fiction and in fact, as it is expressed in art and literature, in the physiques and feats of female athletes and in sexual values and practices. The digest provides information, discussion, and a supportive environment for these values and issues. Gender role traditionalists not welcome.

i ± `amazons-request@math.uio.no` (Thomas Gramstad)

1-68 **amend2-discuss:** Discussion of the implications Colorado's Amendment 2 (see amend2-info).

i `amend2-mod@cs.colorado.edu`

± `majordomo@cs.colorado.edu` [body = `subscribe amend2-discuss`]

Gated: ⇒ `co.politics.amend2.discuss`

1-69 **amend2-info:** Information-related implications and issues surrounding the passing of Amendment 2 to the Colorado constitution, which revokes any existing gay/lesbian/bisexual civil rights legislation and prohibits the drafting of any new legislation.

i `amend2-mod@cs.colorado.edu`

± `majordomo@cs.colorado.edu` [body = `subscribe amend2-info`]

Gated: ⇒ `co.politics.amend2.info`

1-70   **AMERCATH:** On the history of American Catholicism.

i `jccannek@ukcc.bitnet` (Bitnet: JCCANNEK@UKCC) (Anne Kearney)

± `listserv@ukcc.uky.edu` (Bitnet: LISTSERV@UKCC) [body = SUBSCRIBE AMERCATH first-name last-name]

Other: Subscription is limited. Requests will be sent to list owner for approval.

1-71   **AMIGA-TR:** On Amiga computers.

i `sysadm1@trearn.bitnet` (Bitnet: SYSADM1@TREARN) or `oprj50@trearn.bitnet` (Bitnet: OPRJ50@TREARN) (Cem Turgay)

± `listserv@trearn.bitnet` (Bitnet: LISTSERV@TREARN) [body = SUBSCRIBE AMIGA-TR first-name last-name]

Archive: `listserv@trearn.bitnet`

Language: Turkish

1-72   **AMINT-L:** For worldwide links among scholars and practitioners of management.

i `dbi@psuvm.bitnet` (Bitnet: DBI@PSUVM) (Carolyn Dexter)

± `listserv@psuvm.psu.edu` (Bitnet: LISTSERV@PSUVM) [body = SUBSCRIBE AMINT-L first-name last-name]

1-73   **AMLIT-L:** On American literature.

i `engmo@mizzou1.bitnet` (Bitnet: ENGMO@MIZZOU1) (Michael O'Conner)

± `listserv@mizzou1.missouri.edu` (Bitnet: LISTSERV@MIZZOU1) [body = SUBSCRIBE AMLIT-L first-name last-name]

Archive: `listserv@mizzou1.missouri.edu`

1-74   **AMSSIS-L:** On American Management System's Student Information System (AMSSIS), a mainframe software for maintaining student information at colleges and universities.

i `allenf@saturn.uark.edu` (Allen Fields)

± `listserv@uafsysb.uark.edu` (Bitnet: LISTSERV@UAFSYSB) [body = SUBSCRIBE AMSSIS-L first-name last-name]

Archive: `listserv@uafsysb.uark.edu`

1-75   **AMWEST-H:** Scholarly discussion on American history west of the Mississippi from the Lewis and Clark expedition of 1804-05 to the last Indian/white confrontation at Wounded Knee in 1890. Points of view besides the "traditional" are encouraged, especially those that might illuminate Native American views on the events of the period.

± `listserv@umrvmb.umr.edu` (Bitnet: LISTSERV@UMRVMB) [body = SUBSCRIBE AMWEST-H first-name last-name]

Archive: `listserv@umrvmb.umr.edu`

1-76   **ANCANACH:** For the members of the Clan Henderson Society of US/Canada. *Moderated*

i `0004241803@mcimail.com`

± `listserv@uabdpo.dpo.uab.edu` (Bitnet: LISTSERV@UABDPO) [body = SUBSCRIBE ANCANACH first-name last-name]

Archive: `listserv@uabdpo.dpo.uab.edu`

Other: Subscription is limited. Requests will be sent to list owner for approval.

1-77 **ANCIEN-L:** On the history of the ancient Mediterranean.

    i `jacock01@ulkyvm.bitnet` (Bitnet: `JACOCK01@ULKYVM`) (Jim Cocks)

    ± `listserv@ulkyvm.louisville.edu` (Bitnet: `LISTSERV@ULKYVM`) [body = SUBSCRIBE ANCIEN-L first-name last-name]

    Archive: `listserv@ulkyvm.louisville.edu`

    Other: Daily digest

1-78 **ANGLICAN:** On matters pertaining to the Episcopal Church and members of the Anglican Communion.

    i `cms@dragon.com` (Cindy Smith) or `cts@dragon.com` (Charles Smith)

    ± `listserv@american.edu` (Bitnet: `LISTSERV@AUVM`) [body = SUBSCRIBE ANGLICAN first-name last-name]

    Archive: `listserv@american.edu`

1-79 **anneal:** Discussion of simulated annealing techniques and analysis, and related issues (stochastic optimization, Boltzmann machines, metricity of NP-complete move spaces, etc.). Membership restricted to those doing active research in simulated annealing or related areas.

    i ± `anneal-request@cs.ucla.edu` (Daniel R. Greening)

1-80 **ANSAX-L:** Scholarly discussions on topics in Old English (7th to 11th centuries).

    i `u47c2@wvnvm.bitnet` (Bitnet: `U47C2@WVNVM`) (Patrick W. Conner)

    ± `listserv@wvnvm.wvnet.edu` (Bitnet: `LISTSERV@WVNVM`) [body = SUBSCRIBE ANSAX-L first-name last-name]

    Other: Subscription is limited. Requests will be sent to list owner for approval.

1-81 **ANTHRO-L:** On general anthropology.

    i `antowner@ubvm.cc.buffalo.edu` (owners of Anthro-L)

    ± `listserv@ubvm.cc.buffalo.edu` (Bitnet: `LISTSERV@UBVM`) [body = SUBSCRIBE ANTHRO-L first-name last-name]

    Archive: `listserv@ubvm.cc.buffalo.edu`

    Gated: ⇔ `bit.listserv.anthro-l`

    Other: Daily digest

1-82 **Antiquaria:** For rare book dealers to exchange information and books and searches for specific books.

    i `joshuac2@aol.com` (Joshua Capy)

    ± `listserv@aol.com` [body = SUBSCRIBE ANTIQUARIA first-name last-name]

1-83 **ANU-NEWS:** For discussion of the uses, bugs, and fixes for ANU-NEWS software, a Usenet News package for DEC's OpenVMS operating system.

    i `sloane@kuhub.cc.ukans.edu` (Bob Sloane)

    ± `listserv@vm1.nodak.edu` (Bitnet: `LISTSERV@NDSUVM1`) [body = SUBSCRIBE ANU-NEWS first-name last-name]

    Archive: `listserv@vm1.nodak.edu`

    Gated: ⇔ `news.software.anu-news`

1-84 **APASD-L:** On research and funding opportunities for psychologists. *Moderated*

    i `apasddes@gwuvm.bitnet` (Bitnet: `APASDDES@GWUVM`) (Deborah Segal)

± `listserv@vtvml.cc.vt.edu` (Bitnet: `LISTSERV@VTVM1`) [body = `SUBSCRIBE APASD-L` first-name last-name]

1-85 **apc-open:** About SCO Advanced Product Centers. Membership for APC OPEN members or by invitation only.

i ± `apc-open-request@uunet.uu.net` or `fred@compu.com` (Fred Rump)

1-86 **APL-L:** For users of the APL programming language.

i `t4327@unbmvs1.bitnet` (Bitnet: `T4327@UNBMVS1`) (APL list management)

± `listserv@unb.ca` (Bitnet: `LISTSERV@UNBVM1`) [body = `SUBSCRIBE APL-L` first-name last-name]

Archive: `listserv@unb.ca`

1-87 **APLEDU-L:** On using the APL programming language in education.

i `t4327@unbmvs1.bitnet` (Bitnet: `T4327@UNBMVS1`) (D. G. Macneil)

± `listserv@unb.ca` (Bitnet: `LISTSERV@UNBVM1`) [body = `SUBSCRIBE APLEDU-L` first-name last-name]

Archive: `listserv@unb.ca`

1-88 **APO90-L:** For members of Alpha Phi Omega, a national coed service fraternity.

i `asb111@psu.edu` (Amandeep Singh Bawa)

± `listserv@psuvm.psu.edu` (Bitnet: `LISTSERV@PSUVM`) [body = `SUBSCRIBE APO90-L` first-name last-name]

1-89 **APPL-L:** Computer applications in science and education

i `wiecz@pltumk11.bitnet` (Bitnet: `WIECZ@PLTUMK11`) (Kazimierz Wieczorkowski)

± `listserv@pltumk11.bitnet` (Bitnet: `LISTSERV@PLTUMK11`) [body = `SUBSCRIBE APPL-L` first-name last-name]

Archive: `listserv@pltumk11.bitnet`

Language: English, Polish

1-90 **AR-News:** A public news wire for items relating to animal rights and welfare. Informational postings only. For discussions and commentary, see AR-Talk.

i ± `ar-news-request@cygnus.com` (Ian Lance Taylor or Chip Roberson)

1-91 **AR-Talk:** An unmoderated list for the discussion of animal rights.

i ± `ar-talk-request@cygnus.com` (Ian Lance Taylor or Chip Roberson)

1-92 **ARACHNET:** For distribution of the Electronic Journal on Virutal Culture. *Moderated*

i `dkovacs@kentvm.kent.edu` (Diane Kovacs)

± `listserv@kentvm.kent.edu` (Bitnet: `LISTSERV@KENTVM`) [body = `SUBSCRIBE ARACHNET` first-name last-name]

Archive: `listserv@vm1.nodak.edu`

1-93 **ARCH-L:** Scholarly discussions on archaeological problems.

i `carlson@tamvm1.earn` (David Carlson)

± `listserv@tamvm1.tamu.edu` (Bitnet: `LISTSERV@TAMVM1`) [body = `SUBSCRIBE ARCH-L` first-name last-name]

Archive: `listserv@tamvm1.tamu.edu` or `listserv@ibm.gwdg.de` (includes archeology-related shareware)

1-94 **ARCITRON:** For distribution of Architronic, the Electronic Journal of Architecture. *Moderated*

    i `archeds@kentvm.bitnet` (Bitnet: `ARCHEDS@KENTVM`)

    ± `listserv@kentvm.kent.edu` (Bitnet: `LISTSERV@KENTVM`) [body = `SUBSCRIBE ARCITRON` first-name last-name]

    Archive: `listserv@kentvm.kent.edu`

1-95 **ARENAL:** For international communication among Spanish-speaking gays, lesbians, and bisexuals.

    i `dsoto@ucs.indiana.edu` (Daniel Soto)

    ± `listserv@lut.fi` (Bitnet: `LISTSERV@LUT`) [body = `SUBSCRIBE ARENAL` first-name last-name]

    Language: Spanish

1-96 **argentina:** For general discussion and information on Argentine and Latin-American social/political issues.

    i ± `argentina-requests@journal.math.indiana.edu` (Elena Fraboschi/Jorge Gatica) [body = first-name-last-name , e-mail-address, phone number, address, and topics of interest]

    Language: Spanish

1-97 **ARGUS-L:** For users of ARGUS, a Unix-based collections management system used in art, ethnographic, and natural history museums.

    i `lfg@yalevm.bitnet` (Bitnet: `LFG@YALEVM`) (Larry Gall)

    ± `listserv@yalevm.ycc.yale.edu` (Bitnet: `LISTSERV@YALEVM`) [body = `SUBSCRIBE ARGUS-L` first-name last-name]

    Archive: Available to subscribers only.

1-98 **ARIE-L:** For users of Ariel, a document transmission system for the Internet developed by the Research Libraries Group.

    i `alileste@idbsu.bitnet` (Bitnet: `ALILESTE@IDBSU`) (Dan Lester)

    ± `listserv@idbsu.idbsu.edu` (Bitnet: `LISTSERV@IDBSU`) [body = `SUBSCRIBE ARIE-L` first-name last-name]

    Archive: `listserv@idbsu.idbsu.edu`

1-99 **arithmetic:** The SUNDAYS.

    i `ccytsao@uclink.berkeley.edu` (Cynthia C. Y. Tsao)

    ± `arithmetic-request@uclink.berkeley.edu` [subject = `subscribe`]

    Archive: FTP `ftp.uwp.edu` in `/sundays/mail.list`

1-100 **ARMS-L:** For various and sundry comments and questions on policy issues related to peace, war, national security, weapons, the arms race, and the like. *Moderated*

    i `gross@bcvms.bitnet` (Bitnet: `GROSS@BCVMS`) (Rob Gross)

    ± `listserv@buacca.bitnet` (Bitnet: `LISTSERV@BUACCA`) [body = `SUBSCRIBE ARMS-L` first-name last-name]

    Archive: e-mail requests to list owner

    Other: Subscription is limited. Requests will be sent to list owner for approval. In digest format.

1-101   **aroc:** For discussions relating to the Alfa Romeo Owners Club (USA).

     i ± `aroc-request@balltown.cma.com`

1-102   **Ars Magica:** For the discussion of White Wolf's role-playing game, Ars Magica.

     i ± `ars-magica-request@soda.berkeley.edu`

1-103   **Art of Noise:** On the avant-garde British music group. An extensive discography is available.

     i ± `aon-request@overpass.calpoly.edu` (Cliff Tuel)

1-104   **ARTCRIT:** On visual art criticism, including postmodernism, Marxism, feminism, curatorial practices, funding and any issue that affects artists, critics, and art viewers.

     i `macal@nexus.yorku.ca` (Michele Macaluso)

     ± `listserv@yorkvm1.bitnet` (Bitnet: LISTSERV@YORKVM1) [body = SUBSCRIBE ARTCRIT first-name last-name]

     Archive: `listserv@vm1.yorku.ca`

     Gated: ⇔ `bit.listserv.artcrit`

1-105   **ARTIST-L:** For student artists.

     i `ks06054@uafsysb.bitnet` (Bitnet: KS06054@UAFSYSB) (Ken Schriner)

     ± `listserv@uafsysb.uark.edu` (Bitnet: LISTSERV@UAFSYSB) [body = SUBSCRIBE ARTIST-L first-name last-name]

     Archive: `listserv@uafsysb.uark.edu`

1-106   **artist-users:** Discussion group for users and potential users of the software tools from Cadence Design Systems.

     i ± `artist-users-request@uicc.com` (Jeff Putsch)

     Gated: ⇔ `comp.cad.cadence`

1-107   **ASEH-L:** For the discussion of environmental history among environmental historians, geographers, ecologists, land-use planners, and others interested in understanding human interactions with the environment in the past.

     i `williams.dennis@epamail.epa.gov` (Dennis Williams)

     ± `listserv@ttuvm1.bitnet` (Bitnet: LISTSERV@TTUVM1) [body = SUBSCRIBE ASEH-L first-name last-name]

     Archive: `listserv@ttuvm1.bitnet`

1-108   **ASHE-L:** For members of the Association for the Study of Higher Education.

     i `edrsr438@mizzou1.bitnet` (Bitnet: EDRSR438@MIZZOU1) (Irv Cockriel)

     ± `listserv@mizzou1.missouri.edu` (Bitnet: LISTSERV@MIZZOU1) [body = SUBSCRIBE ASHE-L first-name last-name]

     Archive: `listserv@mizzou1.missouri.edu`

1-109   **ASIS-L:** For members of the American Society for Information Science. Information for information science professionals on continuing education, R&D, and increasing public awareness of the benefits of information science.

     i `mlavagni@uvmvm.bitnet` (Bitnet: MLAVAGNI@UVMVM) (Merri Beth Lavagnino)

     ± `listserv@uvmvm.uvm.edu` (Bitnet: LISTSERV@UVMVM) [body = SUBSCRIBE ASIS-L first-name last-name]

     Archive: Available to subscribers only.

1-110 **ASPIRE-L:** For networking among students from Asian nations. *Moderated*

    i `aspirel@ucs.indiana.edu` (Chun-Perng Cheah)

    ± `listserv@iubvm.ucs.indiana.edu` (Bitnet: `LISTSERV@IUBVM`) [body = SUBSCRIBE ASPIRE-L first-name last-name]

    Archive: `listserv@iubvm.ucs.indiana.edu`

    Other: Subscription is limited. Requests will be sent to list owner for approval.

1-111 **ASTR-L:** On theater history (American Society for Theatre Research).

    i `padavis@uiucvmd.bitnet` (Bitnet: `PADAVIS@UIUCVMD`) (Peter Davis)

    ± `listserv@vmd.cso.uiuc.edu` (Bitnet: `LISTSERV@UIUCVMD`) [body = SUBSCRIBE ASTR-L first-name last-name]

    Archive: `listserv@vmd.cso.uiuc.edu`

1-112 **ASYSM-L:** For associate members of the ASM (Association of Systems Management).

    i `wesson@auducvax.bitnet` (Bitnet: `WESSON@AUDUCVAX`) (Rick H. Wesson)

    ± `listserv@ua1vm.ua.edu` (Bitnet: `LISTSERV@UA1VM`) [body = SUBSCRIBE ASYSM-L first-name last-name]

    Archive: Available to subscribers only.

    Other: Subscription is limited. Requests will be sent to list owner for approval.

1-113 **AT-NET:** On approximation theory, a monthly bulletin. *Moderated*

    i `maprx99@technion.technion.ac.il` (Pinkus Allan)

    ± `listserv@technion.ac.il` (Bitnet: `LISTSERV@TECHNION`) [body = SUBSCRIBE AT-NET first-name last-name]

    Archive: `listserv@technion.ac.il`

1-114 **Atavachron:** For topics related to the works of jazz guitarist Allan Holdsworth. *Moderated*

    i `preston@msuacad.morehead-st.edu` (Jeff Preston)

    ± `listserv@msuacad.morehead-st.edu` [body = subscribe atavachron or atavachron-digest first-name last-name]

    Archive: FTP `ftp.uwp.edu`

1-115 **ATHTRN-L:** The discussion list for athletic trainers. *Moderated*

    i `pminger@nurs.indstate.edu` (Chris Ingersoll)

    ± `listserv@iubvm.ucs.indiana.edu` (Bitnet: `LISTSERV@IUBVM`) [body = SUBSCRIBE ATHTRN-L first-name last-name]

    Archive: Available to subscribers only.

1-116 **ATLANTIS:** For members of the American Theological Library Association and others. Emphasis is on librarianship, not theological discussion.

    i `cwill@harvarda.bitnet` (Bitnet: `CWILL@HARVARDA`)

    ± `listserv@harvarda.harvard.edu` (Bitnet: `LISTSERV@HARVARDA`) [body = SUBSCRIBE ATLANTIS first-name last-name]

    Archive: Available to subscribers only.

    Other: Subscription is limited. Requests will be sent to list owner for approval.

1-117 **ATLAS-L:** For users of ATLAS, a library automation system published by Data Research

Associates.

i `mayne@gamma.is.tcu.edu` (Jim Mayne)

± `listserv@tcubvm.bitnet` (Bitnet: LISTSERV@TCUBVM) [body = SUBSCRIBE
ATLAS-L first-name last-name]

Archive: Available to subscribers only.

1-118 **ATP-EMTP:** For users of the Alternative Transients program, an electromagnetic transients
software used in the electrical power industry.

i `bamork@mtu.edu` (Bruce Mork)

± `listserv@vm1.nodak.edu` (Bitnet: LISTSERV@NDSUVM1) [body = SUBSCRIBE
ATP-EMTP first-name last-name]

Archive: Available to subscribers only.

Gated: ⇔ `bit.listserv.ATP-EMTP`

1-119 **att-pc+:** About the AT&T PC 63xx series of computers. Membership must be requested.
Moderated

i ± `bill@wlk.com` (Bill Kennedy)

1-120 **auc-tex:** About the AUC TeX package, which runs under GNU Emacs.

i ± `auc-tex-request@iesd.auc.dk` or `auc-tex_mgr@iesd.auc.dk`

Gated: ⇔ `gnu.emacs.auctex`

1-121 **AUGLBC-L:** Supported by the American University Gay, Lesbian, & Bisexual Community for
students and friends worldwide—support, information, discussion, and contact with the
International Gay and Lesbian Youth Organization (IGLYO).

i `ep4417a@american.edu` (Erik G. Paul)

± `listserv@american.edu` (Bitnet: LISTSERV@AUVM) [body = SUBSCRIBE
AUGLBC-L first-name last-name]

1-122 **Aus-Views:** Australian subset of Cro-Views. All Australian Cro-Views members automatically
included. Only items of relevance to Australian-Croatians.

i ± `joe@mullara.met.unimelb.edu.au` (Joe Stojsic)

1-123 **Auspex:** For administrators of Auspex (NFS file servers).

± `auspex-request@princeton.edu`

1-124 **AUTOCAD:** On AutoCAD.

i `own-auto@jhuvm.hcf.jhu.edu` or `lwatkins@jhuvm.hcf.jhu.edu`

± `listserv@jhuvm.hcf.jhu.edu` (Bitnet: LISTSERV@JHUVM) [body =
SUBSCRIBE AUTOCAD first-name last-name]

Archive: `listserv@jhuvm.hcf.jhu.edu`

Gated: ⇔ `alt.cad.autocad`

1-125 **AUTOCAT:** On library cataloging and authorities, or that part of library cataloging that relates
to the establishment of headings (names, subjects, and uniform titles) used in catalogs.

i `ulcjh@ubvm.bitnet` (Bitnet: ULCJH@UBVM) (Judith Hopkins)

± `listserv@ubvm.cc.buffalo.edu` (Bitnet: LISTSERV@UBVM) [body =
SUBSCRIBE AUTOCAT first-name last-name]

Archive: `listserv@ubvm.cc.buffalo.edu`

1-126 **AUTOS-L:** On classic and sports cars, including racing and concours.

    i `ahmet@tritu.bitnet` (Bitnet: `AHMET@TRITU`) (Ahmet Tekelioglu)

    ± `listserv@tritu.bitnet` (Bitnet: `LISTSERV@TRITU`) [body = SUBSCRIBE AUTOS-L first-name last-name]

    Archive: `listserv@tritu.bitnet`

    Gated: ⇔ `bit.listserv.autos-l`

1-127 **autox:** Discussion of autocrossing, SCCA solo events.

    Other: Also available as a digest.

    i ± `autox-request@autox.team.net` (Mark J. Bradakis)

1-128 **Aviator:** For users of Aviator (tm), the flight simulation program from Artificial Horizons, Inc.

    i ± `aviator-request@icdwest.teradyne.com` (Jim Hickstein)

1-129 **awizard:** On Todd Rundgren.

    i `ed.grieze@ebay.sun.com` (Ed Grieze)

    ± `awizard-request@planning.ebay.sun.com`

1-130 **AXIOM:** For users of AXIOM Computer Algebra System, published by Numerical Algorithms Group, Ltd (NAG), running on IBM Risc System/6000 workstation and SUN Sparc workstation. *Moderated*

    i `axiom@watson.ibm.com` (Timothy Daly)

    ± `listserv@vm1.nodak.edu` (Bitnet: `LISTSERV@NDSUVM1`) [body = SUBSCRIBE AXIOM first-name last-name]

    Archive: `listserv@vm1.nodak.edu`

    Gated: ⇔ `bit.listserv.AXIOM`

1-131 **AYN-EDUC:** For an edited introduction to Ayn Rand's objectivist philosophy. *Moderated*

    i `jwales@iubvm.bitnet` (Bitnet: `JWALES@IUBVM`) (Jimmy -Jimbo- Wales)

    ± `listserv@iubvm.ucs.indiana.edu` (Bitnet: `LISTSERV@IUBVM`) [body = SUBSCRIBE AYN-EDUC first-name last-name]

    Archive: `listserv@iubvm.ucs.indiana.edu`

    Other: Subscription is limited. Requests will be sent to list owner for approval.

1-132 **AYN-RAND:** For scholarly discussion of Ayn Rand's objectivist philosophy. *Moderated*

    i `jwales@iubvm.bitnet` (Bitnet: `JWALES@IUBVM`) (Jimmy -Jimbo- Wales)

    ± `listserv@iubvm.ucs.indiana.edu` (Bitnet: `LISTSERV@IUBVM`) [body = SUBSCRIBE AYN-RAND first-name last-name]

    Archive: `listserv@iubvm.ucs.indiana.edu`

    Other: Subscription is limited. Requests will be sent to list owner for approval.

1-133 **ba-firearms:** Announcement and discussion of California firearms legislation and related issues. Includes discussion local to the San Francisco Bay Area and all ca-firearms messages.

    i ± `ba-firearms-request@shell.portal.com` (Jeff Chan)

1-134 **ba-liberty:** Announcement of local San Francisco Bay Area libertarian meetings, events, activities, etc. Also includes all ca-liberty messages.

    i ± `ba-liberty-request@shell.portal.com` (Jeff Chan)

1-135 **ba-poker-list:** On poker in the San Franciso Bay Area (broadly defined). Topics include upcoming events, unusual games, strategies, comparisons of various venues, and player "networking."

i ± ba-poker-request@netcom.com (Martin Veneroso)

1-136 **babble:** For discussion about the band The Cure.

i owner-babble@bobby.ecst.csuchico.edu

± babble-request@cindy.ecst.csuchico.edu

Other: For digest/moderated version, subscribe to
babble-m-request@bobby.ecst.csuchico.edu

1-137 **BACKS-L:** On low back pain, disability, and rehabilitation.

i e_dow@uvmvax.bitnet (Bitnet: E_DOW@UVMVAX) (Elizabeth H. Dow)

± listserv@uvmvm.uvm.edu (Bitnet: LISTSERV@UVMVM) [body = SUBSCRIBE
BACKS-L first-name last-name]

Archive: Available to subscribers only.

Other: Daily digest

1-138 **backstreets:** For fans of Bruce Springsteen's music.

i ± backstreets-request@virginia.edu

Archive: FTP ftp.uwp.edu in /pub/music/lists/springsteen

1-139 **bagpipe:** On anything related to bagpipes. All manner of Scottish, Irish, English, and other
instruments are discussed.

i ± bagpipe-request@cs.dartmouth.edu

Archives: FTP cs.dartmouth.edu in /pub/bagpipes

1-140 **balloon:** This is a list for balloonists of any sort, be they hot air or gas, commercial or sport.
Discussion topics include just about anything related to ballooning.

i ± balloon-request@lut.ac.uk (Phil Herbert)

1-141 **BALT-L:** On the Baltic Republics. *Moderated*

i a.e.b.bevan@open.ac:uk (Edis Bevan)

± listserv@ib.rl.ac.uk (Bitnet: LISTSERV@UKACRL) [body = SUBSCRIBE
BALT-L first-name last-name] or listserv@ubvm.cc.buffalo.edu (Bitnet:
LISTSERV@UBVM) [body = SUBSCRIBE BALT-L first-name last-name]

Archive: listserv@ib.rl.ac.uk or listserv@ubvm.cc.buffalo.edu

Gated: ⇔ bit.listserv.balt-l

1-142 **BAPTIST:** Open Baptist discussion.

i str002@ukcc.uky.edu (Bob Moore)

± listserv@ukcc.uky.edu (Bitnet: LISTSERV@UKCC) [body = SUBSCRIBE
BAPTIST first-name last-name]

Archive: listserv@ukcc.uky.edu

1-143 **barbershop:** On barbershop harmony, quartets, and choruses, and on organizations promoting
the barbershop singing.

i ± barbershop-request@bigd.cray.com (David Bowen)

1-144   **BASIC programming:** On using the BASIC programming language.

> *i* ± `basic-request@ireq.hydro.qc.ca` (Robert Meunier)

1-145   **bbones:** On the construction of e-mail backbones for organizations and campuses.

> ± `mail-bbones-request@ics.uci.edu`

1-146   **bears:** Digest format list for gay and bisexual men who are bears (men who are variously cuddly, furry, perhaps stocky, or bearded) themselves and for those who enjoy the company of bears. People uncomfortable with discussing sexually explicit topics should not subscribe.

> *i* ± `bears-request@spdcc.com` (Steve Dyer and Brian Gollum)

1-147   **Beats Per Minute:** For professional and semi-professional disc-jockeys. Topics include mixing-beat techniques, software (records, CDs), and hardware (turntables, CD players, mixers, samplers, effects, etc.).

> *i* `sg1q+@andrew.cmu.edu` (Simon Gatrall)
>
> ± `bpm-request@andrew.cmu.edu`

1-148   **BEE-L:** On the biology of bees, including sociobiology, behavior, ecology, adaptation/evolution, genetics, taxonomy, physiology, pollination, and flower nectar and pollen production of bees.

> *i* `erik@acspr1.acs.brockport.edu` (Erik Seielstad)
>
> ± `listserv@uacsc2.albany.edu` (Bitnet: LISTSERV@ALBNYVM1) [body = SUBSCRIBE BEE-L first-name last-name]

Archive: Available to subscribers only.

1-149   **BEEF-L:** For beef specialists.

> *i* `pace@wsuvm1.bitnet` (Bitnet: PACE@WSUVM1) or `wright@wsuvm1.bitnet` (Bitnet: WRIGHT@WSUVM1)
>
> ± `listserv@wsuvm1.csc.wsu.edu` (Bitnet: LISTSERV@WSUVM1) [body = SUBSCRIBE BEEF-L first-name last-name]

Archive: `listserv@wsuvm1.csc.wsu.edu`

1-150   **BEER-L:** Homebrew Digest redistribution list. *Moderated*

> *i* `darren@ua1vm.ua.edu`
>
> ± `listserv@ua1vm.ua.edu` (Bitnet: LISTSERV@UA1VM) [body = SUBSCRIBE BEER-L first-name last-name]

1-151   **Bel Canto:** On all aspects of the pop group Bel Canto.

> *i* ± `dewy-fields-request@ifi.uio.no`

Archive: FTP `ftp.ifi.uio.no` in `pub/bel-canto`

1-152   **BELIEF-L:** For discussing and debating personal beliefs. The tone is rational, discursive, and eclectic; proselytization, or the simple recitation of beliefs, is strongly discouraged by the list guidelines.

> *i* `el406006@brownvm.bitnet` (Bitnet: EL406006@BROWNVM) (David B. O'Donnell)
>
> ± `listserv@brownvm.brown.edu` (Bitnet: LISTSERV@BROWNVM) [body = SUBSCRIBE BELIEF-L first-name last-name] or `listserv@ucf1vm.cc.ucf.edu` (Bitnet: LISTSERV@UCF1VM) [body = SUBSCRIBE BELIEF-L first-name last-name]

Archive: `listserv@brownvm.brown.edu`

Other: Weekly digest

1-153 **BERITA-L:** For news on Malaysia and southeast Asia.

i spectre@uiuc.edu

± listserv@vmd.cso.uiuc.edu (Bitnet: LISTSERV@UIUCVMD) [body = SUBSCRIBE BERITA-L first-name last-name]

Archive: listserv@vmd.cso.uiuc.edu

Other: Weekly digest

1-154 **BETA:** For BETA users. BETA is a modern object-oriented programming language.

i sales@mjolner.dk (Kim Jensen Moller)

± usergroup-request@mjolner.dk

Archive: FTP ftp.daimi.aau.dk in /pub/beta

1-155 **Between the Lines:** All about Debbie Gibson and her music.

i ± mkwong@scf.nmsu.edu (Myra Wong)

Other: In digest format.

1-156 **BGRASS-L:** For discussion of bluegrass and old-time music.

i uka016@ukcc.bitnet (Bitnet: UKA016@UKCC)

± listserv@ukcc.uky.edu (Bitnet: LISTSERV@UKCC) [body = SUBSCRIBE BGRASS-L first-name last-name]

Archive: listserv@ukcc.uky.edu

Other: Daily digest

1-157 **BGUBS-L:** For the Behavioral Sciences Department at Ben Gurion University in Israel.

i chermesh@bgumail.bgu.ac.il (Ran Chermesh)

± listserv@bguvm.bitnet (Bitnet: LISTSERV@BGUVM) [body = SUBSCRIBE BGUBS-L first-name last-name]

Archive: Available to subscribers only.

1-158 **BI-L:** On educating library users to be self-sufficient in using new-technology resources at libraries. *Moderated*

i mraish@bingvmb.bitnet (Bitnet: MRAISH@BINGVMB) (Martin Raish)

± listserv@bingvmb.cc.binghamton.edu (Bitnet: LISTSERV@BINGVMB) [body = SUBSCRIBE BI-L first-name last-name]

Archive: listserv@bingvmb.cc.binghamton.edu

1-159 **BIBSOFT:** About software for citations and bibliographies.

i morganj@indyvax.iupui.edu or stigle@cs.unca.edu

± listserv@indycms.iupui.edu (Bitnet: LISTSERV@INDYCMS) [body = SUBSCRIBE BIBSOFT first-name last-name]

Archive: listserv@indycms.iupui.edu or listserv@indycms.bitnet

1-160 **BICOMPAL:** For members of the Big Computer Pals.

i drz@sjuvm.bitnet (Bitnet: DRZ@SJUVM)

± listserv@stjohns.edu (Bitnet: LISTSERV@SJUVM) [body = SUBSCRIBE BICOMPAL first-name last-name]

Archive: Available to subscribers only.

1-161   **BICYCLE:** All about human-powered cycling.

    i ctanski@nyx.cs.du.edu

    ± listserv@bitnic.educom.edu (Bitnet: LISTSERV@BITNIC) [body =
      SUBSCRIBE BICYCLE first-name last-name]

1-162   **BIG-LAN:** On campus-sized LANs.

    i serveman@ebcesca1.bitnet (Bitnet: SERVEMAN@EBCESCA1) (Caterina Parals)

    ± listserv@ebcesca1.bitnet (Bitnet: LISTSERV@EBCESCA1) [body =
      SUBSCRIBE BIG-LAN first-name last-name]

    Archive: listserv@ebcesca1.bitnet

1-163   **bikecommute:** On bicycle transportation, and the steps necessary for improved bicycling conditions in (sub)urban areas. Mostly for Silicon Valley area, though others may join.

    i ± bikecommute-request@bike2work.eng.sun.com

1-164   **bikepeople:** On bicycle issues—local, state, and national. Mostly for Santa Cruz County, CA,
area.

    i ± bikepeople-request@daizu.ucsc.edu (Kevin Karplus)

1-165   **BILDIL:** On Turkish natural language processing studies.

    i bozsahin@trmetu.bitnet (Bitnet: BOZSAHIN@TRMETU) (Cem Bozsahin) or
      ko@trbilun.bitnet (Bitnet: KO@TRBILUN) (Kemal Oflazer)

    ± listserv@vm.cc.metu.edu.tr (Bitnet: LISTSERV@TRMETU) [body =
      SUBSCRIBE BILDIL first-name last-name]

    Archive: listserv@vm.cc.metu.edu.tr

1-166   **BILLING:** For discussion of principles and techniques for reporting and billing for the use of
computer resources.

    i rcoprob@hdetud2.tudelft.nl

    ± listserv@hearn.nic.surfnet.nl (Bitnet: LISTSERV@HEARN) [body =
      SUBSCRIBE BILLING first-name last-name]

    Archive: listserv@hearn.nic.surfnet.nl

    Gated: ⇔ Bit.listserv.billing

1-167   **billy-bragg:** On the rock musician Billy Bragg.

    i zen@sun.com (Dan Farmer)

    ± billy-bragg-request@death.corp.sun.com

1-168   **BIOMAT-L:** On research and use of biomaterials in medicine and biology, including announcements of conferences and meetings.

    i a.brandwood@unsw.edu.au (Arthur Brandwood)

    ± listserv@hearn.nic.surfnet.nl (Bitnet: LISTSERV@HEARN) [body =
      SUBSCRIBE BIOMAT-L first-name last-name]

    Archive: listserv@hearn.nic.surfnet.nl

1-169   **BIOMCH-L:** On biomechanics and human/animal movement science. *Moderated*

    i bogert@acs.ucalgary.ca (Ton van den Bogert)

    ± listserv@hearn.nic.surfnet.nl (Bitnet: LISTSERV@HEARN) [body =
      SUBSCRIBE BIOMCH-L first-name last-name]

Archive: `listserv@hearn.nic.surfnet.nl`

Gated: ⇔ `bit.listserv.biomch-1`

1-170 **BIOPI-L:** On secondary biology teacher enhancement.

i `tmanney@ksuvm.bitnet` (Bitnet: `TMANNEY@KSUVM`)

± `listserv@ksuvm.ksu.edu` (Bitnet: `LISTSERV@KSUVM`) [body = SUBSCRIBE BIOPI-L first-name last-name]

Archive: `listserv@ksuvm.ksu.edu`

1-171 **biosym:** For users of Biosym Technologies software. (Includes the products InsightII, Discover, Dmol, Homology, Delphi, and Polymer.) List not run by Biosym. No discussion on commercial aspects, restricted to research and maintenance of the software and its use.

i ± `dibug-request@comp.bioz.unibas.ch` (Reinhard Doelz)

Archive: FTP `bioftp.unibas.ch`; gopher `biox.unibas.ch`

1-172 **BIOTECH:** For open discussion of all issues related to biotechnology. *Moderated*

i `dan@umdd.bitnet` (Bitnet: `DAN@UMDD`) (Dan Jacobs)

± `listserv@umdd.umd.edu` (Bitnet: `LISTSERV@UMDD`) [body = SUBSCRIBE BIOTECH first-name last-name]

Archive: `listserv@umdd.umd.edu`

1-173 **Black Sabbath:** On the rock group Black Sabbath and related topics.

i ± `sabbath-request@fa.disney.com`

1-174 **BLINDNWS:** On blindness and visual impairment. *Moderated*

i `info@ndsuvm1.bitnet` (Bitnet: `INFO@NDSUVM1`) (Marty Hoag)

± `listserv@vm1.nodak.edu` (Bitnet: `LISTSERV@NDSUVM1`) [body = SUBSCRIBE BLINDNWS first-name last-name]

Archive: `listserv@vm1.nodak.edu`

Other: Daily digest

Gated: ⇔ `bit.listserv.blindnws`

1-175 **BLISS-L:** On the Barus Lab Interactive Speech System, a DOS software for psychological subject testing using speech and visual displays.

i `mertus@brownvm.bitnet` (Bitnet: `MERTUS@BROWNVM`)

± `listserv@brownvm.brown.edu` (Bitnet: `LISTSERV@BROWNVM`) [body = SUBSCRIBE BLISS-L first-name last-name]

Archive: `listserv@brownvm.brown.edu`

1-176 **blue-eyed-pop:** "The Sugarcubes" mailing list.

i `glocke@morgan.ucs.mun.ca`

± `listserver@morgan.ucs.mun.ca` [body = subscribe blue-eyed-pop first-name last-name]

Archive: FTP `ftp.uwp.edu` in `/pub/music/artists/s/sugarcubes`

Other: Available in digest form; include a line `/set blue-eyed-pop mail digest` in subscription request.

1-177 **BMW:** Discussion of cars made by BMW.

i ± `bmw-request@balltown.cma.com` (Richard Welty)

1-178   **Bobs:** For "fobs" (Friends of the Bobs). The Bobs is a four-person a cappella musical group originating in the San Francisco Bay Area.

i `fobs-owner@netcom.com`

± `fobs-request@netcom.com`

1-179   **boc-l:** On the rock bands Blue Oyster Cult and Hawkwind.

i ± `boc-request@spcvxa.spc.edu`

1-180   **BOGEN-L:** On the Industrial Engineering Department of Bosphorus University.

i `erhan_erkut@mts.ucs.ualberta.ca` (Erhan Erkut)

± `listserv@vm.ucs.ualberta.ca` (Bitnet: `LISTSERV@UALTAVM`) [body = SUBSCRIBE BOGEN-L first-name last-name]

Gated: ⇔ `bit.listserv.bogen-l`

1-181   **BONSAI:** On bonsai, the Asian art of growing trees or shrubs in shallow pots or trays.

i `dcwiert@waynest1.bitnet` (Bitnet: `DCWIERT@WAYNEST1`) (Daniel Cwiertniewicz)

± `listserv@cms.cc.wayne.edu` (Bitnet: `LISTSERV@WAYNEST1`) [body = SUBSCRIBE BONSAI first-name last-name]

Archive: `listserv@cms.cc.wayne.edu`

Gated: ⇔ `rec.arts.bonsai`

1-182   **BosNet:** Daily digest of news and discussions mainly about Bosnia and Herzegovina, including news from the international press. Original contributions by readers encouraged. *Moderated*

i ± and submissions to: `zukicn@wl.aecl.ca` (Nermin Zukic) or `hozo@math.lsa.umich.edu` (Hozo Iztok)

Archive: FTP `ftp.triples.math.mcgill.ca` in `/pub/bosnia`

Language: English and Bosnian

Other: In digest format.

1-183   **Boston-Music:** Boston/New England music and other events in the Boston/New England Area that are of interest to fans of the Grateful Dead.

i `dalton@mtl.mit.edu` (Timothy J. Dalton)

± `boston-music-request@virginia.edu` (Bitnet: `BM-REQ@VIRGINIA`)

1-184   **BRAINTMR:** Brain Tumor Research/Support.

i `samajane@athena.mit.edu` (Samantha J. Scolamiero)

± `listserv@mitvma.mit.edu` (Bitnet: `LISTSERV@MITVMA`) [body = SUBSCRIBE BRAINTMR first-name last-name]

Archive: `listserv@mitvma.mit.edu`

1-185   **bras-net:** All about Brazil—from sports to politics.

Language: Portuguese

i `bras-net-request@cs.ucla.edu`

± `bras-net-request@cs.ucla.edu` [body = first-name last-name e-mail-address]

1-186   **brass:** About brass musical performance and related topics, especially small musical ensembles of all kinds.

i ± `brass-request@geomag.gly.fsu.edu` (Ted Zateslo)

1-187 **BRIDGE-L:** "The Bridge Across Consciousness" on the epistemology of religion and spiritual foundations for a pluralistic society—being used to develop an international database on ecumenical and universal religion.

> *i* origin@coyote.rain.org (Bruce Schuman)
>
> ± listserv@ucsbvm.bitnet (Bitnet: LISTSERV@UCSBVM) [body = SUBSCRIBE BRIDGE-L first-name last-name]
>
> **Archive:** listserv@ucsbvm.bitnet

1-188 **british-cars:** Discussion of owning, repairing, racing, cursing, and loving British cars, predominantly sports cars, some Land Rover and sedan stuff. Also available as a digest.

> *i* ± british-cars-request@autox.team.net (Mark Bradakis)

1-189 **BRS-L:** On the BRS/Search Full Text Retrieval Software package from BRS Information Technologies.

> *i* brsadm@uscvm.bitnet (Karl Geiger)
>
> ± listserv@vm.usc.edu (Bitnet: LISTSERV@USCVM) [body = SUBSCRIBE BRS-L first-name last-name]
>
> **Archive:** listserv@vm.usc.edu

1-190 **BUDDHA-L:** For academic discussion on Buddhism. *Moderated*

> *i* cxev@musica.mcgill.ca (Richard Hayes)
>
> ± listserv@ulkyvm.louisville.edu (Bitnet: LISTSERV@ULKYVM) [body = SUBSCRIBE BUDDHA-L first-name last-name]
>
> **Archive:** listserv@ulkyvm.louisville.edu
>
> **Other:** Daily digest

1-191 **BUDDHIST:** On Buddhism.

> *i* kawazoe@jpntohok.bitnet (Bitnet: KAWAZOE@JPNTOHOK) (Yoshiyuki Kawazoe)
>
> ± listserv@jpntuvm0.bitnet (Bitnet: LISTSERV@JPNTUVM0) [body = SUBSCRIBE BUDDHIST first-name last-name]
>
> **Archive:** listserv@jpntuvm0.bitnet

1-192 **build-a-home:** A forum for discussion and questions related to designing or building one's home.

> *i* ± build-a-home-request@sol.asl.hitachi.com (Joe Augenbraun)

1-193 **BURG-CEN:** On fluid mechanics.

> *i* f.c.visser@wb.utwente.nl (Frank Visser)
>
> ± listserv@hearn.nic.surfnet.nl (Bitnet: LISTSERV@HEARN) [body = SUBSCRIBE BURG-CEN first-name last-name]
>
> **Archive:** listserv@hearn.nic.surfnet.nl

1-194 **BUSFAC-L:** For the international business faculty members.

> *i* 3m3eplg@cmuvm.bitnet (Bitnet: 3M3EPLG@CMUVM) (Syed Shahabuddin)
>
> ± listserv@cmuvm.csv.cmich.edu (Bitnet: LISTSERV@CMUVM) [body = SUBSCRIBE BUSFAC-L first-name last-name]
>
> **Archive:** Available to subscribers only.
>
> **Other:** Subscription is limited. Requests will be sent to list owner for approval.

1-195 **C+HEALTH:** About the health effects of computer use.

> *i* `sheehan@bronze.ucs.indiana.edu` (Mark Sheehan)
>
> ± `listserv@iubvm.ucs.indiana.edu` (Bitnet: `LISTSERV@IUBVM`) [body = `SUBSCRIBE C+HEALTH` first-name last-name]
>
> **Archive:** `listserv@iubvm.ucs.indiana.edu`

1-196 **C18-L:** For interdisciplinary discussion of the 18th century, including professional notices (calls for papers, fellowship information), requests for information, discussion of specialized topics, and bibliographies.

> *i* `bcj@psuvm.bitnet` (Bitnet: `BCJ@PSUVM`)
>
> ± `listserv@psuvm.psu.edu` (Bitnet: `LISTSERV@PSUVM`) [body = `SUBSCRIBE C18-L` first-name last-name]
>
> **Archive:** `listserv@psuvm.psu.edu`
>
> **Language:** English, French

1-197 **C_C++:** On C and C++ programming languages.

> *i* `eince@basalt.mines.colorado.edu` (Erdem Ince)
>
> ± `listserv@tritu.bitnet` (Bitnet: `LISTSERV@TRITU`) [body = `SUBSCRIBE C_C++` first-name last-name]
>
> **Archive:** `listserv@tritu.bitnet`
>
> **Gated:** ⇔ `itu.listserv.c_c++`
>
> **Language:** Turkish, English

1-198 **ca-firearms:** Announcement and discussion of California firearms legislation and related statewide issues. See also ba-firearms.

> *i* ± `ca-firearms-request@shell.portal.com` (Jeff Chan)

1-199 **CA-L:** On cellular automata, including theory, applications, and available software packages.

> *i* `bmb@think.com` (Bruce Boghosian)
>
> ± `listserv@mitvma.mit.edu` (Bitnet: `LISTSERV@MITVMA`) [body = `SUBSCRIBE CA-L` first-name last-name] or `cellular-automata-request@think.com` [body = `subscribe e-mai-address internet-ca-list`]
>
> **Archive:** FTP `think.com` in `/archive`; `maillistserv@mitvma.mit.edu`
>
> **Gated:** ⇔ `comp.theory.cell-automata`

1-200 **ca-liberty:** Announcement of California libertarian meetings, events, activities, etc. See also ba-liberty.

> *i* ± `ca-liberty-request@shell.portal.com` (Jeff Chan)

1-201 **cabot:** Official mailing list of the New York State Institute for Sebastian Cabot Studies.

> *i* ± `cabot-request@balltown.cma.com` (Richard Welty)

1-202 **CACI-L:** General topics in research and advanced study in Canada and Italy.

> *i* `postmast@ualtavm.bitnet` (Bitnet: `POSTMAST@UALTAVM`) (Postmaster)
>
> ± `listserv@vm.ucs.ualberta.ca` (Bitnet: `LISTSERV@UALTAVM`) [body = `SUBSCRIBE CACI-L` first-name last-name]
>
> **Language:** English, French, Italian
>
> **Gated:** ⇔ `bit.listserv.caci-l`

1-203 **CAMEL-L:** For scholarly discussion on camels.

    i `devmtg12@sakfu00.bitnet` (Bitnet: `DEVMTG12@SAKFU00`) (Mustafa Ghazal)

    ± `listserv@sakfu00.bitnet` (Bitnet: `LISTSERV@SAKFU00`) [body = SUBSCRIBE CAMEL-L first-name last-name]

    Archive: `listserv@sakfu00.bitnet`

    Language: English

    Other: Subscription is limited. Requests will be sent to list owner for approval.

1-204 **CAMNET:** For discussion of Cameroon.

    i `hell@vm.cnuce.cnr.it` (Dr. Louis B. Hell)

    ± `listserv@vm.cnuce.cnr.it` (Bitnet: `LISTSERV@ICNUCEVM`) [body = SUBSCRIBE CAMNET first-name last-name]

    Archive: `listserv@vm.cnuce.cnr.it`

    Language: French, English

1-205 **CAMPCLIM:** On college campuses, personal, educational, and physical environments.

    i `cblih@uafsysb.bitnet` (Bitnet: `CBLIH@UAFSYSB`) (C. B. Lih)

    ± `listserv@uafsysb.uark.edu` (Bitnet: `LISTSERV@UAFSYSB`) [body = SUBSCRIBE CAMPCLIM first-name last-name]

    Archive: Available to subscribers only.

1-206 **CANADA-L:** For discussion of political, social, cultural, and economic issues in Canada.

    i `ed22@musica.mcgill.ca` (Anastassia Khouri St-Pierre)

    ± `listserv@vm1.mcgill.ca` (Bitnet: `LISTSERV@MCGILL1`) [body = SUBSCRIBE CANADA-L first-name last-name]

    Archive: `listserv@vm1.mcgill.ca`

1-207 **CANALC:** Canadian Association for Latin American and Caribbean Studies.

    i `lanfran@yorkvm1.bitnet` (Bitnet: `LANFRAN@YORKVM1`) (Sam Lanfranco)

    ± `listserv@yorkvm1.bitnet` (Bitnet: `LISTSERV@YORKVM1`) [body = SUBSCRIBE CANALC first-name last-name]

    Archive: Available to subscribers only.

1-208 **CANARIE:** For associates of the Canada Network for Advancement of Research, Industry and Education (CANARIE).

    i `t4327@unbmvs1.bitnet` (Bitnet: `T4327@UNBMVS1`) (list management)

    ± `listserv@unb.ca` (Bitnet: `LISTSERV@UNBVM1`) [body = SUBSCRIBE CANARIE first-name last-name]

    Archive: Available to subscribers only.

1-209 **CANCHID:** For the Canadian Network on Health in International Development.

    i `lanfran@yorkvm1.bitnet` (Bitnet: `LANFRAN@YORKVM1`) (Sam Lanfranco)

    ± `listserv@yorkvm1.bitnet` (Bitnet: `LISTSERV@YORKVM1`) [body = SUBSCRIBE CANCHID first-name last-name]

    Archive: Available to subscribers only.

1-210 **CANDLE-L:** Candle Products discussion list.
  i darren@ua1vm.ua.edu (Darren Evans-Young)
  ± listserv@ua1vm.ua.edu (Bitnet: LISTSERV@UA1VM) [body = SUBSCRIBE CANDLE-L first-name last-name]
  Archive: listserv@ua1vm.ua.edu

1-211 **CANDRAMA:** For research of Canadian theater.
  i mullaly@unb.ca (Edward Mullaly)
  ± listserv@unb.ca (Bitnet: LISTSERV@UNBVM1) [body = SUBSCRIBE CANDRAMA first-name last-name]
  Archive: listserv@unb.ca

1-212 **CANSPACE:** On space geodesy, including Navstar Global Positioning System (GPS), Glonass, Transit, very long baseline interferometry, satellite laser ranging, satellite altimetry.
  i lang@unb.ca (Richard Langley) or se@unb.ca (Terry Arsenault)
  ± listserv@unb.ca (Bitnet: LISTSERV@UNBVM1) [body = SUBSCRIBE CANSPACE first-name last-name]
  Archive: listserv@unb.ca

1-213 **CAPES-L:** For support of research projects by Brazilian university students.
  i josi@brfapesp.bitnet (Bitnet: JOSI@BRFAPESP) (Josefina Perez Alvarez)
  ± listserv@vm1.lcc.ufmg.br (Bitnet: LISTSERV@BRUFMG) [body = SUBSCRIBE CAPES-L first-name last-name]
  Language: Portuguese

1-214 **Cards (aka sportscards):** On collecting, speculating, and investing in sports and nonsport trading cards and/or memorabilia. Discussion and wantlists are welcome, as are limited sell lists. Auctions are not allowed. Membership is limited, and there is a waiting list to get on. This list will not feed CompuServe, Genie, AOL or any other pay-for-play system. Memberships from public access machines by invitation only.
  i ± cards-request@tanstaafl.uchicago.edu (Keane Arase)

1-215 **CARL-L:** About the CARL system.
  i macmill@uhunix.uhcc.hawaii.edu (Bitnet: MACMILL@UHUNIX)
  ± listserv@uhccvm.uhcc.hawaii.edu (Bitnet: LISTSERV@UHCCVM) [body = SUBSCRIBE CARL-L first-name last-name]
  Archive: Available to subscribers only.

1-216 **CARWAR-L:** On the Steve Jackson game, Car Wars including rules debates, tournament organization, computer versions, and more.
  i psr@acsu.buffalo.edu (Strider)
  ± listserv@ubvm.buffalo.edu [body = sub CARWAR-L first-name last-name]

1-217 **CASE-L:** On Computer Aided Software Engineering.
  i spgrjh@uccvma.bitnet (Bitnet: SPGRJH@UCCVMA) (Richard Hintz)
  ± listserv@uccvma.ucop.edu (Bitnet: LISTSERV@UCCVMA) [body = SUBSCRIBE CASE-L first-name last-name]
  Archive: Available to subscribers only.

1-218   **CASLL:** On the learning and teaching of reading and writing, especially in Canada.

i hunt@academic.stu.stthomasu.ca (Russ Hunt)

± listserv@unb.ca (Bitnet: LISTSERV@UNBVM1) [body = SUBSCRIBE CASLL first-name last-name]

Other: Subscription is limited. Requests will be sent to list owner for approval.

1-219   **CATALA:** For people who want to discuss things in Catalan.

i serveman@ebcesca1.bitnet (Bitnet: SERVEMAN@EBCESCA1) (Caterina Parals)

± listserv@ebcesca1.bitnet (Bitnet: LISTSERV@EBCESCA1) [body = SUBSCRIBE CATALA first-name last-name]

Archive: listserv@ebcesca1.bitnet

Language: Catalan

1-220   **CATHAR-M:** For "Cartharsis," a newsmagazine of personal health, intellect and creativity for the Chronic Fatigue Syndrome community—linked to newsgroup alt.med.cfs.zine.

i cfs-file-request@sjuvm.stjohns.edu (Molly Holzschlag)

± listserv@sjuvm.stjohns.edu (Bitnet: LISTSERV@SJUVM)[body = SUBSCRIBE CATHAR-M first-name last-name]

1-221   **CATHOLIC:** On matters pertaining to the Catholic churches (Anglican, Roman, Orthodox).

i cms@dragon.com (Cindy Smith) or cts@dragon.com (Charles Smith)

± listserv@american.edu (Bitnet: LISTSERV@AUVM) [body = SUBSCRIBE CATHOLIC first-name last-name]

Archive: listserv@american.edu

1-222   **Catholic Doctrine:** For Catholics. On orthodox Catholic theology . *Moderated*

i ± catholic-request@sarto.gaithersburg.md.us (Joe Buehler)

Archive: Mailserver catholic-archives@sarto.gaithersburg.md.us (includes complete archive of all past posts to the list)

1-223   **CAUCE-L:** For discussion of issues (broad, narrow, practical, theoretical, controversial, or mundane) related to university continuing education.

i lihein@uregina1.bitnet (Bitnet: LIHEIN@UREGINA1) (Dr. Larry Hein)

± listserv@max.cc.uregina.ca (Bitnet: LISTSERV@UREGINA1) [body = SUBSCRIBE CAUCE-L first-name last-name]

Archive: listserv@max.cc.uregina.ca

Other: Subscription is limited. Requests will be sent to list owner for approval.

1-224   **CAUSEASM:** On planning administrative computer systems for institutions of higher education, including impacts of new technologies and managing diverse hardware and software environments.

i awdcms@vtvm1.bitnet (Bitnet: AWDCMS@VTVM1) (A. Wayne Donald)

± listserv@vtvm1.cc.vt.edu (Bitnet: LISTSERV@VTVM1) [body = SUBSCRIBE CAUSEASM first-name last-name]

Archive: Available to subscribers only.

1-225   **CBEHIGH :** Computer-based education in higher education.

i laaaa43@blekul11.bitnet (Bitnet: LAAAA43@BLEKUL11)

± listserv@blekul11.bitnet (Bitnet: LISTSERV@BLEKUL11) [body = SUBSCRIBE CBEHIGH: CBEHIGH list first-name last-name]

Archive: listserv@blekul11.bitnet

1-226 **CCDIC-L:** Canadian Centre for the Development of Instructional Computing.

i craig_montgomerie@admin.educ.ualberta.ca

± listserv@vm.ucs.ualberta.ca (Bitnet: LISTSERV@UALTAVM) [body = SUBSCRIBE CCDIC-L first-name last-name]

Archive: Available to subscribers only.

Gated: ⇔ bit.listserv.ccdic-l

Other: Subscription is limited. Requests will be sent to list owner for approval.

1-227 **CCES-L:** For members of the Congress of Canadian Engineering Students (CCES), an organization for engineering students in Canada, although others are welcome to join in.

i cfes@jupiter.sun.csd.unb.ca (Canadian Federation of Engineering Students)

± listserv@unb.ca (Bitnet: LISTSERV@UNBVM1) [body = SUBSCRIBE CCES-L first-name last-name]

1-228 **CCNET-L:** On computing networks in China.

i jiang@ifcss.org (Yuan Jiang)

± listserv@uga.cc.uga.edu (Bitnet: LISTSERV@UGA) [body = SUBSCRIBE CCNET-L first-name last-name]

Archive: listserv@uga.cc.uga.edu

1-229 **CCNL:** On the employment/immigration issues affecting the Chinese community.

i ding@library.uta.edu (Bitnet: B366JDX@UTARLVM1) (Jian Ding)

± listserv@utarlvm1.uta.edu (Bitnet: LISTSERV@UTARLVM1) [body = SUBSCRIBE CCNL first-name last-name]

1-230 **cd-forum:** For the support of cross-dressing, transsexuality, and other gender issues.

i ± cd-request@valis.biocad.com
(UUCP: uunet!sgi!biocad!valis!cd-request)

Other: In digest format.

1-231 **CDMAJOR:** On communication disorders, primarily for students and faculty in speech-language pathology, audiology, speech science, or hearing science programs.

i acaruso@kentvm.bitnet (Bitnet: ACARUSO@KENTVM) (Anthony J. Caruso)

± listserv@kentvm.kent.edu (Bitnet: LISTSERV@KENTVM) [body = SUBSCRIBE CDMAJOR first-name last-name]

Archive: listserv@kentvm.kent.edu

1-232 **CDPub:** On CD-ROM publishing in general and desktop cdrom recorders and publishing systems in particular. *Moderated*

i cdpub-info@knex.via.mind.org

± mail-server@knex.via.mind.org [body = SUBSCRIBE CDPub first-name last-name]

1-233 **CDROM-L:** On uses of CD-ROM.

i opsrjh@uccvma.bitnet (Bitnet: OPSRJH@UCCVMA) (Richard Hintz)

± `listserv@uccvma.ucop.edu` (Bitnet: LISTSERV@UCCVMA) [body = SUBSCRIBE CDROM-L first-name last-name]

Archive: `listserv@uccvma.ucop.edu`

Gated: `alt.cdrom netnews group`

Other: Daily digest

1-234 **cdrom-list:** Discussion of installation and use of CD-ROM drives and discs for the Amiga computer.

i `ben@ben.com` (Ben Jackson)

± `cdrom-list-request@ben.com`

1-235 **CDROMLAN:** On using CD-ROMs on local area networks.

i `alileste@idbsu.bitnet` (Bitnet: ALILESTE@IDBSU) (Dan Lester)

± `listserv@idbsu.idbsu.edu` (Bitnet: LISTSERV@IDBSU) [body = SUBSCRIBE CDROMLAN first-name last-name]

Archive: `listserv@idbsu.idbsu.edu`

1-236 **CDS-ISIS:** For users of Unesco's CDS/ISIS text retrieval program, which is widely used, especially in developing countries, for bibliographic applications and project administration. *Moderated*

i `besemer@jka.wau.nl` (Hugo Besemer) or `nri@ukc.ac.uk` (Chris Addison)

± `listserv@hearn.nic.surfnet.nl` (Bitnet: LISTSERV@HEARN) [body = SUBSCRIBE CDS-ISIS first-name last-name]

Archive: `listserv@hearn.nic.surfnet.nl`

Language: French, English, Spanish

1-237 **CELTIC-L:** Celtic culture mailing list.

i `smaccona@ccvax.ucd.ie`

± `listserv@irlearn.bitnet` (Bitnet: LISTSERV@IRLEARN) [body = SUBSCRIBE CELTIC-L first-name last-name]

Archive: `listserv@irlearn.bitnet`

1-238 **CENASIA:** On all political, eonomic and military issues involving the central Asian republics of the former Soviet Union.

i `czgk@musica.mcgill.ca` (Keith Martin)

± `listserv@vm1.mcgill.ca` (Bitnet: LISTSERV@MCGILL1) [body = SUBSCRIBE CENASIA first-name last-name]

1-239 **CENTAM-L:** For interchange of academically oriented ideas regarding Central America.

i `michaelb@ksgrsch.harvard.edu` (Michael Blackmore)

± `listserv@ubvm.cc.buffalo.edu` (Bitnet: LISTSERV@UBVM) [body = SUBSCRIBE CENTAM-L first-name last-name]

Gated: ⇔ `bit.listserv.centam-l`

1-240 **CERRO-L:** On research of the Central Europe region.

i `gonter@awiwuw11.bitnet` (Bitnet: GONTER@AWIWUW11) (Gerhard Gonter)

± `listserv@helios.edvz.univie.ac.at` (Bitnet: LISTSERV@AEARN) [body = SUBSCRIBE CERRO-L first-name last-name]

Archive: `listserv@helios.edvz.univie.ac.at`

1-241 **CETH:** For postings from the Center for Electronic Texts in the Humanities at Brown University. *Moderated*

i `ceth@zodiac.rutgers.edu` (Christine Bohlen)

± `listserv@pucc.princeton.edu` (Bitnet: `LISTSERV@PUCC`) [body = SUBSCRIBE CETH first-name last-name]

Archive: Available to subscribers only.

1-242 **CFS-FILE:** Chronic Fatigue Syndrome medical files—a database of medical files on CFS and related illnesses.

i `cfs-file-request@sjuvm.stjohns.edu` (Molly Holzschlag)

± `listserv@sjuvm.stjohns.edu` (Bitnet: `LISTSERV@SJUVM`)[body = SUBSCRIBE CFS-FILE first-name last-name]

1-243 **CFS-L:** Chronic Fatigue Syndrome general discussion.

i `cfs-l-request@list.nih.gov` (Roger Burns)

± `listserv@list.nih.gov` (Bitnet: `LISTSERV@NIHLIST`) [body = SUBSCRIBE CFS-L first-name last-name]

Gated: ⇔ `alt.med.cfs`

1-244 **CFS-MED:** For M.D. clinicians to discuss diagnosis and treatment of Chronic Fatigue Syndrome.

i `cfs-med-request@list.nih.gov` (Roger Burns)

± `listserv@list.nih.gov` (Bitnet: `LISTSERV@NIHLIST`) [body = SUBSCRIBE CFS-MED first-name last-name]

1-245 **CFS-NEWS:** For the Chronic Fatigue Syndrome Electronic Newsletter, a monthly that covers CFS/CFIDS/ME medical news.

i `cfs-news@list.nih.gov` (Roger Burns)

± `listserv@list.nih.gov` (Bitnet: `LISTSERV@NIHLIST`) [body = SUBSCRIBE CFS-NEWS first-name last-name]

Gated: ⇔ `bit.listserv.cfs.newsletter`

1-246 **CFS-WIRE:** For newswire-style exchange of news articles and information among Chronic Fatigue Syndrome/CFIDS/ME support groups. *Moderated*

i `cfs-wire-request@sjuvm.stjohns.edu` or `cfs-me@sjuvm.stjohns.edu`

± `listserv@sjuvm.stjohns.edu` (Bitnet: `LISTSERV@SJUVM`)[body = SUBSCRIBE CFS-WIRE first-name last-name]

Gated: ⇔ `alt.med.cfs.wire`

1-247 **CGE:** On visualization and computer graphics.

i `jzem@marist.bitnet` (Bitnet: `JZEM@MARIST`) (William J. Joel)

± `listserv@vm.marist.edu` (Bitnet: `LISTSERV@MARIST`) [body = SUBSCRIBE CGE first-name last-name]

Archive: `listserv@vm.marist.edu`

1-248 **CGSA-L:** On the Chinese Graduate Student Association.

i `gerland@ubvms.cc.buffalo.edu` (Jim Gerland)

± `listserv@ubvm.cc.buffalo.edu` (Bitnet: LISTSERV@UBVM) [body = SUBSCRIBE CGSA-L first-name last-name]

1-249 **chalkhills:** On the music and recordings of the band XTC . *Moderated*

i ± `chalkhills-request@presto.ig.com` (John M. Relph)

Other: In digest format.

Archive: FTP `net.bio.net` in `/pub/misc/chalkhills`

1-250 **Chaosium Digest:** The Chaosium Digest is a weekly forum used to discuss Chaosium's role-playing games, including Call of Cthulhu, Elric!, Elfquest, Pendragon, and many others.

i ± `appel@erzo.berkeley.edu` (Shannon Appel)

1-251 **Chapman Stick:** On a stringed musical instrument called the Chapman, its technique, its players, its manufacturer, etc.

i ± `stick%moliere@uunet.uu.net` (Peter Krausler)

1-252 **CHATBACK:** For the SJU Chatback Planning Group.

i `drz@sjuvm.bitnet` (Bitnet: DRZ@SJUVM)

± `listserv@stjohns.edu` (Bitnet: LISTSERV@SJUVM) [body = SUBSCRIBE CHATBACK first-name last-name]

Archive: Available to subscribers only.

1-253 **chem-eng:** An electronic newsletter on chemical engineering.

i ± `trayms@cc.curtin.edu.au` (Dr. Martyn Ray)

1-254 **CHEMCORD:** For coordinators of general chemistry courses for colleges and universities.

i `wharwood@alsc.umd.edu` (William S. Harwood)

± `listserv@umdd.umd.edu` (Bitnet: LISTSERV@UMDD) [body = SUBSCRIBE CHEMCORD first-name last-name]

Archive: `listserv@umdd.umd.edu`

1-255 **CHEME-L:** On the role of chemical engineering in the world economy, including research trends, public and federal support, and education.

i `r0mira01@ulkyvm.bitnet` (Bitnet: R0MIRA01@ULKYVM) (Raul Miranda)

± `listserv@psuvm.psu.edu` (Bitnet: LISTSERV@PSUVM) [body = SUBSCRIBE CHEME-L first-name last-name]

1-256 **CHEMED-L:** On chemistry education at all grade levels.

i `whalpern@uwf.bitnet` (Bitnet: WHALPERN@UWF) (Bill Halpern)

± `listserv@uwf.cc.uwf.edu` (Bitnet: LISTSERV@UWF) [body = SUBSCRIBE CHEMED-L first-name last-name]

Archive: `listserv@uwf.cc.uwf.edu`

1-257 **CHEMIC-L:** On chemistry in Israel. *Moderated*

i `jo@ilncrd.bitnet` (Bitnet: JO@ILNCRD)

± `listserv@taunivm.tau.ac.il` (Bitnet: LISTSERV@TAUNIVM) [body = SUBSCRIBE CHEMIC-L first-name last-name]

1-258 **CHESS-L:** On chess, including tournaments, chess problems, and interesting games.

i `theodore@knosos.cc.uch.gr` (Theodore J. Soldatos)

± `listserv@grearn.bitnet` (Bitnet: LISTSERV@GREARN) [body = SUBSCRIBE

CHESS-L first-name last-name]

Archive: `listserv@grearn.bitnet`

1-259 **chessnews:** About chess played both by and against computers and humans.

i ± `chessnews-request@tssi.com`

Gated: ⇔ `rec.games.chess`

Other: In digest form.

1-260 **Chicago Area Showslist:** A weekly (usually) listing of upcoming rock and alternative shows in the Chicagoland area.

i ± `lclayton@uhuru.uchicago.edu` (Liz Clayton)

1-261 **CHICLE:** For Chicano Literature and Culture Exchange—includes music, dance, art, and theater. *Moderated*

i `tmarquez@unmb.bitnet` (Bitnet: `TMARQUEZ@UNMB`) (Teresa Marquez)

± `listserv@unmvma.unm.edu` (Bitnet: `LISTSERV@UNMVMA`) [body = SUBSCRIBE CHICLE first-name last-name]

Archive: Available to subscribers only.

Language: English, Spanish

1-262 **CHILE-L:** For discussion on Chile.

i `mladinic@usachvm1.bitnet` (Bitnet: `MLADINIC@USACHVM1`) (Antonio Mladinic)

± `listserv@usachvm1.usach.cl` (Bitnet: `LISTSERV@USACHVM1`) [body = SUBSCRIBE CHILE-L first-name last-name]

Archive: `listserv@usachvm1.usach.cl`

1-263 **CHILEHOY:** For news about Chile.

i `mladinic@usachvm1.bitnet` (Bitnet: `MLADINIC@USACHVM1`) (Antonio Mladinic)

± `listserv@usachvm1.usach.cl` (Bitnet: `LISTSERV@USACHVM1`) [body = SUBSCRIBE CHILEHOY first-name last-name]

Archive: `listserv@usachvm1.usach.cl`

1-264 **CHINA:** Chinese studies list. *Moderated*

i `q4356@pucc.bitnet` (Bitnet: `Q4356@PUCC`) (Tom Nimick and David Wright)

± `listserv@pucc.princeton.edu` (Bitnet: `LISTSERV@PUCC`) [body = SUBSCRIBE CHINA first-name last-name]

Archive: `listserv@pucc.princeton.edu`

Other: Subscription requests will be sent to list owners for approval. Owners require that all participants agree to abide by list guidelines.

1-265 **CHINA-NT:** The Coordination Network for the Independent Federation for Chinese Students and Scholars in USA (IFCSS) and other overseas Chinese student organizations.

i `c258p295@ubvm.bitnet` (Bitnet: `C258P295@UBVM`) (Weihe Guan)

± `listserv@uga.cc.uga.edu` (Bitnet: `LISTSERV@UGA`) [body = SUBSCRIBE CHINA-NT first-name last-name]

Archive: Available to subscribers only.

1-266 **CHMINF-L:** On chemical information sources.

i `wiggins@indiana.edu` (Gary Wiggins)

± `listserv@iubvm.ucs.indiana.edu` (Bitnet: LISTSERV@IUBVM) [body = SUBSCRIBE CHMINF-L first-name last-name]

Archive: `listserv@iubvm.ucs.indiana.edu`

1-267 **chorus:** Lesbian and gay chorus mailing list. Topics of discussion include repertoire, arrangements, staging, costuming, management, fundraising, music, events and concerts, and much more.

± `chorus-request@psych.toronto.edu` or `jschrag@alias.com` (John Schrag) or `jarvis@psych.toronto.edu` (Brian Jarvis)

1-268 **CHRISTIA:** For discussing practical Christian living—wide range of denominations, experiences, and scholarly backgrounds.

i `ispmom@asuacad.bitnet` (Bitnet: ISPMOM@ASUACAD) (Madge McBurney)

± `listserv@asuvm.inre.asu.edu` (Bitnet: LISTSERV@ASUACAD) [body = SUBSCRIBE CHRISTIA first-name last-name]

Archive: `listserv@asuvm.inre.asu.edu`

1-269 **CICS-L:** On CICS, a transaction-oriented system from IBM.

i `reichetz@awiimc12.bitnet` (Bitnet: REICHETZ@AWIIMC12) (Christian Reichetzeder) or
`christian.j.reichetzeder@awiimc12.imc.univie.ac.at`

± `listserv@vm.ucs.ualberta.ca` (Bitnet: LISTSERV@UALTAVM) [body = SUBSCRIBE CICS-L first-name last-name] or `listserv@utarlvm1.uta.edu` (Bitnet: LISTSERV@UTARLVM1) [body = SUBSCRIBE CICS-L first-name last-name] or `listserv@vm.akh-wien.ac.at` (Bitnet: LISTSERV@AWIIMC12) [body = SUBSCRIBE CICS-L first-name last-name] or `listserv@vm.marist.edu` (Bitnet: LISTSERV@MARIST) [body = SUBSCRIBE CICS-L first-name last-name] or `listserv@vm1.cc.uakron.edu` (Bitnet: LISTSERV@AKRONVM) [body = SUBSCRIBE CICS-L first-name last-name] or `listserv@uga.cc.uga.edu` (Bitnet: LISTSERV@UGA) [body = SUBSCRIBE CICS-L first-name last-name]

Archive: `listserv@vm.ucs.ualberta.ca` or `listserv@vm.marist.edu` or `listserv@vm.akh-wien.ac.at` or `listserv@uga.cc.uga.edu` or `listserv@vm1.cc.uakron.edu`

Gated: ⇔ `Bit.listserv.cics-l`

1-270 **CICSUG:** For users of CICS, an IBM product for developing end-user applications, at the Northeast Regional Data Center at the University of Florida.

i `jbigham@nervm.bitnet` (Bitnet: JBIGHAM@NERVM) or `durant@nervm.bitnet` (Bitnet: DURANT@NERVM)

± `listserv@nervm.nerdc.ufl.edu` (Bitnet: LISTSERV@NERVM) [body = SUBSCRIBE CICSUG first-name last-name]

1-271 **CINEMA-L:** Discussions about all aspects of cinema.

i `mike@wvnvm.bitnet` (Bitnet: MIKE@WVNVM) (Mike Karolchik)

± `listserv@american.edu` (Bitnet: LISTSERV@AUVM)[body = SUBSCRIBE

CINEMA-L first-name last-name]

Archive: `listserv@american.edu`

1-272 **CIO-L:** For higher education Chief Information Officers.

i `ricki@wvnvm.bitnet` (Bitnet: `RICKI@WVNVM`) (Ricki Dulin)

± `listserv@wvnvm.wvnet.edu` (Bitnet: `LISTSERV@WVNVM`) [body = SUBSCRIBE CIO-L first-name last-name]

1-273 **CIRCPLUS:** On library circulation issues.

i `alileste@idbsu.bitnet` (Bitnet: `ALILESTE@IDBSU`) (Dan Lester)

± `listserv@idbsu.idbsu.edu` (Bitnet: `LISTSERV@IDBSU`) [body = SUBSCRIBE CIRCPLUS first-name last-name]

Archive: `listserv@idbsu.idbsu.edu`

1-274 **cisco:** About network products from Cisco Systems, Inc.

i ± `cisco-request@spot.colorado.edu` (David Wood)

Archive: FTP `spot.Colorado.EDU` in `cisco`

Gated: ⇒ `comp.dcom.sys.cisco`

1-275 **CISDN-L:** For California ISDN users.

i `opsrjh@uccvma.bitnet` (Bitnet: `OPSRJH@UCCVMA`) (Richard Hintz)

± `listserv@uccvma.ucop.edu` (Bitnet: `LISTSERV@UCCVMA`) [body = SUBSCRIBE CISDN-L first-name last-name]

1-276 **CIVIL-L:** On civil engineering research and education.

i `eldo@unb.ca` (Eldo Hildebrand)

± `listserv@unb.ca` (Bitnet: `LISTSERV@UNBVM1`) [body = SUBSCRIBE CIVIL-L first-name last-name]

Archive: `listserv@unb.ca`

1-277 **CJ-L:** On the beliefs and practices of Conservative Judaism.

i `mark@csc.albany.edu` (Mark Steinberger)

± `listserv@uacsc2.albany.edu` (Bitnet: `LISTSERV@ALBNYVM1`) [body = SUBSCRIBE CJ-L first-name last-name]

Archive: `listserv@uacsc2.albany.edu`

Other: Subscription is limited. Requests will be sent to list owner for approval.

1-278 **CJKLIB-L:** For members of the European Association of Sinological Librarians (EASL) and anyone interested in the subject of librarianship of print materials in the languages of Chinese, Japanese, and Korean.

i `g42@vm.urz.uni-heidelberg.de` (Thomas Hahn)

± `listserv@dhdurz1.bitnet` (Bitnet: `LISTSERV@DHDURZ1`) [body = SUBSCRIBE CJKLIB-L first-name last-name]

1-279 **CJMOVIES:** The Journal of Criminal Justice and Popular Culture (ISSN 1070-8286) publishes reviews of movies with a criminal justice theme and refereed papers on criminal justice and popular culture. *Moderated*

i `sunycrj@albnyvm1.bitnet` (Bitnet: `SUNYCRJ@ALBNYVM1`) (Graeme Newman)

± `listserv@uacsc2.albany.edu` (Bitnet: `LISTSERV@ALBNYVM1`) [body =

SUBSCRIBE CJMOVIES first-name last-name]

    Archive: `listserv@uacsc2.albany.edu`

1-280 **CJUST-L:** Criminal Justice Discussion List.

    i `ahrjj@cunyvm.bitnet` (Bitnet: AHRJJ@CUNYVM) (Alex Rudd)

    ± `listserv@cunyvm.cuny.edu` (Bitnet: LISTSERV@CUNYVM) [body = SUBSCRIBE CJUST-L first-name last-name]

    Archive: Available to subscribers only.

1-281 **CLASSICS:** On all aspects of classical Greek and Latin scholarship.

    i `lwright@cac.washington.edu` (Linda Wright)

    ± `listserv@uwavm.u.washington.edu` (Bitnet: LISTSERV@UWAVM) [body = SUBSCRIBE CLASSICS first-name last-name]

    Archive: `listserv@uwavm.u.washington.edu`

1-282 **CLASSM-L:** On classical music.

    i `cyang@brownvm.bitnet` (Bitnet: CYANG@BROWNVM) (Catherine Yang)

    ± `listserv@brownvm.brown.edu` (Bitnet: LISTSERV@BROWNVM) [body = SUBSCRIBE CLASSM-L first-name last-name]

    Archive: `listserv@brownvm.brown.edu`

1-283 **CLASTALK:** For studying the sociometric relationships that develop using computer-mediated communication.

    i `ttreadwe@wcu.bitnet` (Bitnet: TTREADWE@WCU)

    ± `listserv@wcu.bitnet` (Bitnet: LISTSERV@WCU) [body = SUBSCRIBE CLASTALK first-name last-name]

    Archive: Available to subscribers only.

1-284 **CLEIP94:** For official information about the XX Latin American Informatics Congress, which will take place in Mexico City from September 19 to 23, 1994. *Moderated*

    i `tec-clei@itesmvf1.bitnet` (Bitnet: TEC-CLEI@ITESMVF1) (Sistemas de Informacion)

    ± `listserv@itesmvf1.rzs.itesm.mx` (Bitnet: LISTSERV@ITESMVF1) [body = SUBSCRIBE CLEIP94 first-name last-name]

1-285 **CLGSG-L:** Coalition of Lesbian/Gay Student Groups.

    i `glba@tamu.edu`

    ± `listserv@tamvm1.tamu.edu` (Bitnet: LISTSERV@TAMVM1) [body = SUBSCRIBE CLGSG-L first-name last-name]

    Other: Subscription is limited. Requests will be sent to list owner for approval.

1-286 **CLIMLIST:** For distribution of information to professionals working in the field of climatology, including conferences, research reports, funding and study opportunities, and data availability. *Moderated*

    i `aja+@osu.edu` (John Arnfield)

    ± `listserv@psuvm.psu.edu` (Bitnet: LISTSERV@PSUVM) [body = SUBSCRIBE CLIMLIST first-name last-name]

    Archive: Available to subscribers only.

Other: Weekly digest. Subscription is limited. Requests will be sent to list owner for approval.

1-287 **CLINALRT:** For clinical alerts from the National Institutes of Health, which are issued irregularly (above one every six months), and intended for medical professionals.

   i gfreibur@umab.bitnet (Bitnet: GFREIBUR@UMAB) (Gary Freiburger)

   ± listserv@umab.umd.edu (Bitnet: LISTSERV@UMAB) [body = SUBSCRIBE CLINALRT first-name last-name]

   Archive: listserv@umab.umd.edu

1-288 **CLINTON:** Discussion of the presidency of Bill Clinton.

   i urls@marist.bitnet (Bitnet: URLS@MARIST) (Lee Sakkas)

   ± listserv@vm.marist.edu (Bitnet: LISTSERV@MARIST) [body = SUBSCRIBE CLINTON first-name last-name]

   Archive: listserv@vm.marist.edu

1-289 **CLIOLOGY:** On theories of history.

   i todd.gernes@um.cc.umich (Todd S. Gernes)

   ± listserv@msu.edu (Bitnet: LISTSERV@MSU) [body = SUBSCRIBE CLIOLOGY first-name last-name]

   Archive: listserv@msu.edu

   Other: Subscription is limited. Requests will be sent to list owner for approval.

1-290 **CMSPIP-L:** For users of CMS Pipelines, part of IBM's VM/CMS operating system.

   i reichetz@awiimc12.bitnet (Bitnet: REICHETZ@AWIIMC12) (Christian Reichetzeder)

   ± listserv@vm.akh-wien.ac.at (Bitnet: LISTSERV@AWIIMC12) [body = SUBSCRIBE CMSPIP-L first-name last-name] or listserv@vm.marist.edu (Bitnet: LISTSERV@MARIST) [body = SUBSCRIBE CMSPIP-L first-name last-name]

   Archive: listserv@vm.akh-wien.ac.at or listserv@vm.marist.edu

1-291 **CNC-L:** The China News—Canada.

   i cnc-l-request@uvvm.uvic.ca (China News Canada) or klassen@uvvm.bitnet (Bitnet: KLASSEN@UVVM) (Melvin Klassen)

   ± listserv@uvvm.uvic.ca (Bitnet: LISTSERV@UVVM) [body = SUBSCRIBE CNC-L first-name last-name]

1-292 **CNET-OP:** Information about CINECA (Italian research organization) and its networks (CINECAnet/GARR).

   i anr0@icineca.bitnet (Bitnet: ANR0@ICINECA) (Gabriele Neri)

   ± listserv@icineca.cineca.it (Bitnet: LISTSERV@ICINECA) [body = SUBSCRIBE CNET-OP first-name last-name]

   Archive: Available to subscribers only.

1-293 **CNETIE-L:** For discussion and sharing of information among those involved in international education within or outside of Canada, on matters related to international education of concern to Canada.

  i kt_kwee@ic.ualberta.ca (K. T. Kwee) or barry_tonge@ic.ualberta.ca
  (Barry Tonge)

  ± listserv@vm.ucs.ualberta.ca (Bitnet: LISTSERV@UALTAVM) [body =
  SUBSCRIBE CNETIE-L first-name last-name institution]

  Archive: Available to subscribers only.

  Gated: ⇔ bit.listserv.CNETIE-L

1-294 **CNI-ARCH:** For the Coalition for Networked Information Architecture and Standards

  i opsrjh@uccvma.bitnet (Bitnet: OPSRJH@UCCVMA) (Richard Hintz)

  ± listserv@uccvma.ucop.edu (Bitnet: LISTSERV@UCCVMA) [body = SUBSCRIBE
  CNI-ARCH first-name last-name]

  Archive: Available to subscribers only.

1-295 **CNPQ-L:** For support of research projects by Brazilian university students.

  i josi@brfapesp.bitnet (Bitnet: JOSI@BRFAPESP) (Josefina Perez Alvarez) or
  s.cacp@cnpq.andf.br (Carlos Campana)

  ± listserv@vm1.lcc.ufmg.br (Bitnet: LISTSERV@BRUFMG) [body = SUBSCRIBE
  CNPQ-L first-name last-name]

  Language: Portuguese

1-296 **COAACAD:** On the SUNY COA Academic Subcommittee.

  i gerland@ubvms.cc.buffalo.edu (Jim Gerland)

  ± listserv@ubvm.cc.buffalo.edu (Bitnet: LISTSERV@UBVM) [body =
  SUBSCRIBE COAACAD first-name last-name]

  Archive: listserv@ubvm.cc.buffalo.edu

  Gated: ⇔ bit.listserv.coaacad

1-297 **COASTGIS:** On coastal applications of geographical information systems (GIS)—to further the
  work of the International Geographical Union Commission on Coastal Systems.

  i stgg8004@iruccvax.ucc.ie (Darius Bartlett)

  ± listserv@irlearn.bitnet (Bitnet: LISTSERV@IRLEARN) [body = SUBSCRIBE
  COASTGIS first-name last-name]

  Archive: Available to subscribers only.

1-298 **COCAMED:** On computers in Canadian medical education.

  i grace.paterson@dal.ca (Grace Paterson)

  ± listserv@utoronto.bitnet (Bitnet: LISTSERV@UTORONTO) [body =
  SUBSCRIBE COCAMED first-name last-name]

  Archive: listserv@utoronto.bitnet

1-299 **COCO:** All about all models of the Tandy Color Computer. Includes software reviews, helpful
  hints, assembly language, support for Microware's OS9 and OSK operating system, and discussion on the various OSK upgrade platforms for the CoCo.

  i steve@wuarchive.wustl.edu (Steve Wegert)

  ± listserv@pucc.princeton.edu (Bitnet: LISTSERV@PUCC) [body =
  SUBSCRIBE COCO first-name last-name]

Archive: `listserv@pucc.princeton.edu`

Gated: ⇔ `bit.listserv.coco`

1-300 **coins:** On numismatics and collecting in general but with limited talk on trading and exchange of collectable items.

± `coins-request@uni.edu`

Other: New members are asked to provide the other list members with a very brief biographical sketch and information about their numismatic collecting, writing, etc. interests.

1-301 **COLA-L:** For academics and practitioners who are interested in analytical models for locating facilities.

i `erhan_erkut@mts.ucs.ualberta.ca` (Erhan Erkut)

± `listserv@vm.ucs.ualberta.ca` (Bitnet: `LISTSERV@UALTAVM`) [body = SUBSCRIBE COLA-L first-name last-name]

Gated: ⇔ `bit.listserv.cola-l`

1-302 **COLEXT:** For Columbians who live outside Columbia.

i `jfarjona@andescol.bitnet` (Bitnet: `JFARJONA@ANDESCOL`) (Juan Felipe Arjona) or `jauus@cuvmb.bitnet` (Bitnet: `JAUUS@CUVMB`) (Jerry Altzman)

± `listserv@cuvmb.cc.columbia.edu` (Bitnet: `LISTSERV@CUVMB`) [body = SUBSCRIBE COLEXT first-name last-name] or `listserv@andescol.uniandes.edu.co` (Bitnet: `LISTSERV@ANDESCOL`) [body = SUBSCRIBE COLEXT first-name last-name]

1-303 **COMEDIA:** A discussion of Spanish Golden Age theater.

i `jabraham@ccit.arizona.edu` (James Abraham) or `vwilliam@ccit.arizona.edu` (Vern Williamsen)

± `listserv@arizvm1.ccit.arizona.edu` (Bitnet: `LISTSERV@ARIZVM1`) [body = SUBSCRIBE COMEDIA first-name last-name]

Archive: `listserv@arizvm1.ccit.arizona.edu`

Language: English, Spanish

1-304 **COMICS-L:** About comics. *Moderated*

i `ianr012@unlvm.bitnet` (Bitnet: `IANR012@UNLVM`) (Bill Hayes)

± `listserv@unlvm.unl.edu` (Bitnet: `LISTSERV@UNLVM`) [body = SUBSCRIBE COMICS-L first-name last-name]

1-305 **COMICW-L:** The Comic Writers Workshop.

i `ianr012@unlvm.bitnet` (Bitnet: `IANR012@UNLVM`) (Bill Hayes)

± `listserv@unlvm.unl.edu` (Bitnet: `LISTSERV@UNLVM`) [body = SUBSCRIBE COMICW-L first-name last-name]

Other: Subscription is limited. Requests will be sent to list owner for approval.

1-306 **comix:** On non-mainstream and independent comic books. Little about superheroes and nothing about Marvel Mutants.

i ± `comix-request@world.std.com` (Elizabeth Lear Newman)

1-307 **COMMCOLL:** For community and/or junior colleges.

    i `jccannek@ukcc.bitnet` (Bitnet: JCCANNEK@UKCC) (Anne Kearney)

    ± `listserv@ukcc.uky.edu` (Bitnet: LISTSERV@UKCC) [body = SUBSCRIBE COMMCOLL first-name last-name]

    Other: Subscription is limited. Requests will be sent to list owner for approval.

1-308 **COMMODOR:** On Commodore computers.

    i `bpoelln1@ua1vm.bitnet` (Bitnet: BPOELLN1@UA1VM) (Brian W. Poellnitz / Gandalf)

    ± `listserv@ubvm.cc.buffalo.edu` (Bitnet: LISTSERV@UBVM) [body = SUBSCRIBE COMMODOR first-name last-name]

    Archive: `listserv@ubvm.cc.buffalo.edu`

1-309 **COMMUNET:** On community computer networks, including Free-Nets, city BBSes, information kiosks, and downtown information systems, Indian reservation networks, community computer conferencing systems, interactive systems run by newspapers, rural and regional area networks.

    i `sjc@uvmvm.uvm.edu` (Steve Cavrak)

    ± `listserv@uvmvm.uvm.edu` (Bitnet: LISTSERV@UVMVM) [body = SUBSCRIBE COMMUNET first-name last-name]

    Archive: Available to subscribers only.

1-310 **COMP-CEN:** On computer center managers' issues.

    i `opsrjh@uccvma.bitnet` (Bitnet: OPSRJH@UCCVMA) (Richard Hintz)

    ± `listserv@uccvma.ucop.edu` (Bitnet: LISTSERV@UCCVMA) [body = SUBSCRIBE COMP-CEN first-name last-name]

    Archive: Available to subscribers only.

1-311 **COMPMED:** All about comparative medicine, laboratory animals (all species), and related subjects.

    i `ken@wudcm.wustl.edu` (Ken Boschert)

    ± `listserv@wuvmd.wustl.edu` (Bitnet: LISTSERV@WUVMD) [body = SUBSCRIBE COMPMED first-name last-name]

    Archive: Available to subscribers only.

    Other: Subscription is limited. Requests will be sent to list owner for approval.

1-312 **COMSOC-L:** Discussion of the social impact of computers and computer-related technologies.

    Moderated

    i `socicom@auvm.american.edu` (Greg Welsh)

    ± `listserv@american.edu` (Bitnet: LISTSERV@AUVM) [body = SUBSCRIBE COMSOC-L first-name last-name]

    Archive: `listserv@american.edu`

    Other: Daily digest

1-313 **concrete-blonde:** On the rock group Concrete Blonde and related artists and issues.

    i `rearl@oinker.ucsb.edu` (Robert Earl)

    ± `concrete-blonde-request@oinker.ucsb.edu` [subject = subscribe]

Archive: `concrete-blonde-request@oinker.ucsb.edu` [subject = `send archive` or `discography` or `charter` or `list`]

1-314 **CONFOCAL:** On confocal microscopy.

i `summers@ubmed.buffalo.edu` (Robert Summers)

± `listserv@ubvm.cc.buffalo.edu` (Bitnet: LISTSERV@UBVM) [body = `SUBSCRIBE CONFOCAL` first-name last-name]

Archive: `listserv@ubvm.cc.buffalo.edu`

Gated: ⇔ `bit.listserv.confocal`

1-315 **CONSBIO:** Society for Conservation Biology list on conservation biology and biodiversity.

i `pdh@stein.u.washington.edu` (Preston D. Hardison)

± `listserv@uwavm.u.washington.edu` (Bitnet: LISTSERV@UWAVM) [body = `SUBSCRIBE CONSBIO` first-name last-name]

Archive: `listserv@uwavm.u.washington.edu`

1-316 **CONSGIS:** On biological conservation and geographical information systems.

i `pete@edcserv.edc.uri.edu`

± `listserv@uriacc.uri.edu` (Bitnet: LISTSERV@URIACC) [body = `SUBSCRIBE CONSGIS` first-name last-name]

Archive: `listserv@uriacc.uri.edu`

1-317 **CONSIM-L:** On conflict simulation games.

i `hgerber@vm.ucs.ualberta.ca` (Hjalmar Gerber) or `postmast@vm.ucs.ualberta.ca` (Postmaster)

± `listserv@vm.ucs.ualberta.ca` (Bitnet: LISTSERV@UALTAVM) [body = `SUBSCRIBE CONSIM-L` first-name last-name]

Gated: ⇔ `bit.listserv.consim-1`

1-318 **CONSLINK:** On biological conservation.

i `nzpem001@sivm.bitnet` (Bitnet: NZPEM001@SIVM) (Michael Stuwe)

± `listserv@sivm.si.edu` (Bitnet: LISTSERV@SIVM) [body = `SUBSCRIBE CONSLINK` first-name last-name]

Archive: `listserv@sivm.si.edu`

1-319 **CONSLT-L:** For members of the International Mentoring Association for discussion on issues, research, practical applications, and funding for mentoring programs.

i `brescia@iubacs.bitnet` (Bitnet: BRESCIA@IUBACS) (Bill Brescia)

± `listserv@iubvm.ucs.indiana.edu` (Bitnet: LISTSERV@IUBVM) [body = `SUBSCRIBE CONSLT-L` first-name last-name]

Archive: Available to subscribers only.

Other: Subscription is limited. Requests will be sent to list owner for approval.

1-320 **COOPCAT:** On cooperative cataloging.

i `carwalt@nervm.bitnet` (Bitnet: CARWALT@NERVM)

± `listserv@nervm.nerdc.ufl.edu` (Bitnet: LISTSERV@NERVM) [body = `SUBSCRIBE COOPCAT` first-name last-name]

Archive: `listserv@nervm.nerdc.ufl.edu`

1-321 **CORRYFEE:** On economics, econometrics, and management science. *Moderated*

　　i a608hans@hasara11.bitnet (Bitnet: A608HANS@HASARA11)

　　± listserv@hasara11.bitnet (Bitnet: LISTSERV@HASARA11) [body = SUBSCRIBE CORRYFEE first-name last-name]

　　Archive: listserv@hasara11.bitnet

1-322 **COUNCIL:** For the Global Council Forum on moving beyond the nation-state.

　　i lefevre@sjsuvm1.bitnet (Bitnet: LEFEVRE@SJSUVM1) (Martin Lefevre)

　　± listserv@sjsuvm1.sjsu.edu (Bitnet: LISTSERV@SJSUVM1) [body = SUBSCRIBE COUNCIL first-name last-name]

　　Archive: listserv@sjsuvm1.sjsu.edu

1-323 **COUNTY-L:** Representatives from all counties in Virginia on LGNET, a local government network.

　　i harngton@vtvm1.bitnet (Bitnet: HARNGTON@VTVM1) (Marcia A. Harrington)

　　± listserv@vtvm1.cc.vt.edu (Bitnet: LISTSERV@VTVM1) [body = SUBSCRIBE COUNTY-L first-name last-name]

　　Archive: Available to subscribers only.

1-324 **CPE-LIST:** Computer Performance Evaluation.

　　i lyman@unchmvs.unch.unc.edu (Lyman Ripperton)

　　± listserv@uncvm1.oit.unc.edu (Bitnet: LISTSERV@UNCVM1) [body = SUBSCRIBE CPE-LIST first-name last-name]

　　Archive: listserv@uncvm1.oit.unc.edu

1-325 **CPGIS-L:** On Chinese geographic information systems.

　　i esrixia@ubvms.bitnet (Bitnet: ESRIXIA@UBVMS) (Fuxiang Xia) or c258p295@ubvm.bitnet (Bitnet: C258P295@UBVM) (Weihe Guan)

　　± listserv@ubvm.cc.buffalo.edu (Bitnet: LISTSERV@UBVM) [body = SUBSCRIBE CPGIS-L first-name last-name]

　　Archive: listserv@ubvm.cc.buffalo.edu

1-326 **CPRI-L:** On computerized patient records and telecommunications in healthcare/social services.

　　i dv02@academia.swt.edu (Deanie French)

　　± listserv@ukanaix.cc.ukans.edu [body = subscribe cpri-l first-name last-name]

　　Other: Unix list processor software and not LISTSERV.

1-327 **CREAD:** Latin American and Caribbean electronic distance education forum.

　　i lanfran@yorkvm1.bitnet (Bitnet: LANFRAN@YORKVM1) (Sam Lanfranco)

　　± listserv@yorkvm1.bitnet (Bitnet: LISTSERV@YORKVM1) [body = SUBSCRIBE CREAD first-name last-name]

　　Archive: Available to subscribers only.

1-328 **CREWRT-L:** Creative writing in education for teachers and students.

　　i lceric@mizzou1.bitnet (Bitnet: LCERIC@MIZZOU1) (Eric Crump)

　　± listserv@mizzou1.missouri.edu (Bitnet: LISTSERV@MIZZOU1) [body = SUBSCRIBE CREWRT-L first-name last-name]

Archive: `listserv@mizzou1.missouri.edu`

1-329 **CRIC-L:** On semiotics of culture, or the study of culture as a sign and as a composite of systems of signifiers.

i `mbeaudoi@muskwa.ucs.ualberta.ca` (Martin Beaudoin)

± `listserv@vm.ucs.ualberta.ca` (Bitnet: `LISTSERV@UALTAVM`) [body = `SUBSCRIBE CRIC-L` first-name last-name]

Archive: Available to subscribers only.

Gated: ⇔ `bit.listserv.cric-1`

Language: English, French

1-330 **Cro-News:** News coming from Croatia.

Language: Croatian, English, and occasionally Slovene

i ± `cro-news-request@medphys.ucl.ac.uk` (Nino Margetic)

1-331 **Cro-Views:** Discussions on Croatia and other former-Yugoslav republics. Sometimes heated. Civility required.

i ± `joe@mullara.met.unimelb.edu.au` (Joe Stojsic)

1-332 **CROMED-L:** On current events in Croatia, particularly in the sphere of medicine. *Moderated*

i `neven.henigsberg@x400.srce.hr`

± `listserv@helios.edvz.univie.ac.at` (Bitnet: `LISTSERV@AEARN`) [body = `SUBSCRIBE CROMED-L` first-name last-name]

Archive: Available to subscribers only.

Other: Subscription is limited. Requests will be sent to list owner for approval.

1-333 **CROSS-L:** On research in cross-cultural information systems.

i `evaristo@diana.cair.du.edu` (Roberto Evaristo)

± `listserv@vm1.spcs.umn.edu` (Bitnet: `LISTSERV@UMINN1`) [body = `SUBSCRIBE CROSS-L` first-name last-name]

Archive: Available to subscribers only.

Other: Subscription is limited. Requests will be sent to list owner for approval.

1-334 **crossfire:** On the developement of the multiplayer graphical arcade game for X-windows environments.

i `owner-crossfire@ifi.uio.no` (Frank Tore Johansen)

± `crossfire-request@ifi.uio.no`

Archive: FTP `ftp.ifi.uio.no` in `/pub/crossfire/archive/`

1-335 **Crowded House:** On Crowded House and related rock groups (Split Enz, Tim Finn, The Makers, etc.).

i `marck@nwu.edu` (Marck L. Bailey)

± `house-request@casbah.acns.nwu.edu`

Archive: FTP `ftp.acns.nwu.edu` in `/pub/crowded-house/` (includes articles, discography, lyrics, chords, and tablature of all songs)

Other: For digest version, send subscription request to `house-digest-request@casbah.acns.nwu.edu`

1-336   **CRTNET:** A magazine about communication research and theory. *Moderated*

     i `t3b@psuvm.bitnet` (Bitnet: `T3B@PSUVM`) (Tom Benson)

     ± `listserv@psuvm.psu.edu` (Bitnet: `LISTSERV@PSUVM`) [body = `SUBSCRIBE CRTNET` first-name last-name]

     Archive: `listserv@psuvm.psu.edu`

1-337   **CRUST-L:** On crustacean systematics, distribution, and ecology.

     i `mnhiv002@sivm.bitnet` (Bitnet: `MNHIV002@SIVM`) (Jan Clark) or `mnhiv040@sivm.bitnet` (Bitnet: `MNHIV040@SIVM`) (Jim Thomas)

     ± `listserv@sivm.si.edu` (Bitnet: `LISTSERV@SIVM`) [body = `SUBSCRIBE CRUST-L` first-name last-name]

1-338   **cryonics:** The cryonics mailing list includes the news from the Usenet `sci.cryonics` newsgroup (biochemistry of memory, low temperature biology, new research and publications, conferences, cryonics facility design, nanotechnology ,and cell repair machines) plus many cryonics issues not appropriate for a Usenet `sci.*` newsgroup (organizational issues confronting the cryonics groups, mass media coverage of cryonics, local cryonics group meetings, legal status of cryonics, and cryonically suspended people).

     i ± `kqb@whscad1.att.com` (Kevin Q. Brown)

     Archive: Available to list members.

1-339   **CRYPTO-L:** On cryptology and related mathematics. *Moderated*

     i `shizuya@jpntuvm0.bitnet` (Bitnet: `SHIZUYA@JPNTUVM0`) (Hiroki Shizuya)

     ± `listserv@jpntuvm0.bitnet` (Bitnet: `LISTSERV@JPNTUVM0`) [body = `SUBSCRIBE CRYPTO-L` first-name last-name]

     Archive: `listserv@jpntuvm0.bitnet`

     Other: Subscription is limited. Requests will be sent to list owner for approval.

1-340   **CS1OBJ-L:** On teaching object-oriented programming to first-year students. *Moderated*

     i `rhm1@psuvm.bitnet` (Bitnet: `RHM1@PSUVM`) (Richard Mercer)

     ± `listserv@psuvm.psu.edu` (Bitnet: `LISTSERV@PSUVM`) [body = `SUBSCRIBE CS1OBJ-L` first-name last-name]

     Archive: `listserv@psuvm.psu.edu`

1-341   **CSAA:** Announcements for Amiga users. Includes posts on product releases, updates, shows and events, etc. *Moderated*

     Gated: ⇔ `Comp.Sys.Amiga.Announce`

     i `zerkle@cs.ucdavis.edu` (Dan Zerkle)

     ± `announce-request@cs.ucdavis.edu` (Carlos Amezaga)

     Archive: FTP `litamiga.epfl.ch`

1-342   **CSEA-L:** On visual arts education in Canada.

     i `dsoucy@unb.ca` (Don Soucy)

     ± `listserv@unb.ca` (Bitnet: `LISTSERV@UNBVM1`) [body = `SUBSCRIBE CSEA-L` first-name last-name]

1-343   **CSEMLIST:** On computational methods in economics and econometrics. *Moderated*

     i `a608hans@hasara11.bitnet` (Bitnet: `A608HANS@HASARA11`)

± `listserv@hasara11.bitnet` (Bitnet: `LISTSERV@HASARA11`) [body = SUBSCRIBE CSEMLIST first-name last-name]

Archive: `listserv@hasara11.bitnet`

1-344 **CSG-L:** For discussion among the Control Systems Group Network (CSGnet), a behavioral science group interested inPerceptual Control Theory (PCT).

i `cziko@uiucvmd.bitnet` (Bitnet: `CZIKO@UIUCVMD`) (Gary A. Cziko)

± `listserv@vmd.cso.uiuc.edu` (Bitnet: `LISTSERV@UIUCVMD`) [body = SUBSCRIBE CSG-L first-name last-name]

Archive: `listserv@vmd.cso.uiuc.edu`

1-345 **CSP-L:** For users of Cross System Product, an IBM mainframe 4GL application development and execution environment that allows embedding of SQL/DS, DB/2, VSAM databases.

i `sysadm4@trearn.bitnet` (Bitnet: `SYSADM4@TREARN`) (Suleyman N. Kutlu)

± `listserv@trearn.bitnet` (Bitnet: `LISTSERV@TREARN`) [body = SUBSCRIBE CSP-L first-name last-name]

Archive: `listserv@trearn.bitnet`

1-346 **CSSE-L:** For members of the Canadian Society for the Study of Education, for discussion of Society issues, educational issues in Canada, and how international educational issues might effect Canadian education.

i `craig_montgomerie@admin.educ.ualberta.ca`

± `listserv@vm.ucs.ualberta.ca` (Bitnet: `LISTSERV@UALTAVM`) [body = SUBSCRIBE CSSE-L first-name last-name]

Archive: Available to subscribers only.

Gated: ⇔ `bit.listserv.csse-l`

Other: Subscription is limited. Requests will be sent to list owner for approval.

1-347 **CTURTLE:** On sea turtle biology and conservation.

i `abb@gnv.ifas.ufl.edu`

± `listserv@nervm.nerdc.ufl.edu` (Bitnet: `LISTSERV@NERVM`) [body = SUBSCRIBE CTURTLE first-name last-name]

1-348 **CTYTWN-L:** Representatives from cities and towns in Virginia on LGNET, a local government network.

i `harngton@vtvm1.bitnet` (Bitnet: `HARNGTON@VTVM1`) (Marcia A. Harrington)

± `listserv@vtvm1.cc.vt.edu` (Bitnet: `LISTSERV@VTVM1`) [body = SUBSCRIBE CTYTWN-L first-name last-name]

Archive: `listserv@vtvm1.cc.vt.edu`

1-349 **CUBA-L:** On contemporary Cuba.

i `nvaldes@unmb.bitnet` (Bitnet: `NVALDES@UNMB`) (Nelson Valdes)

± `listserv@unmvma.unm.edu` (Bitnet: `LISTSERV@UNMVMA`) [body = SUBSCRIBE CUBA-L first-name last-name]

Archive: Available to subscribers only.

Language: Spanish, English

1-350 **CUFMA-L:** On the College and University Facilities Management Association/NYS.

> *i* kskenyon@suvm.bitnet (Bitnet: KSKENYON@SUVM) (Kevin S. Kenyon, 2272)

> ± listserv@suvm.acs.syr.edu (Bitnet: LISTSERV@SUVM) [body = SUBSCRIBE CUFMA-L first-name last-name]

> **Other:** Subscription is limited. Requests will be sent to list owner for approval.

1-351 **CUFS-L:** A discussion of the CUFS system.

> *i* jelipnic@miamiu.bitnet (Bitnet: JELIPNIC@MIAMIU) (Jim Lipnickey)

> ± listserv@miamiu.acs.muohio.edu (Bitnet: LISTSERV@MIAMIU) [body = SUBSCRIBE CUFS-L first-name last-name]

> **Archive:** Available to subscribers only.

1-352 **CURIA-L:** On the Curia database of Irish literature (the Thesaurus Linguarum Hiberniae).

> *i* cbts8001@iruccvax.bitnet (Bitnet: CBTS8001@IRUCCVAX)

> ± listserv@irlearn.bitnet (Bitnet: LISTSERV@IRLEARN) [body = SUBSCRIBE CURIA-L first-name last-name]

> **Archive:** listserv@irlearn.bitnet

1-353 **CUSSNET:** CUSSNET is Computer Users in the Social Sciences. About the use of computers by social workers, counselors, and human service workers of all disciplines.

> *i* cussnet-request@stat.com

> ± [body = subscribe cussnet]

1-354 **CYAN-TOX:** For exchange of information about cyanobacterial toxins, toxic cyanobacteria (blue-green algae) and related topics.

> *i* cdaz02@grtheun1.bitnet (Bitnet: CDAZ02@GRTHEUN1) (Tom Lanaras)

> ± listserv@grearn.bitnet (Bitnet: LISTSERV@GREARN) [body = SUBSCRIBE CYAN-TOX first-name last-name]

> **Archive:** Available to subscribers only.

1-355 **CYBERLAW-L:** On the law and policy of computer networks

> *i* thardy@mail.wm.edu (Trotter Hardy)

> ± listserv@listserv.cc.wm.edu (Bitnet: LISTSERV@WMVM1) [body = SUBSCRIBE CYBERLAW first-name last-name]

> **Archive:** Available to subscribers only.

1-356 **CYBSYS-L:** For interdisciplinary discussion of systems science, cybernetics, and related fields.
> *Moderated*

> *i* cybsys@bingsuns.cc.binghamton.edu (CYBSYS-L Moderator)

> ± listserv@bingvmb.cc.binghamton.edu (Bitnet: LISTSERV@BINGVMB) [body = SUBSCRIBE CYBSYS-L first-name last-name]

1-357 **CYCOOP-L:** On cooperation between industry and universities.

> *i* plonski2@bruspvm.bitnet (Guilherme Ary Plonski)

> ± listserv@bruspvm.bitnet (Bitnet: LISTSERV@BRUSPVM) [body = SUBSCRIBE CYCOOP-L first-name last-name]

> **Archive:** Available to subscribers only.

> **Language:** Portugese, Spanish, English

1-358 **CZ:** The Convergence Zone (CZ). For discussion of the Harpoon naval wargame series and related topics.

 Other: In digest format.

 i ± `cz-request@stsci.edu` (Tom Comeau)

 Archive: FTP in USA: `sunbane.engrg.uwo.ca` in `pub/harpoon` Europe: `ftp.cs.vu.nl` in `harpoon` or `jumi.lut.fi` in `pub/harpoon` (CZ and Computer Scenarios for Amiga, Mac, PC)

1-359 **CZE-ITP:** Discussion on problems of capillary electrophoretic methods.

 i `vdolnik@csbrmu11.bitnet`

 ± `listserv@csbrmu11.bitnet` (Bitnet: `LISTSERV@CSBRMU11`) [body = SUBSCRIBE CZE-ITP first-name last-name]

 Archive: `listserv@csbrmu11.bitnet`

1-360 **DAL-L:** On DAL (data access language), a "middleware" product for databases sold by Apple Computer that is used to add syntax for procedures, conditionals, and control structures.

 i `repa@mitvma.mit.edu` (Jim Repa) or `rosenberg@mit.edu` (David Rosenberg)

 ± `listserv@mitvma.mit.edu` (Bitnet: `LISTSERV@MITVMA`) [body = SUBSCRIBE DAL-L first-name last-name]

 Archive: `listserv@mitvma.mit.edu`

1-361 **DALNET:** On the Detroit area library network, primarily concerned with the NOTIS installation. *Moderated*

 i `wkane@waynest1.bitnet` (Bitnet: `WKANE@WAYNEST1`) (William Kane)

 ± `listserv@cms.cc.wayne.edu` (Bitnet: `LISTSERV@WAYNEST1`) [body = SUBSCRIBE DALNET first-name last-name]

 Archive: `listserv@cms.cc.wayne.edu`

1-362 **Dan Hicks:** On Dan Hicks (Hot Licks, Acoustic Warriors), past and present.

 i ± `sramirez@sedona.intel.com` (Steve Ramirez)

1-363 **DANCE-L:** On international folk- and traditional dance

 i `xyz@rcl.wau.nl` (Leo A.M. van der Heijden)

 ± `listserv@hearn.nic.surfnet.nl` (Bitnet: `LISTSERV@HEARN`) [body = SUBSCRIBE DANCE-L first-name last-name]

 Archive: `listserv@hearn.nic.surfnet.nl`

1-364 **DARGON-L:** For writers for the Dargon Project, a shared world writing project.

 i `white@duvm.bitnet` (Bitnet: `WHITE@DUVM`) (Dafydd, Dargon Project Coordinator)

 ± `listserv@brownvm.brown.edu` (Bitnet: `LISTSERV@BROWNVM`) [body = SUBSCRIBE DARGON-L first-name last-name]

 Other: Subscription is limited. Requests will be sent to list owner for approval.

1-365 **DARS-L:** Degree Audit Reporting System, which tracks a college student's progress towards an academic degree.

 i `southard@miamiu.bitnet` (Bitnet: `SOUTHARD@MIAMIU`) (Jack Southard)

 ± `listserv@miamiu.acs.muohio.edu` (Bitnet: `LISTSERV@MIAMIU`) [body = SUBSCRIBE DARS-L first-name last-name]

Archive: Available to subscribers only.

Language: English

1-366 **DARWIN-L:** Methodologies of the Historical Sciences

   i lhnelson@ukanvm.bitnet (Bitnet: LHNELSON@UKANVM) or
     dawin@iris.uncg.edu

   ± listserv@ukanaix.cc.ukans.edu (Bitnet: LISTSERV@UKANAIX) [body =
     SUBSCRIBE DARWIN-L first-name last-name]

   Archive: listserv@ukanaix.cc.ukans.edu

1-367 **DASP-L:** On digital acoustic signal processing.

   i fkadlec@csearn.bitnet (Bitnet: FKADLEC@CSEARN) (Frantisek Kadlec)

   ± listserv@csearn.bitnet (Bitnet: LISTSERV@CSEARN) [body = SUBSCRIBE
     DASP-L first-name last-name]

   Archive: listserv@csearn.bitnet

   Language: English

1-368 **DATANET:** On social sciences in Israel, emphasis on empirical research.

   i keumb@hujivm1.bitnet (Bitnet: KEUMB@HUJIVM1) (Michael Beenstock) or
     michalp@hujivms.bitnet (Bitnet: MICHALP@HUJIVMS) (Michal Peleg)

   ± listserv@taunivm.tau.ac.il (Bitnet: LISTSERV@TAUNIVM) [body =
     SUBSCRIBE DATANET first-name last-name]

   Archive: Available to subscribers only.

1-369 **DATAPERF:** For users of the DataPerfect software, created to facilitate communication among
   users of the database software. *Moderated*

   i harness@wsuvm1.bitnet (Bitnet: HARNESS@WSUVM1)

   ± listserv@wsuvm1.csc.wsu.edu (Bitnet: LISTSERV@WSUVM1) [body =
     SUBSCRIBE DATAPERF first-name last-name]

   Archive: listserv@wsuvm1.csc.wsu.edu

1-370 **datsun-roadsters:** To discuss any and all aspects of owning, showing, repairing, driving, etc.
   Datsun roadsters.

   i ± datsun-roadsters-request@autox.team.net (Mark J. Bradakis)

1-371 **David Bowie:** For fans of David Bowie.

   ± spiders@phoenix.imag.fr [subject = Bowie subscription]

   Other: Weekly digest

   Archive: FTP phoenix.imag.fr in /pub/morel/

1-372 **DBLIST:** On computers and infomatics issues related to dentistry.

   i jlz4@columbia.edu (John Zimmerman, D.D.S.)

   ± listserv@umab.umd.edu (Bitnet: LISTSERV@UMAB) [body = SUBSCRIBE
     DBLIST first-name last-name]

1-373 **DDMS-L:** On the Display Device Management System for 3270 CMS consoles.

   i dwight@ucsbvm.bitnet (Bitnet: DWIGHT@UCSBVM) (Dwight McCann)

   ± listserv@ucsbvm.bitnet (Bitnet: LISTSERV@UCSBVM) [body = SUBSCRIBE
     DDMS-L first-name last-name]

Archive: `listserv@ucsbvm.bitnet`

1-374 **DDTs-Users:** On the DDTs defect-tracking software from QualTrak.

    i `ddts-users-request@bigbird.bu.edu`

    ± `majordomo@bigbird.bu.edu` [body = subscribe ddts-users]

1-375 **DEAFBLND:** About dual sensory impairment (deaf-blindness).

    i `str002@ukcc.uky.edu` (Bob Moore)

    ± `listserv@ukcc.uky.edu` (Bitnet: LISTSERV@UKCC) [body = SUBSCRIBE DEAFBLND first-name last-name]

    Archive: `listserv@ukcc.uky.edu`

1-376 **Deborah Harry/Blondie Information Service:** An information service for anything and everything regarding Blondie/Deborah Harry, anything you ever wanted to know from the latest tour info/recording info to other projects, films, etc.

    i ± `gunter@yarrow.wt.uwa.edu.au`

1-377 **Decision Power:** On the Decision Power product of ICL Computers Limited. DP is comprised of a logic programming language Prolog, a constraint handling system Chip, a data base interface Seduce (runs on top of Ingres), a development environment Kegi (runs on X) and an end-user graphical display environment KHS (also runs on X).

    i ± `dp-friends-request@aiai.ed.ac.uk` (Tim Duncan)

1-378 **DECMCC-L:** On DEC DECmcc (a network monitoring tool from DEC) and related software.

    i `sloane@ukanvax.bitnet` (Bitnet: SLOANE@UKANVAX) (Bob Sloane)

    ± `listserv@american.edu` (Bitnet: LISTSERV@AUVM) [body = SUBSCRIBE DECMCC-L first-name last-name]

    Archive: `listserv@american.edu`

1-379 **decstation-managers:** Fast-turnaround troubleshooting tool for managers of RISC DECstations.

    i `decstation-managers-request@ornl.gov` [body = help]

    ± `majordomo@ornl.gov` [body subscribe = decstation-managers]

1-380 **DECTEI-L:** On Digital Equipment Corporation's Education Initiative program of discounts and services for educational institutions.

    i `kathy@wugate.wustl.edu` (Kathy A. Atnip)

    ± `listserv@ubvm.cc.buffalo.edu` (Bitnet: LISTSERV@UBVM) [body = SUBSCRIBE DECTEI-L first-name last-name]

    Archive: `listserv@ubvm.cc.buffalo.edu`

    Gated: ⇔ `bit.listserv.esl-1`

1-381 **DEEPSEA:** For deep-sea and hydrothermal vent biologists.

    i `amcarthu@uvvm.uvic.ca` (Andrew McArthur)

    ± `listserv@uvvm.uvic.ca` (Bitnet: LISTSERV@UVVM) [body = SUBSCRIBE DEEPSEA first-name last-name]

    Archive: Available to subscribers only.

1-382 **DELTACHI:** For the members of Delta Chi Fraternity.

    i `jwales@iubvm.bitnet` (Bitnet: JWALES@IUBVM) (Jimbo Wales)

    ± `listserv@ubvm.cc.buffalo.edu` (Bitnet: LISTSERV@UBVM) [body =

SUBSCRIBE DELTACHI first-name last-name]

Archive: `listserv@ubvm.cc.buffalo.edu`

1-383 **DEMING-L:** On the theories of W. Edwards Deming.

i `chadwick@uhunix.uhcc.hawaii.edu`

± `listserv@uhccvm.uhcc.hawaii.edu` (Bitnet: LISTSERV@UHCCVM) [body = SUBSCRIBE DEMING-L first-name last-name]

Archive: Available to subscribers only.

Other: Subscription is limited. Requests will be sent to list owner for approval.

1-384 **DENTAL-L:** On encouraging e-mail use by oral/dental researchers.

i `stpd8008@iruccvax.ucc.ie` (Ruben Keane)

± `listserv@irlearn.bitnet` (Bitnet: LISTSERV@IRLEARN) [body = SUBSCRIBE DENTAL-L first-name last-name]

Archive: `listserv@irlearn.bitnet`

1-385 **depot:** On the 'depot' software installation framework, a strategy for installing software packages that facilitates sharing across hardware platforms and corporate (i.e., political) organizations.

i ± `depot-request@cme.nist.gov`

1-386 **derby:** About horse racing, mostly thoroughbred handicapping, but other racing-related topics welcome.

i ± `derby-request@ekrl.com` (John Wilkes)

1-387 **DERRIDA:** On Jacques Derrida and deconstruction.

i `erben@chuma.cas.usf.edu` (David Erben)

± `listserv@cfrvm.bitnet` (Bitnet: LISTSERV@CFRVM) [body = SUBSCRIBE DERRIDA first-name last-name]

Archive: `listserv@cfrvm.bitnet`

1-388 **deryni-l:** For fans of Katherine Kurtz' novels and other works.

i `elendil@mintir.new-orleans.la.us` (Edward J. Branley)

± `mail-server@mintir.new-orleans.la.us` [body = SUBSCRIBE DERYNI-L]

1-389 **DEVEL-L:** On technology transfer in international development.

i `vita@gmuvax.bitnet` (Bitnet: VITA@GMUVAX) (Dania Granados)

± `listserv@american.edu` (Bitnet: LISTSERV@AUVM) [body = SUBSCRIBE DEVEL-L first-name last-name]

1-390 **deviants:** On the workings of the Great Wok and all things deviant from accepted social norm. Occasionally, but not always disgusting, ranting, experimental reports, news clippings, medical curiosities, cults, murders, and other phenomena are well in place here.

i ± `deviants-request@csv.warwick.ac.uk`

1-391 **DIATOM-L:** About the research on the diatom algae.

i `sweets@ucs.indiana.edu` (P. Roger Sweets)

± `listserv@iubvm.ucs.indiana.edu` (Bitnet: LISTSERV@IUBVM) [body = SUBSCRIBE DIATOM-L first-name last-name]

1-392   **DIET:** On the support and discussion of weight loss.

> *i* `campbell@ubvm.bitnet` (Bitnet: `CAMPBELL@UBVM`) (Roger Campbell)
>
> ± `listserv@ubvm.cc.buffalo.edu` (Bitnet: `LISTSERV@UBVM`) [body = SUBSCRIBE DIET first-name last-name]
>
> **Archive:** `listserv@ubvm.cc.buffalo.edu`

1-393   **DIGIT-L:** For members of the Diffusion Interest Group in Information Systems, who are primarily academics in business schools researching information technology adoption, diffusion, and implementation.

> *i* `mary@cfrvm.bitnet` (Bitnet: `MARY@CFRVM`) (Mary Alexander)
>
> ± `listserv@cfrvm.bitnet` (Bitnet: `LISTSERV@CFRVM`) [body = SUBSCRIBE DIGIT-L first-name last-name]
>
> **Other:** Subscription is limited. Requests will be sent to list owner for approval.

1-394   **dinosaur:** Discussion of dinosaurs and other archosaurs.

> *i* ± `dinosaur-request@donald.wichitaks.ncr.com` (John Matrow)

1-395   **DIPL-L:** On the game Diplomacy.

> *i* `nick@watfrost.uwaterloo.ca` (Nick Fitzpatrick)
>
> ± `listserv@mitvma.mit.edu` (Bitnet: `LISTSERV@MITVMA`) [body = SUBSCRIBE DIPL-L first-name last-name]
>
> **Gated:** ⇔ `rec.games.diplomacy`

1-396   **dire-straits:** On the musical group Dire Straits and associated side projects.

> *i* `rand@merrimack.edu`
>
> ± `dire-straits-request@merrimack.edu` [body = subscribe]

1-397   **direct:** On the musical artist Vangelis.

> *i* ± `direct-request@celtech.com`
>
> **Archive:** FTP `ftp.uwp.edu` in `/pub/music/lists/direct`
>
> **Other:** Available as digest or mail-reflector, specify preference in body of mail when subscribing.

1-398   **DIRECT-L:** On the MacroMedia Director software for the Macintosh.

> *i* `cblih@uafsysb.bitnet` (Bitnet: `CBLIH@UAFSYSB`) (CB Lih)
>
> ± `listserv@uafsysb.uark.edu` (Bitnet: `LISTSERV@UAFSYSB`) [body = SUBSCRIBE DIRECT-L first-name last-name]
>
> **Archive:** Available to subscribers only.

1-399   **DISARM-D:** On disarmament, including military and political strategy, technology, sociology, and peace activism, conventional, chemical and biological weapons, superpower intervention and exploitation of the Third World, the economic disruption and nonaggressive forms of security and defense. *Moderated*

> *i* `dfp10@albnyvm1.bitnet` (Bitnet: `DFP10@ALBNYVM1`) (Donald F. Parsons)
>
> ± `listserv@uacsc2.albany.edu` (Bitnet: `LISTSERV@ALBNYVM1`) [body = SUBSCRIBE DISARM-D first-name last-name]
>
> **Archive:** `listserv@uacsc2.albany.edu`

1-400   **DISARM-L:** On disarmament, a monthly digest of materials mostly from DISARM-D.

    i `dfp10@albnyvm1.bitnet` (Bitnet: `DFP10@ALBNYVM1`) (Donald F. Parsons)

    ± `listserv@uacsc2.albany.edu` (Bitnet: `LISTSERV@ALBNYVM1`) [body = SUBSCRIBE DISARM-L first-name last-name]

    Archive: `listserv@uacsc2.albany.edu`

    Other: Monthly digest

1-401   **Discipline:** For Robert Fripp and King Crimson enthusiasts.

    i ± `toby@cs.man.ac.uk` (Toby Howard)

    Archive: FTP `ftp.uwp.edu` in `/pub/music/lists/discipline`

    Other: Weekly digest

1-402   **disney-afternoon:** Discussion of the Disney Afternoon and other related topics. This is a very high-volume, low-noise mailing list. *Moderated*

    Other: available in digest form.

    i ± `ranger-list-request@taronga.com` (Stephanie da Silva)

1-403   **disney-comics:** Discussion of Disney comics.

    i ± `disney-comics-request@student.docs.uu.se` (Per Starbäck)

    Archive: FTP: `ftp.lysator.liu.se` in `/pub/comics/disney`

1-404   **DIST-CPM:** INFO-CPM Mailing List.

    i `fisher@rpitsvm.bitnet` (Bitnet: `FISHER@RPITSVM`) (John S. Fisher)

    ± `listserv@vm.its.rpi.edu` (Bitnet: `LISTSERV@RPITSVM`) [body = SUBSCRIBE DIST-CPM first-name last-name]

    Archive: `listserv@vm.its.rpi.edu`

1-405   **DIST-MDM:** INFO-MODEMS mailing list. *Moderated*

    i `fisher@rpitsvm.bitnet` (Bitnet: `FISHER@RPITSVM`) (John S. Fisher)

    ± `listserv@vm.its.rpi.edu` (Bitnet: `LISTSERV@RPITSVM`) [body = SUBSCRIBE DIST-MDM first-name last-name]

    Archive: `listserv@vm.its.rpi.edu`

1-406   **DIST-MIC:** Distribution on the Info-Micro mailing list *Moderated*

    i `fisher@rpitsvm.bitnet` (Bitnet: `FISHER@RPITSVM`) (John S. Fisher)

    ± `listserv@vm.its.rpi.edu` (Bitnet: `LISTSERV@RPITSVM`) [body = SUBSCRIBE DIST-MIC first-name last-name]

    Archive: `listserv@vm.its.rpi.edu`

1-407   **DITTO-L:** For users of DITTO (Data Interfile Transfer, Testing, and Operations), an IBM product used to move data between various media.

    i `reichetz@awiimc12.bitnet` (Bitnet: `REICHETZ@AWIIMC12`) (Christian Reichetzeder)

    ± `listserv@vm.akh-wien.ac.at` (Bitnet: `LISTSERV@AWIIMC12`) [body = SUBSCRIBE DITTO-L first-name last-name]

    Archive: `listserv@vm.akh-wien.ac.at`

1-408 **DJ-L:** For discussions of interest to campus radio station disk jockeys.

    i `lefty@mtu.edu` (Douglas J. Coffman)

    ± `listserv@vm1.nodak.edu` (Bitnet: `LISTSERV@NDSUVM1`) [body = SUBSCRIBE DJ-L first-name last-name]

    Archive: `listserv@vm1.nodak.edu`

    Gated: ⇔ `bit.listserv.DJ-L`

    Other: listserv@vm1.nodak.edu digest

1-409 **DLDG-L:** For dance librarians and other scholars, students, or teachers of dance who wish to discuss or ask questions about dance resources.

    i `boppm@iubacs.bitnet` (Bitnet: `BOPPM@IUBACS`) (Mary Bopp)

    ± `listserv@iubvm.ucs.indiana.edu` (Bitnet: `LISTSERV@IUBVM`) [body = SUBSCRIBE DLDG-L first-name last-name]

    Archive: Available to subscribers only.

1-410 **DMA-LIST:** On the mathematical analysis of discrete structures and the design of discrete algorithms and their applications in operations research, computer science, and engineering.
Moderated

    i `u.faigle@math.utwente.nl` (Ulrich Faigle)

    ± `listserv@hearn.nic.surfnet.nl` (Bitnet: `LISTSERV@HEARN`) [body = SUBSCRIBE DMA-LIST first-name last-name]

    Archive: `listserv@hearn.nic.surfnet.nl`

    Other: Subscription is limited. Requests will be sent to list owner for approval.

1-411 **dmtf-info:** For discussing the DMTF (Desktop Management Task Force), a technology to help those who manage computer networks or who build software and hardware that run with/on computer systems make those products manageable.

    i ± `dmtf-info-request@sun.com`

1-412 **DNN-L:** The Volunteers in Technical Assistance's DevelopNet.

    i `vita@gmuvax.bitnet` (Bitnet: `VITA@GMUVAX`) (Dania Granados)

    ± `listserv@american.edu` (Bitnet: `LISTSERV@AUVM`) [body = SUBSCRIBE DNN-L first-name last-name]

1-413 **DOCDIS:** For informal discussion and support among doctoral students in library and information science, topics including reasons for getting a doctorate, choosing committee members, job interview.

    i `vyoung@ua1vm.bitnet` (Bitnet: `VYOUNG@UA1VM`) (Virginia Young)

    ± `listserv@ua1vm.ua.edu` (Bitnet: `LISTSERV@UA1VM`) [body = SUBSCRIBE DOCDIS first-name last-name]

    Archive: `listserv@ua1vm.ua.edu`

1-414 **Dodge Stealth/Mitsubishi 3000GT:** Discussion of anything related to these cars.

    i ± `stealth-request%jim@wupost.wustl.edu`

1-415 **Dokken/Lynch Mob:** Articles, questions, and discussions on the Dokken and Lynch Mob pop music groups.

    i ± `kydeno00@ukpr.uky.edu` or `kirsten@mik.uky.edu`

Archive: FTP `f.ms.uky.edu` in `pub3/mailing.lists/dokken`

1-416 **dominion:** On The Sisters of Mercy rock group and related music.

i `pete@ohm.york.ac.uk`

± `dominion-request@ohm.york.ac.uk`

1-417 **Donosy:** Distribution of a news bulletin from Poland.

Other: English and Polish versions are both available, please specify in subscription request.

i ± `donosy@fuw.edu.pl` or `przemek@ndcvx.cc.nd.edu` (Przemek Klosowski)

1-418 **DOROTHYL:** On mystery literature. *Moderated*

i `dkovacs@kentvm.bitnet` (Bitnet: `DKOVACS@KENTVM`)

± `listserv@kentvm.kent.edu` (Bitnet: `LISTSERV@KENTVM`) [body = `SUBSCRIBE DOROTHYL` first-name last-name]

Archive: `listserv@kentvm.kent.edu`

Other: Daily digest

1-419 **DPMAST-L:** For the members of the Data Processing Management Association.

i `ed6704@cmsuvmb.bitnet` (Bitnet: `ED6704@CMSUVMB`)

± `listserv@cmsuvmb.bitnet` (Bitnet: `LISTSERV@CMSUVMB`) [body = `SUBSCRIBE DPMAST-L` first-name last-name]

1-420 **draker8:** For users of the Draker 8 shortwave radio receiver. *Moderated*

i ± `draker8-request@hpsesuka.pwd.hp.com` (Mik Butler, moderator)

1-421 **DRIV-L:** On defining the behavior of TeX DVI driver interpreters.

i `dhosek@hmcvax.bitnet` (Bitnet: `DHOSEK@HMCVAX`) (Don Hosek)

± `listserv@tamvm1.tamu.edu` (Bitnet: `LISTSERV@TAMVM1`) [body = `SUBSCRIBE DRIV-L` first-name last-name]

Archive: `listserv@tamvm1.tamu.edu`

1-422 **DRP-L:** On Disaster Recovery Plans for Computing Services.

i `urmm@marist.bitnet` (Bitnet: `URMM@MARIST`) (Martha McConaghy)

± `listserv@vm.marist.edu` (Bitnet: `LISTSERV@MARIST`) [body = `SUBSCRIBE DRP-L` first-name last-name]

Archive: Available to subscribers only.

1-423 **DRS:** The Dead Runners Society. On the psychological, philosophical, and personal aspects of running.

i ± `drs-request@dartcms1.dartmouth.edu` (Christopher Mark Conn)

1-424 **drum:** Discussion of anything related to percussion instruments.

i `boarjas@elof.acc.iit.edu` (Jason Boardman)

± `drum-request@elof.acc.iit.edu`

1-425 **DVI-list:** On Intel's DVI (Digital Video Interactive) system. Covers both applications and programming with DVI.

i `server@calvin.dgbt.doc.ca`

± `listserv@calvin.dgbt.doc.ca` [body = `subscribe dvi-list` first-name last-name]

Archive: FTP `debra.dgbt.doc.ca` in `pub/dvi`

1-426 **dynsys:** The dynamical systems mailing list. On ergodic theory and dynamical systems.

    i `karl_petersen@unc.edu`

    ± `listserv@gibbs.oit.unc.edu` [body = `subscribe dynsys`]

1-427 **E-EUROPE:** Eastern Europe business communication network for studying the CEE/CIS (Central and Eastern Europe/Commonwealth of Independent States) business and economic systems, to help these countries in their transition to market economies. *Moderated*

    i `r505040@univscvm.bitnet` (Bitnet: `R505040@UNIVSCVM`) (James W. Reese)

    ± `listserv@pucc.princeton.edu` (Bitnet: `LISTSERV@PUCC`) [body = `SUBSCRIBE E-EUROPE` first-name last-name]

    Archive: `listserv@pucc.princeton.edu`

    Other: Weekly digest

1-428 **E-HUG:** On all things relating to use of Hebrew, Yiddish, Judesmo, and Aramaic on computers. *Moderated*

    i `ari@well.sf.ca.us` (Ari Davidow, Oakland, CA, US)

    ± `listserv@dartcms1.dartmouth.edu` (Bitnet: `LISTSERV@DARTCMS1`) [body = `SUBSCRIBE E-HUG` first-name last-name]

    Archive: `listserv@dartcms1.dartmouth.edu`

1-429 **E-List:** News and discussion on Estonia.

    i ± `vilo@cs.helsinki.fi` (Jaak Vilo)

    Language: Estonian (mostly), English (some)

1-430 **EARAM-L:** On early American history, i.e., before circa 1820, including Native Americans, "discovery" documents, colonial and federal materials.

    i `rcraig2@kentvm.bitnet` (Bitnet: `RCRAIG2@KENTVM`)

    ± `listserv@kentvm.kent.edu` (Bitnet: `LISTSERV@KENTVM`) [body = `SUBSCRIBE EARAM-L` first-name last-name]

    Archive: `listserv@kentvm.kent.edu`

1-431 **EARN-UG:** For EARN users.

    i `grange@frors12.bitnet` (Bitnet: `GRANGE@FRORS12`) (Nadine Grange) or `trumpy@icnucevm.bitnet` (Bitnet: `TRUMPY@ICNUCEVM`) (Stefano Trumpy)

    ± `listserv@irlearn.bitnet` (Bitnet: `LISTSERV@IRLEARN`) [body = `SUBSCRIBE EARN-UG` first-name last-name]

    Archive: `listserv@irlearn.bitnet`

1-432 **EARNEWS:** For news on EARN, the European Academic and Research Network, the European counterpart of CREN/BITNET. *Moderated*

    i `grange@frors12.bitnet` (Bitnet: `GRANGE@FRORS12`) (Nadine Grange)

    ± `listserv@frmop11.cnusc.fr` (Bitnet: `LISTSERV@FRMOP11`) [body = `SUBSCRIBE EARNEWS` first-name last-name]

    Archive: `listserv@frmop11.cnusc.fr`

1-433 **EC:** About the European Community.

    i `turan@vm.cc.metu.edu.tr` (egemen (Metin Turan)

± `listserv@vm.cc.metu.edu.tr` (Bitnet: LISTSERV@TRMETU) [body = SUBSCRIBE EC first-name last-name]

Archive: `listserv@vm.cc.metu.edu.tr`

1-434 **ECENET-L:** The ERIC Clearinghouse on Elementary and Early Childhood Education.

i `pmeyer@vmd.cso.uiuc.edu` (Phil Meyer)

± `listserv@vmd.cso.uiuc.edu` (Bitnet: LISTSERV@UIUCVMD) [body = SUBSCRIBE ECENET-L first-name last-name]

Archive: `listserv@vmd.cso.uiuc.edu`

1-435 **ECEOL-L:** Early Childhood Education On Line. Idea and information exchange for early childhood educators.

i `bonnieb@maine.bitnet` (Bitnet: BONNIEB@MAINE) (Bonnie Blagojevic)

± `listserv@maine.edu` (Bitnet: LISTSERV@MAINE) [body = SUBSCRIBE ECEOL-L first-name last-name]

Archive: `listserv@maine.edu`

1-436 **echoes:** Info and commentary on the musical group Pink Floyd as well as other projects members of the group have been involved with.

i ± `echoes-request@fawnya.tcs.com` (H.W. Neff)

1-437 **ECONED-L:** Economic education discussion group.

i `kberon@utdallas.bitnet` (Bitnet: KBERON@UTDALLAS) (Kurt Beron)

± `listserv@utdallas.edu` (Bitnet: LISTSERV@UTDALLAS) [body = SUBSCRIBE ECONED-L first-name last-name]

Archive: Available to subscribers only.

1-438 **ECONHIST:** On teaching and research in economic history. *Moderated*

i `cliomets@miamiu.bitnet` (Bitnet: CLIOMETS@MIAMIU) (Sam Williamson)

± `listserv@miamiu.acs.muohio.edu` (Bitnet: LISTSERV@MIAMIU) [body = SUBSCRIBE ECONHIST first-name last-name]

Archive: `listserv@miamiu.acs.muohio.edu`

Other: Subscription is limited. Requests will be sent to list owner for approval.

1-439 **ECOTHEOL:** On environmental issues from a theological or ethical perspective.

i `i.j.tilsed@cen.ex.ac.uk` (Ian Tilsed)

± `mailbase@mailbase.ac.uk` [body = SUBSCRIBE ECOTHEOL first-name last-name]

Archive: `mailbase@mailbase.ac.uk` [body = INDEX ECOTHEOL]

1-440 **ECOVIS-L:** On trends in ecology of vision—for scientists working within biology, ecology, and visual science.

i `palacios-adrian@yale.edu` (Adrian Palacios)

± `listserv@yalevm.ycc.yale.edu` (Bitnet: LISTSERV@YALEVM) [body = SUBSCRIBE ECOVIS-L first-name last-name]

Archive: Available to subscribers only.

Other: Subscription is limited. Requests will be sent to list owner for approval.

1-441 **ECTL:** The "Electronic Communal Temporal Lobe" for researchers interested in computer speech interfaces. *Moderated*

i ectl-request@snowhite.cis.uoguelph.ca (David Leip)

± ectl-request@snowhite.cis.uoguelph.ca [body = first-name last-name, institute, department, daytime phone, and e-mail-address]

Archive: FTP snowhite.cis.uoguelph.ca in /pub/ectl

1-442 **ecto:** On Happy Rhodes (and other music, books, films, art).

i jessica@noc.rutgers.edu

± ecto-request@ns1.rutgers.edu

Archive: FTP hardess.rutgers.edu in /pub/hr

1-443 **ECU-L:** For computer users at East Carolina University.

i ssbsc@ecuvm1.bitnet (Bitnet: SSBSC@ECUVM1) (Brad Carson)

± listserv@ecuvm.cis.ecu.edu (Bitnet: LISTSERV@ECUVM1) [body = SUBSCRIBE ECU-L first-name last-name]

Archive: listserv@ecuvm.cis.ecu.edu

1-444 **EDAD-L:** For discussions between departments of educational administration internationally.

i u5b35@wvnvm.bitnet (Bitnet: U5B35@WVNVM) (Ed Lilley)

± listserv@wvnvm.wvnet.edu (Bitnet: LISTSERV@WVNVM) [body = SUBSCRIBE EDAD-L first-name last-name]

1-445 **EDLAW:** On law and education.

i nordin@ukcc.uky.edu (Virginia Davis-Nordin)

± listserv@ukcc.uky.edu (Bitnet: LISTSERV@UKCC) [body = SUBSCRIBE EDLAW first-name last-name]

Archive: listserv@ukcc.uky.edu

1-446 **EDPOLYAN:** For discussion of education policy analysis.

i glass@asu.edu (Gene V. Glass)

± listserv@asuvm.inre.asu.edu (Bitnet: LISTSERV@ASUACAD) [body = SUBSCRIBE EDPOLYAN first-name last-name]

Archive: listserv@asuvm.inre.asu.edu

1-447 **EDPOLYAR:** On education policy analysis. *Moderated*

i glass@asu.edu (Gene V. Glass)

± listserv@asuvm.inre.asu.edu (Bitnet: LISTSERV@ASUACAD) [body = SUBSCRIBE EDPOLYAR first-name last-name]

Archive: listserv@asuvm.inre.asu.edu

1-448 **EDSTYLE:** On learning styles theory and research.

i drz@sjuvm.bitnet (Bitnet: DRZ@SJUVM)

± listserv@stjohns.edu (Bitnet: LISTSERV@SJUVM) [body = SUBSCRIBE EDSTYLE first-name last-name]

Archive: Available to subscribers only.

1-449 **EDUCOM-W:** On women and information technology. *Moderated*

i eloise@maine.bitnet (Bitnet: ELOISE@MAINE)

± listserv@bitnic.educom.edu (Bitnet: LISTSERV@BITNIC) [body = SUBSCRIBE EDUCOM-W first-name last-name]

1-450 **EDUSIG-L:** On education and the Digital Equipment Corporation.

i gerland@ubvms.cc.buffalo.edu (Jim Gerland)

± listserv@ubvm.cc.buffalo.edu (Bitnet: LISTSERV@UBVM) [body = SUBSCRIBE EDUSIG-L first-name last-name]

Archive: listserv@ubvm.cc.buffalo.edu

Gated: ⇔ bit.listserv.edusig-l

1-451 **EEC-L:** On European training and technology.

i dstruppa@gmuvax.gmu.edu (Daniele Struppa)

± listserv@american.edu (Bitnet: LISTSERV@AUVM) [body = SUBSCRIBE EEC-L first-name last-name]

Archive: listserv@american.edu

1-452 **EGRET-L:** For users of EGRET, an epidemiological software package that runs on CMS. *Moderated*

i sbaker@umassmed.bitnet (Bitnet: SBAKER@UMASSMED) (Stephen P. Baker)

± listserv@dartcms1.dartmouth.edu (Bitnet: LISTSERV@DARTCMS1) [body = SUBSCRIBE EGRET-L first-name last-name]

Archive: listserv@dartcms1.dartmouth.edu

1-453 **ELDNET-L:** American Society for Engineering Education (ASEE) Engineering Libraries Division Network. *Moderated*

i desart@uiucvmd.bitnet (Bitnet: DESART@UIUCVMD)

± listserv@vmd.cso.uiuc.edu (Bitnet: LISTSERV@UIUCVMD) [body = SUBSCRIBE ELDNET-L first-name last-name]

Archive: listserv@vmd.cso.uiuc.edu

1-454 **ELEASAI:** The Open Library/Information Science Research Forum.

i gwhitney@arizvms.bitnet (Bitnet: GWHITNEY@ARIZVMS) (Gretchen Whitney)

± listserv@arizvm1.ccit.arizona.edu (Bitnet: LISTSERV@ARIZVM1) [body = SUBSCRIBE ELEASAI first-name last-name]

Archive: listserv@arizvm1.ccit.arizona.edu

1-455 **Electric Light Orchestra:** On the music of the Electric Light Orchestra rock group, and of its members, both solo and with other groups.

i db74@andrew.cmu.edu (Derrick J. Brashear)

± elo-list-request@andrew.cmu.edu

1-456 **electromagnetics:** On electromagnetics. Includes discussion of practical electromagnetics, theory, numerical solutions to problems, books and information sources, and more.

i ± em-request@decwd.ece.uiuc.edu

1-457 **ELED-L:** On elementary education.

i dzollman@ksuvm.bitnet (Bitnet: DZOLLMAN@KSUVM)

± listserv@ksuvm.ksu.edu (Bitnet: LISTSERV@KSUVM) [body = SUBSCRIBE ELED-L first-name last-name]

Archive: `listserv@ksuvm.ksu.edu`

1-458　**elements:** The purpose of the Shuttle Elements mailing list is to get Keplerian Elements out as quickly as possible during flights. We send out pre-launch elements and post launch elements based on Flight Dynamics Office predictions, Shuttle computer state vector data, or NORAD radar tracking data. Anyone may subscribe but prior approval is required before sending submissions to the list. Element data, tracking software and information, are available through an automated e-mail archive server, send e-mail to `listserv@alsys.com` to get information about the server.

　　i ± `elements-request@alsys.com` (Gary Morris, KK6YB)

1-459　**ELP:** News, opinions, discussions, etc. on the musical group Emerson, Lake & Palmer as well as related bands (e.g., The Nice) and ELP solo projects.

　　i ± `j.arnold@ma30.bull.com` (John Arnold)

　　Archive: FTP `ftp.uwp.edu` in `/pub/music/lists/elp/digests`

　　Other: Digest (once every 2-3 weeks)

1-460　**ELTMAG-L:** Discussions on applied electromagnism in Brazil.

　　i `renatocm@brufmg.bitnet` (Bitnet: `RENATOCM@BRUFMG`) (Renato Cardoso Mesquita)

　　± `listserv@vm1.lcc.ufmg.br` (Bitnet: `LISTSERV@BRUFMG`) [body = `SUBSCRIBE ELTMAG-L` first-name last-name]

　　Language: Portuguese

　　Other: Subscription is limited. Requests will be sent to list owner for approval.

1-461　**Elton-John:** For fans of the musician Elton John.

　　i `barfmaster@uiuc.edu` (Dan Blanchard)

　　± `elton-john-request@uiuc.edu` [subject = `subscribe-service` or `subscribe-digest`]

　　Other: Digest available

1-462　**Elvis Costello:** Discussions and news of the music of Declan Patrick Aloysius MacManus, better known as Elvis Costello. Topics about the King (of America) are always welcomed, as are other artists and music.

　　i ± `costello-request@gnu.ai.mit.edu` (Danny Hernandez)

　　Archive: FTP `Archive` in cs.uwp.edu (131.210.1.4)

1-463　**EMBINFO:** For EMBNet (European Molecular Biology Network).

　　i `turso@vm.csata.it` (Giovanni Turso)

　　± `listserv@ibacsata.bitnet` (Bitnet: `LISTSERV@IBACSATA`) [body = `SUBSCRIBE EMBINFO` first-name last-name]

　　Archive: `listserv@ibacsata.bitnet` or `listserv@vm.csata.it`

1-464　**emdreams:** "emdreams" (proper lowercase "e") is a discussion forum exclusively for members of the organization Electronic Dreams. Their focus is upon the progressive, instrumental electronic music of artists/groups such as Tangerine Dream, Jean-Michel Jarre, Klaus Schulze, and Vangelis.

　　i ± `elana@netcom.com` (Elana Mell Beach)

　　Archive: FTP `ftp.uwp.edu`

Other: The list is available as a daily digest and reflector. To join this list, you must first become a paid member of Electronic Dreams—a fairly simple and inexpensive process. E-mail elana@netcom.com for a membership information kit. (Include your snail mail address.)

1-465 **EMEDCH-L:** On Early Medieval China (the period between the end of the Han and the beginning of the Tang dynasties, roughly 3rd through 6th centuries).

   i kklein@uscvm.bitnet (Bitnet: KKLEIN@USCVM) (Ken Klein)

   ± listserv@vm.usc.edu (Bitnet: LISTSERV@USCVM) [body = SUBSCRIBE EMEDCH-L first-name last-name]

1-466 **EMPLOY:** Forum to assist federal employees and others in the sharing of job opportunities and ideas on gaining employment. The primary emphasis is on DoD jobs and employment-related issues. The list is restricted to U.S. federal and federal-related sites (.gov and .mil domains).

   i ± employ-request@oti.disa.mil (Jeff Roth)

1-467 **EMSNY-L:** On emergency medical services for providers in the state of New York.

   i meg04@albnydh2.bitnet (Bitnet: MEG04@ALBNYDH2) (Michael Gilbertson)

   ± listserv@albnydh2.bitnet (Bitnet: LISTSERV@ALBNYDH2) [body = SUBSCRIBE EMSNY-L first-name last-name]

   Archive: listserv@albnydh2.bitnet

1-468 **EMUNIM:** On the Jewish campus network in Michigan.

   i 23163msf@msu.edu (Mark Finkelstein)

   ± listserv@msu.edu (Bitnet: LISTSERV@MSU) [body = SUBSCRIBE EMUNIM first-name last-name]

   Archive: listserv@msu.edu

   Other: Daily digest

1-469 **ENGLISH:** Discussions for departments of English faculty in the U.S. and Canada on using computers to teach literature and composition, and general discussions on literary studies.

   i b399tary@utarlvm1.bitnet (Bitnet: B399TARY@UTARLVM1) (Tom Ryan)

   ± listserv@utarlvm1.uta.edu (Bitnet: LISTSERV@UTARLVM1) [body = SUBSCRIBE ENGLISH first-name last-name]

   Other: Subscription is limited. Requests will be sent to list owner for approval.

1-470 **ENTOBR-L:** On entomology in Brazil.

   i dbaxpsff@brufv.bitnet (Bitnet: DBAXPSFF@BRUFV) (Paulo Sergio Fiuza Ferreira)

   ± listserv@vm1.lcc.ufmg.br (Bitnet: LISTSERV@BRUFMG) [body = SUBSCRIBE ENTOBR-L first-name last-name]

   Language: Portuguese

1-471 **ENTOMO-L:** For scientists (and others) interested in insects and terrestrial arthropods.

   i evbkevan@vm.uoguelph.ca (PETER KEVAN)

   ± listserv@vm.uoguelph.ca (Bitnet: LISTSERV@UOGUELPH) [body = SUBSCRIBE ENTOMO-L first-name last-name]

   Archive: Available to subscribers only.

1-472 **enya:** Discussion of Enya's music.

    i `tim@boulder.colorado.edu` (Tim Hunter)

    ± `enya-request@boulder.colorado.edu`

    Archive: FTP `refuge.colorado.edu` in `/pub/enya`

1-473 **EOCHR-L:** On Eastern Orthodox Christianity.

    i `vukomano@qucdn.queensu.ca` (Dragic Vukomanovic)

    ± `listserv@qucdn.queensu.ca` (Bitnet: `LISTSERV@QUCDN`) [body = `SUBSCRIBE EOCHR-L` first-name last-name]

    Archive: Available to subscribers only.

    Other: Subscription is open to anybody who has interest in East Orthodox Christianity. Requests will be sent to list owner for approval.

1-474 **eps:** On Ensoniq EPS Digital Samplers.

    ± `eps-request@reed.edu`

    Archive: FTP `ftp.reed.edu` in `/pub/mailing-lists/eps/`

1-475 **equestrians:** About anything and everything related to equestrian activities.

    Gated: ⇔ `rec.equestrian`

    i `kovar@nda.com` (David C. Kovar)

    ± `equestrians-request@world.std.com`

1-476 **ERCIM:** For news on European research and developments in information technology and applied mathematics.

    i `beltrame@icnucevm.bitnet` (Bitnet: `BELTRAME@ICNUCEVM`) (Renzo Beltrame)

    ± `listserv@vm.cnuce.cnr.it` (Bitnet: `LISTSERV@ICNUCEVM`) [body = `SUBSCRIBE ERCIM` first-name last-name]

    Archive: Available to subscribers only.

    Language: Italian, English

    Other: Subscription is limited. Requests will be sent to list owner for approval.

1-477 **ERL-L:** On educational research, including discussion and updates from Washington on education-related proposals.

    i `p30jwp1@niu.bitnet` (Bitnet: `P30JWP1@NIU`) (Jean Pierce)

    ± `listserv@asuvm.inre.asu.edu` (Bitnet: `LISTSERV@ASUACAD`) [body = `SUBSCRIBE ERL-L` first-name last-name]

    Archive: `listserv@asuvm.inre.asu.edu`

1-478 **ESAPRESS:** Distribution of European Space Agency press releases.

    i `pregan@esoc.bitnet` (Bitnet: `PREGAN@ESOC`) (Phil Regan) or `fbonacin@esa.bitnet` (Bitnet: `FBONACIN@ESA`) or `mailrp@esa.bitnet` (Bitnet: `MAILRP@ESA`)

    ± `listserv@esoc.bitnet` (Bitnet: `LISTSERV@ESOC`) [body = `SUBSCRIBE ESAPRESS` first-name last-name]

    Archive: Available to subscribers only.

    Gated: ⇔ `sci.space.news`

1-479   **esperanto:** On the neutral international language Esperanto. Often in Esperanto.

     i ± `esperanto-request@rand.org` (Mike Urban)

1-480   **ESPORA-L:** On the history of the Iberian Peninsula.

     i `lhnelson@ukanvm.bitnet` (Bitnet: `LHNELSON@UKANVM`)

     ± `listserv@ukanvm.cc.ukans.edu` (Bitnet: `LISTSERV@UKANVM`) [body = SUBSCRIBE ESPORA-L first-name last-name]

1-481   **ETHMUS-L:** EthnoFORUM, a global ethnomusicology forum. *Moderated*

     i `signell@umdd.bitnet` (Bitnet: `SIGNELL@UMDD`) (Dr. Karl Signell)

     ± `listserv@umdd.umd.edu` (Bitnet: `LISTSERV@UMDD`) [body = SUBSCRIBE ETHMUS-L first-name last-name]

     Archive: Available to subscribers only.

     Other: Subscription is limited to networkers with a professional interest in ethnomusicology: professors, graduate students, researchers, and librarians. Requests will be sent to list owner for approval.

1-482   **ETHOLOGY:** On animal behavior and behavioral ecology. Topics include new or controversial theories, new research methods and equipment, announcements of books, papers, conferences, new software for behavioral analysis, etc.

     i `jarmo.saarikko@helsinki.fi`

     ± `listserv@searn.sunet.se` or `listserv@searn.bitnet` [body = subscribe ethology first-name last-name]

     Archive: `listserv@searn.sunet.se`

     Gated: ⇔ `bit.listserv.ethology`

1-483   **EUDKRB-L:** On Kerberized Eudora, a Macintosh/PC mail client that uses Kerberos authentication.

     i `dascher@brownvm.bitnet` (Bitnet: `DASCHER@BROWNVM`) (David Ascher)

     ± `listserv@brownvm.brown.edu` (Bitnet: `LISTSERV@BROWNVM`) [body = SUBSCRIBE EUDKRB-L first-name last-name]

     Archive: Available to subscribers only.

1-484   **EUDORA:** For announcements relating to the Eudora SMTP/POP mail software for Macintosh and PC computers. *Moderated*

     i `sdorner@qualcomm.com` (Steve Dorner)

     ± `listserv@vmd.cso.uiuc.edu` (Bitnet: `LISTSERV@UIUCVMD`) [body = SUBSCRIBE EUDORA first-name last-name]

     Archive: `listserv@vmd.cso.uiuc.edu`

1-485   **EUEARN-L:** On Eastern Europe Telecommunications.

     i `gfrajkor@ccs.carleton.ca` (Jan George Frajkor)

     ± `listserv@ubvm.cc.buffalo.edu` (Bitnet: `LISTSERV@UBVM`) [body = SUBSCRIBE EUEARN-L first-name last-name]

     Archive: `listserv@ubvm.cc.buffalo.edu`

     Gated: ⇔ `bit.listserv.euearn-l`

1-486   **EURO-LEX:** All EUROpean Legal Information EXchange List, which allows the exchange of, and mutual assistance with, legal information research in all European countries.

i `bbweidin@dknkurz1.bitnet` (Bitnet: `BBWEIDIN@DKNKURZ1`) (Renate Weidinger)

± `listserv@vm.gmd.de` (Bitnet: `LISTSERV@DEARN`) [body = SUBSCRIBE EURO-LEX first-name last-name]

Archive: `listserv@vm.gmd.de`

Language: English, multilingual

1-487 **European Top 20 Charts:** Distribution of the MTV European Top 20 charts.

i ± `a3@rivm.nl` (Adri Verhoef)

1-488 **EV:** On the state of the art and future directions for electric vehicles.

i `dodeca!clyde@ucrmath.ucr.edu` (Clyde Visser)

± `listserv@sjsuvm1.sjsu.edu` (Bitnet: `LISTSERV@SJSUVM1`) [body = SUBSCRIBE EV first-name last-name]

Archive: `listserv@sjsuvm1.sjsu.edu`

1-489 **exhibitionists:** For cinema managers and/or projectionists, but open also to anyone working or interested in a cinema or film society, etc.

i ± `exhibitionists-request@jvnc.net`

1-490 **EXLIBRIS:** For users of the UMR Library. *Moderated*

i `psgraham@gandalf.rutgers.edu` (Paul Graham)

± `listserv@umrvmb.umr.edu` (Bitnet: `LISTSERV@UMRVMB`) [body = SUBSCRIBE EXLIBRIS first-name last-name]

Archive: `listserv@umrvmb.umr.edu`

1-491 **Extropians:** Spinoff of the "Extropy" journal. Topics include "anarchocapitalist politics, cryonics (and other life extension techniques), the technological extension of human intelligence and perception, nanotechnology, and spontaneous orders, and a number of other related ideas."

i `extropians-request@extropy.org`

± `extropians-request@extropy.org` [body = `user@domain`]

Other: Available as digest or reflector (specify which in subscription request)

1-492 **EZTRV-L:** On EZTreieve.

i `slhatf01@ulkyvm.bitnet` (Bitnet: `SLHATF01@ULKYVM`) (Sherry Hatfield)

± `listserv@ulkyvm.louisville.edu` (Bitnet: `LISTSERV@ULKYVM`) [body = SUBSCRIBE EZTRV-L first-name last-name]

Archive: Available to subscribers only.

1-493 **FACINTL:** A scholarly, international bulletin board, listing funding opportunities, calls for papers, relevant seminars and conferences, and the exchange of ideas.

i `pcr1@psuadmin.bitnet` (Bitnet: `PCR1@PSUADMIN`) (Patricia Ryan)

± `listserv@psuvm.psu.edu` (Bitnet: `LISTSERV@PSUVM`) [body = SUBSCRIBE FACINTL first-name last-name]

1-494 **FACSER-L:** On facilities and services departments in universities.

i `u42b5@wvnvm.bitnet` (Bitnet: `U42B5@WVNVM`) (Kate Bingham)

± `listserv@wvnvm.wvnet.edu` (Bitnet: `LISTSERV@WVNVM`) [body = SUBSCRIBE

      FACSER-L first-name last-name]

      Gated: ⇔ bit.listserv.facser-l

1-495   **FACXCH-L:** For establishing faculty exchanges between departments of architecture throughout the world.

      i hrl@psuarch.bitnet (Bitnet: HRL@PSUARCH) (Howard Lawrence)

      ± listserv@psuvm.psu.edu (Bitnet: LISTSERV@PSUVM) [body = SUBSCRIBE FACXCH-L first-name last-name]

      Archive: listserv@psuvm.psu.edu

1-496   **FAD-L:** About the Full Acceptance Detector (FAD), a proposed form of detector for use at the Superconducting Supercollider in Texas.

      i bjorken@slacvm.slac.stanford.edu (James Bjorken) or achim@slacvm.slac.stanford.edu (Achim Weidemann)

      ± listserv@slacvm.slac.stanford.edu (Bitnet: LISTSERV@SLACVM) [body = SUBSCRIBE FAD-L first-name last-name]

1-497   **Fall:** Any discussion concerning the fall and the various offspring of it, plus any related subjects.

      i ± fall-request@wg.estec.esa.nl

1-498   **FAMILY-L:** On academic family medicine.

      i fcmjoe@mizzou1.bitnet (Bitnet: FCMJOE@MIZZOU1) (Joe Stanford)

      ± listserv@mizzou1.missouri.edu (Bitnet: LISTSERV@MIZZOU1) [body = SUBSCRIBE FAMILY-L first-name last-name]

      Archive: listserv@mizzou1.missouri.edu

      Other: Subscription is limited. Requests will be sent to list owner for approval.

1-499   **FAMLYSCI:** For the Family Science Network.

      i gwbrock@ukcc.uky.edu (Greg Brock)

      ± listserv@ukcc.uky.edu (Bitnet: LISTSERV@UKCC) [body = SUBSCRIBE FAMLYSCI first-name last-name]

      Archive: listserv@ukcc.uky.edu

1-500   **FAMULUS:** On Famulus software.

      i charamza@csearn.bitnet (Bitnet: CHARAMZA@CSEARN) (Pavel Charamza)

      ± listserv@csearn.bitnet (Bitnet: LISTSERV@CSEARN) [body = SUBSCRIBE FAMULUS first-name last-name]

      Archive: listserv@csearn.bitnet

      Language: Czech, English

1-501   **FASTBS-L:** On FASTBUS, a standardised modular 32-bit wide data-bus system for data aquisition, data processing and control, used mainly by high-energy nuclear physics researchers.

      i rosk@sscvx1.bitnet (Bitnet: ROSK@SSCVX1) (Robert Skegg)

      ± listserv@vm.ucs.ualberta.ca (Bitnet: LISTSERV@UALTAVM) [body = SUBSCRIBE FASTBS-L first-name last-name]

      Archive: Available to subscribers only.

1-502   **FASTLN-L:** Virginia Tech Computing Center News. *Moderated*

      i fastline@vtvm1.bitnet (Bitnet: FASTLINE@VTVM1) (Peggy Morgan)

± `listserv@vtvm1.cc.vt.edu` (Bitnet: `LISTSERV@VTVM1`) [body = `SUBSCRIBE`
`FASTLN-L` first-name last-name]

Other: Subscription is limited. Requests will be sent to list owner for approval.

1-503 **fear:** On the rock band "disappear fear."

i `zen@sun.com` (Dan Farmer)

± `fear-request@death.corp.sun.com`

1-504 **fegmaniax:** On music, news, and whatnot about Robyn Hitchcock with some ties to the ex-offi-
cial Robyn Hitchcock fan club Fegmaniax.

i `fegmaniax-request@gnu.ai.mit.edu` or `cutter@gnu.ai.mit.edu` or
`woj@remus.rutgers.edu`

± `fegmaniax-request@gnu.ai.mit.edu` [body = `help`]

Archive: FTP `cs.uwp.edu` in `pub/music/lists/fegmaniax/digest`

1-505 **feminism-digest:** Digest version of newsgroup soc.feminism. (All posts must be approved.)
Moderated

i ± `feminism-digest@ncar.ucar.edu` (Cindy Tittle Moore)

Gated: ⇔ `soc.feminism`

1-506 **FEMINIST:** American Library Association's Feminist Task Force. On all aspects of feminism,
but especially on how it relates to the tasks and work of librarians.

i `tat@athena.mit.edu` (Theresa A. Tobin)

± `listserv@mitvma.mit.edu` (Bitnet: `LISTSERV@MITVMA`) [body = `SUBSCRIBE`
`FEMINIST` first-name last-name]

1-507 **FEMREL-L:** Women, religion, and feminist theology.

i `c497487@mizzou1.bitnet` (Bitnet: `C497487@MIZZOU1`) (Cathy Quick) or
`bfvegiar@midway.uchicago.edu` (Bonnie Vegiard)

± `listserv@mizzou1.missouri.edu` (Bitnet: `LISTSERV@MIZZOU1`) [body =
`SUBSCRIBE FEMREL-L` first-name last-name]

Archive: `listserv@mizzou1.missouri.edu`; Gopher: `gopher.gac.edu`

1-508 **ferrets:** All about domestic pet ferrets (Mustela Furo). Topics include suitability as pets, health
information, funny ferret stories, etc.

i ± `ferret-request@ferret.ocunix.on.ca` (Chris Lewis)

1-509 **FIBROM-L:** For patients, family, and friends of patients, researchers, and others interested in
the disease/syndrome known as Fibromyalgia/Fibrositis. Emphasis is on support for those
who suffer from Fibromyalgia.

i `sbott@vmd.cso.uiuc.edu` (Sandra Bott)

± `listserv@vmd.cso.uiuc.edu` (Bitnet: `LISTSERV@UIUCVMD`) [body =
`SUBSCRIBE FIBROM-L` first-name last-name]

Archive: `listserv@vmd.cso.uiuc.edu`

1-510 **FICTION:** For the Fiction Writers Workshop, where people who are interested in writing fiction professionally can share and critique works in progress and discuss the art and craft of
writing.

i `sascmc@unx.sas.com` (Christopher Mark Conn)

± listserv@psuvm.psu.edu (Bitnet: LISTSERV@PSUVM) [body = SUBSCRIBE FICTION first-name last-name]

Other: Daily digest. Subscription is limited. Requests will be sent to list owner for approval.

1-511 **filmmakers:** On all aspects of motion picture (not video) production, with an emphasis on technical issues especially construction and design issues for those working on tight budgets.

i ± filmmakers-request@grissom.larc.nasa.gov

1-512 **FILMUS-L:** Discussion on film music.

i c60hsw1@niu.bitnet (Bitnet: C60HSW1@NIU) (H. Stephen Wright, Principal Owner) or papakhi@iubvm.bitnet (Bitnet: PAPAKHI@IUBVM) (A. Ralph Papakhian, Associate Owner)

± listserv@iubvm.ucs.indiana.edu (Bitnet: LISTSERV@IUBVM) [body = SUBSCRIBE FILMUS-L first-name last-name]

Archive: listserv@iubvm.ucs.indiana.edu

Other: Daily digest

1-513 **FINAID-L:** For discussing student financial aid administration, including automation, federal regulations, professional judgement, and policies and procedures. It is not a mechanism for applying for financial aid or private business solicitation.

i req1@psuadmin.bitnet (Bitnet: REQ1@PSUADMIN) (Robert Quinn)

± listserv@psuvm.psu.edu (Bitnet: LISTSERV@PSUVM) [body = SUBSCRIBE FINAID-L first-name last-name]

Archive: Available to subscribers only.

Other: Daily digest

1-514 **FINANCE:** On finance, an e-journal.

i jfried@templevm.bitnet (Bitnet: JFRIED@TEMPLEVM) (Dr. Joseph Friedman)

± listserv@vm.temple.edu (Bitnet: LISTSERV@TEMPLEVM) [body = SUBSCRIBE FINANCE first-name last-name]

Archive: listserv@vm.temple.edu

Language: English

1-515 **finewine:** On the rock music group God Street Wine.

i ± finewine-request@world.std.com (Eric Budke)

1-516 **firewalls:** On the Internet "firewall" security systems and related issues.

i firewalls-owner@greatcircle.com

± majordomo@greatcircle.com [body = subscribe firewalls]

Archive: FTP ftp.greatcircle.com in pub/archive

1-517 **FISC-L:** For members of the Fee-based Information Service Centers in Academic Libraries (F.I.S.C.A.L.) discussion group of the American Library Association. *Moderated*

i nu146901@ndsuvm1.bitnet (Bitnet: NU146901@NDSUVM1) (Diane Richards)

± listserv@vm1.nodak.edu (Bitnet: LISTSERV@NDSUVM1) [body = SUBSCRIBE FISC-L first-name last-name]

Archive: listserv@vm1.nodak.edu

Gated: ⇔ bit.listserv.fisc-l

1-518 **FISICA-L:** For scholarly discussion of physics.

i migueltr@brufmg.bitnet (Bitnet: MIGUELTR@BRUFMG) (Miguel Tostes Ribeiro) or peb@ukacrl.bitnet (Bitnet: PEB@UKACRL) (Paul Edgar Bryant)

± listserv@ib.rl.ac.uk (Bitnet: LISTSERV@UKACRL) [body = SUBSCRIBE FISICA-L first-name last-name]

Language: Portuguese, English, French

1-519 **FIT-L:** On exercise, diet, and wellness.

i jones@etsuadmn.bitnet (Bitnet: JONES@ETSUADMN) (Chris Jones)

± listserv@etsuadmn.etsu.edu (Bitnet: LISTSERV@ETSUADMN) [body = SUBSCRIBE FIT-L first-name last-name]

Archive: listserv@etsuadmn.etsu.edu

1-520 **FITNESS:** On fitness and the IUPUI campus.

i ijvw100@indycms.iupui.edu (Betty Evenbeck)

± listserv@indycms.iupui.edu (Bitnet: LISTSERV@INDYCMS) [body = SUBSCRIBE FITNESS first-name last-name]

Archive: listserv@indycms.iupui.edu

1-521 **FLADOCS:** For Southeast U.S. document librarians.

i garcorn@nervm.bitnet (Bitnet: GARCORN@NERVM)

± listserv@nervm.nerdc.ufl.edu (Bitnet: LISTSERV@NERVM) [body = SUBSCRIBE FLADOCS first-name last-name]

1-522 **flamingo:** For fans of the (now defunct) T.V. series "Parker Lewis" (formerly "Parker Lewis Can't Lose") on the Fox television network.

i ± flamingo-request@lenny.corp.sgi.com

Other: Available both as a mail reflector and as a digest. State your preference when you subscribe.

1-523 **FLEXWORK:** On the flexible work environment, including telecommuting, job-sharing, and flex-time.

i psweinha@psuhmc.bitnet (Bitnet: PSWEINHA@PSUHMC) (Paul Sweinhart for Maria Holcomb)

± listserv@psuhmc.hmc.psu.edu (Bitnet: LISTSERV@PSUHMC) [body = SUBSCRIBE FLEXWORK first-name last-name]

Archive: listserv@psuhmc.hmc.psu.edu

1-524 **FLIPPER:** For Florida Librarians Interested in Preservation Programs, Education, and Resources (FLIPPER).

i erikess@nervm.bitnet (Bitnet: ERIKESS@NERVM)

± listserv@nervm.nerdc.ufl.edu (Bitnet: LISTSERV@NERVM) [body = SUBSCRIBE FLIPPER first-name last-name]

1-525 **FLN:** For scholarly discussion of figurative language—discussion is international and interdisciplinary (psychology, linguistics, AI, computational linguistics, literary studies).

i g77boqr1@icineca.bitnet (Bitnet: G77BOQR1@ICINECA) (Cristina Cacciari)

± listserv@icineca.cineca.it (Bitnet: LISTSERV@ICINECA) [body = SUBSCRIBE FLN first-name last-name]

Archive: Available to subscribers only.

1-526 **FNORD-L:** For the discussion and implementation of various views presented by such minds as those of Robert Anton Wilson, Timothy Leary, John Lilly, Antero Alli, and Christopher Hyatt.

   i `majcher@acsu.buffalo.edu` (Marc Majcher)

   ± `listserv@ubvm.cc.buffalo.edu` (Bitnet: LISTSERV@UBVM) [body = SUBSCRIBE FNORD-L first-name last-name]

   Archive: `listserv@ubvm.cc.buffalo.edu`

   Gated: ⇔ `Bit.Listserv.Fnord-l`

1-527 **folk-dancing:** All issues about folk dancing and related music are welcome. Also, this list is the place to find where folk dancing groups and clubs meet. All forms of folk dancing are welcome including, but not limited to, international, contra, square, cajun, barn dancing, etc.

   i ± `tjw+@pitt.edu` or `tjw@vms.cis.pitt.edu` (Terry J. Wood)+@pitt.edu for posting address.

   Gated: ⇔ `rec.folk-dancing`

1-528 **Folk Music:** All about new American folk music. Includes tour schedules, reviews, album release info, and other information on artists like Shawn Colvin, Mary Chapin Carpenter, David Wilcox, Nanci Griffith, Darden Smith, Cheryl Wheeler, John Gorka, Ani DiFranco, and others. *Moderated*

   i `alanr@nysernet.net` (Alan Roworth)

   ± `listserv@nysernet.org` [body = SUBSCRIBE `folk_music` first-name last-name]

   Archive: gopher `nysernet.org`

1-529 **FOLKTALK:** On folk music.

   i `shammer@leo.vsla.edu` (Scott Hammer)

   ± `listserv@wmvm1.cc.wm.edu` (Bitnet: LISTSERV@WMVM1) [body = SUBSCRIBE FOLKTALK first-name last-name]

   Archive: Available to subscribers only.

1-530 **FOODWINE:** On food and wine.

   i `32hyfev@cmuvm.bitnet` (Bitnet: 32HYFEV@CMUVM) or `32hyfev@cmuvm.csv.cmich.edu` (Musa Knickerbocker) or `3zlufur@cmuvm.bitnet` (Bitnet: 3ZLUFUR@CMUVM) or `3zlufur@cmuvm.csv.cmich.edu` (Elliott Parker)

   ± `listserv@cmuvm.csv.cmich.edu` (Bitnet: LISTSERV@CMUVM) [body = SUBSCRIBE FOODWINE first-name last-name]

   Archive: Available to subscribers only.

   Other: Daily digest

1-531 **FORAGE-L:** On foraging.

   i `agro121@unlvm.bitnet` (Bitnet: AGRO121@UNLVM) (Ken Moore)

   ± `listserv@unlvm.unl.edu` (Bitnet: LISTSERV@UNLVM) [body = SUBSCRIBE FORAGE-L first-name last-name]

   Other: Subscription is limited. Requests will be sent to list owner for approval.

1-532 **FoxPro-L:** For users of the FoxPro (tm) database development environment from Microsoft. This list is not affiliated with Microsoft Corp.

   i `coneill@polarbear.rankin-inlet.nt.ca` (Chris O'Neill)

   ± `fileserv@polarbear.rankin-inlset.nt.ca` [body = `join foxpro-l`]

1-533 **framers:** For users of the FrameMaker desktop publishing package from Frame Technology.

   i `framers-request@uunet.uu.net` (Mark Lawrence)

   ± `majordomo@drd.com` [body = `subscribe framers`]

1-534 **FRANCEHS:** On the history of France.

   i `jonas@stein.u.washington.edu` (Raymond Jonas)

   ± `listserv@uwavm.u.washington.edu` (Bitnet: LISTSERV@UWAVM) [body = SUBSCRIBE FRANCEHS first-name last-name]

   Archive: `listserv@uwavm.u.washington.edu`

1-535 **freaks:** About Marillion and related rock groups.

   i `brian@qualcomm.com`

   ± `freaks-request@bnf.com` [body = `subscribe freaks` first-name last-name]

1-536 **FREE-L:** On fathers' rights and equality, including parenting, divorce law, mediation, child support, false charges of sex abuse, and child custody.

   i `itog400@indycms.bitnet` (Bitnet: ITOG400@INDYCMS) (Dale Marmaduke)

   ± `listserv@indycms.iupui.edu` (Bitnet: LISTSERV@INDYCMS) [body = SUBSCRIBE FREE-L first-name last-name]

   Archive: `listserv@indycms.iupui.edu`

   Other: Daily digest

1-537 **FREETALK:** For free discussion, with no restriction on topic matters.

   i `snallen@lsuvm.bitnet` (Bitnet: SNALLEN@LSUVM) (Allen Gordon)

   ± `listserv@brownvm.brown.edu` (Bitnet: LISTSERV@BROWNVM) [body = SUBSCRIBE FREETALK first-name last-name] or `listserv@krsnucc1.bitnet` (Bitnet: LISTSERV@KRSNUCC1) [body = SUBSCRIBE FREETALK first-name last-name]

1-538 **fsp-discussion:** On the new FSP protocol which like anonymous-FTP provides public-access archives but is connectionless and virtually stateless.

   i `listmaster@germany.eu.net`

   ± `listserv@germany.eu.net` [body = `subscribe fsp-discussion user@domain`]

1-539 **fsuucp:** Everything about FSUUCP, an MSDOS UUCP/mail/news shareware package.

   i ± `fsuucp-request@toys.fubarsys.com` (Christopher J. Ambler)

1-540 **FSVS-L:** On using freeware, shareware and public domain software in university education and research, particularly for nuclear sciences and physical engineering.

   i `malusek@csearn.bitnet` (Bitnet: MALUSEK@CSEARN) (Alexandr Malusek)

   ± `listserv@csearn.bitnet` (Bitnet: LISTSERV@CSEARN) [body = SUBSCRIBE FSVS-L first-name last-name]

   Archive: `listserv@csearn.bitnet`

Language: Czech

1-541 **FTPADM-L:** For administrators of FTP archives.

   i `il@cspuni12.bitnet` (Bitnet: IL@CSPUNI12) (Ingrid Ledererova)

   ± `listserv@csearn.bitnet` (Bitnet: LISTSERV@CSEARN) [body = SUBSCRIBE
     FTPADM-L first-name last-name]

   Archive: `listserv@csearn.bitnet`

   Language: Czech

1-542 **FUNDLIST:** On university fund-raising issues.

   ± `listserv@jhuvm.hcf.jhu.edu` (Bitnet: LISTSERV@JHUVM) [body =
     SUBSCRIBE FUNDLIST first-name last-name]

   Archive: `listserv@jhuvm.hcf.jhu.edu`

1-543 **funky-music:** On funk music, as well as rap, hip-hop, soul, rhythm and blues, and related vari-
eties. Discussions of zydeco, reggae, salsa, soca, and similar gutsy street music are also welcome.

   i ± `funky-music-request@athena.mit.edu`

1-544 **FUSION:** Redistribution of `sci.physics.fusion`. *Moderated*

   i `fusion-request@zorch.sf-bay.org` (Scott Hazen Mueller)

   ± `listserv@vm1.nodak.edu` (Bitnet: LISTSERV@NDSUVM1) [body = SUBSCRIBE
     FUSION first-name last-name]

   Archive: `listserv@vm1.nodak.edu`

1-545 **fuzzy-ramblings:** On the British girl group "We've Got a Fuzzbox and We're Going to Use It!"

   i `rearl@oinker.ucsb.edu`

   ± `fuzzy-ramblings-request@oinker.ucsb.edu` [subject = subscribe]

   Archive: `fuzzy-ramblings-request@oinker.ucsb.edu` [subject = send
     `archive` or `discography` or `charter` or `list`]

1-546 **GALACTIC:** For users of software published by Galactic Industries, including SpectraCalc,
LabCalc, and GRAMS, which are used for the presentation of spectroscopic data.

   i `dehaseth@dehsrv.chem.uga.edu` (James de Haseth)

   ± `listserv@uga.cc.uga.edu` (Bitnet: LISTSERV@UGA) [body = SUBSCRIBE
     GALACTIC first-name last-name]

   Other: Subscription is limited. Requests will be sent to list owner for approval.

1-547 **gamekit:** On Don Yacktman's "GameKit," discussions, new release announcements, and general
talk on developing games for Next Step.

   i ± `gamekit-request@byu.edu`

1-548 **GAMES-L:** On computer games, from micro to mainframe.

   i `dwb@brownvm.bitnet` (Bitnet: DWB@BROWNVM) (David W. Baker)

   ± `listserv@brownvm.brown.edu` (Bitnet: LISTSERV@BROWNVM) [body =
     SUBSCRIBE GAMES-L first-name last-name] or `listserv@grearn.bitnet`
     (Bitnet: LISTSERV@GREARN) [body = SUBSCRIBE GAMES-L first-name last-name]
     or `listserv@krsnucc1.bitnet` (Bitnet: LISTSERV@KRSNUCC1) [body =
     SUBSCRIBE GAMES-L first-name last-name] or `listserv@twnmoe10.bitnet`
     (Bitnet: LISTSERV@TWNMOE10) [body = SUBSCRIBE GAMES-L first-name last-

name] or `listserv@utarlvm1.uta.edu` (Bitnet: `LISTSERV@UTARLVM1`) [body = SUBSCRIBE GAMES-L first-name last-name]

Archive: `listserv@brownvm.brown.edu` or `listserv@krsnucc1.bitnet` or `listserv@utarlvm1.uta.edu`

1-549 **GAMS-L:** On the General Algebraic Modeling System.

  i `une50f@dbnrhrz1.bitnet` (Bitnet: `UNE50F@DBNRHRZ1`) (Prof. S. Bauer and F. Nelihsen)

  ± `listserv@vm.gmd.de` (Bitnet: `LISTSERV@DEARN`) [body = SUBSCRIBE GAMS-L first-name last-name]

  Archive: `listserv@vm.gmd.de`

1-550 **GARDENS:** On gardens and gardening.

  i `crovo@ukcc.uky.edu`

  ± `listserv@ukcc.uky.edu` (Bitnet: `LISTSERV@UKCC`) [body = SUBSCRIBE GARDENS first-name last-name]

  Archive: `listserv@ukcc.uky.edu`

  Other: Daily digest

1-551 **GARR-BO:** GARR (Italian research network) for the metropolitan area Bologna and Romagna.

  i `anr0@icineca.bitnet` (Bitnet: `ANR0@ICINECA`) (Gabriele Neri)

  ± `listserv@icineca.cineca.it` (Bitnet: `LISTSERV@ICINECA`) [body = SUBSCRIBE GARR-BO first-name last-name]

  Archive: Available to subscribers only.

  Other: Subscription is limited. Requests will be sent to list owner for approval.

1-552 **GARR-OP:** For the network operation center of GARR.

  i `anr0@icineca.bitnet` (Bitnet: `ANR0@ICINECA`) (Gabriele Neri)

  ± `listserv@vm.cnuce.cnr.it` (Bitnet: `LISTSERV@ICNUCEVM`) [body = SUBSCRIBE GARR-OP first-name last-name]

  Archive: Available to subscribers only.

  Language: English, Italian

  Other: Subscription is limited. Requests will be sent to list owner for approval.

1-553 **GC-L:** On the global classroom, international student e-mail, and debates.

  i `chaikim@uriacc.uri.edu`

  ± `listserv@uriacc.uri.edu` (Bitnet: `LISTSERV@URIACC`) [body = SUBSCRIBE GC-L first-name last-name]

1-554 **GCT:** On the Generic Coverage Tool (GCT), a freeware package that measures how thoroughly tests exercise C programs.

  i ± `gct-request@cs.uiuc.edu`

1-555 **gender:** On gender issues. Open-minded forum for discussion of gender stereotypes vs. individuality, gender roles and particularly how people can get beyond these restrictions.

  i ± `owner-mail.gender@indiana.edu` [subject = add me mail.gender]

1-556 **GEODESIC:** On Buckminster Fuller.

  i `majcher@acsu.buffalo.edu` (Marc Majcher)

± `listserv@ubvm.cc.buffalo.edu` (Bitnet: `LISTSERV@UBVM`) [body = `SUBSCRIBE GEODESIC` first-name last-name]

Archive: `listserv@ubvm.cc.buffalo.edu`

Gated: ⇔ `Bit.Listserv.Geodesic`

1-557 **GEOGED:** On geography education.

i `jajone02@ukcc.uky.edu` (Jeff Jones)

± `listserv@ukcc.uky.edu` (Bitnet: `LISTSERV@UKCC`) [body = `SUBSCRIBE GEOGED` first-name last-name]

Archive: Available to subscribers only.

1-558 **GEOGFEM:** On feminism in geography

i `jajone02@ukcc.uky.edu` (Jeff Jones)

± `listserv@ukcc.uky.edu` (Bitnet: `LISTSERV@UKCC`) [body = `SUBSCRIBE GEOGFEM` first-name last-name]

Archive: Available to subscribers only.

1-559 **GEOGRAPH:** For academic discussions concerning geographical matters.

i `pellervo.kokkonen@helsinki.fi` (Pellervo Kokkonen) or `pyyhtia@finuh.bitnet` (Bitnet: `PYYHTIA@FINUH`)

± `listserv@searn.sunet.se` (Bitnet: `LISTSERV@SEARN`) [body = `SUBSCRIBE GEOGRAPH` first-name last-name]

Archive: `listserv@searn.sunet.se`

1-560 **GEONET-L:** For geoscience librarians and information specialists, including problem reference questions, shared resources, and developments in publishing books, journals, maps.
Moderated

i `heiser@iubacs.bitnet` (Bitnet: `HEISER@IUBACS`) (Lois Heiser)

± `listserv@iubvm.ucs.indiana.edu` (Bitnet: `LISTSERV@IUBVM`) [body = `SUBSCRIBE GEONET-L` first-name last-name]

Archive: Available to subscribers only.

1-561 **GER-RUS:** On Germans from Russia.

i `nu021140@ndsuvm1.bitnet` (Bitnet: `NU021140@NDSUVM1`) (Michael Miller)

± `listserv@vm1.nodak.edu` (Bitnet: `LISTSERV@NDSUVM1`) [body = `SUBSCRIBE GER-RUS` first-name last-name]

Archive: `listserv@vm1.nodak.edu`

Gated: ⇔ `bit.listserv.GER-RUS`

1-562 **GERINET:** On geriatric health care.

i `phil@wubios.wustl.edu` (J. Phillip Miller)

± `listserv@ubvm.cc.buffalo.edu` (Bitnet: `LISTSERV@UBVM`) [body = `SUBSCRIBE GERINET` first-name last-name]

Archive: `listserv@ubvm.cc.buffalo.edu`

1-563 **GEV List:** On Steve Jackson's classic OGRE/GEV board game of tactical warfare in the 21st century.

i ± `hcobb@fly2.berkeley.edu` (Henry J. Cobb)

1-564   **gibraltar:** A weekly digest dedicated to all forms of progressive, psychedelic, and electronic rock.

    i ± `gib@mailhost.tcs.tulane.edu`

1-565   **GIK2-L:** For users of Graphics Interface Kit/2, an OS/2 tool used to build applications that manipulate network diagrams.

    i `reichetz@awiimc12.bitnet` (Bitnet: `REICHETZ@AWIIMC12`) (Christian Reichetzeder)

    ± `listserv@vm.akh-wien.ac.at` (Bitnet: `LISTSERV@AWIIMC12`) [body = `SUBSCRIBE GIK2-L` first-name last-name]

    Archive: `listserv@vm.akh-wien.ac.at`

1-566   **GLB-NEWS:** For news, issues, and information of concern to lesbians, gay men, bisexuals, transsexuals, and transgendered persons. Heterosexuals are welcome, but anti-gay activity is prohibited. Membership is confidential.

    i `el406006@brownvm.bitnet` (Bitnet: `EL406006@BROWNVM`) (David B. O'Donnell) or `julie@drycas.club.cc.cmu.edu` (Julie Waters)

    ± `listserv@brownvm.brown.edu` (Bitnet: `LISTSERV@BROWNVM`)[body = `SUBSCRIBE GLB-NEWS` first-name last-name]

    Archive: Available to subscribers only.

1-567   **GLED:** On economic development in the Great Lakes region.

    i `u42762@uicvm.bitnet` (Bitnet: `U42762@UICVM`)

    ± `listserv@uicvm.bitnet` (Bitnet: `LISTSERV@UICVM`) [body = `SUBSCRIBE GLED` first-name last-name]

    Archive: Available to subscribers only.

    Other: Subscription is limited. Requests will be sent to list owner for approval.

1-568   **GLFR92-L:** On the ecology conference held in Brazil in 1992.

    i `josi@brfapesp.bitnet` (Bitnet: `JOSI@BRFAPESP`) (Josefina Perez Alvarez) or `tadao@ethos1.ansp.br` (Tadao Takahashi)

    ± `listserv@vm1.lcc.ufmg.br` (Bitnet: `LISTSERV@BRUFMG`) [body = `SUBSCRIBE GLFR92-L` first-name last-name]

    Language: Portuguese

1-569   **GLOMOD-L:** On global modeling.

    i `chadwick@uhunix.uhcc.hawaii.edu`

    ± `listserv@uhccvm.uhcc.hawaii.edu` (Bitnet: `LISTSERV@UHCCVM`) [body = `SUBSCRIBE GLOMOD-L` first-name last-name]

    Archive: Available to subscribers only.

    Other: Subscription is limited. Requests will be sent to list owner for approval.

1-570   **GLOSAS-L:** GLObal Systems Analysis and Simulation List.

    i `anton@vax2.concordia.ca` (Anton Ljutic)

    ± `listserv@acadvm1.uottawa.ca` (Bitnet: `LISTSERV@UOTTAWA`) [body = `SUBSCRIBE GLOSAS-L` first-name last-name]

    Archive: Available to subscribers only.

    Other: Subscription is limited. Requests will be sent to list owner for approval.

1-571   **GLRC:** For researchers on scholarly or scientific topics related to the Great Lakes region of the U.S. *Moderated*

> *i* `jmanno@suvm.bitnet` (Bitnet: `JMANNO@SUVM`) (Jack Manno)
>
> ± `listserv@suvm.acs.syr.edu` (Bitnet: `LISTSERV@SUVM`) [body = `SUBSCRIBE GLRC` first-name last-name]
>
> **Other:** Subscription is limited. Requests will be sent to list owner for approval.

1-572   **GMAST-L:** For general discussion on role-playing games.

> *i* `jeff@utcvm.bitnet` (Bitnet: `JEFF@UTCVM`) (Jeff Kell)
>
> ± `listserv@utcvm.utc.edu` (Bitnet: `LISTSERV@UTCVM`) [body = `SUBSCRIBE GMAST-L` first-name last-name]
>
> **Archive:** `listserv@utcvm.utc.edu`

1-573   **gnu-objc:** For active GNU Objective-C users and developers.

> ± `gnu-objc-request@prep.ai.mit.edu`

1-574   **GodlyGraphics:** On Christian uses of computer graphics and animations, especially using the Amiga computer, and for related trading of ideas, objects, images, and even joint projects, such as the design of a Christian computer game.

> *i* `pacheco@acs.harding.edu` (Ron Pacheco)
>
> ± `godlygraphics-request@acs.harding.edu` [body = `subscribe`]
>
> **Archive:** `listserv@acs.harding.edu`

1-575   **GOLF-L:** On golf.

> *i* `ctanski@onondaga.bitnet` (Bitnet: `CTANSKI@ONONDAGA`) (Chris Tanski)
>
> ± `listserv@ubvm.cc.buffalo.edu` (Bitnet: `LISTSERV@UBVM`) [body = `SUBSCRIBE GOLF-L` first-name last-name]
>
> **Other:** Daily digest

1-576   **GOVDOC-L:** All about government documents. *Moderated*

> *i* `raed@vmd.cso.uiuc.edu` (Raeann Dossett) or `dkovacs@kentvm.bitnet` (Bitnet: `DKOVACS@KENTVM`) (Diane Kovacs)
>
> ± `listserv@vm.ucs.ualberta.ca` (Bitnet: `LISTSERV@UALTAVM`) [body = `SUBSCRIBE GOVDOC-L` first-name last-name] or `listserv@psuvm.psu.edu` (Bitnet: `LISTSERV@PSUVM`) [body = `SUBSCRIBE GOVDOC-L` first-name last-name]
>
> **Archive:** Public

1-577   **GPNDG:** On the Great Pacific Northwest Gather, an annual rally for motorcycle enthusiasts to meet, generally in early August someplace in the Pacific Northwest to ride and tell truths.

> *i* `johnsw@wsuvm1.bitnet` (Bitnet: `JOHNSW@WSUVM1`)
>
> ± `listserv@wsuvm1.csc.wsu.edu` (Bitnet: `LISTSERV@WSUVM1`) [body = `SUBSCRIBE GPNDG` first-name last-name]
>
> **Archive:** `listserv@wsuvm1.csc.wsu.edu`

1-578   **GRADNRSE:** On nursing practice situations. *Moderated*

> *i* `lthede@kentvm.bitnet` (Bitnet: `LTHEDE@KENTVM`)
>
> ± `listserv@kentvm.kent.edu` (Bitnet: `LISTSERV@KENTVM`) [body = `SUBSCRIBE GRADNRSE` first-name last-name]

Archive: `listserv@kentvm.kent.edu`

1-579 **GRAFIK-L:** Discussions on computer graphics. *Moderated*

 i `ruediger.kolb@gmd.de` (Ruediger Kolb)

 ± `listserv@vm.gmd.de` (Bitnet: `LISTSERV@DEARN`) [body = `SUBSCRIBE`
 `GRAFIK-L` first-name last-name]

 Archive: `listserv@vm.gmd.de`

 Language: German

 Other: Subscription is limited. Requests will be sent to list owner for approval.

1-580 **GRAFOS-L:** On the mathematical and computational aspects of graphs.

 i `cerioli@ufrj.bitnet` (Bitnet: `CERIOLI@UFRJ`) (Cerioli, Marcia—COPPE
 SISTEMAS)

 ± `listserv@ufrj.bitnet` (Bitnet: `LISTSERV@UFRJ`) [body = `SUBSCRIBE`
 `GRAFOS-L` first-name last-name]

 Archive: Available to subscribers only.

 Language: Portuguese

 Other: Subscription is limited. Requests will be sent to list owner for approval.

1-581 **GRANT:** Fulbright Awards and grants for faculty and professionals.

 i `cies1@gwuvm.bitnet` (Bitnet: `CIES1@GWUVM`) (Jutta Hagner)

 ± `listserv@gwuvm.gwu.edu` (Bitnet: `LISTSERV@GWUVM`) [body = `SUBSCRIBE`
 `GRANT` first-name last-name]

1-582 **GRAPHNET:** For discussions of graph theory by mathematicians, including Hamiltonian problems, extremal graph theory, coloring problems, factorization, enumeration problems.

 i `shreve@plains.nodak.edu` (Warren Shreve)

 ± `listserv@vm1.nodak.edu` (Bitnet: `LISTSERV@NDSUVM1`) [body = `SUBSCRIBE`
 `GRAPHNET` first-name last-name]

 Archive: `listserv@vm1.nodak.edu`

 Gated: ⇔ `bit.listserv.graphnet`

1-583 **GRASS:** Generic Religions and Secret Societies (GRASS) is a forum for the development of religions and secret societies for use in role-playing games. Before being admitted to the list,
 prospective members must submit an essay on a religion or secret society which adds subtan-
 tially to the collective knowledge of the list.

 i `grass-server@wharton.upenn.edu` [subject = `help`]

 ± `grass-server@wharton.upenn.edu` [subject = `SUBSCRIBE` first-name last-
 name]

 Archive: `grass-server@wharton.upenn.edu` [subject = `dir` for index or `get`
 file-name]

1-584 **GRMNHIST:** Scholarly dicussions on all aspects of German history.

 i `113355@vmxa.hrz.uni-oldenburg.de` (Bitnet: `113355@DOLUNI1`) (Thomas
 Zielke) or `rehbock@cats.ucsc.edu` (Gary Lease)

 ± `listserv@vm.usc.edu` (Bitnet: `LISTSERV@USCVM`) [body = `SUBSCRIBE`
 `GRMNHIST` first-name last-name] or `listserv@ibm.gwdg.de` (Bitnet:
 `LISTSERV@DGOGWDG1`) [body = `SUBSCRIBE` `GRMNHIST` first-name last-name]

Archive: `listserv@ibm.gwdg.de`

1-585 **GRNSD-XX:** For the Global Research Network on Sustainable Development, a worldwide, independent forum of researchers who aim to increase the effectiveness and efficiency of the global sustainable development research process.

   i `grnsd@kub.nl` ("Aldo de Moor")

   ± `listserv@hearn.nic.surfnet.nl` (Bitnet: LISTSERV@HEARN) [body = SUBSCRIBE GRNSD-SC first-name last-name] or `listserv@hearn.nic.surfnet.nl` (Bitnet: LISTSERV@HEARN) [body = SUBSCRIBE GRNSD-SD first-name last-name] or `listserv@hearn.nic.surfnet.nl` (Bitnet: LISTSERV@HEARN) [body = SUBSCRIBE GRNSD-TU first-name last-name]

   Archive: Available to subscribers only.

   Other: Subscription is limited. Requests will be sent to list owner for approval.

1-586 **GRUNGE-L:** On grunge rock.

   i `rockin@mudhoney.micro.umn.edu` (Hilgreen)

   ± `listserv@ubvm.cc.buffalo.edu` (Bitnet: LISTSERV@UBVM) [body = SUBSCRIBE GRUNGE-L first-name last-name]

   Other: Daily digest

1-587 **GSA:** For genetic stock administrators.

   i `matthewk@fly.bio.indiana.edu` (Kathy Matthews)

   ± `listserv@iubvm.ucs.indiana.edu` (Bitnet: LISTSERV@IUBVM) [body = SUBSCRIBE GSA first-name last-name]

1-588 **GSP-List:** For alumni of Kentucky Governor's Scholars Program to participate in intellectual discussions on various topics, while also promoting the spirit of "community" fostered by GSP.

   i ± `gsp-list-request@ms.uky.edu` from the Internet or `gsp-list-request@ukma.bitnet` (Bitnet: REQUEST@UKMA) from Bitnet (David W. Rankin, Jr.)

1-589 **GSS-L:** For group support systems researchers, covering research, products, facilitation, and conferences.

   i `rwatson@uga.bitnet` (Bitnet: RWATSON@UGA) (Richard Watson)

   ± `listserv@uga.cc.uga.edu` (Bitnet: LISTSERV@UGA) [body = SUBSCRIBE GSS-L first-name last-name]

   Archive: `listserv@uga.cc.uga.edu`

   Other: Daily digest

1-590 **GTGUN:** On marksmanship, or competive gun shooting, at Georgia Tech.

   i `cc100dr@gitvm1.bitnet` (Bitnet: CC100DR@GITVM1) (Dave Re)

   ± `listserv@gitvm1.gatech.edu` (Bitnet: LISTSERV@GITVM1) [body = SUBSCRIBE GTGUN first-name last-name]

   Archive: `listserv@gitvm1.gatech.edu`

   Other: Subscription is limited. Requests will be sent to list owner for approval.

1-591   **GTRTI-L:** On research and teaching in global information technology.

      i `strouble@acad.udallas.edu` (Dennis Strouble)

      ± `listserv@gsuvm1.gsu.edu` (Bitnet: `LISTSERV@GSUVM1`) [body = `SUBSCRIBE GTRTI-L` first-name last-name]

      Archive: `listserv@gsuvm1.gsu.edu`

1-592   **Gunk'l'dunk:** A forum for discussing and promoting *Tales of the Beanworld*, an unusual black-and-white comic published by Eclipse comics. *Moderated*

      i ± `jeremy@stat.cmu.edu` (Jeremy York)

1-593   **gurps-announce-ext:** Announcements relating to the Generic Universal Role-Playing System from Steve Jackson Games.

      ± `owner-gurps-announce-ext@think.com` (Laird Popkin)

1-594   **gurps-ext:** General discussion of the Generic Universal Role-Playing System from Steve Jackson Games. All of the announcements are also sent to this list, so you don't need to be on both lists.

      ± `owner-gurps-ext@think.com` (Laird Popkin)

1-595   **GUTNBERG:** On Project Gutenberg, an effort to create large numbers of publically accessible texts on-line. *Moderated*

      i `hart@vmd.cso.uiuc.edu` (Michael Hart)

      ± `listserv@vmd.cso.uiuc.edu` (Bitnet: `LISTSERV@UIUCVMD`) [body = `SUBSCRIBE GUTNBERG` first-name last-name]

      Archive: `listserv@vmd.cso.uiuc.edu`

1-596   **gymn:** For the discussion of all aspects of gymnastics.

      i ± `owner-gymn@athena.mit.edu`

1-597   **H-DIPLO:** On diplomatic history, international affairs, and foreign policy. *Moderated*

      i `mmccarth@muvms6.bitnet` (Bitnet: `MMCCARTH@MUVMS6`)

      ± `listserv@uicvm.bitnet` (Bitnet: `LISTSERV@UICVM`) [body = `SUBSCRIBE H-DIPLO` first-name last-name institution]

      Archive: `listserv@uicvm.bitnet`

1-598   **H-RURAL:** On the history of agriculture and rural areas. *Moderated*

      i `joberly@cnsvax.uwec.edu`

      ± `listserv@uicvm.bitnet` (Bitnet: `LISTSERV@UICVM`) [body = `SUBSCRIBE H-RURAL` first-name last-name]

      Archive: `listserv@uicvm.bitnet`

1-599   **HABSBURG:** On Austrian history since 1500.

      i `ingrao@purccvm.bitnet` (Bitnet: `INGRAO@PURCCVM`) (Charles Ingrao)

      ± `listserv@vm.cc.purdue.edu` (Bitnet: `LISTSERV@PURCCVM`) [body = `SUBSCRIBE HABSBURG` first-name last-name]

1-600   **hang-gliding:** Topics covering all aspects of hang-gliding and para-gliding.

      i ± `hang-gliding-request@virginia.edu` (Jose A. Fernandez)

1-601   **Harleys:** Discussion about the bikes, politics, lifestyles, and anything else of interest to Harley-

Davidson motorcycle lovers.

i ± harley-request@thinkage.on.ca (Ken Dykes) or harley-request@thinkage.com

Other: In digest format (twice daily)

1-602 **hats:** A forum for discussions about the Montreal band Men Without Hats. The discussions are not moderated but they should have something to do with the band or ex-band members.

i ± hats-request@cs.uwp.edu (Dave Datta)

Other: Available as a daily digest and reflector. Archived at ftp.uwp.edu

1-603 **HEALTHRE:** On healthcare reform.

i str002@ukcc.uky.edu (Bob Moore)

± listserv@ukcc.uky.edu (Bitnet: LISTSERV@UKCC) [body = SUBSCRIBE HEALTHRE first-name last-name]

Archive: listserv@ukcc.uky.edu

1-604 **HEGEL:** For discussion and queries on the philosophy of G.W.F. Hegel.

i stepelev@vuvaxcom.bitnet (Bitnet: STEPELEV@VUVAXCOM) (Dr. Stepelevich)

± listserv@villvm.bitnet (Bitnet: LISTSERV@VILLVM) [body = SUBSCRIBE HEGEL first-name last-name]

Other: Subscription is limited. Requests will be sent to list owner for approval.

Archive: listserv@villvm.bitnet

1-605 **HELLAS:** For communication between Greeks on Bitnet.

i george@pop.psu.edu (Nikos George) or sda106@psuvm.psu.edu (Spyros Antoniou)

± listserv@uga.cc.uga.edu (Bitnet: LISTSERV@UGA) [body = SUBSCRIBE HELLAS first-name last-name] or listserv@american.edu (Bitnet: LISTSERV@AUVM) [body = SUBSCRIBE HELLAS first-name last-name] or listserv@psuvm.psu.edu (Bitnet: LISTSERV@PSUVM) [body = SUBSCRIBE HELLAS first-name last-name]

Archive: Available to subscribers only.

Language: Greek (with Latin characters).

Gated: ⇔ Bit.Listserv.Hellas

Other: Daily digest. Subscription is limited. Requests will be sent to list owner for approval.

1-606 **HELP-NET:** For users of Bitnet/Internet, a help resource including document files on Bitnet/Internet usage.

i stan@templevm.bitnet (Bitnet: STAN@TEMPLEVM) (Stan Horwitz)

± listserv@vm.temple.edu (Bitnet: LISTSERV@TEMPLEVM) [body = SUBSCRIBE HELP-NET first-name last-name]

Archive: listserv@vm.temple.edu

1-607 **HELWA-L:** For discussing topics of interest to Malaysian women in the United States and Canada.

i axh113@psuvm.bitnet (Bitnet: AXH113@PSUVM) (Azmi Hashim)

± listserv@psuvm.psu.edu (Bitnet: LISTSERV@PSUVM) [body = SUBSCRIBE HELWA-L first-name last-name]

Archive: Available to subscribers only.

Language: Malay

Other: Subscription is limited. Requests will be sent to list owner for approval.

1-608   **HEPDB:** For users of HEPDB, a database package designed to store and retrieve detector geometry, calibration information, production control, and perhaps also slow control.

i `jamie@cernvm.cern.ch` (Jamie Shiers)

± `listserv@crnvma.cern.ch` (Bitnet: `LISTSERV@CERNVM`) [body = `SUBSCRIBE HEPDB` first-name last-name]

Archive: Available to subscribers only.

1-609   **HEPIX-F:** On Unix-based high-energy physics applications.

i `jon@frcpn11.bitnet` (Bitnet: `JON@FRCPN11`)

± `listserv@frcpn11.in2p3.fr` (Bitnet: `LISTSERV@FRCPN11`) [body = `SUBSCRIBE HEPIX-F` first-name last-name]

Archive: Available to subscribers only.

Language: French

1-610   **hey-joe:** For fans of Jimi Hendrix and his music.

i ± `hey-joe-request@ms.uky.edu` (Joel Abbott)

Archive: FTP `ftp.ms.uky.edu` in `/pub/mailing.lists/hey-joe`

1-611   **HINDU-D:** On the Hinduism. *Moderated*

i `hindu.students.council@um.cc.umich.edu` (HSC)

± `listserv@arizvm1.ccit.arizona.edu` (Bitnet: `LISTSERV@ARIZVM1`) [body = `SUBSCRIBE HINDU-D` first-name last-name]

Archive: `listserv@arizvm1.ccit.arizona.edu`

Gated: ⇔ `bit.listserv.hindu-d`

1-612   **HIRIS-L:** On high-resolution infrared spectroscopy, including utility programs for handling high-resolution spectra. *Moderated*

i `g1wudd32@icineca.bitnet` (Bitnet: `G1WUDD32@ICINECA`) (Alberto Gambi)

± `listserv@icineca.cineca.it` (Bitnet: `LISTSERV@ICINECA`) [body = `SUBSCRIBE HIRIS-L` first-name last-name]

Archive: Available to subscribers only.

1-613   **HISTEC-L:** History of evangelical Christianity.

i `bays@ukanvm.bitnet` (Bitnet: `BAYS@UKANVM`)

± `listserv@ukanvm.cc.ukans.edu` (Bitnet: `LISTSERV@UKANVM`) [body = `SUBSCRIBE HISTEC-L` first-name last-name]

Archive: `listserv@ukanvm.cc.ukans.edu`

Other: Subscription is limited. Requests will be sent to list owner for approval.

1-614   **HISTORY:** Scholarly dicussion of history, topics include history as a science, computers and historians, cultural development, cultural differences, and philosophy.

± `listserv@ukanvm.cc.ukans.edu` (Bitnet: `LISTSERV@UKANVM`) [body = `SUBSCRIBE HIST-L` first-name last-name] or `listserv@umrvmb.umr.edu` (Bitnet: `LISTSERV@UMRVMB`) [body = `SUBSCRIBE HISTORY` first-name last-name]

Archive: FTP `ra.msstate.edu:/docs/history Listserv`
`listserv@ukanvm.cc.ukans.edu` or `listserv@umrvmb.umr.edu`

Other: Weekly digest

1-615 **HIT:** Highly Imaginative Tech and science fiction. (Discussions about any technology that can/can't be implemented in the near/far future).

i `xexeo@guarani.cos.ufrj.br` (Geraldo Xexeo/Jerry/MindWeb in VR)

± `listserv@ufrj.bitnet` (Bitnet: `LISTSERV@UFRJ`) [body = `SUBSCRIBE HIT` first-name last-name]

Archive: Available to subscribers only.

1-616 **HLPCMD-L:** For discussing HELP commands for the VM/CMS computer operating system.

i `cmsmaint@brownvm.bitnet` (Bitnet: `CMSMAINT@BROWNVM`) (Peter DiCamillo)

± `listserv@brownvm.brown.edu` (Bitnet: `LISTSERV@BROWNVM`) [body = `SUBSCRIBE HLPCMD-L` first-name last-name]

Archive: Available to subscribers only.

1-617 **HN-ASK-L:** For members of the History Network, an international volunteer organization of individuals committed to enhancing the role of computer telecommunications in historical research. *Moderated*

i `lhnelson@ukanvm.bitnet` (Bitnet: `LHNELSON@UKANVM`)

± `listserv@ukanvm.cc.ukans.edu` (Bitnet: `LISTSERV@UKANVM`) [body = `SUBSCRIBE HN-ASK-L` first-name last-name]

Archive: `listserv@ukanvm.cc.ukans.edu`

1-618 **HN-ORG-L:** The History Network subtopic dicussion list.

i `lhnelson@ukanvm.bitnet` (Bitnet: `LHNELSON@UKANVM`)

± `listserv@ukanvm.cc.ukans.edu` (Bitnet: `LISTSERV@UKANVM`) [body = `SUBSCRIBE HN-ORG-L` first-name last-name]

Archive: Available to subscribers only.

Other: Subscription is limited. Requests will be sent to list owner for approval.

1-619 **HOCKEY-L:** On collegiate ice hockey, including scores, team info, schedules, etc.

i `wts@maine.bitnet` (Bitnet: `WTS@MAINE`) (Wayne T. Smith) or `wts@maine.maine.edu`

± `listserv@maine.edu` (Bitnet: `LISTSERV@MAINE`) [body = `SUBSCRIBE HOCKEY-L` first-name last-name]

Archive: `listserv@maine.edu`

Digest: Daily

1-620 **HOLMESGP:** For members of the Holmes Group, a national consortium of research universities committed to making programs of educator preparation more rigorous.

i `hgmod@msu.bitnet` (Bitnet: `HGMOD@MSU`) (Ann E. Williams)

± `listserv@msu.edu` (Bitnet: `LISTSERV@MSU`) [body = `SUBSCRIBE HOLMESGP` first-name last-name]

Archive: `listserv@msu.edu`

1-621   **homebrew:** On the amateur production of beer. Includes all aspects of brewing. Though the main focus is on malt beverages (beer), we welcome discussions on homemade wine, mead, and cider, as well as other fermented (but not distilled) beverages.

    i ± `homebrew-request@hpfcmi.fc.hp.com`

    Archive: FTP `sierra.stanford.edu`

    Other: Digest format

1-622   **HONDA-L:** On Honda and Acura automobiles, including information and advice on purchases, and repair or parts. *Moderated*

    i `mjv@brownvm.bitnet` (Bitnet: `MJV@BROWNVM`) (Marshall Vale)

    ± `listserv@brownvm.brown.edu` (Bitnet: `LISTSERV@BROWNVM`) [body = SUBSCRIBE HONDA-L first-name last-name]

    Archive: `listserv@brownvm.brown.edu`

1-623   **HOPOS-L:** On the history of the philosophy of science.

    i `einphil@ukcc.uky.edu` (Don Howard)

    ± `listserv@ukcc.uky.edu` (Bitnet: `LISTSERV@UKCC`) [body = SUBSCRIBE HOPOS-L first-name last-name]

    Archive: `listserv@ukcc.uky.edu`

1-624   **HORROR:** On horror films and fiction.

    i `vman@pacevm.bitnet` (Bitnet: `VMAN@PACEVM`) (Cliff Brenner)

    ± `listserv@pacevm.dac.pace.edu` (Bitnet: `LISTSERV@PACEVM`) [body = SUBSCRIBE HORROR first-name last-name]

    Archive: Available to subscribers only.

1-625   **HORTPGM:** For the Virginia Tech Horticulture Department's programs in consumer horticulture.

    i `pdrelf@vtvm1.bitnet` (Bitnet: `PDRELF@VTVM1`) (Diane Relf) or `xnet@vtvm1.bitnet` (Bitnet: `XNET@VTVM1`) (Extension Information Systems)

    ± `listserv@vtvm1.cc.vt.edu` (Bitnet: `LISTSERV@VTVM1`) [body = SUBSCRIBE HORTPGM first-name last-name]

1-626   **HOSPEX:** The HOSPitality EXchange (homestays) database. *Moderated*

    i `wojsyl@plearn.bitnet` (Bitnet: `WOJSYL@PLEARN`) (Wojtek Sylwestrzak)

    ± `listserv@plearn.edu.pl` (Bitnet: `LISTSERV@PLEARN`) [body = SUBSCRIBE HOSPEX first-name last-name]

    Archive: Available to subscribers only.

    Other: Subscription is limited. Requests will be sent to list owner for approval.

1-627   **HOSPEX-L:** For discussion on HOSPitality EXchange (homestays) program.

    i `wojsyl@plearn.bitnet` (Bitnet: `WOJSYL@PLEARN`) (Wojtek Sylwestrzak)

    ± `listserv@plearn.edu.pl` (Bitnet: `LISTSERV@PLEARN`) [body = SUBSCRIBE HOSPEX-L first-name last-name]

    Archive: `listserv@plearn.edu.pl`

1-628   **HOTEL-L:** For hotel and restaurant educators and students.

    i `foodmatt@mizzou1.bitnet` (Bitnet: `FOODMATT@MIZZOU1`) (Matt Lonam)

± listserv@mizzou1.missouri.edu (Bitnet: LISTSERV@MIZZOU1) [body = SUBSCRIBE HOTEL-L first-name last-name]

Archive: listserv@mizzou1.missouri.edu

1-629 **hotrod:** Forum for people interested in high-performance vehicles.

i jgd@dixie.com

± hotrod-request@dixie.com [subject = subscribe user@domain]

Archive: FTP ece.rutgers.edu (for list) and ftp.nau.edu (for hotrod GIFs)

Gated: ⇔ alt.hotrod

1-630 **HP Patch:** For announcements of patches from Hewlett Packard (unofficial).

i owner-hpux-patch@cv.ruu.nl

± hpux-patch-request@cv.ruu.nl [subject = subscribe]

1-631 **HP3000-L:** For information exchange, discussion, questions, and answers dealing with the use and/or management of HP-3000 computers.

i jeff@utcvm.bitnet (Bitnet: JEFF@UTCVM) (Jeff Kell)

± listserv@utcvm.utc.edu (Bitnet: LISTSERV@UTCVM) [body = SUBSCRIBE HP3000-L first-name last-name]

Archive: listserv@utcvm.utc.edu

1-632 **HPSST-L:** On the history and philosophy of science and science teaching.

i hillss@qucdn.bitnet (Bitnet: HILLSS@QUCDN) (Skip Hills) or farquhad@qucdn.bitnet (Bitnet: FARQUHAD@QUCDN) (Doug Farquhar)

± listserv@qucdn.queensu.ca (Bitnet: LISTSERV@QUCDN) [body = SUBSCRIBE HPSST-L first-name last-name]

Archive: listserv@qucdn.queensu.ca

1-633 **hs-modem:** On high-speed modems and radios.

i ± hs-modem-request@wb3ffv.ampr.org

1-634 **HSPNET-L:** On the way computer wide-area networks can be used for remote diagnosis and treatment, transfer of patient records, and supplementing rural health care.

i dfp10@albnydh2.bitnet (Bitnet: DFP10@ALBNYDH2) or dfp10@albnyvm1.bitnet (Bitnet: DFP10@ALBNYVM1) (Donald F. Parsons, M.D.)

± listserv@albnydh2.bitnet (Bitnet: LISTSERV@ALBNYDH2) [body = SUBSCRIBE HSPNET-L first-name last-name]

Archive: listserv@albnydh2.bitnet

Gated: ⇔ sci.med.telemedicine

1-635 **HTECH-L:** On the history of technology.

i mah0h06@sivm.bitnet (Bitnet: MAH0H06@SIVM) (Steven Lubar)

± listserv@sivm.si.edu (Bitnet: LISTSERV@SIVM) [body = SUBSCRIBE HTECH-L first-name last-name]

Archive: listserv@sivm.si.edu

1-636 **humans:** Bruce Cockburn.

i zen@sun.com (Dan Farmer)

± humans-request@death.corp.sun.com

1-637 **HUMBUL:** Online bulletin board for arts and humanities. *Moderated*

i humbul@vax.oxford.ac.uk

± listserv@ib.rl.ac.uk (Bitnet: LISTSERV@UKACRL) [body = SUBSCRIBE
HUMBUL first-name last-name]

1-638 **HUMOR:** Funny things (warning required for sensitive content).

i bedwards@uga.bitnet (Bitnet: BEDWARDS@UGA) (Bill Edwards)

± listserv@uga.cc.uga.edu (Bitnet: LISTSERV@UGA) [body = SUBSCRIBE
HUMOR first-name last-name]

Archive: listserv@uga.cc.uga.edu

Other: Daily digest

1-639 **HUNTING:** On hunting. *Moderated*

i cbarnes@tamvm1.tamu.edu

± listserv@tamvm1.tamu.edu (Bitnet: LISTSERV@TAMVM1) [body = SUBSCRIBE
HUNTING first-name last-name]

Archive: listserv@tamvm1.tamu.edu

Gated: ⇔ rec.hunting

Other: Daily digest

1-640 **huskers:** On University of Nebraska sports.

± huskers-request@tssi.com

1-641 **HYPBAR-L:** About hyperbaric and diving medicine.

i al@ccvs4.technion.ac.il

± listserv@technion.ac.il (Bitnet: LISTSERV@TECHNION) [body =
SUBSCRIBE HYPBAR-L first-name last-name]

Archive: listserv@technion.ac.il

1-642 **HYPERCRD:** On the Macintosh Hypercard software.

i alleng@msu.bitnet (Bitnet: ALLENG@MSU) (George D. Allen)

± listserv@msu.edu (Bitnet: LISTSERV@MSU) [body = SUBSCRIBE HYPERCRD
first-name last-name]

Archive: listserv@msu.edu

1-643 **hypnodrone:** For droney guitar bands like Spacemen 3 and Galaxie 500 and Mercury Rev and
Medicine.

i ± hypnodrone-request@gnu.ai.mit.edu

1-644 **HYTEL-L:** The Hytelnet updates distribution list.

i aa375@freenet.carleton.ca (Peter Scott)

± listserv@kentvm.kent.edu (Bitnet: LISTSERV@KENTVM) [body = SUBSCRIBE
HYTEL-L first-name last-name]

Archive: listserv@kentvm.bitnet (Bitnet: LISTSERV@KENTVM) [body = INDEX
HYTEL-L]

Gated: ⇔ bit.listserv.hytel-l

1-645 **I-AMIGA:** All about the Amiga computer with a technical bent, including product releases and reviews, software development, etc.

i owner-i-amiga@ubvm.cc.buffalo.edu

± listserv@vm.ucs.ualberta.ca (Bitnet: LISTSERV@UALTAVM) [body = SUBSCRIBE AMIGA-L first-name last-name] or listserv@rutvm1.rutgers.edu (Bitnet: LISTSERV@RUTVM1) [body = SUBSCRIBE I-AMIGA first-name last-name] or listserv@ubvm.cc.buffalo.edu (Bitnet: LISTSERV@UBVM) [body = SUBSCRIBE I-AMIGA first-name last-name] or listserv@utarlvm1.uta.edu (Bitnet: LISTSERV@UTARLVM1) [body = SUBSCRIBE I-AMIGA first-name last-name]

Gated: ⇔ bit.listserv.i-amiga

1-646 **I-KERMIT:** KERMIT File transfer protocol discussion/digest. *Moderated*

i cmg@watsun.cc.columbia.edu (Christine Gianone)

± listserv@cuvmb.cc.columbia.edu (Bitnet: LISTSERV@CUVMB) [body = SUBSCRIBE I$KERMIT first-name last-name]

Archive: listserv@ebcesca1.bitnet or listserv@vtvm1.cc.vt.edu or listserv@utoronto.bitnet or listserv@vm.tcs.tulane.edu or listserv@vm.tcs.tulane.edu or listserv@vm.tcs.tulane.edu or listserv@uga.cc.uga.edu or listserv@bnandp11.bitnet

1-647 **I-VIDTEK:** On video technology, including Home Satellite (TVRO, DBS), Teletext, Cable Television, Stereo Television, Video Disc Technology, HighRes Television, Video Tape Recorders (Beta/VHS/UMatic).

i wancho@wsmr-simtel20.army.mil

± listserv@vmd.cso.uiuc.edu (Bitnet: LISTSERV@UIUCVMD) [body = SUBSCRIBE I-VIDTEK first-name last-name]

1-648 **IAFA-L:** For scholarly discussion of fantastic literature.

i hatt@vtvm1.bitnet (Bitnet: HATT@VTVM1) (Len Hatfield)

± listserv@vtvm1.cc.vt.edu (Bitnet: LISTSERV@VTVM1) [body = SUBSCRIBE IAFA-L first-name last-name]

Archive: listserv@vtvm1.cc.vt.edu

1-649 **IARPE-L:** Radiation protection mailing list. *Moderated*

± listserv@slacvm.slac.stanford.edu (Bitnet: LISTSERV@SLACVM) [body = SUBSCRIBE IARPE-L first-name last-name]

1-650 **IAUG-L:** For members of the International AIX Users Group of AIX(IAUG). AIX is a Unix operating system for IBM computers.

i meo@pencom.com (Miles O'Neal)

± listserv@psuvm.psu.edu (Bitnet: LISTSERV@PSUVM) [body = SUBSCRIBE IAUG-L first-name last-name]

Archive: listserv@psuvm.psu.edu

Other: Subscription is limited. Requests will be sent to list owner for approval.

1-651 **IB:** Forum for teachers, IB coordinators, and administrators involved wtih the International

Baccalaureate Diploma Program.

i `hreha@vax2.concordia.ca` (Dr. Steve Hreha)

± `listserv@proteus.qc.ca` [body = `subscribe IB` first-name last-name]

1-652 **IBDlist:** On Inflammatory Bowel Diseases, with particular emphasis on Crohn's disease and ulcerative colitis. *Moderated*

i ± `ibdlist-request%mvac23@udel.edu` (Thomas Lapp)

1-653 **IBM$KERM:** On IBM 370 Series KERMIT development.

i `jchbn@cuvmb.bitnet` (Bitnet: JCHBN@CUVMB) (John Chandler)

± `listserv@cuvmb.cc.columbia.edu` (Bitnet: LISTSERV@CUVMB) [body = `SUBSCRIBE IBM$KERM` first-name last-name institution country]

Archive: `listserv@cuvmb.cc.columbia.edu`

1-654 **IBM-HESC:** For discussion among the IBM Higher Education Software Consortium, which tries to enhance the academic process by making available IBM software and by sharing information on its effective use.

i `a1rw@psuorvm.bitnet` (Bitnet: A1RW@PSUORVM) (Ron Wills)

± `listserv@psuorvm.cc.pdx.edu` (Bitnet: LISTSERV@PSUORVM) [body = `SUBSCRIBE IBM-HESC` first-name last-name]

Archive: `listserv@psuorvm.cc.pdx.edu`

1-655 **IBM-MAIN:** All about IBM mainframes.

i `darren@ua1vm.ua.edu` (Darren Evans-Young)

± `listserv@ua1vm.ua.edu` (Bitnet: LISTSERV@UA1VM) [body = `SUBSCRIBE IBM-MAIN` first-name last-name] or `listserv@rutvm1.rutgers.edu` (Bitnet: LISTSERV@RUTVM1) [body = `SUBSCRIBE IBM-MAIN` first-name last-name] or `listserv@vm1.cc.uakron.edu` (Bitnet: LISTSERV@AKRONVM) [body = `SUBSCRIBE IBM-MAIN` first-name last-name] or `listserv@vm.gmd.de` (Bitnet: LISTSERV@DEARN) [body = `SUBSCRIBE IBM-MAIN` first-name last-name]

Archive: `listserv@ua1vm.ua.edu` or `listserv@vm1.cc.uakron.edu` or `listserv@vm.gmd.de` or `listserv@rutvm1.rutgers.edu`

Other: Daily digest

Gated: ⇔ `bit.listserv.ibm-main`

1-656 **IBM-NETS:** On IBM mainframes and networking including Tcp/Ip and VM or MVS, Wiscnet, Knet, X.25, Ethernet, Pronet, SNA, Vnet, Bitnet NJE protocols, etc.

i `jim@american.edu` (Jim McIntosh)

± `listserv@bitnic.educom.edu` (Bitnet: LISTSERV@BITNIC) [body = `SUBSCRIBE IBM-NETS` first-name last-name] or `listserv@uga.cc.uga.edu` (Bitnet: LISTSERV@UGA) [body = `SUBSCRIBE IBM-NETS` first-name last-name]

Archive: `listserv@bitnic.educom.edu` or `listserv@uga.cc.uga.edu`

1-657 **IBM-SRD:** For users of the IBM-SRD screen reader.

i `nu079509@ndsuvm1.bitnet` (Bitnet: NU079509@NDSUVM1) (Brett Person)

± `listserv@ndsuvm1.nodak.edu` (Bitnet: LISTSERV@NDSUVM1) [body = `SUBSCRIBE IBM-SRD` first-name last-name]

Archive: `listserv@vm1.nodak.edu`

Gated: ⇔ `bit.listserv.IBM-SRD`

1-658 **IBMAS-L:** On IBM's application system.

i `nlaflamm@irishvma.bitnet` (Bitnet: `NLAFLAMM@IRISHVMA`) (Nick Laflamme)

± `listserv@vma.cc.nd.edu` (Bitnet: `LISTSERV@IRISHVMA`) [body = `SUBSCRIBE IBMAS-L` first-name last-name]

Archive: `listserv@vma.cc.nd.edu`

1-659 **IBMTCP-L:** All about IBM TCP/IP software products for VM, MVS, OS/2, and for associated IBM TCP/IP hardware such as the 8232 LAN Channel Station, 3172 Interconnect Controller, 9370 Ethernet adapter, and other similar products.

i `gettes@pucc.princeton.edu` (Michael Gettes)

± `listserv@pucc.princeton.edu` (Bitnet: `LISTSERV@PUCC`) [body = `SUBSCRIBE IBMTCP-L` first-name last-name]

Archive: `listserv@pucc.princeton.edu`

Gated: ⇔ `bit.listserv.ibmtcp-l`

1-660 **IBSCG:** For members of International Business Schools Computing Association.

i `rajkumar@miamiu.bitnet` (Bitnet: `RAJKUMAR@MIAMIU`) (Rajkumar)

± `listserv@miamiu.acs.muohio.edu` (Bitnet: `LISTSERV@MIAMIU`) [body = `SUBSCRIBE IBSCG` first-name last-name]

Archive: `listserv@miamiu.acs.muohio.edu`

1-661 **IBYCUS-L:** On the Ibycus Computer, a microcomputer created for scholarly computing and word processing primarily in classics and in Biblical studies. It is integrated with CD-ROMs to search and display texts in Greek, Hebrew, Coptic, as well as the Roman alphabet).

i `bjorndahl@augustana.ab.ca` (Sterling G. Bjorndahl) or `mccarthy@cu4500.cua.edu` (William J. McCarthy)

± `listserv@vm.usc.edu` (Bitnet: `LISTSERV@USCVM`) [body = `SUBSCRIBE IBYCUS-L` first-name last-name]

Archive: `listserv@vm.usc.edu`

1-662 **icf-2010:** For users of the Sony CF-2010 shortwave radio receiver.

± `icf-2010-request@cup.hp.com`

1-663 **ICIS-L:** On the International Conference on Information Systems (whatever that is), including papers, conference registration details, program information.

i `rwatson@uga.bitnet` (Bitnet: `RWATSON@UGA`) (Richard Watson)

± `listserv@uga.cc.uga.edu` (Bitnet: `LISTSERV@UGA`) [body = `SUBSCRIBE ICIS-L` first-name last-name]

Archive: `listserv@uga.cc.uga.edu`

Other: Daily digest

1-664 **ICONEWS:** On optical physics, including optoelectronics, electrooptics, and photonics.
Moderated

i `chavel@fropt11.bitnet` (Bitnet: `CHAVEL@FROPT11`) (Pierre Chavel)

± `listserv@frmop11.cnusc.fr` (Bitnet: `LISTSERV@FRMOP11`) [body = `SUBSCRIBE ICONEWS` first-name last-name]

Archive: Available to subscribers only.

Other: Subscription is limited. Requests will be sent to list owner for approval.

1-665 **ICS-L:** On the International Chemometrics Society.

    i `thomas_c_ohaver@umail.umd.edu` (Tom O'Haver)

    ± `listserv@umdd.umd.edu` (Bitnet: `LISTSERV@UMDD`) [body = `SUBSCRIBE ICS-L` first-name last-name]

    Archive: `listserv@umdd.umd.edu`

1-666 **ID-LINE:** An idea exchange for Chinese communication scholars.

    i `cqm101@uriacc.bitnet` (Bitnet: `CQM101@URIACC`) (Guo-Ming Chen)

    ± `listserv@uriacc.uri.edu` (Bitnet: `LISTSERV@URIACC`) [body = `SUBSCRIBE ID-LINE` first-name last-name]

    Archive: Available to subscribers only.

1-667 **IDAHONET:** For networking among colleges, universities, and secondary schools in Idaho—primarily for the social sciences and public affairs.

    i `gsobilli@idbsu.bitnet` (Bitnet: `GSOBILLI@IDBSU`)

    ± `listserv@idbsu.idbsu.edu` (Bitnet: `LISTSERV@IDBSU`) [body = `SUBSCRIBE IDAHONET` first-name last-name]

    Archive: `listserv@idbsu.idbsu.edu`

1-668 **IDFORUM:** On industrial/product design and design education.

    i `gl250267@venus.yorku.ca` (Maurice Barnwell)

    ± `listserv@yorkvm1.bitnet` (Bitnet: `LISTSERV@YORKVM1`) [body = `SUBSCRIBE IDFORUM` first-name last-name]

    Archive: Available to subscribers only.

1-669 **IEEE-EGE:** For engineering students at Ege University.

    i `bilako@trearn.bitnet` (Bitnet: `BILAKO@TREARN`) (Ahmet Koltuksuz)

    ± `listserv@trearn.bitnet` (Bitnet: `LISTSERV@TREARN`) [body = `SUBSCRIBE IEEE-EGE` first-name last-name]

    Archive: `listserv@trearn.bitnet`

    Language: Turkish

1-670 **IEEE-L:** For students and professionals involved in electrical engineering.

    i `ba08034@bingsuns.cc.binghamton.edu` (Curt Coulter)

    ± `listserv@bingvmb.cc.binghamton.edu` (Bitnet: `LISTSERV@BINGVMB`) [body = `SUBSCRIBE IEEE-L` first-name last-name]

1-671 **IES-L:** On illumination engineering, or the design of the lighted environment. Participants include architects, engineers, students, contractors, educators, manufacturers, scientists.

    i `rns@psuecl.bitnet` (Bitnet: `RNS@PSUECL`) (Riad Saraiji)

    ± `listserv@psuvm.psu.edu` (Bitnet: `LISTSERV@PSUVM`) [body = `SUBSCRIBE IES-L` first-name last-name]

1-672 **IFER-L:** Institute for Educational Renewal.

    i `bedwards@miamiu.bitnet` (Bitnet: `BEDWARDS@MIAMIU`) (Barb Edwards)

    ± `listserv@miamiu.acs.muohio.edu` (Bitnet: `LISTSERV@MIAMIU`) [body =

SUBSCRIBE IFER-L first-name last-name]

Archive: Available to subscribers only.

1-673 **IFIP82-L:** On social and organizational factors implied by information technology and information systems. This list serves members and friends of Working Group 8.2 of The International Federation for Information Processing.

i rbask@bingsuns.cc.binghamton.edu (Richard L. Baskerville)

± listserv@bingvmb.cc.binghamton.edu (Bitnet: LISTSERV@BINGVMB)
[body = SUBSCRIBE IFIP82-L first-name last-name]

1-674 **Igor:** Forum for users of Igor (an integrated graphing and data analysis environment for the Macintosh) to share problems and solutions, as well as for potential users to seek opinions on the utility and performance of the application.

i ± igor-request@pica.army.mil (Tom Coradeschi)

1-675 **ihc:** International Harvester mailing list, devoted to the discussion of the line of utility vehicles (scout, travel all, pickup trucks) once sold by the International Harvester corporation.

i ± ihc-request@balltown.cma.com

1-676 **IHOUSE-L:** For free discussion on draft submissions before final printing of Washington University International House newsletter; also a resource to other groups serving internationals.

i c73221dc@wuvmd.bitnet (Bitnet: C73221DC@WUVMD) (Doyle Cozadd)

± listserv@wuvmd.wustl.edu (Bitnet: LISTSERV@WUVMD) [body = SUBSCRIBE IHOUSE-L first-name last-name]

Archive: listserv@wuvmd.wustl.edu

1-677 **IIRS:** For information retrieval specialists in Israel.

i rafarber@weizmann.bitnet (Bitnet: RAFARBER@WEIZMANN) (Miriam Farber)

± listserv@taunivm.tau.ac.il (Bitnet: LISTSERV@TAUNIVM) [body = SUBSCRIBE IIRS first-name last-name]

Archive: listserv@taunivm.tau.ac.il

1-678 **IL-ADS:** Israel bulletin board for single-party, noncommercial advertisements, such as selling a personal car or computer or providing piano lessons.

i hank@taunivm.bitnet (Bitnet: HANK@TAUNIVM) (Hank Nussbacher)

± listserv@taunivm.tau.ac.il (Bitnet: LISTSERV@TAUNIVM) [body = SUBSCRIBE IL-ADS first-name last-name]

Gated: ⇔ il.ads

1-679 **ILL-L:** Interlibrary loans and document supply.

i pmardeus@uvmvm.bitnet (Bitnet: PMARDEUS@UVMVM) (Patricia Mardeusz)

± listserv@uvmvm.uvm.edu (Bitnet: LISTSERV@UVMVM) [body = SUBSCRIBE ILL-L first-name last-name]

Archive: listserv@uvmvm.uvm.edu

1-680 **ILSPEEDE:** For discussion among a group of secondary and postsecondary school administrators who have developed an ANSI standard for electronic transmission of the kinds of academic records data found on high school and college transcripts.

i `axablwn@uicvmc.bitnet` (Bitnet: `AXABLWN@UICVMC`) (Brian Wallen)

± `listserv@vmd.cso.uiuc.edu` (Bitnet: `LISTSERV@UIUCVMD`) [body = `SUBSCRIBE ILSPEEDE` first-name last-name]

Archive: `listserv@vmd.cso.uiuc.edu`

1-681 **Imagen-L:** Imagen Laser Printer discussions, including software compatibility, hardware interfacing, LAN attachment capabilities, imPRESS programming, or methods used to create spooling and accounting software, etc.

i `amillar@bolis.sf-bay.org` (Alan Millar)

± `listserv@bolis.sf-bay.org` [body = `subscribe Imagen-L`]

1-682 **Imagine:** On the 3D computer rendering package "Imagine" by Impulse Inc.

i `dave@email.sp.paramax.com` (Dave Wickard)

± `imagine-request@email.sp.paramax.com` [subject = `subscribe`]

Archive: FTP `wuarchive.wustl.edu` in `/pub/amiga/boing/video/imagine/archive`

1-683 **IMAGRS-L:** On digital-image processing of remotely-sensed data

i `sincak@ccsun.tuke.cs` (Peter Sincak)

± `listserv@csearn.bitnet` (Bitnet: `LISTSERV@CSEARN`) [body = `SUBSCRIBE IMAGRS-L` first-name last-name]

Archive: `listserv@csearn.bitnet`

1-684 **IMMNET-L:** On medical immunization tracking systems. *Moderated*

i `jlevin@simvax.labmed.umn.edu` (Bitnet: `JLEVIN@UMNHCS`) (James E. Levin)

± `listserv@dartcms1.dartmouth.edu` (Bitnet: `LISTSERV@DARTCMS1`) [body = `SUB IMMNET-L` first-name last-name]

1-685 **immune:** A support group for people with immune-system breakdowns (and their symptoms) such as Chronic Fatigue Syndrome, lupus, candida, hypoglycemia, multiple allergies, chemical sensitivities, etc. No diagnosis turned away. Friends and family, medical and disability professionals, etc,. are also welcome.

i `cnorman@ucsd.edu` (Cyndi Norman)

± `immune-request@weber.ucsd.edu`

1-686 **improv:** Questions, comments, and bug-reports relating to the Improv spreadsheet for NeXTStep and Windows, published by Lotus Corp.

i ± `improv-request@gun.com` (Timothy Reed)

1-687 **INDEX-L:** On indexing, including the intellectual, philosophical, and technical aspects of index preparation. *Moderated*

i `skuster@bingvmb.bitnet` (Bitnet: `SKUSTER@BINGVMB`) (Charlotte Skuster)

± `listserv@bingvmb.cc.binghamton.edu` (Bitnet: `LISTSERV@BINGVMB`) [body = `SUBSCRIBE INDEX-L` first-name last-name]

Archive: `listserv@bingvmb.cc.binghamton.edu`

1-688 **INDIA-D:** For discussion on the affairs of the Indian subcontinent. *Moderated*

i `kvrao@trapper.bitnet` (Bitnet: `KVRAO@TRAPPER`) (Prof. K. Vaninadha Rao)

± `listserv@ukcc.uky.edu` (Bitnet: `LISTSERV@UKCC`) [body = `SUBSCRIBE INDIA-D` first-name last-name] or `listserv@utarlvm1.uta.edu` (Bitnet: `LISTSERV@UTARLVM1`) [body = `SUBSCRIBE INDIA-D` first-name last-name] or `listserv@vm.temple.edu` (Bitnet: `LISTSERV@TEMPLEVM`) [body = `SUBSCRIBE INDIA-D` first-name last-name]

Archive: `listserv@utarlvm1.uta.edu` or `listserv@vm.temple.edu`

1-689 **INDIA-L:** For news on the Indian subcontinent. *Moderated*

i `kvrao@trapper.bitnet` (Bitnet: `KVRAO@TRAPPER`) (Prof. K. Vaninadha Rao)

± `listserv@ukcc.uky.edu` (Bitnet: `LISTSERV@UKCC`) [body = `SUBSCRIBE INDIA-L` first-name last-name] or `listserv@utarlvm1.uta.edu` (Bitnet: `LISTSERV@UTARLVM1`) [body = `SUBSCRIBE INDIA-L` first-name last-name] or `listserv@vm.temple.edu` (Bitnet: `LISTSERV@TEMPLEVM`) [body = `SUBSCRIBE INDIA-L` first-name last-name]

Archive: `listserv@utarlvm1.uta.edu` or `listserv@vm.temple.edu`

1-690 **INDIANS:** For Asian Indians in the central New York region, especially cultural activities.

i `sanjay@suvm.bitnet` (Bitnet: `SANJAY@SUVM`) (Sanjay K. Pandey)

± `listserv@suvm.acs.syr.edu` (Bitnet: `LISTSERV@SUVM`) [body = `SUBSCRIBE INDIANS` first-name last-name]

1-691 **Indie-List:** A weekly magazine-style digest of local reports and live reviews of shows, records, anecdotes, news, and various information about "indie" music—generally defined as the current underground (sometimes called "alternative" or "grunge") music that is not generally associated with major labels such as WEA, Sony, etc. Bands that might fall into this category are Fugazi, Pavement, Sebadoh, etc.

i `mcornick@delphi.com` (Mark Cornick)

± `lclayton@uhuru.uchicago.edu` (Liz Clayton)

Submissions to: `keb@carson.u.washington.edu` (Kathleen Bennett)

Other: Weekly digest.

1-692 **indigo-girls:** Concerning the "Indigo Girls" musical group. Tour information, concert reviews, discussion of lyrics and music.

i ± `indigo-girls-request@cgrg.ohio-state.edu` (Stephen Spencer) [body = user@domain, "regular" or "digest"]

Other: digest available

1-693 **indigo-home:** Silicon Graphics Indigo.

i ± `indigo-home-request@world.std.com`

1-694 **INDKNOW:** For indigenous knowledge systems, traditional ecological knowledge and development.

i `pdh@stein.u.washington.edu` (Preston D. Hardison)

± `listserv@uwavm.u.washington.edu` (Bitnet: `LISTSERV@UWAVM`) [body = `SUBSCRIBE INDKNOW` first-name last-name]

Archive: `listserv@uwavm.u.washington.edu`

1-695 **INFO-APP:** For information on Apple II computers.

i `info-apple-request@apple.com`

± `listserv@vm1.nodak.edu` (Bitnet: `LISTSERV@NDSUVM1`) [body = `SUBSCRIBE INFO-APP` first-name last-name]

1-696 **info-fortune:** For users of Unix-based microcomputers produced by Fortune Systems.

i ± `info-fortune-request@csd4.csd.uwm.edu` (Thomas Krueger)

1-697 **info-gnu:** Progress reports from the GNU Project and requests for help. *Moderated*

i ± `info-gnu-request@prep.ai.mit.edu`

Gated: ⇔ `gnu.announce`

1-698 **info-high-audio:** About high-end audio equipment and modifications performed to high-end pieces. Techniques used to modify equipment, especially, but not limited to, vacuum tube electronics, are exchanged. Some comments may be subjective or intuitive and may not yet have a measurable basis.

i ± `info-high-audio-request@csd4.csd.uwm.edu` (Thomas Krueger)

Archive: FTP `csd4.csd.uwm.edu` in `pub/high-audio`

Gated: ⇔ `rec.audio.high-end` newsgroup

1-699 **info-ingres:** To discuss the commercial version of Ingres.

i ± `info-ingres-request@math.ams.org`

1-700 **info-labview:** For users of National Instruments' LabVIEW package (Mac, Sparc, and Windows).

i ± `info-labview-request@pica.army.mil`

1-701 **INFO-MAC:** INFO-MAC Digest. *Moderated*

i `info-mac-request@sumex-aim.stanford.edu` (Moderator)

± `listserv@vmd.cso.uiuc.edu` (Bitnet: `LISTSERV@UIUCVMD`) [body = `SUBSCRIBE INFO-MAC` first-name last-name] or `listserv@bnandp11.bitnet` (Bitnet: `LISTSERV@BNANDP11`) [body = `SUBSCRIBE INFO-MAC` first-name last-name] or `listserv@cearn.cern.ch` (Bitnet: `LISTSERV@CEARN`) [body = `SUBSCRIBE INFO-MAC` first-name last-name] or `listserv@ebcesca1.bitnet` (Bitnet: `LISTSERV@EBCESCA1`) [body = `SUBSCRIBE INFO-MAC` first-name last-name] or `listserv@hearn.nic.surfnet.nl` (Bitnet: `LISTSERV@HEARN`) [body = `SUBSCRIBE INFO-MAC` first-name last-name] or `listserv@irlearn.bitnet` (Bitnet: `LISTSERV@IRLEARN`) [body = `SUBSCRIBE INFO-MAC` first-name last-name] or `listserv@utoronto.bitnet` (Bitnet: `LISTSERV@UTORONTO`) [body = `SUBSCRIBE INFO-MAC` first-name last-name] or `listserv@ricevm1.rice.edu` (Bitnet: `LISTSERV@RICEVM1`) [body = `SUBSCRIBE INFO-MAC` first-name last-name] or `listserv@vm.cnuce.cnr.it` (Bitnet: `LISTSERV@ICNUCEVM`) [body = `SUBSCRIBE INFO-MAC` first-name last-name] or `listserv@vm.gmd.de` (Bitnet: `LISTSERV@DEARN`) [body = `SUBSCRIBE INFO-MAC` first-name last-name]

Archive: `listserv@vmd.cso.uiuc.edu` or `listserv@vm.cnuce.cnr.it` or `listserv@ebcesca1.bitnet` or `listserv@utoronto.bitnet` or `listserv@bnandp11.bitnet` or `listserv@irlearn.bitnet`

1-702 **info-oda:** On the ISO 8613 standard for Office Document Architecture, and ODIF (Office

Document Interchange Format).

i ± info-oda-request@andrew.cmu.edu

1-703 **Info-Russ:** Informal communication in Russian-speaking (or having related interests) community of (mostly) emigrants from the former USSR.

i ± info-russ-request@smarty.ece.jhu.edu (Alexander Kaplan)

1-704 **info-solbourne:** Discussions and information about Solbourne computers.

i ± info-solbourne-request@acsu.buffalo.edu (Paul Graham)

1-705 **info-stratus:** User-centered and user-conducted forum for discussing the fault-tolerant machines produced by Stratus Computer Corporation and also their cousins, the IBM System/88 and Olivetti CPS-32.

i ± info-stratus-request@mike.lrc.edu (Richard Shuford)

Gated: ⇔comp.sys.stratus

1-706 **info-vm:** Discussion and information exchange about the VM mail reader, which runs under GNU Emacs.

i ± info-vm-request@uunet.uu.net (Kyle Jones)

1-707 **INFOCD:** On the Compact Audio Disc medium and related hardware.

i ± mikey@cperch.nosc.mil (Michael Pawka)

1-708 **INFOCHIM:** On computing in chemistry in Italy.

i g1wudd32@icineca.bitnet (Bitnet: G1WUDD32@ICINECA) (Alberto Gambi)

± listserv@icineca.cineca.it (Bitnet: LISTSERV@ICINECA) [body = SUBSCRIBE INFOCHIM first-name last-name]

Archive: Available to subscribers only.

Language: Italian

Other: Subscription is limited. Requests will be sent to list owner for approval.

1-709 **INNS-L:** On the International Neural Network Society. *Moderated*

i metzger@umbc.bitnet (Bitnet: METZGER@UMBC) (Mary Ann Metzger)

± listserv@umdd.umd.edu (Bitnet: LISTSERV@UMDD) [body = SUBSCRIBE INNS-L first-name last-name]

Archive: listserv@umdd.umd.edu

1-710 **INSEA-L:** On education through the arts internationally.

i dsoucy@unb.ca (Don Soucy)

± listserv@unb.ca (Bitnet: LISTSERV@UNBVM1) [body = SUBSCRIBE INSEA-L first-name last-name]

1-711 **INT-LAW:** On foreign and international law librarianship.

i m-rush@uminn1.bitnet (Bitnet: M-RUSH@UMINN1) (Milagros Rush)

± listserv@vm1.spcs.umn.edu (Bitnet: LISTSERV@UMINN1) [body = SUBSCRIBE INT-LAW first-name last-name]

Archive: listserv@vm1.spcs.umn.edu

1-712 **INTDEV-L:** On international development and global education.

i david@uriacc.bitnet (Bitnet: DAVID@URIACC) (David Abedon)

± `listserv@uriacc.uri.edu` (Bitnet: `LISTSERV@URIACC`) [body = `SUBSCRIBE INTDEV-L` first-name last-name]

Archive: `listserv@uriacc.uri.edu`

1-713 **INTER-L:** For members of the Association of International Educators (formerly National Association of Foreign Student Affairs)—mainly admissions officers with questions about evaluation of foreign credentials and foreign student advisers with questions about interpretation of immigration laws and regulations.

i `jgraham@lamar.colostate.edu` (Jim Graham)

± `listserv@vtvm1.cc.vt.edu` (Bitnet: `LISTSERV@VTVM1`) [body = `SUBSCRIBE INTER-L` first-name last-name]

Archive: Available to subscribers only.

1-714 **INTERDIS:** On interdisciplinary studies.

i `crwolfe@miavx1.bitnet` (Bitnet: `CRWOLFE@MIAVX1`) or `scduncan@miavx1.bitnet` (Bitnet: `SCDUNCAN@MIAVX1`)

± `listserv@miamiu.acs.muohio.edu` (Bitnet: `LISTSERV@MIAMIU`) [body = `SUBSCRIBE INTERDIS` first-name last-name]

Archive: Available to subscribers only.

1-715 **INTERF-L:** The Israeli interest group on interfacial phenomena, an area of physics, chemistry, and engineering concerned with studies of surfaces and interfaces between different phases and states of matter (gas, liquid, solid). *Moderated*

i `andelman@taunivm.tau.ac.il` (David Andelman)

± `listserv@taunivm.tau.ac.il` (Bitnet: `LISTSERV@TAUNIVM`) [body = `SUBSCRIBE INTERF-L` first-name last-name]

1-716 **intergraph:** Discussion of all Intergraph CADCAM software and hardware.

i ± `ndsimpso@ingr.com`

Gated: ⇔ `alt.sys.intergraph`

1-717 **INTERQ-L:** For discussion of Internet applications at university libraries in Quebec.

i `ed22@musica.mcgill.ca` (Anastassia Khouri St-Pierre)

± `listserv@vm1.mcgill.ca` (Bitnet: `LISTSERV@MCGILL1`) [body = `SUBSCRIBE INTERQ-L` first-name last-name]

Archive: `listserv@vm1.mcgill.ca`

Language: French

Other: Subscription is limited. Requests will be sent to list owner for approval.

1-718 **InterText:** Bi-monthly fiction magazine with over 1,000 subscribers worldwide.

i ± Submissions `intertxt@network.ucsd.edu` (Jason Snell)

Archive: FTP `network.ucsd.edu` in `/intertext`

Other: In ASCII and PostScript

1-719 **INXS:** An unmoderated forum for the discussion of the Australian rock group INXS.

i ± `inxs-list-request@iastate.edu`

1-720 **IOUDAIOS:** For scholarly discussion of first-century Judaism, especially the writings of Philo of

Alexandria and Flavius Josephus.

i dreimer@ox.ac.uk (David Reimer)

± listserv@yorkvm1.bitnet (Bitnet: LISTSERV@YORKVM1) [body = SUBSCRIBE IOUDAIOS first-name last-name]

Archive: listserv@yorkvm1.bitnet

Language: English, Ancient Greek

1-721 **IPCT-L:** Broad ranging discussion on interpersonal computing and technology used in education. *Moderated*

i ipct@guvax.bitnet (Bitnet: IPCT@GUVAX)

± listserv@guvm.ccf.georgetown.edu (Bitnet: LISTSERV@GUVM) [body = SUBSCRIBE IPCT-L first-name last-name]

Archive: listserv@guvm.ccf.georgetown.edu

Language: English

1-722 **IR-L:** On information retrieval.

i ncgur@uccmvsa.bitnet (Bitnet: NCGUR@UCCMVSA) (Nancy Gusack)

± listserv@uccvma.ucop.edu (Bitnet: LISTSERV@UCCVMA) [body = SUBSCRIBE IR-L first-name last-name]

Archive: listserv@uccvma.ucop.edu

1-723 **IRAZU:** For Costa Ricans living abroad.

i listext@ucrvm2.bitnet (Bitnet: LISTEXT@UCRVM2)

± listserv@ucrvm2.bitnet (Bitnet: LISTSERV@UCRVM2) [body = SUBSCRIBE IRAZU first-name last-name]

Language: Spanish

Other: Subscription is limited. Requests will be sent to list owner for approval.

1-724 **IRL-POL:** On current Irish politics.

i fin@irlearn.bitnet (Bitnet: FIN@IRLEARN)

± listserv@irlearn.bitnet (Bitnet: LISTSERV@IRLEARN) [body = SUBSCRIBE IRL-POL first-name last-name]

Archive: listserv@irlearn.bitnet

1-725 **IROQUOIS:** For discussion on the Iroquois language.

i cdyck@epas.utoronto.ca (Carrie Dyck)

± listserv@utoronto.bitnet (Bitnet: LISTSERV@UTORONTO) [body = SUBSCRIBE IROQUOIS first-name last-name]

Archive: listserv@utoronto.bitnet

1-726 **IRTRAD-D:** On Irish traditional music. *Moderated*

i arar6013@iruccvax.ucc.ie (Paul McGettrick)

± listserv@irlearn.bitnet (Bitnet: LISTSERV@IRLEARN) [body = SUBSCRIBE IRTRAD-D first-name last-name]

Archive: listserv@irlearn.bitnet

Other: Digest

1-727 **IRTRAD-L:** On Irish traditional music.

   i `arar6013@iruccvax.ucc.ie` (Paul McGettrick)

   ± `listserv@irlearn.bitnet` (Bitnet: `LISTSERV@IRLEARN`) [body = `SUBSCRIBE`
      `IRTRAD-L` first-name last-name]

   Archive: `listserv@irlearn.bitnet`

1-728 **ISAGA-L:** For members of the International Simulation and Gaming Association.

   i `chadwick@uhunix.uhcc.hawaii.edu`

   ± `listserv@uhccvm.uhcc.hawaii.edu` (Bitnet: `LISTSERV@UHCCVM`) [body =
      `SUBSCRIBE ISAGA-L` first-name last-name]

   Archive: Available to subscribers only.

   Other: Subscription is limited. Requests will be sent to list owner for approval.

1-729 **ISDN:** The emerging telephony ISDN standard. The primary focus is on political and economic
      issues related to ISDN deployment (tariffs, compatibility, etc.) rather than on technical mat-
      ters. However, the list is unmoderated and all contributions are welcome.

   ± `isdn-request@csn.org`

1-730 **ISDN-ITA:** On the use of ISDN in Italy.

   i `pirovano@sparc10.siam.mi.cnr.it` (Marco Pirovano)

   ± `listserv@vm.cnuce.cnr.it` (Bitnet: `LISTSERV@ICNUCEVM`) [body =
      `SUBSCRIBE ISDN-ITA` first-name last-name]

   Archive: `listserv@vm.cnuce.cnr.it`

1-731 **ISIS-L:** For users of ISIS student information software products, published by SCT.

   i `dholmes@utdallas.edu` (David Holmes)

   ± `listserv@utdallas.edu` (Bitnet: `LISTSERV@UTDALLAS`) [body = `SUBSCRIBE`
      `ISIS-L` first-name last-name]

   Archive: `listserv@utdallas.edu`

1-732 **ISLAM-L:** On the history of Islam.

   i `jacock01@ulkyvm.bitnet` (Bitnet: `JACOCK01@ULKYVM`) (Jim Cocks)

   ± `listserv@ulkyvm.louisville.edu` (Bitnet: `LISTSERV@ULKYVM`) [body =
      `SUBSCRIBE ISLAM-L` first-name last-name]

   Archive: `listserv@ulkyvm.louisville.edu`

   Other: Daily digest

1-733 **ISO8859:** On 1-byte coded-character-set issues related to (1) the ISO/IEC 8859 coded-charac-
      ter-set standard, and (2) conversion between the family of 8-bit EBCDIC codes, and both
      the 7-bit ASCII (ISO/IEC 646) and 8-bit ASCII (ISO/IEC 8859-1) codes.

   i `hart@aplvm.bitnet` (Bitnet: `HART@APLVM`) (Ed Hart)

   ± `listserv@jhuvm.hcf.jhu.edu` (Bitnet: `LISTSERV@JHUVM`) [body =
      `SUBSCRIBE ISO8859` first-name last-name]

   Archive: `listserv@jhuvm.hcf.jhu.edu`

1-734 **ISO9000:** For discussion of standards for ISO 9000, a quality management system for businesses
      or organizations. *Moderated*

   i `jennejohnn@uwstout.edu` (Nancy Jennejohn)

± listserv@vm1.nodak.edu (Bitnet: LISTSERV@NDSUVM1) [body = SUBSCRIBE ISO9000 first-name last-name]

Archive: listserv@vm1.nodak.edu

Gated: ⇔ bit.listserv.ISO9000

1-735 **ISO10646:** On multibyte coded-character-set issues related to the ISO/IEC 10646 Universal Coded Character Set standard and the Unicode implementation of ISO/IEC 10646.

i hart@aplvm.bitnet (Bitnet: HART@APLVM) (Ed Hart)

± listserv@jhuvm.hcf.jhu.edu (Bitnet: LISTSERV@JHUVM) [body = SUBSCRIBE ISO10646 first-name last-name]

Archive: listserv@jhuvm.hcf.jhu.edu

1-736 **ISPF-L:** On programming and advanced usage techniques of IBM's ISPF and ISPF/PDF products for MVS and VM.

i ldw@usc.edu (Leonard Woren)

± listserv@vm.usc.edu (Bitnet: LISTSERV@USCVM) [body = SUBSCRIBE ISPF-L first-name last-name]

Archive: listserv@vm.usc.edu

1-737 **italian-cars:** Discussion of Italian-made automobiles.

i ± italian-cars-request@balltown.cma.com (Richard Welty)

1-738 **ITALIC-L:** On the use of Irish TeX and LaTeX.

i cbts8001@iruccvax.bitnet (Bitnet: CBTS8001@IRUCCVAX) (Peter Flynn)

± listserv@irlearn.bitnet (Bitnet: LISTSERV@IRLEARN) [body = SUBSCRIBE ITALIC-L first-name last-name]

Archive: listserv@irlearn.bitnet

1-739 **iti151:** For users of Imaging Technology's series 150 and 151 image processing systems and ITEX151 software.

i ± iti151-request@oce.orst.edu (Paul O'Neill)

1-740 **ITIG-L:** On information technology in libraries, especially for members of the Information Technology Interest Group of the Canadian Library Association.

i sloan@unb.ca (Stephen Sloan)

± listserv@unb.ca (Bitnet: LISTSERV@UNBVM1) [body = SUBSCRIBE ITIG-L first-name last-name]

Archive: Available to subscribers only.

1-741 **ITISALAT:** On Arabic computing. *Moderated*

i roochnik@guvax.bitnet (Bitnet: ROOCHNIK@GUVAX) (Paul Roochnik)

± listserv@guvm.ccf.georgetown.edu (Bitnet: LISTSERV@GUVM) [body = SUBSCRIBE ITISALAT first-name last-name]

Archive: listserv@guvm.ccf.georgetown.edu

Language: English

1-742 **IUFIS-L:** On the financial information system project at Indiana University.

i bgarrett@ucs.indiana.edu (Betty Garrett)

± listserv@iubvm.ucs.indiana.edu (Bitnet: LISTSERV@IUBVM) [body =

SUBSCRIBE IUFIS-L first-name last-name]
Archive: Available to subscribers only.

1-743 **jackson-list:** On the music of Joe Jackson, and members of his band over time, including sound-track work.

i thurlow@convex.com

± jackson-list-request@convex.com

1-744 **jamie-l:** On Jamie Notarthomas.

i jta1@cornell.edu (Jeffrey Anbinder)

± listserv@cornell.edu [body = subscribe jamie-l first-name last-name]

1-745 **janes-addiction:** On the defunct music group Jane's Addiction and its former members' current projects.

i ± janes-addiction-request@ms.uky.edu (Joel Abbot)

Archive: FTP ftp.ms.uky.edu in /pub/mailing.lists/janes-addiction

1-746 **JANITORS:** College and university housekeeping information.

i supervisor@sweep.fo.ukans.edu

± listserv@ukanvm.cc.ukans.edu (Bitnet: LISTSERV@UKANVM) [body = SUBSCRIBE JANITORS first-name last-name]

Archive: listserv@ukanvm.cc.ukans.edu

Other: Weekly digest

1-747 **JAPAN:** For the discussion of Japanese business, industry, and economic systems. *Moderated*

i r505040@univscvm.csd.scarolina.edu (Bitnet: R505040@UNIVSCVM) (James W. Reese)

± listserv@pucc.princeton.edu (Bitnet: LISTSERV@PUCC) [body = SUBSCRIBE JAPAN first-name last-name]

Archive: listserv@pucc.princeton.edu

1-748 **jarre:** A forum for discussions about music of the Jarre family. Primary discussion is of Jean-Michel and artists that work with him. The discussions are not moderated, but the discussions have some small relation to Jarre.

i ± jarre-request@cs.uwp.edu (Dave Datta)

Archive: ftp.uwp.edu

Other: The list is available as a daily digest and reflector.

1-749 **Jazz Butcher Conspiracy:** On the English pop musician Pat Fish and his group, the Jazz Butcher Conspiracy. Inside and firsthand information about forthcoming tours, tales, and projects. Also covers bootleg trading, creation records, David J. Max Eider, the black eg.

± jbc-list-request@pasture.ecn.purdue.edu

1-750 **JCMST-L:** Journal of Computer in Mathematics and Science Teaching.

i lehman@purccvm.bitnet (Bitnet: LEHMAN@PURCCVM) (James Lehman)

± listserv@vm.cc.purdue.edu (Bitnet: LISTSERV@PURCCVM) [body = SUBSCRIBE JCMST-L first-name last-name]

1-751 **JEI-L:** Technology in education.

i keane@earthsun.umd.edu (Christopher Keane)

± `listserv@umdd.umd.edu` (Bitnet: `LISTSERV@UMDD`) [body = `SUBSCRIBE JEI-L` first-name last-name]

Archive: `listserv@umdd.umd.edu`

1-752 **JES2-L:** Technical discussions on JES2, a component of the IBM MVS operating system.

i `p85025@barilvm.bitnet` (Bitnet: `P85025@BARILVM`) (Doron Shikmoni)

± `listserv@cearn.cern.ch` (Bitnet: `LISTSERV@CEARN`) [body = `SUBSCRIBE JES2-L` first-name last-name] or `listserv@vm1.nodak.edu` (Bitnet: `LISTSERV@NDSUVM1`) [body = `SUBSCRIBE JES2-L` first-name last-name] or `listserv@vtvm1.cc.vt.edu` (Bitnet: `LISTSERV@VTVM1`) [body = `SUBSCRIBE JES2-L` first-name last-name]

Archive: `listserv@vtvm1.cc.vt.edu` or `listserv@vm1.nodak.edu` or `listserv@cearn.cern.ch`

1-753 **JES3-L:** For programmers using JES3, IBM's job entry subsystem 3 for MVS.

i `b19141@anlvm.bitnet` (Bitnet: `B19141@ANLVM`) (Barry Finkel)

± `listserv@uga.cc.uga.edu` (Bitnet: `LISTSERV@UGA`) [body = `SUBSCRIBE JES3-L` first-name last-name]

Archive: Available to subscribers only.

1-754 **JESSE:** On Open Library/Information Science Education.

i `gwhitney@arizvms.bitnet` (Bitnet: `GWHITNEY@ARIZVMS`) (Gretchen Whitney)

± `listserv@arizvm1.ccit.arizona.edu` (Bitnet: `LISTSERV@ARIZVM1`) [body = `SUBSCRIBE JESSE` first-name last-name]

Archive: `listserv@arizvm1.ccit.arizona.edu`

1-755 **Jesus & Mary Chain:** Discussion about the music group The Jesus & Mary Chain.

i ± `21329ks@ibm.cl.msu.edu` (Karl Stuber)

1-756 **Jethro Tull Digest:** On the music of the Jethro Tull rock group.

i ± `jtull-request@remus.rutgers.edu`

Other: In digest format

1-757 **JEWISHGT:** For members of the Jewish community at Georgia Tech and other interested Jews.

i `gt5549d@prism.gatech.edu` (Aviva Starkman)

± `listserv@gitvm1.gatech.edu` (Bitnet: `LISTSERV@GITVM1`) [body = `SUBSCRIBE JEWISHGT` first-name last-name]

Archive: Available to subscribers only.

Other: Subscription is limited. Requests will be sent to list owner for approval.

1-758 **JNET-L:** JNET Discussion Group.

i `gerland@ubvms.cc.buffalo.edu` (Jim Gerland)

± `listserv@bitnic.educom.edu` (Bitnet: `LISTSERV@BITNIC`) [body = `SUBSCRIBE JNET-L` first-name last-name] or `listserv@hearn.nic.surfnet.nl` (Bitnet: `LISTSERV@HEARN`) [body = `SUBSCRIBE JNET-L` first-name last-name] or `listserv@vm.marist.edu` (Bitnet: `LISTSERV@MARIST`) [body = `SUBSCRIBE JNET-L` first-name last-name] or `listserv@uga.cc.uga.edu` (Bitnet: `LISTSERV@UGA`) [body = `SUBSCRIBE JNET-L` first-name last-name] or `listserv@vm.gmd.de` (Bitnet:

LISTSERV@DEARN) [body = SUBSCRIBE JNET-L first-name last-name]

Archive: `listserv@vmd.cso.uiuc.edu`

1-759 **JOBPLACE:** On self-directed job search techniques and job placement issues. This is not a place to list or look for job openings.

i `dkhowa01@ukcc.uky.edu` (Drema Howard)

± `listserv@ukcc.uky.edu` (Bitnet: LISTSERV@UKCC) [body = SUBSCRIBE JOBPLACE first-name last-name]

Archive: `listserv@ukcc.uky.edu`

1-760 **JOURNET:** On journalism and journalism education.

i `gfrajkor@ccs.carleton.ca` (George Frajkor)

± `listserv@qucdn.queensu.ca` (Bitnet: LISTSERV@QUCDN) [body = SUBSCRIBE JOURNET first-name last-name]

Archive: `listserv@qucdn.queensu.ca`

1-761 **JTIT-L:** For Japanese teachers and instructional technology.

i `tomita@kenyon.edu` (Hideo Tomita)

± `listserv@psuvm.psu.edu` (Bitnet: LISTSERV@PSUVM) [body = SUBSCRIBE JTIT-L first-name last-name]

Archive: `listserv@psuvm.psu.edu`

1-762 **Jugo:** News, editorials, views, and public actions regarding the events in ex-Yugoslavia.

i ± `dimitrije@buenga.bu.edu` (Dimitrije Stamenovic)

1-763 **jump-in-the-river:** On the music, recordings, lyrics, and tour information of Sinead O'Connor.

i ± `jump-in-the-river-request@presto.ig.com` (Michael C. Berch)

Archive: FTP `net.bio.net` in `/misc/jitr/`

1-764 **JURIST-L:** For Dutch legal researchers.

i `l.dejong@strafr.rulimburg.nl` (Leo de Jong)

± `listserv@hearn.nic.surfnet.nl` (Bitnet: LISTSERV@HEARN) [body = SUBSCRIBE JURIST-L first-name last-name]**Archive:** `listserv@hearn.nic.surfnet.nl`

1-765 **JURIX-L:** On legal knowledge based systems of the Dutch Foundation for Legal Knowledge Based Systems, JURIX.

i `romix@bsk.utwente.nl`

± `listserv@hearn.nic.surfnet.nl` (Bitnet: LISTSERV@HEARN) [body = SUBSCRIBE JURIX-L first-name last-name]

Archive: `listserv@hearn.nic.surfnet.nl`

1-766 **KANSAS-L:** Kansas history and life.

i `lhnelson@ukanm.bitnet` (Bitnet: LHNELSON@UKANM) or `karmita@ukanvm.bitnet` (Bitnet: KARMITA@UKANVM)

± `listserv@ukanaix.cc.ukans.edu` (Bitnet: LISTSERV@UKANAIX) [body = SUBSCRIBE KANSAS-L first-name last-name]

Archive: `listserv listserv@ukanaix.cc.ukans.edu`

1-767   **KATALIST:** On library systems and databases.

     i `h1192dro@ella.hu` (Drotos Laszlo) or `ib001ara@huearn.bitnet` (Bitnet: `IB001ARA@HUEARN`) (Sandor Aranyi)

     ± `listserv@huearn.sztaki.hu` (Bitnet: `LISTSERV@HUEARN`) [body = `SUBSCRIBE KATALIST last-name first-name`]

     Archive: `listserv@huearn.sztaki.hu`

     Language: Hungarian, English

1-768   **KENTUCKY:** For discussion of civic affairs and politics in Kentucky.

     i `str002@ukcc.uky.edu` (Bob Moore)

     ± `listserv@ukcc.uky.edu` (Bitnet: `LISTSERV@UKCC`) [body = `SUBSCRIBE KENTUCKY first-name last-name`]

     Archive: `listserv@ukcc.uky.edu`

1-769   **kgs:** Distributes announcements of the Kurt Goedel Society, an international association for symbolic logic and philosophy, to members and others interested in its activities.

     i ± `kgs@logic.tuwien.ac.at`

1-770   **khoros:** On khoros software package an X-Windows integrated software development environment for information processing and visualization.

     i ± `khoros-request@chama.unm.edu`

1-771   **KIDLINK:** For learning about, and signing up for, the Kidlink network, which spans several other lists. This network coordinates worldwide dialogue among youth in several age groups and many areas of interest. Other KIDLINK lists are KIDCAFE, KIDLEADR, KIDNEWS, KINDEX, KINDEXW, KIDFORUM, KIDCAFEP. *Moderated*

     i `kidlink-info@vm1.nodak.edu` or `opresno@extern.uio.no` (Odd de Presno)

     ± `listserv@vm1.nodak.edu` (Bitnet: `LISTSERV@NDSUVM1`) [body = `SUBSCRIBE KIDLINK first-name last-name`]

     Archive: `listserv@vm1.nodak.edu`

     Language: English, Portuguese, Japanese

1-772   **KIDLIT-L:** For educators, librarians, researchers, authors, and others interested in literature for children and youths, including teaching strategies, innovative course ideas, current research. *Moderated*

     i `pstellin@bingvmb.bitnet` (Prue Stelling)

     ± `listserv@bingvmb.cc.binghamton.edu` (Bitnet: `LISTSERV@BINGVMB`) [body = `SUBSCRIBE KIDLIT-L first-name last-name`]

     Archive: `listserv@bingvmb.cc.binghamton.edu`

1-773   **KIMYA-L:** For communication on chemistry and chemical engineering.

     i `h.c.yatmaz@newcastle.ac.uk` (Cengiz Yatmaz)

     ± `listserv@tritu.bitnet` (Bitnet: `LISTSERV@TRITU`) [body = `SUBSCRIBE KIMYA-L first-name last-name`]

     Archive: `listserv@tritu.bitnet`

     Language: Turkish

     Gated: ⇔ `itu.listserv.kimya-l`

1-774 **kites:** On kite and kite activities, including, but not limited to, kite making and flying, and reports of kite events.

    i `mss@das.harvard.edu` (Marty Sasaki)

    ± (USA/Canada/Europe): `kites-request@das.harvard.edu` (Japan): `koscvax.keio.junet!kites-request`

    Gated: ⇔ `rec.kites`

1-775 **KLARINET:** For clarinettists.

    i `nvfayxj@vccswest.bitnet` (Bitnet: NVFAYXJ@VCCSWEST) (Jim Fay)

    ± `listserv@vccscent.bitnet` (Bitnet: LISTSERV@VCCSCENT) [body = SUBSCRIBE KLARINET first-name last-name]

    Archive: `listserv@vccscent.bitnet`

1-776 **KONFER-L:** For schedules and related data of Turkish conferences, seminars, workshops all around the world.

    i `bilsay@trearn.bitnet` (Bitnet: BILSAY@TREARN) (Dr. Sitki Aytac) or `turgut@trearn.bitnet` (Bitnet: TURGUT@TREARN) (Turgut Kalfaoglu)

    ± `listserv@trearn.bitnet` (Bitnet: LISTSERV@TREARN) [body = SUBSCRIBE KONFER-L first-name last-name]

    Archive: `listserv@trearn.bitnet`

1-777 **kraftwerk:** A forum for discussions about the German band Kraftwerk and other related German electronic artists. The discussions are not moderated.

    i ± `kraftwerk-request@cs.uwp.edu` (Dave Datta)

    Other: The list is available as a daily digest and reflector. Archives are stored at `ftp.uwp.edu`

1-778 **Kuharske Bukve:** Weekly posting of a recipe previously tested by a member of editorial board. The recipes are formatted. Feedback requested. *Moderated*

    Language: Slovene.

    i ± & submissions to: `kuharske-bukve@krpan.arnes.si` or `kuharske.bukve@uni-lj.si` (Polona Novak and Andrej Brodnik)

1-779 **KUHIST-L:** History at Kansas University.

    i `lhnelson@ukanvm.bitnet` (Bitnet: LHNELSON@UKANVM) (Lynn H. Nelson)

    ± `listserv@ukanvm.cc.ukans.edu` (Bitnet: LISTSERV@UKANVM) [body = SUBSCRIBE KUHIST-L first-name last-name]

1-780 **kundera-list:** On the works of Milan Kundera.

    i ± `kundera-request@anat3d1.anatomy.upenn.edu`

1-781 **L-CHA:** The Canadian Historical Association Conference on Computing.

    i `r12270@er.uqam.ca` (José Igartua)

    ± `listserv@uqam.bitnet.ca` (Bitnet: LISTSERV@UQAM) [body = SUBSCRIBE L-CHA first-name last-name]

    Archive: Available to subscribers only.

    Other: Subscription is limited. Requests will be sent to list owner for approval.

1-782 **L-HCAP:** For discussion of issues related to handicapped people in education, including access to computers, buildings, and employment. *Moderated*

i wtm@bunker.shel-isc-br.com

± listserv@vm1.nodak.edu (Bitnet: LISTSERV@NDSUVM1) [body = SUBSCRIBE
L-HCAP first-name last-name]

Archive: listserv@vm1.nodak.edu

Gated: ⇔ bit.listserv.l-hcap

Other: Daily digest

1-783 **LABOR-L:** On labor in the emerging global economy.

i lanfran@yorkvm1.bitnet (Bitnet: LANFRAN@YORKVM1) (Sam Lanfranco)

± listserv@yorkvm1.bitnet (Bitnet: LISTSERV@YORKVM1) [body = SUBSCRIBE
LABOR-L first-name last-name]

Archive: Available to subscribers only.

1-784 **LACTACID:** On lactic acid bacteria.

i eng-leong_foo_mircen-ki%micforum@mica.mic.ki.se

± listserv@searn.sunet.se (Bitnet: LISTSERV@SEARN) [body = SUBSCRIBE
LACTACID first-name last-name]

Archive: listserv@searn.sunet.se

1-785 **lang-lucid:** On Lucid, Lu+, and other indexical programming languages.

i ± lang-lucid-request@csl.sri.com (R. Jagannathan)

1-786 **LANGIT:** On linguistics in Italy.

i dolci@iveuncc.bitnet (Bitnet: DOLCI@IVEUNCC) (Roberto Dolci)

± listserv@icineca.cineca.it (Bitnet: LISTSERV@ICINECA) [body =
SUBSCRIBE LANGIT first-name last-name]

Archive: Available to subscribers only.

Language: Italian

1-787 **LANMAN-L:** For users of Microsoft LAN Manager and Windows NT Advanced Server.

i chriso@nih.gov (Chris Ohlandt)

± listserv@list.nih.gov (Bitnet: LISTSERV@NIHLIST) [body = SUBSCRIBE
LANMAN-L first-name last-name]

Archive: listserv@list.nih.gov

1-788 **LARCH-L:** On landscape architecture.

i zooey@suvm.bitnet (Bitnet: ZOOEY@SUVM) (James F. Palmer)

± listserv@suvm.acs.syr.edu (Bitnet: LISTSERV@SUVM) [body = SUBSCRIBE
LARCH-L first-name last-name]

1-789 **LARCHNET:** On landscape architecture.

i ccsgrimm@vm.uoguelph.ca (Paul Graham)

± listserv@vm.uoguelph.ca (Bitnet: LISTSERV@UOGUELPH) [body =
SUBSCRIBE LARCHNET first-name last-name]

Archive: Available to subscribers only.

1-790 **LASPAU-L:** For announcements of conferences and seeking help with research projects in or about Latin America and the Caribbean. *Moderated*

i `laspau@harvarda.bitnet` (Bitnet: `LASPAU@HARVARDA`)

± `listserv@harvarda.harvard.edu` (Bitnet: `LISTSERV@HARVARDA`) [body = SUBSCRIBE LASPAU-L first-name last-name]

Archive: `listserv@harvarda.harvard.edu`

Language: English, Spanish, French

1-791 **LATAMMUS:** For discussion of all aspects and styles of music in Latin American countries. *Moderated*

i `icrjh@asuacad.bitnet` (Bitnet: `ICRJH@ASUACAD`) (J. Richard Haefer)

± `listserv@asuvm.inre.asu.edu` (Bitnet: `LISTSERV@ASUACAD`) [body = SUBSCRIBE LATAMMUS first-name last-name]

Archive: Available to subscribers only.

Other: Subscription is limited. Requests will be sent to list owner for approval.

1-792 **LATEX-L:** On the development of the successor to LaTeX version 2.09.

i `jl2@dhdurz1.bitnet` (Bitnet: `JL2@DHDURZ1`) (Rainer Schoepf) or `schoepf@sc.zib-berlin.de` (Rainer Schoepf) or `jl2@vm.urz.uni-heidelberg.de` (Rainer Schoepf)

± `listserv@dhdurz1.bitnet` (Bitnet: `LISTSERV@DHDURZ1`) [body = SUBSCRIBE LATEX-L first-name last-name]

1-793 **LATEX-UG:** On the LaTeX typsetting system.

i `facy009@saupm00.bitnet` (Bitnet: `FACY009@SAUPM00`) (Dr. Sadiq M. Sait)

± `listserv@saupm00.bitnet` (Bitnet: `LISTSERV@SAUPM00`) [body = SUBSCRIBE LATEX-UG first-name last-name]

Other: Subscription is limited. Requests will be sent to list owner for approval.

1-794 **LATIN-L:** For Latin and NeoLatin discussions.

i `bcj@psuvm.bitnet` (Bitnet: `BCJ@PSUVM`)

± `listserv@psuvm.psu.edu` (Bitnet: `LISTSERV@PSUVM`) [body = SUBSCRIBE LATIN-L first-name last-name]

Archive: `listserv@psuvm.psu.edu`

Language: Latin and any other vulgar tongue

1-795 **LAWAID:** For financial aid and related personnel of law schools.

i `u740026@rutadmin.bitnet` (Bitnet: `U740026@RUTADMIN`) (Rich Woodland)

± `listserv@rutvm1.rutgers.edu` (Bitnet: `LISTSERV@RUTVM1`) [body = SUBSCRIBE LAWAID first-name last-name]

1-796 **LDBASE-L:** A discussion of Listserv database search capability.

i `supervisor@sweep.fo.ukans.edu`

± `listserv@ukanvm.cc.ukans.edu` (Bitnet: `LISTSERV@UKANVM`) [body = SUBSCRIBE LDBASE-L first-name last-name]

Archive: `listserv@ukanvm.cc.ukans.edu`

Other: Weekly digest

1-797 **lds-net:** For members of The Church of Jesus Christ of Latter-day Saints (Mormons) to discuss church doctrine, Mormon culture, and life in general.

i ± `lds-net-request@andrew.cmu.edu`

Archive: FTP `carnot.itc.cmu.edu` in `pub`

1-798 **LEADTCHR:** For networking lead teachers.

i `jdp115@psuvm.bitnet` (Bitnet: `JDP115@PSUVM`) (Dave Popp)

± `listserv@psuvm.psu.edu` (Bitnet: `LISTSERV@PSUVM`) [body = `SUBSCRIBE LEADTCHR` first-name last-name]

Archive: `listserv@psuvm.psu.edu`

1-799 **LEXX-L:** On the LEXX parsing editor.

i `nlaflamm@irishvma.bitnet` (Bitnet: `NLAFLAMM@IRISHVMA`) (Nick Laflamme)

± `listserv@vma.cc.nd.edu` (Bitnet: `LISTSERV@IRISHVMA`) [body = `SUBSCRIBE LEXX-L` first-name last-name]

Archive: Available to subscribers only.

1-800 **LFATMEN:** On FATMEN, a distributed file and tape management system that is based on the IEEE computer society mass storage system reference model.

i `jamie@cernvm.cern.ch` (Jamie Shiers)

± `listserv@crnvma.cern.ch` (Bitnet: `LISTSERV@CERNVM`) [body = `SUBSCRIBE LFATMEN` first-name last-name]

Archive: Available to subscribers only.

1-801 **LIBADMIN:** On library administration and management.

i `pbluh@umab.bitnet` (Bitnet: `PBLUH@UMAB`) (Pamela Bluh)

± `listserv@umab.umd.edu` (Bitnet: `LISTSERV@UMAB`) [body = `SUBSCRIBE LIBADMIN` first-name last-name]

1-802 **liberal-judaism:** For nonjudgmental discussions of liberal judaism (Reform, Reconstructionist, Conservative, Secular Humanist, etc.) and liberal Jewish issues, its practices, opinions, and beliefs.

i ± `faigin@nysernet.org` (Daniel Faigin)

Other: In digest format.

1-803 **libernet:** Libertarian-related information distribution list (not for discussion).

i `owner-libernet@dartmouth.edu` (Barry S. Fagin)

± `libernet-request@dartmouth.edu` [body = `subscribe libernet-batch-list` or `subscribe libernet-reflected-list`]

Archive: FTP `coos.dartmouth.edu` in `/pub/Libernet`

Other: Available as mail reflector or digest.

1-804 **libernet-d:** Libertarian discussion list.

i `owner-libernet@dartmouth.edu` (Barry S. Fagin)

± `libernet-request@dartmouth.edu` [body = `subscribe libernet-d-batch-list` or `subscribe libernet-d-reflected-list`]

Archive: FTP `coos.dartmouth.edu` in `/pub/Libernet`

Other: Available as mail reflector or digest.

1-805   **LIBEVENT:** On library events in Southern California. *Moderated*

     i `rwallach@uscvm.bitnet` (Bitnet: RWALLACH@USCVM) (Ruth Wallach)

     ± `listserv@vm.usc.edu` (Bitnet: LISTSERV@USCVM) [body = SUBSCRIBE LIBEVENT first-name last-name]

     Archive: `listserv@vm.usc.edu`

1-806   **LIBPLN-L:** University library planning discussion.

     i `cnoble@ukanvm.bitnet` (Bitnet: CNOBLE@UKANVM) or `kerber@ukanvm.bitnet` (Bitnet: KERBER@UKANVM)

     ± `listserv@ukanvm.cc.ukans.edu` (Bitnet: LISTSERV@UKANVM) [body = SUBSCRIBE LIBPLN-L first-name last-name]

     Archive: `listserv@ukanvm.cc.ukans.edu` [body = INDEX LIBPLN-L]

1-807   **LIBRARY:** Libraries and librarians.

     i `library@carat.arizona.edu` (Libraries and Librarians) or `jbharlan@carat.arizona.edu` (John B. Harlan)

     ± `listserv@arizvm1.ccit.arizona.edu` (Bitnet: LISTSERV@ARIZVM1) [body = SUBSCRIBE LIBRARY first-name last-name]

     Archive: `listserv@arizvm1.ccit.arizona.edu`

     Other: Daily digest

1-808   **LIBREF-L:** On library reference issues. *Moderated*

     i `librefed@kentvm.bitnet` (Bitnet: LIBREFED@KENTVM)

     ± `listserv@kentvm.kent.edu` (Bitnet: LISTSERV@KENTVM) [body = SUBSCRIBE LIBREF-L first-name last-name]

     Archive: `listserv@kentvm.kent.edu`

1-809   **Linda:** On Linda-based parallel programming systems. Linda is a set of operators that are added to various conventional programming languages to produce a parallel programming language.

     i ± `linda-users-request@cs.yale.edu` or `linda-users-request@yalecs.bitnet`

1-810   **LINES-L:** For discussing enhancements to LifeLines Genealogical Database and Report Generator, an experimental genealogical software for Unix.

     i `cmanis@csoftec.csf.com`

     ± `listserv@vm1.nodak.edu` (Bitnet: LISTSERV@NDSUVM1) [body = SUBSCRIBE LINES-L first-name last-name]

     Archive: `listserv@vm1.nodak.edu`

     Gated: ⇔ `bit.listserv.LINES-L`

1-811   **LINGUA:** About linguistics at the University of Arizona

     i `langendt@arizvm1.bitnet` (Bitnet: LANGENDT@ARIZVM1) (Terry Langendoen)

     ± `listserv@arizvm1.ccit.arizona.edu` (Bitnet: LISTSERV@ARIZVM1) [body = SUBSCRIBE LINGUA first-name last-name]

     Archive: `listserv@arizvm1.ccit.arizona.edu`

     Other: Subscription is limited. Requests will be sent to list owner for approval.

1-812 **LINKFAIL:** Bitnet link failure announcements.

    i `listmgr@bitnic.educom.edu`

    ± `listserv@bitnic.educom.edu` (Bitnet: `LISTSERV@BITNIC`) [body = `SUBSCRIBE LINKFAIL` first-name last-name] or `listserv@cearn.cern.ch` (Bitnet: `LISTSERV@CEARN`) [body = `SUBSCRIBE LINKFAIL` first-name last-name] or `listserv@hearn.nic.surfnet.nl` (Bitnet: `LISTSERV@HEARN`) [body = `SUBSCRIBE LINKFAIL` first-name last-name] or `listserv@vm.marist.edu` (Bitnet: `LISTSERV@MARIST`) [body = `SUBSCRIBE LINKFAIL` first-name last-name] or `listserv@uga.cc.uga.edu` (Bitnet: `LISTSERV@UGA`) [body = `SUBSCRIBE LINKFAIL` first-name last-name] or `listserv@vm.gmd.de` (Bitnet: `LISTSERV@DEARN`) [body = `SUBSCRIBE LINKFAIL` first-name last-name]

    Archive: `listserv@bitnic.educom.edu` or `listserv@uga.cc.uga.edu` or `listserv@vm.gmd.de` or `listserv@vm.marist.edu` or `listserv@cearn.cern.ch`

1-813 **Linux-Activists:** On Linux operating system hacking.

    i `linux-activists-request@niksula.hut.fi` [body = `X-Mn-Info: linux-activists`]

    ± `linux-activists-request@niksula.hut.fi` [body = `X-Mn-Admin: join normal`]

    Archive: FTP `nic.funet.fi` in `/pub/OS/Linux`

1-814 **List-Managers:** On managing Internet mailing lists, including software, methods, mechanisms, techniques, and policies.

    i `brent@greatcircle.com` (Brent Chapman)

    ± `majordomo@greatcircle.com` [body = `subscribe list-managers` or `subscribe list-managers-digest`]

    Archive: FTP `ftp.GreatCircle.COM` in `pub/archive`

1-815 **LITSCI-L:** Society for Literature and Science—philosophy, technology, cyber discussion

    i `jamato@ux1.cso.uiuc.edu` (Joe Amato)

    ± `listserv@vmd.cso.uiuc.edu` (Bitnet: `LISTSERV@UIUCVMD`) [body = `SUBSCRIBE LITSCI-L` first-name last-name]

    Archive: `listserv@vmd.cso.uiuc.edu`

1-816 **LLTI:** For information on language learning and technology, including language lab technology, computer-supported language learning, and interactive video and audio. *Moderated*

    i `otmar.k.e.foelsche@dartmouth.edu` (Otmar Foelsche, Director, LRC)

    ± `listserv@dartcms1.dartmouth.edu` (Bitnet: `LISTSERV@DARTCMS1`) [body = `SUBSCRIBE LLTI` first-name last-name]

    Archive: `listserv@dartcms1.dartmouth.edu`

1-817 **LM_NET:** School library media and network communications.

    i `mike@suvm.bitnet` (Bitnet: `MIKE@SUVM`) (Mike Eisenberg) or `pmilbur@eis.calstate.edu` (Peter Milbury)

    ± `listserv@suvm.acs.syr.edu` (Bitnet: `LISTSERV@SUVM`) [body = `SUBSCRIBE LM_NET` first-name last-name]

Other: Daily digest. Subscription is limited. Requests will be sent to list owner for approval.

1-818 **LMAIL-L:** The LMail give-and-take forum.

i `eric@searn.bitnet` (Bitnet: `ERIC@SEARN`) (Eric Thomas)

± `listserv@searn.sunet.se` (Bitnet: `LISTSERV@SEARN`) [body = `SUBSCRIBE LMAIL-L` first-name last-name]

Archive: `listserv@searn.sunet.se`

1-819 **LNGTEACH:** For Linguistics Instructors, University of Arizona.

i `langendt@arizvm1.bitnet` (Bitnet: `LANGENDT@ARIZVM1`) (Terry Langendoen)

± `listserv@arizvm1.ccit.arizona.edu` (Bitnet: `LISTSERV@ARIZVM1`) [body = `SUBSCRIBE LNGTEACH` first-name last-name]

Archive: Available to subscribers only.

Other: Subscription is limited. Requests will be sent to list owner for approval.

1-820 **LOJBAN:** On Lojban, a language constructed to be culturally neutral, grammatically logical, phonetically spelled. Uses include cross-cultural communication, creative and scientific discussion, and possibly, communication with computers.

i `lojban-list-request@snark.thyrsus.com`

± `listserv@cuvmb.cc.columbia.edu` (Bitnet: `LISTSERV@CUVMB`) [body = `SUBSCRIBE LOJBAN` first-name last-name]

1-821 **Loop:** For people who like music that drones. Bands include The Loop, their offshoots such as Hair and Skin Trading Company, Main, and others like Spacemen 3, Telescopes, Ozric Tentacles, Orb, etc.

i ± `bp094@cleveland.freenet.edu`

1-822 **LORE:** For discussion of all aspects of folklore.

i `carey@plains.nodak.edu` (Pat Carey)

± `listserv@vm1.nodak.edu` (Bitnet: `LISTSERV@NDSUVM1`) [body = `SUBSCRIBE LORE` first-name last-name]

Archive: `listserv@vm1.nodak.edu`

1-823 **lost-chords:** Dicussion and information on the Moody Blues rock group.

i ± `lost-chords-request@mit.edu`

1-824 **lotus-cars:** Discussion of cars built and designed by Colin Chapman, Lotus Cars Ltd., or Team Lotus.

± `lotus-cars-request@netcom.com`

Archive: FTP `ftp.netcom.com` in `pub/lotus-cars`

1-825 **loureed:** On music, etc. related to the career of Mr. Lou Reed, including Velvet Underground matters.

i ± `loureed-request@cvi.hahnemann.edu` or `sylvia@cvi.hahnemann.edu` (Sylvia)

1-826 **love-hounds:** On Kate Bush and related musicians.

i `wisner@uunet.uu.net` (Bill Wisner)

± `love-hounds-request@uunet.uu.net`

1-827 **LPN-L:** For scientists doing research on or with nonhuman primates, including care and breeding, research news, requests for information or materials, and conservation. *Moderated*

i primate@brownvm.bitnet (Bitnet: PRIMATE@BROWNVM) (Judith Schrier)

± listserv@brownvm.brown.edu (Bitnet: LISTSERV@BROWNVM) [body = SUBSCRIBE LPN-L first-name last-name]

Archive: listserv@brownvm.brown.edu

1-828 **LSTOWN-L:** For owners, editors, and coordinators of LISTSERV-based discussion and distribution lists.

i eric@searn.bitnet (Bitnet: ERIC@SEARN) (Eric Thomas)

± listserv@searn.sunet.se (Bitnet: LISTSERV@SEARN) [body = SUBSCRIBE LSTOWN-L first-name last-name]

Archive: listserv@searn.sunet.se

1-829 **LSTSRV-L:** Give-and-take forum on LISTSERV software.

i eric@searn.bitnet (Bitnet: ERIC@SEARN) (Eric Thomas)

± listserv@searn.sunet.se (Bitnet: LISTSERV@SEARN) [body = SUBSCRIBE LSTSRV-L first-name last-name]

Archive: listserv@listserv@searn.sunet.se

1-830 **LTEST-L:** On language testing research and practice.

i iyg9lfb@mvs.oac.ucla.edu or iyg9lfb@uclamvs.bitnet

± listserv@uclacn1.bitnet (Bitnet: LISTSERV@UCLACN1) [body = SUBSCRIBE LTEST-L first-name last-name]

1-831 **lute:** For lute players and researchers of lute music.

i ± lute-request@cs.dartmouth.edu (Wayne B. Cripps)

1-832 **LWUSERS:** For users of LANWatch, a local area network analyzer for IBM compatibles. *Moderated*

i info@ndsuvm1.bitnet (Bitnet: INFO@NDSUVM1) (Marty Hoag)

± listserv@vm1.nodak.edu (Bitnet: LISTSERV@NDSUVM1) [body = SUBSCRIBE LWUSERS first-name last-name]

Archive: listserv@vm1.nodak.edu

Other: Daily digest

1-833 **LYH-L:** For members of the Queen's Chinese Friendship Association.

i tan@mips2.phy.queensu.ca (Jin Tan)

± listserv@qucdn.queensu.ca (Bitnet: LISTSERV@QUCDN) [body = SUBSCRIBE LYH-L first-name last-name]

1-834 **mac-security:** All about Macintosh security issues. Topics have included tracking printer usage, security holes in commercial applications, data security (on disks and on networks), and physical hardware security.

i (David C. Kovar)

± majordomo@nda.com [body = subscribe mac-security]

FTP ftp.nda.com

1-835 **macgyver:** For fans of the MacGyver T.V. show.
　　i ± `shari@cc.gatech.edu` (Shari Feldman)

1-836 **MACIRC-L:** On Macintosh Internet Relay Chat (IRC) client design.
　　i `peter@brownvm.bitnet` (Bitnet: PETER@BROWNVM) (Peter DiCamillo)
　　± `listserv@brownvm.brown.edu` (Bitnet: LISTSERV@BROWNVM) [body = SUBSCRIBE MACIRC-L first-name last-name]
　　Archive: Available to subscribers only.
　　Other: Subscription is limited. Requests will be sent to list owner for approval.

1-837 **madonna:** On the rock and movie star Madonna.
　　i ± `madonna-request@athena.mit.edu` (Joe Barco)

1-838 **madonna-digest:** Daily summary of posts sent to the madonna mailing list.
　　i ± `madonna-digest-request@athena.mit.edu` (Joe Barco)

1-839 **MAES-L:** Society of Mexican-American Engineers and Scientists.
　　i `x211km@tamvm1.bitnet` (Bitnet: X211KM@TAMVM1) (Keith A. Marrocco)
　　± `listserv@tamvm1.tamu.edu` (Bitnet: LISTSERV@TAMVM1) [body = SUBSCRIBE MAES-L first-name last-name]
　　Archive: `listserv@tamvm1.tamu.edu`
　　Other: Weekly digest

1-840 **magic:** On sleight of hand and the art of magic. Membership to the list is restricted. You must fill out a questionnaire to qualify.
　　i ± `magic-request@maillist.crd.ge.com` (Bruce Barnett)
　　Archive: Available to subscriber by request.

1-841 **magyar:** On pre-1600 Hungary and "living history" recreation thereof.
　　± `dl-server@bransle.ucs.mun.ca` [body = subscribe magyar first-name last-name]

1-842 **MAIL-ITA:** On e-mail developments in Italy.
　　i `turso@ibacsata.bitnet` (Bitnet: TURSO@IBACSATA) (Giovanni Turso)
　　± `listserv@vm.cnuce.cnr.it` (Bitnet: LISTSERV@ICNUCEVM) [body = SUBSCRIBE MAIL-ITA first-name last-name]

1-843 **mail-men:** Forum for men and women to discuss men's issues (those problems and experiences that affect male humans) in an atmosphere of openness and support. *Moderated*
　　i ± `mail-men-request@usl.com`

1-844 **Mailing Lists:** Information on mailing lists from South Slavic countries.
　　i ± `mailing-lists@krpan.arnes.si`

1-845 **Majordomo-Announce:** This list is for announcements of new releases of the Majordomo mailing list manager.
　　i `majordomo-announce-owner@greatcircle.com`
　　± `majordomo@greatcircle.com` [body = subscribe Majordomo-Announce]
　　Archive: FTP `greatcircle.com` in `/pub/archives`

1-846 **Majordomo-Users:** This list is for discussions (including bug reports, enhancement reports, and general usage tips) concerning the Majordomo mailing list manager.

i `majordomo-users-owner@greatcircle.com`

± `majordomo@greatcircle.com` [body = `subscribe Majordomo-Users`]

Archive: FTP `ftp.greatcircle.com` in `pub/archive`

1-847 **MALACHI:** For the exchange of ideas and information about graduate courses among the universities in the Washington D.C. metropolitan area.

i `kent_norman@umail.umd.edu` (Kent Norman) or `sobiloff@lap.umd.edu` (Blake Sobiloff)

± `listserv@umdd.umd.edu` (Bitnet: LISTSERV@UMDD) [body = SUBSCRIBE MALACHI first-name last-name]

Archive: `listserv@umdd.umd.edu`

1-848 **MAPS-L:** On Maps and Air Photo Systems. For map librarians, cartographers, geographers, and people interested in remote sensing. *Moderated*

i `jsutherl@uga.bitnet` (Bitnet: JSUTHERL@UGA) (Johnnie D. Sutherland, Curator of Maps)

± `listserv@uga.cc.uga.edu` (Bitnet: LISTSERV@UGA) [body = SUBSCRIBE MAPS-L first-name last-name]

Archive: `listserv@uga.cc.uga.edu`

1-849 **Margaret's Eyes:** On the musical group King Missile.

i `mrosco@pigeon.creighton.edu`

± `mrosco@pigeon.creighton.edu` [subject = `sign me up please!`]

Other: In digest format.

1-850 **Mariah Carey:** On Mariah's music, musical projects, and to share information about concerts, paraphernalia, and other miscellaneous topics about Mariah's music.

i ± `skul_ltd@uhura.cc.rochester.edu` (Seemant Kulleen)

1-851 **MARIO:** For Italians living abroad.

i `ffavata@estsa2.estec.esa.nl` (Fabio Favata)

± `listserv@searn.sunet.se` (Bitnet: LISTSERV@SEARN) [body = SUBSCRIBE MARIO first-name last-name]

Archive: Available to subscribers only.

Language: Italian

Other: Subscription is limited. Requests will be sent to list owner for approval.

1-852 **MARKET-L:** For discussions among marketing academics and practitioners.

i `chofack@cob.fsu.edu` (Charles Hofacker)

± `listserv@ucf1vm.cc.ucf.edu` (Bitnet: LISTSERV@UCF1VM) [body = SUBSCRIBE MARKET-L first-name last-name]

Archive: `listserv@ucf1vm.cc.ucf.edu`

1-853 **martial-arts:** All about martial arts, including teaching and training techniques, philosophy, self-defense, traditional and non-traditional styles, etc.

i `martial-arts-owner@listserv.cso.uiuc.edu`

± `majordomo@listserv.cso.uiuc.edu` [body = `subscribe martial-arts`]

1-854 **Masonic Digest:** Forum for discussion of Free Masonry, affiliated groups, and other fraternal orders. *Moderated*

i ± `ptrei@mitre.org` (Peter Trei)

Other: Digest format

1-855 **MasPar:** On all models of MasPar SIMD parallel machines. These machines have a full-featured data-parallel instruction set and are programmable in Fortran90 and MPL, an ANSI C with parallel data types.

± `mp-users-request@thunder.mcrcim.mcgill.edu` (Lee Iverson)

1-856 **MAT-DSGN:** On materials design by computer.

i `kawazoe@jpntohok.bitnet` (Bitnet: `KAWAZOE@JPNTOHOK`) (Yoshiyuki Kawazoe)

± `listserv@jpntuvm0.bitnet` (Bitnet: `LISTSERV@JPNTUVM0`) [body = `SUBSCRIBE MAT-DSGN` first-name last-name]

Archive: `listserv@jpntuvm0.bitnet`

1-857 **MATHDEP:** For notices on mathematical science seminars in Ireland, and mathematics with some Irish connection.

i `wsulivan@irlearn.bitnet` (Bitnet: `WSULIVAN@IRLEARN`) (UCD Maths Department)

± `listserv@irlearn.bitnet` (Bitnet: `LISTSERV@IRLEARN`) [body = `SUBSCRIBE MATHDEP` first-name last-name]

1-858 **Matlab:** For users and potential users of the MATLAB numeric computation software from The MathWorks. MATLAB is an interactive matrix-oriented product for linear algebra, digital signal processing, equation solving, control system design, and other engineering and scientific applications.

i `matlab-users-request@mcs.anl.gov` (Chris Bischof)

± `subscribe@mathworks.com`

1-859 **Mayberry:** On the TV shows featuring Andy Griffith, including The Andy Griffith Show and Mayberry RFD.

i `amillar@bolis.sf-bay.org` (Alan Millar)

± `listserv@bolis.sf-bay.org` [body = `subscribe Mayberry`]

1-860 **mazda-list:** Technical correspondance and discussion of Mazda-designed vehicles.

i ± `mazda-list-request@ms.uky.edu` (Joel Abbott)

Archive: FTP `ftp.ms.uky.edu` in `/pub/mailing.lists/mazda-list`

1-861 **MC68HC11:** Discussions about the Motorola MC68HC11 family of microcontrollers.

i ± `mc68hc11-request@hipp.etsu.edu` (Bob Wier)

Archive: FTP `hipp.etsu.edu`

1-862 **MCJRNL:** MC Journal—The Journal of Academic Media Librarianship. This is an electronic peer reviewed journal. *Moderated*

i `hslljw@ubvm.bitnet` (Bitnet: `HSLLJW@UBVM`) (Lori Widzinski)

± `listserv@ubvm.cc.buffalo.edu` (Bitnet: `LISTSERV@UBVM`) [body = `SUBSCRIBE MCJRNL` first-name last-name]

Archive: `listserv@ubvm.cc.buffalo.edu`

1-863 MCLR-L: For the Midwest Consortium for Latino Research. *Moderated*

i 22429bsc@msu.edu (Belinda S. Cook)

± listserv@msu.edu (Bitnet: LISTSERV@MSU) [body = SUBSCRIBE MCLR-L first-name last-name]

Archive: listserv@msu.edu

1-864 MCRIT-L: On multicriteria analysis, a discipline that helps to formulate decisions in the face of (sometimes) conflicting criteria.

i mcrit@sjaan.fbk.eur.nl

± listserv@hearn.nic.surfnet.nl (Bitnet: LISTSERV@HEARN) [body = SUBSCRIBE MCRIT-L first-name last-name]

1-865 MDPHD-L: On dual degree programs, for example, pursuing an M.D. along with a Ph.D. or a J.D.

i jvmg9796@uxa.cso.uiuc.edu (doc)

± listserv@ubvm.cc.buffalo.edu (Bitnet: LISTSERV@UBVM) [body = SUBSCRIBE MDPHD-L first-name last-name]

Archive: listserv@ubvm.cc.buffalo.edu

1-866 MEANING: On the meaning of life and other weighty contemplations.

i idsak@asuacad.bitnet (Bitnet: IDSAK@ASUACAD)

± listserv@asuvm.inre.asu.edu (Bitnet: LISTSERV@ASUACAD) [body = SUBSCRIBE MEANING first-name last-name]

Archive: Available to subscribers only.

1-867 MECH-L: On mechanical engineering.

i b470ssn@utarlvm1.bitnet (Bitnet: B470SSN@UTARLVM1) (S. Nomura)

± listserv@utarlvm1.uta.edu (Bitnet: LISTSERV@UTARLVM1) [body = SUBSCRIBE MECH-L first-name last-name]

Archive: listserv@utarlvm1.uta.edu

1-868 MEDEVLIT: For open discussion of medieval English literature.

i gr4302@siucvmb.bitnet (Bitnet: GR4302@SIUCVMB) (Jeff Taylor)

± listserv@siucvmb.bitnet (Bitnet: LISTSERV@SIUCVMB) [body = SUBSCRIBE MEDEVLIT first-name last-name]

Archive: Available to subscribers only.

1-869 MEDFEM-L: An open discussion for medievalist feminists and others interested in topics related to feminism and the Middle Ages.

i jrondeau@oregon.uoregon.edu (Jennifer Rondeau)

± listserv@uwavm.u.washington.edu (Bitnet: LISTSERV@UWAVM) [body = SUBSCRIBE MEDFEM-L first-name last-name]

Archive: listserv@indycms.iupui.edu

1-870 MEDFORUM: The Med Student Organization/Policy Forum.

i manchest@gas.uug.arizona.edu (Troy Manchester) or teytan@gas.uug.arizona.edu (Ted Eytan)

± listserv@arizvm1.ccit.arizona.edu (Bitnet: LISTSERV@ARIZVM1) [body

= SUBSCRIBE MEDFORUM first-name last-name]

Archive: Available to subscribers only.

1-871 **MEDGAY-L:** On Gay-Lesbian Medieval Studies—official list of the Society for the Study of Homosexuality in the Middle Ages.

i rclark@ksuvm.bitnet (Bitnet: RCLARK@KSUVM) (Robert Clark)

± listserv@ksuvm.ksu.edu (Bitnet: LISTSERV@KSUVM) [body = SUBSCRIBE MEDGAY-L first-name last-name]

Archive: listserv@ksuvm.ksu.edu

1-872 **MEDIEV-L:** Scholarly discussion of medieval history (from AD 285 to 1500).

i lhnelson@ukanvm.bitnet (Bitnet: LHNELSON@UKANVM)

± listserv@ukanvm.cc.ukans.edu (Bitnet: LISTSERV@UKANVM) [body = SUBSCRIBE MEDIEV-L first-name last-name]

Archive: listserv@ukanvm.cc.ukans.edu

1-873 **MEDLIB-L:** For medical and health sciences librarians. Not for reference questions from non-librarians.

i hslstart@ubvm.bitnet (Bitnet: HSLSTART@UBVM) (Nancy Start)

± listserv@ubvm.cc.buffalo.edu (Bitnet: LISTSERV@UBVM) [body = SUBSCRIBE MEDLIB-L first-name last-name]

Archive: listserv@ubvm.cc.buffalo.edu

Gated: ⇔ bit.listserv.medlib-1

1-874 **MEDNETS:** On the role of global computer networks in the clinical, research, and administrative areas of medicine.

i info@ndsuvm1.bitnet (Bitnet: INFO@NDSUVM1) (Marty Hoag)

± listserv@vm1.nodak.edu (Bitnet: LISTSERV@NDSUVM1) [body = SUBSCRIBE MEDNETS first-name last-name]

Archive: listserv@vm1.nodak.edu

Other: Daily digest

1-875 **MEDNEWS:** Health Info-Com Network Newsletter, carrying the latest MMWR, FDA News, AIDS News, and information from major health organizations. *Moderated*

i david@stat.com

± listserv@asuvm.inre.asu.edu (Bitnet: LISTSERV@ASUACAD) [body = SUBSCRIBE MEDNEWS first-name last-name]

Other: Weekly digest

1-876 **medphys:** On the physics of the diagnostic and therapeutic use of radiation in medicine.

i ± medphys-request@radonc.duke.edu

1-877 **MEDSCI-L:** On medieval and Renaissance science.

i st001424@brownvm.bitnet (Bitnet: ST001424@BROWNVM) (Josh Brandon)

± listserv@brownvm.brown.edu (Bitnet: LISTSERV@BROWNVM) [body = SUBSCRIBE MEDSCI-L first-name last-name]

Archive: listserv@brownvm.brown.edu

1-878 **MEDSEA-L:** On processes controlling life in the Adriatic Sea, especially interactions between eutrophication phenomenon and food web structures.

i a8721gaj@awiuni11.bitnet (Bitnet: A8721GAJ@AWIUNI11) (Osiander Meixner)

± listserv@helios.edvz.univie.ac.at (Bitnet: LISTSERV@AEARN) [body = SUBSCRIBE MEDSEA-L first-name last-name]

Archive: listserv@helios.edvz.univie.ac.at

Other: Subscription is limited. Requests will be sent to list owner for approval.

1-879 **MEH2O-L:** On water in the Middle East, including limnology, oceanograpy, marine biotechnology, aquaculture, conservation, reclamation, ecology, international shared resource management.

i chasan73@matrix.newpaltz.edu (Robert Chasan)

± listserv@taunivm.tau.ac.il (Bitnet: LISTSERV@TAUNIVM) [body = SUBSCRIBE MEH2O-L first-name last-name]

Archive: listserv@taunivm.tau.ac.il

1-880 **Melissa Etheridge:** On Melissa Etheridge's career and music, as well as various other artists with similar styles.

i etheridge-owner@cnd.mcgill.ca (David Johnson and Glenna Vinokur)

± etheridge-request@cnd.mcgill.ca

Archive: FTP ftp.uwp.edu in /pub/music/artists/e/etheridge.melissa (list and discography)

1-881 **mensatalk:** For members of Mensa (membership will be verified). Mensatalk is NOT supported, endorsed, or approved by MENSA. For Information on joining MENSA e-mail to *i* address or see newsgroup rec.org.mensa. *Moderated*

i ± mensatalk-request@psg.com (Ed Wright)

1-882 **MERPL:** Discussion list for players and gamemasters of MERP, a role-playing game.

i zielony@plszus11.bitnet (Bitnet: ZIELONY@PLSZUS11) (Tomasz W. Stepien)

± listserv@plearn.edu.pl (Bitnet: LISTSERV@PLEARN) [body = SUBSCRIBE MERPL first-name last-name]

Archive: Available to subscribers only.

1-883 **Mesa:** For users (and potential users) of Mesa, Athena Design's award winning spreadsheet for NeXTStep.

i ± mesa-request@athena.com

1-884 **metacard-list:** Discussion of all aspects of the MetaCard computer program from MetaCard Corporation. MetaCard is an application development system, similar to Apple's HyperCard program, which runs on a variety of popular platforms in a Unix/X11/Motif environment.

i metacard-list-owner@grot.starconn.com (Brian Smithson)

± listserv@grot.starconn.com [body = subscribe metacard-list first-name last-name]

1-885 **METALIB:** On Metalibrary.

i kawazoe@jpntohok.bitnet (Bitnet: KAWAZOE@JPNTOHOK) (Yoshiyuki Kawazoe)

± listserv@jpntuvm0.bitnet (Bitnet: LISTSERV@JPNTUVM0) [body = SUBSCRIBE METALIB first-name last-name]

Archive: `listserv@jpntuvm0.bitnet`

1-886 **Metallica:** On the Metallica rock group.

i ± `affouj@rpi.edu` [subject = subscribe or help] (Jason Affourtit)

Archive: FTP `pc10868.pc.cc.cmu.edu`; e-mail: `aj2ny2@greenwich.ac.uk`

Other: In digest format.

1-887 **Meteorology Students:** On latest research results in meteorology and current weather events as well as student-related topics in meteorology such as scholarships, summer schools, conferences, and conditions of studying meteorology at a particular university, etc.

i ± `dennis@metw3.met.fu-berlin.de`

1-888 **METU-L:** For Middle East technical university graduates.

i `halkilis@trmetu.bitnet` (Bitnet: `HALKILIS@TRMETU`) (ODTU Halkla Iliskiler Birimi)

± `listserv@vm.cc.metu.edu.tr` (Bitnet: `LISTSERV@TRMETU`) [body = SUBSCRIBE METU-L first-name last-name]

Archive: `listserv@vm.cc.metu.edu.tr`

1-889 **MEXICO-L:** All about Mexico—its people, places, culture.

i `mpinones@netmon.mty.itesm.mx` (Marco A. Pinones)

± `listserv@tecmtyvm.mty.itesm.mx` (Bitnet: `LISTSERV@TECMTYVM`) [body = SUBSCRIBE MEXICO-L first-name last-name]

Archive: Available to subscribers only.

Other: Weekly digest

1-890 **MFJ-L:** On MFJ International add-ons for CA's DATACOM/DB database.

i `rondot@ipfwvm.bitnet` (Bitnet: `RONDOT@IPFWVM`) (Larry Rondot)

± `listserv@ipfwvm.bitnet` (Bitnet: `LISTSERV@IPFWVM`) [body = SUBSCRIBE MFJ-L first-name last-name]

Archive: `listserv@ipfwvm.bitnet`

1-891 **MGARDEN:** On the master gardening program and all aspects of gardening.

i `pace@wsuvm1.bitnet` (Bitnet: `PACE@WSUVM1`) or `wright@wsuvm1.bitnet` (Bitnet: `WRIGHT@WSUVM1`)

± `listserv@wsuvm1.csc.wsu.edu` (Bitnet: `LISTSERV@WSUVM1`) [body = SUBSCRIBE MGARDEN first-name last-name]

Archive: `listserv@wsuvm1.csc.wsu.edu`

1-892 **MGSA-L:** For scholars of modern Greek culture, society, literature, etc.—of special interest to graduate students in Modern Greek studies.

i `moore@qal.berkeley.edu`

± `listserv@cmsa.berkeley.edu` (Bitnet: `LISTSERV@UCBCMSA`) [body = SUBSCRIBE MGSA-L first-name last-name]

Archive: Available to subscribers only.

1-893 **MHCARE-L:** On managed health care and clinical process management.

i `medinfab@mizzou1.bitnet` (Bitnet: `MEDINFAB@MIZZOU1`) (Andrew Balas)

± `listserv@mizzou1.missouri.edu` (Bitnet: `LISTSERV@MIZZOU1`) [body =

SUBSCRIBE MHCARE-L first-name last-name]

Archive: listserv@mizzou1.missouri.edu

Other: Subscription is limited. Requests will be sent to list owner for approval.

1-894   **MIA-L:** For discussion of information access offered by libraries at McGill University.

i ed22@musica.mcgill.ca (Anastassia Khouri St-Pierre)

± listserv@vm1.mcgill.ca (Bitnet: LISTSERV@MCGILL1) [body = SUBSCRIBE MIA-L first-name last-name]

Archive: listserv@vm1.mcgill.ca

Other: Subscription is limited. Requests will be sent to list owner for approval.

1-895   **miata:** For owners and fans of Mazda Miata cars.

i andy@jhunix.hcf.jhu.edu (andy S. Poling)

± miata-request@jhunix.hcf.jhu.edu [body = subscribe miata]

Archive: FTP jhunix.hcf.jhu.edu in mailing_lists/miata; gopher jhunix.hcf.jhu.edu in Academic Computing/JHUNIX Archive/mailing-lists/miata Mail Server send e-mail to miata-request@jhunix.hcf.jhu.edu [body = index miata for index or get miata file-name]

1-896   **MICRO-EL:** On microelectronics research in Israel. *Moderated*

i jo@ilncrd.bitnet (Bitnet: JO@ILNCRD) (Jo van Zwaren) or wolff@ilncrd.bitnet (Bitnet: WOLFF@ILNCRD)

± listserv@taunivm.tau.ac.il (Bitnet: LISTSERV@TAUNIVM) [body = SUBSCRIBE MICRO-EL first-name last-name]

1-897   **MICRONET:** On fungus and root interaction—for mycorrhizae researchers around the world.

i botlew@uoguelph.bitnet (Bitnet: BOTLEW@UOGUELPH) (Lewis Melville)

± listserv@vm.uoguelph.ca (Bitnet: LISTSERV@UOGUELPH) [body = SUBSCRIBE MICRONET first-name last-name]

Archive: Available to subscribers only.

Other: Subscription is limited. Requests will be sent to list owner for approval.

1-898   **MicroPhone Pro for NeXTStep:** On the MicroPhone Pro communications software running on NeXTStep (not for PC or Mac versions of MicroPhone Pro).

± mpro-request@netcom.com

Archive: FTP netcom.com in /pub/mpro

1-899   **MICROSCALE-L:** The Microscale Chemistry List.

i rand@merrimack.edu

± microscale-l-request@merrimack.edu

1-900   **MICS-L:** For technical discussion about the MICS Information Control System, from Morino Inc., including accounting, performance analysis and general reporting in MVS and VM, and other non-IBM systems supported by MICS.

i rcoprob@hdetud2.tudelft.nl

± listserv@hearn.nic.surfnet.nl (Bitnet: LISTSERV@HEARN) [body = SUBSCRIBE MICS-L first-name last-name]

Archive: `listserv@hearn.nic.surfnet.nl`

Gated: ⇔ `Bit.listserv.mics-l`

1-901 **Middle-Eastern Music:** On music originating from the Middle-East.

i ± `middle-eastern-music-request@nic.funet.fi` (Juhana Kouhia)

1-902 **MIDEUR-L:** About Middle Europe.

i `gfrajkor@ccs.carleton.ca` (Jan George Frajkor)

± `listserv@ubvm.cc.buffalo.edu` (Bitnet: LISTSERV@UBVM) [body = SUBSCRIBE MIDEUR-L first-name last-name]

Archive: `listserv@ubvm.cc.buffalo.edu`

Gated: ⇔ `bit.listserv.mideur-l`

1-903 **MIDWPDE:** Information on the Midwest Partial Differential Equations Seminar, a semiannual meeting on recent developments in partial differential equations. *Moderated*

i `u12585@uicvm.bitnet` (Bitnet: U12585@UICVM)

± `listserv@uicvm.bitnet` (Bitnet: LISTSERV@UICVM) [body = SUBSCRIBE MIDWPDE first-name last-name]

Archive: Available to subscribers only.

1-904 **Migra-List:** All about international migration issues.

i ± `migra-list-request@cc.utah.edu` or `moliva@cc.utah.edu` (Maurizio Oliva)

1-905 **MILES:** For discussing jazz trumpeter Miles Davis.

i `miles-request@hearn.bitnet` (Bitnet: MILES-REQUEST@HEARN)

± `listserv@hearn.nic.surfnet.nl` (Bitnet: LISTSERV@HEARN) [body = SUBSCRIBE MILES first-name last-name]

Archive: `listserv@hearn.nic.surfnet.nl`

1-906 **MILHST-L:** Scholarly discussion of military history.

i `jphughes@ukanvm.bitnet` (Bitnet: JPHUGHES@UKANVM)

± `listserv@ukanvm.cc.ukans.edu` (Bitnet: LISTSERV@UKANVM) [body = SUBSCRIBE MILHST-L first-name last-name]

Archive: `listserv@ukanvm.cc.ukans.edu`

1-907 **Minor League Baseball:** All about minor league baseball.

i ± `minors-request@medraut.apple.com` (Chuq von Rospach)

1-908 **MIS-L:** On management information systems (MIS).

i `stu1a0e@saupm00.bitnet` (Bitnet: STU1A0E@SAUPM00) (Tareq F. Al-Yahya)

± `listserv@saupm00.bitnet` (Bitnet: LISTSERV@SAUPM00) [body = SUBSCRIBE MIS-L first-name last-name]

Other: Subscription is limited. Requests will be sent to list owner for approval.

1-909 **misckit:** A collaborative net-wide project of software development of miscellaneous, Objective-C objects, primarily for use under NEXTSTEP. The misckit currently includes a string object and objects for managing times and dates.

i ± `misckit-request@byu.edu`

1-910 **MISCONF:** On the Mid-America Informational Conference (MISC) for information science students, faculty, and researchers.

i amundson@fairview.cc.ndsu.nodak.edu (Dennis Amundson)

± listserv@vm1.nodak.edu (Bitnet: LISTSERV@NDSUVM1) [body = SUBSCRIBE MISCONF first-name last-name]

Archive: listserv@vm1.nodak.edu

1-911 **MISG-L:** For members of the Malaysian Islamic Study Group, an association to help Muslim students cope with the non-Islamic living environment.

i axh113@psuvm.bitnet (Bitnet: AXH113@PSUVM) (Azmi Hashim)

± listserv@psuvm.psu.edu (Bitnet: LISTSERV@PSUVM) [body = SUBSCRIBE MISG-L first-name last-name]

Archive: listserv@psuvm.psu.edu

Other: Subscription is limited. Requests will be sent to list owner for approval.

1-912 **MIT-TV-L:** MIT cable television schedule. *Moderated*

i randy@mit.edu (Randall W. Winchester)

± listserv@mitvma.mit.edu (Bitnet: LISTSERV@MITVMA) [body = SUBSCRIBE MIT-TV-L first-name last-name]

1-913 **MIT1962:** MIT Class of 1962 e-mail network. *Moderated*

i 0004241803@mcimail.com (Henry N. McCarl)

± listserv@mitvma.mit.edu (Bitnet: LISTSERV@MITVMA) [body = SUBSCRIBE MIT1962 first-name last-name]

1-914 **MIT1966:** MIT Class of 1966 e-mail network.

i jblake@mitvmc.bitnet (Bitnet: JBLAKE@MITVMC) (John Blake)

± listserv@mitvma.mit.edu (Bitnet: LISTSERV@MITVMA) [body = SUBSCRIBE MIT1966 first-name last-name]

1-915 **MIT1972:** MIT Class of 1972 e-mail network.

i jblake@mitvmc.bitnet (Bitnet: JBLAKE@MITVMC) (John Blake)

± listserv@mitvma.mit.edu (Bitnet: LISTSERV@MITVMA) [body = SUBSCRIBE MIT1972 first-name last-name]

1-916 **MIT1988:** MIT Class of 1988 e-mail network. *Moderated*

i jblake@mitvmc.bitnet (Bitnet: JBLAKE@MITVMC) (John Blake)

± listserv@mitvma.mit.edu (Bitnet: LISTSERV@MITVMA) [body = SUBSCRIBE MIT1988 first-name last-name]

1-917 **MITBAY:** MIT Bay Area Club E-Mail Network. *Moderated*

i jblake@mitvmc.bitnet (Bitnet: JBLAKE@MITVMC) (John Blake)

± listserv@mitvma.mit.edu (Bitnet: LISTSERV@MITVMA) [body = SUBSCRIBE MITBAY first-name last-name]

1-918 **MMNUG-L:** For Mid-Missouri Network users.

i medinfjc@mizzou1.bitnet (Bitnet: MEDINFJC@MIZZOU1) (James H. Cutts III)

± listserv@mizzou1.missouri.edu (Bitnet: LISTSERV@MIZZOU1) [body = SUBSCRIBE MMNUG-L first-name last-name]

Archive: listserv@mizzou1.missouri.edu

1-919 **mmos2-l:** On programming, authoring tools and peripherals, for producing multimedia for IBM's OS/2.

i `mmos2-info@knex.via.mind.org` [body = `empty`]

± `mail-server@knex.via.mind.org` [body = `subscribe mmos2-l` first-name last-name]

1-920 **MOBILITY:** On mobility disablities.

i `drz@sjuvm.bitnet` (Bitnet: `DRZ@SJUVM`)

± `listserv@stjohns.edu` (Bitnet: `LISTSERV@SJUVM`) [body = `SUBSCRIBE MOBILITY` first-name last-name]

Archive: `listserv@stjohns.edu`

1-921 **MOCAVES:** On exploring caves in the midwest U.S.

i `sjalaws@umslvma.bitnet` (Bitnet: `SJALAWS@UMSLVMA`)

± `listserv@umslvma.umsl.edu` (Bitnet: `LISTSERV@UMSLVMA`) [body = `SUBSCRIBE MOCAVES` first-name last-name]

Archive: `listserv@umslvma.umsl.edu`

1-922 **MODBRITS:** On modern British and Irish literature from 1895 to 1955. *Moderated*

i `modbreds@kentvm.bitnet` (Bitnet: `MODBREDS@KENTVM`)

± `listserv@kentvm.kent.edu` (Bitnet: `LISTSERV@KENTVM`) [body = `SUBSCRIBE MODBRITS` first-name last-name]

Archive: `listserv@kentvm.kent.edu`

Other: Subscription is limited. Requests will be sent to list owner for approval.

1-923 **Modesty Blaise:** On Peter O'Donnell's *Modesty Blaise* books and comics.

i ± `modesty-blaise-request@math.uio.no` (Thomas Gramstad)

1-924 **MOPOLY-L:** About Missouri political issues.

± `listserv@mizzou1.missouri.edu` (Bitnet: `LISTSERV@MIZZOU1`) [body = `SUBSCRIBE MOPOLY-L` first-name last-name]

Archive: `listserv@mizzou1.missouri.edu`

1-925 **MORPHMET:** On biological morphometrics, the study of size and shape of organisms.

i `lamqc@cunyvm.bitnet` (Bitnet: `LAMQC@CUNYVM`) (Leslie F. Marcus)

± `listserv@cunyvm.cuny.edu` (Bitnet: `LISTSERV@CUNYVM`) [body = `SUBSCRIBE MORPHMET` first-name last-name]

Archive: Available to subscribers only.

1-926 **MORRIS:** On Morris dancing, a celebrational English folk dance.

i `libhtk@suvm.bitnet` (Bitnet: `LIBHTK@SUVM`) (Tom Keays)

± `listserv@suvm.acs.syr.edu` (Bitnet: `LISTSERV@SUVM`) [body = `SUBSCRIBE MORRIS` first-name last-name]

Other: Daily digest

1-927 **MOTORDEV:** About human motor skill development.

i `jane_e_clark@umail.umd.edu` (Jane Clark)

± `listserv@umdd.umd.edu` (Bitnet: `LISTSERV@UMDD`) [body = `SUBSCRIBE MOTORDEV` first-name last-name]

Archive: `listserv@umdd.umd.edu`

1-928 **MOUNT-L:** On mountaineering.

 i `turan@vm.cc.metu.edu.tr` (egemen Metin Turan)

 ± `listserv@vm.cc.metu.edu.tr` (Bitnet: `LISTSERV@TRMETU`) [body = SUBSCRIBE MOUNT-L first-name last-name]

 Archive: `listserv@vm.cc.metu.edu.tr`

1-929 **mpeg-list:** Discussions about MPEG standards and U.C. Berkeley MPEG decoder and encoder.

 i ± `mpeg-list-request@cs.berkeley.edu`

1-930 **MPG-L:** For the Yale multiprotocol gateway discussion group.

 i `susan@yalevm.bitnet` (Bitnet: `SUSAN@YALEVM`) (Susan Bramhall)

 ± `listserv@yalevm.ycc.yale.edu` (Bitnet: `LISTSERV@YALEVM`) [body = SUBSCRIBE MPG-L first-name last-name]

 Archive: `listserv@yalevm.ycc.yale.edu`

1-931 **MPSYCH-L:** Announcements from the Society for Mathematical Psychology. *Moderated*

 i `metzger@umbc.bitnet` (Bitnet: `METZGER@UMBC`) (Mary Ann Metzger) or `bi599088@brownvm.bitnet` (Bitnet: `BI599088@BROWNVM`) (Bob Stout)

 ± `listserv@brownvm.brown.edu` (Bitnet: `LISTSERV@BROWNVM`) [body = SUBSCRIBE MPSYCH-L first-name last-name]

 Archive: Available to subscribers only.

1-932 **mr2-interest:** Discussion of Toyota MR2's, old and new.

 i ± `mr2-interest-request@validgh.com` (David Hough)

1-933 **MS-Access:** An unmoderated list for MS Access topics, including Access Basic questions, reviews, rumors, etc.

 i ± `ms-access-request@eunet.co.at` (Martin Hilger)

1-934 **MSA-L:** For news and discussion on Islam.

 i `axh113@psuvm.bitnet` (Bitnet: `AXH113@PSUVM`) (Azmi Hashim)

 ± `listserv@psuvm.psu.edu` (Bitnet: `LISTSERV@PSUVM`) [body = SUBSCRIBE MSA-L first-name last-name]

1-935 **MSP-L:** On RFC-1312 (Message Send Protocol 2), an experimental protocol that proposes a method to provide the ability to communicate one-on-one in "real time" under TCP/IP.

 i `bec@albany.bitnet` (Bitnet: `BEC@ALBANY`) (Ben Chi)

 ± `listserv@albany.edu` (Bitnet: `LISTSERV@ALBANY`) [body = SUBSCRIBE MSP-L first-name last-name]

 Archive: Available to subscribers only.

1-936 **MT3270-L:** On beta test for Macintosh TN3270, a version of Telnet that emulates IBM 3270 terminals.

 i `cmsmaint@brownvm.bitnet` (Bitnet: `CMSMAINT@BROWNVM`) (Peter DiCamillo)

 ± `listserv@brownvm.brown.edu` (Bitnet: `LISTSERV@BROWNVM`) [body = SUBSCRIBE MT3270-L first-name last-name]

 Archive: Available to subscribers only.

1-937   **MTN:** On training by midwest college and university physical plant staffs.

     i   `stonec@iubacs.bitnet` (Bitnet: `STONEC@IUBACS`) (Cindy Stone) or `schnelle@iubacs.bitnet` (Bitnet: `SCHNELLE@IUBACS`) (Paul Schneller)

     ±   `listserv@iubvm.ucs.indiana.edu` (Bitnet: `LISTSERV@IUBVM`) [body = SUBSCRIBE MTN first-name last-name]

     Archive: `listserv@iubvm.ucs.indiana.edu`

1-938   **MUDA-L:** For players of MUDA, multi-user interactive game.

     i   `theodore@knosos.cc.uch.gr` (Theodore J. Soldatos)

     ±   `listserv@grearn.bitnet` (Bitnet: `LISTSERV@GREARN`) [body = SUBSCRIBE MUDA-L first-name last-name]

     Archive: Available to subscribers only.

     Language: English

1-939   **MULTI-L:** On language and education in multi-lingual educational settings.

     ±   `listserv@vm.biu.ac.il` (Bitnet: `LISTSERV@BARILVM`) [body = SUBSCRIBE MULTI-L first-name last-name]

     Archive: Available to subscribers only.

     Other: Subscription is limited. Requests will be sent to list owner for approval.

1-940   **MUNIX-L:** Discussion about Unix at Masaryk University, Brno, Czechoslovakia.

     i   `milos@varda.ics.muni.cs`

     ±   `listserv@csbrmu11.bitnet` (Bitnet: `LISTSERV@CSBRMU11`) [body = SUBSCRIBE MUNIX-L first-name last-name]

     Archive: `listserv@csbrmu11.bitnet`

     Language: Czech

1-941   **murmur-digest:** On the R.E.M. rock group.

     i   `murmur-mgr@lynchburg.edu`

     ±   `murmur-digest-request@lynchburg.edu` [body = subscribe]

     Archive: Fileserver `fables@lynchburg.edu` [body = `sendme` FAQ (for Frequently Asked Questions File), or `SENDME LYRICS.x` where x is one of AUTOMATIC, `CHRONIC_TOWN`, `DEAD_LETTER`, DOCUMENT, FABLES, GREEN, MURMUR, `OUT_OF_TIME`, PAGEANT, RECKONING]

     Other: High volume of mail.

1-942   **MUSEUM-L:** On museums.

     i   `chadwick@unmb.bitnet` (Bitnet: `CHADWICK@UNMB`) (John Chadwick)

     ±   `listserv@unmvma.unm.edu` (Bitnet: `LISTSERV@UNMVMA`) [body = SUBSCRIBE MUSEUM-L first-name last-name]

     Archive: Available to subscribers only.

1-943   **Music Developer:** On The Music Kit, an object-oriented software package for playing music and sound-related tasks under NeXTStep (available by FTP from `ccrma-ftp.stanford.edu`)

     i ±   `mkdist-request@ccrma.stanford.edu`

1-944   **Music-Research:** For musicologists, music analysts, computer scientists, and others working on applications of computers in music research. NOT about electronic music, synthesizers, MIDI, etc. *Moderated*

   i ± `music-research-request@prg.oxford.ac.uk` (Stephen Page) or `music-research-request@cattell.psych.upenn.edu`

   Gated: ⇒ `comp.music`

   Archive: FTP `ftp.comlab.ox.ac.uk`

1-945 **musicals:** Forum for the general discussions on musical theater.

   i ± `musicals-request@world.std.com` (Elizabeth Lear Newman)

   Gated: ⇔ `rec.arts.theatre` newsgroup

1-946 **MUSLIMS:** Academic and non-political education on issues relating to Islam and Muslims, including news, conferences, Muslim student groups, discussion of books by and about Muslims. *Moderated*

   i `mughal@alumni.caltech.edu` (Asim Mughal) or `pakeditr@asuacad.bitnet` (Nauman Mysorewala)

   ± `listserv@asuvm.inre.asu.edu` (Bitnet: LISTSERV@ASUACAD) [body = SUBSCRIBE MUSLIMS first-name last-name]

   Archive: `listserv@asuacad.bitnet` (Bitnet: LISTSERV@ASUACAD)

   Gated: ⇔ `bit.listserv.muslims`

1-947 **mustangs:** On technical and performance issues, problems, solutions, and modifications relating to late model (~1980+) Ford Mustangs. Flames and "my car is faster than your car" mailings are discouraged. *Moderated*

   i ± `mustangs-request@cup.hp.com` (Gary Gitzen)

1-948 **MUTEX:** For discussions and support of TeX typesetting system with emphasis typesetting in Czech and Slovak—ran by Masaryk University.

   i `sojka@rumil.ics.muni.cs`

   ± `listserv@csbrmu11.bitnet` (Bitnet: LISTSERV@CSBRMU11) [body = SUBSCRIBE MUTEX first-name last-name]

   Archive: `listserv@csbrmu11.bitnet`

   Language: Czech

1-949 **MuTeX:** A community resource for users of MuTeX and MusicTeX (writing music notation with TeX).

   i ± `mutex-request@stolaf.edu`

1-950 **MVSGOPHER:** On the MVS implementation of the Gopher client and server.

   ± `listserver@lists.acs.ohio-state.edu` [body = SUBSCRIBE MVSGOPHER first-name last-name]

1-951 **MWTOPSEM:** For announcements of topology seminars in the midwest U.S. *Moderated*

   i `taylor@laotse.helios.nd.edu` (Laurence Taylor)

   ± `listserv@vma.cc.nd.edu` (Bitnet: LISTSERV@IRISHVMA) [body = SUBSCRIBE MWTOPSEM first-name last-name]

   Archive: `listserv@vma.cc.nd.edu`

1-952 **My Dad Is Dead:** On the Scat recording artists, My Dad Is Dead, and other independent rock bands, particularly, those on the Scat label.

i ± bp094@cleveland.freenet.edu

1-953 **mystery:** On mystery and detective fiction (all media). Reviews of works and discussions of plot, characterization, and other aspects will are discussed.

i ± mystery-request@csd4.csd.uwm.edu (Thomas Krueger)

1-954 **NA-net:** Numerical analysis discussions.

± na.join@na-net.ornl.gov [body = join last-name first-name e-mail-address]

1-955 **NABOKV-L:** For scholarly discussion on the English and Russian writings of Vladimir Nabokov. *Moderated*

i chtodel@humanitas.ucsb.edu (D. Barton Johnson)

± listserv@ucsbvm.bitnet (Bitnet: LISTSERV@UCSBVM) [body = SUBSCRIBE NABOKV-L first-name last-name]

Archive: listserv@ucsbvm.bitnet

1-956 **NAHIA-L:** For North American historians of Islamic art.

i alan@ah2.cal.msu.edu (Alan Fisher)

± listserv@msu.edu (Bitnet: LISTSERV@MSU) [body = SUBSCRIBE NAHIA-L first-name last-name]

Archive: listserv@msu.edu

1-957 **NARST-L:** On improving the education of science teachers through research.

i jpeters@uwf.bitnet (Bitnet: JPETERS@UWF) (Joe Peters)

± listserv@uwf.cc.uwf.edu (Bitnet: LISTSERV@UWF) [body = SUBSCRIBE NARST-L first-name last-name]

Archive: Available to subscribers only.

Other: Subscription is limited. Requests will be sent to list owner for approval.

1-958 **NASPA1-L:** Distribution on the National Association of Student Personnel Administrators and related subjects.

i danielw@maine.bitnet (Bitnet: DANIELW@MAINE) (Daniel Williams)

± listserv@maine.edu (Bitnet: LISTSERV@MAINE) [body = SUBSCRIBE NASPA1-L first-name last-name]

1-959 **NASSR-L:** For members of the North American Society for the Study of Romanticism (NASSR). Scholarly discussions on Romantic literature.

i dcstewa@wvnvm.bitnet (Bitnet: DCSTEWA@WVNVM) (David C. Stewart)

± listserv@wvnvm.wvnet.edu (Bitnet: LISTSERV@WVNVM) [body = SUBSCRIBE NASSR-L first-name last-name]

Other: Subscription is limited. Requests will be sent to list owner for approval.

1-960 **NAT-1492:** On the Columbus Quincentenary. *Moderated*

i gst@gnosys.svle.ma.us (Gary S. Trujillo)

± listserv@tamvm1.tamu.edu (Bitnet: LISTSERV@TAMVM1) [body = SUBSCRIBE NAT-1492 first-name last-name]

Archive: listserv@tamvm1.tamu.edu

1-961 **NAT-LANG:** On the languages of aboriginal peoples. *Moderated*

    i `gst@gnosys.svle.ma.us` (Gary S. Trujillo)

    ± `listserv@tamvm1.tamu.edu` (Bitnet: `LISTSERV@TAMVM1`) [body = `SUBSCRIBE NAT-LANG` first-name last-name]

    Archive: `listserv@tamvm1.tamu.edu`

1-962 **NATCHAT:** On issues pertaining to aboriginal peoples. *Moderated*

    i `gst@gnosys.svle.ma.us` (Gary S. Trujillo) or
    `mkkuhner@genetics.washington.edu`

    ± `listserv@tamvm1.tamu.edu` (Bitnet: `LISTSERV@TAMVM1`) [body = `SUBSCRIBE NATCHAT` first-name last-name]

1-963 **NATIVE-L:** On issues pertaining to aboriginal peoples. *Moderated*

    i `gst@gnosys.svle.ma.us` (Gary S. Trujillo)

    ± `listserv@tamvm1.tamu.edu` (Bitnet: `LISTSERV@TAMVM1`) [body = `SUBSCRIBE NATIVE-L` first-name last-name]

    Archive: `listserv@tamvm1.tamu.edu`

1-964 **NATODATA:** For distribution of public data from the North Atlantic Treaty Organization, including press releases, communiques, NATO Review Articles, NATO factsheets, NATO Fellowship Programmes, Secretary General Speeches, NATO handbook. *Moderated*

    i `scheurwe@stc.nato.int`

    ± `listserv@blekul11.bitnet` (Bitnet: `LISTSERV@BLEKUL11`) [body = `SUBSCRIBE NATODATA` first-name last-name]

    Archive: `listserv@blekul11.bitnet`

1-965 **NAUSICAA:** For discussing manga (Japanese comics) and anime (Japanese animation), especially work by Hayao Miyazaki or other anime which are of a quasi-serious and/or progressive nature.

    i `ar402004@brownvm.bitnet` (Bitnet: `AR402004@BROWNVM`) (Steven Feldman) or
    `mauricio@mozart.aero.ufl.edu` (Mauricio Tavares)

    ± `listserv@brownvm.brown.edu` (Bitnet: `LISTSERV@BROWNVM`) [body = `SUBSCRIBE NAUSICAA` first-name last-name]

    Archive: `listserv@brownvm.brown.edu`

    Other: Subscription is limited. Requests will be sent to list owner for approval.

1-966 **navnews:** E-mail distribution of the weekly Navy News Service (NAVNEWS), published by the Navy Internal Relations Activity in Washington. Contains official news and information about fleet operations and exercises, personnel policies, budget actions, and more.

    i ± `navnews@nctamslant.navy.mil`

1-967 **NBS-AEP:** For members of National Broadcasting Society—Alpha Epsilon Rho, an organization for bridging school and careers in broadcasting.

    i `regbc@cunyvm.bitnet` (Bitnet: `REGBC@CUNYVM`) (Reg Gamar)

    ± `listserv@cunyvm.cuny.edu` (Bitnet: `LISTSERV@CUNYVM`) [body = `SUBSCRIBE NBS-AEP` first-name last-name]

    Archive: `listserv@cunyvm.cuny.edu`

    Other: Subscription is limited. Requests will be sent to list owner for approval.

1-968 **NCC-L:** For National Communication Coordinators residence hall student government organizations and their advisors. Topics of discussion focus on business and procedural issues for NCCs.

i `n018gh@tamvm1.bitnet` (Bitnet: `N018GH@TAMVM1`) (Michael Osterbuhr)

± `listserv@tamvm1.tamu.edu` (Bitnet: `LISTSERV@TAMVM1`) [body = SUBSCRIBE NCC-L first-name last-name]

Archive: `listserv@tamvm1.tamu.edu`

1-969 **NCE-RESP:** On respiratory research topics.

i `whitney@christie.meakins.mcgill.ca` (Whitney Devries)

± `listserv@vm1.mcgill.ca` (Bitnet: `LISTSERV@MCGILL1`) [body = SUBSCRIBE NCE-RESP first-name last-name]

1-970 **NCS-L:** For discussing the design and use of the National Crime Survey to produce national estimates of criminal victimization.

i `brianw@umdd.bitnet` (Bitnet: `BRIANW@UMDD`) (Brian Wiersema)

± `listserv@umdd.umd.edu` (Bitnet: `LISTSERV@UMDD`) [body = SUBSCRIBE NCS-L first-name last-name]

Archive: `listserv@umdd.umd.edu`

1-971 **NDDESIGN:** For graphic and industrial design educators.

i `john.f.sherman.1@nd.edu` (John Sherman)

± `listserv@vma.cc.nd.edu` (Bitnet: `LISTSERV@IRISHVMA`) [body = SUBSCRIBE NDDESIGN first-name last-name]

Archive: `listserv@vma.cc.nd.edu`

1-972 **ne-raves:** For information about the N.E. USA rave scene.

i ± `ne-raves-request@gnu.ai.mit.edu`

1-973 **ne-social-motss:** Announcements of social and other events and other happenings in the North Eastern United States of interest to of interest to lesbian, gay, and bisexual people.

i `ne-social-motss-request@plts.org`

± `majordomo@plts.org` [body = subscribe ne-social-motss]

1-974 **NEDER-L:** An e-journal for the study of Dutch language and literature. *Moderated*

i `u216013@hnykun11.bitnet` (Bitnet: `U216013@HNYKUN11`) (Ben Salemans)

± `listserv@hearn.nic.surfnet.nl` (Bitnet: `LISTSERV@HEARN`) [body = SUBSCRIBE NEDER-L first-name last-name]

Archive: `listserv@hearn.nic.surfnet.nl`

Language: Dutch

1-975 **neph:** On the defunct rock group Fields of the Nephilim, the current bands The Nefilim and Rubicon, and related issues.

i `rearl@oinker.ucsb.edu` (Robert Earl)

± `neph-request@oinker.ucsb.edu`

Archive: mail-serv `neph-request@oinker.ucsb.edu` [body = send archive]

1-976 **Nerdnosh:** A list which describes itself as "a gathering of friends around a campfire, except there is no packing, no mosquitos, no moving, even. A network neighborhood for the sharing of journals and stories; it's flame-free, frivolous, friendly, and informative, in roughly that order."

i `nerdnosh-request@scruz.ucsc.edu` (Tim Bowden)

± `majordomo@scruz.ucsc.edu` [body = `subscribe nerdnosh`]

1-977 **NESUG-L:** For users of SAS in the northeast U.S.

i `mscerbo@umab.bitnet` (Bitnet: `MSCERBO@UMAB`) (Marge Scerbo)

± `listserv@umab.umd.edu` (Bitnet: `LISTSERV@UMAB`) [body = `SUBSCRIBE NESUG-L` first-name last-name]

1-978 **NET_LIC:** On managing applications software licenses in a networked environment. Issues include metering systems, concurrent licensing, software distribution, software piracy control, software management.

i `acdrlk@suvm.bitnet` (Bitnet: `ACDRLK@SUVM`) (Ron Kalinoski)

± `listserv@suvm.acs.syr.edu` (Bitnet: `LISTSERV@SUVM`) [body = `SUBSCRIBE NET_LIC` first-name last-name]

1-979 **netblazer-users:** Forum for users of Telebit NetBlazer products.

i `netblazer-users-request@telebit.com`

± `majordomo@telebit.com` [body = `subscribe netblazer-users`]

1-980 **NETCON-L:** For NetCon 94 information. *Moderated*

i `rebat@vtvm1.bitnet` (Bitnet: `REBAT@VTVM1`) or `ahrjj@cunyvm.bitnet` (Bitnet: `AHRJJ@CUNYVM`)

± `listserv@vtvm1.cc.vt.edu` (Bitnet: `LISTSERV@VTVM1`) [body = `SUBSCRIBE NETCON-L` first-name last-name]

1-981 **NetJam:** Discussion and execution of remote musical collaboration.

± `netjam-request@xcf.berkeley.edu` [subject = `request for info`]

Archive: FTP `xcf.berkeley.edu` in `misc/netjam`

1-982 **NETNWS-L:** For operators and developers of various Netnews programs on non-Unix-to-Unix networks. *Moderated*

i `nu021172@ndsuvm1.bitnet` (Bitnet: `NU021172@NDSUVM1`) (Marty Hoag)

± `listserv@vm1.nodak.edu` (Bitnet: `LISTSERV@NDSUVM1`) [body = `SUBSCRIBE NETNWS-L` first-name last-name]

Archive: `listserv@vm1.nodak.edu`

Gated: ⇔ `bit.listserv.netnws-l`

1-983 **NETTRAIN:** About Internet/BITNET network trainers. *Moderated*

i `millesjg@sluvca.slu.edu` (Jim Milles)

± `listserv@ubvm.cc.buffalo.edu` (Bitnet: `LISTSERV@UBVM`) [body = `SUBSCRIBE NETTRAIN` first-name last-name]

Archive: `listserv@ubvm.cc.buffalo.edu`

Other: Weekly digest

1-984 **NETV-L:** On IBM's NETView

i `urmm@marist.bitnet` (Bitnet: `URMM@MARIST`) (Martha McConaghy)

± `listserv@vm.marist.edu` (Bitnet: `LISTSERV@MARIST`) [body = `SUBSCRIBE`

NETV-L first-name last-name]

Archive: `listserv@vm.marist.edu`

1-985 **Network-Audio-Bits:** Bi-monthly electronic magazine that features reviews of and information about current rock, pop, new age, jazz, funk, folk, and other musical genres.

i ± `murph@maine.bitnet` (Michael A. Murphy)

1-986 **NEUCHILE:** For Chilean neurosciences.

i `palacios-adrian@yale.edu` (Adrian Palacios)

± `listserv@yalevm.ycc.yale.edu` (Bitnet: LISTSERV@YALEVM) [body = SUBSCRIBE NEUCHILE first-name last-name] or `listserv@uchcecvm.bitnet` (Bitnet: LISTSERV@UCHCECVM) [body = SUBSCRIBE NEUCHILE first-name last-name]

Archive: `listserv@yalevm.ycc.yale.edu` or `listserv@uchcecvm.bitnet`

Language: Spanish

Other: Subscription is limited. Requests will be sent to list owner for approval.

1-987 **neuron:** On all aspects of neural networks. Topics include both artificial neural networks and biological systems. *Moderated*

i ± `neuron-request@psych.upenn.edu` (Peter Marvit)

Archive: FTP `psych.upenn.edu`

Gated: ⇔ `comp.ai.neural-nets`

Other: Digest format

1-988 **NEW-LIST:** For distributing announcements of new public mailing lists on the Internet.

i `info@vm1.nodak.edu` (Bitnet: INFO@NDSUVM1) (Marty Hoag)

± `listserv@vm1.nodak.edu` (Bitnet: LISTSERV@NDSUVM1) [body = SUBSCRIBE NEW-LIST first-name last-name] or `listserv@irlearn.bitnet` (Bitnet: LISTSERV@IRLEARN) [body = SUBSCRIBE NEW-LIST first-name last-name]

Other: Weekly digest

Gated: ⇔ `bit.listserv.NEW-LIST`

1-989 **new-orleans:** Any discussion related to the city of New Orleans, Louisiana

i `elendil@mintir.new-orleans.la.us`

± `mail-server@mintir.new-orleans.la.us` [body = SUBSCRIBE NEW-ORLEANS]

1-990 **new-releases:** A distribution list for the weekly New and Upcoming Releases listing compiled by `dld30@quts.ccc.amdahl.com` (Dave Dooley)

i ± `new-releases-request@cs.uwp.edu` (Dave Datta)

Other: The list is available as a weekly digest. Archives are stored at `ftp.uwp.edu`

1-991 **NeXT Managers:** A community resource for NeXT managers to help each other with quick answers to techincal problems.

± `listserv@vm1.nodak.edu` [body = subscribe new-list first-name last-name] or `next-managers-request@stolaf.edu`

1-992 **next-classroom:** NeXT Courseware.

± `mailserv@gac.edu` [body = SUBSCRIBE next-classroom first-name last-name]

1-993 **NeXT-Graphics:** All about high-end graphics on computers running the NeXTStep operating system.

± `next-graphics-request@gun.com`

1-994 **NeXT-icon:** For distribution of 64 x 64 or 48 x 48 pixel icons (2-, 8-, 12-, 24- and/or 32-bit) compatible with the NeXT Computer's NeXTStep software. Most posts contain attachments and font-formatting that may be read with NeXTmail-compatible mail readers only.

i ± `next-icon-request@gun.com` (Timothy Reed)

Archives: FTP `cs.orst.edu` in `/pub/next/graphics/`

1-995 **NeXT-Med:** On medical uses of NeXT computers.

± `next-med-request@ms.uky.edu`

1-996 **next-nihongo:** Kanji and Japanese on NeXTStep.

± `next-nihongo-request@pinoko.berkeley.edu`

Archive: FTP `pinoko.berkeley.edu` in `/pub/next/nihongo`

1-997 **next-prog:** Forum for items of interest, and Q and A for NeXTStep programmers.

± `next-prog-request@cpac.washington.edu`

1-998 **Next/Apple II:** On the NeXTStep application "zaniWok," an Apple II simulator.

± `na2sig-request@byu.edu`

1-999 **Nextcomm:** On NeXTStep telecommunications.

i ± `nextcomm-request@marble.com`

1-1000 **NeXTmusic:** On music related topics for users of NeXTStep, including MusicKit, DSP expansion options, MIDI, and software announcements..

± `nextmusic-request@horowitz.eecs.umich.edu`

1-1001 **NEXTSTEP News:** NEXTSTEP General Information

i ± `conrad@rmnug.org`

1-1002 **NFDL-L:** The Nordic Forum for Computer Aided Higher Education.

i `karlsson@mech.kth.se` (Goeran Karlsson)

± `listserv@searn.sunet.se` (Bitnet: LISTSERV@SEARN) [body = SUBSCRIBE NFDL-L first-name last-name]

Archive: `listserv@searn.sunet.se`

Language: various Scandinavian, English

1-1003 **NHILLEL:** For Jewish students.

i `hilleln@gwuvm.bitnet` (Bitnet: HILLELN@GWUVM) (Shamir Caplan)

± `listserv@gwuvm.gwu.edu` (Bitnet: LISTSERV@GWUVM) [body = SUBSCRIBE NHILLEL first-name last-name]

Archive: `listserv@gwuvm.gwu.edu`

1-1004 **NIHDIS-L:** For institutional hubs who are participating in the NIH E-Guide program.

i `jimj@jhuvm.bitnet` (Bitnet: JIMJ@JHUVM) (Jim Jones)

± `listserv@jhuvm.hcf.jhu.edu` (Bitnet: LISTSERV@JHUVM) [body = SUBSCRIBE NIHDIS-L first-name last-name]

Archive: `listserv@jhuvm.hcf.jhu.edu`

1-1005 **NIHGDE-L:** NIH Guide for Grants and Contracts Primary Distribution List. *Moderated*

i `q2c@nihcu.bitnet` (Bitnet: `Q2C@NIHCU`) (Myra Brockett)

± `listserv@jhuvm.hcf.jhu.edu` (Bitnet: `LISTSERV@JHUVM`) [body = `SUBSCRIBE NIHGDE-L` first-name last-name]

Archive: `listserv@jhuvm.hcf.jhu.edu`

Other: Subscription is limited. Requests will be sent to list owner for approval.

1-1006 **NIS-REP:** The GARR NIS report.

i `vannozzi@vm.cnuce.cnr.it` (Daniele Vannozzi)

± `listserv@vm.cnuce.cnr.it` (Bitnet: `LISTSERV@ICNUCEVM`) [body = `SUBSCRIBE NIS-REP` first-name last-name]

Archive: `listserv@vm.cnuce.cnr.it`

1-1007 **NISO-L:** For distribution of press releases and informational items from the National Information Standards Organization. *Moderated*

i `fclmth@nervm.bitnet` (Bitnet: `FCLMTH@NERVM`)

± `listserv@nervm.nerdc.ufl.edu` (Bitnet: `LISTSERV@NERVM`) [body = `SUBSCRIBE NISO-L` first-name last-name]

1-1008 **NNLM-SEA:** On improving access to biomedical information for health professionals nation-wide—a project of the Southeastern/Atlantic Region of the National Network of Libraries of Medicine.

i `sbailey@umab.bitnet` (Bitnet: `SBAILEY@UMAB`) (Susan Bailey)

± `listserv@umab.umd.edu` (Bitnet: `LISTSERV@UMAB`) [body = `SUBSCRIBE NNLM-SEA` first-name last-name]

Archive: `listserv@umab.umd.edu`

Other: Subscription is limited. Requests will be sent to list owner for approval.

1-1009 **NNMVS-L:** MVS/TSO NNTP News Reader (NNMVS) Discussion.

i `seb1@mvs.draper.com` (Stephen E. Bacher) or `ldw@uscvm.bitnet` (Leonard D. Woren)

± `listserv@vm.usc.edu` (Bitnet: `LISTSERV@USCVM`) [body = `SUBSCRIBE NNMVS-L` first-name last-name]

Archive: `listserv@vm.usc.edu`

1-1010 **NNRP-L:** On network news reading protocol, which splits server/server interactions and server/client interactions.

i `david_ascher@brown.edu`

± `listserv@brownvm.brown.edu` (Bitnet: `LISTSERV@BROWNVM`) [body = `SUBSCRIBE NNRP-L` first-name last-name]

Archive: Available to subscribers only.

1-1011 **NONLIN-L:** On economic nonlinear dynamics.

i `xum@nihcu.bitnet` (Bitnet: `XUM@NIHCU`)

± `listserv@list.nih.gov` (Bitnet: `LISTSERV@NIHLIST`) [body = `SUBSCRIBE NONLIN-L` first-name last-name]

Archive: `listserv@list.nih.gov`

1-1012 **nonserv:** Discussions on the philosophy of Max Stirner and other rebellious spirits.

i ± `nonserv-request@math.uio.no`

1-1013 **NORDBALT:** About networking between Nordic and Baltic countries.

i `ber@sunic.sunet.se` (Bjorn Eriksen)

± `listserv@searn.sunet.se` (Bitnet: `LISTSERV@SEARN`) [body = SUBSCRIBE NORDBALT first-name last-name]

Archive: `listserv@searn.sunet.se`

1-1014 **nordic-skiing:** Discussion of nordic skiing sports, including cross-country, , ski-orienteering, biathlon, ski jumping, nordic combined, telemark, and back-country.

i ± `nordic-ski-request@graphics.cornell.edu` (Mitch Collinsworth)

1-1015 **NORML-L:** National Organization for the Reform of Marijuana Laws (NORML), Texas A & M chapter.

i `norml@tamu.edu`

± `listserv@tamvm1.tamu.edu` (Bitnet: `LISTSERV@TAMVM1`) [body = SUBSCRIBE NORML-L first-name last-name]

Other: Subscription is limited. Requests will be sent to list owner for approval.

1-1016 **NOVELL:** On Novell LANs.

i `noveladm@suvm.bitnet` (Bitnet: `NOVELADM@SUVM`) (Bruce Riddle)

± `listserv@suvm.acs.syr.edu` (Bitnet: `LISTSERV@SUVM`) [body = SUBSCRIBE NOVELL first-name last-name]

Archive: `listserv@suvm.acs.syr.edu`

1-1017 **Novice-MZT (News from MZT):** News of Ministry for Science and Technology of the Republic of Slovenia.

i ± `novice-mzt@krpan.arnes.si,novice.mzt@uni-lj.si`

Language: Slovene

Other: published several times a month.

1-1018 **nqthm-users:** On theorem proving using the Boyer-Moore theorem prover, NQTHM.

i `dww@informatik.tfh-berlin.d400.de` (Debora Weber-Wulff)

± `nqthm-users-request@cli.com` or `nqthm-users-request@inf.fu-berlin.de`

1-1019 **NRSING-L:** On nursing informatics and other nursing topics.

i `larrivee@umassmed.ummed.edu` (Gordon Larrivee)

± `listproc@nic.umass.edu` [body = SUBSCRIBE NRSING-L first-name last-name]

Archive: Mailserv `listproc@nic.umass.edu`

1-1020 **NRSOCSCI:** For discussing relationships between people and natural resources, including conflict resolution, sustainable development, eco-tourism, and ecological economics.

i `jc30102@coyote.cfr.washington.edu` (John Chmelik)

± `listserv@uwavm.u.washington.edu` (Bitnet: `LISTSERV@UWAVM`) [body = SUBSCRIBE NRSOCSCI first-name last-name]

Archive: `listserv@uwavm.u.washington.edu`

1-1021 **NSP-L:** Noble Savage Philosophers mailing list.

    i `userf98f@rpitsmts.bitnet` (Bitnet: `USERF98F@RPITSMTS`) (Barry B. Floyd)

    ± `listserv@vm.its.rpi.edu` (Bitnet: `LISTSERV@RPITSVM`) [body = SUBSCRIBE NSP-L first-name last-name]

    Archive: `listserv@vm.its.rpi.edu`

1-1022 **ntp:** Discussion of the Network Time Protocol.

    i ± `ntp-request@ni.umd.edu`

    Gated: ⇔ `comp.protocols.time.ntp`

1-1023 **NTS-L:** On the New Typesetting System (NTS), a project organised under the aegis of DANTE (the German-speaking TeX Users' Group) to consider how best the philosophy and strengths of the TeX typesetting system might be preserved for future generations.

    i `chaa006@vax.rhbnc.ac.uk` (Philip Taylor)

    ± `listserv@dhdurz1.bitnet` (Bitnet: `LISTSERV@DHDURZ1`) [body = SUBSCRIBE NTS-L first-name last-name]

1-1024 **nucmed:** A discussion of nuclear medicine and related issues. Of particular concern is the Interfile format for nuclear medicine digital images.

    i ± `nucmed-request@irus.rri.uwo.ca` or `cradduck@uwo.ca` (Trevor Cradduck)

1-1025 **numeric-interest:** On floating-point correctness and performance with respect to hardware, operating systems, languages, and standard libraries.

    i ± `numeric-interest-request@validgh.com` (David Hough)

1-1026 **NUTEPI:** On nutritional epidemiology.

    i `mensink@db0tui11.bitnet` (Bitnet: `MENSINK@DB0TUI11`) (Gert Mensink)

    ± `listserv@db0tui11.bitnet` (Bitnet: `LISTSERV@DB0TUI11`) [body = SUBSCRIBE NUTEPI first-name last-name]

    Archive: `listserv@db0tui11.bitnet`

1-1027 **NV6000-L:** For users of NetView/6000.

    i `x28@vm.urz.uni-heidelberg.de` (Matthias Melcher)

    ± `listserv@dhdurz1.bitnet` (Bitnet: `LISTSERV@DHDURZ1`) [body = SUBSCRIBE NV6000-L first-name last-name]

    Language: German

1-1028 **nwu-sports:** On Northwestern University sports, also known as "da cats."

    i (Michael Nolan)

    ± `nwu-sports-request@tssi.com`

1-1029 **NYSLUX-L:** Forum on the NY Consortium for Model European Community Simulation.

    i `psceagle@ubvms.bitnet` (Bitnet: `PSCEAGLE@UBVMS`) (Munroe Eagles)

    ± `listserv@ubvm.cc.buffalo.edu` (Bitnet: `LISTSERV@UBVM`) [body = SUBSCRIBE NYSLUX-L first-name last-name]

1-1030 **NYSO-L:** For members of the New York State/Ontario Chapter of the Music Library

Association.

i `mmlrick@ubvm.bitnet` (Bitnet: `MMLRICK@UBVM`) (Rick McRae)

± `listserv@ubvm.cc.buffalo.edu` (Bitnet: `LISTSERV@UBVM`) [body = `SUBSCRIBE NYSO-L` first-name last-name]

Archive: `listserv@ubvm.cc.buffalo.edu`

1-1031 **objectivism:** For students of objectivism to discuss their ideas, concrete issues, exchange news, etc.

i ± `objectivism-request@vix.com` (Paul Vixie)

1-1032 **OFFCAMP:** On off-campus library services.

i `blessin@waynest1.bitnet` (Bitnet: `BLESSIN@WAYNEST1`) (Barton Lessin)

± `listserv@cms.cc.wayne.edu` (Bitnet: `LISTSERV@WAYNEST1`) [body = `SUBSCRIBE OFFCAMP` first-name last-name]

1-1033 **offroad:** For owners, users, or enthusiasts of four wheel drive vehicles.

Other: Available as reflector or digest.

i ± `offroad-request@ai.gtri.gatech.edu` (Stefan Roth)

Archive: Mailserv `offroad-server@ai.gtri.gatech.edu` [body = `help`]

1-1034 **oh-motss:** The Ohio Members Of The Same Sex mailing list is for open discussion of lesbian, gay, and bisexual issues in and affecting Ohio.

i ± `oh-motss-request@cps.udayton.edu`

1-1035 **OICISNET:** Support network for development activities of OICA Member Countries and their institutions.

i `amin@sairti00.bitnet` (Bitnet: `AMIN@SAIRTI00`) (Amin Abdullah Said)

± `listserv@sairti00.bitnet` (Bitnet: `LISTSERV@SAIRTI00`) [body = `SUBSCRIBE OICISNET` first-name last-name]

Other: Subscription is limited. Requests will be sent to list owner for approval.

1-1036 **OISNEWS:** News for Indiana University International Students and Scholars. *Moderated*

i `intlcent@indiana.edu`

± `listserv@iubvm.ucs.indiana.edu` (Bitnet: `LISTSERV@IUBVM`) [body = `SUBSCRIBE OISNEWS` first-name last-name]

Archive: `listserv@iubvm.ucs.indiana.edu`

1-1037 **OLYMPUCK:** For the discussion of Olympic ice hockey. Discussion concerning players, coaches, teams, and the games themselves are welcome and encouraged. Related topics such as the interaction between the Olympic competition and college or NHL hockey are also acceptable.

i `slavin@maine.bitnet` (Bitnet: `SLAVIN@MAINE`) (Charlie Slavin)

± `listserv@maine.edu` (Bitnet: `LISTSERV@MAINE`) [body = `SUBSCRIBE OLYMPUCK` first-name last-name]

Archive: `listserv@maine.edu`

Other: Daily digest

1-1038 **on-this-day:** Subscribers to on-this-day receive a daily listing of interesting birthdays, events, religious holidays, astronomical events, etc. The messages are sent out in the wee hours of the morning, so you should have it for your morning coffee.

i ± geiser@pictel.com (Wayne Geiser)

1-1039 **on-u:** All about Adrian Sherwood's On-U Sound label and the artists that record on it. This includes Tack>Head, Gary Clail, The Dub Syndicate, African Head Charge, Bim Sherman, Mark Stewart, etc.

i ± on-u-request@pyramid.com.au (Ben Golding)

1-1040 **ONE-L:** On the mutual impact of organizations and the environment.

i throop@clvm.bitnet (Bitnet: THROOP@CLVM) (Gary Throop)

± listserv@clvm.clarkson.edu (Bitnet: LISTSERV@CLVM) [body = SUBSCRIBE ONE-L first-name last-name]

Archive: listserv@clvm.clarkson.edu

1-1041 **ONS-L:** For democratic decisionmaking and political discussion among students at the University of Nijmegen in the Netherlands. *Moderated*

i u211297@hnykun11.bitnet (Bitnet: U211297@HNYKUN11)

± listserv@hearn.nic.surfnet.nl (Bitnet: LISTSERV@HEARN) [body = SUBSCRIBE ONS-L first-name last-name]

Archive: Available to subscribers only.

Language: Dutch

Other: Subscription is limited. Requests will be sent to list owner for approval.

1-1042 **operlist:** For discussions on Internet Relay Chat, especially on irc routing, the irc protocol, and announcements of new versions of irc clients and servers.

i ± operlist-request@eff.org (Helen Trillian Rose)

1-1043 **OPERS-L:** On mainframe computer operations.

i o1evert@akronvm.bitnet (Bitnet: O1EVERT@AKRONVM) (Tom Evert)

± listserv@pccvm.bitnet (Bitnet: LISTSERV@PCCVM) [body = SUBSCRIBE OPERS-L first-name last-name] or listserv@vm1.cc.uakron.edu (Bitnet: LISTSERV@AKRONVM) [body = SUBSCRIBE OPERS-L first-name last-name]

Archive: listserv@vm1.cc.uakron.edu

Gated: ⇔ bit.listserv.opers-l

1-1044 **OPT-PROC:** On holography and optical computing. *Moderated*

i feglaser@weizmann.bitnet (Bitnet: FEGLASER@WEIZMANN) (Shelly Glaser)

± listserv@taunivm.tau.ac.il (Bitnet: LISTSERV@TAUNIVM) [body = SUBSCRIBE OPT-PROC first-name last-name]

1-1045 **OPTICS-L:** On optics, electro optics, and lasers in Israel. *Moderated*

i jo@ilncrd.bitnet (Bitnet: JO@ILNCRD) (Jo van Zwaren)

± listserv@taunivm.tau.ac.il (Bitnet: LISTSERV@TAUNIVM) [body = SUBSCRIBE OPTICS-L first-name last-name]

1-1046 **ORCS-L:** On the interface between operations research and computer science.

i sharda@osuvm1.bitnet (Bitnet: SHARDA@OSUVM1)

± listserv@vm1.ucc.okstate.edu (Bitnet: LISTSERV@OSUVM1) [body = SUBSCRIBE ORCS-L first-name last-name]

Archive: Available to subscribers only.

1-1047 **orienteering:** Discussion of the sport of orienteering and related topics such as map-making, land access, the sport of ROGAINE, etc.

    i ± `orienteering-request@graphics.cornell.edu` (Mitch Collinsworth)

1-1048 **origami:** On the Japanese art of paper folding.

    ± `origami-l-request@nstn.ns.ca` [body = `subscribe origami-l`]

    Archive: FTP `rugcis.rug.nl` in `origami`

1-1049 **OUTDOR-L:** On the outdoors.

    i `jacock01@ulkyvm.bitnet` (Bitnet: `JACOCK01@ULKYVM`) (Jim Cocks)

    ± `listserv@ulkyvm.louisville.edu` (Bitnet: `LISTSERV@ULKYVM`) [body = `SUBSCRIBE OUTDOR-L` first-name last-name]

    Archive: Available to subscribers only.

1-1050 **OXYGEN-L:** On oxygen free radical biology and medicine.

    i `c467414@mizzou1.bitnet` (Bitnet: `C467414@MIZZOU1`) (Lillian Novela)

    ± `listserv@mizzou1.missouri.edu` (Bitnet: `LISTSERV@MIZZOU1`) [body = `SUBSCRIBE OXYGEN-L` first-name last-name]

    Archive: `listserv@mizzou1.missouri.edu`

1-1051 **oysters:** For discussion of the British folk-rock band The Oyster band and related topics.

    i ± `oysters-request@blowfish.taligent.com`

1-1052 **PACE-L:** For users of the PACE computer-assisted advisement and degree audit system.

    i `regmse@gsuvm1.bitnet` (Bitnet: `REGMSE@GSUVM1`) (Mark Elliott)

    ± `listserv@gsuvm1.gsu.edu` (Bitnet: `LISTSERV@GSUVM1`) [body = `SUBSCRIBE PACE-L` first-name last-name]

    Archive: `listserv@gsuvm1.gsu.edu`

1-1053 **PACES-L:** For Publications Association of Canadian Engineering Students (PACES), an organization for editors of student engineering publications in Canada.

    i `cfes@jupiter.sun.csd.unb.ca` (Canadian Federation of Engineering Students)

    ± `listserv@unb.ca` (Bitnet: `LISTSERV@UNBVM1`) [body = `SUBSCRIBE PACES-L` first-name last-name]

1-1054 **PACS-L:** Public access computer systems discussion and distribution of four electronic journals—Current Cites, LITA Newsletter, Public-Access Computer Systems News, and The Public-Access Computer Systems Review.

    i `libpacs@uhupvm1.bitnet` (Bitnet: `LIBPACS@UHUPVM1`)

    ± `listserv@uhupvm1.uh.edu` (Bitnet: `LISTSERV@UHUPVM1`) [body = `SUBSCRIBE PACS-L` first-name last-name]

    Archive: `listserv@uhupvm1.uh.edu`

1-1055 **PACS-P:** Distribution of four electronic journals—Current Cites, LITA Newsletter, Public-Access Computer Systems News, and The Public-Access Computer Systems Review.

    i `libpacs@uhupvm1.bitnet` (Bitnet: `LIBPACS@UHUPVM1`)

    ± `listserv@uhupvm1.uh.edu` (Bitnet: `LISTSERV@UHUPVM1`) [body = `SUBSCRIBE PACS-P` first-name last-name]

Archive: `listserv@uhupvm1.uh.edu`

1-1056 **PACV-L:** On computer vision, artificial intelligence, life, neural networks, and automation.

i `heping@ipb1.ipb.uni-bonn.de` (Dr. Ing He-Ping Pan)

± `listserv@vm.gmd.de` (Bitnet: `LISTSERV@DEARN`) [body = `SUBSCRIBE PACV-L` first-name last-name]

Archive: `listserv@vm.gmd.de`

1-1057 **pagan:** On the religions, philosophy, etc. of paganism.

i ± `pagan-request@drycas.bitnet`

Archive: by mail from `uther@drycas.bitnet` or `dstalder@gmuvax.bitnet`

1-1058 **PAGEMAKR:** On desktop publishing using Pagemaker for Macintosh or PC-compatibles.

i `stonec@iubacs.bitnet` (Bitnet: `STONEC@IUBACS`) (Cindy Stone) or `jbone@dopig.uab.edu` (Jeff Bone)

± `listserv@indycms.iupui.edu` (Bitnet: `LISTSERV@INDYCMS`) [body = `SUBSCRIBE PAGEMAKR` first-name last-name]

Archive: `listserv@indycms.iupui.edu`

1-1059 **PAKISTAN:** The Pakistan News Service. *Moderated*

i `mysorenk@ucbeh.bitnet` (Bitnet: `MYSORENK@UCBEH`) (Nauman K. Mysorewala)

± `listserv@psuvm.psu.edu` (Bitnet: `LISTSERV@PSUVM`) [body = `SUBSCRIBE PAKISTAN` first-name last-name] or `listserv@asuvm.inre.asu.edu` (Bitnet: `LISTSERV@ASUACAD`) [body = `SUBSCRIBE PAKISTAN` first-name last-name]

Archive: `listserv@asuvm.inre.asu.edu`

Gated: ⇔ `bit.listserv.pakistan`

1-1060 **Papa:** On the life and works of Ernest Hemingway.

i ± `dgross@polyslo.calpoly.edu` (Dave Gross)

1-1061 **PARAGUAY:** For people interested in all aspects of Paraguay, including its culture, its native language (Guarani), and everyday events.

i `horacio.recalde@sdrc.com` (Horacio Recalde)

± `listserv@vm.usc.edu` (Bitnet: `LISTSERV@USCVM`) [body = `SUBSCRIBE PARAGUAY` first-name last-name]

1-1062 **parallax:** Discussions about products from Parallax Inc, in particular the XVIDEO board, which is a graphics frame buffer with video capture, compression, and decompression.

i ± `parallax-request@cs.berkeley.edu`

1-1063 **parker-list:** On the music of Graham Parker, with or without the Rumour, and members of that band.

i `thurlow@convex.com` (Rob Thurlow)

± `parker-list-request@convex.com`

1-1064 **ParNET:** On installation, use and modification of ParNET, an Amiga`<->`Amiga networking program.

i `ben@ben.com` (Ben Jackson)

± `parnet-list-request@ben.com`

1-1065 **PAYHR-L:** On payroll, benefits, and human resources in higher education.

> *i* upsxxas@okway.okstate.edu
>
> ± listserv@vm1.ucc.okstate.edu (Bitnet: LISTSERV@OSUVM1) [body = SUBSCRIBE PAYHR-L first-name last-name]
>
> **Archive:** listserv@vm1.ucc.okstate.edu

1-1066 **pc532:** For people interested in the pc532 project, a National Semiconductor NS32532 based system, offered for a very low cost.

> ± pc532-request@bungi.com (Dave Rand)

1-1067 **PCARAB-L:** On the various tools used for applying Arabic letters to personal computers.

> *i* devmtg12@sakfu00.bitnet (Bitnet: DEVMTG12@SAKFU00) (Mustafa Alghazal)
>
> ± listserv@sakfu00.bitnet (Bitnet: LISTSERV@SAKFU00) [body = SUBSCRIBE PCARAB-L first-name last-name]
>
> **Archive:** Available to subscribers only.
>
> **Language:** English
>
> **Other:** Weekly digest. Subscription is limited. Requests will be sent to list owner for approval.

1-1068 **PCBR-L:** For members of Paciber, an organization interested in research and development of business activities that span the Pacific basin.

> *i* morton@uhunix.uhcc.hawaii.edu (Bitnet: MORTON@UHUNIX)
>
> ± listserv@uhccvm.uhcc.hawaii.edu (Bitnet: LISTSERV@UHCCVM) [body = SUBSCRIBE PCBR-L first-name last-name]
>
> **Archive:** Available to subscribers only.
>
> **Other:** Subscription is limited. Requests will be sent to list owner for approval.

1-1069 **PCBUILD:** On building PCs.

> *i* gomberg@ucsfvm.bitnet (Bitnet: GOMBERG@UCSFVM) (Dave Gomberg)
>
> ± listserv@tscvm.trenton.edu (Bitnet: LISTSERV@TSCVM) [body = SUBSCRIBE PCBUILD first-name last-name]
>
> **Archive:** listserv@tscvm.trenton.edu

1-1070 **PCORPS-L:** For international volunteers.

> *i* 3zlufur@cmuvm.bitnet (Bitnet: 3ZLUFUR@CMUVM) (Elliott Parker)
>
> ± listserv@cmuvm.csv.cmich.edu (Bitnet: LISTSERV@CMUVM) [body = SUBSCRIBE PCORPS-L first-name last-name]
>
> **Archive:** Available to subscribers only.

1-1071 **PDC-L:** For users of PDC Prolog, a Prolog compiler that runs unde DOS, Extended DOS, OS/2, Unix and Xenix. Applications include gaming simulation, genetic pedigree analysis, and databases.

> *i* de_boer@eco.rug.nl (Thomas de Boer)
>
> ± listserv@hearn.nic.surfnet.nl (Bitnet: LISTSERV@HEARN) [body = SUBSCRIBE PDC-L first-name last-name]
>
> **Archive:** listserv@hearn.nic.surfnet.nl

1-1072 **perfect-beat:** Discussion of early 1980s synth-pop music and groups

    i `rnovak@nyx.cs.du.edu` (Robert Novak)

    ± `perfect-beat-request@gnu.ai.mit.edu`

    Archive: FTP `ftp.uwp.edu`

    Other: Digest available from archives.

1-1073 **PERFORM:** On Medieval performing arts.

    i `flanigan@iubvm.bitnet` (Bitnet: `FLANIGAN@IUBVM`) (Clifford Flanigan)

    ± `listserv@iubvm.ucs.indiana.edu` (Bitnet: `LISTSERV@IUBVM`) [body = `SUBSCRIBE PERFORM` first-name last-name]

    Archive: Available to subscribers only.

1-1074 **PERSON-L:** On personal and micro computers.

    i `mnorris@irlearn.bitnet` (Bitnet: `MNORRIS@IRLEARN`) (Mike Norris)

    ± `listserv@irlearn.bitnet` (Bitnet: `LISTSERV@IRLEARN`) [body = `SUBSCRIBE PERSON-L` first-name last-name]

    Archive: `listserv@irlearn.bitnet`

    Other: Subscription is limited. Requests will be sent to list owner for approval.

1-1075 **Peru:** Interchange of information on matters of interest to Peruvians and friends of Peru.

    i ± `owner-peru@cs.sfsu.edu` (Herbert Koller)

    Languages: Spanish, English, Quechua.

    Gated: ⇒`soc.culture.peru`

1-1076 **Peter Gabriel:** On the music and art of Peter Gabriel.

    i `listserv@listserv.acns.nwu.edu` [body = `help`]

    ± `listserv@listserv.acns.nwu.edu` [body = `subscribe gabriel`]

    Archive: FTP `ftp.acns.nwu.edu` in `/pub/gabriel`

1-1077 **PFUG-L:** Parallel FORTRAN Users' Group newsletter.

    i `jimj@jhuvm.bitnet` (Bitnet: `JIMJ@JHUVM`)

    ± `listserv@jhuvm.hcf.jhu.edu` (Bitnet: `LISTSERV@JHUVM`) [body = `SUBSCRIBE PFUG-L` first-name last-name]

    Archive: `listserv@jhuvm.hcf.jhu.edu`

    Other: Weekly digest

1-1078 **PH-BSG:** For the biological sciences group of the Philippines Science and Technology Advisory Council Electronic Network.

    i `eng-leong_foo_mircen-ki%micforum@mica.mic.ki.se` or `joe@credit.erin.utoronto.ca` (Joe Lim)

    ± `listserv@searn.sunet.se` (Bitnet: `LISTSERV@SEARN`) [body = `SUBSCRIBE PH-BSG` first-name last-name]

    Archive: `listserv@searn.sunet.se`

1-1079 **PH-PSG:** On the physical sciences group of the Philippines Science and Technology Advisory Council Electronic Network.

    i `eng-leong_foo_mircen-ki%micforum@mica.mic.ki.se` or `joe@credit.erin.utoronto.ca` (Joe Lim)

± listserv@searn.sunet.se (Bitnet: LISTSERV@SEARN) [body = SUBSCRIBE PH-PSG first-name last-name]

Archive: listserv@searn.sunet.se

1-1080 **ph7:** A list which talks about Peter Hammill and related rock groups.

i jester@qualcomm.com

± ph7-request@bnf.com [body = subscribe ph7 first-name last-name]

1-1081 **pharm:** For pharmacists and workers in related fields. A directory of e-mail users is maintained, and subscribers receive details of access to the Pharmacy section of the NISS BBS service on JANET via Telnet and IXI (see also the newsgroup sci.med.pharmacy).

i ± pharm-request@dmu.ac.uk (Paul Hodgkinson)

1-1082 **PHIKAP-L:** For members of Phi Kappa Theta, a national social fraternity.

i phikap-r@sruvm.sru.edu

± listserv@psuvm.psu.edu (Bitnet: LISTSERV@PSUVM) [body = SUBSCRIBE PHIKAP-L first-name last-name]

Other: Subscription is limited. Requests will be sent to list owner for approval.

1-1083 **PHIL-L:** Dedicated to the philosophical/technical aspects of parallel distributed processing (PDP). *Moderated*

i iberkele@vm.ucs.ualberta.ca

± listserv@vm.ucs.ualberta.ca (Bitnet: LISTSERV@UALTAVM) [body = SUBSCRIBE PHIL-L first-name last-name]

Other: Subscription is limited. Requests will be sent to list owner for approval.

1-1084 **PHILOSED:** For students and teachers discussing the philosophy of education, an unofficial service of the Philosophy of Education Society.

i tfgreen@suvm.bitnet (Bitnet: TFGREEN@SUVM) (Thomas F. Green)

± listserv@suvm.acs.syr.edu (Bitnet: LISTSERV@SUVM) [body = SUBSCRIBE PHILOSED first-name last-name]

Archive: listserv@suvm.acs.syr.edu

1-1085 **PHILOSOP:** For scholarly discussion of philosophy, and for sharing information relevant to the discipline.

i gl250011@yuorion.bitnet (Bitnet: GL250011@YUORION) (Nollaig MacKenzie)

± listserv@yorkvm1.bitnet (Bitnet: LISTSERV@YORKVM1) [body = SUBSCRIBE PHILOSOP first-name last-name]

Archive: Available to subscribers only.

1-1086 **PHOTOHST:** On the history of photography.

i iacrpm@asuacad.bitnet (Bitnet: IACRPM@ASUACAD) (Richard Pearce-Moses)

± listserv@asuvm.inre.asu.edu (Bitnet: LISTSERV@ASUACAD) [body = SUBSCRIBE PHOTOHST first-name last-name]

Archive: listserv@asuvm.inre.asu.edu

1-1087 **PHYS-STU:** For discussion of physics and related topics by physics students.

i mrichich@drunivac.bitnet (Bitnet: MRICHICH@DRUNIVAC) (Mike Richichi)

± listserv@uwf.cc.uwf.edu (Bitnet: LISTSERV@UWF) [body = SUBSCRIBE

`PHYS-STU first-name last-name]`

Archive: `listserv@uwf.cc.uwf.edu`

1-1088 **PHYSHARE:** Resources sharing on high school physics.

i `jdp115@psuvm.bitnet` (Bitnet: `JDP115@PSUVM`) (Dave Popp)

± `listserv@psuvm.psu.edu` (Bitnet: `LISTSERV@PSUVM`) [body = SUBSCRIBE PHYSHARE first-name last-name]

Archive: `listserv@psuvm.psu.edu`

1-1089 **PHYSIC-L:** On physics in Israel. *Moderated*

i `jo@ilncrd.bitnet` (Bitnet: `JO@ILNCRD`) (Jo van Zwaren)

± `listserv@taunivm.tau.ac.il` (Bitnet: `LISTSERV@TAUNIVM`) [body = SUBSCRIBE PHYSIC-L first-name last-name]

1-1090 **PIADAS:** Humor distribution forum.

i `walter@rain.com` (Walter Morales)

± `listserv@pccvm.bitnet` (Bitnet: `LISTSERV@PCCVM`) [body = SUBSCRIBE PIADAS first-name last-name]

Language: Portuguese

1-1091 **pipes:** For all those who enjoy smoking, collecting, or sharing information on pipes, tobacco, and related topics. *Moderated*

i ± `pipes-request@paul.rutgers.edu` (Steve Masticola)

Archive: available on request to *i* address

Other: In digest format.

1-1092 **PIPORG-L:** For discussion of musical, technical, and historical aspects of organs of all kinds—classical, theater, electronic, reed, tracker, electropneumatic, etc. Stoplists, recitals (past and future), recordings, jobs (wanted and available), restoration hints, news of progress in restoration projects are all interesting.

i `schutt@netcom.com` (Dave Schutt)

± `listserv@uacsc2.albany.edu` (Bitnet: `LISTSERV@ALBNYVM1`) [body = SUBSCRIBE PIPORG-L first-name last-name]

Archive: Available to subscribers only.

Other: Daily digest

1-1093 **Pisma Bralcev:** "Pisma bralcev" is an edited (not moderated) mailing list which provides the possibility of publishing readers' opinions, questions, inquiries for help, answers, etc. There are also published travel tips and book reviews.

i ± `pisma-bralcev@krpan.arnes.si` or `pisma.bralcev@uni-lj.si` (Andrej Brodnik and Srecko Vidmar)

Language: Slovene

1-1094 **PJ Harvey:** For fans of PJ Harvey.

i ± `pj-request@langmuir.eecs.berkeley.edu`

1-1095 **PNWMLA-L:** For music librarians who are members of the Pacific Northwest Chapter of the Music Library Association.

i `gibbs@carson.u.washington.edu` (John Gibbs)

± `listserv@uwavm.u.washington.edu` (Bitnet: `LISTSERV@UWAVM`) [body = SUBSCRIBE PNWMLA-L first-name last-name]

Archive: `listserv@uwavm.u.washington.edu`

1-1096 **POET:** A workshop/critique forum for poetic works of all descriptions in progress.

i `poet-request@scruz.ucsc.edu`

± `majordomo@scruz.ucsc.edu` [body = subscribe poet]

1-1097 **POFP-J:** Public Opinion and Foreign Policy Journal. *Moderated*

i `chittick@uga.bitnet` (Bitnet: `CHITTICK@UGA`) (William Chittick)

± `listserv@uga.cc.uga.edu` (Bitnet: `LISTSERV@UGA`) [body = SUBSCRIBE POFP-J first-name last-name]

Archive: `listserv@uga.cc.uga.edu`

Other: Daily digest

1-1098 **POLAND-L:** Discussion of Polish culture.

i `michal@gs58.sp.cs.cmu.edu` (Michal Prussak)

± `listserv@ubvm.cc.buffalo.edu` (Bitnet: `LISTSERV@UBVM`) [body = SUBSCRIBE POLAND-L first-name last-name]

Archive: `listserv@ubvm.cc.buffalo.edu`

1-1099 **POLAR-L:** On the subject of polar issues in the broadest sense —science, humanities, arts, news, views, questions, answers—for people interested in arctic and antarctic.

i `evbkevan@uoguelph.bitnet` (Bitnet: `EVBKEVAN@UOGUELPH`) (Peter Kevan)

± `listserv@vm.uoguelph.ca` (Bitnet: `LISTSERV@UOGUELPH`) [body = SUBSCRIBE POLAR-L first-name last-name]

Archive: Available to subscribers only.

1-1100 **Police:** For fans of the music group The Police and its members Sting, Stewart Copeland, and Andy Summers.

i `police-request@cindy.ecst.csuchico.edu` [body = help] or `police-owner@cindy.ecst.csuchico.edu` (Pete Ashdown)

± `police-request@cindy.ecst.csuchico.edu` [body = subscribe]

Archive: `police-request@cindy.ecst.csuchico.edu` [body = get file-name]

1-1101 **POLITICS:** For the serious discussion of political issues.

i `anderson@ucf1vm.bitnet` (Bitnet: `ANDERSON@UCF1VM`) (Eric Anderson)

± `listserv@ucf1vm.cc.ucf.edu` (Bitnet: `LISTSERV@UCF1VM`) [body = SUBSCRIBE POLITICS first-name last-name]

Archive: `listserv@ucf1vm.cc.ucf.edu`

Other: Subscription is limited. Requests will be sent to list owner for approval.

1-1102 **POLPAL-L:** For scientists (and others) interested in pollination and palynology.

i `evbkevan@uoguelph.bitnet` (Bitnet: `EVBKEVAN@UOGUELPH`) (Peter Kevan)

± `listserv@vm.uoguelph.ca` (Bitnet: `LISTSERV@UOGUELPH`) [body = SUBSCRIBE POLPAL-L first-name last-name]

Archive: Available to subscribers only.

1-1103   **PolymerP:** On polymer physics.

    i `peter@fenk.wau.nl` (Peter Barneveld)

    ± `listserv@hearn.nic.surfnet.nl` (Bitnet: `LISTSERV@HEARN`) [body = `SUBSCRIBE POLYMERP` first-name last-name] or `listserv@rutvm1.rutgers.edu` (Bitnet: `LISTSERV@RUTVM1`) [body = `SUBSCRIBE POLYMERP` first-name last-name]

    Archive: `listserv@hearn.nic.surfnet.nl` or `listserv@rutvm1.rutgers.edu`

1-1104   **POP:** On the Post Office Protocol (POP2 and POP3—described in RFCs 918, 937, 1081, and 1082) and implimentations thereof.

    i `andy@jhunix.hcf.jhu.edu` (Andy S. Poling)

    ± `pop-request@jhunix.hcf.jhu.edu` [body = `subscribe pop`]

    Archive: FTP `jhunix.hcf.jhu.edu` in `mailing_lists/pop`; gopher `jhunix.hcf.jhu.edu` in `Academic Computing/JHUNIX Archive/mailing-lists/pop`; Mail Server send e-mail to `pop-request@jhunix.hcf.jhu.edu` [body = `index pop` for an index or `get pop` file-name to retrieve archive files]

1-1105   **por:** For academics and professionals interested in public opinion research.

    i `cassell@gibbs.oit.unc.edu` (James Cassell)

    ± `listserv@gibbs.oit.unc.edu` [body = `SUBSCRIBE por` first-name last-name]

    Archive: `listserv@gibbs.oit.unc.edu` [body = `index por`]

1-1106   **POSCIM:** Forum for those researching, teaching or studying the subject as well as the practicians of politics. Not a public list.

    i ± `ps500@ibm.rhrz.uni-bonn.de` or `markus@uni-bonn.de` (Bitnet: `UPS500@DBNRHRZ1`) (Markus Schlegel)

    Archive: `listserv@csearn.bitnet`

    Language: English, German

1-1107   **posix-ada:** On the Ada binding of the Posix standard. This is the IEEE P1003.5 working group.

    ± `posix-ada-request@verdix.com`

1-1108   **POSTCARD:** For discussing and exchanging picture postcards.

    i `alileste@idbsu.bitnet` (Bitnet: `ALILESTE@IDBSU`) (Dan Lester)

    ± `listserv@idbsu.idbsu.edu` (Bitnet: `LISTSERV@IDBSU`) [body = `SUBSCRIBE POSTCARD` first-name last-name]

    Archive: `listserv@idbsu.idbsu.edu`

1-1109   **powderworks:** On the musical group Midnight Oil.

    i `tim@boulder.colorado.edu` (Tim Hunter)

    ± `powderworks-request@boulder.colorado.edu`

    Archive: FTP `refuge.colorado.edu` in `/pub/powderworks`

1-1110   **POWER-L:** For discussing the IBM RISC System/6000 family based on the Performance Optimization with Enhanced RISC (POWER) architecture.

    i `info@ndsuvm1.bitnet` (Bitnet: `INFO@NDSUVM1`) (Marty Hoag)

± `listserv@vm1.nodak.edu` (Bitnet: `LISTSERV@NDSUVM1`) [body = `SUBSCRIBE POWER-L` first-name last-name]

Archive: `listserv@vm1.nodak.edu`

Other: Daily digest

1-1111 **POWERH-L:** For users of PowerHouse, a fourth generation application development language published by Cognos.

i `bourgeg@umoncton.ca` (Georges M. Bourgeois)

± `listserv@unb.ca` (Bitnet: `LISTSERV@UNBVM1`) [body = `SUBSCRIBE POWERH-L` first-name last-name]

Archive: Available to subscribers only.

1-1112 **PPP:** Discussion between users of Morning Star PPP, and announcements from Morning Star Technologies about new versions, features, etc.

i ± `ppp-users-request@morningstar.com`

Archive: `ftp.morningstar.com` in `pub/ppp/ppp-users-mail-archive`

1-1113 **PRENAT-L:** For data and information on perinatal outcomes, primarily for New York State.

i `cmb04@albnydh2.bitnet` (Bitnet: `CMB04@ALBNYDH2`) (Colene Byrne) or `msz03@albnydh2.bitnet` (Bitnet: `MSZ03@ALBNYDH2`) (Michael Zdeb)

± `listserv@albnydh2.bitnet` (Bitnet: `LISTSERV@ALBNYDH2`) [body = `SUBSCRIBE PRENAT-L` first-name last-name]

Archive: Available to subscribers only.

1-1114 **Prince:** On the musician Prince and related artists.

i ± `prince-request@icpsr.umich.edu`

1-1115 **PRO-CITE:** About personal bibliographic software.

i `daym@ucs.indiana.edu` (Mark T. Day)

± `listserv@iubvm.ucs.indiana.edu` (Bitnet: `LISTSERV@IUBVM`) [body = `SUBSCRIBE PRO-CITE` first-name last-name]

Archive: Available to subscribers only.

1-1116 **Prog-Pubs:** For people interested in progressive and/or alternative publications and other media.

i ± `prog-pubs-request@fuggles.acc.virginia.edu`

1-1117 **Progress:** Discussion of the Progress RDBMS.

i ± `progress-list-request@math.niu.edu`

Archives FTP `ftp.math.niu.edu` in `/pub/progress`

1-1118 **proof:** On the left-associative natural language parser "proof."

± `proof-request@xcf.berkeley.edu` [subject = `ADD ME`]

Archive: FTP `XCF.Berkeley.EDU` in `src/local/proof`

1-1119 **PROP-L:** For users of programmable operators, a utility that comes with VM that can automate much of the console operator's duties.

i `c133ges@utarlvm1.bitnet` (Bitnet: `C133GES@UTARLVM1`) (Gary Samek)

± `listserv@utarlvm1.uta.edu` (Bitnet: `LISTSERV@UTARLVM1`) [body = `SUBSCRIBE PROP-L` first-name last-name]

Archive: `listserv@utarlvm1.uta.edu`

1-1120 **PROSODY:** About prosody, the rhythm, intonation, and phrasing of spoken language.

i `alleng@msu.bitnet` (Bitnet: `ALLENG@MSU`) (George D. Allen)

± `listserv@msu.edu` (Bitnet: `LISTSERV@MSU`) [body = SUBSCRIBE PROSODY first-name last-name]

Archive: `listserv@msu.edu`

1-1121 **PROSTAFF:** For discussion of matters of common concern to professional staff at universities, particularly employment issues.

i `roseth@u.washington.edu`

± `listserv@uwavm.u.washington.edu` (Bitnet: `LISTSERV@UWAVM`) [body = SUBSCRIBE PROSTAFF first-name last-name]

Archive: Available to subscribers only.

1-1122 **PROTOCOL:** Discussion on computer protocol.

i `david@campfire.stl.mo.us`

± `listserv@vmd.cso.uiuc.edu` (Bitnet: `LISTSERV@UIUCVMD`) [body = SUBSCRIBE PROTOCOL first-name last-name]

Archive: `listserv@vmd.cso.uiuc.edu`

1-1123 **PSATC-L:** For use by attendees at the Annual National Conference on Problem Solving Across The Curriculum.

i `gerland@ubvms.cc.buffalo.edu` (Jim Gerland)

± `listserv@ubvm.cc.buffalo.edu` (Bitnet: `LISTSERV@UBVM`) [body = SUBSCRIBE PSATC-L first-name last-name]

Archive: `listserv@ubvm.cc.buffalo.edu`

1-1124 **PSI-L:** Discussion on the nature of parapsychology, not its existence. Topics include ESP, out-of-body experiences, dream experiences, altered states of consciousness, etc.

i `lnaqc@cunyvm.cuny.edu` (Lusi N. Altman)

± `listserv@vm.its.rpi.edu` (Bitnet: `LISTSERV@RPITSVM`) [body = SUBSCRIBE PSI-L first-name last-name]

Archive: `listserv@vm.its.rpi.edu`

1-1125 **PSTAT-L:** On data management and statistics using P-STAT.

i `cbts8001@iruccvax.bitnet` (Bitnet: `CBTS8001@IRUCCVAX`) (Peter Flynn)

± `listserv@irlearn.bitnet` (Bitnet: `LISTSERV@IRLEARN`) [body = SUBSCRIBE PSTAT-L first-name last-name]

Archive: Available to subscribers only.

1-1126 **PSUTOOLS:** For discussion of VM related tools available from Penn State.

i `lrl@psuvm.bitnet` (Bitnet: `LRL@PSUVM`)

± `listserv@psuvm.psu.edu` (Bitnet: `LISTSERV@PSUVM`) [body = SUBSCRIBE PSUTOOLS first-name last-name]

1-1127 **PSYART:** On the psychological study of the arts, especially literature. *Moderated*

i `nnh@nervm.bitnet` (Bitnet: `NNH@NERVM`)

± `listserv@nervm.nerdc.ufl.edu` (Bitnet: `LISTSERV@NERVM`) [body = SUBSCRIBE PSYART first-name last-name]

1-1128 **PSYC: PSYCOLOQUY**—Refereed Electronic Journal of Peer Discussion on psychology, cognitive science, neuroscience and behavioral science, linguistics and philosophy. *Moderated*

    i harnad@psycho.princeton.edu (Stevan Harnad)

    ± listserv@pucc.princeton.edu (Bitnet: LISTSERV@PUCC) [body = SUBSCRIBE PSYC first-name last-name]

    Archive: listserv@pucc.princeton.edu

    Gated: ⇔ sci.psychology.digest

1-1129 **PSYCGRAD:** Psychology graduate students discussion group list.

    i 054340@acadvm1.uottawa.ca (Matthew Simpson)

    ± listserv@acadvm1.uottawa.ca (Bitnet: LISTSERV@UOTTAWA) [body = SUBSCRIBE PSYCGRAD first-name last-name]

    Archive: listserv@acadvm1.uottawa.ca

    Other: Daily digest

1-1130 **PSYCHE-D:** Discussions on the electronic journal PSYCHE.

    i x91007@pitvax.xx.rmit.edu.au (Patrick Wilken)

    ± listserv@nki.bitnet (Bitnet: LISTSERV@NKI) [body = SUBSCRIBE PSYCHE-D first-name last-name]

    Archive: listserv@nki.bitnet

1-1131 **PSYCHE-L:** An interdisciplinary journal of research on consciousness.

    i x91007@pitvax.xx.rmit.edu.au (Patrick Wilken)

    ± listserv@nki.bitnet (Bitnet: LISTSERV@NKI) [body = SUBSCRIBE PSYCHE-L first-name last-name]

    Archive: listserv@nki.bitnet

1-1132 **PSYGRD-J:** The Psychology Graduate-Student Journal—The PSYCGRAD Journal. *Moderated*

    i 054340@acadvm1.uottawa.ca (Matthew Simpson)

    ± listserv@acadvm1.uottawa.ca (Bitnet: LISTSERV@UOTTAWA) [body = SUBSCRIBE PSYGRD-J first-name last-name]

    Archive: Available to subscribers only.

1-1133 **PSYSTS-L:** For discussion of statistical techniques used in psychology, with particular emphasis on structural equation modeling, factor analysis, and configural frequency analysis, and for new users of statistics in psychology to field their questions.

    i psywood@mizzou1.bitnet (Bitnet: PSYWOOD@MIZZOU1) (Phil Wood)

    ± listserv@mizzou1.missouri.edu (Bitnet: LISTSERV@MIZZOU1) [body = SUBSCRIBE PSYSTS-L first-name last-name]

1-1134 **Publish:** On the "high-end" use of computer workstations, in book, magazine, newspaper, and other publishing.

    i ± publish-request@chron.com

1-1135 **pubnet:** On the administration and use of public access computer systems—primarily Unix systems. Do NOT send mail here to find out how to get access to the Internet.

    i ± pubnet-request@chinacat.unicom.com (Chip Rosenthal)

1-1136 **PUBPOL-L:** For graduate students, faculty, and professionals of public policy. *Moderated*

i clif0005@student.tc.umn.edu (Steven L. Clift)

± listserv@vm1.spcs.umn.edu (Bitnet: LISTSERV@UMINN1) [body = SUBSCRIBE PUBPOL-L first-name last-name]

Archive: listserv@vm1.spcs.umn.edu

1-1137 **PUBS-L:** For the staff of publications offices at educational and non-profit institutions.

i kelly@utkvx.bitnet (Bitnet: KELLY@UTKVX) (Jim Kelly)

± listserv@utkvm1.utk.edu (Bitnet: LISTSERV@UTKVM1) [body = SUBSCRIBE PUBS-L first-name last-name]

Archive: listserv@utkvm1.utk.edu

1-1138 **PURTOPOI:** On rhetoric, language, and professional writing.

i nvo@mace.cc.purdue.edu (Pat Sullivan)

± listserv@vm.cc.purdue.edu (Bitnet: LISTSERV@PURCCVM) [body = SUBSCRIBE PURTOPOI first-name last-name]

Archive: listserv@vm.cc.purdue.edu

Other: Subscription is limited. Requests will be sent to list owner for approval.

1-1139 **PVM-L:** On PVM, an IBM communications/networking package that runs under the various VM operating systems.

i jimj@jhuvm.bitnet (Bitnet: JIMJ@JHUVM)

± listserv@jhuvm.hcf.jhu.edu (Bitnet: LISTSERV@JHUVM) [body = SUBSCRIBE PVM-L first-name last-name]

Archive: listserv@jhuvm.hcf.jhu.edu

Other: Weekly digest

1-1140 **Python:** On Python, an object-oriented, interpreted, extensible programming language.

i python-list-request@cwi.nl (Guido van Rossum)

± python-list-request@cwi.nl [body = e-mail-address]

Archive: FTP ftp.cwi.nl in /pub/python

1-1141 **Q-METHOD:** On Q methodology, a general approach to the scientific study of subjectivity.

i sbrown@kentvm.bitnet (Bitnet: SBROWN@KENTVM) (Steven R. Brown)

± listserv@kentvm.kent.edu (Bitnet: LISTSERV@KENTVM) [body = SUBSCRIBE Q-METHOD first-name last-name]

Archive: Available to subscribers only.

Other: Subscription is limited. Requests will be sent to list owner for approval.

1-1142 **qn:** For members and those interested in Queer Nation, an activist group devoted to furthering gay rights.

i qn-request@queernet.org

± majordomo@queernet.org [body = subscribe qn]

1-1143 **QNTEVA-L:** On the theory and design of quantitative methods to evaluate social, educational, psychological, and other forms of programs and policies.

i m5m@psuvm.bitnet (Bitnet: M5M@PSUVM)

± listserv@psuvm.psu.edu (Bitnet: LISTSERV@PSUVM) [body = SUBSCRIBE

QNTEVA-L first-name last-name]

Archive: `listserv@psuvm.psu.edu`

1-1144 **qnx2:** On all aspects of versions 2.15/2.20 of the QNX realtime operating system.

　i `qnx2-request@dlogtech.cuc.ab.ca`[subject = `username@domain`, body = `help`]

　± `qnx2-request@dlogtech.cuc.ab.ca` [subject = `path username@domain`, body = `subscribe username@domain`]

1-1145 **qnx4:** On all aspects of the 4.x POSIX version of the QNX realtime operating system.

　i `qnx4-request@dlogtech.cuc.ab.ca`[subject = `username@domain`, body = `help`]

　± `qnx4-request@dlogtech.cuc.ab.ca` [subject = `path username@domain`, body = `subscribe username@domain`]

1-1146 **Quadraverb:** Discussion of the Alesis Quadraverb family of effects boxes.

　i ± `qv-interest-request@swap.eng.sun.com` (Bob Page)

1-1147 **QUAKE-L:** On earthquakes.

　i `info@ndsuvm1.bitnet` (Bitnet: `INFO@NDSUVM1`) (Marty Hoag)

　± `listserv@vm1.nodak.edu` (Bitnet: `LISTSERV@NDSUVM1`) [body = `SUBSCRIBE QUAKE-L` first-name last-name]

　Archive: `listserv@vm1.nodak.edu`

　Gated: ⇔ `bit.listserv.QUAKE-L`

　Other: Daily digest

1-1148 **QUAKER-L:** On Quaker concerns for community, consensus process, spirituality, more.

　i `ap430001@brownvm.bitnet` (Bitnet: `AP430001@BROWNVM`) (Richard Ristow) or `bdienes@psych.uiuc.edu` (Bruce Dienes) or `thompson@pobox.upenn.edu` (Stephen W. Thompson)

　± `listserv@vmd.cso.uiuc.edu` (Bitnet: `LISTSERV@UIUCVMD`) [body = `SUBSCRIBE QUAKER-L` first-name last-name]

　Archive: `listserv@vmd.cso.uiuc.edu`

　Other: Weekly digest

1-1149 **QUAKER-P:** On Quaker concerns related to peace and social justice issues.

　i `ap430001@brownvm.bitnet` (Bitnet: `AP430001@BROWNVM`) (Richard Ristow) or `bdienes@psych.uiuc.edu` (Bruce Dienes) or `thompson@pobox.upenn.edu` (Stephen W. Thompson)

　± `listserv@vmd.cso.uiuc.edu` (Bitnet: `LISTSERV@UIUCVMD`) [body = `SUBSCRIBE QUAKER-P` first-name last-name]

　Archive: `listserv@vmd.cso.uiuc.edu`

1-1150 **QUALRS-L:** On qualitative research for the human sciences, any method of studying human beings that depends on accounts and interpretations of what is seen, heard, tasted, touched, smelled, and experienced, including field research, case study research, ethnography, document and content analysis, interview and observational research, community study, and life history and biographical studies.

i jude@uga.bitnet (Bitnet: JUDE@UGA) (Judith Preissle)

± listserv@uga.cc.uga.edu (Bitnet: LISTSERV@UGA) [body = SUBSCRIBE QUALRS-L first-name last-name]

Archive: listserv@uga.cc.uga.edu

Gated: ⇔ bit.listserv.qualrs-l

1-1151 **Quanta:** Science fiction magazine, typically published bi-monthly, containing mostly short fiction with articles and editorials by authors around the world and across the net.

i quanta@andrew.cmu.edu

± quanta+requests-ascii@andrew.cmu.edu or quanta+requests-postscript@andrew.cmu.edu

Archive: FTP export.acs.cmu.edu and ftp.eff.org

Other: Available in ASCII and PostScript.

1-1152 **QUARKXPR:** On desktop publishing using QuarkXpress on the Macintosh.

i stonec@iubacs.bitnet (Bitnet: STONEC@IUBACS) (Cindy Stone)

± listserv@iubvm.ucs.indiana.edu (Bitnet: LISTSERV@IUBVM) [body = SUBSCRIBE QUARKXPR first-name last-name]

Archive: listserv@iubvm.ucs.indiana.edu

1-1153 **Queen-Digest:** All about the rock group Queen.

i barfmaster@uiuc.edu (Dan Blanchard)

± barfmaster@uiuc.edu [subject = subscribe queen digest]

Other: Weekly digest

1-1154 **QUEENS-L:** On the QK-MHS/VM X.400 Message Handling System.

i juan@dearn.bitnet (Bitnet: JUAN@DEARN) (Juan Pizzorno) or mabogen@dearn.bitnet (Bitnet: MABOGEN@DEARN) (Manfred Bogen)

± listserv@vm.gmd.de (Bitnet: LISTSERV@DEARN) [body = SUBSCRIBE QUEENS-L first-name last-name]

Archive: listserv@vm.gmd.de

Other: Subscription is limited. Requests will be sent to list owner for approval.

1-1155 **racefab:** To discuss racing fabrication and engineering. Suitable topics include suspension geometry and configurations, anti-drive, anti-squat, control arm placement, shock and strut valving, spindle design, floating rear ends, pan-hard bars and watts linkages, cage construction, chassis reinforcement, bearing specs, sources for information and materials, etc.

± racefab-request@pms706.pms.ford.com [body = Type of racing you're involved in (autox, circle track, road race) and the type of race cars/bikes you work/race]

1-1156 **RADCH-L:** For chemists studying radiochemistry, nuclear chemistry, nuclear analytical techniques.

i abbe@frcpn11.bitnet (Bitnet: ABBE@FRCPN11)

± listserv@frcpn11.in2p3.fr (Bitnet: LISTSERV@FRCPN11) [body = SUBSCRIBE RADCH-L first-name last-name]

1-1157 **RATION-L:** For academic discussions of theories of rational behavior.

  i zamir@shum.cc.huji.ac.il (Prof. Shmuel Zamir)

  ± listserv@taunivm.tau.ac.il (Bitnet: LISTSERV@TAUNIVM) [body = SUBSCRIBE RATION-L first-name last-name]

1-1158 **Ravenloft:** Discussion of Gothic Horror with respect to the Ravenloft Accessory to Advanced Dungeons & Dragons.

  i roshne@faerun.mi.org (Rod Shelton) or alvalent@husc.harvard.edu (Lee Valentine) or jgostin@eternal.chi.il.us (Jeff Gostin)

  ± raven+request@drycas.club.cc.cmu.edu

  Archive: Mailserv mail-server@faerun.mi.org [body = get /public/readme RET dir RET help RET quit RET]

1-1159 **RCUG:** On real Coke (the one true soda).

  i t_wade@ccvax.bitnet (Bitnet: T_WADE@CCVAX) (Tom Wade)

  ± listserv@irlearn.bitnet (Bitnet: LISTSERV@IRLEARN) [body = SUBSCRIBE RCUG first-name last-name]

  Archive: Available to subscribers only.

1-1160 **really-deep-thoughts:** Tori Amos.

  ± really-deep-thoughts-request@gradient.cis.upenn.edu

  Archive: FTP ftp.uwp.edu in /pub/music/lists/rdt (list and discography)

  Other: 24-hour digest format available. State which format you want.

1-1161 **RECMGMT:** For records and archival management professionals.

  i mph@hbll1.byu.edu (Maralyn Harmston)

  ± listserv@suvm.acs.syr.edu (Bitnet: LISTSERV@SUVM) [body = SUBSCRIBE RECMGMT first-name last-name]

1-1162 **recovery:** Support group for survivors of childhood sexual abuse/incest and/or their significant others (SO's) and professionals who treat survivors of childhood abuse.

  i ± recovery@wvnvm.wvnet.edu (Jeff Brooks)

  Other: In digest format. Contributors may post anonymously.

1-1163 **RED-NET:** On research in education and didactics.

  i conrad@cidoc.iuav.unive.it (Corrado Petrucco)

  ± listserv@icineca.cineca.it (Bitnet: LISTSERV@ICINECA) [body = SUBSCRIBE RED-NET first-name last-name]

  Archive: Available to subscribers only.

1-1164 **REDALC:** On spreading computer mediated communication (networks) in the Latin American and Carribean regions.

  i ulat-rd@frmop11.bitnet (Bitnet: ULAT-RD@FRMOP11) (Christian Matias)

  ± listserv@frmop11.cnusc.fr (Bitnet: LISTSERV@FRMOP11) [body = SUBSCRIBE REDALC first-name last-name]

  Archive: listserv@frmop11.cnusc.fr

  Language: Spanish, French, English, Portuguese

1-1165 **REDEMG-L:** On the "Minas" network, a regional internet that covers education, research, and development instituitions in the state of Minas Gerais in Brazil.

i jmarcos@dcc.ufmg.br (José Marcos Silva Nogueira)

± listserv@vm1.lcc.ufmg.br (Bitnet: LISTSERV@BRUFMG) [body = SUBSCRIBE REDEMG-L first-name last-name]

Archive: Available to subscribers only.

Language: Portuguese, English

Other: Subscription is limited. Requests will be sent to list owner for approval.

1-1166 **REED-L:** For discussion of early English drama.

i reed@epas.utoronto.ca (Dr. Abigail Young)

± listserv@utoronto.bitnet (Bitnet: LISTSERV@UTORONTO) [body = SUBSCRIBE REED-L first-name last-name]

Archive: listserv@utoronto.bitnet

Other: Subscription is limited. Requests will be sent to list owner for approval.

1-1167 **REGIST-L:** For sharing of information, experiences, concerns, and advice about issues affecting records and registration professionals at colleges and universities.

i regjeg@gsuvm1.bitnet (Bitnet: REGJEG@GSUVM1) (Jim Greene) or aucoin@evansville.edu (Paul Aucoin) or sreg1004@altair.selu.edu (Janet Busekist)

± listserv@gsuvm1.gsu.edu (Bitnet: LISTSERV@GSUVM1) [body = SUBSCRIBE REGIST-L first-name last-name]

Archive: listserv@gsuvm1.gsu.edu

1-1168 **RELIGCOM:** On religious communication and communication in religious contexts.

i tukey@nkuvax.bitnet (Bitnet: TUKEY@NKUVAX) (David D. Tukey)

± listserv@ukcc.uky.edu (Bitnet: LISTSERV@UKCC) [body = SUBSCRIBE RELIGCOM first-name last-name]

Archive: listserv@ukcc.uky.edu

1-1169 **RELUSR-L:** Relay Users Forum.

i rebat@vtvm1.bitnet (Bitnet: REBAT@VTVM1) (Reba Taylor) or valdis@vtvm1.bitnet (Bitnet: VALDIS@VTVM1) (Valdis Kletnieks)

± listserv@vtvm1.cc.vt.edu (Bitnet: LISTSERV@VTVM1) [body = SUBSCRIBE RELUSR-L first-name last-name]

Gated: ⇔ bit.listserv.relusr-l

1-1170 **RENAIS-L:** On Early Modern History —Renaissance.

i jacock01@ulkyvm.bitnet (Bitnet: JACOCK01@ULKYVM) (Jim Cocks)

± listserv@ulkyvm.louisville.edu (Bitnet: LISTSERV@ULKYVM) [body = SUBSCRIBE RENAIS-L first-name last-name]

Archive: listserv@ulkyvm.louisville.edu

Other: Daily digest

1-1171 **rend386-announce:** Announcements of new versions of the rend386 software, new utilities, new PLG files, and worlds, etc.

i rend386-request@sunee.uwaterloo.ca

± `majordomo@sunee.uwaterloo.ca` [body = subscribe rend386-announce]

1-1172 **rend386-discuss:** Discussion by and for users of the REND386 software package (fast polygon-based graphics on 386 and 486 systems).

i `rend386-request@sunee.uwaterloo.ca`

± `majordomo@sunee.uwaterloo.ca` [body = subscribe rend386-discuss]

1-1173 **REPUB-L:** On Republican Party politics.

i `urmm@marist.bitnet` (Bitnet: URMM@MARIST) (Martha McConaghy) or Quiet: `harry@marist.bitnet` (Bitnet: HARRY@MARIST) (A. Harry Williams)

± `listserv@vm.marist.edu` (Bitnet: LISTSERV@MARIST) [body = SUBSCRIBE REPUB-L first-name last-name]

Archive: `listserv@vm.marist.edu`

1-1174 **REPUBLIC:** On the Republican Party, its ideologies, and candidates—maintained as a way of quickly spreading the news of the party discussing the party.

i `ph279hr@prism.gatech.edu` (Hank Roark)

± `listserv@gitvm1.gatech.edu` (Bitnet: LISTSERV@GITVM1) [body = SUBSCRIBE REPUBLIC first-name last-name]

Archive: `listserv@gitvm1.gatech.edu`

1-1175 **REXSYM-L:** On the REXX procedural and macro programming language designed by Michael Cowlishaw.

i `bebo@slacvm.bitnet` (Bitnet: BEBO@SLACVM) (Bebo White)

± `listserv@slacvm.slac.stanford.edu` (Bitnet: LISTSERV@SLACVM) [body = SUBSCRIBE REXSYM-L first-name last-name]

1-1176 **RFERL-L:** The RFE/RL Daily Report is a digest of the latest developments in the former Soviet Union and Eastern Europe. *Moderated*

i `reedb@rferl.org` (Brian Reed)

± `listserv@ubvm.cc.buffalo.edu` (Bitnet: LISTSERV@UBVM) [body = SUBSCRIBE RFERL-L first-name last-name]

Archive: `listserv@ubvm.cc.buffalo.edu`

Other: Daily digest

1-1177 **RHA-L:** On issues for residence hall student government and their advisors.

i `n018gh@tamvm1.bitnet` (Bitnet: N018GH@TAMVM1) (Michael D. Osterbuhr)

± `listserv@tamvm1.tamu.edu` (Bitnet: LISTSERV@TAMVM1) [body = SUBSCRIBE RHA-L first-name last-name]

Archive: `listserv@tamvm1.tamu.edu`

1-1178 **RIGHTS-L:** For persons interested in the ongoing effort to create a bill of rights and responsibilities for elctronic citizens.

i `frank@american.edu` (Frank Connolly)

± `listserv@american.edu` (Bitnet: LISTSERV@AUVM) [body = SUBSCRIBE RIGHTS-L first-name last-name]

Archive: `listserv@american.edu`

1-1179 **RISK:** Risk and insurance issues.

> *i* fixv626@utxvm.bitnet (Bitnet: FIXV626@UTXVM) or
> garven@utxvm.cc.utexas.edu

> ± majordomo@bongo.cc.utexas.edu [body = SUBSCRIBE RISK first-name last-name]

> **Archive:** Majordomo majordomo@bongo.cc.utexas.edu

1-1180 **RISKS:** Risks List

> *i* neumann@kl.sri.com (Peter G. Neumann)

> ± listserv@uga.cc.uga.edu (Bitnet: LISTSERV@UGA) [body = SUBSCRIBE RISKS first-name last-name] or listserv@ubvm.cc.buffalo.edu (Bitnet: LISTSERV@UBVM) [body = SUBSCRIBE RISKS first-name last-name] or listserv@vm.marist.edu (Bitnet: LISTSERV@MARIST) [body = SUBSCRIBE RISKS first-name last-name]

> **Archive:** listserv@uga.cc.uga.edu or listserv@vm.marist.edu

> **Gated:** ⇔ bit.listserv.risks

1-1181 **RLIN-L:** On the RLIN database.

> *i* bl.tss@rlg.bitnet (Bitnet: TSS@RLG) (John Eilts)

> ± listserv@rutvm1.rutgers.edu (Bitnet: LISTSERV@RUTVM1) [body = SUBSCRIBE RLIN-L first-name last-name]

> **Archive:** listserv@rutvm1.rutgers.edu

1-1182 **RMUSIC-L:** On music—designed to help expand and discuss different tastes in music. Owner wants a list where people can feel comfortable discussing their likes and dislikes, without being flamed.

> *i* pharris@umkcvax1.bitnet (Bitnet: PHARRIS@UMKCVAX1)

> ± listserv@gitvm1.gatech.edu (Bitnet: LISTSERV@GITVM1) [body = SUBSCRIBE RMUSIC-L first-name last-name]

> **Archive:** listserv@gitvm1.gatech.edu

1-1183 **Robin-Lane:** On the music of Robin Lane.

> *i* ± robin-lane-request@cs.wpi.edu

1-1184 **rockhounds:** For gem and mineral collectors.

> *i* ± rockhounds-request@infodyn.com (Tom Corson)

1-1185 **RokPress:** News from Slovenia, Croatia, Serbia, Bosnia and Macedonia. *Moderated*

> ± From Europe: rokpress-list-request@uni-lj.si [body = SUBSCRIBE], from other locations and for more info e-mail to ibenko@maveric0.uwaterloo.ca (Igor Benko) or rokpress@krpan.arnes.si or rokpress@uni-lj.si

> **Language:** Slovene (principal), English, Croatian, Serbian

1-1186 **romanians:** Discussions, news, and information in the Romanian language.

> *i* ± mihai@sep.stanford.edu (Mihai Popovici)

1-1187 **ROOTS-L:** On geneological matters.

> *i* cmanis@csoftec.csf.com (Cliff Manis)

± `listserv@vm1.nodak.edu` (Bitnet: LISTSERV@NDSUVM1) [body = SUBSCRIBE ROOTS-L first-name last-name]

Archive: `listserv@vm1.nodak.edu`

1-1188 **RRA-L:** Romance Readers Anonymous. *Moderated*

i `jlangend@kentvm.bitnet` (Bitnet: JLANGEND@KENTVM) (Jeanne Langendorfer)

or `lhaas@kentvm.bitnet` (Bitnet: LHAAS@KENTVM) (Leslie M. Haas) or `krobinso@kentvm.bitnet` (Bitnet: KROBINSO@KENTVM) (Kara Robinson)

± `listserv@kentvm.kent.edu` (Bitnet: LISTSERV@KENTVM) [body = SUBSCRIBE RRA-L first-name last-name]

Archive: `listserv@kentvm.kent.edu`

Other: Daily digest

1-1189 **RS1-L:** For users of RS/1, a research and data analysis software package running on VMS, Unix, and MS-DOS, and published by Bolt, Beranek, and Newman, Inc.

i `mcmahon@ac.grin.edu` (Brian McMahon)

± `listserv@vm1.nodak.edu` (Bitnet: LISTSERV@NDSUVM1) [body = SUBSCRIBE RS1-L first-name last-name]

Archive: `listserv@vm1.nodak.edu`

1-1190 **RSCS-L:** All about RSCS.

i `gettes@pucc.princeton.edu` (Michael Gettes)

± `listserv@pucc.princeton.edu` (Bitnet: LISTSERV@PUCC) [body = SUBSCRIBE RSCS-L first-name last-name]

Archive: `listserv@pucc.princeton.edu`

Gated: ⇔ `bit.listserv.rscs-l`

1-1191 **RuneQuest Daily:** Discussion of themes related to the RuneQuest role-playing game and the game world and mythology of Glorantha. Glorantha is the creation of Greg Stafford. RuneQuest is a trademark of Avalon Hill.

i ± `runequest-request@glorantha.holland.sun.com` (Henk Langeveld)

Archvie: FTP `soda.berkeley.edu`

Other: Daily digest format (20k parts)

1-1192 **RuneQuest Digest:** Excerpts from the RuneQuest Daily, plus additional materials submitted separately. Same subject matter.

i ± `runequest-request@glorantha.holland.sun.com` (Henk Langeveld)

Archvie: FTP `soda.berkeley.edu`

Other: Digest format (irregular)

1-1193 **RURALAM:** On development issues for rural America.

i `22331mom@msu.bitnet` (Bitnet: 22331MOM@MSU) (Shawn T. Lock)

± `listserv@msu.edu` (Bitnet: LISTSERV@MSU) [body = SUBSCRIBE RURALAM first-name last-name]

Archive: `listserv@msu.edu`

Other: Subscription is limited. Requests will be sent to list owner for approval.

1-1194 **RURALDEV:** On community and rural economic development.

    i `rcyoung@ksuvm.bitnet` (Bitnet: RCYOUNG@KSUVM)

    ± `listserv@ksuvm.ksu.edu` (Bitnet: LISTSERV@KSUVM) [body = SUBSCRIBE RURALDEV first-name last-name]

    Archive: `listserv@ksuvm.ksu.edu`

1-1195 **rush:** For fans of the Canadian rock group Rush.

    i `rush-mgr@syrinx.umd.edu`

    ± `rush-request@syrinx.umd.edu`

    Archive: FTP `syrinx.umd.edu`; gopher `syrinx.umd.edu 2112`

    Other: In digest format (~5 times a week)

1-1196 **RUSHIST:** For scholarly dicussion on Russian history from the beginning of the reign of Ivan III (1462-1505) to the end of the Romanov dynasty in 1917. Topics include Russian culture, politics, wars, industrial development, ruling styles, relationships of the tsars to the populace, law and codification of law, the various tsars and pretenders and more.

    i `cdell@umkcvax1.bitnet` (Bitnet: CDELL@UMKCVAX1) (Valentine M. Smith)

    ± `listserv@vm.usc.edu` (Bitnet: LISTSERV@USCVM) [body = SUBSCRIBE RUSHIST first-name last-name] or `listserv@csearn.bitnet` (Bitnet: LISTSERV@CSEARN) [body = SUBSCRIBE RUSHIST first-name last-name] or `listserv@umrvmb.umr.edu` (Bitnet: LISTSERV@UMRVMB) [body = SUBSCRIBE RUSHIST first-name last-name] or `listserv@dosuni1.rz.uni-osnabrueck.de` (Bitnet: LISTSERV@DOSUNI1) [body = SUBSCRIBE RUSHIST first-name last-name]

    Archive: `listserv@dosuni1.rz.uni-osnabrueck.de,` `listserv@csearn.bitnet, listserv@umrvmb.umr.edu`

1-1197 **rust:** On the rock musician Neil Young.

    i `zen@sun.com` (Dan Farmer)

    ± `rust-request@death.corp.sun.com`

1-1198 **RUSTEX-L:** About Russian TeX and Cyrillic text processing.

    i `dlv@dm.com` (Dimitri Vulis)

    ± `listserv@ubvm.cc.buffalo.edu` (Bitnet: LISTSERV@UBVM) [body = SUBSCRIBE RUSTEX-L first-name last-name]

    Archive: `listserv@ubvm.cc.buffalo.edu`

    Gated: ⇔ `bit.listserv.rustex-l`

1-1199 **RXIRC-L:** About the Internet Relay Chat client for VM/CMS.

    i `carl.von.loesch@arbi.informatik.uni-oldenburg.de` (Carl von Loesch)

    ± `listserv@vmtecqro.qro.itesm.mx` (Bitnet: LISTSERV@VMTECQRO) [body = SUBSCRIBE RXIRC-L first-name last-name]

    Archive: `listserv@vmtecqro.qro.itesm.mx`

    Gated: ⇔ `bit.listserv.rxirc-l`

    Other: Weekly digest

1-1200 **S-news:** Information and discussion about the S language for data analysis and graphics.
i ± s-news-request@utstat.toronto.edu (Tom Glinos)

1-1201 **SAFETY:** On environmental health and safety at university and college campuses, including life safety issues (fire protection and other general safety issues), chemical safety issues (waste disposal, laboratory safety, regulatory compliance), biological hazards, and radiation safety.
i rstuart@moose.uvm.edu (Ralph Stuart)
± listserv@uvmvm.uvm.edu (Bitnet: LISTSERV@UVMVM) [body = SUBSCRIBE SAFETY first-name last-name]
Archive: listserv@uvmvm.uvm.edu

1-1202 **SAG-L:** For users of Software AG products, including ADABAS, a database management system; NATURAL, a 4th generation programming language; PREDICT, a data dictionary; ENTIRE, enterprise/networking products; and SUPERNATURAL, a report generator/inquiry system
i dm06900@uafsysb.bitnet (Bitnet: DM06900@UAFSYSB) (David L. Merrifield)
± listserv@uafsysb.uark.edu (Bitnet: LISTSERV@UAFSYSB) [body = SUBSCRIBE SAG-L first-name last-name]
Archive: listserv@uafsysb.uark.edu

1-1203 **SAIS-L:** On promoting science to students.
i sais@jupiter.sun.csd.unb.ca (Keith W. Wilson)
± listserv@unb.ca (Bitnet: LISTSERV@UNBVM1) [body = SUBSCRIBE SAIS-L first-name last-name]
Archive: listserv@unb.ca
Other: Subscription is limited. Requests will be sent to list owner for approval.

1-1204 **SAM-L:** For members of Sigma Alpha Mu, a college fraternity.
i v1845g@templevm.bitnet (Bitnet: V1845G@TEMPLEVM) (David Crawford)
± listserv@vm.temple.edu (Bitnet: LISTSERV@TEMPLEVM) [body = SUBSCRIBE SAM-L first-name last-name]

1-1205 **SAMATH:** For the Saudi Association for Mathematical Sciences.
i f40m001@saksu00.bitnet (Bitnet: F40M001@SAKSU00) (Dr. Omar Hamed)
± listserv@saksu00.bitnet (Bitnet: LISTSERV@SAKSU00) [body = SUBSCRIBE SAMATH first-name last-name]

1-1206 **San Fran Concert Lists:** Lists of upcoming funk/punk/thrash/ska shows in the S.F. Bay Area.
i ± the-list-request@violet.berkeley.edu (Steve Koepke)

1-1207 **San Francisco Giants:** Discussion and information exchange on the San Francisco Giants baseball team.
i ± giants-request@medraut.apple.com (Chuq Von Rospach)

1-1208 **San Jose Sharks:** Discussion and information exchange on the San José Sharks hockey team.
i ± sharks-request@medraut.apple.com (Laurie Sefton)
Archive: FTP ftp.apple.com in /pub/lsefton/sharks (list contents, GIFs, and more)

1-1209 **SAO-L:** For student affairs officers.

  i morton@uhunix.uhcc.hawaii.edu (Bitnet: MORTON@UHUNIX)

  ± listserv@uhccvm.uhcc.hawaii.edu (Bitnet: LISTSERV@UHCCVM) [body = SUBSCRIBE SAO-L first-name last-name]

  Archive: Available to subscribers only.

  Other: Subscription is limited. Requests will be sent to list owner for approval.

1-1210 **sappho:** A discussion group for gay and bisexual women. All women are invited to join, but only women may join.

  i ± sappho-request@lcs.mit.edu (Regis M. Donovan)

  Other: Available in reflector and digest format.

1-1211 **SAS-L:** On SAS, a statistical analysis package.

  i harold@uga.bitnet (Bitnet: HAROLD@UGA) (Harold Pritchett) or harry@marist.bitnet (Bitnet: HARRY@MARIST) (A. Harry Williams) or lsvmaint@uga.bitnet (Bitnet: LSVMAINT@UGA) (Listserv Postmaster)

  ± listserv@vtvm2.cc.vt.edu (Bitnet: LISTSERV@VTVM2) [body = SUBSCRIBE SAS-L first-name last-name] or listserv@sakaau03.bitnet (Bitnet: LISTSERV@SAKAAU03) [body = SUBSCRIBE SAS-L first-name last-name] or listserv@vm.akh-wien.ac.at (Bitnet: LISTSERV@AWIIMC12) [body = SUBSCRIBE SAS-L first-name last-name] or listserv@vm.marist.edu (Bitnet: LISTSERV@MARIST) [body = SUBSCRIBE SAS-L first-name last-name] or listserv@vm.tcs.tulane.edu (Bitnet: LISTSERV@TCSVM) [body = SUBSCRIBE SAS-L first-name last-name] or listserv@vtvm1.cc.vt.edu (Bitnet: LISTSERV@VTVM1) [body = SUBSCRIBE SAS-L first-name last-name] or listserv@uga.cc.uga.edu (Bitnet: LISTSERV@UGA) [body = SUBSCRIBE SAS-L first-name last-name] or listserv@vm.ucs.ualberta.ca (Bitnet: LISTSERV@UALTAVM) [body = SUBSCRIBE SAS-L first-name last-name]

  Archive: listserv@vtvm2.cc.vt.edu or listserv@vm.ucs.ualberta.ca or listserv@sakaau03.bitnet or listserv@vtvm1.cc.vt.edu or listserv@vm.marist.edu or listserv@uga.cc.uga.edu

  Gated: ⇔ bit.listserv.sas-l

1-1212 **SASH-L:** For discussion on forming policy and organizing against sexual harassment.

  i azpxs@asuacad.bitnet (Bitnet: AZPXS@ASUACAD) (Phoebe Stambaugh)

  ± listserv@asuvm.inre.asu.edu (Bitnet: LISTSERV@ASUACAD) [body = SUBSCRIBE SASH-L first-name last-name]

  Archive: Available to subscribers only.

1-1213 **SASPAC-L:** For users of the SAS software package to access census and other public data files.

  i c1921@umslvma.bitnet (Bitnet: C1921@UMSLVMA)

  ± listserv@umslvma.umsl.edu (Bitnet: LISTSERV@UMSLVMA) [body = SUBSCRIBE SASPAC-L first-name last-name]

  Archive: listserv@umslvma.umsl.edu

1-1214 **SATURN:** On jazz composer and musician Sun Ra and his Arkestra.

  i saturn-request@hearn.bitnet (Bitnet: SATURN-REQUEST@HEARN)

± `listserv@hearn.nic.surfnet.nl` (Bitnet: `LISTSERV@HEARN`) [body = SUBSCRIBE SATURN first-name last-name]

Archive: `listserv@hearn.nic.surfnet.nl`

1-1215 **SBDC-L:** For those interested in small business development—part of LGNET, a local government network in Virginia.

i `harngton@vtvm1.bitnet` (Bitnet: `HARNGTON@VTVM1`) (Marcia Harrington)

± `listserv@vtvm1.cc.vt.edu` (Bitnet: `LISTSERV@VTVM1`) [body = SUBSCRIBE SBDC-L first-name last-name]

Archive: `listserv@vtvm1.cc.vt.edu`

1-1216 **sca:** Discussions related to the Society for Creative Anachronism, a worldwide medievalist organization.

i ± `sca-request@mc.lcs.mit.edu` (Danulf Donaldson, MKA Dana Groff; Eowyn Eilonwy of Alewife Brook MKA Pandora Berman)

Gated: ⇔ `rec.org.sca`

1-1217 **sca-west:** On topics of interests to the Society of Creative Anachronism members in the West (including Northern and Central California, Northern Nevada, Alaska, Australia, and Japan).

i `sca-west-owner@ecst.csuchico.edu`

± `sca-west-request@ecst.csuchico.edu` [body = subscribe yourname]

Archive: FTP `mrfrostie.ecst.csuchico.edu` in `/sca-west`; gopher `mrfrostie.ecst.csuchico.edu` or `trln.lib.unc.edu`

1-1218 **SCAHRLDS:** Discussion among members of the Society for Creative Anachronism, an international educational group interested in recreating aspects of European Middle Ages and Renaissance, about heralds and their functions, including coats-of-arms, ceremony and diplomacy.

i `vnend@phoenix.princeton.edu`

± `listserv@pucc.princeton.edu` (Bitnet: `LISTSERV@PUCC`) [body = SUBSCRIBE SCAHRLDS first-name last-name]

Archive: Available to subscribers only.

1-1219 **SCCE-L:** On supercomputing in Central Europe.

i `andma@pltumk11.bitnet` (Bitnet: `ANDMA@PLTUMK11`) (Andrzej Marecki)

± `listserv@pltumk11.bitnet` (Bitnet: `LISTSERV@PLTUMK11`) [body = SUBSCRIBE SCCE-L first-name last-name]

Archive: `listserv@pltumk11.bitnet`

1-1220 **SCCro-Digest:** Mailing list for people without access to the USENET newsgroup soc.culture.croatia.

i ± `cro-news-request@medphys.ucl.ac.uk` (Nino Margetic)

Language: English (mostly)

Gated: ⇐ `soc.culture.croatia`

1-1221 **SCGREEK:** On the social culture of Greece. *Moderated*

i `mt@cs.wisc.edu` (Manolis Tsangaris)

± `listserv@grearn.bitnet` (Bitnet: `LISTSERV@GREARN`) [body = SUBSCRIBE

SCGREEK first-name last-name]

Language: Greek, English

Gated: ⇔ `soc.culture.greek`

1-1222 **SCHOLAR:** On natural language processing. *Moderated*

i `jqrqc@cunyvm.bitnet` (Bitnet: `JQRQC@CUNYVM`) (Joseph Raben)

± `listserv@cunyvm.cuny.edu` (Bitnet: `LISTSERV@CUNYVM`) [body = SUBSCRIBE SCHOLAR first-name last-name]

Archive: `listserv@cunyvm.cuny.edu`

1-1223 **school:** high-performance driving school mailing list.

i ± `school-request@balltown.cma.com`

1-1224 **SCHOOL-L:** On primary and post-primary schools.

i `mnorris@irlearn.bitnet` (Bitnet: `MNORRIS@IRLEARN`) (Mike Norris, UCD Computing Services) or `cbts8001@iruccvax.bitnet` (Bitnet: `CBTS8001@IRUCCVAX`) (Peter Flynn, UCC Computer Centre)

± `listserv@irlearn.bitnet` (Bitnet: `LISTSERV@IRLEARN`) [body = SUBSCRIBE SCHOOL-L first-name last-name]

1-1225 **Science Tools Group (Sci-Tools):** On the development of a group of object-oriented science oriented software tools in the NeXTStep environment.

i `sci-tools-help@embl-heidelberg.de`

± `sci-tools-request@embl-heidelberg`

1-1226 **Sciences NeXTStep User Group (SNUG):** Discussion and information on topics relating to the use of NeXTStep in the physical and bio-sciences.

± `snug-requests@whitewater.chem.wisc.edu`

Other: In digest format.

Archive: `sonata.cc.purdue.edu`

1-1227 **SCIFRAUD:** On fraud in science.

i `ach13@albnyvms.bitnet` (Bitnet: `ACH13@ALBNYVMS`) (A. C. Higgins)

± `listserv@uacsc2.albany.edu` (Bitnet: `LISTSERV@ALBNYVM1`) [body = SUBSCRIBE SCIFRAUD first-name last-name]

Archive: Available to subscribers only.

1-1228 **scoann:** SCO and SCO Developer product announcements of interest to current and future users of SCO products, and to SCO developers, resellers, and distributors. *Moderated*

i ± `scoann-request@xenitec.on.ca` (Ed Hew)

Archive: FTP `ftp.xenitec.on.ca` in `/pub/news/scoann`

Gated: ⇔ Usenet newsgroup: `biz.sco.announce`

1-1229 **scogen:** For users of all products from The Santa Cruz Operation.

i ± `scogen-request@xenitec.on.ca` (Geoff Scully)

Archive: FTP `ftp.xenitec.on.ca` in `/pub/news/scogen`

Gated: ⇔ Usenet newsgroup: `biz.sco.general`

1-1230 **scomag:** Interaction between the SCO Magazine readers, writers, and publishers.

    i `scomag-admin@xenitec.on.ca` (Ed Hew)

    ± `scomag-request@xenitec.on.ca` (Ed Hew)

    Archive: FTP `ftp.xenitec.on.ca` in `/pub/news/scomag`

    Gated: ⇔ `biz.sco.magazine`

1-1231 **scoodt:** Technical questions and answers and information on the SCO OpenDesktop operating environment and its various bundled components.

    i ± `scoodt-request@xenitec.on.ca` (Ed Hew)

    Archive: FTP `ftp.xenitec.on.ca` in `/pub/news/scoodt`

    Gated: ⇔ `biz.sco.opendesktop`

1-1232 **SCR-L:** On cognitive rehabilitation.

    i `birpjoe@mizzou1.bitnet` (Bitnet: `BIRPJOE@MIZZOU1`) (Joe Silsby)

    ± `listserv@mizzou1.missouri.edu` (Bitnet: `LISTSERV@MIZZOU1`) [body = SUBSCRIBE SCR-L first-name last-name]

    Archive: `listserv@mizzou1.missouri.edu`

1-1233 **Screaming in Digital:** For fans of the band Queensryche.

    i `queensryche-owner@pilot.njin.net` (Dan "Shag" Birchall)

    ± `queensryche-request@pilot.njin.net`

    Archive: FTP `glia.biostr.washington.edu` in `/pub/queensryche/` and `cs.uwp.edu` in `/pub/music/lists/queensryche/`

    Other: Weekly digest

1-1234 **SCRIB-L:** For academic and industrial researchers and developers in the field of computerized handwriting recognition, including communication, graphs, pen-based interfaces, and forensic applications.

    i `schomaker@hnykun53.bitnet` (Bitnet: `SCHOMAKER@HNYKUN53`) (Lambert Schomaker)

    ± `listserv@hearn.nic.surfnet.nl` (Bitnet: `LISTSERV@HEARN`) [body = SUBSCRIBE SCRIB-L first-name last-name]

    Archive: `listserv@hearn.nic.surfnet.nl`

1-1235 **SCTEAC-L:** Discussions on teaching science in Brazil.

    i `bizzo@bruspvm.bitnet` (Bitnet: `BIZZO@BRUSPVM`) (Nelio Marco Vincenzo Bizzo)

    ± `listserv@bruspvm.bitnet` (Bitnet: `LISTSERV@BRUSPVM`) [body = SUBSCRIBE SCTEAC-L first-name last-name]

    Archive: Available to subscribers only.

1-1236 **SCUBA-L:** For discussing scuba diving.

    i `cyang@brownvm.bitnet` (Bitnet: `CYANG@BROWNVM`) (Catherine Yang)

    ± `listserv@brownvm.brown.edu` (Bitnet: `LISTSERV@BROWNVM`) [body = SUBSCRIBE SCUBA-L first-name last-name]

    Archive: `listserv@brownvm.brown.edu`

1-1237 **SCYU-Digest:** For people without access to the Usenet newsgroup.

    i ± `cro-news-request@medphys.ucl.ac.uk` (Nino Margetic)

Language: English (mostly)

Gated: ⇐ `soc.culture.yugoslavia`

1-1238 **SDAnet:** Discussion about Seventh-day Adventists for members and those who are interested. *Moderated*

i ± `st0o+sda@andrew.cmu.edu` (Steve Timm) `+sda@andrew.cmu.edu`

1-1239 **SDOMINGO:** On the culture and society of the Dominican Republic.

i `fmoncion@pucmm.edu.do` (Flavio Moncion)

± `listserv@enlace.bitnet` (Bitnet: LISTSERV@ENLACE) [body = SUBSCRIBE SDOMINGO first-name last-name]

Language: Spanish

1-1240 **SEANET-L:** .For discussion by academics and others interested in the field of Southeast Asian Studies, including information on conferences, research projects, and new publications, but not current affairs.

i `hispaulk@nusvm.bitnet` (Bitnet: HISPAULK@NUSVM) (Dr. Paul H. Kratoska)

± `listserv@nusvm.nus.sg` (Bitnet: LISTSERV@NUSVM) [body = SUBSCRIBE SEANET-L first-name last-name]

Archive: `listserv@nusvm.nus.sg`

1-1241 **SEASIA-L:** About Southeast Asia, including current events.

i `3zlufur@cmuvm.bitnet` (Bitnet: 3ZLUFUR@CMUVM) (Elliott Parker)

± `listserv@msu.edu` (Bitnet: LISTSERV@MSU) [body = SUBSCRIBE SEASIA-L first-name last-name]

Archive: `listserv@msu.edu`

Other: Daily digest

1-1242 **SEBSEL:** For international networking of Black engineers and scientists.

i `geobro@delphi.com` (George Brooks)

± `listserv@arizvm1.ccit.arizona.edu` (Bitnet: LISTSERV@ARIZVM1) [body = SUBSCRIBE SEBSEL first-name last-name]

Archive: `listserv@arizvm1.ccit.arizona.edu`

1-1243 **SEDS-L:** For communications among Students for the Exploration and Development of Space (SEDS)—very active!

i `fhd@tamvm1.bitnet` (Bitnet: FHD@TAMVM1) (H. Alan Montgomery)

± `listserv@tamvm1.tamu.edu` (Bitnet: LISTSERV@TAMVM1) [body = SUBSCRIBE SEDS-L first-name last-name]

Archive: `listserv@tamvm1.tamu.edu`

Gated: ⇔ `bit.listserv.seds-l`

1-1244 **SEDSNEWS:** Distribution of informational from several space research facilities, as well as a mirroring of sci.space.shuttle and sci.space.news from Usenet. NASA is primarily covered, but there is some coverage of European Space Agency and Russian space program.

i `fhd@tamvm1.bitnet` (Bitnet: FHD@TAMVM1) (H. Alan Montgomery)

± `listserv@tamvm1.tamu.edu` (Bitnet: LISTSERV@TAMVM1) [body = SUBSCRIBE SEDSNEWS first-name last-name]

Archive: `listserv@tamvm1.tamu.edu`

Gated: ⇔ `bit.listserv.sedsnews`

1-1245 **SEELANGS:** On Slavic and Eastern European languages and literatures.

i `ahrjj@cunyvm.bitnet` (Bitnet: AHRJJ@CUNYVM) (Alex Rudd) or
`rtwlc@cunyvm.bitnet` (Bitnet: RTWLC@CUNYVM) (Robert Whitaker)

± `listserv@cunyvm.cuny.edu` (Bitnet: LISTSERV@CUNYVM) [body = SUBSCRIBE
SEELANGS first-name last-name]

Archive: Available to subscribers only.

1-1246 **SEMIOS-L:** Semiotics.

i `s0skag01@ulkyvm.bitnet` (Bitnet: S0SKAG01@ULKYVM) (Steve Skaggs)

± `listserv@ulkyvm.louisville.edu` (Bitnet: LISTSERV@ULKYVM) [body =
SUBSCRIBE SEMIOS-L first-name last-name]

Archive: Available to subscribers only.

Other: Daily digest

1-1247 **SEMNET:** Structural Equation Modeling Special Interest Group (SEMSIG), a multidiscipli-
nary special interest group organized to support the application of structural equation modeling with latent variables across the social and behavioral sciences.

i `cferguso@alston.cba.ua.edu` (Carl Ferguson)

± `listserv@ua1vm.ua.edu` (Bitnet: LISTSERV@UA1VM) [body = SUBSCRIBE
SEMNET first-name last-name]

Archive: `listserv@ua1vm.ua.edu`

1-1248 **SENFONI:** Monthly politics magazine in Turkish. *Moderated*

i `sysadm1@trearn.bitnet` (Bitnet: SYSADM1@TREARN) or
`oprj50@trearn.bitnet` (Bitnet: OPRJ50@TREARN)

± `listserv@trearn.bitnet` (Bitnet: LISTSERV@TREARN) [body = SUBSCRIBE
SENFONI first-name last-name]

1-1249 **SERAVES:** On techno music and the rave scene associated with it, particularly in the southeastern U.S.

i `tiffanyde@urvax.urich.edu` (Derek Tiffany)

± `listserv@american.edu` (Bitnet: LISTSERV@AUVM) [body = SUBSCRIBE
SERAVES first-name last-name]

Archive: `listserv@american.edu`

1-1250 **SERCITES:** Citations for Serial Literature. *Moderated*

i `mgeller@athena.mit.edu` (Marilyn Geller)

± `listserv@mitvma.mit.edu` (Bitnet: LISTSERV@MITVMA) [body = SUBSCRIBE
SERCITES first-name last-name]

Archive: `listserv@mitvma.mit.edu`

1-1251 **SERIALST:** On serial publications in libraries, including cataloging, acquisitions collection management, budgets and pricing issues, binding, preservation, microfilm, union list activities,
news, announcements, and job postings. *Moderated*

i `bmaclenn@uvmvm.bitnet` (Bitnet: BMACLENN@UVMVM) (Birdie MacLennan)

± `listserv@uvmvm.uvm.edu` (Bitnet: LISTSERV@UVMVM) [body = SUBSCRIBE SERIALST first-name last-name]

Archive: `listserv@uvmvm.uvm.edu`

Other: Daily digest

1-1252 **sf-lovers:** On all topics in science fiction and fantasy in general, including SF and fantasy books, SF movies, and SF conventions, reviews of books, movies, television shows, and more.

> *i* ± `sf-lovers-request@rutgers.edu` (Saul Jaffe) or `listserv@vm.tcs.tulane.edu` (Bitnet: LISTSERV@TCSVM) [body = SUBSCRIBE SFLOVERS first-name last-name] or `listserv@rutvm1.rutgers.edu` (Bitnet: LISTSERV@RUTVM1) [body = SUBSCRIBE SFLOVERS first-name last-name]

> Posting Addresses—for Written SF: `sf-lovers-written@rutgers.edu` for SF on Television: `sf-lovers-tv@rutgers.edu`, for SF Films: `sf-lovers-movies@rutgers.edu`, For general discussions that don't fit specifically in the other topic headings: `sf-lovers-misc@rutgers.edu`

> **Archive:** FTP `gandalf.rutgers.edu` (for archive help send e-mail to `sf-lovers-ftp@gandalf.rutgers.edu` [body = help]); `listserv@vm.tcs.tulane.edu` or `listserv@uga.cc.uga.edu`

> **Other:** In digest format.

1-1253 **SFRaves:** About the "rave" club scene in San Francisco. Even though it's locally focused, people from all over the world are on SFRaves.

> *i* `bbehlen@sfraves.stanford.edu` (Brian Behlendorf)

> ± `sfraves-request@sfraves.stanford.edu`

> **Archive:** FTP `sfraves.stanford.edu` in `/pub/sfraves` (old postings and more)

1-1254 **SGML-L:** Structured Generalized Markup Language (SGML), used to code documents in a logical structure.

> *i* `wendt@vax.ntp.springer.de` (Holger Wendt) or `x92@dhdurz1.bitnet` (Bitnet: X92@DHDURZ1) (Joachim Lammarsch)

> ± `listserv@dhdurz1.bitnet` (Bitnet: LISTSERV@DHDURZ1) [body = SUBSCRIBE SGML-L first-name last-name]

1-1255 **shadows:** On the late sixties ABC daily soap opera "Dark Shadows."

> *i* `shadows-request@sunee.uwaterloo.ca` (automated reply), `shadows-owner@sunee.uwaterloo.ca` (human)

> ± `majordomo@sunee.uwaterloo.ca` [body = subscribe shadows]

1-1256 **shadows-updates:** Regular synopses of the episodes of the television series "Dark Shadows," currently being show on the "Sci-Fi" cable channel (see also "dark-shadows" in the list).

> *i* `shadows-update-request@sunee.uwaterloo.ca` (automated reply), `shadows-owner@sunee.uwaterloo.ca` (human)

> ± `majordomo@sunee.uwaterloo.ca` [body = subscribe shadows-update]

1-1257 **SHADOWTK:** For posting to Shadowrun, an ever evolving storyline involving personal characters who simulate the communication systems of the Shadowrun universe.

> *i* `hayden@krypton.mankato.msus.edu` (Robert Hayden)

± listserv@hearn.nic.surfnet.nl (Bitnet: LISTSERV@HEARN) [body = SUBSCRIBE SHADOWTK first-name last-name]

Archive: listserv@hearn.nic.surfnet.nl

1-1258 **SHAKER:** About the United Society of Believers (Shakers).

i rhorer@ukcc.uky.edu (Marc Rhorer)

± listserv@ukcc.uky.edu (Bitnet: LISTSERV@UKCC) [body = SUBSCRIBE SHAKER first-name last-name]

Archive: listserv@ukcc.uky.edu

1-1259 **SHAKSPER:** For discussion of Shakespeare. *Moderated*

i hmcook@boe00.minc.umd.edu (Hardy Cook)

± listserv@utoronto.bitnet (Bitnet: LISTSERV@UTORONTO) [body = SUBSCRIBE SHAKSPER first-name last-name]

Archive: Available to subscribers only.

Other: Potential subscribers are requested to submit a brief biography to the list owner prior admission to the list.

1-1260 **SHAPE-L:** For users of the "Shapetools" collection of Unix tools for revision control and configuration management.

i andy@desaster.cs.tu-berlin.de (Andreas Lampen)

± listserv@db0tui11.bitnet (Bitnet: LISTSERV@DB0TUI11) [body = SUBSCRIBE SHAPE-L first-name last-name]

Archive: listserv@db0tui11.bitnet

Gated: ⇔ bit.listserv.shape-l

1-1261 **SHARP-L:** For scholars in all disciplines interested in furthering the study of the history of the printed word.

i pleary@iubacs.bitnet (Bitnet: PLEARY@IUBACS) (Patrick Leary)

± listserv@iubvm.ucs.indiana.edu (Bitnet: LISTSERV@IUBVM) [body = SUBSCRIBE SHARP-L first-name last-name]

Archive: listserv@iubvm.ucs.indiana.edu

1-1262 **SHOGI-L:** On the strategic Japanese board game Shogi.

i stoutepf@lldmpc.dnet.dupont.com or kenney@embl-heidelberg.de

± listserv@technion.ac.il (Bitnet: LISTSERV@TECHNION) [body = SUBSCRIBE SHOGI-L first-name last-name]

Archive: listserv@technion.ac.il

1-1263 **SHOTHC-L:** On history of computing issues.

i nasem001@sivm.bitnet (Bitnet: NASEM001@SIVM) (Paul Ceruzzi)

± listserv@sivm.si.edu (Bitnet: LISTSERV@SIVM) [body = SUBSCRIBE SHOTHC-L first-name last-name]

Archive: listserv@sivm.si.edu

1-1264 **SHS:** For the medical and administrative staffs of student health services of institutions of higher education.

i sweet@utkvx.bitnet (Bitnet: SWEET@UTKVX) (Dr. Jo G. Sweet)

± `listserv@utkvm1.utk.edu` (Bitnet: `LISTSERV@UTKVM1`) [body = `SUBSCRIBE SHS` first-name last-name]

1-1265 **siege:** On pre-black powder methods of attack and defense of fortified positions. Include physics, mechanics, materials, construction, transportation, terminology, historic evidence of use, and historical reconstruction of siege engines.

i `siege-request@bransle.ucs.mun.ca` [body = `help`]

± `siege-request@bransle.ucs.mun.ca` [body = `subscribe siege` first-name last-name]

Archive: FTP `bransle.ucs.mun.ca` in `/pub/sca`

1-1266 **SIGTEL-L:** On classroom use of telecommunications. *Moderated*

i `kathyk@tenet.edu` (Kathy Kothmann)

± `listserv@unmvma.unm.edu` (Bitnet: `LISTSERV@UNMVMA`) [body = `SUBSCRIBE SIGTEL-L` first-name last-name]

Archive: Available to subscribers only.

1-1267 **SII:** Forum on the current events in ex-Yugoslavia, centered around those involving or affecting Serbs.

i ± `owner@moumee.calstatela.edu`

1-1268 **SILS-L:** On the SUNY at Buffalo School of Information and Library Studies.

i `lisyerke@ubvm.bitnet` (Bitnet: `LISYERKE@UBVM`) (Neil Yerkey)

± `listserv@ubvm.cc.buffalo.edu` (Bitnet: `LISTSERV@UBVM`) [body = `SUBSCRIBE SILS-L` first-name last-name]

Archive: `listserv@ubvm.cc.buffalo.edu`

1-1269 **SIMEDU-L:** On simulation applications in business/education.

i `rheadric@nmsuvm1.bitnet` (Bitnet: `RHEADRIC@NMSUVM1`) (Wayne Hedrick)

± `listserv@nmsuvm1.nmsu.edu` (Bitnet: `LISTSERV@NMSUVM1`) [body = `SUBSCRIBE SIMEDU-L` first-name last-name]

1-1270 **SINFONIA:** For members of Phi Mu Alpha Sinfonia, a music fraternity.

i `ben.goren@asu.edu` or `robert.d.reynolds@asu.edu`

± `listserv@asuvm.inre.asu.edu` (Bitnet: `LISTSERV@ASUACAD`) [body = `SUBSCRIBE SINFONIA` first-name last-name]

Archive: Available to subscribers only.

Other: Daily digest. Subscription is limited. Requests will be sent to list owner for approval.

1-1271 **SLA-PAM:** For the discussion of library/information related issues in the fields on physics, astronomy, and mathematics.

i `jmgoode@ukcc.bitnet` (Bitnet: `JMGOODE@UKCC`) (Joanne Goode)

± `listserv@ukcc.uky.edu` (Bitnet: `LISTSERV@UKCC`) [body = `SUBSCRIBE SLA-PAM` first-name last-name]

Archive: Available to subscribers only.

1-1272 **SLA-TECH:** On technical services in small and special libraries and information centers of any sort.

i `lmesner@ukcc.bitnet` (Bitnet: `LMESNER@UKCC`) (Lillian Mesner) or klidsh@ukcc.bitnet (Bitnet: KLIDSH@UKCC) (Debbie Hatfield)

± listserv@ukcc.uky.edu (Bitnet: LISTSERV@UKCC) [body = SUBSCRIBE SLA-TECH first-name last-name]

1-1273 **slade:** On the English glamrock group Slade.

i a3@rivm.nl (Adri Verhoef)

± slade-request@rivm.nl

1-1274 **SLAJOB:** On employment opportunities in special libraries. *Moderated*

i clmonnie@ucs.indiana.edu (Cindy Monnier)

± listserv@iubvm.ucs.indiana.edu (Bitnet: LISTSERV@IUBVM) [body = SUBSCRIBE SLAJOB first-name last-name]

Archive: listserv@iubvm.ucs.indiana.edu

1-1275 **SLART-L:** For scholarly discussion and exchange of information on second or foreign language education.

i abthc@cunyvm.bitnet (Bitnet: ABTHC@CUNYVM) (Anthea Tillyer) or kgakb@cunyvm.cuny.edu (Kate Garretson)

± listserv@cunyvm.cuny.edu (Bitnet: LISTSERV@CUNYVM) [body = SUBSCRIBE SLART-L first-name last-name]

Archive: Available to subscribers only.

1-1276 **SLLING-L:** For the discussion of sign language linguistics.

i cromano@uconnvm.bitnet (Bitnet: CROMANO@UCONNVM) (Christine Romano)

± listserv@yalevm.ycc.yale.edu (Bitnet: LISTSERV@YALEVM) [body = SUBSCRIBE SLLING-L first-name last-name]

Archive: listserv@yalevm.ycc.yale.edu

1-1277 **SLOVAK-L:** Discussion of Slovak issues.

i gfrajkor@ccs.carleton.ca (Jan George Frajkor)

± listserv@ubvm.cc.buffalo.edu (Bitnet: LISTSERV@UBVM) [body = SUBSCRIBE SLOVAK-L first-name last-name]

Archive: listserv@ubvm.cc.buffalo.edu

Gated: ⇔ bit.listserv.slovak-l

1-1278 **smail3-users:** For administrators of smail3.X based mailers. Covers operational aspects, i.e., installation and administration.

i ± smail3-users-request@cs.athabascau.ca

1-1279 **smail3-wizards:** For developers of smail3.X.

i ± smail3-wizards-request@cs.athabascau.ca

1-1280 **Smallmusic:** Discussion and development of object-oriented music software systems using the Smalltalk computing environment.

± smallmusic-request@xcf.berkeley.edu [subject = add me]

Archive: FTP XCF.Berkeley.EDU in misc/smalltalk/smallmusic

1-1281 **SMCDCME:** On continuing medical education.

i rbollin@cms.cc.wayne.edu (Robert Bollinger)

± listserv@cms.cc.wayne.edu (Bitnet: LISTSERV@WAYNEST1) [body =

SUBSCRIBE SMCDCME first-name last-name]

Archive: listserv@cms.cc.wayne.edu

1-1282 **SMDM-L:** On decision-making in medicine, from clinical practice to healthcare policies and programs. *Moderated*

i jlevin@umnhcs.bitnet (Bitnet: JLEVIN@UMNHCS) (James E. Levin, M.D., Ph.D.)

± listserv@dartcms1.dartmouth.edu (Bitnet: LISTSERV@DARTCMS1) [body = SUBSCRIBE SMDM-L first-name last-name]

Archive: listserv@dartcms1.dartmouth.edu

1-1283 **SNAMGT-L:** SNA Network Management discussion.

i maintlst@umrvmb.bitnet (Bitnet: MAINTLST@UMRVMB) (Listserv Postmaster)

± listserv@umrvmb.umr.edu (Bitnet: LISTSERV@UMRVMB) [body = SUBSCRIBE SNAMGT-L first-name last-name]

Archive: listserv@umrvmb.umr.edu

1-1284 **SNSTCP-L:** On Interlink SNS/TCPaccess products for MVS.

i raf@nihcu.bitnet (Bitnet: RAF@NIHCU) (Roger Fajman)

± listserv@list.nih.gov (Bitnet: LISTSERV@NIHLIST) [body = SUBSCRIBE SNSTCP-L first-name last-name]

Archive: listserv@list.nih.gov

1-1285 **SNURSE-L:** For student nurses.

i fisherd@scsud.ctstateu.edu (Dan Fisher)

± listserv@ubvm.cc.buffalo.edu (Bitnet: LISTSERV@UBVM) [body = SUBSCRIBE SNURSE-L first-name last-name]

Archive: listserv@ubvm.cc.buffalo.edu

Other: Subscription is limited. Requests will be sent to list owner for approval.

1-1286 **SOAP-L:** On Student Opportunities for Academic Publishing.

i morton@uhunix.uhcc.hawaii.edu

± listserv@uhccvm.uhcc.hawaii.edu (Bitnet: LISTSERV@UHCCVM) [body = SUBSCRIBE SOAP-L first-name last-name]

Archive: Available to subscribers only.

Other: Subscription is limited. Requests will be sent to list owner for approval.

1-1287 **SOBER-L:** The Brazilian Rural Economy Society's discussion forum.

i usercabs@brlncc.bitnet (Bitnet: USERCABS@BRLNCC) (Carlos Arthur B. da Silva)

± listserv@vm1.lcc.ufmg.br (Bitnet: LISTSERV@BRUFMG) [body = SUBSCRIBE SOBER-L first-name last-name]

Language: Portuguese

1-1288 **SOCCER-L:** For discussion of soccer-related issues and news—lots of scores are posted from subscribers worldwide.

i systrent@ukcc.uky.edu (Trent Fraebel) or crovo@ukcc.uky.edu (Bob Crovo)

± listserv@ukcc.uky.edu (Bitnet: LISTSERV@UKCC) [body = SUBSCRIBE SOCCER-L first-name last-name]

Other: Daily digest

1-1289 **Societies:** Discussion of Greek letter societies of all sorts, primarily those which are at American colleges.

    i ± `societies-request@athena.mit.edu`

1-1290 **SOCINSCT:** For university-level discussion of the biology of social insects (bees, wasps, ants, and termites).

    i `erik@acspr1.acs.brockport.edu` (Erik Seielstad)

    ± `listserv@uacsc2.albany.edu` (Bitnet: `LISTSERV@ALBNYVM1`) [body = SUBSCRIBE SOCINSCT first-name last-name]

    Archive: Available to subscribers only.

1-1291 **SOCWORK:** On social work.

    i `inmate@umab.bitnet` (Bitnet: `INMATE@UMAB`) (Harris Chaiklin)

    ± `listserv@umab.umd.edu` (Bitnet: `LISTSERV@UMAB`) [body = SUBSCRIBE SOCWORK first-name last-name]

1-1292 **softpub:** Forum on entrepreneural software publishing, including (but not limited to) shareware.

    i ± `softpub-request@toolz.atl.ga.us` (Todd Merriman)

1-1293 **SOFTREVU:** For users of software for personal computers. All microcomputer platforms are covered, as well as all software categories.

    i `el406006@brownvm.bitnet` (Bitnet: `EL406006@BROWNVM`) (David B. O'Donnell)

    ± `listserv@brownvm.brown.edu` (Bitnet: `LISTSERV@BROWNVM`) [body = SUBSCRIBE SOFTREVU first-name last-name]

    Archive: Available to subscribers only.

1-1294 **SOMACHI:** For members of the Mathematical Society of Chile.

    i `coryan@mat.puc.cl` or `rubi@mat.puc.cl`

    ± `listserv@usachvm1.usach.cl` (Bitnet: `LISTSERV@USACHVM1`) [body = SUBSCRIBE SOMACHI first-name last-name]

    Archive: Available to subscribers only.

    Other: Subscription is limited. Requests will be sent to list owner for approval.

1-1295 **SOPHIA:** On ancient philosophy (from Hesiod to Iamblichus, Spain to Palestine).

    i `srlclark@liverpool.ac.uk` (Stephen Clark)

    ± `listserv@liverpool.ac.uk` [body = SUBSCRIBE SOPHIA your name]

1-1296 **sos-data:** On any topic related to social science data.

    i `cassell@gibbs.oit.unc.edu` (James Cassell)

    ± `listserv@gibbs.oit.unc.edu` [body = SUBSCRIBE sos first-name last-name]

    Archive: `listserv@gibbs.oit.unc.edu` [body = index sos-data]

1-1297 **soundtracks:** For people interested in film soundtracks. Includes reviews, availability info, trading lists, and more. Not for the casually interested.

    i ± `soundtracks-request@ifi.unizh.ch` (Michel Hafner)

    Archive: FTP `ftp.uwp.edu` in `/pub/music/lists/`

1-1298 **Southern_Cultures:** For students and scholars of Southern history, literature, folklore, and related topics.

i `cassell@gibbs.oit.unc.edu` (James Cassell)

± `listserv@gibbs.oit.unc.edu` [body = SUBSCRIBE `sthcult` first-name last-name]

Archive: `listserv@gibbs.oit.unc.edu` [body = `index sthcult`]

1-1299 **southside-list:** On the music of Southside Johnny, with and without the Asbury Jukes, and members of that band.

i `thurlow@convex.com` (Rob Thurlow)

± `southside-list-request@convex.com`

1-1300 **SOVHIST:** Scholarly dicussion on the politics, cultural events, and history of the Soviet period in the former USSR from the February Revolution of 1917 to the fall of Communist rule in 1991.

i `cdell@umkcvax1.bitnet` (Bitnet: CDELL@UMKCVAX1) (Valentine M. Smith)

± `listserv@vm.usc.edu` (Bitnet: LISTSERV@USCVM) [body = SUBSCRIBE SOVHIST first-name last-name] or `listserv@csearn.bitnet` (Bitnet: LISTSERV@CSEARN) [body = SUBSCRIBE SOVHIST first-name last-name] or `listserv@umrvmb.umr.edu` (Bitnet: LISTSERV@UMRVMB) [body = SUBSCRIBE SOVHIST first-name last-name] or `listserv@dosuni1.rz.uni-osnabrueck.de` (Bitnet: LISTSERV@DOSUNI1) [body = SUBSCRIBE SOVHIST first-name last-name]

Archive: `listserv@dosuni1.rz.uni-osnabrueck.de`, `listserv@csearn.bitnet`, `listserv@umrvmb.umr.edu`

1-1301 **SPACE:** For discussing all types of space-related topics.

i `harold@uga.bitnet` (Bitnet: HAROLD@UGA) (Harold C. Pritchett) or `space-request@isu.isunet.edu`

± `listserv@ubvm.cc.buffalo.edu` (Bitnet: LISTSERV@UBVM) [body = SUBSCRIBE SPACE first-name last-name] or `listserv@uga.cc.uga.edu` (Bitnet: LISTSERV@UGA) [body = SUBSCRIBE SPACE first-name last-name]

Archive: `listserv@uga.cc.uga.edu`

Other: Daily digest

1-1302 **Space 1999:** For fans of the 1975-1976 TV show "Space 1999."

i ± `space-1999-request@quack.kfu.com`

1-1303 **Spandex Handjob:** Drink. Rock. Fuck.

i ± `i261%nemomus.bitnet@academic.nemostate.edu`

1-1304 **SPEEDE-L:** For members of the American Association of Collegiate Registrars and Admissions Officers (AACRAO).

i `carson@vtvm1.bitnet` (Bitnet: CARSON@VTVM1) (E. W. Carson)

± `listserv@vtvm1.cc.vt.edu` (Bitnet: LISTSERV@VTVM1) [body = SUBSCRIBE SPEEDE-L first-name last-name]

Archive: `listserv@vtvm1.cc.vt.edu`

1-1305 **SPORTMGT:** On sport management.

i `haggerty@jupiter.sun.csd.unb.ca` (Terry R. Haggerty)

± listserv@unb.ca (Bitnet: LISTSERV@UNBVM1) [body = SUBSCRIBE SPORTMGT first-name last-name]

1-1306 **SPORTPC:** On the use of computers in sports

i haggerty@jupiter.sun.csd.unb.ca (Terry R. Haggerty)

± listserv@unb.ca (Bitnet: LISTSERV@UNBVM1) [body = SUBSCRIBE SPORTPC first-name last-name]

1-1307 **SPORTPSY:** On exercise and sport psychology.

i v5289e@templevm.bitnet (Bitnet: V5289E@TEMPLEVM) (Michael Sachs)

± listserv@vm.temple.edu (Bitnet: LISTSERV@TEMPLEVM) [body = SUBSCRIBE SPORTPSY first-name last-name]

Archive: listserv@vm.temple.edu

1-1308 **SPUD:** For potato researchers and specialists.

i pace@wsuvm1.bitnet (Bitnet: PACE@WSUVM1) or wright@wsuvm1.bitnet (Bitnet: WRIGHT@WSUVM1)

± listserv@wsuvm1.csc.wsu.edu (Bitnet: LISTSERV@WSUVM1) [body = SUBSCRIBE SPUD first-name last-name]

1-1309 **SQL-sybase:** On the Sybase SQL server and related products, including programming hints, tricks, for Open Client, and stored procedure programming, and dba discussions of administering Sybase SQL Server database systems.

i ± sybase-request@apple.com

1-1310 **SRVREQ-L:** For discussion on resolving conflicts between any network operating system and workstation software, for example, Novell Netware to Novell workstation (IPX, NETX, ODI, etc.).

i itms400@indycms.bitnet (Bitnet: ITMS400@INDYCMS) (Manjit Trehan)

± listserv@indycms.iupui.edu (Bitnet: LISTSERV@INDYCMS) [body = SUBSCRIBE SRVREQ-L first-name last-name]

Archive: listserv@indycms.iupui.edu

1-1311 **SSREL-L:** For scholarly discussion of issues relevant to scientific study of religion—similar to content of journals like Journal for the Scientific Study of Religion, Sociological Analysis, Review of Religious Research, Social Compass.

i ploch@utkvx.bitnet (Bitnet: PLOCH@UTKVX) (Donald R. Ploch)

± listserv@utkvm1.utk.edu (Bitnet: LISTSERV@UTKVM1) [body = SUBSCRIBE SSREL-L first-name last-name]

Archive: listserv@utkvm1.utk.edu

1-1312 **SSSSTALK:** For scholarly discussion of issues relating to sexuality.

i b659bh@tamvm1.bitnet (Bitnet: B659BH@TAMVM1) (Betty Harris)

± listserv@tamvm1.tamu.edu (Bitnet: LISTSERV@TAMVM1) [body = SUBSCRIBE SSSSTALK first-name last-name]

Archive: Available to subscribers only.

Other: Subscription is limited. Requests will be sent to list owner for approval.

1-1313 **SSW-L:** About Soft-Switch products.

    i `$jld@pccjes2.bitnet` (Bitnet: `JLD@PCCJES2`)

    ± `listserv@list.nih.gov` (Bitnet: `LISTSERV@NIHLIST`) [body = SUBSCRIBE
       `SSW-L` first-name last-name]

    Archive: `listserv@list.nih.gov`

1-1314 **stagecraft:** On all aspects of stage work (special effects, sound effects, stage management, set
    design, lighting, hall management, show production, etc.). Not about acting, video, or film.

    i ± `stagecraft-request@jaguar.cs.utah.edu` (Brad Davis)

    Archive: FTP `cs.utah.edu` in `pub/Stagecraft`. e-mail by request from *i* address

1-1315 **Star Fleet Battles:** On the Star Fleet Battles role-playing game.

    i ± `hcobb@fly2.berkeley.edu` (Henry J. Cobb)

1-1316 **STATEPOL:** For scholarly discussion of the study of politics in the U.S. states.

    i `hoefler@dickinsn.bitnet` (Bitnet: `HOEFLER@DICKINSN`) (Jim Hoefler)

    ± `listserv@umab.umd.edu` (Bitnet: `LISTSERV@UMAB`) [body = SUBSCRIBE
       `STATEPOL` first-name last-name]

1-1317 **Steve Morse and the Dixie Dregs:** On the guitarist Steve Morse and his band the Dregs. Topics
    include album and concert reviews, upcoming releases and concert dates, interviews with
    Morse and his bandmates, etc.

    i ± `blickstein@dregs.enet.dec.com`

1-1318 **STKACS-L:** On the Storage Tek Automated Cartridge System.

    i `karl@uscvm.bitnet` (Bitnet: `KARL@USCVM`) (Karl P. Geiger) or
       `vincenc@uscvm.bitnet` (Michael Vincenc)

    ± `listserv@vm.usc.edu` (Bitnet: `LISTSERV@USCVM`) [body = SUBSCRIBE
       `STKACS-L` first-name last-name]

    Archive: `listserv@vm.usc.edu`

1-1319 **STLHE-L:** On teaching and learning in higher education.

    i `rgair@unb.ca` (Reavley Gair)

    ± `listserv@unb.ca` (Bitnet: `LISTSERV@UNBVM1`) [body = SUBSCRIBE `STLHE-L`
       first-name last-name]

    Archive: `listserv@unb.ca`

1-1320 **stormcock:** For discussion and news on the music of folk-rocker Roy Harper.

    i ± `stormcock-request@dcs.qmw.ac.uk` (Paul Davison)

1-1321 **STROKE-L:** For exchange of ideas and information on strokes (cerebrovascular disease) among
    professionals, stroke survivors, and their supporters.

    i `str002@ukcc.uky.edu` (Bob Moore)

    ± `listserv@ukcc.uky.edu` (Bitnet: `LISTSERV@UKCC`) [body = SUBSCRIBE
       `STROKE-L` first-name last-name]

    Archive: `listserv@ukcc.uky.edu`

1-1322 **STU-DEV:** Open discussion about campus problems, student affairs, and practical student devel-
    opment theory—for student services practitioners, university-level educators, graduate stu-

dents in student personnel programs, and others.

i `slingre@waynest1.bitnet` (Bitnet: `SLINGRE@WAYNEST1`) (Scot Lingrell)

± `listserv@cms.cc.wayne.edu` (Bitnet: `LISTSERV@WAYNEST1`) [body = SUBSCRIBE `STU-DEV` first-name last-name]

Archive: `listserv@cms.cc.wayne.edu`

Other: Subscription is limited. Requests will be sent to list owner for approval.

1-1323 **STUD-VM:** Students discussion on VM and EARN.

i `jzp0113@huszeg11.bitnet` (Bitnet: `JZP0113@HUSZEG11`) (Pamer Robert)

± `listserv@huearn.sztaki.hu` (Bitnet: `LISTSERV@HUEARN`) [body = SUBSCRIBE `STUD-VM` first-name last-name]

Archive: `listserv@huearn.sztaki.hu`

Language: Hungarian

1-1324 **STUDEMP:** On issues related to student employment.

i `hebertde@arizvm1.ccit.arizona.edu` (Dean Hebert)

± `listserv@arizvm1.ccit.arizona.edu` (Bitnet: `LISTSERV@ARIZVM1`) [body = SUBSCRIBE `STUDEMP` first-name last-name]

Archive: `listserv@arizvm1.ccit.arizona.edu`

1-1325 **STUNET-L:** For Dutch students.

i `u055098@kunrc1.urc.kun.nl` (D. Hendriks)

± `listserv@hearn.nic.surfnet.nl` (Bitnet: `LISTSERV@HEARN`) [body = SUBSCRIBE `STUNET-L` first-name last-name]

Archive: `listserv@hearn.nic.surfnet.nl`

Language: Dutch

1-1326 **STUTT-X:** On the research of communication disorders.

i `atdnm@asuacad.bitnet` (Bitnet: `ATDNM@ASUACAD`) (Don Mowrer)

± `listserv@asuvm.inre.asu.edu` (Bitnet: `LISTSERV@ASUACAD`) [body = SUBSCRIBE `STUTT-X` first-name last-name]

Archive: `listserv@asuvm.inre.asu.edu`

1-1327 **STUXCH-L:** For establishing student exchanges between architecture departments throughout the world.

i `hrl@psuarch.bitnet` (Bitnet: `HRL@PSUARCH`) (Howard Lawrence)

± `listserv@psuvm.psu.edu` (Bitnet: `LISTSERV@PSUVM`) [body = SUBSCRIBE `STUXCH-L` first-name last-name]

Archive: `listserv@psuvm.psu.edu`

1-1328 **sun-386i:** For owners and users of Sun Microsystems 386i "Roadrunner" computers. Topics include support issues (Sun Microsystems no longer sells or supports this system), sources for spares, and adaptation of existing Unix software to the 386i.

i ± `sun-386i-request@ssg.com`

1-1329 **sun-managers:** For managers of sites with Sun workstations or servers.

i `sun-managers-request@eecs.nwu.edu` [body = help]

± `sun-managers-request@eecs.nwu.edu` [body = add e-mail-address]

1-1330 **sunflash (aka "The Florida SunFlash"):** Press releases, product announcements, and technical articles from Sun Inc. This is a one-way mailing list.

    i `info-sunflash@sun.com`.

    ± `sunflash-request@sun.com`

1-1331 **SUNYEC-L:** For communication among the staffs of the State University of New York's Educational Communications Centers and Instructional Resources Centers.

    i `jdonahue@bingsuns.cc.binghamton.edu` (Jeff Donahue)

    ± `listserv@bingvmb.bitnet@bingsuns.cc.binghamton.edu` (Bitnet: LISTSERV@BINGVMB) [body = SUBSCRIBE SUNYEC-L first-name last-name]

    Other: Subscription is limited. Requests will be sent to list owner for approval.

1-1332 **SUNYLA-L:** On libraries within the SUNY system.

    i `fmols@bingvmb.bitnet` (Bitnet: FMOLS@BINGVMB) (Frank Mols)

    ± `listserv@bingvmb.cc.binghamton.edu` (Bitnet: LISTSERV@BINGVMB) [body = SUBSCRIBE SUNYLA-L first-name last-name]

1-1333 **SUNYSPHL:** For the State University of New York School of Public Health. *Moderated*

    i `vml04@albnydh2.bitnet` (Bitnet: VML04@ALBNYDH2) (Vito M. Logrillo)

    ± `listserv@albnydh2.bitnet` (Bitnet: LISTSERV@ALBNYDH2) [body = SUBSCRIBE SUNYSPHL first-name last-name]

    Archive: `listserv@albnydh2.bitnet`

1-1334 **SUP-COND:** On superconductivity research in Israel. *Moderated*

    i `jo@ilncrd.bitnet` (Bitnet: JO@ILNCRD) (Jo van Zwaren)

    ± `listserv@taunivm.tau.ac.il` (Bitnet: LISTSERV@TAUNIVM) [body = SUBSCRIBE SUP-COND first-name last-name]

1-1335 **SUPERESP:** Supercomputing in Spain.

    i `montanan@evalun11.bitnet` (Bitnet: MONTANAN@EVALUN11) (Rogelio Montanana) or `serveman@ebcesca1.bitnet` (Bitnet: SERVEMAN@EBCESCA1)

    ± `listserv@ebcesca1.bitnet` (Bitnet: LISTSERV@EBCESCA1) [body = SUBSCRIBE SUPERESP first-name last-name]

    Archive: Available to subscribers only.

    Language: Spanish

1-1336 **SUPERGUY:** For participants in SUPERGUY, a multi-author, shared multiverse that focuses on humorous, superhero genre stories, but includes serious superhero, science fiction, and related stories.

    i `simmons@ucf1vm.bitnet` (Bitnet: SIMMONS@UCF1VM) (Tad Simmons)

    ± `listserv@ucf1vm.cc.ucf.edu` (Bitnet: LISTSERV@UCF1VM) [body = SUBSCRIBE SUPERGUY first-name last-name]

    Archive: `listserv@ucf1vm.cc.ucf.edu`

1-1337 **SUPERIBM:** For users of IBM equipment for high performance scientific applications (super-computing).

    i `crovo@ukcc.bitnet` (Bitnet: CROVO@UKCC) (Bob Crovo)

    ± `listserv@ukcc.uky.edu` (Bitnet: LISTSERV@UKCC) [body = SUBSCRIBE

SUPERIBM first-name last-name]

Archive: Available to subscribers only.

1-1338 **SUPEUR:** On supercomputing in Europe.

i delhaye@frmop11.bitnet (Bitnet: DELHAYE@FRMOP11) (Jean-Loic Delhaye)

± listserv@frmop11.cnusc.fr (Bitnet: LISTSERV@FRMOP11) [body = SUBSCRIBE SUPEUR first-name last-name]

Archive: listserv@frmop11.cnusc.fr

Other: Subscription is limited. Requests will be sent to list owner for approval.

1-1339 **SWIM-L:** On all aspects of swimming.

i ks06054@uafsysb.bitnet (Bitnet: KS06054@UAFSYSB) (Ken Schriner)

± listserv@uafsysb.uark.edu (Bitnet: LISTSERV@UAFSYSB) [body = SUBSCRIBE SWIM-L first-name last-name]

Archive: Available to subscribers only.

1-1340 **SWIP-L:** For members of the Society for Women in Philosophy and others involved in the field of feminist philosophy.

i dllafaa@cfrvm.bitnet (Bitnet: DLLAFAA@CFRVM) (Linda Lopez McAlister)

± listserv@cfrvm.bitnet (Bitnet: LISTSERV@CFRVM) [body = SUBSCRIBE SWIP-L first-name last-name]

Archive: Available to subscribers only.

Other: Subscription is limited. Requests will be sent to list owner for approval.

1-1341 **SWL$L:** For shortwave radio listeners.

i npape@trinity.bitnet (Bitnet: NPAPE@TRINITY) (Neal Pape)

± listserv@cuvmb.cc.columbia.edu (Bitnet: LISTSERV@CUVMB) [body = SUBSCRIBE SWL$L first-name last-name]

1-1342 **SYSCI-L:** On the Program of Systems Science at the University of Ottawa, including seminars, newsletter, research/teaching assistantships. *Moderated*

i jmyhg@acadvm1.uottawa.ca (Jean-Michel Thizy)

± listserv@acadvm1.uottawa.ca (Bitnet: LISTSERV@UOTTAWA) [body = SUBSCRIBE SYSCI-L first-name last-name]

Archive: listserv@acadvm1.uottawa.ca

1-1343 **T-ASSIST:** For university teaching assistants.

i jgruene@bootes.unm.edu (Jennifer Gruenewald) or dicker@acc.fau.edu (Todd J. Dicker)

± listserv@unmvma.unm.edu (Bitnet: LISTSERV@UNMVMA) [body = SUBSCRIBE T-ASSIST first-name last-name]

Archive: Available to subscribers only.

1-1344 **T_LEVAL:** For identifying and compiling a database of projects that use networking and networked information resources for education.

i rapagnani@arizona.edu (Larry Rapagnani)

± listserv@arizvm1.ccit.arizona.edu (Bitnet: LISTSERV@ARIZVM1) [body = SUBSCRIBE T_LEVAL first-name last-name]

Archive: `listserv@arizvm1.ccit.arizona.edu`

Other: Subscription is limited. Requests will be sent to list owner for approval.

1-1345 **TACT-L:** For users of Textual Analysis Computing Tools (TACT), a system of MS-DOS programs for producing word-lists, concordances, graphs, and statistical information about texts.

  i `mccarty@epas.utoronto.ca` (Dr. Willard McCarty)

  ± `listserv@utoronto.bitnet` (Bitnet: `LISTSERV@UTORONTO`) [body = SUBSCRIBE TACT-L first-name last-name]

  Archive: `listserv@utoronto.bitnet`

  Other: Subscription is limited. Requests will be sent to list owner for approval.

1-1346 **tadream:** On the Tangerine Dream music group and related artists.

  Other: Digest Format and reflector available.

  i ± `tadream-request@cs.uwp.edu` (Dave Datta)

1-1347 **TALKBACK:** For children in Project Chatback.

  i `drz@sjuvm.bitnet` (Bitnet: `DRZ@SJUVM`)

  ± `listserv@stjohns.edu` (Bitnet: `LISTSERV@SJUVM`) [body = SUBSCRIBE TALKBACK first-name last-name]

  Archive: Available to subscribers only.

1-1348 **talking-heads:** On the Talking Heads rock group.

  i `milo@athena.mit.edu` (Cole Robison)

  ± `talking-heads-request@athena.mit.edu`

1-1349 **Talon-Eclipse-Laser:** For owners and admirers of Talon, Eclipse, or Laser automobiles.

  i ± `talon@di.com` (Todd Day)

1-1350 **tcldp-list:** Discussions about the Tcl Distributed Programming package.

  i ± `tcldp-list-request@cs.berkeley.edu`

1-1351 **TCLTK:** On the Tcl/Tk interpreted computer language.

  i `tcltkman@itcaspur.bitnet` (Bitnet: `TCLTKMAN@ITCASPUR`) (Tcl/Tk Mailing List Manager)

  ± `listserv@crnvma.cern.ch` (Bitnet: `LISTSERV@CERNVM`) [body = SUBSCRIBE TCLTK first-name last-name]

  Archive: Available to subscribers only.

  Gated: ⇔ `comp.lang.tcl`

1-1352 **tcp-digest:** Digest version of tcp-group.

  ± `listserv@ucsd.edu` [body = `subscribe tcp-digest`]

1-1353 **tcp-group:** Discussion about promoting TCP/IP use on Ham packet radio.

  ± `tcp-group-request@ucsd.edu` [body = `subscribe tcp-group`]

1-1354 **TCP-ITA:** Forum for Italian Internet users.

  i `vannozzi@icnucevm.bitnet` (Bitnet: `VANNOZZI@ICNUCEVM`) (Daniele Vannozzi)

  ± `listserv@vm.cnuce.cnr.it` (Bitnet: `LISTSERV@ICNUCEVM`) [body = SUBSCRIBE TCP-ITA first-name last-name]

  Archive: `listserv@vm.cnuce.cnr.it`

Archive: `listserv@vm.cnuce.cnr.it`

1-1355 **TEACHEFT:** On "centers for teaching effectiveness" at universities, including polls, feedback on research, program proposals, calls for papers, meetings, and job announcements, more.

i `cradich@wcu.bitnet` (Bitnet: CRADICH@WCU)

± `listserv@wcu.bitnet` (Bitnet: LISTSERV@WCU) [body = SUBSCRIBE TEACHEFT first-name last-name]

Archive: Available to subscribers only.

1-1356 **tears4-fears:** Discussion of the music group Tears For Fears.

i ± `tears4-fears-request@ms.uky.edu` (Joel Abbot)

Archive: FTP `ftp.ms.uky.edu` in `/pub/mailing.lists/tears4-fears`

1-1357 **TECHMATH:** About mathematical activity in Israel. *Moderated*

i `mar23aa@technion.technion.ac.il` (Danny Hershkowitz)

± `listserv@technion.ac.il` (Bitnet: LISTSERV@TECHNION) [body = SUBSCRIBE TECHMATH first-name last-name]

Archive: `listserv@technion.ac.il`

1-1358 **TECHTR:** For discussion of technology transfer, patent, and licensing issues as they relate to an academic insitutition, including the NSF and NIH guidelines on conflict of interest and commitment.

i `cdhurt@ccit.arizona.edu` (C. D. Hurt)

± `listserv@arizvm1.ccit.arizona.edu` (Bitnet: LISTSERV@ARIZVM1) [body = SUBSCRIBE TECHTR first-name last-name]

Archive: `listserv@arizvm1.ccit.arizona.edu`

1-1359 **TECHWR-L:** For technical writers on all technical communication issues.

i `ejray@osuvm1.bitnet` (Bitnet: EJRAY@OSUVM1)

± `listserv@vm1.ucc.okstate.edu` (Bitnet: LISTSERV@OSUVM1) [body = SUBSCRIBE TECHWR-L first-name last-name]

Archive: `listserv@vm1.ucc.okstate.edu`

Other: Daily digest

1-1360 **TECMAT-L:** About technology in secondary math.

i `lcrtroy@ubvms.bitnet` (Bitnet: LCRTROY@UBVMS) (Beth Troy)

± `listserv@ubvm.cc.buffalo.edu` (Bitnet: LISTSERV@UBVM) [body = SUBSCRIBE TECMAT-L first-name last-name]

1-1361 **TeleUSErs:** Technical information, examples, tips, etc., or users of TeleUSE. For technical support, use `guisupport@alsys.com` instead.

i ± `teleusers-request@alsys.com` (Kent Allen)

1-1362 **TELXCH-L:** On telecomunications in the state of New York and national telecommunications and policy issues related to digital infrastructure.

i `pbachman@skidmore.edu` (Peter Bachman)

± `listserv@albnydh2.bitnet` (Bitnet: LISTSERV@ALBNYDH2) [body = SUBSCRIBE TELXCH-L first-name last-name]

Archive: `listserv@albnydh2.bitnet`

1-1363 **TESL-L:** For entering into a group of lists for teachers of English as a second language. Subsidiary lists cover job information, classroom practices, writing materials, pen pals, and more. Lists include TESLCA-L, TESLEC-L, TESLFF-L, TESLIE-L, TESLIT-L, TESLJB-L, TESLMW-L.

 i `abthc@cunyvm.bitnet` (Bitnet: `ABTHC@CUNYVM`) (Anthea Tillyer) or `rushing@wsuvm1.bitnet` (Tim Rushing)

 ± `listserv@cunyvm.cuny.edu` (Bitnet: `LISTSERV@CUNYVM`) [body = `SUBSCRIBE TESL-L` first-name last-name]

 Archive: Available to subscribers only.

1-1364 **Testing-Research:** For researchers in the field of software testing.

 i ± `testing-research-request@cs.uiuc.edu` (Brian Marick)

1-1365 **The Bottom Line:** Bass players' digest.

 i ± `bass-request@uwplatt.edu`

1-1366 **The Cleveland Sports Mailing List:** On anything related to the Cleveland sports scene.

 i ± `sports-request@wariat.org`

 Gated: ⇔`cle.sports`

1-1367 **The Learning List:** Forum for discussing child-centered learning. Members must agree with the Charter of the Learning List to subscribe.

 i `learning-request@sea.east.sun.com` [subject = `help`]

 ± `learning-request@sea.east.sun.com` [subject = `subscribe`]

1-1368 **The Replacements:** On the Replacements rock group.

 i ± `e149%nemomus.bitnet@academic.nemostate.edu`

1-1369 **The Silent Planet:** Newletter and discussions about the bands King's X and Galactic Cowboys.

 i ± `n8846069@henson.cc.wwu.edu` (BarryB)

 Archive: FTP `cs.uwp.edu` in `/pub/music/artists/k/kingsx/`

1-1370 **The Skyway:** Mailing list and support group for fans of The Replacements.

 i ± `i261%nemomus@academic.nemostate.edu`

 Other: available in digest format.

1-1371 **THEATRE:** For people involved in theater.

 i `theodore@knosos.cc.uch.gr` (Theodore J. Soldatos)

 ± `theatre-request@world.std.com` (Elizabeth Lear Newman) or `listserv@grearn.bitnet` (Bitnet: `LISTSERV@GREARN`) [body = `SUBSCRIBE THEATRE` first-name last-name]

 Archive: `listserv@grearn.bitnet`

 Gated: ⇔ `rec.arts.theatre` newsgroup

1-1372 **THEORIST:** For users of the Theorist math software program

 i `koch@ece.engr.utk.edu` (Dan Koch)

 ± `listserv@utkvm1.utk.edu` (Bitnet: `LISTSERV@UTKVM1`) [body = `SUBSCRIBE THEORIST` first-name last-name]

 Archive: `listserv@utkvm1.utk.edu`

1-1373 **THEORYNT:** On computer science theory.

    i `u14780@uicvm.bitnet` (Bitnet: `U14780@UICVM`) or `u32799@uicvm.bitnet` (Bitnet: `U32799@UICVM`) or `u08208@uicvm.bitnet` (Bitnet: `U08208@UICVM`)

    ± `listserv@vm1.nodak.edu` (Bitnet: `LISTSERV@NDSUVM1`) [body = SUBSCRIBE THEORYNT first-name last-name]

    Archive: `listserv@vm1.nodak.edu`

1-1374 **THETAXI:** For discussions pertaining to the Theta Xi Fraternity.

    i `cc100pg@gitvm1.bitnet` (Bitnet: `CC100PG@GITVM1`) (Paul Goodwin)

    ± `listserv@gitvm1.gatech.edu` (Bitnet: `LISTSERV@GITVM1`) [body = SUBSCRIBE THETAXI first-name last-name]

    Archive: `listserv@gitvm1.gatech.edu`

1-1375 **they-might-be:** Official discussion of the musical group They Might Be Giants.

    i `owner-they-might-be@gnu.ai.mit.edu`

    ± `they-might-be-request@super.org` [body = `subscribe they-might-be`]

    Archive: FTP `insti.physics.sunysb.edu` in `/pub/tmbg`(contains everything from list, sound samples, pictures of the band, lyrics to all the albums, discography/FAQ, and more)

1-1376 **think-c:** For users of the Think C and C++ compiler for the Macintosh. Includes problems and solutions/workarounds, discussion of object-oriented programming and Macintosh programming, and the sharing of source code.

    i ± `think-c-request@ics.uci.edu` (Mark Nagel)

    Archive: FTP `ftp.ics.uci.edu` Mail Archive Server: `archive-server@ics.uci.edu` Archive submissions: `think-c-request@ics.uci.edu`

1-1377 **TIBET-L:** On Tibet

    i `sdhargay@ucs.indiana.edu` (Sonam Dargyay)

    ± `listserv@iubvm.ucs.indiana.edu` (Bitnet: `LISTSERV@IUBVM`) [body = SUBSCRIBE TIBET-L first-name last-name]

    Archive: Available to subscribers only.

1-1378 **TIDBITS:** A newsletter for users of Macintosh computers. *Moderated*

    i `ace@tidbits.com` (Adam C. Engst)

    ± `listserv@ricevm1.rice.edu` (Bitnet: `LISTSERV@RICEVM1`) [body = SUBSCRIBE TIDBITS first-name last-name]

    Archive: `sumex-aim.stanford.edu`

1-1379 **tiffany:** On the music and career of Tiffany Darswisch.

    i `rnovak@nyx.cs.du.edu` (Robert Novak)

    ± `tiffany-request@nyx.cs.du.edu`

    Archive: FTP `ftp.uwp.edu` (discography and lyrics)

    Gated: Fidonet's TIFFandDEB echo via 1:380/7.

    Other: Digest available (subscribe to `tiffany-digest-request@nyx.cs.du.edu`)

1-1380 **tiger:** On the rock group Duran Duran.

 i `tiger-request@cs.unca.edu` [body = `help`]

 ± `tiger-request@cs.unca.edu` [body = `sub`]

1-1381 **tinymuck-sloggers:** For programmers, and users of the TinyMUCK Multiple User Dungeon (MUD) environment.

 i `rearl@piggy.ucsb.edu` (Robert Earl)

 ± `tinymuck-sloggers-request@piggy.ucsb.edu` [subject = `subscribe`]

 Archive: Mailserv `tinymuck-sloggers-request@piggy.ucsb.edu` [subject = `send archive`]

1-1382 **tinymush-programmers:** For programmers of the TinyMUSH Multiple User Dungeon (MUD) environment.

 i ± `tinymush-programmers-request@cygnus.com`

1-1383 **TIP:** For theoretical computer science researchers in Poland, supporting organization of local meetings, exchange of literature, and distribution of local news.

 i `jurekty@mimuw.edu.pl` (Jerzy Tyszkiewicz)

 ± `listserv@plearn.edu.pl` (Bitnet: LISTSERV@PLEARN) [body = `SUBSCRIBE TIP` first-name last-name]

 Archive: `listserv@plearn.edu.pl`

 Other: Subscription is limited. Requests will be sent to list owner for approval.

1-1384 **TIPSHEET:** Computer Help and Tip Exchange.

 i `pace@wsuvm1.bitnet` (Bitnet: PACE@WSUVM1)

 ± `listserv@wsuvm1.csc.wsu.edu` (Bitnet: LISTSERV@WSUVM1) [body = `SUBSCRIBE TIPSHEET` first-name last-name]

 Archive: `listserv@wsuvm1.csc.wsu.edu`

1-1385 **TKE-INFO:** Discussions relating to Tau Kappa Epsilon social fraternity.

 i `rand@merrimack.edu`

 ± `mxserver@merrimack.edu`

1-1386 **TML-L:** For a database of text and graphics on Latin music theory.

 i `mathiese@iubvm.bitnet` (Bitnet: MATHIESE@IUBVM) (Thomas J. Mathiesen)

 ± `listserv@iubvm.ucs.indiana.edu` (Bitnet: LISTSERV@IUBVM) [body = `SUBSCRIBE TML-L` first-name last-name]

 Archive: `listserv@iubvm.ucs.indiana.edu`

 Language: Latin

1-1387 **TNC:** On technoculture, or the broad and complex relationships between technology and culture—particularly the political and cultural implications of information, communication, and entertainment technologies.

 i `lceric@mizzou1.bitnet` (Bitnet: LCERIC@MIZZOU1) (Eric Crump)

 ± `listserv@gitvm1.gatech.edu` (Bitnet: LISTSERV@GITVM1) [body = `SUBSCRIBE TNC` first-name last-name]

 Archive: `listserv@gitvm1.gatech.edu`

1-1388 **TNNG:** On neural networks and artificial intelligence.

  i `ko@trbilun.bitnet` (Bitnet: KO@TRBILUN) (Kemal Oflazer)

  ± `listserv@vm.cc.metu.edu.tr` (Bitnet: LISTSERV@TRMETU) [body = SUBSCRIBE TNNG first-name last-name]

  Archive: `listserv@vm.cc.metu.edu.tr`

  Language: Turkish

1-1389 **TOLKIEN:** For fans of J.R.R.Tolkien's books.

  i `jimj@jhuvm.bitnet` (Bitnet: JIMJ@JHUVM)

  ± `listserv@jhuvm.hcf.jhu.edu` (Bitnet: LISTSERV@JHUVM) [body = SUBSCRIBE TOLKIEN first-name last-name]

  Archive: `listserv@jhuvm.hcf.jhu.edu`

1-1390 **TolkLang:** On the linguistic aspects (from Elvish vocabulary and grammar to the use of Old English) in J.R.R. Tolkien's works. *Moderated*

  i ± `tolklang-request@dcs.ed.ac.uk` (Julian Bradfield) or `tolklang-request=server@dcs.ed.ac.uk` [body = subscribe tolklang first-name last-name]

  Archive: FTP `ftp.dcs.ed.ac.uk` in `/export/TolkLang`

1-1391 **TOOLB-L:** On the Asymetrix "Toolbook" for MS/Windows (an interface design toolbox).

  i `ks06054@uafsysb.bitnet` (Bitnet: KS06054@UAFSYSB) (Ken Schriner)

  ± `listserv@uafsysb.uark.edu` (Bitnet: LISTSERV@UAFSYSB) [body = SUBSCRIBE TOOLB-L first-name last-name]

  Archive: `listserv@uafsysb.uark.edu`

1-1392 **Top 10 Charts:** Distribution of Billboard's Top 10.

  i ± `buckmr@rpi.edu` (Ron Buckmire)

1-1393 **top:** On the musical group Tower of Power and associated side projects.

  i `owner-top@cv.ruu.nl`

  ± `top-request@cv.ruu.nl`

  Archive: Available by request.

1-1394 **topology:** Topology Eprints is a mailing list for distributiog abstracts of recent results in topology, including geometric topology, low dimensional topology, infinite dimensional topology, manifolds, dynamical systems, transformation group actions, point set topology, and general topology.

  i `listserv@math.ufl.edu` [body = FAQ topology] or `topology-request@math.ufl.edu`

  ± `listserv@math.ufl.edu` [body = suscribe topology]

1-1395 **Toronto Blue Jays:** On the Toronto Blue Jays baseball club.

  i ± `jays-request@hivnet.ubc.ca`

  Other: there is a weekly list (called jaysweek) that carrys highlights and standings. Subscribe via `jays-request@hivnet.ubc.ca` [body = subscribe to jaysweek]

1-1396 **TOUCHTON:** On Touch-Tone/Voice Response Systems.

  i `sroka@sjsuvm1.sjsu.edu` (John Sroka)

± listserv@sjsuvm1.sjsu.edu (Bitnet: LISTSERV@SJSUVM1) [body =
    SUBSCRIBE TOUCHTON first-name last-name]

Archive: listserv@sjsuvm1.sjsu.edu

1-1397 **towers:** All about NCR Tower computers.

i ± bill@wlk.com (Bill Kennedy)

Gated: ⇔ comp.sys.ncr

1-1398 **toyota:** For owners and prospective owners of all models of Toyota consumer passenger vehicles and light trucks.

i ± toyota-request@quack.kfu.com

1-1399 **TQM-L:** Total Quality Management in higher education.

i supervisor@sweep.fo.ukans.edu

± listserv@ukanvm.cc.ukans.edu (Bitnet: LISTSERV@UKANVM) [body =
    SUBSCRIBE TQM-L first-name last-name]

Archive: listserv@ukanvm.cc.ukans.edu

Other: Daily digest

1-1400 **TRANSGEN:** For and about people who are transsexual, transgendered, and/or transvestites.

i owner-transgen@brownvm.brown.edu or
    julie@drycas.club.cc.cmu.edu

± listserv@brownvm.brown.edu (Bitnet: LISTSERV@BROWNVM) [body =
    SUBSCRIBE TRANSGEN first-name last-name]

Archive: Available to subscribers only.

Other: Daily digest. Subscription is limited. Requests will be sent to list owner for approval.

1-1401 **TRASHCAN:** For fans of the Trash Can Sinatras (lotta guitars, very atmospheric).

i u52549@uicvm.bitnet (Bitnet: U52549@UICVM)

± listserv@uicvm.bitnet (Bitnet: LISTSERV@UICVM) [body = SUBSCRIBE
    TRASHCAN first-name last-name]

Archive: listserv@uicvm.bitnet

1-1402 **traveller:** On the TRAVELLER science-fiction role-playing game, published by Game Designers' Workshop.

i ± traveller-request@engrg.uwo.ca (James T. Perkins)

Archive: FTP ftp.engrg.uwo.ca in /pub/traveller

1-1403 **TRKNWS-L:** News and articles used by the "Turkish Cultural Program" broadcast by the KUSF Radio. Mostly in English and some in Turkish. Covers the entire Turkish-speaking world, including Turkey, Azerbaijan, Turkmenistan, Kazakhstan, Uzbekistan, Kirgizistan.
Moderated

i toprak@mcimail.com (A.A. Toprak)

± listserv@vm.usc.edu (Bitnet: LISTSERV@USCVM) [body = SUBSCRIBE
    TRKNWS-L first-name last-name]

1-1404 **TRNSPLNT:** For organ transplant recipients and anyone else intested in the issues.

i flasar@wugcrc.wustl.edu (Dan Flasar)

± listserv@wuvmd.wustl.edu (Bitnet: LISTSERV@WUVMD) [body = SUBSCRIBE

TRNSPLNT first-name last-name]

Archive: listserv@wuvmd.wustl.edu

1-1405 **TSA-L:** For the Turkish Studies Association.

i alan@ah2.cal.msu.edu (Alan Fisher) or

± listserv@msu.edu (Bitnet: LISTSERV@MSU) [body = SUBSCRIBE TSA-L first-name last-name]

Archive: listserv@msu.edu

1-1406 **TSSACT-L:** About activities of the Tunisian Scientific Society.

i jomaa@utkvx1.bitnet (Bitnet: JOMAA@UTKVX1) (Jomaa Ben-Hassine)

± listserv@utkvm1.utk.edu (Bitnet: LISTSERV@UTKVM1) [body = SUBSCRIBE TSSACT-L first-name last-name]

Other: Subscription is limited. Requests will be sent to list owner for approval.

1-1407 **TUNINFO:** For the Tunisian Information Office in Washington, D.C. *Moderated*

i bnj@psuecl.bitnet (Bitnet: BNJ@PSUECL) (Bilel N. Jamoussi)

± listserv@psuvm.psu.edu (Bitnet: LISTSERV@PSUVM) [body = SUBSCRIBE TUNINFO first-name last-name]

Language: French

Other: Subscription is limited. Requests will be sent to list owner for approval.

1-1408 **TURBVIS :** For users of TurboVision, a free library that comes with Borland C++ and Borland Pascal programming languages. *Moderated*

i daves@vt.edu (Dave Sisson)

± listserv@vtvm1.cc.vt.edu (Bitnet: LISTSERV@VTVM1) [body = SUBSCRIBE TURBVIS first-name last-name]

Archive: listserv@vtvm1.cc.vt.edu

Gated: comp.os.msdos.programmer.turbovision

1-1409 **TURKMATH:** About Turkish mathematics.

i akgul@trbilun.bitnet (Bitnet: AKGUL@TRBILUN) (Mustafa Akgul)

± listserv@vm.cc.metu.edu.tr (Bitnet: LISTSERV@TRMETU) [body = SUBSCRIBE TURKMATH first-name last-name]

Archive: listserv@vm.cc.metu.edu.tr

1-1410 **TWAIN-L:** The Mark Twain Forum, for scholarly interest in the life and writings of Mark Twain. Postings may include queries, discussion, conference announcements, calls for papers, information on new publications.

i robertst@unixg.ubc.ca (Taylor Roberts)

± listserv@yorkvm1.bitnet (Bitnet: LISTSERV@YORKVM1) [body = SUBSCRIBE TWAIN-L first-name last-name]

Archive: listserv@yorkvm1.bitnet

1-1411 **twins:** Forum on twin/triplets/etc. Topics include research on twin-related issues, parenting issues as well as issues concerning adult twins.

i owner-twins@athena.mit.edu

± owner-twins@athena.mit.edu [subject = Twins Subscription, body =

subscribe/unsubscribe]

1-1412 **Two-Strokes:** On two-stroke motorcycle technology, maintenance, and riding. (Mostly about street and road-racing, with some dirt bike discussion.)

i ± 2strokes-request@microunity.com

Archive: Available upon request to 2strokes-request@microunity.com

1-1413 **TXDXN-L:** For discussion of availability and dissemination of government information to the public, "needs and offers" of specific publications, reference questions, guides and bibliographies—particularly for Texas and U.S.

i law7@uhupvm1.bitnet (Bitnet: LAW7@UHUPVM1)

± listserv@uhupvm1.uh.edu (Bitnet: LISTSERV@UHUPVM1) [body = SUBSCRIBE TXDXN-L first-name last-name]

Archive: Available to subscribers only.

1-1414 **TYPO-L:** On typography, type, and typographic design.

i pflynn@curia.ucc.ie (Peter Flynn)

± listserv@irlearn.bitnet (Bitnet: LISTSERV@IRLEARN) [body = SUBSCRIBE TYPO-L first-name last-name]

Archive: listserv@irlearn.bitnet

1-1415 **u2:** On the rock band U2.

i tjordan@hub.cs.jmu.edu (Thomas Jordan)

± u2-request@hub.cs.jmu.edu [subject = sub u2 or digest]

Archive: FTP hub.cs.jmu.edu in pub/u2

1-1416 **UCEA-L:** For members of the University Council for Educational Administration, an institutional consortium dedicated to the improvement of administrator preparation.

i pbf2@psuvm.bitnet (Bitnet: PBF2@PSUVM) (Patrick Forsyth)

± listserv@psuvm.psu.edu (Bitnet: LISTSERV@PSUVM) [body = SUBSCRIBE UCEA-L first-name last-name]

Archive: listserv@psuvm.psu.edu

1-1417 **UCP-L:** The University Computing Project.

i gerland@ubvms.cc.buffalo.edu (Jim Gerland)

± listserv@ubvm.cc.buffalo.edu (Bitnet: LISTSERV@UBVM) [body = SUBSCRIBE UCP-L first-name last-name]

Archive: listserv@ubvm.cc.buffalo.edu

Gated: ⇔ bit.listserv.ucp-l

1-1418 **UCSMON:** The UCS MONITOR Computing News from Indiana University *Moderated*

i eschlene@ucs.indiana.edu (Eric Schlene)

± listserv@iubvm.ucs.indiana.edu (Bitnet: LISTSERV@IUBVM) [body = SUBSCRIBE UCSMON first-name last-name]

Archive: listserv@iubvm.ucs.indiana.edu

1-1419 **UD-L:** For the Ultimate Dungeon, where the overworked make up questionnaires—a fantasy-spinning collective.

i opus@uriacc.bitnet (Bitnet: OPUS@URIACC) (Mark Oliver)

± `listserv@uriacc.uri.edu` (Bitnet: LISTSERV@URIACC) [body = SUBSCRIBE
   UD-L first-name last-name]

Archive: `listserv@uriacc.uri.edu`

Other: Subscription is limited. Requests will be sent to list owner for approval.

1-1420 **UFO-L:** On UFO-related phenomenon.

i `srk106@psuvm.bitnet` (Bitnet: SRK106@PSUVM) (Senthil Kumar)

± `listserv@psuvm.psu.edu` (Bitnet: LISTSERV@PSUVM) [body = SUBSCRIBE
   UFO-L first-name last-name]

Archive: `listserv@psuvm.psu.edu`

1-1421 **uk-hockey:** About ice hockey as played in and by Great Britain. Includes news, gossip, league
   tables, match reports, and results. Open to all interested in British hockey.

i ± `uk-hockey-request@cee.hw.ac.uk` (Steve Salvini)

1-1422 **ultralite-list:** For users or potential users of the original NEC UltraLite PC1701 and PC1702
   computers.

i `ultralite-list-owner@grot.starconn.com` (Brian Smithson)

± `listserv@grot.starconn.com` [body = subscribe ultralite-list first-
   name last-name]

1-1423 **undercover:** All about the Rolling Stones rock group, and associated artists.

i ± `undercover-request@snowhite.cis.uoguelph.ca.` (Steve Portigal)

Other: Also available in digest format.

1-1424 **UNIRAS:** For users of UNIRAS, device-independent computer graphics software package used
   for visualization of technical and scientific data.

i `vannes@ecn.nl` (Gerard van Nes, ECN, The Netherlands)

± `listserv@nic.surfnet.nl` (Bitnet: LISTSERV@SURFNET) [body = SUBSCRIBE
   UNIRAS first-name last-name]

Archive: `listserv@nic.surfnet.nl`

Language: English

1-1425 **Unisys:** Discussion of all Unisys products and equipment.

i ± `unisys-request@bcm.tmc.edu` (Richard H. Miller)

1-1426 **UNIVOC:** For vocational education researchers and teacher educators, managed by the National
   Center for Research in Vocational Education at UC Berkeley.

i `dissemn8@ucbcmsa.bitnet` (Bitnet: DISSEMN8@UCBCMSA)

± `listserv@cmsa.berkeley.edu` (Bitnet: LISTSERV@UCBCMSA) [body =
   SUBSCRIBE UNIVOC first-name last-name]

Archive: Monthly notebooks on `listserv@cmsa.berkeley.edu`

1-1427 **UNIX-SRC:** Unix-Sources Mailing List—redistribution.

i `unix-sources-request@pa.dec.com`

± `listserv@vm1.nodak.edu` (Bitnet: LISTSERV@NDSUVM1) [body = SUBSCRIBE
   UNIX-SRC first-name last-name]

Other: Daily digest

1-1428 **UNIX-WIZ:** Unix-Wizards mailing list—redistribution.

    i `unix-wizards-request@brl.mil`

    ± `listserv@vm1.nodak.edu` (Bitnet: `LISTSERV@NDSUVM1`) [body = `SUBSCRIBE UNIX-WIZ` first-name last-name]

    Other: Daily digest

1-1429 **UPCDATA:** On using store, chain, and market-level Universal Price Code (UPC) scanner data in econometric time series analysis, including functional forms of price elasticities, isolation of promotions, and measurement of retailer compliance with promotional agreements.

    i `sbmeade@umslvma.bitnet` (Bitnet: `SBMEADE@UMSLVMA`) (Bill Meade, Ph.D.)

    ± `listserv@umslvma.umsl.edu` (Bitnet: `LISTSERV@UMSLVMA`) [body = `SUBSCRIBE UPCDATA` first-name last-name]

    Archive: `listserv@umslvma.umsl.edu`

1-1430 **UPGRADE:** On IBM hardware upgrades for computer centers.

    i `rondot@ipfwvm.bitnet` (Bitnet: `RONDOT@IPFWVM`) (Larry Rondot)

    ± `listserv@ipfwvm.bitnet` (Bitnet: `LISTSERV@IPFWVM`) [body = `SUBSCRIBE UPGRADE` first-name last-name]

    Archive: `listserv@ipfwvm.bitnet`

1-1431 **UPS-alumni:** For alumni of the University of Puget Sound (located in Tacoma, Washington). Please note that this list is not sponsored by the University.

    ± `ups_alumni-request@stephsf.com` (Bill England)

    Other: Please include year of graduation in subscription request.

1-1432 **URANTIAL:** On the ideas in "The URANTIA Book." Topics include holism, the integration of knowledge, and consolidations of worldviews.

    i `mm24681@uafsysb.uark.edu` (Michael Million)

    ± `listserv@uafsysb.uark.edu` (Bitnet: `LISTSERV@UAFSYSB`) [body = `SUBSCRIBE URANTIAL` first-name last-name]

    Archive: Available to subscribers only.

1-1433 **URBANET:** The Urban Planning Student Network.

    i `22633urb@msu.bitnet` (Bitnet: `22633URB@MSU`) (Urban Planning)

    ± `listserv@msu.edu` (Bitnet: `LISTSERV@MSU`) [body = `SUBSCRIBE URBANET` first-name last-name]

    Archive: Available to subscribers only.

    Other: Subscription is limited. Requests will be sent to list owner for approval.

1-1434 **US-State-Department Travel Advisories:** This list is the Internet and Bitnet distribution point of the official U.S. State Department Travel Warnings and Consular Information Sheets.

    i ± `travel-advisories-request@stolaf.edu`

1-1435 **usenet-oracle:** An active, cooperative effort for creative humor. The Usenet Oracle answers any questions posed to it.

    i `oracle@cs.indiana.edu` [subject = help], `oracle-admin@cs.indiana.edu` (Steve Kinzler)

    ± `oracle-request@cs.indiana.edu` [subject = subscribe] (or subscribe to usenet newsgroup `rec.humor.oracle`)

Questions to: `oracle@cs.indiana.edu` [subject = `tell me`; body = your question]

Archive: FTP `cs.indiana.edu` in `/pub/oracle` or `mailserv@cs.indiana.edu` [body = `help`]

1-1436 **USMARC-L:** The USMARC Advisory Group Forum, on the implementation, maintenance, changes, and development of the USMARC formats and other related topics. Includes discussions on proposals and discussion papers prepared for the Machine-Readable Bibliographic Information Committee (MARBI). Also a distribution list for MARBI meeting agendas. Maintains a file archive that includes proposals and discussion papers prepared for MARBI, MARBI minutes, and some USMARC format documentation. *Moderated*

i `rgue@seq1.loc.gov` (Rebecca Guenther)

± `listserv@maine.edu` [body = `SUBSCRIBE USMARC-L` first-name last-name]

Archive: `listserv@sun7.loc.gov`

1-1437 **USNPLIST:** On the United States Newspaper Program (USNP).

i `tmccarty@leo.vsla.edu` (Trudy McCarty)

± `listserver@leo.vsla.edu` [body = `Subscribe USNPLIST` first-name last-name]

Other: listserver NOT LISTSERV

1-1438 **USTC85-L:** For discussion among past and current students at the University of Science and Technology in China.

i `snow@owlnet.rice.edu` (Jun Wu)

± `listserv@ricevm1.rice.edu` (Bitnet: `LISTSERV@RICEVM1`) [body = `SUBSCRIBE USTC85-L` first-name last-name]

1-1439 **utne-salon-list:** Discussion relating to the Utne Reader Neighborhoood Salon Association, a group facilitating community discussion groups around the country where interested citizens can meet with other neighbors and community members to discuss any topics of interest, be they deeply philosophical or trivially important.

i ± `utne-salon-request@netcom.com` (Bill Sheppard)

Other: Inquiries regarding the Utne Reader or joining a salon should be addressed to `utnereader@mr.net`

1-1440 **UTS-L:** On Amdahl/UTS environment.

i `doug@ysub.bitnet` (Bitnet: `DOUG@YSUB`) (Doug Sewell)

± `listserv@vm.gmd.de` (Bitnet: `LISTSERV@DEARN`) [body = `SUBSCRIBE UTS-L` first-name last-name]

Archive: `listserv@vm.gmd.de`

1-1441 **UUG-dist:** Discussion of Unify Corporations Database products including Unify, Accell/IDS, Accell/SQL and Accell/"generic database engine."

i `uug-dist-request@dsi.com` (Syd Weinstein)

± `uug-dist-request@dsi.com` [subject = `add`]

1-1442 **UVP-D:** For discussions of new or potential features in the Update Verification Program (UVP). The UVP accepts updates to the BITNET network database (BITEARN NODES) in a specified format, allowing BITNET node, site, and member adminstrators to control their own network database information.

i robinson@bitnic.bitnet (Bitnet: ROBINSON@BITNIC) (Andy Robinson)

± listserv@bitnic.educom.edu (Bitnet: LISTSERV@BITNIC) [body = SUBSCRIBE UVP-D first-name last-name]

Archive: listserv@bitnic.educom.edu

1-1443 **VAMPYRES:** On Vampiric lore, fact and fiction, including original stories, movie reviews, group original stories (multiple authors to the same story), and lists of movies, TV shows, books, articles, stories.

i wilder@guvax.bitnet (Bitnet: WILDER@GUVAX) (Jim Wilderotter)

± listserv@guvm.ccf.georgetown.edu (Bitnet: LISTSERV@GUVM) [body = SUBSCRIBE VAMPYRES first-name last-name]

1-1444 **van:** On the rock musician Van Morrison.

i zen@sun.com (Dan Farmer)

± van-request@death.corp.sun.com

1-1445 **VECSRV-L:** For users of the vector facilities of the IBM 3090 computer at Ege University.

i bilako@trearn.bitnet (Bitnet: BILAKO@TREARN) (Ahmet Koltuksuz)

± listserv@trearn.bitnet (Bitnet: LISTSERV@TREARN) [body = SUBSCRIBE VECSRV-L first-name last-name]

Archive: listserv@trearn.bitnet

Language: Turkish

1-1446 **VECTOR-L:** For users of the IBM 3090 vector facility at any location.

i t4327@unbmvs1.bitnet (Bitnet: T4327@UNBMVS1) (List Management)

± listserv@unb.ca (Bitnet: LISTSERV@UNBVM1) [body = SUBSCRIBE VECTOR-L first-name last-name]

Archive: listserv@unb.ca

1-1447 **VETCAI-L:** On computer-assisted instruction in veterinary medicine.

i oblandr@ksuvm.bitnet (Bitnet: OBLANDR@KSUVM)

± listserv@ksuvm.ksu.edu (Bitnet: LISTSERV@KSUVM) [body = SUBSCRIBE VETCAI-L first-name last-name]

Archive: listserv@ksuvm.ksu.edu

1-1448 **VETLIB-L:** On veterinary medicine library issues and information.

i kok@vtvm1.bitnet (Bitnet: KOK@VTVM1) (Vicki Kok)

± listserv@vtvm2.cc.vt.edu (Bitnet: LISTSERV@VTVM2) [body = SUBSCRIBE VETLIB-L first-name last-name]

Archive: listserv@vtvm2.cc.vt.edu

1-1449 **VETTE-L:** On Corvettes, including shows around the country, service information, and more.

i osdtm@emuvm1.bitnet (Bitnet: OSDTM@EMUVM1)

± listserv@emuvm1.cc.emory.edu (Bitnet: LISTSERV@EMUVM1) [body = SUBSCRIBE VETTE-L first-name last-name]

Archive: listserv@emuvm1.cc.emory.edu

1-1450 **vettes:** For Corvette owners and enthusiasts to talk about anything about America's great sports car.

i hackney@compaq.com (Greg Hackney)

± vettes-request@chiller.compaq.com

Archive: FTP chiller.compaq.com in /pub/vettes, Listserv listserv@asuvm.inre.asu.edu

1-1451 **VFORT-L:** For users of VS-Fortran, a Fortran compiler distributed by IBM that runs under VM, MVS, and AIX.

i jimj@jhuvm.bitnet (Bitnet: JIMJ@JHUVM) (Jim Jones)

± listserv@jhuvm.hcf.jhu.edu (Bitnet: LISTSERV@JHUVM) [body = SUBSCRIBE VFORT-L first-name last-name] or listserv@ebcesca1.bitnet (Bitnet: LISTSERV@EBCESCA1) [body = SUBSCRIBE VFORT-L first-name last-name]

Archive: listserv@jhuvm.hcf.jhu.edu or listserv@ebcesca1.bitnet

1-1452 **VICTORIA:** For sharing of ideas and information about all aspects of 19th-century British culture and society.

i pleary@ucs.indiana.edu (Patrick Leary)

± listserv@iubvm.ucs.indiana.edu (Bitnet: LISTSERV@IUBVM) [body = SUBSCRIBE VICTORIA first-name last-name]

Archive: listserv@iubvm.ucs.indiana.edu

Other: Digest

1-1453 **VIDNET-L:** Specifically for the exchange of information between professionals who operate video networks at college campuses.

i jstephen@uga.bitnet (Bitnet: JSTEPHEN@UGA) (John Stephens, IRC)

± listserv@uga.cc.uga.edu (Bitnet: LISTSERV@UGA) [body = SUBSCRIBE VIDNET-L first-name last-name]

Archive: listserv@uga.cc.uga.edu

Other: Subscription is limited. Requests will be sent to list owner for approval.

1-1454 **VIETNET:** Gateway to Usenet forum on Vietnamese culture and News. Please use only if you don't have Usenet access.

i hho@scf.usc.edu (Hung P. Ho, Jr.) or anh@media.mit.edu (Viet Anh)

± listserv@vm.usc.edu (Bitnet: LISTSERV@USCVM) [body = SUBSCRIBE VIETNET first-name last-name]

Gated: ⇔ soc.cuture.vietnamese

1-1455 **VIFLIS:** The Virtual Int'l Faculty in Library and Information Science.

i gwhitney@arizvms.bitnet (Bitnet: GWHITNEY@ARIZVMS) (Gretchen Whitney)

± listserv@arizvm1.ccit.arizona.edu (Bitnet: LISTSERV@ARIZVM1) [body = SUBSCRIBE VIFLIS first-name last-name]

Archive: listserv@arizvm1.ccit.arizona.edu

1-1456 **VIGIS-L:** On virtual reality and geographical information systems. *Moderated*

i navanax@u.washington.edu (Thomas M. Edwards)

± listserv@uwavm.u.washington.edu (Bitnet: LISTSERV@UWAVM) [body = SUBSCRIBE VIGIS-L first-name last-name]

Archive: `listserv@uwavm.u.washington.edu`

1-1457 **VISBAS-L:** On Microsoft's Visual Basic computer programming language.

i `x005rh@tamvm1.bitnet` (Bitnet: X005RH@TAMVM1) (Rick Huff)

± `listserv@tamvm1.tamu.edu` (Bitnet: LISTSERV@TAMVM1) [body = SUBSCRIBE VISBAS-L first-name last-name]

Archive: Available to subscribers only.

1-1458 **Vision:** For Christians to discuss visions, prophecies, and spiritual gifts. *Moderated*

i ± `pruss@math.ubc.ca`

Archive: e-mail to *i*

Other: Anonymous posting available to `an22936@anon.penet.fi`

1-1459 **Vivisect - Australian Industrial and Electronic Music:** "Industrial-culture" events are announced and discussed. Radio, band, nightclub lists distributed regularly.

i ± `joe@mullara.met.unimelb.edu.au` (Joe Stojsic)

1-1460 **VIZANTIJA:** News, editorials, views, public actions focused on Serbian issues.

i ± `dimitrije@buenga.bu.edu` (Dimitrije Stamenovic)

1-1461 **VM-SHOW:** Monthly comics magazine in Turkish. *Moderated*

i `sysadm1@trearn.bitnet` (Bitnet: SYSADM1@TREARN) or `oprj50@trearn.bitnet` (Bitnet: OPRJ50@TREARN)

± `listserv@trearn.bitnet` (Bitnet: LISTSERV@TREARN) [body = SUBSCRIBE VM-SHOW first-name last-name]

Archive: `listserv@trearn.bitnet`

Language: Turkish

1-1462 **VMS-L:** The VMS give-and-take forum.

i `eric@searn.bitnet` (Bitnet: ERIC@SEARN) (Eric Thomas)

± `listserv@searn.sunet.se` (Bitnet: LISTSERV@SEARN) [body = SUBSCRIBE VMS-L first-name last-name]

Archive: `listserv@searn.sunet.se`

1-1463 **VMS-STOR:** For VMS Store administrators.

i `eric@searn.bitnet` (Bitnet: ERIC@SEARN) (Eric Thomas)

± `listserv@searn.sunet.se` (Bitnet: LISTSERV@SEARN) [body = SUBSCRIBE VMS-STOR first-name last-name]

Archive: Available to subscribers only.

1-1464 **VMSLSV-L:** The VAX/VMS LISTSERV.

i `gerland@ubvms.cc.buffalo.edu` (Jim Gerland)

± `listserv@ubvm.cc.buffalo.edu` (Bitnet: LISTSERV@UBVM) [body = SUBSCRIBE VMSLSV-L first-name last-name]

Archive: `listserv@ubvm.cc.buffalo.edu`

Gated: ⇔ `bit.listserv.vmslsv-l`

1-1465 **VMSTEX-L:** For users of TeX on VAX/VMS systems.

i `dhosek@hmcvax.bitnet` (Bitnet: DHOSEK@HMCVAX)

± `listserv@uicvm.bitnet` (Bitnet: `LISTSERV@UICVM`) [body = `SUBSCRIBE VMSTEX-L first-name last-name`]

Archive: `listserv@uicvm.bitnet`

1-1466 **VNEWS-L:** On VNEWS.

i `gerland@ubvms.cc.buffalo.edu` (Jim Gerland)

± `listserv@ubvm.cc.buffalo.edu` (Bitnet: `LISTSERV@UBVM`) [body = `SUBSCRIBE VNEWS-L first-name last-name`]

1-1467 **VNIX-L:** On running a virtual copy of the Unix operating system under the VM operating system.

i `troth@rice.edu` (Rick Troth)

± `listserv@tamvm1.tamu.edu` (Bitnet: `LISTSERV@TAMVM1`) [body = `SUBSCRIBE VNIX-L first-name last-name`] or `listserv@ricevm1.rice.edu` (Bitnet: `LISTSERV@RICEVM1`) [body = `SUBSCRIBE VNIX-L first-name last-name`]

1-1468 **VOCNET:** For vocational education practioners, managed by the National Center for Research in Vocational Education at UC Berkeley.

i `dissemn8@ucbcmsa.bitnet` (Bitnet: `DISSEMN8@UCBCMSA`)

± `listserv@cmsa.berkeley.edu` (Bitnet: `LISTSERV@UCBCMSA`) [body = `SUBSCRIBE VOCNET first-name last-name`]

Archive: Monthly notebooks on `listserv@cmsa.berkeley.edu`

1-1469 **VOLCANO:** On volcanology, the study of volcanoes. *Moderated*

i `aijhf@asuacad.bitnet` (Bitnet: `AIJHF@ASUACAD`)

± `listserv@asuvm.inre.asu.edu` (Bitnet: `LISTSERV@ASUACAD`) [body = `SUBSCRIBE VOLCANO first-name last-name`]

Archive: Available to subscribers only.

Other: Subscription is limited. Requests will be sent to list owner for approval.

1-1470 **volvo:** Discussion of Volvo automobiles —ownership, repair, maintenance, performance driving. International membership.

i ± `volvo-net-request@me.rochester.edu` (Tim Takahashi)

Language: English

1-1471 **VPIEJ-L:** A discussion list for electronic publishing issues, especially those related to Scholarly Electronic Journals. Topics for discussion include SGML, PostScript, and other e-journal formats; as well as software and hardware considerations for creation of, storage of, and access to e-journals.

i `jpowell@vtvm1.cc.vt.edu`

± `listserv@vtvm1.bitnet` [body = `SUB VPIEJ-L first-name last-name`]

Archive: `listserv@vtvm1.bitnet` (Bitnet: `LISTSERV@VTVM1`) [body = `INDEX VPIEJ-L`]

Gated: ⇔ `bit.listserv.vpiej-1`; WAIS VPIEJ-L (in the directory-of-servers list); WWW `http://borg.lib.vt.edu/z-borg/www/scholar.html`

1-1472 **VRA-L:** For members of the Visual Resources Association.

i `chilker@uafsysb.bitnet` (Bitnet: `CHILKER@UAFSYSB`) (Christine Hilker)

± listserv@uafsysb.uark.edu (Bitnet: LISTSERV@UAFSYSB) [body = SUBSCRIBE VRA-L first-name last-name]

Archive: Available to subscribers only.

1-1473 **VRAPP-L:** Scholarly discussion on the applications of virtual reality. *Moderated*

i gbnewby@uiucvmd.bitnet (Bitnet: GBNEWBY@UIUCVMD) (Gregory B. Newby)

± listserv@vmd.cso.uiuc.edu (Bitnet: LISTSERV@UIUCVMD) [body = SUBSCRIBE VRAPP-L first-name last-name]

Archive: listserv@vmd.cso.uiuc.edu

Other: Weekly digest

1-1474 **VTLSLIST:** For users of VTLS, a library software package used to manage the operations of libraries. *Moderated*

i buddyl@vtvm1.bitnet (Bitnet: BUDDYL@VTVM1) (Buddy Litchfield)

± listserv@vtvm1.cc.vt.edu (Bitnet: LISTSERV@VTVM1) [body = SUBSCRIBE VTLSLIST first-name last-name]

Archive: Available to subscribers only.

Gated: ⇔ sci.virtual-worlds.apps

Other: Subscription is limited. Requests will be sent to list owner for approval.

1-1475 **VWAR-L:** For communication among veterans, scholars, and students of the Vietnam War—the networking component of the Vietnam Veterans Oral History and Folklore Project.

i fishlm@snybufva.bitnet (Bitnet: FISHLM@SNYBUFVA) (Lydia Fish)

± listserv@ubvm.cc.buffalo.edu (Bitnet: LISTSERV@UBVM) [body = SUBSCRIBE VWAR-L first-name last-name]

Archive: listserv@ubvm.cc.buffalo.edu

Other: Daily digest

1-1476 **W5AC:** For members of the Amateur Radio Club at Texas AandM, and others interested in ham radios.

i jwj2047@sigma.tamu.edu (Joe Jurecka - N5PYK) or troth@rice.edu (Rick Troth - N5VDC)

± listserv@tamvm1.tamu.edu (Bitnet: LISTSERV@TAMVM1) [body = SUBSCRIBE W5AC first-name last-name]

1-1477 **WAC-L:** Writing Across the Curriculum, an open forum for college-level administrators, faculty, and staff to exchange ideas about writing in the disciplines.

i hawisher@ux1.cso.uiuc.edu (Gail E. Hawisher)

± listserv@vmd.cso.uiuc.edu (Bitnet: LISTSERV@UIUCVMD) [body = SUBSCRIBE WAC-L first-name last-name] Manager = mhocks@ux1.cso.uiuc.edu (Mary Hocks)

Archive: listserv@vmd.cso.uiuc.edu

1-1478 **wais-discussion:** On electronic publishing issues in general and Wide Area Information Servers (WAIS) in particular. *Moderated*

± wais-discussion-request@think.com [body = add wais-discussion]

Archive: FTP quake.think.com

Other: Digest format (~ weekly)

1-1479 **wais-talk:** For implementors and developers of Wide Area Information Servers (WAIS). This is a techie "talk" list; please use the `alt.wais` newsgroup for support, and send bug fixes, etc. to `bug-wais@think.com`.

± `wais-talk-request@think.com` [body = `add wais-talk`]

Archive: FTP `quake.think.com`

1-1480 **WAKONS-L:** For discussion among individuals who have participated in the Wakonse Conference on improving teaching at the undergraduate level.

i `psywood@mizzou1.bitnet` (Bitnet: `PSYWOOD@MIZZOU1`) (Phil Wood)

± `listserv@mizzou1.missouri.edu` (Bitnet: `LISTSERV@MIZZOU1`) [body = SUBSCRIBE WAKONS-L first-name last-name]

1-1481 **walkers-in-darkness:** For sufferers from depression and/or bipolar disorder, and affected friends.

i ± `walkers-request@world.std.com` (David Harmon)

1-1482 **WATER-L:** For Washington State water quality agents.

i `pace@wsuvm1.bitnet` (Bitnet: `PACE@WSUVM1`) or `wright@wsuvm1.bitnet` (Bitnet: `WRIGHT@WSUVM1`)

± `listserv@wsuvm1.csc.wsu.edu` (Bitnet: `LISTSERV@WSUVM1`) [body = SUBSCRIBE WATER-L first-name last-name]

Archive: `listserv@wsuvm1.csc.wsu.edu`

1-1483 **weights:** On all aspects of using weights in exercise.

i ± `weights-request@fa.disney.com` (Michael Sullivan)

1-1484 **WEIRD-L:** For disturbing/bizarre/offensive short stories, poetry, and ramblings. Not for humor or jokes. Only postings original with the submittor will be accepted. *Moderated*

i `jeremy@apple.com` (Dep Settlement)

± `listserv@brownvm.brown.edu` (Bitnet: `LISTSERV@BROWNVM`) [body = SUBSCRIBE WEIRD-L first-name last-name]

Archive: `listserv@brownvm.brown.edu`

1-1485 **WELSH-L:** On the Welsh, Breton, and Cornish languages.

i `briony@cstr.edinburgh.ac.uk` (Briony Williams)

± `listserv@irlearn.bitnet` (Bitnet: `LISTSERV@IRLEARN`) [body = SUBSCRIBE WELSH-L first-name last-name]

Archive: `listserv@irlearn.bitnet`

Language: Welsh, Breton, Cornish, English

1-1486 **WFW-L:** On Microsoft Windows for Workgroups.

i `greg_bean@umbcadmn.bitnet` (Bitnet: `GREG_BEAN@UMBCADMN`) (Greg Bean)

± `listserv@umdd.umd.edu` (Bitnet: `LISTSERV@UMDD`) [body = SUBSCRIBE WFW-L first-name last-name]

Archive: `listserv@umdd.umd.edu`

1-1487 **WH-NEWS:** A newsletter about women's health.

i `shirlee@carson.u.washington.edu` (Shirlee Cooper)

± `listserv@uwavm.u.washington.edu` (Bitnet: `LISTSERV@UWAVM`) [body =

SUBSCRIBE WH-NEWS first-name last-name]

    Archive: `listserv@uwavm.u.washington.edu`

1-1488 **wheel-to-wheel:** For people interested in participation in auto racing as driver, worker, or crew.

    i ± `wheeltowheel-request@abingdon.eng.sun.com` (Andy Banta)

1-1489 **wildnet:** On computing, statistics, and other quantitative issues in fisheries and wildlife biology. Topics include Geographic Information Systems (GIS), ecological modelling, conference announcements, software reviews, etc.

    i ± `zaphod!pnwc!wildnet-request@access.usask.ca` or `wildnet-request@access.usask.ca` (Eric Woodsworth)

1-1490 **WIN-VAX:** On MS-Windows interfaces to VAX-Rdb

    i `mis5000@umbcadmn.bitnet`

    ± `listserv@umdd.umd.edu` (Bitnet: `LISTSERV@UMDD`) [body = SUBSCRIBE WIN-VAX first-name last-name]

    Archive: `listserv@umdd.umd.edu`

1-1491 **WIN3-L:** For users of Microsoft Windows, version 3.+.

    i `ctct100@uicvmc.bitnet` (Bitnet: `CTCT100@UICVMC`) (Tom Cervenka)

    ± `listserv@uicvm.bitnet` or `uicvm.uic.edu` (Bitnet: `LISTSERV@UICVM`) [body = SUBSCRIBE WIN3-L first-name last-name]

    Archive: Available to subscribers only.

1-1492 **windsurfing:** For boardsailing enthusiasts all over the world.

    i ± `windsurfing-request@gcm.com`

1-1493 **WINTCP-L:** On the Wollongong WIN/TCP (TCP/IP for VMS) software package.

    i `gerland@ubvms.cc.buffalo.edu` (Jim Gerland)

    ± `listserv@ubvm.cc.buffalo.edu` (Bitnet: `LISTSERV@UBVM`) [body = SUBSCRIBE WINTCP-L first-name last-name]

    Gated: ⇔ `vmsnet.networks.tcp-ip.wintcp`

1-1494 **WIOLE-L:** On writing intensive online learning environments.

    i `lceric@mizzou1.bitnet` (Bitnet: `LCERIC@MIZZOU1`) (Eric Crump)

    ± `listserv@mizzou1.missouri.edu` (Bitnet: `LISTSERV@MIZZOU1`) [body = SUBSCRIBE WIOLE-L first-name last-name]

    Archive: `listserv@mizzou1.missouri.edu`

1-1495 **WISE:** Workshop on Information Systems Economics.

    i `u26300@uicvm.bitnet` (Bitnet: `U26300@UICVM`)

    ± `listserv@uicvm.bitnet` (Bitnet: `LISTSERV@UICVM`) [body = SUBSCRIBE WISE first-name last-name]

    Archive: Available to subscribers only.

1-1496 **WITSENDO:** For women who suffer from endometriosis, emphasizing coping with the disease and its treatment, and sharing information on current treatments, research and educational literature. *Moderated*

    i `roihar@crl.aecl.ca` (Pamela Thompson)

    ± `listserv@dartcms1.dartmouth.edu` (Bitnet: `LISTSERV@DARTCMS1`) [body =

SUBSCRIBE WITSENDO first-name last-name]

Archive: listserv@dartcms1.dartmouth.edu

1-1497 **WMN-HLTH:** For discussion of women's health issues, including researchers, healthcare professionals, and educators as well as lay people.

i shirlee@carson.u.washington.edu (Shirlee Cooper)

± listserv@uwavm.u.washington.edu (Bitnet: LISTSERV@UWAVM) [body = SUBSCRIBE WMN-HLTH first-name last-name]

Archive: listserv@uwavm.u.washington.edu

1-1498 **WMST-L:** For scholarly discussion of women's studies teaching, research, and program administration.

i korenman@umbc.bitnet (Bitnet: KORENMAN@UMBC) (Joan Korenman)

± listserv@umdd.umd.edu (Bitnet: LISTSERV@UMDD) [body = SUBSCRIBE WMST-L first-name last-name]

Archive: listserv@umdd.umd.edu

1-1499 **WMUN-L:** About the World Model United Nations 1993. *Moderated*

i ups500@dbnrhrz1.bitnet (Bitnet: UPS500@DBNRHRZ1) (Markus Schlegel)

± listserv@csearn.bitnet (Bitnet: LISTSERV@CSEARN) [body = SUBSCRIBE WMUN-L first-name last-name]

Archive: listserv@csearn.bitnet

1-1500 **WOODWORK:** On woodworking.

i rondot@ipfwvm.bitnet (Bitnet: RONDOT@IPFWVM) (Larry Rondot)

± listserv@ipfwvm.bitnet (Bitnet: LISTSERV@IPFWVM) [body = SUBSCRIBE WOODWORK first-name last-name]

Archive: listserv@ipfwvm.bitnet

Other: Daily digest. For weekly digest, send SUBSCRIBE WOODWEEK instead.

1-1501 **WORLD-L:** On non-Eurocentric world history.

i brownh@ccsua.ctstateu.edu (Haines Brown)

± listserv@ubvm.cc.buffalo.edu (Bitnet: LISTSERV@UBVM) [body = SUBSCRIBE WORLD-L first-name last-name]

1-1502 **WPCORP-L:** On WordPerfect Corporation Products.

i gerland@ubvms.cc.buffalo.edu (Jim Gerland)

± listserv@ubvm.cc.buffalo.edu (Bitnet: LISTSERV@UBVM) [body = SUBSCRIBE WPCORP-L first-name last-name]

Archive: listserv@ubvm.cc.buffalo.edu

Gated: ⇔ bit.listserv.wpcorp-l

1-1503 **WPWIN-L:** On WordPerfect for Windows.

i srsch@mvax.cc.conncoll.edu

± listserv@ubvm.cc.buffalo.edu (Bitnet: LISTSERV@UBVM) [body = SUBSCRIBE WPWIN-L first-name last-name]

Archive: listserv@ubvm.cc.buffalo.edu

Gated: ⇔ bit.listserv.wpwin-l

Other: Weekly digest

1-1504 **WRITERS:** For professional writers and those who aspire to write, featuring announcements of conferences, workshops, new publication opportunities.

i carey@plains.nodak.edu (Pat Carey)

± listserv@vm1.nodak.edu (Bitnet: LISTSERV@NDSUVM1) [body = SUBSCRIBE WRITERS first-name last-name]

Archive: Available to subscribers only.

1-1505 **WROCLAW:** For the alumni of Wroclaw Universities.

i misiak@kchf.ch-pwr.wroc.edu.pl (Pawel Misiak)

± listserv@plearn.edu.pl (Bitnet: LISTSERV@PLEARN) [body = SUBSCRIBE WROCLAW first-name last-name]

Archive: Available to subscribers only.

Language: Polish

1-1506 **wxsat:** Distribution of NOAA status and prediction bulletins for the GOES and polar weather satellites, and discussions on weather satellites, direct readout ground stations, and related topics. The list is open to professional, educational, and amateur direct readout users, and those planning to use of direct readout systems.

i ± wxsat-request@ssg.com (Richard B. Emerson)

1-1507 **x-ada:** On interfaces and bindings for an Ada interface to the X window system.

i ± x-ada-request@expo.lcs.mit.edu

1-1508 **XCULT-L:** For discussing intercultural communication. Topics range from non-dominant cultures in the U.S. to corporate cultures to the use of nonverbal methods in international communication.

i oliver@dhvx20.csudh.edu (Oliver Seely)

± listserv@psuvm.psu.edu (Bitnet: LISTSERV@PSUVM) [body = SUBSCRIBE XCULT-L first-name last-name]

Archive: listserv@psuvm.psu.edu

1-1509 **XCULT-X:** For interdisciplinary discussions of communication philosophy, theory, and practice via computer-mediated communication.

± listserv@umrvmb.umr.edu (Bitnet: LISTSERV@UMRVMB) [body = SUBSCRIBE XCULT-X first-name last-name]

Archive: Available to subscribers only.

1-1510 **XEROX-L:** On Xerox centralized and decentralized printing systems. Topics for discussion include host interfaces (hardware and software issues), printer control languages, fonts, printing technology, and host-based software products.

i x066tr@tamvm1.bitnet (Bitnet: X066TR@TAMVM1) (Tom Reid)

± listserv@tamvm1.tamu.edu (Bitnet: LISTSERV@TAMVM1) [body = SUBSCRIBE XEROX-L first-name last-name]

Archive: listserv@tamvm1.tamu.edu

1-1511 **XF-L:** On the XF software which is used to build X-Windows interfaces for Tcl/Tk based software. For further information on Tcl/Tk, see Usenet group `comp.lang.tcl`.

i `axel@avalanche.cs.tu-berlin.de` (Axel Mahler)

± `listserv@db0tui11.bitnet` (Bitnet: `LISTSERV@DB0TUI11`) [body =
`SUBSCRIBE XF-L` first-name last-name]

Archive: `listserv@db0tui11.bitnet`

1-1512 **XF-PATCH:** Patches for XF-L list.

i `axel@avalanche.cs.tu-berlin.de` (Axel Mahler)

± `listserv@db0tui11.bitnet` (Bitnet: `LISTSERV@DB0TUI11`) [body =
`SUBSCRIBE XF-PATCH` first-name last-name]

Archive: `listserv@db0tui11.bitnet`

1-1513 **XGKS:** On the University of Illinois XGKS package (a level 2C implementation of GKS for the
X Window System.

i ± `xgks-request@unidata.ucar.edu` (Steve Emmerson)

Archive: gopher `unidata.ucar.edu`

1-1514 **XMAILBUG:** Mailer release 2.0 bug list.

i `johnw@pucc.bitnet` (Bitnet: `JOHNW@PUCC`)

± `listserv@pucc.princeton.edu` (Bitnet: `LISTSERV@PUCC`) [body =
`SUBSCRIBE XMAILBUG` first-name last-name]

Archive: `listserv@pucc.princeton.edu`

1-1515 **xopen-testing:** Forum on testing operating systems for conformance to the X/OPEN Portability
Guide (XPG), including Issue 3 (XPG3) and later.

i ± `xopen-testing-request@uel.co.uk` (Andrew Josey)

1-1516 **xpress-list:** Forum for users of the X*Press X*Change (an information service for personal computers, delivered over some cable television systems in the US and Canada).

i `xpress-list-owner@grot.starconn.com` (Brian Smithson)

± `listserv@grot.starconn.com` [body = subscribe `xpress-list` first-name
last-name]

Archive: Mailserv `listserv@grot.starconn.com`

1-1517 **XTROPY-L:** Discussion of extropian ideas such as life extension, nanotechnology, libertarian-
ism, and technology.

i `majcher@acsu.buffalo.edu` (Marc Majcher)

± `listserv@ubvm.cc.buffalo.edu` (Bitnet: `LISTSERV@UBVM`) [body =
`SUBSCRIBE XTROPY-L` first-name last-name]

Archive: `listserv@ubvm.cc.buffalo.edu`

Gated: ⇔ `Bit.Listserv.XTROPY-L`

1-1518 **XXI:** For posting articles on science that may be of interest to XXI, a weekly Chilean magazine,
and other mass media outlets. *Moderated*

i `nluco@uchcecvm.bitnet` (Bitnet: `NLUCO@UCHCECVM`) (Nicolas Luco)

± `listserv@uchcecvm.bitnet` (Bitnet: `LISTSERV@UCHCECVM`) [body =
`SUBSCRIBE XXI` first-name last-name]

Archive: `listserv@uchcecvm.bitnet`

Language: Spanish, Portugese, English

1-1519 **Y-RIGHTS:** On Kid/Teen rights.

i drz@sjuvm.bitnet (Bitnet: DRZ@SJUVM)

± listserv@stjohns.edu (Bitnet: LISTSERV@SJUVM) [body = SUBSCRIBE Y-RIGHTS first-name last-name]

Archive: listserv@stjohns.edu

1-1520 **YACHT-L:** On yachting and amateur boat-building.

i gandalf@grearn.bitnet (Bitnet: GANDALF@GREARN) (Kostas Antonopoulos)

± listserv@grearn.bitnet (Bitnet: LISTSERV@GREARN) [body = SUBSCRIBE YACHT-L first-name last-name]

Archive: listserv@grearn.bitnet

1-1521 **YARDIMCI:** Discussions about IBM 3090 systems.

i nur@trearn.bitnet (Bitnet: NUR@TREARN) (Nur Zincir)

± listserv@trearn.bitnet (Bitnet: LISTSERV@TREARN) [body = SUBSCRIBE YARDIMCI first-name last-name]

Archive: listserv@trearn.bitnet

Language: Turkish

1-1522 **YESCAMP:** For organizers of YESCamps, which are summer camps intended to make math and science fun to learn for students in grades 5 to 8.

i cfes@jupiter.sun.csd.unb.ca (Canadian Federation of Engineering Students)

± listserv@unb.ca (Bitnet: LISTSERV@UNBVM1) [body = SUBSCRIBE YESCAMP first-name last-name]

1-1523 **YONEYLEM:** For discussion of operations research among Turkish scientists and engineers.

i eince@basalt.mines.colorado.edu (Erdem Ince) or h.r.yazgan@qmw.ac.uk (Harun Yazgan)tex5had@cms1.leeds.ac.uk (Haluk Demirbag)

± listserv@tritu.bitnet (Bitnet: LISTSERV@TRITU) [body = SUBSCRIBE YONEYLEM first-name last-name]

Archive: listserv@tritu.bitnet

Language: Turkish

Gated: ⇔ itu.listserv.yoneylem

1-1524 **YOUTHNET:** For researchers, therapists, and other service providers concerned with youth and adolescence.

i inme100@indycms.bitnet (Bitnet: INME100@INDYCMS) (Sue Steinmetz)

± listserv@indycms.iupui.edu (Bitnet: LISTSERV@INDYCMS) [body = SUBSCRIBE YOUTHNET first-name last-name]

Archive: listserv@indycms.iupui.edu

1-1525 **YSN (The Young Scientists' Network):** Activism on employment issues for scientists just beginning their careers. No requirements to join.

i ysn-request@zoyd.ee.washington.edu [subject = help]

± ysn-adm@zoyd.ee.washington.edu (John Sahr)

Archive: FTP `lupulus.ssc.gov`

1-1526 **ytsejam:** About the rock group Dream Theater.

 i `jhough@qualcomm.com`

 ± `ytsejam-request@bnf.com` [body = `subscribe ytsejam` first-name last-name]

1-1527 **YUNUS:** For Turkish TeX users.

 i `akgul@trbilun.bitnet` (Bitnet: `AKGUL@TRBILUN`) (Mustafa Akgul)

 ± `listserv@vm.cc.metu.edu.tr` (Bitnet: `LISTSERV@TRMETU`) [body = `SUBSCRIBE YUNUS` first-name last-name]

 Archive: `listserv@vm.cc.metu.edu.tr`

1-1528 **Z-cars:** For those interested in Datsun/Nissan Z cars.

 i ± `z-car-request@dixie.com` (John De Armond)

1-1529 **Z-SENATU:** Reports from sessions of Nicolaus Copernicus University Senate.

 i `jkob@risc.phys.torun.edu.pl` (Jacek Kobus)

 ± `listserv@pltumk11.bitnet` (Bitnet: `LISTSERV@PLTUMK11`) [body = `SUBSCRIBE Z-SENATU` first-name last-name]

 Archive: Available to subscribers only.

 Other: Subscription is limited. Requests will be sent to list owner for approval.

1-1530 **Z3950IW:** On implementation of Z39.50, a national standard protocol that defining rules for search and retrieval of information and using a client/server model.

 i `fclmth@nervm.bitnet` (Bitnet: `FCLMTH@NERVM`)

 ± `listserv@nervm.nerdc.ufl.edu` (Bitnet: `LISTSERV@NERVM`) [body = `SUBSCRIBE Z3950IW` first-name last-name]

 Archive: `listserv@nervm.nerdc.ufl.edu`

1-1531 **ZForum:** On the formal specification notation "Z."

 i ± `zforum-request@comlab.ox.ac.uk` (Jonathan Bowen)

 Archive: FTP `ftp.comlab.ox.ac.uk` in `/pub/Zforum`

 Gated: ⇔ `comp.specification.z`

1-1532 **ZINES-L:** On zines, and other alternative publications, both electronic and contemporary, including publication methods, subscription bases, and critiques.

 i `opus@uriacc.bitnet` (Bitnet: `OPUS@URIACC`) (Mark Oliver)

 ± `listserv@uriacc.uri.edu` (Bitnet: `LISTSERV@URIACC`) [body = `SUBSCRIBE ZINES-L` first-name last-name]

 Archive: `listserv@uriacc.uri.edu`

2. USENET NEWSGROUPS

Entry Format: Groups are listed indented hierarchically and in alphabetical order by the left-most subname in the group's name. For example, the group `rec.audio.car` would be found doubly indented under `.car` in the `.audio` section of the `rec` listings, like this:

Item
Number

2-n   **rec**   **Groups on recreational topics**

     ...

2-q   **.audio** High fidelity audio

       ...

2-s   **.car**   Discussions of automobile audio systems.

In some cases, the intermediate group name is descriptive only, and does not represent a group in itself. These entries are in sans-serif type, and the description of the class of groups represented by the subgroup name will be in square brackets. For instance:

2-n   **rec**   **Groups on recreational topics**

     ...

2-q   **.arts**   **[Groups about the "arts" (broadly defined)]**

       ...

2-s   **.bodyart**   tattoos and body decoration discussions.

Where to Find It: A complete list of the Usenet newsgroups is maintained by David Lawrence and posted monthly to the newsgroups `news.announce.newusers`, `news.groups`, and others. Newsgroups are being added and deleted all the time, so please check that list for the most up-to-date information. The list in this book was taken from the September 1993 posting, was edited, and is reprinted here by permission. You can retrieve a copy of the current list by FTP from `ftp.uu.net` in the `/networking/news/config` directory.

Netiquette: Netnews is a public forum. Anything you post may be read by hundreds, if not thousands, of people. Chris Anderson wrote the following in his article on Netnews etiquette: "Imagine a stadium with every seat filled. Now imagine that you have to get up in front of this crowd and that you have to read OUT LOUD anything you post in news. Would that make you nervous? Would you be willing to stand by your words under that scrutiny? No? Then don't post the article to Netnews. E-mail it instead."

Netnews provides true freedom of the press. For the first time in history you don't have to own a press to publish. But any freedom entails a complementary set of responsibilities. Below is a list of some of the things you should keep in mind when posting to the newsgroups. Many of these points are taken directly from the article "A Primer on How to Work With the Usenet Community" by Chuq Von Rospach, which is posted monthly to the `news.newusers` newsgroup. Make sure to read the entire article before posting an article on Netnews.

- Never forget that the person on the other side is human.
- Be careful what you say about others; your voice may be louder than you expect.
- Be brief.
- Your postings reflect upon you; be proud of them, from content to spelling.
- Use descriptive titles.
- Think about your audience.
- Be careful with humor and sarcasm.
- Check the FAQ before you post a question.
- Post a message only once.
- Please scramble (rotate) material with questionable content.
- Summarize what you are following up. Don't quote the whole article.
- Use e-mail; don't post a follow-up.
- Read all follow-ups and don't repeat what has already been said.
- Double-check follow-up newsgroups and distributions to prevent spurious reposting.
- E-mail is private; don't post someone else's without explicit permission.
- Be careful about copyrights and licenses.
- Cite appropriate references.
- Mark or rotate answers or spoilers.
- Spelling flames are considered harmful. Many contain spelling errors themselves!
- Don't overdo signatures; it's a waste of bandwidth. Three lines or less is nice.
- Don't flame. If you disagree with someone, be civil.
- When someone does flame, *don't* respond in kind.
- Familiarize yourself with a group before you post articles to it. Each group has its own rules of order and its own limits as to what is appropriate to discuss. Follow these rules.

Entries:

2-1 **alt Groups on various topics, serious and not**

2-2　　　**.1d** one-dimensional imaging and the thinking behind it

2-3　　　**.3d** three-dimensional imaging

2-4　　　**.59.79.99** hut, hut, hike!

2-5　　　**.abortion.inequity** paternal obligations of failing to abort unwanted child

2-6　　　**.abuse**

2-7　　　　　**.offender.recovery** for those trying no longer to abuse

2-8　　　　　**.recovery** helping victims of abuse to recover

2-9　　　**.activism** activities for activists

2-10　　　　**.d** a place to discuss issues in alt.activism

2-11　　　　**.death-penalty** for people opposed to capital punishment

2-12　　　**.adjective.noun.verb.verb.verb** the penultimate alt group

2-13　　　**.adoption** for those involved with or contemplating adoption

2-14　　　**.agriculture**

2-15　　　　**.fruit** fruit, fruit trees, etc.

2-16　　　　**.misc** general discussions of agriculture, farming etc.

2-17　　　**.aldus**

2-18　　　　**.freehand** Aldus freehand

2-19　　　　**.pagemaker** don't use expensive user support, come here instead

2-20　　　**.alien.visitors** space aliens on earth! Abduction! Government cover-up!

2-21　　　**.amateur-comp** discussion and input for Amateur Computerist Newsletter

2-22　　　**.amiga.demos** demo programs for Amiga

2-23　　　**.angst** anxiety in the modern world

2-24　　　**.answers** as if anyone on alt has the answers (moderated)

2-25　　　**.appalachian** Appalachian region awareness, events and culture

2-26　　　**.aquaria** the aquarium and related as a hobby

2-27　　　**.archery** Robin Hood had the right idea

2-28　　　**.architecture** building design/construction and related topics

2-29　　　**.artcom** artistic community, arts and communication

2-30　　　**.asian-movies** movies from Hong Kong, Taiwan, and the Chinese mainland

2-31　　　**.astrology** twinkle, twinkle, little planet

2-32　　　**.atheism** godless heathens

2-33　　　　**.moderated** focused godless heathens (moderated)

2-34　　　**.authorware** software marketed by its author

2-35　　　**.autos**

2-36　　　　**.antique** on all facets of older automobiles

2-37	.**rod-n-custom**	vehicles with modified engines and/or appearance
2-38	.**bacchus**	joys of wine, but mostly aimless chatter
2-39	.**backrubs**	lower...to the right...aaaah!
2-40	.**basement.graveyard**	another side of the do-it-yourself movement
2-41	.**bbs**	computer BBS systems and software
2-42	.**ads**	ads for various computer BBSs
2-43	.**allsysop**	SysOp concerns of ALL networks and technologies
2-44	.**first-class**	the First Class Mac GUI BBS
2-45	.**internet**	BBSs that are hooked up to the Internet
2-46	.**lists**	postings of regional BBS listings
2-47	.**lists.d**	lists of bulletin boards
2-48	.**metal**	discussions of BBSs
2-49	.**pcboard**	technical support for the PCBoard BBS
2-50	.**pcbuucp**	the commerical PCBoard gateway, PCB-UUCP
2-51	.**searchlight**	searchlight BBS
2-52	.**unixbbs**	on the BBS package UnixBBS
2-53	.**unixbbs.uniboard**	uniboard BBS for Unix
2-54	.**uupcb**	PCB? I used to do that in the sixties, man...
2-55	.**beer**	good for what ales ya
2-56	.**best.of.internet**	it was a time of sorrow, it was a time of joy
2-57	.**bigfoot**	Dr. Scholl's gone native
2-58	.**binaries**	**[Groups with "use at your own risk" downloadable materials]**
2-59	.**multimedia**	sound, text and graphics data rolled in one
2-60	.**pictures**	additional volume in the form of huge image files
2-61	.**pictures.d**	on picture postings
2-62	.**pictures.erotica**	gigabytes of copyright violations
2-63	.**pictures.erotica.blondes**	just what it says
2-64	.**pictures.erotica.d**	discussing erotic copyright violations
2-65	.**pictures.erotica.female**	copyright violations featuring females
2-66	.**pictures.erotica.male**	copyright violations featuring males
2-67	.**pictures.erotica.orientals**	copyright violations featuring Asians
2-68	.**pictures.fine-art.d**	on the fine-art binaries (moderated)
2-69	.**pictures.fine-art.digitized**	art from conventional media (moderated)
2-70	.**pictures.fine-art.graphics**	art created on computers (moderated)
2-71	.**pictures.fractals**	cheaper just to send the program parameters
2-72	.**pictures.misc**	have we saturated the network yet?
2-73	.**pictures.supermodels**	yet more copyright violations

2-74	`.pictures.tasteless` "Eccchh, that last one was *sick...*"
2-75	`.pictures.utilities` posting of pictures-related utilities
2-76	`.sounds.d` sounding off
2-77	`.sounds.erotica` just what it sounds like
2-78	`.sounds.misc` digitized audio adventures
2-79	`.sounds.music` music samples in MOD/669 format
2-80	`.bitch.pork` complaints about pork
2-81	`.bitterness` no matter what it's for, you know how it'll turn out
2-82	**`.books`**
2-83	`.deryni` Katherine Kurtz's books, especially the Deryni series
2-84	`.isaac-asimov` fans of the late SF/science author Isaac Asimov
2-85	`.reviews` "If you want to know how it turns out, read it!"
2-86	`.technical` on technical books
2-87	`.boomerang` boomerangs, finding, buying, throwing
2-88	`.brother-jed` the born-again minister touring US campuses
2-89	`.buddha.short.fat.guy` religion. And not religion. Both. Neither
2-90	**`.business`**
2-91	`.misc` entrepreneurial discussions
2-92	`.multi-level` multilevel (network) marketing businesses
2-93	`.cable-tv.re-regulate` seeking reregulation of cable TV
2-94	`.cad` computer-aided design
2-95	`.autocad` CAD as practiced by customers of Autodesk
2-96	`.california` the state and the state of mind
2-97	`.callahans` Callahan's Bar for puns and fellowship
2-98	`.cascade` art or litter— you decide
2-99	`.cd-rom` on optical storage media
2-100	`.censorship` on restricting speech/press
2-101	`.cereal` breakfast cereals and their (m)ilk
2-102	`.cesium` College-educated Students In Universal Mainland
2-103	`.chess.ics` about the Internet chess server at `coot.lcs.mit.edu`
2-104	`.child-support` raising children in a split family
2-105	`.chinchilla` the nature of chinchilla farming in America today
2-106	**`.chinese`**
2-107	`.text` postings in Chinese; Chinese-language software
2-108	`.text.big5` posting in Chinese [BIG 5]
2-109	`.clearing.technology` renegades from the Church of Scientology
2-110	`.clubs.compsci` computer-science clubs

2-111	**.co-evolution** theories of co-evolution
2-112	**.co-ops** on co-operatives
2-113	**.cobol** relationship between programming and stone axes
2-114	**.collecting.autographs** WOW! You got Pete Rose's? What about Kibo's?
2-115	**.college**
2-116	**.college-bowl** on the College Bowl competition
2-117	**.food** dining halls, cafeterias, mystery meat and more
2-118	**.comedy**
2-119	**.british** on British comedy in a variety of media
2-120	**.firesgn-thtre** Firesign Theatre in all its flaming glory
2-121	**.comics**
2-122	**.batman** marketing mania
2-123	**.buffalo-roam** comics miscellany
2-124	**.lnh** interactive net.madness in the superhero genre
2-125	**.superman** no one knows it is also alt.clark kent
2-126	**.comp**
2-127	**.acad-freedom.news** academic freedom issues related to computers (moderated)
2-128	**.acad-freedom.talk** academic freedom issues related to computers
2-129	**.fsp** a file transport protocol
2-130	**.hardware.homebuilt** homebuilt computers, etc.
2-131	**.computer.consultants** geeks on patrol
2-132	**.config** alternative subnet discussions and connectivity
2-133	**.consciousness** on the study of the human consciousness
2-134	**.conspiracy** be paranoid—they're out to get you
2-135	**.jfk** the Kennedy assassination
2-136	**.control-theory** devoted to control theory
2-137	**.cows.moo.moo.moo** like cows would cluck or something
2-138	**.crackers** edible *and* jailable
2-139	**.cult-movies** movies with a cult following
2-140	**.rocky-horror** Virgin! Virgin! Virgin! Virgin!
2-141	**.culture**
2-142	**.alaska** is this where the ice weasels come from?
2-143	**.argentina** don't cry for me
2-144	**.austrian** all aspects of Austrian culture
2-145	**.hawaii** Ua Mau Ke Ea O Ka 'Aina I Ka Pono
2-146	**.indonesia** Indonesian culture, news, etc.
2-147	**.internet** the culture(s) of the Internet

2-148	**.karnataka** culture and language of the Indian state of Karnataka
2-149	**.kerala** people of Keralite origin and the Malayalam language
2-150	**.ny-upstate** New York State, above Westchester
2-151	**.oregon** on the state of Oregon
2-152	**.tuva** all aspects of Feynmann's obsession
2-153	**.us.asian-indian** Asian Indians in the US and Canada
2-154	**.us.southwest** basking in the sun of the US's lower left
2-155	**.usenet** a self-referential oxymoron
2-156	**.current-events**
2-157	**.bosnia** the strife of Bosnia-Herzegovina
2-158	**.flood-of-93** how the midwest U.S. was turned into a sea
2-159	**.somalia** news about Somalia
2-160	**.wtc-explosion** about the World Trade Center explosion
2-161	**.cyberpunk** high-tech low-life
2-162	**.chatsubo** literary virtual reality in a cyberpunk hangout
2-163	**.movement** William Gibson's spawn
2-164	**.tech** cyberspace and cyberpunk technology
2-165	**.cyberspace** cyberspace and how it should work
2-166	**.dads-rights** rights of fathers trying to win custody in court
2-167	**.data.bad.bad.bad** evil androids siding with the Borg
2-168	**.dcom.telecom** on telecommunications technology
2-169	**.dear.whitehouse** when Hints from Heloise aren't enough
2-170	**.decathena** digital's DEC Athena product (moderated)
2-171	**.desert-storm** news and views about Operation Desert Storm
2-172	**.facts** the *real* background of Desert Storm
2-173	**.destroy.the.earth** how-tos, suggestions, antimatter, etc.
2-174	**.dev.null** the ultimate in moderated newsgroups (moderated)
2-175	**.devilbunnies** probably better left undescribed
2-176	**.discordia** all hail Eris, etc.
2-177	**.discrimination** quotas, affirmative action, bigotry, persecution
2-178	**.divination** divination techniques (e.g., I Ching, Tarot, runes)
2-179	**.dreams** what do they mean?
2-180	**.lucid** all about lucid dreaming
2-181	**.drugs** recreational pharmaceuticals and related flames
2-182	**.caffeine** all about the world's most-used stimulant
2-183	**.drumcorps** drum and bugle corps discussion (and related topics)
2-184	**.drwho.creative** writing about long scarfs and time machines

2-185	**.education**
2-186	**.disabled** education and the disabled
2-187	**.distance** computer and telecom technology as applied to education
2-188	**.research** discussions of research in education
2-189	**.elvis**
2-190	**.king** Costello. Not!
2-191	**.sighting** sightings of Elvis Costello. Not!
2-192	**.emulators.ibmpc.apple2** Apple II on the IBM PC
2-193	**.emusic** ethnic, exotic, electronic, elaborate, etc. music
2-194	**.engr.explosives** building backyard bombs
2-195	**.ensign.wesley.die.die.die** we just can't get enough of him
2-196	**.etext** online e-texts, announcements, postings, etc.
2-197	**.evil** tales from the dark side
2-198	**.exotic-music** exotic music discussions
2-199	**.extropians** life extension
2-200	**.fan** [Groups for those who are especially fond of some weird thing]
2-201	**.BIFF** Biff Henderson
2-202	**.alok.vijayvargia** vote early and vote often
2-203	**.amy-fisher** Amy Furiosa
2-204	**.asprin** the works of Robert Lynn Asprin
2-205	**.bgcrisis** Priss, the Replicants, the ADP and Bubblegum Crisis
2-206	**.bill-gates** fans of the original micro-softie
2-207	**.chris-elliott** Chris Elliott
2-208	**.dan-quayle** for discussion of the U.S. Vice President
2-209	**.dave_barry** electronic fan club for humorist Dave Barry
2-210	**.debbie.gibson** the world's oldest cheerleader
2-211	**.devo** funny hats do not a band make
2-212	**.dice-man** discussions of the comedian
2-213	**.dick-depew** dump on Dick
2-214	**.disney.afternoon** Disney afternoon characters and shows
2-215	**.douglas-adams** author of "The Meaning of Life" and other fine works
2-216	**.eddings** the works of writer David Eddings
2-217	**.enya** for Enya fandom
2-218	**.firesign-theatre** the first try for alt.comedy.firesgn-thtre
2-219	**.frank-zappa** is that a Sears poncho?
2-220	**.furry** fans of funny animals, ala Steve Gallacci's book
2-221	**.g-gordon-liddy** y'know, I saw him and Rush holding hands in a bar once

2-222	**.gene-scott** Gene Scott
2-223	**.goons** careful Neddy, it's that dastardly Moriarty again
2-224	**.greaseman** fans of Doug Tracht, the DJ
2-225	**.harry-mandel** Harry Mandel
2-226	**.hofstadter** Douglas Hofstadter and *Godel, Escher, Bach*
2-227	**.holmes** elementary, my dear Watson. Like he ever said that.
2-228	**.howard-stern** fans of the abrasive radio and TV personality
2-229	**.james-bond** on his Majesty's Secret Service (and secret linen, too)
2-230	**.jen-coolest** gosh, isn't she just wonderful?
2-231	**.jimmy-buffett** a white sports coat and a pink crustacean
2-232	**.john-palmer** John Palmer
2-233	**.karla-homolka** Why are there so few hot, exhibitionist, S&M women?
2-234	**.kent-montana** Kent Montana
2-235	**.kevin-darcy** Kevin Darcy
2-236	**.laurie.anderson** will it be a music concert or a lecture this time?
2-237	**.lemurs** little critters with BIG eyes
2-238	**.letterman** one of the top ten reasons to get the alt. groups
2-239	**.lightbulbs** a hardware problem
2-240	**.madonna** nice tits, eh... And how about that puppy?
2-241	**.maria-callas** Maria Callas
2-242	**.max-headroom** Max Headroom
2-243	**.mike-jittlov** electronic fan club for animator Mike Jittlov
2-244	**.monty-python** electronic fan club for those wacky Brits
2-245	**.naked-guy** naked guy at Berkeley
2-246	**.oingo-boingo** Oingo Boingo
2-247	**.pern** Anne McCaffrey's s-f oeuvre
2-248	**.piers-anthony** for fans of the s-f author Piers Anthony
2-249	**.pratchett** for fans of Terry Pratchett, s-f humor writer
2-250	**.q** q of Star Trek and Deep Space 9
2-251	**.robert.mcelwaine** another favorite net-personality
2-252	**.ronald-reagan** jellybeans and all
2-253	**.rumpole** Rumpole of the bailey
2-254	**.rush-limbaugh** derogation of others for fun and profit
2-255	**.rush-limbaugh.tv-show** fans of the conservative writer and comic
2-256	**.serdar-argic** all about Armenia, Turkey, genocide and robot-posting
2-257	**.shostakovich** Shostakovich
2-258	**.spinal-tap** down on the sex farm

2-259	**.suicide-squid** suicide squid
2-260	**.tank-girl** no, she doesn't make noises like a squirrel. Really.
2-261	**.thunder-thumbs** thunder thumbs
2-262	**.tolkien** ...and in the dark shall find them
2-263	**.tom-robbins** Tom Robbins
2-264	**.tom_peterson** Tom Peterson
2-265	**.wal-greenslade** Wal Greenslade
2-266	**.warlord** the War Lord of the West Preservation Fan Club
2-267	**.wodehouse** on the works of humor author P.G. Wodehouse
2-268	**.woody-allen** Woody Allen
2-269	**.fandom**
2-270	**.cons** announcements of conventions (science fiction and others)
2-271	**.misc** other topics for fans of various kinds
2-272	**.fashion** all facets of the fashion industry discussed
2-273	**.feminism** like `soc.feminism`, only different
2-274	**.filesystems.afs** on AFS, from deployment to development
2-275	**.fishing** fishing as a hobby and sport
2-276	**.flame** alternative, literate, pithy, succinct screaming
2-277	**.faggots** ignore the homophobic twits and they'll go away
2-278	**.fucking.faggots** for especially intellectual homophobes
2-279	**.hall-of-flame** best flames
2-280	**.roommate** putting the pig on a spit
2-281	**.sean-ryan** Sean Ryan
2-282	**.spelling** flames about poor spelling
2-283	**.folklore**
2-284	**.college** collegiate humor
2-285	**.computers** stories and anecdotes about computers (some true!)
2-286	**.ghost-stories** boo!
2-287	**.herbs** on all aspects of herbs and their uses
2-288	**.science** the folklore of science, not the science of folklore
2-289	**.urban** urban legends, a la Jan Harold Brunvand
2-290	**.fondle.vomit** people who like having sticky fingers
2-291	**.food** health, additives, etc.
2-292	**.cocacola** and Royal Crown, Pepsi, Dr. Pepper, NEHI etc...
2-293	**.dennys** fans or frequenters of the Dennys' chain
2-294	**.mcdonalds** Carl Sagan's favorite burger place
2-295	**.sugar-cereals** discussions of bad breakfast foods

2-296   **.fractals** better you should go to `sci.fractals`

2-297   **.french.captain.borg.borg.borg**

2-298   **.funk-you** the altnet, so full of wit!

2-299   **.gambling** all aspects of games of chance

2-300   **.games**

2-301   **.frp.dnd-util** discussion and creation of utility programs for Advanced Dungeons and Dragons (AD&D)

2-302   **.frp.live-action** on all forms of live-action gaming

2-303   **.galactic-bloodshed** galactic bloodshed

2-304   **.gb** the Galactic Bloodshed conquest game

2-305   **.lynx** the Atari Lynx

2-306   **.mk** struggling in Mortal Kombat!

2-307   **.mornington.cresent** Mornington Crescent

2-308   **.omega** the computer game Omega

2-309   **.sf2** the video game Street Fighter 2

2-310   **.tiddlywinks** tiddlywinks

2-311   **.torg** gateway for TORG mailing list

2-312   **.vga-planets** on Tim Wisseman's VGA Planets

2-313   **.video.classic** classic video games

2-314   **.xpilot** on all aspects of the X11 game Xpilot

2-315   **.gathering.rainbow** for discussing the annual Rainbow Gathering

2-316   **.geek** to fulfill an observed need

2-317   **.genealogy** finding your roots, genealogy

2-318   **.good**

2-319   **.morning** Would you like coffee with that?

2-320   **.news** a place for some news that's good news

2-321   **.gopher** on the gopher information service

2-322   **.gothic** the Gothic movement: things mournful and dark

2-323   **.gourmand** recipes and cooking info (moderated)

2-324   **.grad-student.tenured** most prison terms are finished sooner

2-325   **.graffiti** found literature, graffiti

2-326   **.graphics.pixutils** on Pixmap utilities

2-327   **.great-lakes** on the Great Lakes and adjacent places

2-328   **.great.ass.paulina** name in poor taste, though accurate

2-329   **.guitar** you axed for it, you got it

2-330   **.bass** bass guitars

2-331   **.tab** on guitar tablature music

2-332   **.hackers** descriptions of projects currently under development (moderated)

2-333	`.malicious` evil folk with keyboards, hackers
2-334	`.happy.birthday.to.me` the loneliest number
2-335	`.health.ayurveda` really old medicine from India
2-336	`.hemp` It's about knot-tying with rope. Knot!
2-337	`.hi.are.you.cute` are there a lot of pathetic people on the net or what?
2-338	`.hindu` the Hindu religion (moderated)
2-339	**.history**
2-340	`.living` a forum for discussing the hobby of living history
2-341	`.what-if` what would the net have been like without this group?
2-342	`.homosexual` same as `alt.sex.homosexual`
2-343	`.horror` the horror genre
2-344	`.cthulhu` on H.P Lovecraft's stories of the Cthulhu Mythos
2-345	`.werewolves` they were wolves, now they're something to be wary of
2-346	`.hotrod` high speed automobiles (moderated)
2-347	`.housing.nontrad` nontraditional housing
2-348	**.humor**
2-349	`.best-of-usenet` what the moderator thinks is funniest (moderated)
2-350	`.best-of-usenet.d` why everyone else doesn't think it's funny
2-351	`.hypertext` on hypertext—uses, transport etc.
2-352	`.hypnosis` when you awaken, you will forget about this newsgroup
2-353	`.illuminati` see `alt.cabal.Fnord`
2-354	`.image.medical` medical image exchange discussions
2-355	`.india.progressive` progressive politics in the Indian subcontinent (moderated)
2-356	`.individualism` philosophies in which individual rights are paramount
2-357	`.industrial` computing, not music
2-358	`.info-science` discussions of information science
2-359	`.info-theory` discussions of information theory
2-360	**.internet**
2-361	`.access.wanted` "Oh. Okay, how about just an MX record for now?"
2-362	`.services` not available in the UUCP world, even via e-mail
2-363	`.talk-radio` Internet talk radio
2-364	`.irc` Internet Relay Chat material
2-365	`.ircii` Internet Relay Chat
2-366	`.lamers` see `alt.hi.are.you.cute`
2-367	`.recovery` recovering from Internet Relay Chat abuse
2-368	`.is.too` NOT!
2-369	`.japanese.text` postings in Japanese; Japanese language software

2-370	**.journalism** general hangout for journalists
2-371	**.criticism** discussions of journalism
2-372	**.gonzo** Hunter Thompson and his ilk
2-373	**.ketchup** whak*...whak*...shake...whak* Damn, all over my tie
2-374	**.kids-talk** a place for the precollege set on the net
2-375	**.kill.the.whales** this newsgroup is evidence for the coming apocalypse
2-376	**.lang [Groups on alternate computer languages]**
2-377	**.asm** assembly languages of various flavors
2-378	**.awk** about AWK
2-379	**.basic** the Language That Would Not Die
2-380	**.intercal** a joke language with a real compiler
2-381	**.law-enforcement** no, ossifer, there's nothing illegal going on in alt
2-382	**.lawyers.sue.sue.sue** questions about initiating lawsuits
2-383	**.life**
2-384	**.internet** one big throbbing mass of life, we are
2-385	**.sucks** and then you shrivel up
2-386	**.locksmithing** you locked your keys in *where*?
2-387	**.lucid-emacs**
2-388	**.bug** bug reports about Lucid Emacs
2-389	**.help** questions and answers and general discussion of Lucid Emacs
2-390	**.magic** for discussion about stage magic
2-391	**.magick** for discussion about supernatural arts
2-392	**.sex** sexuality, spirituality and magick
2-393	**.manga** on non-Western comics
2-394	**.mcdonalds** can I get fries with that?
2-395	**.med.cfs** Chronic Fatigue Syndrome information
2-396	**.meditation** general discussion of meditation
2-397	**.transcendental** contemplation of states beyond the teeth
2-398	**.memetics** the evolution of ideas in societies
2-399	**.messianic** messianic traditions
2-400	**.military.cadet** preparing for the coming apocalypse
2-401	**.mindcontrol** cults, cult-awareness, analysis, etc.
2-402	**.misanthropy** anger directed at people in general
2-403	**.misc** anything
2-404	**.missing-kids** locating missing children
2-405	**.models** mannequins or constructs
2-406	**.msdos.programmer** for the serious MS/DOS programmer (no for-sale ads)

2-407   **.mud** same as rec.games.mud

2-408   **.cyberworld** "Made for some student," the clueless newgroup said.

2-409   **.mudders.anonymous** you might as well face it, you're addicted to MUD

2-410   **.music**

2-411   **.a-cappella** voice only, no /dev/sound

2-412   **.alternative** for groups having two or fewer platinum-selling albums

2-413   **.bela-fleck** Bela Fleck

2-414   **.canada** oh, Canada, eh?

2-415   **.ebm** EBM

2-416   **.enya** Gaelic set to spacey music

2-417   **.filk** folk music based on themes in science fiction and fantasy

2-418   **.hardcore** could be porno set to music

2-419   **.karaoke** karaoke

2-420   **.marillion** a progressive band. The Silmarillion is a book.

2-421   **.prince** So my Prince came. Make him go away.

2-422   **.progressive** yes, Marillion, Asia, King Crimson, etc.

2-423   **.queen** he's dead, Jim

2-424   **.rush** for Rushheads

2-425   **.ska** on ska (skank) music, bands, and suchlike

2-426   **.the.police** the Police

2-427   **.tmbg** They Might Be Giants

2-428   **.world** on music from around the world

2-429   **.my.head.hurts** after things go bump in the night

2-430   **.mythology** Zeus rules

2-431   **.national.enquirer** for enquiring minds

2-432   **.native** Native Americans

2-433   **.necktie** wearing apparel

2-434   **.necromicon** yet another sign of the coming apocalypse

2-435   **.net.personalities** about prominent personalities on the net

2-436   **.netgames.bolo** a multiplayer tank game for the Macintosh

2-437   **.news-media** don't believe the hype

2-438   **.news.macedonia** news concerning Macedonia in the Balkan Region

2-439   **.nick.sucks** probably

2-440   **.non.sequitur** Richard Nixon

2-441   **.online-service** large commercial online services and the Internet

2-442   **.org.food-not-bombs** progressive, organic, social activists

2-443   **.os**

2-444	**.bsdi** bsd Unix
2-445	**.multics** 30 years old and going strong
2-446	**.out-of-body** out-of-body experiences
2-447	**.overlords** office of the Omnipotent Overlords of the Omniverse
2-448	**.pagan** on paganism and religion
2-449	**.pantyhose** whaddaya call a trashbag and two rubber bands
2-450	**.paranet** [Groups on all aspects of parapsycology and the paranormal]
2-451	**.abduct** "They replaced Jim-Bob with a look-alike!"
2-452	**.paranormal** "If it exists, how can supernatural be beyond natural?"
2-453	**.science** "Maybe if we dissect the psychic …"
2-454	**.skeptic** "I don't believe they turned you into a newt."
2-455	**.ufo** "Heck, I guess naming it 'UFO' identifies it."
2-456	**.paranormal** phenomena which are not scientifically explicable
2-457	**.parents-teens** parent-teenager relationships
2-458	**.party** parties, celebration and general debauchery
2-459	**.pave.the.earth** one world, one people, one slab of asphalt
2-460	**.pcnews** Usenet on the PC and clones
2-461	**.peace-corps** about the Peace Corps, experiences, etc.
2-462	**.peeves** on peeves and related issues
2-463	**.periphs.pcmcia** credit-card size peripherals, pcmcia
2-464	**.personals** do you really want to meet someone this way?
2-465	**.ads** Geek seeks dweeb. Object: low-level interfacing.
2-466	**.bondage** are you tied up this evening?
2-467	**.misc** Dweeb seeks geek. Object: low-level interfacing.
2-468	**.poly** Hi there, do you multiprocess?
2-469	**.pets.chia** stoneware with hair, chia pets
2-470	**.philosophy.objectivism** a product of the Ayn Rand corporation
2-471	**.planning.urban** how and why to build a city
2-472	**.politics**
2-473	**.british** politics and a real queen, too
2-474	**.bush** politics and George Bush
2-475	**.clinton** discussing Slick Willie and Co.
2-476	**.correct** a Neil Bush fan club
2-477	**.ec** ?European community?
2-478	**.economics** war = poverty, and other discussions
2-479	**.elections** everyone who voted for Quayle gets a free lollipop
2-480	**.equality** equality and discrimination

2-481	**.greens** Green Party politics and activities worldwide
2-482	**.homosexuality** as the name implies
2-483	**.india.progressive** all about Progressive politics in India
2-484	**.libertarian** the libertarian ideology
2-485	**.media** there's lies, damn lies, statistics, and news reports
2-486	**.org.misc** political organizations
2-487	**.org.un** about the United Nations
2-488	**.perot** on the non-candidate
2-489	**.radical-left** who remains after the radicals left?
2-490	**.reform** political reform
2-491	**.sex** not a good idea to mix them, sez Marilyn and Profumo
2-492	**.usa.constitution** U.S. Constitutional politics
2-493	**.usa.misc** miscellaneous U.S politics
2-494	**.usa.republican** on the U.S. Republican Party
2-495	**.vietnamese** governing the Vietnamese
2-496	**.polyamory** for those who maintain multiple love relationships
2-497	**.postmodern** postmodernism, semiotics, deconstruction, and the like
2-498	**.president.clinton** will the CIA undermine his efforts?
2-499	**.prisons** can I get an **alt.*** feed in the slammer?
2-500	**.privacy** privacy issues in cyberspace
2-501	**.anon-server** technical and policy matters of anonymous contact servers
2-502	**.clipper** no, really, we can't read it. (Snicker)
2-503	**.prophecies.nostradamus** Nostradamus
2-504	**.prose** postings of original writings, fictional and otherwise
2-505	**.d** writing divertissements
2-506	**.psychoactives** better living through chemistry
2-507	**.psychology.personality** personality taxonomy, such as Myers-Briggs
2-508	**.pub**
2-509	**.cloven-shield** SF role-playing
2-510	**.dragons-inn** fantasy virtual-reality pub similar to **alt.callahans**
2-511	**.havens-rest** even more SF role-playing
2-512	**.pulp** pulp fiction
2-513	**.punk** burning them keeps insects away
2-514	**.ql.creative** the "Quantum Leap" TV show
2-515	**.quotations** quotations, quips, .sig lines, witticisms, et al.
2-516	**.radio**
2-517	**.pirate** hide the gear, here come the magic station-wagons

2-518	**.scanner** on scanning radio receivers
2-519	**.rap** for fans of rap music
2-520	**.rap-gdead** Grateful Dead
2-521	**.rave** technoculture: music, dancing, drugs, dancing...
2-522	**.recovery** for people in recovery programs (e.g., AA, ACA, GA)
2-523	**.codependency** recovering from the disease of codependency
2-524	**.religion**
2-525	**.all-worlds** general discussion of religion
2-526	**.computers** people who worship computers
2-527	**.emacs** Emacs. Umacs. We all macs.
2-528	**.kibology** he's Fred, Jim
2-529	**.monica** on net-Venus Monica and her works
2-530	**.santaism** worship of St. Nick, an American affliction
2-531	**.scientology** he's dead, Jim
2-532	**.restaurants** places to eat, restaurants
2-533	**.revisionism** "It CAN'T be that way 'cause here's the FACTS."
2-534	**.revolution.counter** on counterrevolutionary issues
2-535	**.rhode_island** on the great little state
2-536	**.rock-n-roll** counterpart to alt.sex and alt.drugs
2-537	**.acdc** dirty deeds done dirt cheap
2-538	**.classic** classic rock, both the music and its marketing
2-539	**.hard** music where stance is everything
2-540	**.metal** for the headbangers on the net
2-541	**.metal.gnr** "Axl Rose" is an anagram for "Oral Sex"
2-542	**.metal.heavy** nonsissyboy metal bands
2-543	**.metal.ironmaiden** sonic torture methods
2-544	**.metal.metallica** sort of like Formica with more hair
2-545	**.metal.progressive** Slayer teams up with Tom Cora
2-546	**.oldies** *good* rock-n-roll
2-547	**.stones** gathering plenty of moss by now
2-548	**.symphonic** Moody Blues, Deep Purple, etc.
2-549	**.romance** on the romantic side of love
2-550	**.chat** talk about no sex
2-551	**.rush-limbaugh** fans of the conservative activist radio announcer
2-552	**.satanism** not such a bad dude once you get to know him
2-553	**.satellite**
2-554	**.tv.europe** all about European satellite TV

2-555	`.tv.forsale` satellite TV equipment classifieds
2-556	`.save.the.earth` environmentalist causes
2-557	`.sb.programmer` sound-blaster programming and use
2-558	**`.sci`**
2-559	`.physics.acoustics` sound advice
2-560	`.physics.new-theories` scientific theories you won't find in journals
2-561	`.planetary` studies in planetary science
2-562	`.sociology` people are really interesting when you watch them
2-563	`.security` security issues on computer systems
2-564	`.index` pointers to good stuff in `alt.security` (moderated)
2-565	`.keydist` keyed encryption systems
2-566	`.pgp` the Pretty Good Privacy package
2-567	`.ripem` encryption using Ripem
2-568	`.sega.genesis` another addiction
2-569	`.self-improve` self-improvement in less than 14 characters
2-570	`.sewing` a group that is not as it seams
2-571	`.sex` postings of a prurient nature
2-572	`.bestiality` happiness is a warm puppy
2-573	`.bestiality.barney` for people with big-purple-newt fetishes
2-574	`.bondage` tie me, whip me, make me read the net!
2-575	`.bondage.particle.physics`
2-576	`.boredom`
2-577	`.fetish.amputee` they're as sexual as anyone else
2-578	`.fetish.fa` the group creator couldn't spell "fat" right
2-579	`.fetish.feet` Kiss them. Now
2-580	`.fetish.hair` it worked for Rapunsel
2-581	`.fetish.orientals` the mysteries of Asia are a potent lure
2-582	`.homosexual`
2-583	`.masturbation` where one's SO is oneself
2-584	`.motss` Jesse Helms would not subscribe to this group
2-585	`.movies` discussing the ins and outs of certain movies
2-586	`.pictures` gigabytes of copyright violations
2-587	`.pictures.d`
2-588	`.pictures.female` copyright violations featuring, mostly, females
2-589	`.pictures.male` copyright violations featuring, mostly, males
2-590	`.sounds`
2-591	`.stories` for those who need it *now*

2-592	**.stories.d** for those who talk about needing it *now*
2-593	**.voyeurism**
2-594	**.wanted** requests for erotica, either literary or in the flesh
2-595	**.watersports**
2-596	**.wizards** questions for only true sex wizards
2-597	**.sexual**
2-598	**.abuse.recovery** helping others deal with traumatic experiences
2-599	**.abuse.recovery.d** recovering from sexual abuse
2-600	**.sexy.bald.captains** more Stardrek
2-601	**.sf4m** miscellaneous complaints
2-602	**.shenanigans** practical jokes, pranks, randomness, etc.
2-603	**.showbiz.gossip** showbiz gossip
2-604	**.shut.the.hell.up.geek** group for Usenet motto
2-605	**.skate** skating (or fishing)
2-606	**.skate-board** on all aspects of skate-boarding
2-607	**.skinheads** the skinhead culture/anticulture
2-608	**.slack** postings relating to the Church of the Subgenius
2-609	**.slick.willy.tax.tax.tax** not just for rich people anymore
2-610	**.snowmobiles** winter sports, snowmobiles
2-611	**.soc.ethics** discussions of ethics
2-612	**.society**
2-613	**.anarchy** societies without rulers
2-614	**.ati** the Activist Times Digest. (moderated)
2-615	**.civil-disob** discussions of civil disobedience
2-616	**.civil-liberties** individual rights
2-617	**.civil-liberty** same as `alt.society.civil-liberties`
2-618	**.conservatism** social, cultural and political conservatism
2-619	**.foia** Freedom of Information Act
2-620	**.futures** trends in society's development
2-621	**.resistance** resistance against governments
2-622	**.revolution** on revolutions
2-623	**.soft-sys.tooltalk** forum for ToolTalk-related issues
2-624	**.soulmates** but what if Richard Bach's true love lived in Mongolia?
2-625	**.sources** alternative source code, unmoderated. *Caveat emptor*
2-626	**.amiga** Commodore programming and service
2-627	**.d** on posted sources
2-628	**.index** pointers to source code in `alt.sources.*` (moderated)

2-629   `.wanted` requests for source code

2-630   `.spam` what is that stuff that doth jiggle in the breeze?

2-631   `.tin` spam-lovers' support group

2-632   **`.sport`**

2-633   `.bowling` in the gutter again

2-634   `.bungee` bungee-jumping

2-635   `.darts` look what you've done to the wall!

2-636   `.foosball` table soccer and dizzy little men

2-637   `.lasertag` indoor splatball with infrared lasers

2-638   `.paintball` paintball

2-639   `.pool` knock your balls into your pockets for fun

2-640   **`.sports`**

2-641   `.baseball.atlanta-braves` Atlanta Braves major league baseball

2-642   `.baseball.balt-orioles` Baltimore Orioles major league baseball

2-643   `.baseball.chicago-cubs` Chicago Cubs major league baseball

2-644   `.baseball.cinci-reds` Cincinnati Reds major league baseball

2-645   `.baseball.col-rockies` Colorado Rockies major league baseball

2-646   `.baseball.fla-marlins` Florida Marlins major league baseball

2-647   `.baseball.houston-astros` Houston Astros major league baseball

2-648   `.baseball.la-dodgers` Los Angeles Dodgers major league baseball

2-649   `.baseball.mke-brewers` for discussion of the Milwaukee Brewers...

2-650   `.baseball.mke-brewers.suck.suck.suck` ...and why they suck

2-651   `.baseball.mn-twins` Minnesota Twins major league baseball

2-652   `.baseball.montreal-expos` Montreal Expos major league baseball

2-653   `.baseball.ny-mets` New York Mets baseball talk

2-654   `.baseball.oakland-as` Oakland A's major league baseball talk

2-655   `.baseball.phila-phillies` Philadelphia Phillies baseball talk

2-656   `.baseball.pitt-pirates` Pittsburgh Pirates baseball talk

2-657   `.baseball.sf-giants` San Francisco Giants baseball talk

2-658   `.baseball.stl-cardinals` St. Louis Cardinals baseball talk

2-659   `.football.mn-vikings` Minnesota Vikings football talk

2-660   `.football.pro.wash-redskins` Washington Redskins football talk

2-661   `.stagecraft` technical theater issues

2-662   `.startrek.creative` stories and parodies related to Star Trek

2-663   `.stupid.religious.discussion` `talk.religion.misc`'s no-nonsense name

2-664   `.stupidity` on stupid newsgroups

2-665   `.suburbs` discussions of the burbs

2-666	**.suicide.holiday** why suicides increase at holidays
2-667	**.suit.att-bsdi** the ATT&T vs. BDSI lawsuit over Unix code
2-668	**.super.nes** on the Super Nintendo video game
2-669	**.supermodels** discussing famous and beautiful models
2-670	**.support** dealing with emotional situations and experiences
2-671	**.big-folks** sizeism can be as awful as sexism or racism
2-672	**.cancer** support for victims of cancer
2-673	**.diet** seeking enlightenment through weight loss
2-674	**.mult-sclerosis** on living with multiple sclerosis
2-675	**.step-parents** difficulties of being a step-parent
2-676	**.surfing** riding the ocean waves
2-677	**.sustainable.agriculture** such as the Mekong Delta before Agent Orange
2-678	**.swedish.chef.bork.bork.bork** the beginning of the end
2-679	**.sys**
2-680	**.amiga.demos** code and talk to show off the Amiga
2-681	**.amiga.uucp** Amiga UUCP
2-682	**.amiga.uucp.patches** patches for UUCP on the Amiga
2-683	**.hp48** the Hewlett-Packard handheld hp48 calculator
2-684	**.intergraph** support for Intergraph machines
2-685	**.pc-clone.gateway2000** Gateway 2000 pc clones
2-686	**.perq** keeping the antiques working
2-687	**.sun** technical discussion of Sun Microsystems products
2-688	**.tasteless** truly disgusting
2-689	**.johan.wevers** the OETLUL of the year
2-690	**.jokes** sometimes insulting rather than disgusting or humorous
2-691	**.penis** poor analogy for a bad hotdog
2-692	**.techno-shamanism** but can they make the name work on SYSV systems?
2-693	**.technology**
2-694	**.misc** another well-focused alt. group
2-695	**.mkt-failure** promising technologies that failed to sell
2-696	**.obsolete** things that work
2-697	**.test** alternative subnetwork testing
2-698	**.my.new.group** created by a fool on his day
2-699	**.test** more from the people who brought you "BBS systems."
2-700	**.text.dwb** about dwb, where to get it, what to do with it
2-701	**.thinking.hurts** Barbie was right
2-702	**.thrash** thrashlife

2-703	**.timewasters** a Dutch computer club; perhaps a microcosm of Usenet...
2-704	**.toolkits.xview** the XWindows XView toolkit
2-705	**.toon-pics** computer graphics of cartoon characters
2-706	**.toys**
2-707	**.hi-tech** Optimus Prime is my hero
2-708	**.lego** snap 'em together
2-709	**.transgendered** boys will be girls, and vice-versa
2-710	**.true-crime** discussions of lurid crimes
2-711	**.tv**
2-712	**.babylon-5** Casablanca in space
2-713	**.beakmans-world** Beakman's world
2-714	**.beavis-n-butthead** the MTV success
2-715	**.bh90210** fans of "Beverly Hills 90210" TV show
2-716	**.dinosaurs** the best show on TV
2-717	**.dinosaurs.barney.die.die.die** squish the saccharine newt
2-718	**.fifteen** fifteen
2-719	**.infomercials** program-length (and -like) commercials
2-720	**.la-law** for the folks out in la-law land
2-721	**.liquid-tv** liquid TV
2-722	**.mash** nothing like a good comedy about war and dying
2-723	**.melrose-place** Melrose Place
2-724	**.mst3k** Hey, you robots! Down in front!
2-725	**.muppets** Miss Piggy on the tube
2-726	**.mwc** "Married... With Children"
2-727	**.northern-exp** for the TV show with moss growing on it
2-728	**.prisoner** the Prisoner television series from years ago
2-729	**.red-dwarf** the British science-fiction comedy show
2-730	**.ren-n-stimpy** some change from Lassie, eh?
2-731	**.rockford-files** but he won't do windows
2-732	**.saved-bell** saved by the bell
2-733	**.seinfeld** a funny guy
2-734	**.simpsons** don't have a cow, man!
2-735	**.simpsons.itchy-scratchy** Simpsons and Itchy & Scratchy
2-736	**.snl** Saturday Night Live
2-737	**.time-traxx** if you run into Nyssa, let us know
2-738	**.tiny-toon** on the "Tiny Toon Adventures" show
2-739	**.tiny-toon.fandom** apparently one fan group could not bind them all

2-740	**.twin-peaks** on the popular (and unusual) TV show
2-741	**.unix.wizards** people who can change permissions
2-742	**.unsubscribe-me** just strap right in to this electric chair here
2-743	**.usage.english** English grammar, word usages, and related topics
2-744	**.usenet**
2-745	**.offline-reader** getting your fix offline
2-746	**.recovery** for people addicted to news
2-747	**.uu**
2-748	**.future** Usenet University/global network academy developments
2-749	**.lang.esperanto.misc** study of Esperanto in Usenet University
2-750	**.lang.misc** about language and usage
2-751	**.lang.russian.misc** miscellany about Russian language
2-752	**.virtual-worlds.misc** virtual reality in education
2-753	**.vampyres** on vampires and related writings, films etc.
2-754	**.video**
2-755	**.games.reviews** what's hot and what's not in video games
2-756	**.laserdisc** LD players and selections available for them
2-757	**.visa.us** discussion/information on visas pertaining to US
2-758	**.war** not just collateral damage
2-759	**.civil.usa** on the U.S. Civil War (1861-1865)
2-760	**.vietnam** on all aspects of the Vietnam War
2-761	**.wedding** til death or our lawyers do us part
2-762	**.wesley.crusher.die.die.die** ensigns just get no respect
2-763	**.whine** why me?
2-764	**.whistleblowing** whistleblowing on fraud, abuse and other corruption
2-765	**.winsock** windows sockets
2-766	**.wolves** discussing wolves and wolf-mix dogs
2-767	**.wonderment.bgjw** By gosh, Judge Wapner!
2-768	**.zima** not to be confused with zuma
2-769	**.zines** small magazines, mostly noncommercial
2-770	**.znet** [The ZNET online magazine.]
2-771	**.aeo** Atari Explorer Online magazine (moderated)
2-772	**.pc** z*NET International ASCII Magazines (Weekly) (moderated)

2-773 **bionet** Groups of interest to professional biologists

2-774	**.agroforestry** on agroforestry
2-775	**.announce** announcements of widespread interest to biologists (moderated)

2-776	**.biology**
2-777	**.computational** computer and mathematical applications (moderated)
2-778	**.n2-fixation** research issues on biological nitrogen fixation
2-779	**.tropical** on tropical biology
2-780	**.cellbiol** discussions of cell biology
2-781	**.chlamydomonas** on the green alga Chlamydomonas
2-782	**.drosophila** on the biology of fruit flies
2-783	**.general** general BIOSCI discussion
2-784	**.genome**
2-785	**.arabidopsis** information about the Arabidopsis project.
2-786	**.chrom22** on Chromosome 22
2-787	**.chromosomes** mapping and sequencing of eucaryote chromosomes
2-788	**.immunology** on research in immunology
2-789	**.info-theory** on biological information theory
2-790	**.jobs** scientific job opportunities
2-791	**.journals**
2-792	**.contents** contents of biology journal publications (moderated)
2-793	**.note** advice on dealing with journals in biology
2-794	**.metabolic-reg** science of metabolic regulation
2-795	**.molbio**
2-796	**.ageing** on cellular and organismal ageing
2-797	**.bio-matrix** computer applications to biological databases
2-798	**.embldatabank** info about the EMBL Nucleic acid database
2-799	**.evolution** how genes and proteins have evolved
2-800	**.gdb** messages to and from the GDB database staff
2-801	**.genbank** info about the GenBank Nucleic acid database
2-802	**.genbank.updates** hot off the presses! (moderated)
2-803	**.gene-linkage** on genetic linkage analysis
2-804	**.genome-program** on Human Genome Project issues
2-805	**.hiv** on the molecular biology of HIV
2-806	**.methds-reagnts** requests for information and lab reagents
2-807	**.proteins** research on proteins and protein databases
2-808	**.rapd** research on Randomly Amplified Polymorphic DNA
2-809	**.yeast** the molecular biology and genetics of yeast
2-810	**.n2-fixation** research issues on biological nitrogen fixation
2-811	**.neuroscience** research issues in the neurosciences
2-812	**.photosynthesis** on research on photosynthesis

bionet

2-813	**.plants** on all aspects of plant biology
2-814	**.population-bio** technical discussions about population biology
2-815	**.sci-resources** information about funding agencies etc (moderated)
2-816	**.software** information about software for biology
2-817	**.acedb** discussions by users of genome databases using ACEDB
2-818	**.gcg** on using the ACEDB software
2-819	**.sources** software source relating to biology (moderated)
2-820	**.users.addresses** who's who in biology
2-821	**.virology** on research in virology
2-822	**.women-in-bio** on women in biology
2-823	**.xtallography** on protein crystallography

2-824
bit Groups that are redistributions of Bitnet mailing lists

2-825	**.admin** Bit.* Newgroups discussions
2-826	**.general** discussions relating to BitNet/Usenet
2-827	**.lang.neder-l** Dutch Language and Literature list (moderated)
2-828	**.listserv**
2-829	**.3com-l** 3Com Products Discussion list
2-830	**.9370-l** IBM 9370 and VM/IS specific topics list
2-831	**.ada-law** ADA Law Discussions
2-832	**.advanc-l** Geac Advanced Integrated Library System Users
2-833	**.advise-l** user Services List
2-834	**.aix-l** IBM AIX Discussion List
2-835	**.allmusic** on all forms of music
2-836	**.appc-l** APPC Discussion List
2-837	**.apple2-l** Apple II List
2-838	**.applicat** applications under Bitnet
2-839	**.arie-l** RLG Ariel Document Transmission Group
2-840	**.ashe-l** Higher Education Policy and Research
2-841	**.asm370** IBM 370 Assembly Programming Discussions
2-842	**.autism** Autism and Developmental Disabilities List
2-843	**.banyan-l** Banyan Vines Network Software Discussions
2-844	**.big-lan** Campus-Size LAN Discussion Group (moderated)
2-845	**.billing** Chargeback of Computer Resources
2-846	**.biosph-l** Biosphere, Ecology, Discussion List
2-847	**.bitnews** Bitnet news
2-848	**.blindnws** Blindness Issues and Discussions (moderated)

2-849	`.buslib-1` Business Libraries List
2-850	`.c+health` Computers and Health Discussion List
2-851	`.c18-1` 18th-Century Interdisciplinary Discussion
2-852	`.c370-1` c/370 Discussion List
2-853	`.candle-1` Candle Products Discussion List
2-854	`.catala` Catalan Discussion List
2-855	`.catholic` Free Catholics mailing list
2-856	`.cdromlan` CD-ROM on Local Area Networks
2-857	`.cfs.newsletter` Chronic Fatigue Syndrome Newsletter (moderated)
2-858	`.christia` Practical Christian Life (moderated)
2-859	`.cics-1` CICS Discussion List
2-860	`.cinema-1` on all forms of cinema
2-861	`.circplus` Circulation Reserve and Related Library Issues
2-862	`.cmspip-1` VM/SP CMS Pipelines Discussion List
2-863	`.commed` Communication Education
2-864	`.csg-1` Control System Group Network
2-865	`.cumrec-1` CUMREC-L administrative computer use
2-866	`.cw-email` Campus-Wide E-mail Discussion List
2-867	`.cwis-1` Campus-Wide Information Systems
2-868	`.cyber-1` CDC Computer Discussion
2-869	`.dasig` database administration
2-870	`.db2-1` DB2 Data Base Discussion List
2-871	`.dbase-1` On the use of the dBase IV
2-872	`.deaf-1` Deaf List
2-873	`.decnews` Digital Equipment Corporation News List
2-874	`.dectei-1` DECUS Education Software Library Discussions
2-875	`.devel-1` Technology Transfer in International Development
2-876	`.disarm-1` Disarmament Discussion List
2-877	`.domain-1` Domains Discussion Group
2-878	`.earntech` EARN Technical Group
2-879	`.ecolog-1` Ecological Society of America List
2-880	`.edi-1` Electronic Data Interchange Issues
2-881	`.edpolyan` Professionals and Students Discuss Education
2-882	`.edstat-1` Statistics Education Discussion List
2-883	`.edtech` EDTECH - Educational Technology (moderated)
2-884	`.edusig-1` EDUSIG Discussions
2-885	`.emusic-1` Electronic Music Discussion List

2-886	**.endnote** Bibsoft Endnote Discussions
2-887	**.envbeh-1** forum on Environment and Human Behavior
2-888	**.erl-1** Educational Research List
2-889	**.ethics-1** On ethics in computing
2-890	**.ethology** Ethology List
2-891	**.euearn-1** computers in Eastern Europe
2-892	**.film-1** Film Making and Reviews List
2-893	**.fnord-1** New Ways of Thinking List
2-894	**.frac-1** Fractal Discussion List
2-895	**.free-1** Fathers' Rights and Equality Discussion List
2-896	**.games-1** Computer Games List
2-897	**.gaynet** GayNet Discussion List (moderated)
2-898	**.gddm-1** the GDDM Discussion List
2-899	**.geodesic** list for the Discussion of Buckminster Fuller
2-900	**.gguide** BITNIC GGUIDE List
2-901	**.govdoc-1** on Government Document Issues
2-902	**.gutnberg** on Project Gutenberg Discussion List
2-903	**.hellas** the Hellenic Discussion List (moderated)
2-904	**.help-net** help on Bitnet and the Internet
2-905	**.hindu-d** Hindu Digest (moderated)
2-906	**.history** History List
2-907	**.hp3000-1** HP-3000 Computer Systems Discussion List
2-908	**.hytel-1** HYTELNET Discussions (moderated)
2-909	**.i-amiga** Info-Amiga List
2-910	**.ibm-hesc** IBM Higher Education Consortium
2-911	**.ibm-main** IBM Mainframe Discussion List
2-912	**.ibm-nets** BITNIC IBM-NETS List
2-913	**.ibm7171** Protocol Converter List
2-914	**.ibmtcp-1** IBM TCP/IP List
2-915	**.india-d** India Interest Group (moderated)
2-916	**.info-gcg** INFO-GCG: GCG Genetics Software Discussion
2-917	**.ingrafx** Information Graphics
2-918	**.innopac** Innovative Interfaces Online Public Access
2-919	**.ioob-1** Industrial Psychology
2-920	**.ipct-1** Interpersonal Computing and Technology List (moderated)
2-921	**.isn** ISN Data Switch Technical Discussion Group
2-922	**.jes2-1** JES2 Discussion group

2-923	**.jnet-l** BITNIC JNET-L List
2-924	**.l-hcap** Handicap List (moderated)
2-925	**.l-vmctr** VMCENTER Components Discussion List
2-926	**.lawsch-l** Law School Discussion List
2-927	**.liaison** BITNIC LIAISON
2-928	**.libref-l** Library Reference Issues (moderated)
2-929	**.libres** Library and Information Science Research (moderated)
2-930	**.license** Software Licensing List
2-931	**.linkfail** Link Failure Announcements
2-932	**.literary** On Literature
2-933	**.lstsrv-l** Forum on LISTSERV
2-934	**.mail-l** BITNIC MAIL-L List
2-935	**.mailbook** MAIL/MAILBOOK subscription list
2-936	**.mba-l** MBA Student Curriculum Discussion
2-937	**.mbu-l** megabyte University—Computers and Writing
2-938	**.mdphd-l** Dual-Degree Programs Discussion List
2-939	**.medforum** Medical Student Discussions (moderated)
2-940	**.medlib-l** Medical Libraries Discussion List
2-941	**.mednews** Health Info-Com Network Newsletter (moderated)
2-942	**.mideur-l** Middle Europe Discussion List
2-943	**.netnws-l** NETNWS-L Netnews List
2-944	**.nettrain** Network Trainers List
2-945	**.new-list** NEW-LIST—New List Announcements (moderated)
2-946	**.next-l** NeXT Computer List
2-947	**.nodmgt-l** node management
2-948	**.notabene** Nota Bene List
2-949	**.notis-l** NOTIS/DOBIS Discussion Group List
2-950	**.novell** Novell LAN Interest Group
2-951	**.omrscan** NMR Scanner Discussion
2-952	**.os2-l** OS/2 Discussion
2-953	**.ozone** OZONE Discussion List
2-954	**.pacs-l** Public-Access Computer System Forum (moderated)
2-955	**.page-l** IBM 3812/3820 Tips and Problems Discussion List
2-956	**.pagemakr** PageMaker for Desktop Publishers
2-957	**.physhare** K-12 Physics List
2-958	**.pmdf-l** PMDF Distribution List
2-959	**.politics** Forum for the Discussion of Politics

2-960	**.postcard**	Postcard Collectors Discussion Group
2-961	**.power-l**	POWER-L IBM RS/6000 POWER Family
2-962	**.powerh-l**	PowerHouse Discussion List
2-963	**.psycgrad**	Psychology Grad Student Discussions
2-964	**.qualrs-l**	Qualitative Research of the Human Sciences
2-965	**.relusr-l**	Relay Users Forum
2-966	**.rhetoric**	Rhetoric, social movements, persuasion
2-967	**.rra-l**	Romance Readers Anonymous (moderated)
2-968	**.rscs-l**	VM/RSCS Mailing List
2-969	**.rscsmods**	The RSCS Modifications List
2-970	**.s-comput**	Supercomputers List
2-971	**.sas-l**	SAS Discussion
2-972	**.script-l**	IBM vs Waterloo SCRIPT Discussion Group
2-973	**.scuba-l**	Scuba-diving Discussion List
2-974	**.seasia-l**	Southeast Asia Discussion List
2-975	**.seds-l**	Interchapter SEDS Communications
2-976	**.sfs-l**	VM Shared File System Discussion List
2-977	**.sganet**	Student Government Global Mail Network
2-978	**.simula**	the SIMULA Language List
2-979	**.slart-l**	SLA Research and Teaching
2-980	**.slovak-l**	Slovak Discussion List
2-981	**.snamgt-l**	SNA Network Management Discussion
2-982	**.sos-data**	Social Science Data List
2-983	**.spires-l**	SPIRES Conference List
2-984	**.sportpsy**	Exercise and Sports Psychology
2-985	**.spssx-l**	SPSSX Discussion
2-986	**.sqlinfo**	Forum for SQL/DS and Related Topics
2-987	**.stat-l**	Statistical Consulting
2-988	**.tech-l**	BITNIC TECH-L List
2-989	**.techwr-l**	Technical Writing List
2-990	**.tecmat-l**	Technology in Secondary Math
2-991	**.test**	Test Newsgroup
2-992	**.tex-l**	the TeXnical Topics List
2-993	**.tn3270-l**	tn3270 Protocol Discussion List
2-994	**.toolb-l**	Asymetrix Toolbook List
2-995	**.trans-l**	BITNIC TRANS-L List
2-996	**.travel-l**	Tourism Discussions

2-997	**.tsorexx** REXX for TSO List
2-998	**.ucp-l** University Computing Project Mailing List
2-999	**.ug-l** Usage Guidelines
2-1000	**.uigis-l** User Interface for Geographical Info Systems
2-1001	**.urep-l** UREP-L Mailing List
2-1002	**.usrdir-l** User Directory List
2-1003	**.uus-l** Unitarian-Universalist List
2-1004	**.valert-l** Virus Alert List (moderated)
2-1005	**.vfort-l** VS-Fortran Discussion List
2-1006	**.vm-util** VM Utilities Discussion List
2-1007	**.vmesa-l** VM/ESA Mailing List
2-1008	**.vmslsv-l** VAX/VMS LISTSERV Discussion List
2-1009	**.vmxa-l** VM/XA Discussion List
2-1010	**.vnews-l** VNEWS Discussion List
2-1011	**.vpiej-l** Electronic Publishing Discussion List
2-1012	**.win3-l** Microsoft Windows Version 3 Forum
2-1013	**.words-l** English Language Discussion Group
2-1014	**.wpcorp-l** WordPerfect Corporation Products Discussions
2-1015	**.wpwin-l** WordPerfect for Windows
2-1016	**.wx-talk** Weather Issues Discussions
2-1017	**.x400-l** X.400 Protocol List
2-1018	**.xcult-l** International Intercultural Newsletter
2-1019	**.xedit-l** VM System Editor List
2-1020	**.xerox-l** The Xerox Discussion List
2-1021	**.xmailer** Crosswell Mailer
2-1022	**.xtropy-l** Extopian List
2-1023	**.mailserv**
2-1024	**.word-mac** Word Processing on the Macintosh
2-1025	**.word-pc** Word Processing on the IBM PC
2-1026	**.org.peace-corps** International Volunteers Discussion Group
2-1027	**.software.international** International Software List (moderated)

biz Groups where businesses are allowed to post information on their products

2-1028	
2-1029	**.americast** AmeriCast announcements
2-1030	**.samples** samples of AmeriCast (moderated)
2-1031	**.books.technical** technical bookstore and publisher advertising and information
2-1032	**.clarinet** announcements about ClariNet

2-1033	**.sample**	samples of ClariNet newsgroups for the outside world
2-1034	**.comp**	
2-1035	**.hardware**	generic commercial hardware postings
2-1036	**.services**	generic commercial service postings
2-1037	**.software**	generic commercial software postings
2-1038	**.telebit**	support of the Telebit modem
2-1039	**.telebit.netblazer**	the Telebit Netblazer
2-1040	**.config**	biz Usenet configuration and administration
2-1041	**.control**	control information and messages
2-1042	**.dec**	DEC equipment and software
2-1043	**.decathena**	DECathena discussions
2-1044	**.decnews**	the DECNews newsletter (moderated)
2-1045	**.ip**	IP networking on DEC machines
2-1046	**.workstations**	DEC workstation discussions and info
2-1047	**.digex.announce**	announcements from Digex (moderated)
2-1048	**.jobs.offered**	position announcements
2-1049	**.misc**	miscellaneous postings of a commercial nature
2-1050	**.next.newprod**	new product announcements for the NeXT
2-1051	**.pagesat**	for discussion of the Pagesat Satellite Usenet Newsfeed
2-1052	**.sco**	**[Groups on the SCO Unix package]**
2-1053	**.announce**	SCO and related product announcements (moderated)
2-1054	**.binaries**	binary packages for SCO Xenix, Unix or ODT (moderated)
2-1055	**.general**	questions and answers, discussions and comments on SCO products
2-1056	**.magazine**	to discuss SCO Magazine and its contents
2-1057	**.opendesktop**	ODT environment and applications tech info, questions and answers
2-1058	**.sources**	source code ported to an SCO operating environment
2-1059	**.stolen**	postings about stolen merchandise
2-1060	**.tadpole.sparcbook**	on the Sparcbook portable computer
2-1061	**.test**	biz newsgroup test messages
2-1062	**.univel.misc**	Univel software
2-1063	**.zeos**	
2-1064	**.announce**	zeos Product Announcements (moderated)
2-1065	**.general**	zeos technical support and general information.

2-1066   clari   Groups from the clariNet company (Your site must be licensed!)

2-1067	**.biz**	
2-1068	**.commodity**	commodity news and price reports (moderated)

2-1069	**.courts** lawsuits and business-related legal matters (moderated)
2-1070	**.economy** economic news and indicators (moderated)
2-1071	**.economy.world** economy stories for non-US countries (moderated)
2-1072	**.features** business feature stories (moderated)
2-1073	**.finance** finance, currency, corporate finance (moderated)
2-1074	**.finance.earnings** earnings and dividend reports (moderated)
2-1075	**.finance.personal** personal investing and finance (moderated)
2-1076	**.finance.services** banks and financial industries (moderated)
2-1077	**.invest** news for investors (moderated)
2-1078	**.labor** strikes, unions and labor relations (moderated)
2-1079	**.market** general stock market news (moderated)
2-1080	**.market.amex** American Stock Exchange reports and news (moderated)
2-1081	**.market.dow** Dow Jones NYSE reports (moderated)
2-1082	**.market.ny** NYSE reports (moderated)
2-1083	**.market.otc** NASDAQ reports (moderated)
2-1084	**.market.report** general market reports, S&P etc (moderated)
2-1085	**.mergers** mergers and acquisitions (moderated)
2-1086	**.misc** other business news (moderated)
2-1087	**.products** important new products and services (moderated)
2-1088	**.top** top business news (moderated)
2-1089	**.urgent** breaking business news (moderated)
2-1090	**.canada**
2-1091	**.biz** Canadian Business Summaries (moderated)
2-1092	**.briefs** regular updates of Canadian News in Brief (moderated)
2-1093	**.briefs.ont** news briefs for Ontario and Toronto (moderated)
2-1094	**.briefs.west** news briefs for Alberta, the Prairies and B.C. (moderated)
2-1095	**.features** Alamanac, Ottawa Special, Arts (moderated)
2-1096	**.general** short items on Canadian news stories (moderated)
2-1097	**.gov** government related news (all levels) (moderated)
2-1098	**.law** crimes, the courts, and the law (moderated)
2-1099	**.newscast** regular newscast for Canadians (moderated)
2-1100	**.politics** political and election items (moderated)
2-1101	**.trouble** mishaps, accidents, and serious problems (moderated)
2-1102	**.feature**
2-1103	**.dave_barry** columns of humorist Dave Barry (moderated)
2-1104	**.mike_royko** Chicago Opinion Columnist Mike Royko (moderated)
2-1105	**.miss_manners** Judith Martin's Humorous Etiquette Advice (moderated)

2-1106	**.local**
2-1107	**.alberta.briefs** local news briefs (moderated)
2-1108	**.arizona** local news (moderated)
2-1109	**.arizona.briefs** local news briefs (moderated)
2-1110	**.bc.briefs** local news briefs (moderated)
2-1111	**.california** local news (moderated)
2-1112	**.california.briefs** local news briefs (moderated)
2-1113	**.chicago** local news (moderated)
2-1114	**.chicago.briefs** local news briefs (moderated)
2-1115	**.florida** local news (moderated)
2-1116	**.florida.briefs** local news briefs (moderated)
2-1117	**.georgia** local news (moderated)
2-1118	**.georgia.briefs** local news briefs (moderated)
2-1119	**.headlines** various local headline summaries (moderated)
2-1120	**.illinois** local news (moderated)
2-1121	**.illinois.briefs** local news briefs (moderated)
2-1122	**.indiana** local news (moderated)
2-1123	**.indiana.briefs** local news briefs (moderated)
2-1124	**.iowa** local news (moderated)
2-1125	**.iowa.briefs** local news briefs (moderated)
2-1126	**.los_angeles** local news (moderated)
2-1127	**.los_angeles.briefs** local news briefs (moderated)
2-1128	**.louisiana** local news (moderated)
2-1129	**.manitoba.briefs** local news briefs (moderated)
2-1130	**.maritimes.briefs** local news briefs (moderated)
2-1131	**.maryland** local news (moderated)
2-1132	**.maryland.briefs** local news briefs (moderated)
2-1133	**.massachusetts** local news (moderated)
2-1134	**.massachusetts.briefs** local news briefs (moderated)
2-1135	**.michigan** local news (moderated)
2-1136	**.michigan.briefs** local news briefs (moderated)
2-1137	**.minnesota** local news (moderated)
2-1138	**.minnesota.briefs** local news briefs (moderated)
2-1139	**.missouri** local news (moderated)
2-1140	**.missouri.briefs** local news briefs (moderated)
2-1141	**.nebraska** local news (moderated)
2-1142	**.nebraska.briefs** local news briefs (moderated)

2-1143	`.nevada` local news (moderated)
2-1144	`.nevada.briefs` local news briefs (moderated)
2-1145	`.new_england` local news (moderated)
2-1146	`.new_hampshire` local news (moderated)
2-1147	`.new_jersey` local news (moderated)
2-1148	`.new_jersey.briefs` local news briefs (moderated)
2-1149	`.new_york` local news (moderated)
2-1150	`.new_york.briefs` local news briefs (moderated)
2-1151	`.nyc` local news (New York City) (moderated)
2-1152	`.nyc.briefs` local news briefs (moderated)
2-1153	`.ohio` local news (moderated)
2-1154	`.ohio.briefs` local news briefs (moderated)
2-1155	`.ontario.briefs` local news briefs (moderated)
2-1156	`.oregon` local news (moderated)
2-1157	`.oregon.briefs` local news briefs (moderated)
2-1158	`.pennsylvania` local news (moderated)
2-1159	`.pennsylvania.briefs` local news briefs (moderated)
2-1160	`.saskatchewan.briefs` local news briefs (moderated)
2-1161	`.sfbay` stories datelined San Francisco Bay Area (moderated)
2-1162	`.texas` local news (moderated)
2-1163	`.texas.briefs` local news briefs (moderated)
2-1164	`.utah` local news (moderated)
2-1165	`.utah.briefs` local news briefs (moderated)
2-1166	`.virginia+dc` local news (moderated)
2-1167	`.virginia+dc.briefs` local news briefs (moderated)
2-1168	`.washington` local news (moderated)
2-1169	`.washington.briefs` local news briefs (moderated)
2-1170	`.wisconsin` local news (moderated)
2-1171	`.wisconsin.briefs` local news briefs (moderated)
2-1172	`.matrix_news` monthly journal on the Internet (moderated)
2-1173	**`.nb`**
2-1174	`.apple` newsbytes Apple/Macintosh news (moderated)
2-1175	`.business` newsbytes business and industry news (moderated)
2-1176	`.general` newsbytes general computer news (moderated)
2-1177	`.govt` newsbytes legal and government computer news (moderated)
2-1178	`.ibm` newsbytes IBM PC world coverage (moderated)
2-1179	`.review` newsbytes new product reviews (moderated)

2-1180   **.telecom** newsbytes telecom and online industry news (moderated)

2-1181   **.top** newsbytes top stories (crossposted) (moderated)

2-1182   **.trends** newsbytes new developments and trends (moderated)

2-1183   **.unix** newsbytes Unix news (moderated)

2-1184   **.net**

2-1185   **.admin** announcements for news admins at ClariNet sites (moderated)

2-1186   **.announce** announcements for all ClariNet readers (moderated)

2-1187   **.newusers** online info about ClariNet (moderated)

2-1188   **.products** new ClariNet products (moderated)

2-1189   **.talk** on ClariNet—only unmoderated group

2-1190   **.news**

2-1191   **.almanac** daily almanac—quotes, "this date in history," etc. (moderated)

2-1192   **.arts** stage, drama, and other fine arts (moderated)

2-1193   **.aviation** aviation industry and mishaps (moderated)

2-1194   **.books** books and publishing (moderated)

2-1195   **.briefs** regular news summaries (moderated)

2-1196   **.bulletin** major breaking stories of the week (moderated)

2-1197   **.canada** news related to Canada (moderated)

2-1198   **.cast** regular U.S. news summary (moderated)

2-1199   **.children** stories related to children and parenting (moderated)

2-1200   **.consumer** consumer news, car reviews, etc. (moderated)

2-1201   **.demonstration** demonstrations around the world (moderated)

2-1202   **.disaster** major problems, accidents and natural disasters (moderated)

2-1203   **.economy** general economic news (moderated)

2-1204   **.election** news regarding both US and international elections (moderated)

2-1205   **.entertain** entertainment industry news and features (moderated)

2-1206   **.europe** news related to Europe (moderated)

2-1207   **.features** unclassified feature stories (moderated)

2-1208   **.fighting** clashes around the world (moderated)

2-1209   **.flash** ultra-important once-a-year news flashes (moderated)

2-1210   **.goodnews** stories of success and survival (moderated)

2-1211   **.gov** general government-related stories (moderated)

2-1212   **.gov.agency** government agencies, FBI, etc. (moderated)

2-1213   **.gov.budget** budgets at all levels (moderated)

2-1214   **.gov.corrupt** government corruption, kickbacks, etc. (moderated)

2-1215   **.gov.international** international government-related stories (moderated)

2-1216   **.gov.officials** government officials and their problems (moderated)

2-1217   **.gov.state**   state government stories of national importance (moderated)

2-1218   **.gov.taxes**   tax laws, trials, etc. (moderated)

2-1219   **.gov.usa**   U.S. Federal government news. (high volume) (moderated)

2-1220   **.group**   special interest groups not covered in their own group (moderated)

2-1221   **.group.blacks**   news of interest to black people (moderated)

2-1222   **.group.gays**   homosexuality and Gay Rights (moderated)

2-1223   **.group.jews**   Jews and Jewish interests (moderated)

2-1224   **.group.women**   women's issues and abortion (moderated)

2-1225   **.headlines**   hourly list of the top U.S./World headlines (moderated)

2-1226   **.hot.east_europe**   news from Eastern Europe (moderated)

2-1227   **.hot.somalia**   news from Somalia (moderated)

2-1228   **.hot.ussr**   news from the Soviet Union (moderated)

2-1229   **.interest**   human interest stories (moderated)

2-1230   **.interest.animals**   animals in the news (moderated)

2-1231   **.interest.history**   human interest stories and history in the making (moderated)

2-1232   **.interest.people**   famous people in the news (moderated)

2-1233   **.interest.people.column**   daily "People" column—tidbits on celebs (moderated)

2-1234   **.interest.quirks**   unusual or funny news stories (moderated)

2-1235   **.issues**   stories on major issues not covered in their own group (moderated)

2-1236   **.issues.civil_rights**   freedom, Racism, Civil Rights Issues (moderated)

2-1237   **.issues.conflict**   conflict between groups around the world (moderated)

2-1238   **.issues.family**   family, child abuse, etc. (moderated)

2-1239   **.labor**   unions, strikes (moderated)

2-1240   **.labor.strike**   strikes (moderated)

2-1241   **.law**   general group for law issues (moderated)

2-1242   **.law.civil**   civil trials and litigation (moderated)

2-1243   **.law.crime**   major crimes (moderated)

2-1244   **.law.crime.sex**   sex crimes and trials (moderated)

2-1245   **.law.crime.trial**   trials for criminal actions (moderated)

2-1246   **.law.crime.violent**   violent crime and criminals (moderated)

2-1247   **.law.drugs**   drug-related crimes and drug stories (moderated)

2-1248   **.law.investigation**   investigation of crimes (moderated)

2-1249   **.law.police**   police and law enforcement (moderated)

2-1250   **.law.prison**   prisons, prisoners, and escapes (moderated)

2-1251   **.law.profession**   lawyers, judges, etc. (moderated)

2-1252   **.law.supreme**   U.S. Supreme court rulings and news (moderated)

2-1253   **.lifestyle**   fashion, leisure, etc. (moderated)

2-1254	**.military**	military equipment, people, and issues (moderated)
2-1255	**.movies**	reviews, news, and stories on movie stars (moderated)
2-1256	**.music**	reviews and issues concerning music and musicians (moderated)
2-1257	**.politics**	politicians and politics (moderated)
2-1258	**.politics.people**	politicians and political personalities (moderated)
2-1259	**.religion**	religion, religious leaders, televangelists (moderated)
2-1260	**.sex**	sexual issues, sex-related political stories (moderated)
2-1261	**.terrorism**	terrorist actions and related news around the world (moderated)
2-1262	**.top**	top U.S. news stories (moderated)
2-1263	**.top.world**	top international news stories (moderated)
2-1264	**.trends**	surveys and trends (moderated)
2-1265	**.trouble**	less major accidents, problems and mishaps (moderated)
2-1266	**.tv**	TV news, reviews, and stars (moderated)
2-1267	**.urgent**	major breaking stories of the day (moderated)
2-1268	**.weather**	weather and temperature reports (moderated)
2-1269	**.sfbay**	
2-1270	**.briefs**	twice-daily news roundups for SF Bay Area (moderated)
2-1271	**.entertain**	reviews and entertainment news for SF Bay Area (moderated)
2-1272	**.fire**	stories from Fire Departments of the SF Bay Area (moderated)
2-1273	**.general**	main stories for SF Bay Area (moderated)
2-1274	**.misc**	shorter general items for SF Bay Area (moderated)
2-1275	**.police**	stories from the Police Depts. of the SF Bay (moderated)
2-1276	**.roads**	reports from Caltrans and the CHP (moderated)
2-1277	**.short**	very short items for SF Bay Area (moderated)
2-1278	**.weather**	SF Bay and California weather reports (moderated)
2-1279	**.sports**	
2-1280	**.baseball**	baseball scores, stories, stats (moderated)
2-1281	**.baseball.games**	baseball games and box scores (moderated)
2-1282	**.basketball**	basketball coverage (moderated)
2-1283	**.basketball.college**	college basketball coverage (moderated)
2-1284	**.features**	sports feature stories (moderated)
2-1285	**.football**	pro football coverage (moderated)
2-1286	**.football.college**	college football coverage (moderated)
2-1287	**.hockey**	NHL coverage (moderated)
2-1288	**.misc**	other sports, plus general sports news (moderated)
2-1289	**.motor**	racing, motor sports (moderated)
2-1290	**.olympic**	the Olympic Games (moderated)

2-1291	**.tennis** tennis news and scores (moderated)
2-1292	**.top** top sports news (moderated)
2-1293	**.tw**
2-1294	**.aerospace** aerospace industry and companies (moderated)
2-1295	**.computers** computer industry, applications, and developments (moderated)
2-1296	**.defense** defense-industry issues (moderated)
2-1297	**.education** stories involving universities and colleges (moderated)
2-1298	**.electronics** electronics makers and sellers (moderated)
2-1299	**.environment** environmental news, hazardous waste, forests (moderated)
2-1300	**.health** disease, medicine, health care, sick celebs (moderated)
2-1301	**.health.aids** AIDS stories, research, political issues (moderated)
2-1302	**.misc** general industrial technology stories (moderated)
2-1303	**.nuclear** nuclear power and waste (moderated)
2-1304	**.science** general science stories (moderated)
2-1305	**.space** NASA, astronomy, and spaceflight (moderated)
2-1306	**.stocks** regular reports on computer and technology stock prices (moderated)
2-1307	**.telecom** phones, satellites, media, and general telecom (moderated)

2-1308 **comp** Groups on computer related topics

2-1309	**.admin.policy** on site administration policies
2-1310	**.ai** artificial-intelligence discussions
2-1311	**.edu** applications of artificial intelligence to education
2-1312	**.fuzzy** fuzzy set theory, a.k.a. fuzzy logic
2-1313	**.genetic** genetic algorithms in computing
2-1314	**.jair.announce** announcements of papers in Journal of Artificial Intelligence Research
2-1315	**.nat-lang** natural-language processing by computers
2-1316	**.neural-nets** on neural networks
2-1317	**.nlang-know-rep** natural Language and Knowledge Representation (moderated)
2-1318	**.philosophy** philosophical aspects of artificial intelligence
2-1319	**.shells** artificial intelligence applied to shells
2-1320	**.vision** artificial intelligence vision research (moderated)
2-1321	**.answers** repository for periodic Usenet articles (moderated)
2-1322	**.apps.spreadsheets** spreadsheets on various platforms
2-1323	**.arch** computer architecture
2-1324	**.bus.vmebus** hardware and software for VMEbus Systems
2-1325	**.storage** storage system issues, both hardware and software
2-1326	**.archives** descriptions of public-access archives (moderated)

2-1327	**.admin** issues relating to computer-archive administration
2-1328	**.msdos.announce** announcements about MSDOS archives (moderated)
2-1329	**.msdos.d** on materials available in MSDOS archives
2-1330	**.bbs**
2-1331	**.misc** anything about computer bulletin board systems
2-1332	**.waffle** the Waffle BBS and Usenet system on all platforms
2-1333	**.benchmarks** on benchmarking techniques and results
2-1334	**.binaries** [Groups on Groups with downloadable software (shareware, demos, and freeware!)]
2-1335	**.acorn** binary-only postings for Acorn machines (moderated)
2-1336	**.amiga** encoded public-domain programs in binary (moderated)
2-1337	**.apple2** binary-only postings for the Apple II computer
2-1338	**.atari.st** binary-only postings for the Atari ST (moderated)
2-1339	**.ibm.pc** binary-only postings for IBM PC/MS-DOS (moderated)
2-1340	**.ibm.pc.d** on IBM/PC binary postings
2-1341	**.ibm.pc.wanted** requests for IBM PC and compatible programs
2-1342	**.mac** encoded Macintosh programs in binary (moderated)
2-1343	**.ms-windows** binary programs for Microsoft Windows (moderated)
2-1344	**.os2** binaries for use under the OS/2 API (moderated)
2-1345	**.bugs** [Groups on problem reports for various software packages]
2-1346	**.2bsd** reports of Unix version 2BSD related bugs
2-1347	**.4bsd** reports of Unix version 4BSD related bugs
2-1348	**.4bsd.ucb-fixes** bug reports/fixes for BSD Unix (moderated)
2-1349	**.misc** general Unix bug reports and fixes (incl V7, UUCP)
2-1350	**.sys5** reports of USG (System III, V etc.) bugs
2-1351	**.cad** [Groups on Groups on various Computer Aided Design(CAD) packages]
2-1352	**.cadence** users of Cadence Design Systems products
2-1353	**.compass** Compass Design Automation EDA tools
2-1354	**.pro-engineer** engineering applications of CAD
2-1355	**.synthesis** research and production in the field of logic synthesis
2-1356	**.client-server** topics relating to client/server technology
2-1357	**.cog-eng** cognitive engineering
2-1358	**.compilers** compiler construction, theory, etc. (moderated)
2-1359	**.compression** data-compression algorithms and theory
2-1360	**.research** on data-compression research
2-1361	**.databases** database and data-management issues and theory
2-1362	**.informix** Informix database-management software discussions
2-1363	**.ingres** issues relating to INGRES products

2-1364	`.ms-access`	MS Windows' relational database system, Access
2-1365	`.object`	object-oriented paradigms in database systems
2-1366	`.oracle`	the SQL database products of the Oracle Corporation
2-1367	`.pick`	pick-like, postrelational database systems
2-1368	`.sybase`	implementations of the SQL Server
2-1369	`.theory`	discussing advances in database technology
2-1370	`.xbase.fox`	foxpro
2-1371	`.xbase.misc`	miscellaneous database questions
2-1372	**`.dcom`**	
2-1373	`.cell-relay`	forum for discussion of Cell Relay-based products
2-1374	`.fax`	fax hardware, software, and protocols
2-1375	`.isdn`	the Integrated Services Digital Network (ISDN)
2-1376	`.lans.ethernet`	on the Ethernet/IEEE 802.3 protocols
2-1377	`.lans.fddi`	on the FDDI protocol suite
2-1378	`.lans.hyperchannel`	hyperchannel networks within an IP network
2-1379	`.lans.misc`	local area network hardware and software
2-1380	`.lans.token-ring`	installing and using token ring networks
2-1381	`.modems`	data communications hardware and software
2-1382	`.servers`	selecting and operating data communications servers
2-1383	`.sys.cisco`	info on Cisco routers and bridges
2-1384	`.sys.wellfleet`	Wellfleet bridge and router systems hardware and software
2-1385	`.telecom`	telecommunications digest (moderated)
2-1386	`.doc`	archived public-domain documentation (moderated)
2-1387	`.techreports`	lists of technical reports (moderated)
2-1388	`.dsp`	digital signal processing using computers
2-1389	`.editors`	topics related to computerized text editing
2-1390	`.edu`	computer science education
2-1391	`.composition`	writing instruction in computer-based classrooms
2-1392	`.emacs`	EMACS editors of different flavors
2-1393	`.fonts`	typefonts — design, conversion, use, etc.
2-1394	`.graphics`	computer graphics, art, animation, image processing
2-1395	`.algorithms`	application of algorithms to graphics
2-1396	`.animation`	technical aspects of computer animation
2-1397	`.avs`	the Application Visualization System
2-1398	`.data-explorer`	data explorer
2-1399	`.explorer`	the Explorer Modular Visualisation Environment (MVE)
2-1400	`.gnuplot`	the GNUPLOT interactive function plotter

2-1401	**.opengl** the OpenGL 3D application programming interface
2-1402	**.research** highly technical computer graphics discussion (moderated)
2-1403	**.visualization** info on scientific visualization
2-1404	**.groupware** software and hardware for shared interactive environments
2-1405	**.human-factors** issues related to human-computer interaction (HCI)
2-1406	**.infosystems** any discussion about information systems
2-1407	**.gis** on Geographic Information Systems
2-1408	**.gopher** on the gopher information service
2-1409	**.wais** the Z39.50-based WAIS full-text search system
2-1410	**.www** the World Wide Web information system
2-1411	**.internet.library** discussing electronic libraries (moderated)
2-1412	**.ivideodisc** interactive videodiscs—uses, potential, etc.
2-1413	**.lang** [Groups for discussion of computer languages]
2-1414	**.ada** on Ada
2-1415	**.apl** on APL
2-1416	**.asm370** programming in IBM System/370 Assembly Language
2-1417	**.c** on C
2-1418	**.c++** the object-oriented C++ language
2-1419	**.clos** common Lisp Object System discussions
2-1420	**.clu** the CLU language and related topics
2-1421	**.dylan** for discussion of the Dylan language
2-1422	**.eiffel** the object-oriented Eiffel language
2-1423	**.forth** on Forth
2-1424	**.forth.mac** the CSI MacForth programming environment
2-1425	**.fortran** on FORTRAN
2-1426	**.functional** on functional languages
2-1427	**.hermes** the Hermes language for distributed applications
2-1428	**.icon** topics related to the ICON programming language
2-1429	**.idl** IDL (Interface Description Language) related topics
2-1430	**.idl-pvwave** IDL and PV-Wave language discussions
2-1431	**.lisp** on LISP
2-1432	**.lisp.franz** the Franz Lisp programming language
2-1433	**.lisp.mcl** discussing Apple's Macintosh Common Lisp
2-1434	**.lisp.x** the XLISP language system
2-1435	**.logo** the LOGO teaching and learning language
2-1436	**.misc** different computer languages not specifically listed
2-1437	**.ml** ML languages including Standard ML, CAML, Lazy ML etc (moderated)

2-1438   **.modula2** on Modula-2

2-1439   **.modula3** on the Modula-3 language

2-1440   **.oberon** the Oberon language and system

2-1441   **.objective-c** the Objective-C language and environment

2-1442   **.pascal** on Pascal

2-1443   **.perl** on Larry Wall's Perl system

2-1444   **.pop** pop11 and the Plug user group

2-1445   **.postscript** the PostScript Page Description Language

2-1446   **.prolog** on PROLOG

2-1447   **.rexx** the REXX command language

2-1448   **.sather** the object-oriented computer language Sather

2-1449   **.scheme** the Scheme programming language

2-1450   **.scheme.c** the Scheme language environment

2-1451   **.sigplan** information and announcements from ACM SIGPLAN (moderated)

2-1452   **.smalltalk** on Smalltalk 80

2-1453   **.tcl** the Tcl programming language and related tools

2-1454   **.verilog** discussing Verilog and PLI

2-1455   **.vhdl** VHSIC Hardware Description Language, IEEE 1076/87

2-1456   **.visual** visual programming languages

2-1457   **.laser-printers** laser printers, hardware, and software (moderated)

2-1458   **.lsi** large scale integrated circuits

2-1459   **.cad** electrical Computer Aided Design

2-1460   **.testing** testing of electronic circuits

2-1461   **.mail [Groups on electronic mail and related software]**

2-1462   **.elm** discussion and fixes for ELM mail system

2-1463   **.headers** gatewayed from the Internet header-people list

2-1464   **.maps** various maps, including UUCP maps (moderated)

2-1465   **.mh** the UCI version of the Rand Message Handling system

2-1466   **.mime** multipurpose Internet Mail Extensions of RFC 1341

2-1467   **.misc** general discussions about computer mail

2-1468   **.multi-media** multimedia mail

2-1469   **.mush** the Mail User's Shell (MUSH)

2-1470   **.sendmail** configuring and using the BSD sendmail agent

2-1471   **.uucp** mail in the UUCP network environment

2-1472   **.misc** general topics about computers not covered elsewhere

2-1473   **.multimedia** interactive multimedia technologies of all kinds

2-1474   **.music** applications of computers in music research

2-1475	**.networks**
2-1476	**.noctools** groups on the NOC tools software
2-1477	**.noctools.announce** info and announcements about NOC tools (moderated)
2-1478	**.noctools.bugs** bug reports and fixes for NOC tools
2-1479	**.noctools.d** on NOC tools
2-1480	**.noctools.submissions** for NOC software
2-1481	**.newprod** announcements of new products of interest (moderated)
2-1482	**.object** object-oriented programming and languages
2-1483	**.logic** integrating object-oriented and logic programming
2-1484	**.org [Groups on various Internet related organizations]**
2-1485	**.acm** topics about the Association for Computing Machinery
2-1486	**.decus** Digital Equipment Computer Users' Society newsgroup
2-1487	**.eff.news** news from the Electronic Frontiers Foundation (moderated)
2-1488	**.eff.talk** on EFF goals, strategies, etc.
2-1489	**.fidonet** FidoNews digest, official news of FIDOnet Assoc (moderated)
2-1490	**.ieee** issues and announcements about the IEEE and its members
2-1491	**.isoc.interest** on the Internet Society
2-1492	**.issnnet** the International Student Society for Neural Networks
2-1493	**.sug** talk about/for the The Sun User's Group
2-1494	**.usenix** USENIX Association events and announcements
2-1495	**.usenix.roomshare** finding lodging during Usenix conferences
2-1496	**.os [Groups on computer operating systems]**
2-1497	**.386bsd.announce** announcements relating to the 386bsd operating system(moderated)
2-1498	**.386bsd.apps** applications which run under 386bsd
2-1499	**.386bsd.bugs** bugs and fixes for the 386bsd OS and its clients
2-1500	**.386bsd.development** working on 386bsd internals
2-1501	**.386bsd.misc** general aspects of 386bsd not covered by other groups
2-1502	**.386bsd.questions** general questions about 386bsd
2-1503	**.aos** topics related to Data General's AOS/VS
2-1504	**.coherent** discussion and support of the Coherent operating system
2-1505	**.cpm** on the CP/M operating system
2-1506	**.cpm.amethyst** on Amethyst, CP/M-80 software package
2-1507	**.linux** the free Unix-clone for the 386/486, LINUX
2-1508	**.linux.admin** Linux implementations
2-1509	**.linux.announce** announcements important to the Linux community (moderated)
2-1510	**.linux.development** Linux development
2-1511	**.linux.help** help with Linux installation

2-1512	**.linux.misc** questions about Linux
2-1513	**.mach** the MACH OS from CMU and other places
2-1514	**.minix** on Tanenbaum's MINIX system
2-1515	**.misc** general OS-oriented discussion not carried elsewhere
2-1516	**.ms-windows.advocacy** speculation and debate about Microsoft Windows
2-1517	**.ms-windows.announce** announcements relating to Windows (moderated)
2-1518	**.ms-windows.apps** applications in the Windows environment
2-1519	**.ms-windows.misc** general discussions about Windows issues
2-1520	**.ms-windows.nt.misc** general discussion about Windows NT
2-1521	**.ms-windows.nt.setup** configuring Windows NT systems
2-1522	**.ms-windows.programmer.misc** programming Microsoft Windows
2-1523	**.ms-windows.programmer.tools** development tools in Windows
2-1524	**.ms-windows.programmer.win32** 32-bit Windows programming interfaces
2-1525	**.ms-windows.setup** installing and configuring Microsoft Windows
2-1526	**.msdos.4dos** the 4DOS command processor for MS-DOS
2-1527	**.msdos.apps** on applications that run under MS-DOS
2-1528	**.msdos.desqview** QuarterDeck's Desqview and related products
2-1529	**.msdos.mail-news** administering mail and network-news systems under MS-DOS
2-1530	**.msdos.misc** miscellaneous topics about MS-DOS machines
2-1531	**.msdos.pcgeos** GeoWorks PC/GEOS and PC/GEOS-based packages
2-1532	**.msdos.programmer** programming MS-DOS machines
2-1533	**.msdos.programmer.turbovision** borland's text application libraries
2-1534	**.os2.advocacy** supporting and flaming OS/2
2-1535	**.os2.announce** notable news and announcements related to OS/2 (moderated)
2-1536	**.os2.apps** on applications under OS/2
2-1537	**.os2.beta** on beta releases of OS/2 systems software
2-1538	**.os2.bugs** OS/2 system bug reports, fixes and work-arounds
2-1539	**.os2.misc** miscellaneous topics about the OS/2 system
2-1540	**.os2.multimedia** multi-media on OS/2 systems
2-1541	**.os2.networking** networking in OS/2 environments
2-1542	**.os2.programmer** programming OS/2 machines
2-1543	**.os2.programmer.misc** programming OS/2 machines
2-1544	**.os2.programmer.porting** porting software to OS/2 machines
2-1545	**.os2.setup** installing and configuring OS/2 systems
2-1546	**.os2.ver1x** all aspects of OS/2 versions 1.0 through 1.3
2-1547	**.os9** on the OS/9 operating system
2-1548	**.research** operating systems and related areas (moderated)

2-1549   **.rsts** topics related to the PDP-11 RSTS/E operating system

2-1550   **.v** the V distributed operating system from Stanford

2-1551   **.vms** DEC's VAX line of computers and VMS

2-1552   **.vxworks** the VxWorks real-time operating system

2-1553   **.xinu** the XINU operating system from Purdue (D. Comer)

2-1554   **.parallel** massively parallel hardware/software (moderated)

2-1555   **.pvm** the PVM system of multicomputer parallelization

2-1556   **.patents** discussing patents of computer technology (moderated)

2-1557   **.periphs** peripheral devices

2-1558   **.printers** information on printers

2-1559   **.scsi** on SCSI-based peripheral devices

2-1560   **.programming** programming issues that transcend languages and OSs

2-1561   **.protocols** [Groups on various networking and other protocols]

2-1562   **.appletalk** Applebus hardware and software

2-1563   **.dicom** Digital Imaging and Communications in Medicine

2-1564   **.ibm** networking with IBM mainframes

2-1565   **.iso** the ISO protocol stack

2-1566   **.iso.dev-environ** the ISO Development Environment

2-1567   **.iso.x400** x400 mail protocol discussions

2-1568   **.iso.x400.gateway** x400 mail gateway discussions (moderated)

2-1569   **.kerberos** the Kerberos authentication server

2-1570   **.kermit** info about the Kermit package (moderated)

2-1571   **.misc** various forms and types of FTP protocol

2-1572   **.nfs** on the Network File System protocol

2-1573   **.pcnet** topics related to PCNET (a personal computer network)

2-1574   **.ppp** on the Internet Point to Point Protocol

2-1575   **.snmp** the Simple Network Management Protocol

2-1576   **.tcp-ip** TCP and IP network protocols

2-1577   **.tcp-ip.domains** topics related to Domain Style names

2-1578   **.tcp-ip.ibmpc** TCP/IP for IBM(-like) personal computers

2-1579   **.time.ntp** the network time protocol

2-1580   **.publish.cdrom** [Groups on publishing CD-ROMs]

2-1581   **.hardware** hardware used in publishing with CD-ROM

2-1582   **.multimedia** software for multimedia authoring and publishing

2-1583   **.software** software used in publishing with CD-ROM

2-1584   **.realtime** issues related to real-time computing

2-1585   **.research.japan** the nature of research in Japan (moderated)

2-1586   **.risks** risks to the public from computers and users (moderated)

2-1587   **.robotics** all aspects of robots and their applications

2-1588   **.security**

2-1589   **.announce** announcements from the CERT about security (moderated)

2-1590   **.misc** security issues of computers and networks

2-1591   **.simulation** simulation methods, problems, uses (moderated)

2-1592   **.society** the impact of technology on society (moderated)

2-1593   **.cu-digest** the Computer Underground Digest (moderated)

2-1594   **.development** computer technology in developing countries

2-1595   **.folklore** computer folklore and culture, past and present (moderated)

2-1596   **.futures** events in technology affecting future computing

2-1597   **.privacy** effects of technology on privacy (moderated)

2-1598   **.soft-sys [Groups on software environments]**

2-1599   **.andrew** the Andrew system from CMU

2-1600   **.khoros** the Khoros X11 visualization system

2-1601   **.matlab** the MathWorks calculation and visualization package

2-1602   **.nextstep** the NeXTstep computing environment

2-1603   **.sas** the SAS statistics package

2-1604   **.shazam** the SHAZAM econometrics computer program

2-1605   **.spss** the SPSS statistics package

2-1606   **.software-eng** software engineering and related topics

2-1607   **.software**

2-1608   **.licensing** software licensing technology

2-1609   **.testing** all aspects of testing computer systems

2-1610   **.sources [Groups with source code distribution for many computers]**

2-1611   **.3b1** source code-only postings for the AT&T 3b1 (moderated)

2-1612   **.acorn** source code-only postings for the Acorn (moderated)

2-1613   **.amiga** source code-only postings for the Amiga (moderated)

2-1614   **.apple2** source code and discussion for the Apple2 (moderated)

2-1615   **.atari.st** source code-only postings for the Atari ST (moderated)

2-1616   **.bugs** bug reports, fixes, discussion for posted sources

2-1617   **.d** for any discussion of source postings

2-1618   **.games** postings of recreational software (moderated)

2-1619   **.games.bugs** bug reports and fixes for posted game software

2-1620   **.hp48** programs for the HP48 and HP28 calculators (moderated)

2-1621   **.mac** software for the Apple Macintosh (moderated)

2-1622   **.misc** posting of software (moderated)

2-1623	**.postscript** source code for programs written in PostScript (moderated)
2-1624	**.reviewed** source code evaluated by peer review (moderated)
2-1625	**.sun** software for Sun workstations (moderated)
2-1626	**.testers** finding people to test software
2-1627	**.unix** postings of complete, Unix-oriented sources (moderated)
2-1628	**.wanted** requests for software and fixes
2-1629	**.x** software for the X-Windows system (moderated)
2-1630	**.specification** languages and methodologies for formal specification
2-1631	**.z** on the formal specification notation Z
2-1632	**.speech** research and applications in speech science and technology
2-1633	**.std [Groups on standards in the computer industry]**
2-1634	**.announce** announcements about standards activities (moderated)
2-1635	**.c** on C language standards
2-1636	**.c++** on C++ language, library, standards
2-1637	**.internat** on international standards
2-1638	**.misc** on various standards
2-1639	**.mumps** discussion for the X11.1 committee on Mumps (moderated)
2-1640	**.unix** discussion for the P1003 committee on Unix (moderated)
2-1641	**.wireless** examining standards for wireless network technology (moderated)
2-1642	**.sw.components** software components and related technology
2-1643	**.sys [Groups on various computer systems]**
2-1644	**.3b1** discussion and support of AT&T 7300/3B1/UnixPC
2-1645	**.acorn** on Acorn and ARM-based computers
2-1646	**.acorn.advocacy** why Acorn computers and programs are better
2-1647	**.acorn.announce** announcements for Acorn and ARM users (moderated)
2-1648	**.acorn.tech** software and hardware aspects of Acorn and ARM products
2-1649	**.alliant** info and discussion about Alliant computers
2-1650	**.amiga.advocacy** why an Amiga is better than XYZ
2-1651	**.amiga.announce** announcements about the Amiga (moderated)
2-1652	**.amiga.applications** miscellaneous applications
2-1653	**.amiga.audio** music, MIDI, speech synthesis, other sounds
2-1654	**.amiga.datacomm** methods of getting bytes in and out
2-1655	**.amiga.emulations** various hardware and software emulators
2-1656	**.amiga.games** on games for the Commodore Amiga
2-1657	**.amiga.graphics** charts, graphs, pictures, etc.
2-1658	**.amiga.hardware** Amiga computer hardware, reviews, etc.
2-1659	**.amiga.introduction** group for newcomers to Amigas

2-1660	`.amiga.marketplace` where to find it, prices, etc.
2-1661	`.amiga.misc` discussions not falling in another Amiga group
2-1662	`.amiga.multimedia` animations, video and multimedia
2-1663	`.amiga.programmer` developers and hobbyists discuss code
2-1664	`.amiga.reviews` reviews of Amiga software, hardware (moderated)
2-1665	`.apollo` Apollo computer systems
2-1666	`.apple2` on Apple II micros
2-1667	`.apple2.comm` Apple II data communications
2-1668	`.apple2.gno` the AppleIIgs GNO multitasking environment
2-1669	`.apple2.marketplace` buying, selling and trading Apple II equipment
2-1670	`.apple2.programmer` programming on the Apple II
2-1671	`.apple2.usergroups` all about Apple II user groups
2-1672	`.atari.8bit` on 8-bit Atari micros
2-1673	`.atari.advocacy` attacking and defending Atari computers
2-1674	`.atari.st` on 16-bit Atari micros
2-1675	`.atari.st.tech` technical discussions of Atari ST hard/software
2-1676	`.att` on AT&T microcomputers
2-1677	`.cbm` on Commodore micros
2-1678	`.cdc` control Data Corporation Computers (e.g., Cybers)
2-1679	`.concurrent` the Concurrent/Masscomp line of computers (moderated)
2-1680	`.convex` convex real-time systems
2-1681	`.handhelds` handheld computers and programmable calculators
2-1682	`.hp` on Hewlett-Packard equipment
2-1683	`.hp48` Hewlett-Packard's HP48 and HP28 calculators
2-1684	`.ibm.pc.demos` demonstration programs which showcase programmer skill
2-1685	`.ibm.pc.digest` the IBM PC, PC-XT, and PC-AT (moderated)
2-1686	`.ibm.pc.games` games for IBM PCs and compatibles
2-1687	`.ibm.pc.games.action` arcade-style games on PCs
2-1688	`.ibm.pc.games.adventure` adventure (non-role-playing) games on PCs
2-1689	`.ibm.pc.games.announce` announcements for all PC gamers (moderated)
2-1690	`.ibm.pc.games.flight-sim` flight simulators on PCs
2-1691	`.ibm.pc.games.misc` games not covered by other PC groups
2-1692	`.ibm.pc.games.rpg` role-playing games on the PC
2-1693	`.ibm.pc.games.strategic` strategy/planning games on PCs
2-1694	`.ibm.pc.hardware` XT/AT/EISA hardware, any vendor
2-1695	`.ibm.pc.misc` on IBM personal computers
2-1696	`.ibm.pc.rt` topics related to IBM's RT computer

2-1697   `.ibm.pc.soundcard` hardware and software aspects of PC sound cards

2-1698   `.ibm.ps2.hardware` microchannel hardware, any vendor

2-1699   `.intel` on Intel systems and parts

2-1700   `.intel.ipsc310` anything related to the Intel 310

2-1701   `.isis` the ISIS distributed system from Cornell

2-1702   `.laptops` laptop (portable) computers

2-1703   `.m6809` on the 6809

2-1704   `.m68k` on the 68k series

2-1705   `.m68k.pc` on 68k-based PCs (moderated)

2-1706   `.m88k` on 88k-based computers

2-1707   `.mac.advocacy` the Macintosh computer family compared to others

2-1708   `.mac.announce` important notices for Macintosh users (moderated)

2-1709   `.mac.apps` on Macintosh applications

2-1710   `.mac.comm` on Macintosh communications

2-1711   `.mac.databases` database systems for the Apple Macintosh

2-1712   `.mac.digest` Apple Macintosh: information and uses, but no programs (moderated)

2-1713   `.mac.games` on games on the Macintosh

2-1714   `.mac.hardware` Macintosh hardware issues and discussions

2-1715   `.mac.hypercard` the Macintosh Hypercard: information and uses

2-1716   `.mac.misc` general discussions about the Apple Macintosh

2-1717   `.mac.oop.macapp3` version 3 of the MacApp object-oriented system

2-1718   `.mac.oop.misc` object-oriented programming issues on the Mac

2-1719   `.mac.oop.tcl` Symantec's THINK Class Library for object programming

2-1720   `.mac.portables` discussion particular to laptop Macintoshes

2-1721   `.mac.programmer` discussion by people programming the Apple Macintosh

2-1722   `.mac.scitech` using the Macintosh in scientific and technological work

2-1723   `.mac.system` on Macintosh system software

2-1724   `.mac.wanted` postings of "I want XYZ for my Mac."

2-1725   `.mentor` mentor Graphics products and the Silicon Compiler System

2-1726   `.mips` systems based on MIPS chips

2-1727   `.misc` on computers of all kinds

2-1728   `.ncr` on NCR computers

2-1729   `.next.advocacy` the NeXT religion

2-1730   `.next.announce` announcements related to the NeXT computer system (moderated)

2-1731   `.next.bugs` discussion and solutions for known NeXT bugs

2-1732   `.next.hardware` discussing the physical aspects of NeXT computers

2-1733   `.next.marketplace` NeXT hardware, software and jobs

2-1734	**.next.misc** general discussion about the NeXT computer system
2-1735	**.next.programmer** NeXT-related programming issues
2-1736	**.next.software** function, use, and availability of NeXT programs
2-1737	**.next.sysadmin** discussions related to NeXT system administration
2-1738	**.northstar** Northstar microcomputer users
2-1739	**.novell** on Novell Netware products
2-1740	**.nsc.32k** National Semiconductor 32000 series chips
2-1741	**.palmtops** computers in the palm of your hand
2-1742	**.pen** interacting with computers through pen gestures
2-1743	**.prime** Prime Computer products
2-1744	**.proteon** Proteon gateway products
2-1745	**.pyramid** Pyramid 90x computers
2-1746	**.ridge** Ridge 32 computers and ROS
2-1747	**.sequent** Sequent systems (Balance and Symmetry)
2-1748	**.sgi.admin** system administration on Silicon Graphics's Irises
2-1749	**.sgi.announce** announcements for the SGI community (moderated)
2-1750	**.sgi.apps** applications which run on the Iris
2-1751	**.sgi.bugs** bugs found in the IRIX operating system
2-1752	**.sgi.graphics** graphics packages and issues on SGI machines
2-1753	**.sgi.hardware** base systems and peripherals for Iris computers
2-1754	**.sgi.misc** general discussion about Silicon Graphics's machines
2-1755	**.stratus** Stratus products, incl. System/88, CPS-32, VOS and FTX
2-1756	**.sun.admin** Sun system administration issues and questions
2-1757	**.sun.announce** Sun announcements and Sunergy mailings (moderated)
2-1758	**.sun.apps** software applications for Sun computer systems
2-1759	**.sun.hardware** Sun Microsystems hardware
2-1760	**.sun.misc** miscellaneous discussions about Sun products
2-1761	**.sun.wanted** people looking for Sun products and support
2-1762	**.super** supercomputers
2-1763	**.tahoe** CCI 6/32, Harris HCX/7, and Sperry 7000 computers
2-1764	**.tandy** on Tandy computers, new and old
2-1765	**.ti** on Texas Instruments
2-1766	**.ti.explorer** the Texas Instruments Explorer
2-1767	**.transputer** the Transputer computer and OCCAM language
2-1768	**.unisys** Sperry, Burroughs, Convergent, and Unisys systems
2-1769	**.xerox** Xerox 1100 workstations and protocols
2-1770	**.zenith** heath terminals and related Zenith products

2-1771　　　　**.zenith.z100** the Zenith Z-100 (Heath H-100) family of computers

2-1772　　**.terminals** all sorts of terminals

2-1773　　　　**.bitgraph** the BB&N BitGraph Terminal

2-1774　　　　**.tty5620** AT&T Dot Mapped Display Terminals (5620 and BLIT)

2-1775　　**.text** text-processing issues and methods

2-1776　　　　**.desktop** technology and techniques of desktop publishing

2-1777　　　　**.frame** desktop publishing with FrameMaker

2-1778　　　　**.interleaf** applications and use of Interleaf software

2-1779　　　　**.sgml** ISO 8879 SGML, structured documents, markup languages

2-1780　　　　**.tex** on the TeX and LaTeX systems and macros

2-1781　　**.theory** on Theoretical Computer Science

2-1782　　　　**.cell-automata** on all aspects of cellular automata

2-1783　　　　**.dynamic-sys** ergodic Theory and Dynamical Systems

2-1784　　　　**.info-retrieval** information retrieval topics (moderated)

2-1785　　　　**.self-org-sys** topics related to self-organization

2-1786　　**.unix [Groups on the Unix operating system]**

2-1787　　　　**.admin** administering a Unix-based system

2-1788　　　　**.aix** IBM's version of Unix

2-1789　　　　**.amiga** Minix, SYSV4 and other *nix on an Amiga

2-1790　　　　**.aux** the version of Unix for Apple Macintosh II computers

2-1791　　　　**.bsd** on Berkeley Software Distribution Unix

2-1792　　　　**.cray** Cray computers and their operating systems

2-1793　　　　**.dos-under-unix** MS-DOS running under Unix by whatever means

2-1794　　　　**.internals** on hacking Unix internals

2-1795　　　　**.large** Unix on mainframes and in large networks

2-1796　　　　**.misc** various topics that don't fit other groups

2-1797　　　　**.msdos** Dos under Unix

2-1798　　　　**.osf.misc** various aspects of Open Software Foundation products

2-1799　　　　**.osf.osf1** the Open Software Foundation's OSF/1

2-1800　　　　**.pc-clone.16bit** Unix on 286 architectures

2-1801　　　　**.pc-clone.32bit** Unix on 386 and 486 architectures

2-1802　　　　**.programmer** questions and answers for people programming under Unix

2-1803　　　　**.questions** Unix neophytes group

2-1804　　　　**.shell** using and programming the Unix shell

2-1805　　　　**.solaris** on the Solaris operating system

2-1806　　　　**.sys3** system III Unix discussions

2-1807　　　　**.sys5.misc** versions of System V which predate Release 3

2-1808	**.sys5.r3** discussing System V Release 3
2-1809	**.sys5.r4** discussing System V Release 4
2-1810	**.ultrix** on DEC's Ultrix
2-1811	**.wizards** questions for true Unix wizards only
2-1812	**.xenix.misc** general discussions regarding XENIX (except SCO)
2-1813	**.xenix.sco** XENIX versions from the Santa Cruz Operation
2-1814	**.virus** computer viruses and security (moderated)
2-1815	**.windows** [Groups on window-based human computer interfaces]
2-1816	**.garnet** the Garnet user interface development environment
2-1817	**.interviews** the InterViews object-oriented windowing system
2-1818	**.misc** various issues about windowing systems
2-1819	**.ms** Microsoft Windows
2-1820	**.ms.programmer** programming Microsoft Windows
2-1821	**.news** Sun Microsystems' NeWS Window System
2-1822	**.open-look** on the Open Look GUI
2-1823	**.suit** the SUIT user-interface toolkit
2-1824	**.x** on the XWindow System
2-1825	**.x.announce** X Consortium announcements (moderated)
2-1826	**.x.apps** getting and using, not programming, applications for X
2-1827	**.x.i386unix** the XFree86 Window System and others
2-1828	**.x.intrinsics** on the X toolkit
2-1829	**.x.motif** the Motif GUI for the XWindow System
2-1830	**.x.pex** the PHIGS extension of the XWindow System

2-1831 **courts Groups on the happenings in courts of law**

2-1832	**.usa**
2-1833	**.federal.supreme** the Supreme Court
2-1834	**.state.ohio.appls-8th** Ohio appeals court
2-1835	**.state.ohio.config**
2-1836	**.state.ohio.supreme** Ohio Supreme Court

2-1837 **ddn**

2-1838	**.mgt-bulletin** the DDN Management Bulletin from NIC.DDN.MIL (moderated)
2-1839	**.newsletter** the DDN Newsletter from NIC.DDN.MIL (moderated)

2-1840 **eunet Groups from Europe**

2-1841	**.jokes** jokes about Europeans

2-1842   `.newprod` promoting business in Europe

2-1843   `.politics` politics in the European community

2-1844   `.test` boring test messages

2-1845 # gnu Groups from the GNU Software Foundation

2-1846   `.announce` status and announcements from the Project (moderated)

2-1847   `.bash.bug` Bourne Again SHell bug reports and suggested fixes (moderated)

2-1848   `.chess` announcements about the GNU Chess program

2-1849   **.emacs**

2-1850   `.announce` announcements about GNU Emacs (moderated)

2-1851   `.bug` GNU Emacs bug reports and suggested fixes (moderated)

2-1852   `.gnews` newsreading under GNU Emacs using Weemba's Gnews

2-1853   `.gnus` newsreading under GNU Emacs using GNUS (in English)

2-1854   `.help` user queries and answers

2-1855   `.sources` ONLY (please!) C and Lisp source code for GNU Emacs

2-1856   `.vm.bug` bug reports on the Emacs VM mail package

2-1857   `.vm.info` information about the Emacs VM mail package

2-1858   `.vms` VMS port of GNU Emacs

2-1859   `.epoch.misc` the Epoch X11 extensions to Emacs

2-1860   **.g++**

2-1861   `.announce` announcements about the GNU C++ Compiler (moderated)

2-1862   `.bug` G++ bug reports and suggested fixes (moderated)

2-1863   `.help` GNU C++ compiler (G++) user queries and answers

2-1864   `.lib.bug` G++ library bug reports/suggested fixes (moderated)

2-1865   **.gcc**

2-1866   `.announce` announcements about the GNU C Compiler (moderated)

2-1867   `.bug` GNU C Compiler bug reports/suggested fixes (moderated)

2-1868   `.help` GNU C Compiler (gcc) user queries and answers

2-1869   `.gdb.bug` GCC/G++ DeBugger bugs and suggested fixes (moderated)

2-1870   `.ghostscript.bug` GNU Ghostscript interpreter bugs (moderated)

2-1871   **.gnusenet**

2-1872   `.config` GNU's Not Usenet administration and configuration

2-1873   `.test` GNU's Not Usenet alternative hierarchy testing

2-1874   `.groff.bug` bugs in the GNU roff programs (moderated)

2-1875   `.misc.discuss` serious discussion about GNU and free software

2-1876   `.smalltalk.bug` bugs in GNU Smalltalk (moderated)

2-1877   `.utils.bug` GNU utilities bugs (e.g., make, gawk. ls) (moderated)

2-1878 # hepnet Groups from high-energy and nuclear physics research sites

2-1879   **.admin** discussions among hepnet.* netnews administrators

2-1880   **.announce** announcement of general interest

2-1881   **.conferences** on conference and workshops

2-1882   **.freehep** on the freehep archives

2-1883   **.general** on general interest

2-1884   **.hepix** on the use of Unix

2-1885   **.heplib** on HEPLIB

2-1886   **.jobs** job announcements and discussions

2-1887   **.lang.c++** on the use of C++

2-1888   **.test** test postings

2-1889   **.videoconf** on the use of videoconferencing

2-1890 # ieee Groups from the IEEE engineering association

2-1891   **.announce** general announcements for the IEEE community

2-1892   **.config** postings about managing the ieee.* groups

2-1893   **.general** IEEE—General discussion

2-1894   **.pcnfs** discussion and tips on PC-NFS

2-1895   **.rab**

2-1896   **.announce** Regional Activities Board—announcements

2-1897   **.general** Regional Activities Board—general discussion

2-1898   **.region1** region 1 announcements

2-1899   **.tab**

2-1900   **.announce** Technical Activities Board—announcements

2-1901   **.general** Technical Activities Board—general discussion

2-1902   **.tcos** the Technical Committee on Operating Systems (moderated)

2-1903   **.usab**

2-1904   **.announce** USAB—announcements

2-1905   **.general** USAB—general discussion

2-1906 # info Groups gatewayed from mailing lists

2-1907   **.admin** administrative messages regarding info.* groups. (moderated)

2-1908   **.big-internet** issues facing a huge Internet (moderated)

2-1909   **.bind** the Berkeley BIND server (moderated)

2-1910   **.brl-cad** BRL's Solid-modeling CAD system (moderated)

2-1911 **.bytecounters** NSstat network analysis program (moderated)

2-1912 **.convex** Convex Corp machines (moderated)

2-1913 **.firearms** non-political firearms discussions (moderated)

2-1914 **.politics** political firearms discussions.(moderated)

2-1915 **.gated** Cornell's GATED program (moderated)

2-1916 **.grass**

2-1917 **.programmer** GRASS geographic information system programmer issues (moderated)

2-1918 **.user** GRASS geographic information system user issues (moderated)

2-1919 **.ietf** Internet Engineering Task Force (moderated)

2-1920 **.hosts** IETF host requirements discussions (moderated)

2-1921 **.isoc** Internet Society discussions (moderated)

2-1922 **.njm** JO-MAAN—the Joint Monitoring Access between Adjacent Networks IETF working group (moderated)

2-1923 **.smtp** IETF SMTP extension discussions (moderated)

2-1924 **.isode** the ISO Development Environment package (moderated)

2-1925 **.jethro-tull** on Jethro Tull's music (moderated)

2-1926 **.labmgr** computer lab managers list (moderated)

2-1927 **.mach** the Mach operating system (moderated)

2-1928 **.mh.workers** MH development discussions (moderated)

2-1929 **.nets** inter-network connectivity

2-1930 **.nsf.grants** NSF grant notes (moderated)

2-1931 **.nsfnet**

2-1932 **.cert** computer Emergency Response Team announcements (moderated)

2-1933 **.status** NSFnet status reports (moderated)

2-1934 **.nupop** Northwestern University's POP for PCs (moderated)

2-1935 **.nysersnmp** the SNMP software distributed by PSI.(moderated)

2-1936 **.osf** OSF Electronic Bulletin mailings (moderated)

2-1937 **.pem-dev** IETF privacy-enhanced mail discussions (moderated)

2-1938 **.ph** qi, ph, sendmail/phquery discussions (moderated)

2-1939 **.rfc** announcements of newly released RFCs (moderated)

2-1940 **.slug** care and feeding of Symbolics Lisp machines (moderated)

2-1941 **.snmp** SNMP Simple Gateway/Network Monitoring Protocol (moderated)

2-1942 **.solbourne** discussions and information about Solbourne computers (moderated)

2-1943 **.sun-managers** Sun-managers digest (moderated)

2-1944 **.sun-nets** Sun-nets digest (moderated)

2-1945 **.theorynt** theory list (moderated)

2-1946 **.unix-sw** software available for anonymous FTP (moderated)

2-1947 **.wisenet** Women In Science and Engineering NETwork

2-1948 # k12

2-1949 **.chat**

2-1950 **.elementary** casual conversation for elementary students, grades K-5

2-1951 **.junior** casual conversation for students in grades 6-8

2-1952 **.senior** casual conversation for high school students

2-1953 **.teacher** casual conversation for teachers of grades K-12

2-1954 **.ed**

2-1955 **.art** arts and crafts curricula in K-12 education

2-1956 **.business** business education curricula in grades K-12

2-1957 **.comp.literacy** teaching computer literacy in grades K-12

2-1958 **.health-pe** health and physical education curricula in grades K-12

2-1959 **.life-skills** home economics, career education and school counseling

2-1960 **.math** mathematics curriculum in K-12 education

2-1961 **.music** music and performing arts curriculum in K-12 education

2-1962 **.science** science curriculum in K-12 education

2-1963 **.soc-studies** social studies and history curriculum in K-12 education

2-1964 **.special** educating students with handicaps and/or special needs

2-1965 **.tag** k-12 education for gifted and talented students

2-1966 **.tech** industrial arts and vocational education in grades K-12

2-1967 **.lang**

2-1968 **.art** the art of teaching language skills in grades K-12

2-1969 **.deutsch-eng** bilingual German/English practice with native speakers

2-1970 **.esp-eng** bilingual Spanish/English practice with native speakers

2-1971 **.francais** French practice with native speakers

2-1972 **.russian** bilingual Russian/English practice with native speakers

2-1973 **.library** implementing info technologies in school libraries

2-1974 **.sys**

2-1975 **.ch0** current projects

2-1976 **.ch1** current projects

2-1977 **.ch10** current projects

2-1978 **.ch11** current projects

2-1979 **.ch12** current projects

2-1980 **.ch2** current projects

2-1981 **.ch3** current projects

2-1982 **.ch4** current projects

2-1983 **.ch5** current projects

2-1984 **.ch6** current projects

2-1985	`.ch7` current projects
2-1986	`.ch8` current projects
2-1987	`.ch9` current projects
2-1988	`.projects` on potential projects

misc Groups on all sorts of miscelations topics
2-1989

2-1990	`.activism.progressive` information for Progressive activists (moderated)
2-1991	`.answers` repository for periodic Usenet articles (moderated)
2-1992	`.books.technical` on books about technical topics
2-1993	`.consumers` consumer interests, product reviews, etc.
2-1994	`.house` on owning and maintaining a house
2-1995	`.education` on the educational system
2-1996	`.language.english`
2-1997	`.emerg-services` forum for paramedics and other first responders
2-1998	`.entrepreneurs` on operating a business
2-1999	`.fitness` physical fitness, exercise, etc.
2-2000	`.forsale` short, tasteful postings about items for sale
2-2001	`.computers.d` on misc.forsale.computers.*
2-2002	`.computers.mac` apple Macintosh related computer items
2-2003	`.computers.other` selling miscellaneous computer stuff
2-2004	`.computers.pc-clone` IBM PC related computer items
2-2005	`.computers.workstation` workstation related computer items
2-2006	`.handicap` items of interest for/about the handicapped (moderated)
2-2007	`.headlines` current interest: drug testing, terrorism etc.
2-2008	`.health`
2-2009	`.alternative` alternative, complementary and holistic health care
2-2010	`.diabetes` on diabetes management in daily life
2-2011	`.int-property` on intellectual property rights
2-2012	`.invest` investments and the handling of money
2-2013	`.canada` investment in Canada
2-2014	`.real-estate` property investments
2-2015	`.technical` analyzing market trends with technical methods
2-2016	`.jobs` [Groups on jobs]
2-2017	`.contract` on contract labor
2-2018	`.misc` on employment, workplaces, careers
2-2019	`.offered` announcements of positions available
2-2020	`.offered.entry` job listings only for entry-level positions
2-2021	`.resumes` postings of resumes and "situation wanted" articles

2-2022   **.kids** children, their behavior and activities

2-2023   **.computer** the use of computers by children

2-2024   **.legal** legalities and the ethics of law

2-2025   **.computing** discussing the legal climate of the computing world

2-2026   **.misc** various discussions not fitting into any other group

2-2027   **.news [Groups on "Real World" news distribution]**

2-2028   **.east-europe.rferl** Radio Free Europe/Radio Liberty Daily Report (moderated)

2-2029   **.southasia** news from Bangladesh, India, Nepal, etc (moderated)

2-2030   **.rural** devoted to issues concerning rural living

2-2031   **.taxes** tax laws and advice

2-2032   **.test** For testing of network software. Very boring

2-2033   **.wanted** requests for things that are needed (NOT software)

2-2034   **.writing** on writing in all of its forms

news Groups on Usenet news itself

2-2035

2-2036   **.admin [Groups on the administration of the USENET news network]**

2-2037   **.misc** general topics of network news administration

2-2038   **.policy** policy issues of Usenet

2-2039   **.technical** technical aspects of maintaining network news (moderated)

2-2040   **.announce [Groups with announcements about Usenet news]**

2-2041   **.conferences** calls for papers and conference announcements (moderated)

2-2042   **.important** general announcements of interest to all (moderated)

2-2043   **.newgroups** calls for newgroups and announcements of same (moderated)

2-2044   **.newusers** explanatory postings for new users (moderated)

2-2045   **.answers** repository for periodic Usenet articles (moderated)

2-2046   **.config** postings of system down times and interruptions

2-2047   **.future** the future technology of network news systems

2-2048   **.groups** discussions and lists of newsgroups

2-2049   **.lists** news-related statistics and lists (moderated)

2-2050   **.ps-maps** maps relating to Usenet traffic flows (moderated)

2-2051   **.misc** on Usenet itself

2-2052   **.newsites** postings of new site announcements

2-2053   **.newusers.questions** questions and answers for users new to the Usenet

2-2054   **.software [Groups on the various programs used to read and distribute Usenet news]**

2-2055   **.anu-news** VMS B-news software from Australian National University

2-2056   **.b** on B-news-compatible software

2-2057   **.nn** on the "nn" news reader package

2-2058   **.notes** notesfile software from the University of Illinois

2-2059   **.readers** on software used to read network news.

2-2060 # rec Groups on recreational topics

2-2061   **.answers** repository for periodic Usenet articles (moderated)

2-2062   **.antiques** discussing antiques and vintage items

2-2063   **.aquaria** keeping fish and aquaria as a hobby

2-2064   **.arts [Groups on the arts (broadly defined)]**

2-2065   **.animation** on various kinds of animation

2-2066   **.anime** Japanese animation fen discussion

2-2067   **.anime.info** announcements about Japanese animation (moderated)

2-2068   **.anime.marketplace** things for sale in the Japanese animation world

2-2069   **.anime.stories** all about Japanese comic fanzines (moderated)

2-2070   **.bodyart** tattoos and body decoration discussions

2-2071   **.bonsai** dwarfish trees and shrubbery

2-2072   **.books** books of all genres, and the publishing industry

2-2073   **.books.tolkien** the works of J.R.R. Tolkien

2-2074   **.cinema** on the art of cinema (moderated)

2-2075   **.comics** comic books

2-2076   **.comics.info** reviews, convention information and other comics news (moderated)

2-2077   **.comics.marketplace** the exchange of comics and comic-related items

2-2078   **.comics.misc** comic books, graphic novels, sequential art

2-2079   **.comics.strips** on short-form comics

2-2080   **.comics.xbooks** the Mutant Universe of Marvel Comics

2-2081   **.dance** any aspects of dance not covered in another newsgroup

2-2082   **.disney** on any Disney-related subjects

2-2083   **.drwho** on Dr. Who

2-2084   **.erotica** erotic fiction and verse (moderated)

2-2085   **.fine** fine arts and artists

2-2086   **.int-fiction** on interactive fiction

2-2087   **.manga** all aspects of the Japanese storytelling art form

2-2088   **.marching.drumcorps** drum and bugle corps

2-2089   **.marching.misc** marching-related performance activities

2-2090   **.misc** on the arts not in other groups

2-2091   **.movies** on movies and moviemaking

2-2092   **.movies.reviews** reviews of movies (moderated)

2-2093   **.poems** for the posting of poems

2-2094   **.prose** short works of prose fiction and followup discussion

2-2095   **.sf.announce** major announcements of the SF world (moderated)

2-2096	`.sf.fandom` on SF fan activities
2-2097	`.sf.marketplace` personal for-sale notices of SF materials
2-2098	`.sf.misc` not-so-on-topic discussion from `rec.arts.sf.written`
2-2099	`.sf.movies` discussing SF motion pictures
2-2100	`.sf.reviews` reviews of science fiction/fantasy/horror works (moderated)
2-2101	`.sf.science` real and speculative aspects of SF science
2-2102	`.sf.starwars` on the Star Wars universe
2-2103	`.sf.tv` discussing general television SF
2-2104	`.sf.written` on written science fiction and fantasy
2-2105	`.startrek.current` new Star Trek shows, movies and books
2-2106	`.startrek.fandom` Star Trek conventions and memorabilia
2-2107	`.startrek.info` information about the universe of Star Trek (moderated)
2-2108	`.startrek.misc` general discussions of Star Trek
2-2109	`.startrek.reviews` reviews of Star Trek books, episodes, films etc (moderated)
2-2110	`.startrek.tech` Star Trek's depiction of future technologies
2-2111	`.theatre` on all aspects of stage work and theater
2-2112	`.tv` the boob tube, its history, and past and current shows
2-2113	`.tv.soaps` postings about soap operas
2-2114	`.tv.uk` on telly shows from the UK
2-2115	`.wobegon` discussion of the "A Prairie Home Companion" radio show
2-2116	`.audio` high-fidelity audio
2-2117	`.car` on automobile audio systems
2-2118	`.high-end` high-end audio systems (moderated)
2-2119	`.pro` professional audio recording and studio engineering
2-2120	`.autos` automobiles, automotive products and laws
2-2121	`.antique` discussing all aspects of automobiles over 25 years old
2-2122	`.driving` driving automobiles
2-2123	`.rod-n-custom` high-performance automobiles
2-2124	`.sport` on organized, legal auto competitions
2-2125	`.tech` technical aspects of automobiles, et. al.
2-2126	`.vw` issues pertaining to Volkswagen products
2-2127	**`.aviation` [Groups on airplanes]**
2-2128	`.announce` events of interest to the aviation community (moderated)
2-2129	`.answers` frequently asked questions about aviation (moderated)
2-2130	`.homebuilt` selecting, designing, building, and restoring aircraft
2-2131	`.ifr` flying under Instrument Flight Rules
2-2132	`.military` military aircraft of the past, present, and future

2-2133	**.misc** miscellaneous topics in aviation
2-2134	**.owning** information on owning airplanes
2-2135	**.piloting** general discussion for aviators
2-2136	**.products** reviews and discussion of products useful to pilots
2-2137	**.simulators** flight simulation on all levels
2-2138	**.soaring** all aspects of sailplanes and hang-gliders
2-2139	**.stories** anecdotes of flight experiences (moderated)
2-2140	**.student** learning to fly
2-2141	**.backcountry** activities in the Great Outdoors
2-2142	**.bicycles [Groups on bicycles]**
2-2143	**.marketplace** buying, selling and reviewing items for cycling
2-2144	**.misc** general discussion of bicycling
2-2145	**.racing** bicycle racing techniques, rules, and results
2-2146	**.rides** on tours and training or commuting routes
2-2147	**.soc** social issues of bicycling
2-2148	**.tech** cycling product design, construction, maintenance, etc.
2-2149	**.birds** hobbyists interested in bird watching
2-2150	**.boats** hobbyists interested in boating
2-2151	**.paddle** talk about any boats with oars, paddles, etc.
2-2152	**.climbing** climbing techniques, competition announcements, etc.
2-2153	**.collecting** discussion among collectors of many things
2-2154	**.cards** collecting all sorts of sport and nonsport cards
2-2155	**.crafts**
2-2156	**.brewing** the art of making beers and meads
2-2157	**.metalworking** all aspects of working with metal
2-2158	**.misc** handiwork arts not covered elsewhere
2-2159	**.quilting** quilting
2-2160	**.textiles** sewing, weaving, knitting, and other fiber arts
2-2161	**.equestrian** on things equestrian
2-2162	**.folk-dancing** folk dances, dancers, and dancing
2-2163	**.food**
2-2164	**.cooking** food, cooking, cookbooks, and recipes
2-2165	**.drink** wines and spirits
2-2166	**.historic** the history of food-making arts
2-2167	**.recipes** recipes for interesting food and drink (moderated)
2-2168	**.restaurants** on dining out
2-2169	**.sourdough** making and baking with sourdough

2-2170	**.veg** vegetarians
2-2171	**.gambling** articles on games of chance and betting
2-2172	**.games**
2-2173	**.abstract** perfect information, pure strategy games
2-2174	**.backgammon** on the game of backgammon
2-2175	**.board** discussion and hints on board games
2-2176	**.board.ce** the Cosmic Encounter board game
2-2177	**.bridge** hobbyists interested in bridge
2-2178	**.chess** chess and computer chess
2-2179	**.corewar** the Core War computer challenge
2-2180	**.design** on game-design issues
2-2181	**.diplomacy** the conquest game Diplomacy
2-2182	**.empire** discussion and hints about Empire
2-2183	**.frp** fantasy role-playing games
2-2184	**.frp.advocacy** flames and rebuttals about various role-playing systems
2-2185	**.frp.announce** announcements of happenings in the role-playing world (moderated)
2-2186	**.frp.archives** archivable fantasy stories and other projects (moderated)
2-2187	**.frp.cyber** on cyberpunk-related roleplaying games
2-2188	**.frp.dnd** fantasy role-playing with TSR's Dungeons and Dragons
2-2189	**.frp.marketplace** role-playing game materials wanted and for sale
2-2190	**.frp.misc** general discussions of role-playing games
2-2191	**.go** on Go
2-2192	**.hack** discussion, hints, etc., about the Hack game
2-2193	**.int-fiction** all aspects of interactive-fiction games
2-2194	**.mecha** giant robot games
2-2195	**.miniatures** tabletop wargaming
2-2196	**.misc** games and computer games
2-2197	**.moria** comments, hints and info about the Moria game
2-2198	**.mud** multiple-user role-playing games
2-2199	**.mud.admin** administrative issues of multiuser dungeons
2-2200	**.mud.announce** informational articles about multiuser dungeons (moderated)
2-2201	**.mud.diku** all about DikuMuds
2-2202	**.mud.lp** on the LPMUD computer role-playing game
2-2203	**.mud.misc** various aspects of multiuser computer games
2-2204	**.mud.tiny** on Tiny MUDs, like MUSH, MUSE and MOO
2-2205	**.netrek** on the XWindow system game Netrek (XtrekII)
2-2206	**.pbm** on play-by-mail games

2-2207   **.pinball** discussing pinball-related issues

2-2208   **.programmer** on adventure-game programming

2-2209   **.rogue** discussion and hints about Rogue

2-2210   **.roguelike.announce**

2-2211   **.roguelike.misc**

2-2212   **.trivia** on trivia

2-2213   **.video** video games

2-2214   **.video.arcade** on coin-operated video games

2-2215   **.video.classic** older home video entertainment systems

2-2216   **.video.marketplace** home video game stuff for sale or trade

2-2217   **.video.misc** general discussion about home video games

2-2218   **.video.nintendo** all Nintendo video game systems and software

2-2219   **.video.sega** all Sega video game systems and software

2-2220   **.xtank.play** strategy and tactics for the distributed game Xtank

2-2221   **.xtank.programmer** coding the Xtank game and its robots

2-2222   **.gardens** gardening methods and results

2-2223   **.guns** on firearms (moderated)

2-2224   **.heraldry** on coats of arms

2-2225   **.humor** jokes and the like. May be somewhat offensive

2-2226   **.d** on the content of rec.humor articles

2-2227   **.funny** jokes that are funny (in the moderator's opinion) (moderated)

2-2228   **.oracle** sagacious advice from the Usenet Oracle (moderated)

2-2229   **.oracle.d** comments about the Usenet Oracle's comments

2-2230   **.hunting** on hunting (moderated)

2-2231   **.juggling** juggling techniques, equipment, and events

2-2232   **.kites** talk about kites and kiting

2-2233   **.mag** magazine summaries, tables of contents, etc.

2-2234   **.martial-arts** on the various forms of martial arts

2-2235   **.misc** general topics about recreational/participant sports

2-2236   **.models**

2-2237   **.railroad** model railroads of all scales

2-2238   **.rc** radio-controlled kits for hobbyists

2-2239   **.scale** construction of models

2-2240   **.motorcycles** motorcycles and related products and laws

2-2241   **.dirt** riding motorcycles and ATVs off-road

2-2242   **.harley** all aspects of Harley-Davidson motorcycles

2-2243   **.racing** on all aspects of racing motorcycles

2-2244	**.music**
2-2245	**.a-cappella** vocal music without instrumental accompaniment
2-2246	**.afro-latin** music with Afro-Latin, African, and Latin influences
2-2247	**.beatles** postings about the Fab Four and their music
2-2248	**.bluenote** on jazz, blues and related types of music
2-2249	**.cd** CDs—availability and other discussions
2-2250	**.christian** Christian music, both contemporary and traditional
2-2251	**.classical** on classical music
2-2252	**.classical.guitar** classical music performed on guitar
2-2253	**.classical.performing** playing classical music
2-2254	**.compose** creating musical and lyrical works
2-2255	**.country.western** country and western music, performers, performances, etc.
2-2256	**.dementia** on comedy and novelty music
2-2257	**.dylan** on Bob's works and music
2-2258	**.early** on pre-classical European music
2-2259	**.folk** folks discussing folk music of various sorts
2-2260	**.funky** funk, rap, hip-hop, house, soul, r&b and related
2-2261	**.gaffa** on Kate Bush and other alternative music (moderated)
2-2262	**.gdead** a group for (Grateful) Deadheads
2-2263	**.indian.classical** Hindustani and Carnatic Indian classical music
2-2264	**.indian.misc** discussing Indian music in general
2-2265	**.industrial** on all industrial-related music styles
2-2266	**.info** news and announcements on musical topics (moderated)
2-2267	**.makers** for performers and their discussions
2-2268	**.makers.bass** upright bass and bass guitar techniques and equipment
2-2269	**.makers.guitar** electric and acoustic guitar techniques and equipment
2-2270	**.makers.guitar.tablature** guitar tablature/chords
2-2271	**.makers.marketplace** buying and selling used music-making equipment
2-2272	**.makers.percussion** drum and other percussion techniques and equipment
2-2273	**.makers.synth** synthesizers and computer music
2-2274	**.marketplace** records, tapes, and CDs: wanted, for sale, etc.
2-2275	**.misc** music lovers' group
2-2276	**.newage** "New Age" music discussions
2-2277	**.phish** discussing the musical group Phish
2-2278	**.reggae** roots, rockers, dancehall reggae
2-2279	**.reviews** reviews of music of all genres and mediums (moderated)
2-2280	**.video** on music videos and music video software

2-2281	**.nude** hobbyists interested in naturist/nudist activities
2-2282	**.org**
2-2283	**.mensa** talking with members of the high-IQ society Mensa
2-2284	**.sca** Society for Creative Anachronism
2-2285	**.outdoors.fishing** all aspects of sport and commercial fishing
2-2286	**.parks.theme** theme parks
2-2287	**.pets** pets, pet care and household animals in general
2-2288	**.birds** the culture and care of indoor birds
2-2289	**.cats** on domestic cats
2-2290	**.dogs** any and all subjects relating to dogs as pets
2-2291	**.herp** reptiles, amphibians and other exotic vivarium pets
2-2292	**.photo** hobbyists interested in photography
2-2293	**.puzzles** puzzles, problems and quizzes
2-2294	**.crosswords** making and playing gridded word puzzles
2-2295	**.pyrotechnics** fireworks, rocketry, safety, and other topics
2-2296	**.radio**
2-2297	**.amateur.antenna** antennas: theory, techniques, and construction
2-2298	**.amateur.digital.misc** packet radio and other digital radio modes
2-2299	**.amateur.equipment** all about production of amateur-radio hardware
2-2300	**.amateur.homebrew** amateur-radio construction and experimentation
2-2301	**.amateur.misc** amateur-radio practices, contests, events, rules, etc.
2-2302	**.amateur.packet** on packet radio setups
2-2303	**.amateur.policy** radio use and regulation policy
2-2304	**.amateur.space** amateur-radio transmissions through space
2-2305	**.broadcasting** local-area broadcast radio (moderated)
2-2306	**.cb** citizen-band radio
2-2307	**.info** informational postings related to radio (moderated)
2-2308	**.noncomm** topics relating to noncommercial radio
2-2309	**.shortwave** shortwave radio enthusiasts
2-2310	**.swap** offers to trade and swap radio equipment
2-2311	**.railroad** for fans of real trains
2-2312	**.roller-coaster** roller coasters and other amusement park rides
2-2313	**.running** running for enjoyment, sport, exercise, etc.
2-2314	**.scouting** Scouting youth organizations worldwide
2-2315	**.scuba** hobbyists interested in scuba diving
2-2316	**.skate** ice skating and roller skating
2-2317	**.skiing** hobbyists interested in snow skiing

2-2318	**.skydiving** hobbyists interested in skydiving
2-2319	**.sport**
2-2320	**.baseball** on baseball
2-2321	**.baseball.college** baseball on the collegiate level
2-2322	**.baseball.fantasy** rotisserie (fantasy) baseball play
2-2323	**.basketball.college** hoops on the collegiate level
2-2324	**.basketball.misc** on basketball
2-2325	**.basketball.pro** on of professional basketball
2-2326	**.cricket** on the sport of cricket
2-2327	**.cricket.scores** scores from cricket matches around the globe (moderated)
2-2328	**.disc** on flying-disc (Frisbee) based sports
2-2329	**.fencing** on all aspects of swordplay
2-2330	**.football.australian** on Australian-rules football
2-2331	**.football.canadian** all about Canadian-rules football
2-2332	**.football.college** US-style college football
2-2333	**.football.misc** on American-style football
2-2334	**.football.pro** US-style professional football
2-2335	**.golf** on all aspects of golfing
2-2336	**.hockey** on ice hockey
2-2337	**.hockey.field** on the sport of field hockey
2-2338	**.misc** spectator sports
2-2339	**.olympics** all aspects of the Olympic Games
2-2340	**.paintball** discussing all aspects of the survival game paintball
2-2341	**.pro-wrestling** on professional wrestling
2-2342	**.rowing** crew for competition or fitness
2-2343	**.rugby** on the game of rugby
2-2344	**.soccer** on soccer (Association Football)
2-2345	**.swimming** training for and competing in swimming events
2-2346	**.table-tennis** things related to table tennis (a.k.a. Ping Pong)
2-2347	**.tennis** things related to the sport of tennis
2-2348	**.triathlon** discussing all aspects of multievent sports
2-2349	**.volleyball** on volleyball
2-2350	**.waterski** waterskiing
2-2351	**.travel** traveling all over the world
2-2352	**.air** airline travel around the world
2-2353	**.marketplace** tickets and accommodations wanted and for sale
2-2354	**.video** video and video components

2-2355	**.cable-tv**	technical and regulatory issues of cable television
2-2356	**.production**	making professional-quality video productions
2-2357	**.releases**	prerecorded video releases on laserdisc and videotape
2-2358	**.satellite**	getting shows via satellite
2-2359	**.windsurfing**	riding the waves as a hobby
2-2360	**.woodworking**	hobbyists interested in woodworking

2-2361 # **relcom** Groups from the former Soviet Union

2-2362	**.ads**	non-commercial ads (moderated)
2-2363	**.archives**	messages about new items on archive sites
2-2364	**.d**	discussion on file servers, archives
2-2365	**.bbs**	BBS news
2-2366	**.commerce**	
2-2367	**.audio-video**	audio and video equipment
2-2368	**.chemical**	chemical production
2-2369	**.computers**	computer hardware
2-2370	**.construction**	construction materials and equipment
2-2371	**.consume**	cosmetics, perfumes, dresses, shoes
2-2372	**.energy**	gas, coal, oil, fuel, generators, etc.
2-2373	**.estate**	real estate
2-2374	**.food**	food and drinks (including alcoholic)
2-2375	**.food.drinks**	spirits and soft drinks
2-2376	**.food.sweet**	sweets and sugar
2-2377	**.household**	all for the house—furniture, freezers, ovens, etc.
2-2378	**.infoserv**	information services
2-2379	**.jobs**	jobs offered/wanted
2-2380	**.machinery**	machinery, plant equipment
2-2381	**.medicine**	medical services, equipment, drugs
2-2382	**.metals**	metals and metal products
2-2383	**.money**	credits, deposits, currency
2-2384	**.orgtech**	office equipment
2-2385	**.other**	miscellanea
2-2386	**.software**	software
2-2387	**.stocks**	stocks and bonds
2-2388	**.talk**	on commercial groups
2-2389	**.tobacco**	cigarettes and tobacco
2-2390	**.tour**	tourism, leisure and entertainment opportunities
2-2391	**.transport**	vehicles and spare parts

2-2392	**.comp**
2-2393	**.binaries** binary codes of computer programs (moderated)
2-2394	**.dbms.foxpro** FoxPro database development system
2-2395	**.demo** demo versions of various software (moderated)
2-2396	**.demo.d** on demonstration programs
2-2397	**.lang.pascal** using the Pascal programming language
2-2398	**.os.os2** FIDOnet area, OS/2 operational system
2-2399	**.os.vms** VMS operational system
2-2400	**.os.windows** FIDOnet area, MS-Windows operational system
2-2401	**.os.windows.prog** FIDOnet area, programming under MS-Windows
2-2402	**.sources.d** discussion on sources
2-2403	**.sources.misc** software sources (moderated)
2-2404	**.currency** on currency
2-2405	**.exnet** on ExNet electronic exchange
2-2406	**.quote** ExNet quotes
2-2407	**.expo** exhibitions and fairs, announcements and reviews (moderated)
2-2408	**.fido**
2-2409	**.flirt** FIDOnet, just talking of love
2-2410	**.ru.hacker** FIDOnet, hackers and crackers (legal!)
2-2411	**.ru.modem** inter-network discussion on modems
2-2412	**.ru.networks** inter-network discussion of global nets
2-2413	**.ru.strack** FIDOnet, digitized sound
2-2414	**.ru.unix** FIDOnet, inter-network challenge to OS Unix
2-2415	**.su.books** FIDOnet, for book readers and lovers
2-2416	**.su.c-c++** FIDOnet, C and C++ language
2-2417	**.su.dbms** FIDOnet, database management systems
2-2418	**.su.general** FIDOnet, about everything and nothing
2-2419	**.su.hardw** FIDOnet, computer hardware
2-2420	**.su.magic** FIDOnet, magic and occult sciences
2-2421	**.su.softw** FIDOnet, software in general
2-2422	**.su.tolkien** FIDOnet, creations of J.R.R. Tolkien
2-2423	**.su.virus** FIDOnet, viruses and vaccines
2-2424	**.humor** ha-ha-ha. Jokes, you know them, funny
2-2425	**.infomarket**
2-2426	**.quote** ex-USSR exchanges's quotes /ASMP/ (moderated)
2-2427	**.talk** on market development /ASMP/ (moderated)
2-2428	**.jusinf** information on laws by "Justicinform" (moderated)

2-2429   **.kids** about kids

2-2430   **.lan** inter-network discussion on local area networks

2-2431   **.maps** relcom maps

2-2432   **.msdos** MS-DOS software

2-2433   **.music** music lovers

2-2434   **.netnews** announcements and articles important for all netters

2-2435   **.big** general BIG articles

2-2436   **.newusers** questions and answers of new Relcom users

2-2437   **.penpals** to find friends, colleagues, etc.

2-2438   **.politics** political discussions

2-2439   **.postmasters** for Relcom postmasters, official (moderated)

2-2440   **.d** discussion on postmaster's troubles and bright ideas

2-2441   **.relarn.general** scientific, academic subnet RELARN: general issues (moderated)

2-2442   **.renews** net magazine RENEWS (moderated)

2-2443   **.sources** superseded by `relcom.comp.sources.misc` (moderated)

2-2444   **.spbnews** political and economic news digest by SPB-News Agency (moderated)

2-2445   **.talk** unfettered talk

2-2446   **.tcpip** TCP/IP protocols and their implementation

2-2447   **.terms** on various terms and terminology

2-2448   **.test** "Wow, does it really work?"

2-2449   **.wtc** commercial proposals of World Trade Centers

2-2450   **.x** x Windows discussion

2-2451 # sci Groups for scholarly discussion on various scientific topics

2-2452   **.aeronautics** the science of aeronautics and related technology(moderated)

2-2453   **.airliners** airliner technology (moderated)

2-2454   **.answers** repository for periodic Usenet articles (moderated)

2-2455   **.anthropology** all aspects of studying humankind

2-2456   **.aquaria** only scientifically-oriented postings about aquaria

2-2457   **.archaeology** studying antiquities of the world

2-2458   **.astro** astronomy discussions and information

2-2459   **.fits** issues related to the Flexible Image Transport System

2-2460   **.hubble** processing Hubble Space Telescope data (moderated)

2-2461   **.bio** biology and related sciences

2-2462   **.ecology** ecology

2-2463   **.technology** any topic relating to biotechnology

2-2464   **.chem** chemistry and related sciences

2-2465	**.organomet**	organometallic chemistry
2-2466	**.classics**	studying classical history, languages, art, and more
2-2467	**.cognitive**	perception, memory, judgment, and reasoning
2-2468	**.comp-aided**	the use of computers as tools in scientific research
2-2469	**.cryonics**	theory and practice of biostasis, suspended animation
2-2470	**.crypt**	different methods of data en/decryption
2-2471	**.data.formats**	modeling, storage, and retrieval of scientific data
2-2472	**.econ**	the science of economics
2-2473	**.research**	research in all fields of economics (moderated)
2-2474	**.edu**	the science of education
2-2475	**.electronics**	circuits, theory, electrons, and discussions
2-2476	**.energy**	on energy, science, and technology
2-2477	**.engr**	technical discussions about engineering tasks
2-2478	**.biomed**	discussing the field of biomedical engineering
2-2479	**.chem**	all aspects of chemical engineering
2-2480	**.civil**	topics related to civil engineering
2-2481	**.control**	the engineering of control systems
2-2482	**.manufacturing**	manufacturing technology
2-2483	**.mech**	the field of mechanical engineering
2-2484	**.environment**	on the environment and ecology
2-2485	**.fractals**	objects of nonintegral dimension and other chaos
2-2486	**.games.vectrex**	the Vectrex game system
2-2487	**.geo**	
2-2488	**.fluids**	on geophysical fluid dynamics
2-2489	**.geology**	on solid earth sciences
2-2490	**.meteorology**	on meteorology and related topics
2-2491	**.image.processing**	scientific-image processing and analysis
2-2492	**.lang**	natural languages, communication, etc.
2-2493	**.japan**	the Japanese language, both spoken and written
2-2494	**.life-extension**	slowing, stopping or reversing the aging process
2-2495	**.logic**	logic—math, philosophy and the computational aspects thereof
2-2496	**.mag.fsfnet**	a Science Fiction "fanzine" (moderated)
2-2497	**.materials**	all aspects of materials engineering
2-2498	**.math**	mathematical discussions and pursuits
2-2499	**.num-analysis**	numerical analysis
2-2500	**.research**	on current mathematical research (moderated)
2-2501	**.stat**	statistics discussion

2-2502	**.symbolic** symbolic algebra discussion
2-2503	**.med** medicine and its related products and regulations
2-2504	**.aids** AIDS: treatment, pathology/biology of HIV, prevention (moderated)
2-2505	**.dentistry** dentally related topics; all about teeth
2-2506	**.nutrition** physiological impacts of diet
2-2507	**.occupational** preventing, detecting, and treating occupational injuries
2-2508	**.pharmacy** the teaching and practice of pharmaceutics
2-2509	**.physics** issues of physics in medical testing/care
2-2510	**.telemedicine** clinical consulting through computer networks
2-2511	**.military** on science and the military (moderated)
2-2512	**.misc** short-lived discussions on subjects in the sciences
2-2513	**.nanotech** self-reproducing molecular-scale machines (moderated)
2-2514	**.nonlinear** chaotic systems and other nonlinear scientific study
2-2515	**.optics** discussion relating to the science of optics
2-2516	**.philosophy**
2-2517	**.meta** discussions within the scope of "MetaPhilosophy."
2-2518	**.tech** technical philosophy: math, science, logic, etc.
2-2519	**.physics** physical laws, properties, etc.
2-2520	**.accelerators** particle accelerators
2-2521	**.fusion** info on fusion, esp. "cold" fusion
2-2522	**.research** current physics research (moderated)
2-2523	**.psychology** topics related to psychology
2-2524	**.digest** PSYCOLOQUY: Refereed Psychology Journal and Newsletter (moderated)
2-2525	**.research** research methods, funding, ethics and whatever
2-2526	**.careers** issues relevant to careers in scientific research
2-2527	**.skeptic** skeptics discussing pseudoscience
2-2528	**.software.nntp** the Network News Transfer Protocol
2-2529	**.space** space, space programs, space-related research, etc.
2-2530	**.news** announcements of space-related news items (moderated)
2-2531	**.shuttle** the space shuttle and the STS program
2-2532	**.stat**
2-2533	**.consult** statistical consulting
2-2534	**.edu** statistics education
2-2535	**.math** statistics from a strictly mathematical viewpoint
2-2536	**.systems** the theory and application of systems science
2-2537	**.virtual-worlds** modeling the universe (moderated)
2-2538	**.apps** current and future uses of virtual-worlds technology (moderated)

2-2539 **soc Groups on all things social**

2-2540 **.answers** repository for periodic Usenet articles (moderated)

2-2541 **.bi** on bisexuality

2-2542 **.college** college, college activities, campus life, etc.

2-2543 **.grad** general issues related to graduate schools

2-2544 **.gradinfo** information about graduate schools

2-2545 **.teaching-asst** issues affecting collegiate teaching assistants

2-2546 **.couples** discussions for couples (see soc.singles)

2-2547 **.culture**

2-2548 **.afghanistan** on the Afghan society

2-2549 **.african** on Africa and things African

2-2550 **.african.american** on Afro-American issues

2-2551 **.arabic** technological and cultural issues, *not* politics

2-2552 **.argentina** Argentina, life and ways

2-2553 **.asean** countries of the Association of Southeast Asian Nations

2-2554 **.asian.american** issues and discussion about Asian-Americans

2-2555 **.australian** Australian culture and society

2-2556 **.austria** Austria and its people

2-2557 **.baltics** people of the Baltic states

2-2558 **.bangladesh** issues and discussion about Bangladesh

2-2559 **.bosna-herzgvna** the indepedent state of Bosnia and Herzegovina

2-2560 **.brazil** talking about the people and country of Brazil

2-2561 **.british** issues about Britain and those of British descent

2-2562 **.bulgaria** discussing Bulgarian society

2-2563 **.canada** on Canada and its people

2-2564 **.caribbean** life in the Caribbean

2-2565 **.celtic** Irish, Scottish, Breton, Cornish, Manx, and Welsh

2-2566 **.china** about China and Chinese culture

2-2567 **.croatia** the lives of the people of Croatia

2-2568 **.czecho-slovak** Bohemian, Slovak, Moravian, and Silesian life

2-2569 **.esperanto** the neutral international language Esperanto

2-2570 **.europe** discussing all aspects of pan-European society

2-2571 **.filipino** a group about the Filipino culture

2-2572 **.french** French culture, history and related discussions

2-2573 **.german** on German culture and history

2-2574 **.greek** a group about Greeks

2-2575 **.hongkong** discussions pertaining to Hong Kong

2-2576	**.indian** group for discussion about India and things Indian
2-2577	**.indian.telugu** the culture of the Telugu people of India
2-2578	**.indonesia** all about the Indonesian nation
2-2579	**.iranian** on Iran and things Iranian/Persian
2-2580	**.italian** the Italian people and their culture
2-2581	**.japan** everything Japanese, except the Japanese language
2-2582	**.jewish** Jewish culture and religion. (cf. `talk.politics.mideast`)
2-2583	**.korean** on Korean and things Korean
2-2584	**.latin-america** topics about Latin America
2-2585	**.lebanon** on things Lebanese
2-2586	**.maghreb** North African society and culture
2-2587	**.magyar** the Hungarian people and their culture
2-2588	**.malaysia** all about Malaysian society
2-2589	**.mexican** on Mexico's society
2-2590	**.misc** group for discussion about other cultures
2-2591	**.native** aboriginal people around the world
2-2592	**.nepal** on people and things in and from Nepal
2-2593	**.netherlands** people from the Netherlands and Belgium
2-2594	**.new-zealand** on topics related to New Zealand
2-2595	**.nordic** on culture up north
2-2596	**.pakistan** topics of discussion about Pakistan
2-2597	**.peru** all about the people of Peru
2-2598	**.polish** Polish culture, Polish past, and Polish politics
2-2599	**.portuguese** on the people of Portugal
2-2600	**.romanian** on Romanian and Moldavian people
2-2601	**.singapore** the past, present, and future of Singapore
2-2602	**.soviet** topics relating to Russian or Soviet culture
2-2603	**.spain** on culture on the Iberian peninsula
2-2604	**.sri-lanka** things and people from Sri Lanka
2-2605	**.taiwan** on things Taiwanese
2-2606	**.tamil** Tamil language, history, and culture
2-2607	**.thai** Thai people and their culture
2-2608	**.turkish** on things Turkish
2-2609	**.ukrainian** the lives and times of the Ukrainian people
2-2610	**.usa** the culture of the United States of America
2-2611	**.venezuela** on topics related to Venezuela
2-2612	**.vietnamese** issues and discussions of Vietnamese culture

2-2613   **.yugoslavia** on Yugoslavia and its people

2-2614 **.feminism** on feminism and feminist issues (moderated)

2-2615 **.history** on things historical

2-2616 **.libraries.talk** discussing all aspects of libraries

2-2617 **.men** issues related to men, their problems, and relationships

2-2618 **.misc** socially-oriented topics not in other groups

2-2619 **.motss** issues pertaining to homosexuality

2-2620 **.net-people** announcements, requests, etc., about people on the net

2-2621 **.penpals** in search of net.friendships

2-2622 **.politics** political problems, systems, solutions (moderated)

2-2623   **.arms-d** arms discussion digest (moderated)

2-2624 **.religion**

2-2625   **.bahai** on the Baha'i Faith (moderated)

2-2626   **.christian** Christianity and related topics (moderated)

2-2627   **.christian.bible-study** examining the Holy Bible (moderated)

2-2628   **.eastern** on Eastern religions (moderated)

2-2629   **.islam** on the Islamic faith (moderated)

2-2630   **.quaker** the Religious Society of Friends (Quakers)

2-2631 **.rights.human** human rights and activism (e.g., Amnesty International)

2-2632 **.roots** discussing genealogy and genealogical matters

2-2633 **.singles** newsgroup for single people, their activities, etc.

2-2634 **.veterans** social issues relating to military veterans

2-2635 **.women** issues related to women, their problems, and relationships

2-2636 talk Groups where unending discussion is inevitable

2-2637 **.abortion** all sorts of discussions and arguments on abortion

2-2638 **.answers** repository for periodic Usenet articles (moderated)

2-2639 **.bizarre** the unusual, bizarre, curious and often stupid

2-2640 **.environment** discussion of the state of the environment and what to do

2-2641 **.origins** evolution versus creationism (sometimes hot!)

2-2642 **.philosophy.misc** philosophical musings on all topics

2-2643 **.politics** all aspects of politics

2-2644   **.animals** the use and/or abuse of animals

2-2645   **.china** on political issues related to China

2-2646   **.drugs** the politics of drug issues

2-2647   **.guns** the politics of firearm ownership and (mis)use

2-2648   **.medicine** the politics and ethics involved with health care

2-2649   **`.mideast`** discussion and debate over Middle Eastern events

2-2650   **`.misc`** political discussions and ravings of all kinds

2-2651   **`.soviet`** on Soviet politics, domestic and foreign

2-2652   **`.space`** nontechnical issues affecting space exploration

2-2653   **`.theory`** theory of politics and political systems

2-2654   **`.rape`** on stopping rape; not to be crossposted

2-2655   **`.religion` [Groups on wide-ranging religious conversations]**

2-2656   **`.misc`** religious, ethical, and moral implications

2-2657   **`.newage`** esoteric and minority religions and philosophies

2-2658   **`.rumors`** for the posting of rumors

2-2659   u3b   Groups on ATT&T's 3B computers

2-2660   **`.config`** 3B distribution configuration

2-2661   **`.misc`** 3B miscellaneous discussions

2-2662   **`.sources`** sources for AT&T 3B systems

2-2663   **`.tech`** 3B technical discussions

2-2664   **`.test`** 3B distribution testing

2-2665   vmsnet   Groups of interest to users of VMS computers

2-2666   **`.admin`** administration of the VMSnet newsgroups

2-2667   **`.alpha`** on Alpha AXP architecture, systems, porting, etc.

2-2668   **`.announce`** general announcements of interest to all (moderated)

2-2669   **`.newusers`** orientation info for new users (moderated)

2-2670   **`.databases.rdb`** DEC's Rdb relational DBMS and related topics

2-2671   **`.decus`**

2-2672   **`.journal`** The DECUServe Journal (moderated)

2-2673   **`.lugs`** on DECUS Local User Groups and related issues

2-2674   **`.employment`** jobs sought/offered, workplace and employment related issues

2-2675   **`.internals`** VMS internals, MACRO-32, Bliss, etc., gatewayed to MACRO32 list

2-2676   **`.mail`**

2-2677   **`.misc`** other electronic mail software

2-2678   **`.mx`** MX e-mail system, gatewayed to the MX mailing list

2-2679   **`.pmdf`** PMDF e-mail system, gatewayed to the ipmdf mailing list

2-2680   **`.misc`** general VMS topics not covered elsewhere

2-2681   **`.networks`**

2-2682   **`.desktop.misc`** other desktop integration software

2-2683   **`.desktop.pathworks`** DEC Pathworks desktop integration software

2-2684   **.management.decmcc** DECmcc and related software

2-2685   **.management.misc** other network management solutions

2-2686   **.misc** general networking topics not covered elsewhere

2-2687   **.tcp-ip.cmu-tek** CMU-TEK TCP/IP package, gatewayed to cmu-tek-tcp+

2-2688   **.tcp-ip.misc** other TCP/IP solutions for VMS

2-2689   **.tcp-ip.multinet** TGV's Multinet TCP/IP, gatewayed to info-multinet

2-2690   **.tcp-ip.tcpware** on Process Software's TCPWARE TCP/IP software

2-2691   **.tcp-ip.ucx** DEC's VMS/Ultrix Connection (or TCP/IP services for VMS) product

2-2692   **.tcp-ip.wintcp** the Wollongong Group's WIN-TCP TCP/IP software

2-2693   **.pdp-11** PDP-11 hardware and software, gatewayed to info-pdp11

2-2694   **.sources** source-code postings ONLY (moderated)

2-2695   **.d** discussion on or requests for sources

2-2696   **.games** recreational software postings

2-2697   **.sysmgt** VMS system management

2-2698   **.test** test messages

2-2699   **.tpu** TPU language and applications, gatewayed to info-tpu

2-2700   **.uucp** DECUS uucp software, gatewayed to VMSnet mailing list

2-2701   **.vms-posix** on VMS POSIX

3. LIBRARY CATALOGS (OPACS)

Over a thousand libraries around the world have card catalogs that are accessible via the Internet, and the number increases weekly. You can use online card catalogs to examine the holdings of libraries, browse for books by topic for a research project, and in some cases examine special databases.

To log onto an OPAC (Online Public Access Catalog), you will need to use telnet or TN3270, an enhanced version of telnet that emulates the IBM terminals many online library catalogs require. (For more information on connection services, see "An Internet Refresher" at the beginning of this book.)

Entry Format:

Item
Number

3-n **OPAC or Library Name:** Country *Software Type*
      Access: `host.domain` (telnet or TN3270-reachable address) Login instructions, if any
      Access: Alternate access routes, if any

or

3-m **Library Name:** Country (Access via **Name of OPAC from which library is accessible**)

Where to Find It: The entries in this chapter were taken from the database of a program called Hytelnet, written by Peter Scott. Hytelnet is a powerful program that provides hypertext access to OPACs and other telnet-reachable resources. You can try out this software by telnetting to `access.usask.ca` (login as `hytelnet`). For more information on Hytelnet, including PC and Unix versions of the software, FTP to `ftp.usask.ca` in the `/pub/hytelnet/` directory. There is also a mailing list associated with Hytelnet that distributes updates and information on new OPACs. To subscribe to this mailing list, send e-mail to `listserv@kentvm.kent.edu` with `SUBSCRIBE HYTEL-L` in the body of your message. For other online sources of information on OPACs, please see Chapter 11 (Online Resource Lists).

The entries in this chapter were verified to make sure that access is indeed possible following the instructions listed. A small number of the OPACs listed in Hytlenet could not be verified, so I have not listed them. This does not mean, however, that the OPACs don't exist. OPACs are often unreachable for a number of reasons: libraries sometimes limit access to certain hours, international links go down, host computers crash, etc. A number of the entries listed required many login attempts before access was finally gained.

Comments: Logging in to some of the OPACs in this list can be a bit tricky. No instructions are listed here for OPACs with easy-to-follow online instructions. If the login process is not so easy, instructions are given, and I have tried to make them as clear as possible. Each step in the login process is separated by the ▶ symbol. Text in the `Courier` font is the text that you should type, or, in the case of "wait for the prompt" instructions, text that you will see on your screen. The ↵ symbol indicates that you need to press the return key at a point where you would not automatically do so (for example, before you are presented with a prompt, or at a prompt instead of entering information). Type <control>-`C` (when using TN3270) or <escape>-<shift>-`]` to exit from almost any OPAC (the first screen of the OPAC should give you the exit command if it is neither of these two). If you encounter a "clear the screen" instruction and are not using an IBM terminal with a <clear screen> key, type <escape>-`O-M`. Similarly, if you are prompted to press a PF key and are not using a terminal with PF keys, type <escape> and then the number of the PF key (i.e., if prompted to press PF6, type <escape>-`6`). Access addresses are listed in order of preference; try the top one first.

OPACSs are probably the most confusing resource online. The many OPAC systems were designed by different organizations, use different structures, yet are often linked to one another. It is sometimes difficult to find the particular library catalog you want, even after you've logged on correctly to the OPAC that contains it, and when using some of the larger OPACs it is far too easy to go around in circles without coming across what you're looking for. The instructions given with the entries below should at least get you past the first hurdles and allow you to explore. Keep in mind that many OPACs have help files online; refer to them if you are having problems finding the catalog you want.

OPAC Software Types: A number of OPAC software packages are used by more than one library. Comments and brief instructions on how to use the more common ones are given below. The format of these entries is:

TYPE
> *Comments, explanations, or special instructions, if any.*

> **Help command:** what to enter to access help
> **Searching:**
>> **by author:** instructions on searching by author
>> **by title:** instructions on searching by title
>> **by subject:** instructions on searching by subject

by key word: instructions on searching by key word
by other data: instructions on searching by other data
additional search information: more ways to search, if any

Navigating:
  desired location: navigation keystrokes
  other: navigation keystrokes

Other actions:
  actions: keystrokes

BLCMP

Help command: H
Searching:
  by author: Select A from the menu. Then enter the author's name at the : prompt
  by title: Select T from the menu. Then enter the title at the : prompt
  by subject: Select S from the menu. Enter the subject at the : prompt
  by key word: Select K from the menu and enter the key word at the : prompt

BuCAT

Help command: HELP
Searching:
  by author: find a=author
  by title: find t=title
  by subject: find s=subject
  by author, title, and subject indexes at once: find key word/phrase
  additional search information: You can combine words or phrases using symbols for the boolean operators "and" (symbols "&", "/") "or" (symbol "|"), and "not" (symbol "~"). (example: find united nations & peace)

CATS

Every CATS system has its own site-specific menu system, which is different from that of every other CATS system. All of them are extremely easy to use, so no instructions are provided here.

CLSI

No information available.

DOBIS/LIBIS

No information available.

DRA

Help command: ??.
Searching:
  by author: a=author's last-name first-name
  by title: t=title
  by subject: s=subject
  by call umber: c=call number (example: c=f1897.5)
  by ISBN: i=ISBN (example: i=449908984)

by ISSN: n=ISSN (example: n=0010-0285)
by LCCN: l=LCCN (example: l= 9390457)
by Music Publishers Number: r=MPN (example: r=CD 80096 telarc)
by key word: Enter k=key word (Some DRA sites use the Z39.58 standard for the key word search. See the section on "Using Z39.58.")

DYNIX

The Dynix library package is an entirely different product from the Dynix Operating System used on Sequent Computers.

Searching:

by author: Choose the appropriate number from the main menu
by title: If the exact title is known, select the "Title Alphabetical list" option on the menu. If the exact title is not known, select the "Title Words" option
by subject: Choose the appropriate number from the main menu
by key word: Choose the appropriate number from the main menu. Some systems will look for terms in the subject field, some in the title field, as indicated on the menu
by call number: Choose the appropriate number from the main menu

GEAC

Help command: HELP
Searching:

by author: AUT Author (example: AUT Haring)
by title: TIL Title (example: TIL The Animal Folktales of Africa)
by subject: SUB Subject (example: SUB Folktales)
by key word: KEY Key word/string (example: KEY Animal Folktales)

Navigating:

previously displayed screens: BAC
next screen: FOR

Other actions:

to select an item in a list of items: enter the number to the right of the item

GvB

No information available.

INLEX

Help command: HE= and the desired command (example: HE=AU for author help)
Searching:

by author: au= Author
by title: ti= Title
by subject: su= subject
by call number: ca= call number

Navigating:

next page: NP
previous page: PP
first page: FP
last page: LP

>   **step back:** SB
>   **exit:** EX
Other actions:
>   **to display titles:** dt= line number
>   **to display call numbers:** DC
>   **to display full record:** DF
>   **for instructions:** IN
>   **for bulletin board:** BB

INNOPAC

INNOPAC is very easy to use. Just press the letter or number next to the item that you want. There is no need to press the <enter> or <return> key when choosing one of the menu options.

Searching:
>   **by author:** select A on the main menu
>   **by title:** select T on the main menu
>   **by subject:** select S on the main menu
>   **by key word:** select either K or W, as listed on the menu

Other actions:
>   **to show items with the same subject when looking at a single record:** select S
>   **to show items nearby on the shelf when looking at a single record:** select Z

LIBERTAS

Every Libertas system has its own site-specific menuing system, which is different from that of every other Libertas system. All of them are extremely easy to use, so no instructions are provided here.

LS/2000

Searching:
>   **by author:** enter the number for heading search; when prompted, enter the author name (last-name, first-name)
>   **by title:** enter the number for heading search; when prompted, enter the title
>   **by key word:** enter the number for key word search; when prompted, enter as much of the *beginning* of the heading as you are sure of

Other actions:
>   **to go one step backward in your search:** ^
>   **to see more of a list ending with** more: a
>   **to see previous pages of a list ending with** more: /B

MultiLIS

MultiLIS is menu/prompt driven and is not difficult to use. Status and error messages are usually displayed in the lower right-hand corner of the screen. Press the <return> key to acknowledge these messages.

Help command: press the <help> key or KeyPad7
Searching:
>   **by author:** enter author's last-name first-name (example: haring leigh, haring, leigh, or haring l)
>   **by title:** enter one or more words from the title (in any order)

by subject: enter one or more words that describe the subject (in any order) (example: `folk-tales african animal`)

Navigating:

previous menu/screen: press PF1

previous screen or record: press PF2

next screen or record: press PF3

exit: press PF1

Other actions:

to see the titles listed as the result of a search: enter the number or range of numbers next to the particular title(s). (Once you have selected items from this display, you cannot return to this display without redoing the search)

to start a new search: press PF1

to print a record: press PF4

to limit a search by date or language when a list of titles is displayed: press PF5 or KeyPad5

to display a search history from the searching screen: press PF2 or KeyPad2

NOTIS

Help command: h or HELP for help

Searching:

by author: a= author

by title: t= title

by subject: s= subject

by key word: k= string (example: `k=folktales`)

by subject: SU 4-word heading (example: `SU Folktales of Africa`)

by call number: enter CA call-number (example: `CA QA76.8.I294 1988`)

by combination of fields: CO Author last-name Title firstword (example: `CO Haring Animal` for Leigh Haring's *The Animal Folktales of Africa*)

additional search information: You may use the logical operators (`and`, `or`, `not`) and parentheses to group the operators. Also, `$` is a wildcard character. (Examples: `k=folktales and Anansi; k=folktales and not American; k=folk$ and (Africa or Anansi)`)

Other actions:

to pick an item in a list of items: enter the number to the right of the item

OCLC

Help command: <esc>-H-<return>

Searching:

by author: A

by title: A

by key word: K

by classmark: C

by ISBN (International Standard Book Number): I

by LBN (Library Book Number): L

Navigating:

exit: <esc>-Q-<return>

UNICORN

No information available.

URICA

URICA is menu-driven and very easy to use. However, there are a few things to note.

Help command: \

Other actions:
>   to exit from a menu and return to the last menu: .

UTCAT

Some terminal packages remap the keypad <enter> key to other keys. For example, in Procomm the equivalent to Keypad <enter> is Shift-F10. Keypad <enter> is equivalent to <escape>-O-M.

Help command: HEL or press PF6

Searching:
>   **by author:** a author last-name, first-name (example: a haring, leigh)
>   **by title:** t title (example: t the animal folktales of africa)
>   **by subject:** s subject (example: s folktales)
>   **by key word:** tk key word/string (example: tk animal africa)

Navigating:
>   **previous screen:** BAC (or press PF1)
>   **from brief or full records to the corresponding index:** IND (or press PF3)
>   **Search Choices Menu:** MEN (or press PF7)
>   **exit:** STO (or press PF8)

Other actions:
>   **to repeat the last search:** REP (or press PF2)
>   **to see the index of authors:** AI name of the first author you wish to see (last-name, first-name)
>   (example: ai haring, leigh)
>   **to see the index of titles:** TI followed by the first title you wish to see (example: ti animal
>   folktales of africa)
>   **to view general information about the Online Catalog:** EXP (or press PF4)
>   **to view current information about Online Catalog developments:** NEW (or press PF5)
>   **to send comments to library staff:** COM
>   **to select an item from a list:** enter the number of the desired item

VTLS

VTLS features a Novice User Search System that can be accessed at any time by entering ?. This novice mode is an easy-to-use menu-driven method of searching. In addition, the novice mode also offers training on using the Advanced User Search System. Advanced User Search System commands may be entered at any novice level prompt.

Help command: /HELP

Searching:
>   **by author:** A/Author last-name, first-name (example: A/Haring, Leigh)
>   **by title:** T/title (omit initial articles like "the," "a," and "of") (example: T/animal folk-
>   tales of africa)
>   **by subject:** S/ subject (example: S/folktales)

by key word: W/key word (example: W/africa)
additional search information: To search for key words with boolean operators, use the B/
search command followed by a key word, then an operator, and then the second key word.
(example: B/folktales and africa; B/folktales or anansi)

Navigating:
previous screen: PS
next screen: NS
Novice User Search System: ?

Z39.58

*Z39.58 is a standard from NISO known as the Common Command Language standard. Basic searches are
in the form FIND [index name] [search terms].*

Help command: HELP
Searching:
by author: FIND AU author (example: FIND AU Haring)
by title: FIND TI title (example: FIND TI The Animal Folktales of Africa)
by subject: FIND SU subject (Harvard only) (example: FIND SU folktales)
by topic: FIND TO topic (Dartmouth only) (example: FIND TO africa)
Other actions:
to display results of search: DISPLAY

Entries:

3-1 **Aalborg University:** Denmark *custom*
Access: auboline.bib.dk ▶ press ↵ ▶ wait for the prompt > ▶ enter def

3-2 **Aarhus University:** Denmark *custom*
Access: helios.aau.dk ▶ at the first prompt enter rc9000 ▶ press ↵ ▶ enter press
the ESC key ▶ wait for the prompt att ▶ enter sol ▶ press ↵ ▶ enter sol sol

3-3 **Aberdeen University:** United Kingdom *DYNIX*
Access: sun.nsf.ac.uk ▶ at the first prompt enter janet ▶ wait for the prompt
Password: ▶ press ↵ ▶ wait for the prompt Hostname: ▶ enter uk.ac.abdn.lib
▶ wait for the prompt Selection ▶ enter 3

3-4 **Abilene Christian University:** United States (Access via **Abilene Library Consortium**)

3-5 **Abilene Library Consortium:** United States *DRA*
Access: alcon.acu.edu ▶ at the first prompt enter alcpac

3-6 **Academia Sinica:** Taiwan, Province of China *INNOPAC*
Access: las.as.edu.tw ▶ at the first prompt enter library

3-7 **Acadia University:** Canada *custom*
Access: auls.acadiau.ca ▶ at the first prompt enter opac

3-8 **Access Colorado Library and Information Network:** United States *custom*
Access: teal.csn.org ▶ at the first prompt enter ac

3-9   **Ada Community Library (Idaho):** United States *INNOPAC*
       Access: `192.207.186.1` ◗ at the first prompt enter `library`

3-10   **Adams State College:** United States (Access via **MARMOT Library Network**)

3-11   **Agawam Public Library:** United States (Access via **CARL**)

3-12   **Agnes Scott College—Decatur:** United States (Access via **Georgia On-Line Library Information System**)

3-13   **Air Force Institute of Technology:** United States *DRA*
       Access: `sabre.afit.af.mil` ◗ at the first prompt enter `afitpac` ◗ wait for the prompt `Password:` ◗ enter `library`

3-14   **Albert Einstein College of Medicine:** United States *custom*
       Access: `lis.aecom.yu.edu` ◗ press ↵ ◗ press ↵

3-15   **Allegan Public Library:** United States (Access via **KELLY**)

3-16   **Allegheny College:** United States *INNOPAC*
       Access: `allecat.alleg.edu` ◗ at the first prompt enter `library`

3-17   **Alma College:** United States *DYNIX*
       Access: `mark.alma.edu` ◗ at the first prompt enter `dynixpac`

3-18   **American International College:** United States (Access via **CARL**)

3-19   **American University:** United States (Access via **Washington Research Library Consortium**)

3-20   **Amherst, Jones Library:** United States (Access via **CARL**)

3-21   **Andrews University:** United States *INNOPAC*
       Access: `library.libr.andrews.edu` ◗ at the first prompt enter `library`

3-22   **Anna Maria College:** United States (Access via **CARL**)

3-23   **Appalachian State University:** United States *LS2000*
       Access: `library.appstate.edu`

3-24   **Araphoe Community College:** United States (Access via **CARL**)

3-25   **Arizona State University:** United States *custom*
       Access: `carl.lib.asu.edu`
       Access: `192.153.23.254`
       Access: `victor.umd.edu` ◗ at the first prompt enter `pac` ◗ press ↵ ◗ press ↵

3-26   **Armstrong State College:** United States *DRA*
       Access: `library.armstrong.edu`

3-27   **Aspen Schools:** United States (Access via **MARMOT Library Network**)

3-28 **Aston University:** United Kingdom *GEAC*
    Access: `sun.nsf.ac.uk` ▶ at the first prompt enter `janet` ▶ wait for the prompt
      `Password:` ▶ press ↵ ▶ wait for the prompt `Hostname:` ▶ enter
      `uk.ac.aston.geac` ▶ press ↵ ▶ press ↵

3-29 **Athabasca University:** Canada *BuCAT*
    Access: `aucat.athabascau.ca` ▶ at the first prompt enter `aucat`

3-30 **Atlantic School of Theology:** Canada *GEAC*
    Access: `novanet.dal.ca`

3-31 **Auburn Public Library:** United States (Access via **CARL**)

3-32 **Auburn:** United States *NOTIS*
    Access: `TN3270 auducacd.duc.auburn.edu` ▶ tab to `APPLICATION` ▶ press ↵

3-33 **Audie L. Murphy Memorial Veterans' Administration Hospital:** United States *custom*
    Access: `athena.uthscsa.edu` ▶ at the first prompt enter `lis`

3-34 **Augsburg College:** United States *DYNIX*
    Access: `host.clic.edu` ▶ at the first prompt enter `apac`

3-35 **Augusta College:** United States *PALS*
    Access: `acvax.ac.edu` ▶ at the first prompt enter `acpac`
    Access: `library.gsu.edu`

3-36 **Augusta-Ross Township:** United States (Access via **KELLY**)

3-37 **Augusta/Mckay Library:** United States (Access via **KELLY**)

3-38 **Auraria University:** United States (Access via **CARL**)

3-39 **Aurora University:** United States (Access via **ILLINET On-line Catalog**)

3-40 **Australian Bibliographic Network:** Australia *custom*
    Access: `abn.nla.gov.au` ▶ press ↵ ▶ press ↵

3-41 **Australian Defence Force Academy:** Australia *custom*
    Access: `library.adfa.oz.au` ▶ press ↵

3-42 **Australian National University:** Australia *URICA*
    Access: `library.anu.edu.au`

3-43 **Austrian Academic Library Network:** Austria *custom*
    Access: `opac.univie.ac.at`

3-44 **Ayer Public Library:** United States (Access via **CARL**)

3-45 **Ball State University:** United States *NOTIS*
    Access: `TN3270 lib.cc.purdue.edu` ▶ at the first prompt enter `remote`
      ▶ press ↵ ▶ enter `bsucat`

3-46 **Bangor Public Library:** United States (Access via **University of Maine Library System**)

3-47 **Bar-Ilan University:** Israel *custom*
    Access: `aleph.biu.ac.il` ◗ at the first prompt enter `aleph`

3-48 **Barat College:** United States (Access via **ILLINET On-line Catalog**)

3-49 **Barnes College Library:** United States (Access via **Washington University of St Louis Medical Library**)

3-50 **Bates College:** United States *INNOPAC*
    Access: `ladd.bates.edu`

3-51 **Baylor University:** United States *MultiLIS*
    Access: `library.baylor.edu` ◗ at the first prompt enter `baylis`

3-52 **Baystate Medical Library:** United States (Access via **CARL**)

3-53 **Beaumont Public Library:** United States (Access via **CARL**)

3-54 **Beaumont Royal Oak Hospital Library:** United States (Access via **Detroit Area Library Network**)

3-55 **Beloit College:** United States *DRA*
    Access: `lib.beloit.edu` ◗ at the first prompt enter `belcat`

3-56 **Ben-Gurion University:** Israel (Access via **Hebrew University**)

3-57 **Berrien Springs Community Library:** United States (Access via **KELLY**)

3-58 **Bethel College:** United States *DYNIX*
    Access: `host.clic.edu` ◗ at the first prompt enter `bpac`

3-59 **Biblioteca Nacional de Venezuela:** Venezuela *NOTIS*
    Access: `biblio.iabn.ve` ◗ at the first prompt enter `biblio`

3-60 **Bibliothek St. Gabriel:** Austria (Access via **Austrian Academic Library Network**)

3-61 **Bibliotheken der GMD:** Germany *custom*
    Access: `192.88.108.111` ◗ at the first prompt enter `echo`

3-62 **Bibliotheque Publique et Universitaire de Neuchatel:** Switzerland *GEAC*
    Access: `bpu.unine.ch`

3-63 **Birkbeck College:** United Kingdom (Access via **University of London Central Libertas Consortium**)

3-64 **Boise State University:** United States *GEAC ADVANCE*
    Access: `catalyst.idbsu.edu` ◗ at the first prompt enter `catalyst`

3-65 **Bond University:** Australia *URICA*
    Access: `library.bu.oz.au`

3-66 **Borgess Health Information Library:** United States (Access via **KELLY**)

3-67 **Boston College:** United States (Access via **Boston Library Consortium**)

3-68 **Boston Library Consortium:** United States *custom*
 Access: blc.lrc.northeastern.edu

3-69 **Boston Public Library:** United States (Access via **Boston Library Consortium**)

3-70 **Boston University:** United States *custom*
 Access: bupac.bu.edu ▶ at the first prompt enter library
 Access: blc.lrc.northeastern.edu

3-71 **Botsford Hospital Library:** United States (Access via **Detroit Area Library Network**)

3-72 **Boulder — Carnegie — Manuscripts & Photographs:** United States (Access via **Boulder, Colorado, Public Library System**)

3-73 **Boulder, Colorado, Public Library System:** United States *custom*
 Access: 161.98.1.68
 Access: 192.153.23.254
 Access: pac.carl.org ▶ at the first prompt enter PAC ▶ press ↵ ▶ enter 4
 Access: victor.umd.edu ▶ at the first prompt enter pac ▶ press ↵ ▶ press ↵

3-74 **Bowdoin College:** United States *INNOPAC*
 Access: library.bowdoin.edu ▶ at the first prompt enter library

3-75 **Bowie State University:** United States (Access via **University of Maryland Library System**)

3-76 **Bowling Green State University:** United States *INNOPAC*
 Access: bglink.bgsu.edu ▶ at the first prompt enter library
 Access: cat.ohiolink.edu

3-77 **Bradford University:** United Kingdom *URICA*
 Access: info.brad.ac.uk ▶ at the first prompt enter library

3-78 **Bradley University:** United States (Access via **ILLINET On-line Catalog**)

3-79 **Brandeis University:** United States *custom*
 Access: library.brandeis.edu
 Access: blc.lrc.northeastern.edu

3-80 **Brandon University:** Canada *BuCAT*
 Access: library.brandonu.ca ▶ at the first prompt enter libcat

3-81 **Brevard Community College, Florida:** United States *NOTIS*
 Access: luis.nerdc.ufl.edu ▶ at the first prompt enter luis ▶ select LINCC
  (Florida Community Colleges) from the menu

3-82 **Bridgman Public Library:** United States (Access via **KELLY**)

3-83 **Brigham Young University:** United States *NOTIS*
Access: TN3270 `lib.byu.edu`

3-84 **British Library of Political and Economic Science, University of London:** United Kingdom *LIBERTAS*
Access: `sun.nsf.ac.uk` ▶ at the first prompt enter `janet` ▶ wait for the prompt
`Password:` ▶ press ↵ ▶ wait for the prompt `Hostname:` ▶ enter
`uk.ac.lse.blpes` ▶ wait for the prompt `Username:` ▶ enter `library`

3-85 **Bronson Hospital Health Sciences Library:** United States (Access via **KELLY**)

3-86 **Brookhaven National Laboratory:** United States *custom*
Access: `suntid.bnl.gov` ▶ at the first prompt enter `brookhaven`

3-87 **Broomfield Public Library:** United States (Access via **Boulder, Colorado, Public Library System**)

3-88 **Broward Community College, Florida:** United States *NOTIS*
Access: `luis.nerdc.ufl.edu` ▶ at the first prompt enter `luis` ▶ select LINCC
(Florida Community Colleges) from the menu

3-89 **Brown University:** United States *custom*
Access: TN3270 `brownvm.brown.edu` ▶ tab to COMMAND
▶ enter `dial josiah` ▶ press ↵ ▶ enter PF1

3-90 **Brunel University:** United Kingdom *BLCMP*
Access: `lib.brunel.ac.uk`
Access: `sun.nsf.ac.uk` ▶ at the first prompt enter `janet` ▶ wait for the prompt
`Password:` ▶ press ↵ ▶ wait for the prompt `Hostname:` ▶ enter
`uk.ac.brunel.lib`

3-91 **Brunswick College:** United States (Access via **Georgia On-Line Library Information System**)

3-92 **Bryn Mawr College:** United States *INNOPAC*
Access: `tripod.brynmawr.edu` ▶ at the first prompt enter `library`

3-93 **Buchanan Public Library:** United States (Access via **KELLY**)

3-94 **Bucknell University:** United States *custom*
Access: `quartz.bucknell.edu` ▶ at the first prompt enter `library` ▶ press ↵

3-95 **Bud Werner / Steamboat Public:** United States (Access via **MARMOT Library Network**)

3-96 **Bur Oak Library System:** United States (Access via **ILLINET On-line Catalog**)

3-97 **Butler University:** United States *DRA*
Access: `ruth.butler.edu` ▶ at the first prompt enter `iliad`

3-98 **C.S.I.R.O:** Australia *GEAC*
Access: `library.its.csiro.au` ◗ at the first prompt enter `library`

3-99 **C/W MARS, Inc.:** United States *custom*
Access: `pac.carl.org` ◗ at the first prompt enter `pac`

3-100 **Cal Poly State University:** United States *custom*
Access: `library.calpoly.edu` ◗ at the first prompt enter `polycat`

3-101 **California State University—Chico:** United States *custom*
Access: `libcat.csuchico.edu` ◗ at the first prompt enter `libcat`

3-102 **California State University—Fresno:** United States *GEAC ADVANCE*
Access: `alis.csufresno.edu` ◗ at the first prompt enter `remote` ◗ wait for the prompt `Password:` ◗ press ↵

3-103 **California State University—Fullerton:** United States *INNOPAC*
Access: `137.151.165.2` ◗ at the first prompt enter `library`

3-104 **California State University—Hayward:** United States *INNOPAC*
Access: `library.csuhayward.edu` ◗ at the first prompt enter `library`

3-105 **California State University—Long Beach:** United States *NOTIS*
Access: `coast.lib.csulb.edu`

3-106 **California State University—Sacramento:** United States *INNOPAC*
Access: `eureka.lib.csus.edu` ◗ at the first prompt enter `library`

3-107 **California State University—San Marcos:** United States *INNOPAC*
Access: `pac.csusm.edu` ◗ at the first prompt enter `library`

3-108 **Calvin College:** United States *DYNIX*
Access: `l.calvin.edu` ◗ at the first prompt enter `pub`

3-109 **Cambridge University:** United Kingdom *CATS*
Access: `ipgate.cam.ac.uk` ◗ at the first prompt enter `uk.ac.cam.ul`
Access: `cambl.ixi.ch`

3-110 **Camosun College:** Canada *BuCAT*
Access: `camsrv.camosun.bc.ca` ◗ at the first prompt enter `CATINQ`

3-111 **Canada Centre for Mineral and Energy Technology:** Canada *MultiLIS*
Access: `canlib.emr.ca` ◗ at the first prompt enter `opac`

3-112 **Canisius College:** United States *INNOPAC*
Access: `138.92.8.41` ◗ at the first prompt enter `cando`

3-113 **CARL—Colorado Alliance of Research Libraries:** United States *custom*
Access: `pac.carl.org` ◗ at the first prompt enter `PAC`
Access: `161.98.1.68`

Access: 192.153.23.254

Access: victor.umd.edu ▶ at the first prompt enter pac ▶ press ↵ ▶ press ↵

3-114 **Carleton College:** United States *Z39.58*

Access: lib1.carleton.edu ▶ press ↵

3-115 **Carleton University:** Canada *custom*

Access: library.carleton.ca ▶ press ↵

3-116 **Carnegie Mellon University:** United States *custom*

Access: library.cmu.edu ▶ at the first prompt enter library

3-117 **Case Western Reserve University:** United States *INNOPAC*

Access: catalog.cwru.edu

Access: cat.ohiolink.edu

3-118 **Castleton State College, Vermont:** United States (Access via **Middlebury College**)

3-119 **Catholic Theological Union:** United States (Access via **ILLINET On-line Catalog**)

3-120 **Catholic University of America Law Library:** United States *INNOPAC*

Access: columbo.law.cua.edu ▶ at the first prompt enter library

3-121 **Catholic University of America:** United States (Access via **Washington Research Library Consortium**)

3-122 **Cedar Rapids Public Library:** United States *DRA*

Access: crpl.cedar-rapids.lib.ia.us ▶ at the first prompt enter catalog

3-123 **Cedarville College:** United States *INNOPAC*

Access: library.cedarville.edu ▶ at the first prompt enter library

3-124 **Center for Research Libraries:** United States (Access via **ILLINET On-line Catalog**)

3-125 **Central Florida Community College, Florida:** United States *NOTIS*

Access: luis.nerdc.ufl.edu ▶ at the first prompt enter luis ▶ select LINCC (Florida Community Colleges) from the menu

3-126 **Central Mass Regional Library:** United States (Access via **CARL**)

3-127 **Central Michigan University:** United States *custom*

Access: hme4.merit.edu ▶ at the first prompt enter cmu-ibm

3-128 **Central State University:** United States *INNOPAC*

Access: hallie.ces.edu ▶ at the first prompt enter library

Access: cat.ohiolink.edu

3-129 **Centre for Newfoundland Studies:** Canada (Access via **Memorial University, Newfoundland**)

3-130 **Centro Informatico Cientifico de Andalucia:** Spain *custom*

Access: sevax2.cica.es ▶ at the first prompt enter aleph

3-131 **CERN Scientific Information Service:** Switzerland *custom*
    Access: `vxlib.cern.ch`

3-132 **Chalmers University of Technology:** Sweden *LIBERTAS*
    Access: `cthlib.lib.chalmers.se`

3-133 **Chandler Gilbert Community College Center Library:** United States (Access via **Maricopa Community Colleges Libraries and Media Centers**)

3-134 **Charing Cross & Westminster Medical School—Serials:** United Kingdom (Access via **University of London Central Libertas Consortium**)

3-135 **Charles Sturt University—Mitchell:** Australia *GEAC*
    Access: `opac.clann.edu.au` ▸ press ↵ ▸ enter `CSUMITRIVREG`

3-136 **Charles Sturt University—Riverina:** Australia *custom*
    Access: `opac.clann.edu.au` ▸ at the first prompt enter `CSU-W L122`

3-137 **Charles Sturt University:** Australia (Access via **New South Wales Libraries**)

3-138 **Chicago Public Library:** United States (Access via **ILLINET On-line Catalog**)

3-139 **Chicago State University:** United States (Access via **ILLINET On-line Catalog**)

3-140 **Chicopee Library:** United States (Access via **CARL**)

3-141 **Chinese University of Hong Kong:** Hong Kong *DOBIS/LIBIS*
    Access: TN3270 `vax.csc.cuhk.hk` or `library.cuhk.hk` ▸ at the first prompt enter `library`

3-142 **Chipola Junior College, Florida:** United States *NOTIS*
    Access: `luis.nerdc.ufl.edu` ▸ at the first prompt enter `luis` ▸ select `LINCC` (Florida Community Colleges) from the menu

3-143 **Citadel, the Military College of South Carolina:** United States *DRA*
    Access: `citadel.edu` ▸ at the first prompt enter `info`

3-144 **City Library of Antwerp:** Belgium (Access via **University of Antwerp**)

3-145 **City of Abilene Public Library System:** United States (Access via **Abilene Library Consortium**)

3-146 **City University of New York:** United States *NOTIS*
    Access: TN3270 `cunyvm.cuny.edu` ▸ tab to COMMAND: ▸ enter `dial vtam` ▸ tab or arrow to `CUNYPLUS` or tab twice, arrow to `APPLICATION` => line, and enter `CUNYPLUS` ▸ press ↵ ▸ you will see a CICS-MVS logo screen ▸ clear screen ▸ enter `LNAV` ▸ press ↵ ▸ enter `DPAC`

3-147 **Claremont Colleges:** United States *INNOPAC*
    Access: `blais.claremont.edu` ▸ at the first prompt enter `library`

3-148 **Clarion University of Pennsylvania:** United States *GEAC*
    Access: `vaxa.clarion.edu` ▸ at the first prompt enter `library`

3-149 **Clark University:** United States (Access via **CARL**)

3-150 **Clayton State College—Morrow:** United States (Access via **Georgia On-Line Library Information System**)

3-151 **Clemson University:** United States *NOTIS*
  Access: TN3270 `clemson.clemson.edu` ▶ press ↵

3-152 **Cleveland Public Library:** United States *DRA*
  Access: `library.cpl.org` ▶ at the first prompt enter <ctrl>-z

3-153 **Cleveland State University:** United States *NOTIS*
  Access: TN3270 `vmcms.csuohio.edu`

3-154 **Climax-Scotts Schools:** United States (Access via **KELLY**)

3-155 **Climax/Lawrence Memorial Library:** United States (Access via **KELLY**)

3-156 **Clinton, Bigelow Public Library:** United States (Access via **CARL**)

3-157 **Colby College:** United States *INNOPAC*
  Access: `library.colby.edu` ▶ at the first prompt enter `library`

3-158 **Colgate University:** United States *INNOPAC*
  Access: `library.colgate.edu` ▶ at the first prompt enter `library`

3-159 **College of Cardiff, University of Wales:** United Kingdom *LIBERTAS*
  Access: `sun.nsf.ac.uk` ▶ at the first prompt enter `janet` ▶ wait for the prompt `Password:` ▶ press ↵ ▶ wait for the prompt `Hostname:` ▶ enter `uk.ac.cf.liby` ▶ wait for the prompt `Username:` ▶ enter `library`

3-160 **College of Charleston:** United States *DRA*
  Access: `ashley.cofc.edu` ▶ at the first prompt enter `library`

3-161 **College of Physicians of Philadelphia Library:** United States (Access via **HSLC HealthNET Health Sciences Information Network**)

3-162 **College of St. Catherine—Main Campus:** United States *DYNIX*
  Access: `host.clic.edu` ▶ at the first prompt enter `scpac`

3-163 **College of St. Catherine—St. Mary's Campus:** United States *DYNIX*
  Access: `host.clic.edu` ▶ at the first prompt enter `smpac`

3-164 **College of the Holy Cross:** United States *DRA*
  Access: `hcacad.holycross.edu` ▶ at the first prompt enter `library`

3-165 **College of Wooster:** United States *INNOPAC*
  Access: `woolib.wooster.edu` ▶ at the first prompt enter `library`

3-166 **Coloma Public Library:** United States (Access via **KELLY**)

3-167 **CARL:** United States (See **CARL**)

3-168 **Colorado College:** United States *DYNIX (OP005)*
    Access: 192.70.253.3

3-169 **Colorado Mountain College:** United States (Access via **MARMOT Library Network**)

3-170 **Colorado Northwestern CC:** United States (Access via **MARMOT Library Network**)

3-171 **Colorado School of Mines:** United States (Access via **CARL**)

3-172 **Colorado State University:** United States (Access via **CARL**)

3-173 **Colorado University Health Sciences Center Library:** United States (Access via **CARL**)

3-174 **Columbia College:** United States (Access via **ILLINET On-line Catalog**)

3-175 **Columbia Seminary—Decatur:** United States (Access via **Georgia On-Line Library Information System**)

3-176 **Columbia University Law Library:** United States *INNOPAC*
    Access: pegasus.law.columbia.edu ▶ at the first prompt enter pegasus

3-177 **Columbia University:** United States *NOTIS*
    Access: columbianet.columbia.edu

3-178 **Community College of Rhode Island:** United States (Access via **Rhode Island Higher Education Library Information Network**)

3-179 **Community College of Southern Nevada:** United States (Access via **Nevada Academic Libraries Information System**)

3-180 **Comstock Township Library:** United States (Access via **West Michigan Information Network**)

3-181 **Concordia College:** United States *DYNIX*
    Access: host.clic.edu ▶ at the first prompt enter cpac

3-182 **Concordia University, Canada:** Canada *INNOPAC*
    Access: mercury.concordia.ca ▶ at the first prompt enter clues

3-183 **Concordia University, Illinois:** United States (Access via **ILLINET On-line Catalog**)

3-184 **Connecticut State University:** United States *INNOPAC*
    Access: csulib.ctstateu.edu

3-185 **Consejo Superior de Investigaciones Cientificas:** Spain *custom*
    Access: cti.csic.es ▶ at the first prompt enter aleph

3-186 **Coppin State College:** United States (Access via **University of Maryland Library System**)

3-187 **Corn Belt Library System:** United States (Access via **ILLINET On-line Catalog**)

3-188   **Cornell University Medical College:** United States *custom*
    Access: `lib.med.cornell.edu` ▸ at the first prompt enter `guest`

3-189   **Cornell:** United States *NOTIS*
    Access: TN3270 `cornellc.cit.cornell.edu` ▸ tab twice to COMMAND:
    ▸ enter `library`

3-190   **Cortez Public Library:** United States (Access via **MARMOT Library Network**)

3-191   **Cranfield Institute of Technology:** United Kingdom *LIBERTAS*
    Access: `libvax.ccc.cranfield.ac.uk` ▸ at the first prompt enter EXTERNAL

3-192   **Creighton University:** United States *PALS*
    Access: `owl.creighton.edu` ▸ at the first prompt enter `attach pals`

3-193   **Cumberland College of Health Sciences, University of Sydney:** Australia *VTLS*
    Access: `library.cchs.su.oz.au` ▸ at the first prompt enter `hello`
    `ref.clas01`

3-194   **Cumberland Trails Library System:** United States (Access via **ILLINET On-line Catalog**)

3-195   **Curtin University of Technology:** Australia *custom*
    Access: `cc.curtin.edu.au` ▸ at the first prompt enter `guest`

3-196   **Dalhousie University:** Canada *GEAC*
    Access: `novanet.dal.ca` ▸ press ↵

3-197   **Danish Natural and Medical Science Library:** Denmark *custom*
    Access: `cosmos.dnlb.bib.dk` ▸ at the first prompt enter `cosmos` ▸ wait for the
    prompt CCL> ▸ enter `dia eng`

3-198   **Dansk BiblioteksCenter:** Denmark *custom*
    Access: `bcinfo.bib.dk` ▸ at the first prompt enter `artb`

3-199   **Dartmouth:** United States *Z39.58*
    Access: `lib.dartmouth.edu`

3-200   **De Montfort University:** United Kingdom *BLCMP*
    Access: `sun.nsf.ac.uk` ▸ at the first prompt enter `janet` ▸ wait for the prompt
    Password: ▸ press ↵ ▸ wait for the prompt Hostname: ▸ enter
    `uk.ac.leicp.opac`

3-201   **Deakin University:** Australia *INNOPAC*
    Access: `mips1.lib.deakin.oz.au`

3-202   **DeKalb College—Clarkston/Decatur/Dunwoody:** United States (Access via **Georgia On-Line Library Information System**)

3-203   **Delft University of Technology:** Netherlands *DOBIS/LIBIS*
    Access: `mainf.tudelft.nl` ▸ press ↵ ▸ wait for the prompt userid: ▸ enter nn

3-204 **Denison University:** United States *INNOPAC*
      Access: `dewey.library.denison.edu`

3-205 **Denmarks Technical Library:** Denmark *custom*
      Access: `bib.dtb.dk` ◗ at the first prompt enter `alis`

3-206 **Denver Medical Library:** United States (Access via **CARL**)

3-207 **Denver Public Library:** United States (Access via **CARL**)

3-208 **Denver University:** United States (Access via **CARL**)

3-209 **DePaul University:** United States (Access via **ILLINET On-line Catalog**)

3-210 **Desert Research Institute Libraries:** United States (Access via **Nevada Academic Libraries Information System**)

3-211 **Detroit Area Library Network (DALNET):** United States *NOTIS*
      Access: `hme4.merit.edu` ◗ at the first prompt enter `wsunet`
      Access: TN3270 `cms.cc.wayne.edu` ◗ tab twice to COMMAND: ◗ enter `dial vtam` ◗ press ↵ ◗ enter `luis`

3-212 **Detroit Public Library:** United States (Access via **Detroit Area Library Network**)

3-213 **Dickinson College:** United States *custom*
      Access: `vax.dickinson.edu` ◗ at the first prompt enter `autocat`

3-214 **Dixie University:** United States *DYNIX*
      Access: `lib.dixie.edu` ◗ at the first prompt enter `pub`

3-215 **Dowagiac Public Library:** United States (Access via **KELLY**)

3-216 **Drake University:** United States *DRA*
      Access: `lib.drake.edu`

3-217 **Drew University:** United States *DRA*
      Access: `drew.drew.edu` ◗ at the first prompt enter `library`

3-218 **Drexel University:** United States *DRA*
      Access: `library.drexel.edu` ◗ at the first prompt enter `pac`

3-219 **Dublin City University:** Ireland *DYNIX*
      Access: `library.dcu.ie` ◗ at the first prompt enter `opac`

3-220 **Dudley, Pearle L. Crawford Mem:** United States (Access via **CARL**)

3-221 **Duke University Library:** United States (Access via **Triangle Research Libraries**)

3-222 **Dundee Institute of Technology:** United Kingdom *DYNIX*
      Access: `library.dct.ac.uk` ◗ at the first prompt enter `library`

Access: `sun.nsf.ac.uk` ❯ at the first prompt enter `janet` ❯ wait for the prompt Password: ❯ press ↵ ❯ wait for the prompt `Hostname:` ❯ enter `uk.ac.dct.lib` ❯ press ↵ ❯ enter `library`

3-223 **DuPage Library System:** United States (Access via **ILLINET On-line Catalog**)

3-224 **Durango Public Library:** United States (Access via **MARMOT Library Network**)

3-225 **Durham University:** United Kingdom *custom*
> **Access:** `progate.dur.ac.uk 600`
> **Access:** `sun.nsf.ac.uk` ❯ at the first prompt enter `janet` ❯ wait for the prompt Password: ❯ press ↵ ❯ wait for the prompt `Hostname:` ❯ enter `uk.ac.dur.library`

3-226 **Eagle County Public Library:** United States (Access via **MARMOT Library Network**)

3-227 **East Longmeadow Public:** United States (Access via **CARL**)

3-228 **East Tennessee State University:** United States *NOTIS*
> **Access:** `library.east-tenn-st.edu`

3-229 **East Texas State University:** United States *DRA*
> **Access:** `etsulb.etsu.edu` ❯ at the first prompt enter `pac`

3-230 **Eastern Illinois University:** United States (Access via **ILLINET On-line Catalog**)

3-231 **Eastern Michigan University:** United States *NOTIS*
> **Access:** `hme4.merit.edu` ❯ at the first prompt enter `emu-vax` ❯ wait for the prompt Username: ❯ enter `notis`

3-232 **Eastern New Mexico University:** United States *DRA*
> **Access:** `golden.enmu.edu`

3-233 **Eastern Oregon State College:** United States *INNOPAC*
> **Access:** `eos.eosc.osshe.edu` ❯ at the first prompt enter `eos`

3-234 **Eau Claire District Library:** United States (Access via **KELLY**)

3-235 **Ecole Polytechnique (Montreal):** Canada *GEAC*
> **Access:** `132.207.4.15` ❯ at the first prompt enter `biblio96`

3-236 **Ecole Polytechnique:** France *custom*
> **Access:** `TN3270 frpoly11.polytechnique.fr` ❯ press ↵ ❯ tab twice to COMMAND: ❯ enter `dial vtam` ❯ press ↵ ❯ enter `BI`

3-237 **Edinboro University:** United States *DRA*
> **Access:** `prism.edinboro.edu` ❯ at the first prompt enter `pac`

3-238 **Edinburgh University:** United Kingdom *GEAC*
> **Access:** `geac.ed.ac.uk`

3-239   **Edith Cowan University:** Australia *custom*
    Access: `library.cowan.edu.au` ◗ at the first prompt enter `guest`

3-240   **Eidgenoessiche Technische Hochschule Zuerich (Swiss Federal Institute of Technology, Zurich):** Switzerland *custom*
    Access: `ethics.ethz.ch` ◗ press ↵

3-241   **Elmhurst College:** United States (Access via **ILLINET On-line Catalog**)

3-242   **Elms College:** United States (Access via **CARL**)

3-243   **Elon College:** United States *DRA*
    Access: `vax1.elon.edu` ◗ at the first prompt enter `library`

3-244   **Emerson College:** United States (Access via **Fenway Libraries Online, Inc.**)

3-245   **Emory University:** United States *DOBIS/LIBIS*
    Access: `bigblue.cc.emory.edu` ◗ at the first prompt enter `dobis`
    Access: `library.gsu.edu`

3-246   **Environmental Protection Agency National Online Library System:** United States *custom*
    Access: `epaibm.rtpnc.epa.gov`

3-247   **Erasmus University of Rotterdam:** Netherlands *custom*
    Access: `eurbib.eur.nl`

3-248   **Estes Park Public Library:** United States (Access via **CARL**)

3-249   **European University Institute, Florence, Italy:** Italy *INNOPAC*
    Access: `149.139.6.100`

3-250   **Exeter University:** United Kingdom *LIBERTAS*
    Access: `sun.nsf.ac.uk` ◗ at the first prompt enter `janet` ◗ wait for the prompt
    `Password:` ◗ press ↵ ◗ wait for the prompt `Hostname:` ◗ enter `uk.ac.ex.lax`
    ◗ wait for the prompt `Username:` ◗ enter `library`

3-251   **Fachbibliothek für Biologie an der Universitaet Wien:** Austria (Access via **Austrian Academic Library Network**)

3-252   **Fachbibliothek für Mathematik, Statistik, Informatik Universitaet Wien:** Austria (Access via **Austrian Academic Library Network**)

3-253   **Fairmont State College:** United States (Access via **West Virginia University**)

3-254   **Fakultaetsbibliothek für Medizin an der Universitaet Wien:** Austria (Access via **Austrian Academic Library Network**)

3-255   **Fenway Libraries Online, Inc.:** United States *DRA*
    Access: `flo.org` ◗ at the first prompt enter `guest`

3-256   **Fermi National Accelerator Laboratory:** United States *custom*
    Access: `fnlib.fnal.gov` ◗ at the first prompt enter `library`

3-257 **Finnish National Bibliography (FENNICA): Finland** *VTLS*
> **Access:** `hyk.helsinki.fi` ▶ at the first prompt enter `hello`
> yourname,`user.clas01` ▶ you will see a welcome screen, then a terminal-type menu
> ▶ enter `10` ▶ wait for the prompt that ends in `Anna kokoelma` ▶ enter `100` ▶ press ↵
> ▶ enter `/lang 1` ▶ press ↵ ▶ enter `?`

3-258 **Finnish National Library (HELKA): Finland** *VTLS*
> **Access:** `hyk.helsinki.fi` ▶ at the first prompt enter `hello`
> yourname,`user.clas02` ▶ you will see a welcome screen, then a terminal-type menu
> ▶ enter `10` ▶ wait for the prompt that ends in `Anna kokoelma` ▶ enter `100` ▶ wait for
> the prompt that ends in `komento` ▶ enter `/lang 1` ▶ press ↵ ▶ enter `?`

3-259 **Fitchburg Public Library:** United States (Access via **CARL**)

3-260 **Fitchburg State College:** United States (Access via **CARL**)

3-261 **Flinders University:** Australia *DYNIX*
> **Access:** `library.cc.flinders.edu.au`

3-262 **Florida A&M University:** United States (Access via **Florida State University**)

3-263 **Florida Atlantic University:** United States (Access via **Florida State University**)

3-264 **Florida Community College Jacksonville:** United States *NOTIS*
> **Access:** `luis.nerdc.ufl.edu` ▶ at the first prompt enter `luis` ▶ select LINCC
> (Florida Community Colleges) from the menu

3-265 **Florida International University:** United States (Access via **Florida State University**)

3-266 **Florida Keys Community College, Florida:** United States *NOTIS*
> **Access:** `luis.nerdc.ufl.edu` ▶ at the first prompt enter `luis` ▶ select LINCC
> (Florida Community Colleges) from the menu

3-267 **Florida State University:** United States *NOTIS*
> **Access:** `luis.nerdc.ufl.edu` ▶ at the first prompt enter `luis`

3-268 **Fordham University Law School:** United States *INNOPAC*
> **Access:** `lawpac.fordham.edu` ▶ at the first prompt enter `fullpac`

3-269 **Forschungsinstitut Brenner-Archiv (Innsbruck):** Austria (Access via **Austrian Academic Library Network**)

3-270 **Fort Lewis College Library:** United States (Access via **MARMOT Library Network**)

3-271 **Fort Morgan Public Library:** United States (Access via **CARL**)

3-272 **Franklin and Marshall College:** United States *DRA*
> **Access:** `library.fandm.edu` ▶ at the first prompt enter `libcat`

3-273 **Front Range Community College:** United States (Access via **CARL**)

3-274 **Frostburg State Univ:** United States (Access via **University of Maryland Library System**)

3-275 **Fundacion Romulo Gallegos (CELARG):** Venezuela (Access via **Biblioteca Nacional de Venezuela**)

3-276 **Gainesville College:** United States (Access via **Georgia On-Line Library Information System**)

3-277 **Galesburg Memorial Library:** United States (Access via **West Michigan Information Network**)

3-278 **Galien Township Public Library:** United States (Access via **KELLY**)

3-279 **Gallaudet University:** United States (Access via **Washington Research Library Consortium**)

3-280 **Gardner, Colorado, Library:** United States (Access via **CARL**)

3-281 **Garfield County Public Library:** United States (Access via **MARMOT Library Network**)

3-282 **Gateway Community College Library:** United States (Access via **Maricopa Community Colleges Libraries and Media Centers**)

3-283 **George Mason University:** United States (Access via **Washington Research Library Consortium**)

3-284 **George Washington University:** United States (Access via **Washington Research Library Consortium**)

3-285 **Georgetown University Medical Center:** United States *custom*
Access: `gumedlib2.georgetown.edu` ▶ at the first prompt enter `medlib` ▶ wait for the prompt `Password:` ▶ enter `dahlgren` ▶ wait for the prompt that ends in `Last Name` ▶ enter `netguest`

3-286 **Georgetown University:** United States (Access via **Washington Research Library Consortium**)

3-287 **Georgia College—Milledgeville:** United States (Access via **Georgia On-Line Library Information System**)

3-288 **Georgia On-Line Library Information System (OLLI):** United States *PALS*
Access: `library.gsu.edu`

3-289 **Georgia Southern University—Statesboro:** United States (Access via **Georgia On-Line Library Information System**)

3-290 **Georgia Southern University:** United States *DRA*
Access: `gsvms1.cc.gasou.edu`

3-291 **Georgia Southwestern College:** United States (Access via **Georgia On-Line Library Information System**)

3-292 **Georgia State Department of Archives & History:** United States (Access via **Georgia On-Line Library Information System**)

3-293 **Georgia State Instructional Resource Center—Atlanta:** United States (Access via **Georgia On-Line Library Information System**)

3-294 **Georgia State Law Library—Atlanta:** United States (Access via **Georgia On-Line Library Information System**)

3-295 **Georgia State Pullen Library—Atlanta:** United States (Access via **Georgia On-Line Library Information System**)

3-296 **Georgia Tech Gilbert Library—Atlanta:** United States (Access via **Georgia On-Line Library Information System**)

3-297 **Gettysburg College:** United States *INNOPAC*
    Access: `libcat1.library.gettysburg.edu` ❯ at the first prompt enter `lib`

3-298 **Glasgow University:** United Kingdom *GEAC*
    Access: `sun.nsf.ac.uk` ❯ at the first prompt enter `janet` ❯ wait for the prompt `Password:` ❯ press ↵ ❯ wait for the prompt `Hostname:` ❯ enter `uk.ac.gla.lib`

3-299 **Glen Oaks Community College:** United States (Access via **KELLY**)

3-300 **Glendale Community College Library:** United States (Access via **Maricopa Community Colleges Libraries and Media Centers**)

3-301 **Goldsmiths' College:** United Kingdom (Access via **University of London Central Libertas Consortium**)

3-302 **Gordon Technical College:** Australia *INNOPAC*
    Access: `mips1.lib.deakin.oz.au` ❯ at the first prompt enter `library`

3-303 **Governors State University:** United States (Access via **ILLINET On-line Catalog**)

3-304 **Granby Public Library:** United States (Access via **CARL**)

3-305 **Graz, Universitaetsbibliothek:** Austria (Access via **Austrian Academic Library Network**)

3-306 **Great River Library System:** United States (Access via **ILLINET On-line Catalog**)

3-307 **Greenfield Public Library:** United States (Access via **CARL**)

3-308 **Grenfell College:** Canada (Access via **Memorial University, Newfoundland**)

3-309 **Griffith University:** Australia *GEAC ADVANCE*
    Access: `library.gu.edu.au` ❯ at the first prompt enter `library`

3-310 **Grinnell College:** United States *INNOPAC*
    Access: `132.161.10.60` ❯ at the first prompt enter `library`

3-311 **Guilford College:** United States *DRA*
    Access: `pals.guilford.edu` ❯ at the first prompt enter `hegepac`

3-312 **Gulf Coast Community College, Florida:** United States *NOTIS*
    Access: `luis.nerdc.ufl.edu` ❯ at the first prompt enter `luis` ❯ select `LINCC` (`Florida Community Colleges`) from the menu

3-313 **Gull Lake Community Schools:** United States (Access via **KELLY**)

3-314 **Hackett Catholic Central High School:** United States (Access via **KELLY**)

3-315 **Hahnemann University:** United States *custom*
    Access: `hal.hahnemann.edu` ▶ at the first prompt enter `hal`

3-316 **Haifa University:** Israel (Access via **Hebrew University**)

3-317 **Hamline University Law Library:** United States (Access via **Hamline University**)

3-318 **Hamline University:** United States *DYNIX*
    Access: `host.clic.edu` ▶ at the first prompt enter `lpac`

3-319 **Handelshogeschool (Antwerp):** Belgium (Access via **University of Antwerp**)

3-320 **Hardin Simmons University:** United States (Access via **Abilene Library Consortium**)

3-321 **Harris County Public Library:** United States (Access via **CARL**)

3-322 **Hartford Public Library:** United States (Access via **KELLY**)

3-323 **Hartwick College:** United States *INNOPAC*
    Access: `147.205.85.30` ▶ at the first prompt enter `library`

3-324 **Harvard Public Library:** United States (Access via **CARL**)

3-325 **Harvard University:** United States *custom*
    Access: TN3270 `hollis.harvard.edu` or `hollis.harvard.edu`

3-326 **Haverford College:** United States *INNOPAC*
    Access: `tripod.brynmawr.edu` ▶ at the first prompt enter `library`

3-327 **Hebrew University (Automated Library Expandable Program—ALEPH):** Israel *custom*
    Access: `aleph.huji.ac.il` ▶ at the first prompt enter `aleph`

3-328 **Heriot-Watt University:** United Kingdom *CLSI*
    Access: `sun.nsf.ac.uk` ▶ at the first prompt enter `janet` ▶ wait for the prompt
    Password: ▶ press ↵ ▶ wait for the prompt Hostname: ▶ enter
    `uk.ac.lsply.lib`

3-329 **Hershey Medical Center/Penn State University George T. Harrell Library:** United States
    (Access via **HSLC HealthNET Health Sciences Information Network**)

3-330 **Heythrop College:** United Kingdom (Access via **University of London Central Libertas Consortium**)

3-331 **High Plains Regional Libraries:** United States (Access via **CARL**)

3-332 **Hillsborough Community College, Florida:** United States *NOTIS*
    Access: `luis.nerdc.ufl.edu` ▶ at the first prompt enter `luis` ▶ select LINCC
    (Florida Community Colleges) from the menu

3-333 **Hochschulbibliothek der Hochschule für kuenstlerische und industrielle Gestaltung in Linz:** Austria (Access via **Austrian Academic Library Network**)

3-334 **Hochschule St. Gallen:** Switzerland *DOBIS*
 Access: `gamma.unisg.ch` ▶ at the first prompt enter `opac`

3-335 **Hofstra University:** United States *DRA*
 Access: `vaxa.hofstra.edu` ▶ at the first prompt enter `library`

3-336 **Hogeschool Rotterdam & Omstreken:** Netherlands *custom*
 Access: `hrovx6.hro.nl` ▶ press ↵ ▶ enter `opac`

3-337 **Holden, Gale Free Library:** United States (Access via **CARL**)

3-338 **Holyoke Community College:** United States (Access via **CARL**)

3-339 **Hong Kong Polytechnic:** Hong Kong *DRA*
 Access: `library.hkp.hk` ▶ at the first prompt enter `library`

3-340 **Hong Kong University of Science & Technology:** Hong Kong *INNOPAC*
 Access: `ustlib.ust.hk`

3-341 **Hood College:** United States (Access via **Maryland Interlibrary Consortium**)

3-342 **Houston Area Library Automated Network (HALAN):** United States *custom*
 Access: `pac.carl.org` ▶ at the first prompt enter `PAC` ▶ press ↵ ▶ enter `4`

3-343 **Houston Public Library:** United States (Access via **CARL**)

3-344 **HSLC HealthNET Health Sciences Information Network:** United States *DRA*
 Access: `shrsys.hslc.org` ▶ at the first prompt enter `sal`

3-345 **Hudson Public Library:** United States (Access via **CARL**)

3-346 **Hull University:** United Kingdom *GEAC*
 Access: `sun.nsf.ac.uk` ▶ at the first prompt enter `janet` ▶ wait for the prompt `Password:` ▶ press ↵ ▶ wait for the prompt `Hostname:` ▶ enter `uk.ac.hull.geac`

3-347 **Idaho State University:** United States *VTLS*
 Access: `csc.isu.edu` ▶ at the first prompt enter `hello user.clas01`

3-348 **ILLINET On-line Catalog:** United States *custom*
 Access: `illinet.aiss.uiuc.edu`

3-349 **Illinois Benedictine College:** United States (Access via **ILLINET On-line Catalog**)

3-350 **Illinois Institute of Technology—Chicago Kent Law Library:** United States *INNOPAC*
 Access: `clark.kentlaw.edu` ▶ at the first prompt enter `library`

3-351 **Illinois Institute of Technology:** United States (Access via **ILLINET On-line Catalog**)

3-352 **Illinois Math and Science Academy:** United States (Access via **ILLINET On-line Catalog**)

3-353 **Illinois State Library:** United States (Access via **ILLINET On-line Catalog**)

3-354 **Illinois State University:** United States (Access via **ILLINET On-line Catalog**)

3-355 **Illinois Valley Library System:** United States (Access via **ILLINET On-line Catalog**)

3-356 **Illinois Wesleyan University:** United States (Access via **ILLINET On-line Catalog**)

3-357 **Ilsley, Vermont, Public Library:** United States *custom*
   Access: `lib.middlebury.edu` ▶ at the first prompt enter `lib` ▶ you will see the Middlebury College Library system menu ▶ enter 1 ▶ you will see a `Library resource` menu ▶ enter 1 ▶ press ⏎ until you get to the main catalog menu where you will see a branch library selection menu ▶ press ⏎

3-358 **Imperial College, University of London:** United Kingdom *LIBERTAS*
   Access: `vaxa.lib.ic.ac.uk`

3-359 **Indian River Community College, Florida:** United States *NOTIS*
   Access: `luis.nerdc.ufl.edu` ▶ at the first prompt enter `luis` ▶ select LINCC (Florida Community Colleges) from the menu

3-360 **Indiana Institute of Technology:** United States *NOTIS*
   Access: `iuis.ucs.indiana.edu` ▶ at the first prompt enter `guest` ▶ press ⏎ ▶ enter 3 ▶ press ⏎ ▶ enter OTHER ▶ press ⏎ ▶ enter ITCAT

3-361 **Indiana State University:** United States *NOTIS*
   Access: TN3270 `lib.cc.purdue.edu` ▶ at the first prompt enter `remote` ▶ press ⏎ ▶ enter `isucat`

3-362 **Indiana University of Pennsylvania:** United States *custom*
   Access: `opac.lib.iup.edu` ▶ at the first prompt enter `library`

3-363 **Indiana University:** United States *NOTIS*
   Access: `iuis.ucs.indiana.edu` ▶ at the first prompt enter `guest` ▶ press ⏎ ▶ enter 3

3-364 **INLAN Library System (Spokane, Washington):** United States (Access via **University of Maryland Library System**)

3-365 **Innsbruck, Universitaetsbibliothek:** Austria (Access via **Austrian Academic Library Network**)

3-366 **Institut Fourier:** France *custom*
   Access: `ifbibli.grenet.fr` ▶ at the first prompt enter `bib`

3-367 **Instituto de Altos Estudios de la Defensa Nacional:** Venezuela (Access via **Biblioteca Nacional de Venezuela**)

3-368 **James Cook University:** Australia *DYNIX*
Access: `jculib.jcu.edu.au` ▶ at the first prompt enter `opac`

3-369 **Jewish Hospital Medical Library:** United States (Access via **Washington University of St Louis Medical Library**)

3-370 **Jewish Hospital School of Nursing Library:** United States (Access via **Washington University of St Louis Medical Library**)

3-371 **Jewish Theological Seminary of America:** United States *custom*
Access: `jtsa.edu` ▶ at the first prompt enter `aleph`

3-372 **Joensuu University:** Finland *VTLS*
Access: `joyk.joensuu.fi` ▶ at the first prompt enter `hello yourname,user.clas01` ▶ you will see a welcome screen, then a terminal-type menu ▶ enter `10` ▶ wait for the prompt that ends in `tai?` ▶ enter `100` ▶ wait for the prompt that ends in `komento` ▶ enter `/lang 1` ▶ press ↵ ▶ enter `?`

3-373 **John Carroll University:** United States *DRA*
Access: `jcvaxc.jcu.edu` ▶ at the first prompt enter `jcu_opac` ▶ wait for the prompt `Password:` ▶ enter `grasselli`

3-374 **John Marshall Law School:** United States *INNOPAC*
Access: `catalog.jmls.edu` ▶ at the first prompt enter `catalog`

3-375 **Johns Hopkins University:** United States *NOTIS*
Access: `TN3270 jhuvm.hcf.jhu.edu` ▶ press ↵

3-376 **Johnson State College, Vermont:** United States (Access via **Middlebury College**)

3-377 **Joliet Junior College:** United States (Access via **ILLINET On-line Catalog**)

3-378 **Judson College:** United States (Access via **ILLINET On-line Catalog**)

3-379 **Justus-Liebig-Universitaet Giessen:** Germany *custom*
Access: `nosve.hrz.uni-giessen.de` ▶ at the first prompt enter `gicis` ▶ wait for the prompt `Password:` ▶ enter `cs20` ▶ wait for the prompt `Family:` ▶ press ↵ ▶ enter `H` ▶ you will see a terminal-type menu ▶ enter `41` ▶ press ↵ ▶ press ↵ ▶ enter `BI`

3-380 **Jyvaskyla University:** Finland *VTLS*
Access: `jyk.jyu.fi` ▶ at the first prompt enter `hello yourname,user.clas01` ▶ you will see a welcome screen, then a terminal-type menu ▶ enter `10` ▶ wait for the prompt that ends in `tai?` ▶ enter `100` ▶ wait for the prompt that ends in `komento` ▶ enter `/lang 1` ▶ press ↵ ▶ enter `?`

3-381 **Kalamazoo Christian High School:** United States (Access via **KELLY**)

3-382 **Kalamazoo College:** United States *INNOPAC*
Access: `hme4.merit.edu` ▶ at the first prompt enter `kzoo-lib`

3-383 **Kalamazoo Regional Psychiatric Hospital:** United States (Access via **KELLY**)

3-384 **Kankakee Community College:** United States (Access via **ILLINET On-line Catalog**)

3-385 **Kansas State University:** United States *NOTIS*
> **Access:** TN3270 `ksuvm.ksu.edu` ◗ at the first prompt enter `lynx` ◗ press ↵
> ◗ wait for the prompt `USERID:` ◗ press ↵ ◗ press ↵ ◗ ignore `INVALID SIGN-ON`
> `ATTEMPT` message

3-386 **Karolinska Institute:** Sweden *LIBERTAS*
> **Access:** `kibib.kib.ki.se`

3-387 **Kaskaskia Library System:** United States (Access via **ILLINET On-line Catalog**)

3-388 **Katholieke Universiteit Nijmegen:** Netherlands *custom*
> **Access:** `kunlb1.ubn.kun.nl` ◗ at the first prompt enter `opc`

3-389 **Keene State College/Keene Public Library:** United States *INNOPAC*
> **Access:** `ksclib.keene.edu` ◗ at the first prompt enter `library`

3-390 **KELLY—Western Michigan Regional Online Catalog:** United States *custom*
> **Access:** TN3270 `library.wmich.edu` ◗ tab or arrow to `KELLY` ◗ press ↵
> **Access:** `hme4.merit.edu` ◗ at the first prompt enter `wmu-finder` ◗ tab or arrow to
> `KELLY` ◗ press ↵

3-391 **Kennesaw State College:** United States *PALS*
> **Access:** `ksclib.kennesaw.edu` ◗ at the first prompt enter `library` ◗ wait for the
> prompt `Password:` ◗ enter `library`
> **Access:** `library.gsu.edu`

3-392 **Kent State University:** United States *NOTIS*
> **Access:** `catalyst.kent.edu` ◗ press ↵

3-393 **Kenyon College:** United States *DRA*
> **Access:** `kcvax2.kenyon.edu` ◗ at the first prompt enter `niso`

3-394 **King's College, University of London:** United Kingdom *LIBERTAS*
> **Access:** `sun.nsf.ac.uk` ◗ at the first prompt enter `janet` ◗ wait for the prompt
> `Password:` ◗ press ↵ ◗ wait for the prompt `Hostname:` ◗ enter `uk.ac.kcl.lib` ◗
> wait for the prompt `Username:` ◗ enter `library`

3-395 **Kuopio Reserve Library:** Finland *VTLS*
> **Access:** `varasto.uku.fi` ◗ at the first prompt enter `hello`
> yourname, `user.clas01` ◗ you will see a terminal-type menu ◗ enter `4` ◗ wait for the
> prompt that ends in `tai?` ◗ enter `100` ◗ wait for the prompt that ends in `komento`
> ◗ enter `/lang 1`

3-396 **Kutztown University:** United States *PALS*
> **Access:** `acad.csv.kutztown.edu` ◗ at the first prompt enter `bearcat`

3-397 **La Salle University:** United States *INNOPAC*
    Access: `connelly.lasalle.edu` ▶ at the first prompt enter `library`

3-398 **La Trobe University:** Australia *custom*
    Access: `library.latrobe.edu.au` ▶ at the first prompt enter `catalogue`

3-399 **Labrador Institute of Northern Studies:** Canada (Access via **Memorial University, Newfoundland**)

3-400 **Lafayette College:** United States *INNOPAC*
    Access: `139.147.42.4` ▶ at the first prompt enter `library`

3-401 **Lake City Community College, Florida:** United States *NOTIS*
    Access: `luis.nerdc.ufl.edu` ▶ at the first prompt enter `luis` ▶ select LINCC (Florida Community Colleges) from the menu

3-402 **Lake Forest College:** United States (Access via **ILLINET On-line Catalog**)

3-403 **Lake Sumter Community College, Florida:** United States *NOTIS*
    Access: `luis.nerdc.ufl.edu` ▶ at the first prompt enter `luis` ▶ select LINCC (Florida Community Colleges) from the menu

3-404 **Lakehead University:** Canada *custom*
    Access: `think2.lakeheadu.ca` ▶ at the first prompt enter `faculty`

3-405 **Lamar Community College:** United States (Access via **CARL**)

3-406 **Lamar University:** United States *custom*
    Access: `lub001.lamar.edu or lub002.lamar.edu` ▶ at the first prompt enter `library`

3-407 **Lancaster Town Library:** United States (Access via **CARL**)

3-408 **Lancaster University:** United Kingdom *custom*
    Access: `felix.lancs.ac.uk` ▶ at the first prompt enter `opac`

3-409 **Lapin University:** Finland *VTLS*
    Access: `128.214.30.51` ▶ at the first prompt enter `hello yourname,user.clas01` ▶ you will see a terminal-type menu ▶ enter 4 ▶ wait for the prompt that ends in `tai?` ▶ enter 100 ▶ wait for the prompt that ends in `komento` ▶ enter `/lang 1`

3-410 **Laurentian University:** Canada *MultiLIS*
    Access: `laulibr.laurentian.ca` ▶ at the first prompt enter `netlib`

3-411 **Laval University:** Canada *MultiLIS*
    Access: `ariane.ulaval.ca` ▶ at the first prompt enter `ariane`

3-412 **Lawrence Livermore National Laboratory:** United States *custom*
    Access: `aish.llnl.gov` ▶ at the first prompt enter `patron`

3-413　**Lawrence University:** United States *DRA*
　　　　Access: `lucia.lib.lawrence.edu` ▶ at the first prompt enter `lunet`

3-414　**Lawton Public Library:** United States　(Access via **KELLY**)

3-415　**Lee Library Association:** United States　(Access via **CARL**)

3-416　**Lehigh:** United States *GEAC*
　　　　Access: `asa.lib.lehigh.edu`

3-417　**Leicester University:** United Kingdom *LIBERTAS*
　　　　Access: `sun.nsf.ac.uk` ▶ at the first prompt enter `janet` ▶ wait for the prompt
　　　　`Password:` ▶ press ↵ ▶ wait for the prompt `Hostname:` ▶ enter `uk.ac.le.lib`
　　　　▶ wait for the prompt `Username:` ▶ enter `library`

3-418　**Leiden University:** Netherlands *custom*
　　　　Access: `rulub3.leidenuniv.nl`

3-419　**Leominster Public Library:** United States　(Access via **CARL**)

3-420　**Lesley College:** United States　(Access via **Fenway Libraries Online, Inc.**)

3-421　**Lewis & Clark Library System:** United States　(Access via **ILLINET On-line Catalog**)

3-422　**Lewis University:** United States　(Access via **ILLINET On-line Catalog**)

3-423　**Limburgs Universitair Centrum:** Belgium　(Access via **University of Antwerp**)

3-424　**LINCC (Florida Community Colleges):** United States *NOTIS*
　　　　Access: `luis.nerdc.ufl.edu` ▶ at the first prompt enter `luis` ▶ select LINCC
　　　　`(Florida Community Colleges)` from the menu

3-425　**Lincoln Township Public Library:** United States　(Access via **KELLY**)

3-426　**Lincoln Trail Libraries System:** United States　(Access via **ILLINET On-line Catalog**)

3-427　**Lincoln University:** New Zealand *DYNIX*
　　　　Access: `library.lincoln.ac.nz`　▶ at the first prompt enter `pub`

3-428　**Linz, Universitaetsbibliothek:** Austria　(Access via **Austrian Academic Library Network**)

3-429　**Littleton, Colorado Reuben Hoar Library:** United States　(Access via **CARL**)

3-430　**Liverpool University:** United Kingdom *DOBIS/LIBIS*
　　　　Access: `sun.nsf.ac.uk` ▶ at the first prompt enter `janet` ▶ wait for the prompt
　　　　`Password:` ▶ press ↵ ▶ wait for the prompt `Hostname:` ▶ enter `uk.ac.liv.lib`
　　　　▶ you will see a request for terminal type ▶ enter `VT100` ▶ the screen will clear ▶ press ↵

3-431　**LOCIS—Library of Congress Information System:** United States *custom*
　　　　Access: `locis.loc.gov`

3-432　**Lock Haven University:** United States *DYNIX*
　　　　Access: `owl.lhup.edu` ▶ at the first prompt enter `slpac`

3-433 **Longmeadow, Storrs Library:** United States (Access via **CARL**)

3-434 **Los Alamos National Laboratory:** United States *GEAC Advance*
    Access: `admiral.lanl.gov` ▸ at the first prompt enter `library`

3-435 **Loughborough University:** United Kingdom *BLCMP*
    Access: `sun.nsf.ac.uk` ▸ at the first prompt enter `janet` ▸ wait for the prompt `Password:` ▸ press ↵ ▸ wait for the prompt `Hostname:` ▸ enter `uk.ac.lut.lib`

3-436 **Louisville Public Library:** United States (Access via **Boulder, Colorado, Public Library System**)

3-437 **Loyola College/Notre Dame:** United States (Access via **Maryland Interlibrary Consortium**)

3-438 **Loyola Marymount University:** United States *INNOPAC*
    Access: `linus.lmu.edu` ▸ at the first prompt enter `library`

3-439 **Loyola University:** United States *NOTIS*
    Access: `luc.edu`
    Access: TN3270 `luccpua.it.luc.edu` ▸ at the first prompt enter `guest`

3-440 **Lunar and Planetary Institute:** United States *custom*
    Access: `lpi.jsc.nasa.gov` ▸ at the first prompt enter `lpi`

3-441 **Lund University:** Sweden *VTLS*
    Access: `lolita.lu.se`

3-442 **Luther College:** United States (Access via **CARL**)

3-443 **Luton College of Higher Education:** United Kingdom *LIBERTAS*
    Access: `sun.nsf.ac.uk` ▸ at the first prompt enter `janet` ▸ wait for the prompt `Password:` ▸ press ↵ ▸ wait for the prompt `Hostname:` ▸ enter `uk.ac.` ▸ wait for the prompt `Password:` ▸ press ↵ ▸ wait for the prompt `Username:` ▸ enter `library`

3-444 **Lynchburg Public and College Libraries:** United States *DYNIX (OP005)*
    Access: `lion.edu` ▸ at the first prompt enter `sblib`

3-445 **Lyndon State College, Vermont:** United States (Access via **Middlebury College**)

3-446 **Macalester College:** United States *DYNIX*
    Access: `host.clic.edu` ▸ at the first prompt enter `mpac`

3-447 **Macomb Community College:** United States (Access via **Detroit Area Library Network**)

3-448 **Macon College:** United States (Access via **Georgia On-Line Library Information System**)

3-449 **Macquarie University:** Australia *DYNIX*
    Access: `library.mq.edu.au` ▸ at the first prompt enter `mars`

3-450 **Maine State Law and Legislative Reference Library:** United States (Access via **University of Maine Library System**)

3-451 **Maine State Library:** United States (Access via **University of Maine Library System**)

3-452 **Malaspina College:** Canada *BuCAT*
Access: `mala.bc.ca` ▶ at the first prompt enter `macat`

3-453 **Mallinckrodt Institute of Radiology Library:** United States (Access via **Washington University of St Louis Medical Library**)

3-454 **Manatee Community College, Florida:** United States *NOTIS*
Access: `luis.nerdc.ufl.edu` ▶ at the first prompt enter `luis` ▶ select `LINCC` (`Florida Community Colleges`) from the menu

3-455 **Marcellus/Wood Memorial Library:** United States (Access via **KELLY**)

3-456 **Maricopa Center for Learning & Instruction:** United States (Access via **Maricopa Community Colleges Libraries and Media Centers**)

3-457 **Maricopa Community Colleges Libraries and Media Centers:** United States *custom*
Access: `lib.maricopa.edu` ▶ at the first prompt enter `lib`

3-458 **Marist College:** United States *DOBIS/LIBIS*
Access: TN3270 `vm.marist.edu` ▶ at the first prompt enter `dobis`

3-459 **Marlborough Public Library:** United States (Access via **CARL**)

3-460 **MARMOT Library Network (Colorado Western Slopes):** United States *custom*
Access: `192.245.61.4`
Access: `pac.carl.org` ▶ at the first prompt enter `PAC` ▶ press ↵ ▶ enter `4`
Access: `victor.umd.edu` ▶ at the first prompt enter `pac` ▶ press ↵ ▶ press ↵

3-461 **Marquette University:** United States *INNOPAC*
Access: `libus.csd.mu.edu` ▶ at the first prompt enter `m`

3-462 **Maryland Interlibrary Consortium:** United States *custom*
Access: `144.126.176.78`

3-463 **Marymount University:** United States (Access via **Washington Research Library Consortium**)

3-464 **Massachusetts College of Art:** United States (Access via **Fenway Libraries Online, Inc.**)

3-465 **Massachusetts College of Pharmacy:** United States (Access via **Fenway Libraries Online, Inc.**)

3-466 **Massachusetts Institute of Technology:** United States *custom*
Access: `library.mit.edu`
Access: `blc.lrc.northeastern.edu`

3-467 **Massey University:** New Zealand *custom*
Access: `libserver.massey.ac.nz` ▶ enter any character ▶ press ↵

3-468 **Mattawan Consolidated Schools:** United States (Access via **KELLY**)

3-469 **McGill University:** Canada *NOTIS*
    Access: TN3270 mvs.mcgill.ca

3-470 **McKendree College:** United States (Access via **ILLINET On-line Catalog**)

3-471 **McMaster University:** Canada *NOTIS*
    Access: TN3270 mcmvm1.cis.mcmaster.ca ▶ at the first prompt enter PF9

3-472 **McMurry University:** United States (Access via **Abilene Library Consortium**)

3-473 **Medical College of Ohio:** United States *INNOPAC*
    Access: 136.247.10.14
    Access: cat.ohiolink.edu

3-474 **Medical College of Pennsylvania Eastern Pennsylvania Psychiatric Institute Library Florence A. Moore Library of Medicine:** United States (Access via **HSLC HealthNET Health Sciences Information Network**)

3-475 **Medical College of Wisconsin:** United States *INNOPAC*
    Access: ils.lib.mcw.edu ▶ at the first prompt enter library

3-476 **MELVYL (University of California):** United States *custom*
    Access: melvyl.ucop.edu
    Access: victor.umd.edu
    Access: lib.dartmouth.edu ▶ at the first prompt enter CONNECT MELVYL

3-477 **Memorial University, Newfoundland:** Canada *custom*
    Access: mungate.library.mun.ca ▶ at the first prompt enter mungate

3-478 **Memphis State University:** United States *custom*
    Access: msuvx1.memst.edu ▶ press ↵ ▶ wait for the prompt Title? ▶ enter help

3-479 **Mercer Law Library:** United States (Access via **Georgia On-Line Library Information System**)

3-480 **Mesa Community College Library:** United States (Access via **Maricopa Community Colleges Libraries and Media Centers**)

3-481 **Mesa County Public Library:** United States (Access via **MARMOT Library Network**)

3-482 **Mesa County Schools Library:** United States (Access via **MARMOT Library Network**)

3-483 **Mesa State College Library:** United States (Access via **MARMOT Library Network**)

3-484 **Messiah College:** United States *NOTIS*
    Access: mcis.messiah.edu ▶ at the first prompt enter opac

3-485 **Miami University Library:** United States *INNOPAC*
    Access: watson.lib.muohio.edu ▶ at the first prompt enter library
    Access: cat.ohiolink.edu

3-486 **Miami-Dade Community College, Florida:** United States *NOTIS*
    Access: `luis.nerdc.ufl.edu` ▶ at the first prompt enter `luis` ▶ select `LINCC`
    (`Florida Community Colleges`) from the menu

3-487 **Michigan State University:** United States *NOTIS*
    Access: `TN3270 magic.lib.msu.edu`
    Access: `thorplus.lib.purdue.edu` ▶ at the first prompt enter `catnet`

3-488 **Michigan Technological University:** United States *NOTIS*
    Access: `hme4.merit.edu` ▶ at the first prompt enter `focus`

3-489 **Middle Georgia College:** United States (Access via **Georgia On-Line Library Information System**)

3-490 **Middlebury College:** United States *DRA*
    Access: `lib.middlebury.edu` ▶ at the first prompt enter `lib`

3-491 **Milford Town Library:** United States (Access via **CARL**)

3-492 **Millbury Public Library:** United States (Access via **CARL**)

3-493 **Millikin University:** United States (Access via **ILLINET On-line Catalog**)

3-494 **Mississippi State University:** United States *custom*
    Access: `libserv.msstate.edu` ▶ at the first prompt enter `msu` ▶ wait for the
    prompt `password:` ▶ enter `library`

3-495 **Missouri Western State College:** United States *VTLS*
    Access: `monet.mwsc.edu` ▶ at the first prompt enter `hello gtc.library`
    ▶ press ↵ ▶ press ↵

3-496 **Monash University:** Australia *PALS*
    Access: `library.monash.edu.au`

3-497 **Monson Free Library:** United States (Access via **CARL**)

3-498 **Montana State University:** United States *INLEX*
    Access: `catalog.lib.montana.edu` ▶ at the first prompt enter `hello`
    `msu.library`

3-499 **Montgomery County (Rockville, MD):** United States (Access via **CARL**)

3-500 **Montgomery County Department of Public Libraries (Rockville, MD):** United States (Access via **University of Maryland Library System**)

3-501 **Montrose Public Library:** United States (Access via **MARMOT Library Network**)

3-502 **Morgan Community College:** United States (Access via **CARL**)

3-503 **Mount Allison University:** Canada *DRA*
    Access: `bigmac.mta.ca`

3-504 **Mount Saint Vincent University:** Canada *GEAC*
 Access: `novanet.dal.ca` ▶ press ↵

3-505 **Mount St. Mary's College:** United States (Access via **Maryland Interlibrary Consortium**)

3-506 **Mt. Wachusett Community College:** United States (Access via **CARL**)

3-507 **Multnomah County Library:** United States *DYNIX*
 Access: `192.220.128.20` ▶ at the first prompt enter `fastcat`

3-508 **Murdoch University:** Australia *custom*
 Access: `library.murdoch.edu.au` ▶ press ↵

3-509 **Museum of Fine Arts, Boston:** United States (Access via **Fenway Libraries Online, Inc.**)

3-510 **Nanyang Technological University:** Singapore *DRA*
 Access: `ntuix.ntu.ac.sg` ▶ at the first prompt enter `libopac`

3-511 **National Center for Atmospheric Research:** United States *UNICORN*
 Access: `library.ucar.edu`

3-512 **National Central Library:** Taiwan, Province of China *custom*
 Access: `192.83.186.1` ▶ at the first prompt enter `ltacl`

3-513 **National Chiao Tung University:** Taiwan, Province of China *custom*
 Access: `lib1.nctu.edu.tw` ▶ at the first prompt enter `library`

3-514 **National Institutes of Health:** United States *INNOPAC*
 Access: `nih-library.nih.gov`

3-515 **National Library of Australia:** Australia *DYNIX*
 Access: `janus.nla.gov.au`

3-516 **National Library of Medicine Locator:** United States *custom*
 Access: `locator.nlm.nih.gov` ▶ at the first prompt enter `locator`

3-517 **National Library of Scotland:** United Kingdom *VTLS*
 Access: `sun.nsf.ac.uk` ▶ at the first prompt enter `janet` ▶ wait for the prompt
 `Password:` ▶ press ↵ ▶ wait for the prompt `Hostname:` ▶ enter `uk.nls.opac`
 ▶ wait for the prompt `MPE XL` ▶ enter `hello` yourname, `ref.clas50`

3-518 **National Taiwan University:** Taiwan, Province of China *INNOPAC*
 Access: `140.112.196.20` ▶ at the first prompt enter `library`

3-519 **National Tsing Hua University:** Taiwan, Province of China *custom*
 Access: `140.114.72.2` ▶ at the first prompt enter `search`

3-520 **National University of Singapore:** Singapore *custom*
 Access: `linc.nus.sg`

3-521 **National-Louis University:** United States (Access via **ILLINET On-line Catalog**)

3-522 **Natural Envirement Research Council (NERC):** United Kingdom *LIBERTAS*
    Access: `sun.nsf.ac.uk` ◗ at the first prompt enter `janet` ◗ wait for the prompt
    `Password:` ◗ press ↵ ◗ wait for the prompt `Hostname:` ◗ enter `uk.ac.nkw.vf`
    ◗ wait for the prompt `Username:` ◗ enter `library`

3-523 **Nebraska State Colleges:** United States *INNOPAC*
    Access: `nscs.nscs.edu`

3-524 **Nevada Academic Libraries Information System (NALIS):** United States *INNOPAC*
    Access: `library.nevada.edu`

3-525 **New Buffalo Public Library:** United States (Access via **KELLY**)

3-526 **New England Conservatory:** United States (Access via **Fenway Libraries Online, Inc.**)

3-527 **New Mexico Highlands University:** United States *DRA*
    Access: `venus.nmhu.edu` ◗ at the first prompt enter `atlas`

3-528 **New Mexico State University:** United States *VTLS*
    Access: `hydra.unm.edu`

3-529 **New South Wales Libraries (LIBLINK):** Australia *custom*
    Access: `unilinc.edu.au` ◗ at the first prompt enter `liblink`

3-530 **New York Public Library:** United States *custom*
    Access: `nyplgate.nypl.org` ◗ at the first prompt enter `nypl`

3-531 **New York State Library:** United States *custom*
    Access: `nysl.nysed.gov`

3-532 **New York University Ehrman Medical Library, Waldmann Dental Library, and Environmental Medicine Library:** United States *INNOPAC*
    Access: `mclib0.med.nyu.edu` ◗ at the first prompt enter `library`

3-533 **New York University Law Library (JULIUS):** United States *INNOPAC*
    Access: `mclib0.med.nyu.edu` ◗ at the first prompt enter `library` ◗ press ↵
    ◗ enter `a` ◗ press ↵

3-534 **New York University Library BOBCAT System:** United States *GEAC*
    Access: `bobcat.nyu.edu`
    Access: `mclib0.med.nyu.edu` ◗ at the first prompt enter `library` ◗ press ↵
    ◗ enter `a` ◗ press ↵

3-535 **North Adams Public Library:** United States (Access via **CARL**)

3-536 **North Adams State College:** United States (Access via **CARL**)

3-537 **North Carolina State University Library:** United States (Access via **Triangle Research Libraries**)

3-538 **North Central College:** United States (Access via **ILLINET On-line Catalog**)

3-539 **North Florida Junior College:** United States *NOTIS*
> **Access:** `luis.nerdc.ufl.edu` ▶ at the first prompt enter `luis` ▶ select LINCC (Florida Community Colleges) from the menu

3-540 **North Georgia College—Dahlonega:** United States (Access via **Georgia On-Line Library Information System**)

3-541 **North Suburban Library System:** United States (Access via **ILLINET On-line Catalog**)

3-542 **Northampton, Colorado, Library:** United States (Access via **CARL**)

3-543 **Northborough Free Library:** United States (Access via **CARL**)

3-544 **Northeast Missouri State University:** United States *NOTIS*
> **Access:** TN3270 `academic.nemostate.edu`

3-545 **Northeastern Illinois University:** United States (Access via **ILLINET On-line Catalog**)

3-546 **Northeastern Ohio Universities College of Medicine:** United States *custom*
> **Access:** `scotty.neoucom.edu` ▶ at the first prompt enter `neocat`

3-547 **Northeastern University Law Library:** United States *custom*
> **Access:** `library.lib.northeastern.edu` ▶ at the first prompt enter `catalog`

3-548 **Northeastern University:** United States *custom*
> **Access:** `library.lib.northeastern.edu` ▶ at the first prompt enter `catalog`
> **Access:** `blc.lrc.northeastern.edu`
> **Access:** `pac.carl.org` ▶ at the first prompt enter PAC ▶ press ↵ ▶ enter 4
> **Access:** `victor.umd.edu` ▶ at the first prompt enter `pac` ▶ press ↵ ▶ press ↵

3-549 **Northern Arizona University:** United States (Access via **University of Maryland Library System**)

3-550 **Northern Illinois Library System:** United States (Access via **ILLINET On-line Catalog**)

3-551 **Northern Illinois University:** United States (Access via **ILLINET On-line Catalog**)

3-552 **Northern Nevada Community College:** United States (Access via **Nevada Academic Libraries Information System**)

3-553 **Northern Territory University:** Australia *DYNIX*
> **Access:** `lib2.ntu.edu.au` ▶ at the first prompt enter `libnet`

3-554 **Northwest College:** United States (Access via **CARL**)

3-555 **Northwestern University:** United States *NOTIS*
> **Access:** `nuacvm.acns.nwu.edu` ▶ at the first prompt enter ? ▶ choose terminal type ▶ you will see a sign-on screen ▶ press ↵ ▶ enter `dial vtam` ▶ press ↵ ▶ enter `library`

Access: TN3270 `nuacvm.acns.nwu.edu`   ▶ tab to COMMAND: ▶ enter `dial`
`vtam` ▶ press ↵ ▶ enter `library`

Access: `illinet.aiss.uiuc.edu`

Access: TN3270 `lib.cc.purdue.edu`

Access: `thorplus.lib.purdue.edu`   ▶ at the first prompt enter `catnet`

3-556 **Norwich University Library, Vermont:** United States *custom*

Access: `lib.middlebury.edu` ▶ at the first prompt enter `lib` ▶ you will see the Middlebury College Library system menu ▶ enter 1 ▶ you will see a `Library resource` menu ▶ enter 1 ▶ press ↵ until you get to the main catalog menu where you will see a branch library selection menu ▶ press ↵

3-557 **Nova Scotia College of Art and Design:** Canada *GEAC*

Access: `novanet.dal.ca` ▶ press ↵

3-558 **Oakland, Michigan, Community College:** United States (Access via **Detroit Area Library Network**)

3-559 **Oakland University:** United States (Access via **Detroit Area Library Network**)

3-560 **Oakton Community College:** United States (Access via **ILLINET On-line Catalog**)

3-561 **Oberlin College:** United States *GEAC*

Access: `obis.lib.oberlin.edu`

3-562 **Occidental College:** United States *INNOPAC*

Access: `oasys.lib.oxy.edu`

3-563 **Oesterreichische Nationalbibliothek:** Austria (Access via **Austrian Academic Library Network**)

3-564 **Oesterreichische Phonothek:** Austria (Access via **Austrian Academic Library Network**)

3-565 **Oesterreichisches Bundesinstitut für d. wissenschaftl. Film:** Austria (Access via **Austrian Academic Library Network**)

3-566 **Oglethorpe University—Atlanta:** United States (Access via **Georgia On-Line Library Information System**)

3-567 **Ohio Northern University:** United States *INNOPAC*

Access: `polar.onu.edu` ▶ at the first prompt enter `library`

3-568 **Ohio State University:** United States *NOTIS*

Access: `lcs.us.ohio-state.edu`

Access: TN3270 `lib.cc.purdue.edu`

Access: `thorplus.lib.purdue.edu` ▶ at the first prompt enter `catnet`

3-569 **OhioLink:** United States *custom*

Access: `cat.ohiolink.edu`

3-570 **Okaloosa-Walton Community College, Florida:** United States *NOTIS*
Access: `luis.nerdc.ufl.edu` ▶ at the first prompt enter `luis` ▶ select `LINCC` (Florida Community Colleges) from the menu

3-571 **Old Dominion University:** United States *GEAC*
Access: `geac.lib.odu.edu`

3-572 **Ontario Institute for Studies in Education:** Canada *MultiLIS*
Access: `eloise.oise.on.ca` ▶ at the first prompt enter `eloise`

3-573 **Open University:** United Kingdom *LIBERTAS*
Access: `lib.open.ac.uk`

3-574 **Orange, Colorado, Library:** United States (Access via **CARL**)

3-575 **Oregon Health Sciences University:** United States *VTLS*
Access: `ohsu.edu` ▶ at the first prompt enter `catalog` ▶ wait for the prompt `Password:` ▶ enter `catalog`

3-576 **Oregon State Library:** United States *DRA*
Access: `opac.osl.or.gov` ▶ at the first prompt enter `catalog`

3-577 **Oregon State:** United States *custom*
Access: `oasis.kerr.orst.edu`

3-578 **Otero Junior College:** United States (Access via **CARL**)

3-579 **Otsego District Public Library:** United States (Access via **KELLY**)

3-580 **Ottawa Public Library:** Canada *DRA*
Access: `ottlib.carleton.ca`

3-581 **Oulu University:** Finland *VTLS*
Access: `kirjasto.oulu.fi` ▶ at the first prompt enter `hello yourname,user.clas01` ▶ you will see a terminal-type menu ▶ enter 4 ▶ wait for the prompt that ends in `kokokirjasto` ▶ enter 100 ▶ wait for the prompt that ends in `tai?` ▶ enter `/lang 1`

3-582 **Oxford Free Public Library:** United States (Access via **CARL**)

3-583 **Oxford Polytechnic:** United Kingdom *custom*
Access: `sun.nsf.ac.uk` ▶ at the first prompt enter `janet` ▶ wait for the prompt `Password:` ▶ press ↵ ▶ wait for the prompt `Hostname:` ▶ enter `uk.ac.oxpoly.lib`

3-584 **Oxford University:** United Kingdom *DOBIS/LIBIS*
Access: `library.ox.ac.uk`

3-585 **Oxford Westminster College:** United Kingdom *LIBERTAS*
     Access: `sun.nsf.ac.uk` ◗ at the first prompt enter `janet` ◗ wait for the prompt `Password:` ◗ press ↵ ◗ wait for the prompt `Hostname:` ◗ enter `uk.ac.ox-west.lib` ◗ wait for the prompt `Password:` ◗ press ↵

3-586 **Palm Beach Community College, Florida:** United States *NOTIS*
     Access: `luis.nerdc.ufl.edu` ◗ at the first prompt enter `luis` ◗ select LINCC (Florida Community Colleges) from the menu

3-587 **Palmer Public Library:** United States (Access via **CARL**)

3-588 **Paradise Valley Community College Library:** United States (Access via **Maricopa Community Colleges Libraries and Media Centers**)

3-589 **Parchment Community Library:** United States (Access via **KELLY**)

3-590 **Parchment Public Schools:** United States (Access via **KELLY**)

3-591 **Pasadena Public Library:** United States (Access via **CARL**)

3-592 **Pasco-Hernando Community College, Florida:** United States *NOTIS*
     Access: `luis.nerdc.ufl.edu` ◗ at the first prompt enter `luis` ◗ select LINCC (Florida Community Colleges) from the menu

3-593 **Pathfinder System:** United States (Access via **MARMOT Library Network**)

3-594 **Paw Paw District Library:** United States (Access via **KELLY**)

3-595 **Paw Paw Public Schools:** United States (Access via **KELLY**)

3-596 **Pennsylvania State University:** United States *NOTIS*
     Access: `lias.psu.edu`
     Access: TN3270 `lib.cc.purdue.edu`
     Access: `thorplus.lib.purdue.edu` ◗ at the first prompt enter `catnet`

3-597 **Pepperell, Colorado, Library:** United States (Access via **CARL**)

3-598 **Peru State College:** United States *INNOPAC*
     Access: `nscs.unl.edu`

3-599 **Philadelphia College of Osteopathic Medicine O.L. Snyder Memorial Library:** United States (Access via **HSLC HealthNET Health Sciences Information Network**)

3-600 **Philadelphia College of Pharmacy and Science Joseph W. England Library:** United States (Access via **HSLC HealthNET Health Sciences Information Network**)

3-601 **Phoenix Community College Library:** United States (Access via **Maricopa Community Colleges Libraries and Media Centers**)

3-602 **Pikes Peak Community College:** United States (Access via **CARL**)

3-603 **Pikes Peak Library District:** United States *custom*
     Access: `192.153.23.254`

Access: `192.245.61.4`
Access: `pac.carl.org` ▶ at the first prompt enter `PAC` ▶ press ↵ ▶ enter `4`
Access: `victor.umd.edu` ▶ at the first prompt enter `pac` ▶ press ↵ ▶ press ↵

3-604 **Pima Community College:** United States *INNOPAC*
Access: `libcat.pima.edu`

3-605 **Pitkin County Public Library:** United States (Access via **MARMOT Library Network**)

3-606 **Pittsfield, Colorado, Library:** United States (Access via **CARL**)

3-607 **Plainwell/Charles A. Ransom Public Library:** United States (Access via **KELLY**)

3-608 **Plateau Valley Schools Library:** United States (Access via **MARMOT Library Network**)

3-609 **Point Loma Nazarene College:** United States *INNOPAC*
Access: `192.147.249.103` ▶ at the first prompt enter `public1`

3-610 **Polk Community College, Florida:** United States *NOTIS*
Access: `luis.nerdc.ufl.edu` ▶ at the first prompt enter `luis` ▶ select LINCC
`(Florida Community Colleges)` from the menu

3-611 **Port Arthur Public Library:** United States (Access via **CARL**)

3-612 **Port Neches Public Library:** United States (Access via **CARL**)

3-613 **Portland State University:** United States *UNICORN*
Access: `psulib.cc.pdx.edu` ▶ at the first prompt enter `dialin`

3-614 **Princeton Manuscripts Catalog:** United States *custom*
Access: `TN3270 pucc.princeton.edu` ▶ You will see a VM370 logo screen
▶ press ↵ ▶ enter `folio`

3-615 **Princeton University:** United States *NOTIS*
Access: `catalog.princeton.edu`

3-616 **Providence College:** United States (Access via **Rhode Island Higher Education Library Information Network**)

3-617 **Pueblo Community College:** United States (Access via **CARL**)

3-618 **Purdue University:** United States *NOTIS*
Access: `TN3270 lib.cc.purdue.edu`
Access: `thorplus.lib.purdue.edu` ▶ at the first prompt enter `catnet`

3-619 **Queen Elizabeth II Library:** Canada (Access via **Memorial University, Newfoundland**)

3-620 **Queen Mary and Westfield College, University of London:** United Kingdom *LIBERTAS*
Access: `sun.nsf.ac.uk` ▶ at the first prompt enter `janet` ▶ wait for the prompt
`Password:` ▶ press ↵ ▶ wait for the prompt `Hostname:` ▶ enter `uk.ac.qmw.lib`
▶ wait for the prompt `Username:` ▶ enter `library`

3-621   **Queen's College Library:** Canada (Access via **Memorial University, Newfoundland**)

3-622   **Queen's University:** Canada *NOTIS*
      Access: TN3270 `qucdnadm.queensu.ca`

3-623   **Queensland University of Technology:** Australia *URICA*
      Access: `library.qut.edu.au`

3-624   **Randolph-Macon Woman's College Library:** United States (Access via **Lynchburg Public and College Libraries**)

3-625   **Reading University:** United Kingdom *CLSI*
      Access: `sun.nsf.ac.uk` ❯ at the first prompt enter `janet` ❯ wait for the prompt `Password:` ❯ press ↵ ❯ wait for the prompt `Hostname:` ❯ enter `uk.ac.rdg.linnet` `<ctrl>-O` `<ctrl>-O`

3-626   **Rechenzentrum Der Universitaet Zuerich (University of Zurich):** Switzerland *DOBIS*
      Access: `nuz.unizh.ch` ❯ at the first prompt enter `tso` ❯ wait for the prompt that ends in `Wahl` ❯ enter `1` ❯ wait for the prompt `==>` ❯ enter `dobis`

3-627   **Red Academica Universitaria:** Venezuela (Access via **Biblioteca Nacional de Venezuela**)

3-628   **Red Rocks Community College:** United States (Access via **CARL**)

3-629   **Regis College/Teikyo Loretto University:** United States (Access via **CARL**)

3-630   **Rensselaer Polytechnic Institute:** United States *custom*
      Access: `infotrax.rpi.edu`

3-631   **Research and Reference Centers:** United States (Access via **ILLINET On-line Catalog**)

3-632   **Research Libraries Information Network:** United States *custom*
      Access: `rlin.stanford.edu or rlg.stanford.edu` ❯ An account is required to access this library

3-633   **Rhode Island College:** United States (Access via **Rhode Island Higher Education Library Information Network**)

3-634   **Rhode Island Higher Education Library Information Network (HELIN):** United States *INNOPAC*
      Access: `library.uri.edu` ❯ at the first prompt enter `library`

3-635   **Rhodes University:** South Africa *URICA*
      Access: `library.ru.ac.za`

3-636   **Rice University:** United States *NOTIS*
      Access: TN3270 `library.rice.edu` ❯ press ↵

3-637   **Richland Community Library:** United States (Access via **KELLY**)

3-638   **Rio Salado Community College Library/Media Services:** United States (Access via **Maricopa Community Colleges Libraries and Media Centers**)

3-639 **River Bend Library System:** United States (Access via **ILLINET On-line Catalog**)

3-640 **Rochester Institute of Technology:** United States *INNOPAC*
Access: `ritvax.isc.rit.edu` ▶ at the first prompt enter `library`

3-641 **Rockefeller University:** United States *custom*
Access: `library.rockefeller.edu` ▶ at the first prompt enter `library`

3-642 **Roger Williams University:** United States (Access via **Rhode Island Higher Education Library Information Network**)

3-643 **Rolling Prairie, Illinois, Library System:** United States (Access via **ILLINET On-line Catalog**)

3-644 **Roosevelt University:** United States (Access via **ILLINET On-line Catalog**)

3-645 **Rosary College:** United States (Access via **ILLINET On-line Catalog**)

3-646 **Roskilde University:** Denmark *custom*
Access: `find.uni-c.dk` ▶ at the first prompt enter `find` ▶ wait for the prompt `brugerkode` ▶ enter `rubikon` ▶ you will see a terminal-type menu ▶ enter 1

3-647 **Royal Danish Library:** Denmark *custom*
Access: `129.142.161.005` ▶ at the first prompt enter press the ESC key ▶ wait for the prompt `att` ▶ enter `rex` ▶ wait for the prompt `password:` ▶ enter `kb rex` ▶ press ↵ ▶ enter `dia eng` ▶ press ↵ ▶ enter `?guide`

3-648 **Royal Holloway and Bedford New College, University of London:** United Kingdom *LIBERTAS*
Access: `sun.nsf.ac.uk` ▶ at the first prompt enter `janet` ▶ wait for the prompt `Password:` ▶ press ↵ ▶ wait for the prompt `Hostname:` ▶ enter `uk.ac.rhbnc.lib` ▶ wait for the prompt `Username:` ▶ enter `library`

3-649 **Royal Institute of Technology, Stockholm:** Sweden *LIBERTAS*
Access: `kthbib.lib.kth.se` ▶ at the first prompt enter `tekline`

3-650 **Royal Melbourne Institute of Technology:** Australia *GEAC*
Access: `ccannex02.xx.rmit.oz.au` or `vicnet.xx.rmit.oz.au` ▶ at the first prompt enter `matlas`

3-651 **Royal Postgraduate Medical School:** United Kingdom (Access via **University of London Central Libertas Consortium**)

3-652 **Royal Veterinary College:** United Kingdom (Access via **University of London Central Libertas Consortium**)

3-653 **Rutgers University:** United States *GEAC*
Access: `library.rutgers.edu`

3-654 **Rutherford Appleton Laboratory:** United Kingdom *custom*
    Access: `sun.nsf.ac.uk` ◗ at the first prompt enter `janet` ◗ wait for the prompt
    `Password:` ◗ press ⏎ ◗ wait for the prompt `Hostname:` ◗ enter `uk.ac.rl.ib`
    ◗ you will see a page size menu ◗ enter `24` ◗ wait for the prompt `Login:` ◗ enter `LIB7`

3-655 **Saint Joseph Hospital Library:** United States (Access via **CARL**)

3-656 **Saint Mary's University:** Canada *GEAC*
    Access: `novanet.dal.ca` ◗ press ⏎

3-657 **Saint Xavier University:** United States (Access via **ILLINET On-line Catalog**)

3-658 **Salford University:** United Kingdom *BLCMP*
    Access: `sun.nsf.ac.uk` ◗ at the first prompt enter `janet` ◗ wait for the prompt
    `Password:` ◗ press ⏎ ◗ wait for the prompt `Hostname:` ◗ enter
    `uk.ac.salf.saiso`

3-659 **Salisbury State University:** United States (Access via **University of Maryland Library System**)

3-660 **Salzburg, Universitaetsbibliothek:** Austria (Access via **Austrian Academic Library Network**)

3-661 **San Diego State University:** United States *INNOPAC*
    Access: `library.sdsu.edu 74`

3-662 **San Francisco State University:** United States *GEAC ADVANCE*
    Access: `opac.sfsu.edu` ◗ at the first prompt enter `sfsu` ◗ wait for the prompt
    `Password:` ◗ press ⏎

3-663 **San Miguel County Public Library:** United States (Access via **MARMOT Library Network**)

3-664 **Sangamon State University:** United States (Access via **ILLINET On-line Catalog**)

3-665 **Santa Clara University:** United States *INNOPAC*
    Access: `sculib.scu.edu` ◗ at the first prompt enter `clara`

3-666 **Santa Fe Community College, Florida:** United States *NOTIS*
    Access: `luis.nerdc.ufl.edu` ◗ at the first prompt enter `luis` ◗ select `LINCC`
    `(Florida Community Colleges)` from the menu

3-667 **Santa Rosa Junior College:** United States *DYNIX*
    Access: `santarosa.edu` ◗ at the first prompt enter `library`

3-668 **Saskatoon Public Library:** Canada *DRA*
    Access: `charly.publib.saskatoon.sk.ca` ◗ at the first prompt enter `public`
    `PAC` ◗ wait for the prompt `>>` ◗ enter `pac`

3-669 **School of Oriental and African Studies, University of London:** United Kingdom *LIBERTAS*
    Access: `sun.nsf.ac.uk` ◗ at the first prompt enter `janet` ◗ wait for the prompt
    `Password:` ◗ press ⏎ ◗ wait for the prompt `Hostname:` ◗ enter
    `uk.ac.lon.soas.lib` ◗ wait for the prompt `Username:` ◗ enter `library`

3-670   **School of the Art Institute:** United States (Access via **ILLINET On-line Catalog**)

3-671   **Scott Library:** United States (Access via **Thomas Jefferson University**)

3-672   **Scottsdale Community College Library:** United States (Access via **Maricopa Community Colleges Libraries and Media Centers**)

3-673   **Scuola Normale Superiore di Pisa:** Italy *custom*
     Access: `vaxsns.sns.it` ▶ at the first prompt enter `bib`

3-674   **Seattle Pacific University:** United States *DRA*
     Access: `jerome.spu.edu` ▶ at the first prompt enter `pac`

3-675   **Seminole Community College, Florida:** United States *NOTIS*
     Access: `luis.nerdc.ufl.edu` ▶ at the first prompt enter `luis` ▶ select LINCC (Florida Community Colleges) from the menu

3-676   **Shawnee Library System:** United States (Access via **ILLINET On-line Catalog**)

3-677   **Shawnee State University:** United States *INNOPAC*
     Access: `beartrack.shawnee.edu` ▶ at the first prompt enter `library`

3-678   **Sheffield University:** United Kingdom *BLCMP*
     Access: `sun.nsf.ac.uk` ▶ at the first prompt enter `janet` ▶ wait for the prompt `Password:` ▶ press ↵ ▶ wait for the prompt `Hostname:` ▶ enter `uk.ac.shef.lib`

3-679   **Shepherd College:** United States (Access via **West Virginia University**)

3-680   **Shirley, Colorado, Library:** United States (Access via **CARL**)

3-681   **Shrewsbury, Colorado, Public Library:** United States (Access via **CARL**)

3-682   **Simmons College:** United States *INNOPAC*
     Access: `lib.simmons.edu` ▶ at the first prompt enter `library`

3-683   **Simon Fraser University:** Canada *GEAC*
     Access: `library.sfu.ca` ▶ at the first prompt enter `sfulib`

3-684   **Skidmore College:** United States *DYNIX*
     Access: `lucy.skidmore.edu`

3-685   **Sno-Isle Library System (Marysville, Washington):** United States (Access via **University of Maryland Library System**)

3-686   **Snow College:** United States *DYNIX*
     Access: `lib.snow.edu`

3-687   **Sodus Township Library:** United States (Access via **KELLY**)

3-688   **Sonoma County Library:** United States *DYNIX*
     Access: `sonoma.lib.ca.us`

3-689   **Sonoma State University:** United States *custom*
     Access: `vax.sonoma.edu` ◗ at the first prompt enter `opac`

3-690   **South Bank University:** United Kingdom *DYNIX*
     Access: `sbulib.sbu.ac.uk` ◗ at the first prompt enter `lrlib`

3-691   **South Florida Community College, Florida:** United States *NOTIS*
     Access: `luis.nerdc.ufl.edu` ◗ at the first prompt enter `luis` ◗ select `LINCC`
       `(Florida Community Colleges)` from the menu

3-692   **South Hadley, Colorado, Library System:** United States (Access via **CARL**)

3-693   **South Haven, Michigan, Libraries:** United States (Access via **KELLY**)

3-694   **South Mountain Community College Library:** United States (Access via **Maricopa Community Colleges Libraries and Media Centers**)

3-695   **Southampton University:** United Kingdom *URICA*
     Access: `lib.soton.ac.uk` ◗ at the first prompt enter `library`
     Access: `sun.nsf.ac.uk` ◗ at the first prompt enter `janet` ◗ wait for the prompt
       `Password:` ◗ press ↵ ◗ wait for the prompt `Hostname:` ◗ enter
       `uk.ac.soton.lib` ◗ press ↵ ◗ enter `library`

3-696   **Southbridge, Colorado, Libraries:** United States (Access via **CARL**)

3-697   **Southern Illinois University:** United States (Access via **ILLINET On-line Catalog**)

3-698   **Southern Methodist University:** United States *NOTIS*
     Access: TN3270 `vm.cis.smu.edu` ◗ tab to `COMMAND:` ◗ enter `dial vtam`

3-699   **Southern Oregon State College:** United States *INNOPAC*
     Access: `lib.sosc.osshe.edu` ◗ at the first prompt enter `library`

3-700   **Southern Tech—Marietta:** United States (Access via **Georgia On-Line Library Information System**)

3-701   **Southern Utah University:** United States *DYNIX*
     Access: `lib.li.suu.edu`

3-702   **Southwest Baptist Theological Seminary:** United States *DRA*
     Access: `lib.swbts.edu` ◗ at the first prompt enter `public`

3-703   **Southwest System:** United States (Access via **MARMOT Library Network**)

3-704   **Southwest Texas State University:** United States *DRA*
     Access: `admin.swt.edu` ◗ at the first prompt enter `swtlibrary`
     Access: `panam2.panam.edu` ◗ at the first prompt enter `packey` ◗ pick `Other`
       `Library Catalogs` from the Texas-Pan American Library main menu

3-705   **Southwestern Michigan College:** United States (Access via **KELLY**)

3-706 **Southwick Library:** United States (Access via **CARL**)

3-707 **Springfield, Colorado City Libraries:** United States (Access via **CARL**)

3-708 **St. Andrews University:** United Kingdom *custom*
> **Access:** `sun.nsf.ac.uk` ▸ at the first prompt enter `janet` ▸ wait for the prompt
> `Password:` ▸ press ↵ ▸ wait for the prompt `Hostname:` ▸ enter
> `uk.ac.st-and.lib` ▸ press ↵

3-709 **St. Boniface General Hospital Libraries:** Canada *PALS*
> **Access:** `umopac.umanitoba.ca`

3-710 **St. George's Hospital Medical School:** United Kingdom (Access via **University of London Central Libertas Consortium**)

3-711 **St. John's Mercy Medical Center Library:** United States (Access via **Washington University of St. Louis Medical Library**)

3-712 **St. Johns River Community College, Florida:** United States *NOTIS*
> **Access:** `luis.nerdc.ufl.edu` ▸ at the first prompt enter `luis` ▸ select LINCC
> (Florida Community Colleges) from the menu

3-713 **St. Joseph/Maud Preston Palenske Memorial Library:** United States (Access via **KELLY**)

3-714 **St. Louis Children's Hospital Library:** United States (Access via **Washington University of St. Louis Medical Library**)

3-715 **St. Louis College of Pharmacy Library:** United States (Access via **Washington University of St. Louis Medical Library**)

3-716 **St. Mary's Health Center Library:** United States (Access via **Washington University of St. Louis Medical Library**)

3-717 **St. Mary's University:** United States *DYNIX*
> **Access:** `vax.stmarytx.edu` ▸ at the first prompt enter `dynix` ▸ wait for the prompt
> `Password:` ▸ enter `catalog` ▸ wait for the prompt `Logon:` ▸ enter `dialup`

3-718 **St. Norbert College:** United States *INNOPAC*
> **Access:** `snclib.snc.edu` ▸ at the first prompt enter `library`

3-719 **St. Petersburg Junior College, Florida:** United States *NOTIS*
> **Access:** `luis.nerdc.ufl.edu` ▸ at the first prompt enter `luis` ▸ select LINCC
> (Florida Community Colleges) from the menu

3-720 **Stadsbibliotheek van Antwerpen:** Belgium (Access via **University of Antwerp**)

3-721 **Stanford University:** United States *custom*
> **Access:** `forsythetn.stanford.edu` ▸ at the first prompt enter `socrates`

3-722 **Starved Rock Library System:** United States (Access via **ILLINET On-line Catalog**)

3-723 **State Library of Massachusetts:** United States (Access via **Boston Library Consortium**)

3-724 **State Library of Pennsylvania:** United States *NOTIS*
Access: `192.102.245.100` ▸ press ↵

3-725 **State Library of South Australia:** Australia *INNOPAC*
Access: `ferrari.slsa.sa.gov.au` ▸ at the first prompt enter `library`

3-726 **State Technical Institute:** United States (Access via **KELLY**)

3-727 **Sterling, Colorado, Libraries:** United States (Access via **CARL**)

3-728 **Stockholm University:** Sweden *GEAC*
Access: `fog.tele.su.se` ▸ at the first prompt enter `sub` ▸ wait for the prompt
that ends in `att brja` ▸ enter `1`

3-729 **Strathclyde University:** United Kingdom *GEAC*
Access: `sun.nsf.ac.uk` ▸ at the first prompt enter `janet` ▸ wait for the prompt
`Password:` ▸ press ↵ ▸ wait for the prompt `Hostname:` ▸ enter
`uk.ac.strath.lib`

3-730 **Sturbridge, Colorado, Libraries:** United States (Access via **CARL**)

3-731 **Sturgis Public Schools:** United States (Access via **KELLY**)

3-732 **Suburban Library System:** United States (Access via **ILLINET On-line Catalog**)

3-733 **Suisse Union Catalogue of Foreign Serials:** Switzerland (Access via **Swiss-French Network
Catalogue**)

3-734 **Summit County Public Library:** United States (Access via **MARMOT Library Network**)

3-735 **SUNY College at Buffalo:** United States *INNOPAC*
Access: `snybufvb.cs.snybuf.edu` ▸ at the first prompt enter `library`

3-736 **SUNY College of Environmental Science & Forestry:** United States *NOTIS*
Access: `acsnet.syr.edu` ▸ at the first prompt enter `summit`
Access: TN3270 `suvm.acs.syr.edu` ▸ tab to `COMMAND:` ▸ enter `dial vtam`

3-737 **SUNY—Albany:** United States *GEAC*
Access: `libcat.library.albany.edu` ▸ press ↵

3-738 **SUNY—Binghamton:** United States *NOTIS*
Access: TN3270 `bingvmc.cc.binghamton.edu`

3-739 **SUNY—Brockport:** United States *DYNIX*
Access: `acspr1.acs.brockport.edu` ▸ at the first prompt enter `library`
▸ wait for the prompt `Password?` ▸ enter `drake`

3-740 **SUNY—Fredonia:** United States *PALS*
Access: `library.fredonia.edu` ▸ at the first prompt enter `attach fredcat`

3-741 **SUNY—Stony Brook:** United States *NOTIS*
     Access: TN3270 ccvm.sunysb.edu ◗ tab to COMMAND: ◗ enter STARS

3-742 **Susquehanna University:** United States *INNOPAC*
     Access: ben.susqu.edu ◗ at the first prompt enter library

3-743 **Swarthmore College:** United States *INNOPAC*
     Access: tripod.brynmawr.edu ◗ at the first prompt enter library

3-744 **Swedish Business University:** Finland *VTLS*
     Access: hanna.shh.fi ◗ at the first prompt enter hello yourname,user.clas01
     ◗ you will see a welcome screen, then a terminal-type menu ◗ enter 10 ◗ wait for the
     prompt that ends in Anna kokoelmatunnus tai ? ◗ enter 100 ◗ wait for the
     prompt that ends in komento ◗ enter /lang 1 ◗ press ↵ ◗ enter ?

3-745 **Swedish Medical Center Library:** United States (Access via **CARL**)

3-746 **Swedish University of Agriculture:** Sweden *custom*
     Access: upnod.slu.se ◗ at the first prompt enter lr ◗ wait for the prompt att
     ◗ enter lukas ◗ wait for the prompt > ◗ enter slubib

3-747 **Sweet Briar College Library:** United States (Access via **Lynchburg Public and College
     Libraries**)

3-748 **Swinburne University of Technology:** Australia *DYNIX*
     Access: ollie.xx.swin.oz.au

3-749 **Swiss-French Network Catalogue (SIBIL):** Switzerland *custom*
     Access: sibil.switch.ch ◗ at the first prompt enter 02 ◗ press ↵

3-750 **Sydney College of the Arts, University of Sydney:** Australia (Access via **New South Wales
     Libraries**)

3-751 **Syracuse University:** United States *NOTIS*
     Access: acsnet.syr.edu ◗ at the first prompt enter summit
     Access: TN3270 suvm.acs.syr.edu ◗ tab to COMMAND: ◗ enter dial vtam

3-752 **Tallahassee Community College, Florida:** United States *NOTIS*
     Access: luis.nerdc.ufl.edu ◗ at the first prompt enter luis ◗ select LINCC
     (Florida Community Colleges) from the menu

3-753 **Tampere University:** Finland *VTLS*
     Access: lakka.uta.fi ◗ at the first prompt enter c hilla ◗ wait for the prompt
     MPE XL ◗ enter hello yourname,user.clas01 ◗ you will see a terminal-type
     menu ◗ enter 4 ◗ wait for the prompt that ends in kokoelma ◗ enter 100 ◗ wait for
     the prompt that ends in komento ◗ enter /lang 1

3-754 **Technical University of Budapest:** Hungary *custom*
     Access: tulibb.kkt.bme.hu ◗ at the first prompt enter ?/eng

3-755 **Technical University of Nova Scotia:** Canada *GEAC*
   Access: `novanet.dal.ca` ▶ press ↵

3-756 **Technion:** Israel (Access via **Hebrew University**)

3-757 **Technischen Universitaet Wien:** Austria (Access via **Austrian Academic Library Network**)

3-758 **Tel Aviv University:** Israel (Access via **Hebrew University**)

3-759 **Temple University School of Law Library:** United States *INNOPAC*
   Access: `templ.law.temple.edu` ▶ at the first prompt enter `templaw`

3-760 **Temple University Dental/Allied Health/Pharmacy/Health Sciences Center Library:** United States (Access via **HSLC HealthNET Health Sciences Information Network**)

3-761 **Temple University:** United States *GEAC*
   Access: `library.paley.temple.edu` ▶ press ↵

3-762 **Texas A&M:** United States *NOTIS*
   Access: `venus.tamu.edu` ▶ at the first prompt enter `vtam` ▶ after a long pause you will see a logo screen ▶ enter `notis`
   Access: TN3270 `tamvm1.tamu.edu` ▶ tab to COMMAND: ▶ enter `dial vtam` ▶ you will see an application screen ▶ enter `notis`
   Access: `panam2.panam.edu` ▶ at the first prompt enter `packey` ▶ pick `Other Library Catalogs` from the Texas-Pan American Library main menu
   Access: `panam2.panam.edu` ▶ at the first prompt enter `packey` ▶ pick `Other Library Catalogs` from the Texas-Pan American Library main menu

3-763 **Texas Christian University:** United States *DRA*
   Access: `lib.is.tcu.edu` ▶ at the first prompt enter `tcucat`

3-764 **Texas State Agencies:** United States *CLSI*
   Access: `gabi.tsl.texas.gov`
   Access: `panam2.panam.edu` ▶ at the first prompt enter `packey` ▶ pick `Other Library Catalogs` from the Texas-Pan American Library main menu

3-765 **Texas Tech University:** United States *DRA*
   Access: `ttacs3.ttu.edu` ▶ at the first prompt enter `ttucat`
   Access: `panam2.panam.edu` ▶ at the first prompt enter `packey` ▶ pick `Other Library Catalogs` from the Texas-Pan American Library main menu

3-766 **Texas Woman's University:** United States *GEAC ADVANCE*
   Access: `twu.edu` ▶ at the first prompt enter `iris`

3-767 **Thomas Jefferson University:** United States *custom*
   Access: `jeflin.tju.edu` ▶ at the first prompt enter `jeffline`

3-768 **Three Oaks Township Library:** United States (Access via **West Michigan Information Network**)

3-769 **Three Rivers System:** United States (Access via **MARMOT Library Network**)

3-770 **Tilburg University:** Netherlands *custom*
    Access: `kublib.kub.nl`

3-771 **Towson State University:** United States (Access via **University of Maryland Library System**)

3-772 **Trent University:** Canada *DRA*
    Access: `trentu.ca` ▶ at the first prompt enter `topcat`

3-773 **Tri-College Consortium:** United States *INNOPAC*
    Access: `tripod.brynmawr.edu` ▶ at the first prompt enter `library`

3-774 **Triangle Research Libraries:** United States *custom*
    Access: `librot1.lib.unc.edu`

3-775 **Trinidad State Jr. College:** United States (Access via **CARL**)

3-776 **Trinity Christian College:** United States (Access via **ILLINET On-line Catalog**)

3-777 **Trinity College, Dublin:** Ireland *DYNIX*
    Access: `lib1.tcd.ie` ▶ at the first prompt enter `opac`

3-778 **Trinity College:** United States *NOTIS*
    Access: `library.wesleyan.edu` ▶ press ↵

3-779 **Triton College:** United States (Access via **ILLINET On-line Catalog**)

3-780 **Truckee Meadows Community College:** United States (Access via **Nevada Academic Libraries Information System**)

3-781 **TU-Graz:** Austria *custom*
    Access: `ftub.tu-graz.ac.at` ▶ at the first prompt enter `tub`

3-782 **Tufts University:** United States *DRA*
    Access: `library.tufts.edu` ▶ at the first prompt enter `tulips`
    Access: `blc.lrc.northeastern.edu`

3-783 **Turners Falls, Colorado, Public Library:** United States (Access via **CARL**)

3-784 **Uniformed Services University of the Health Sciences:** United States *INNOPAC*
    Access: `131.158.2.160` ▶ at the first prompt enter `catalog`

3-785 **Union College:** United States *DRA*
    Access: `conan.union.edu` ▶ at the first prompt enter `minerva` ▶ wait for the prompt `Password:` ▶ enter `library`

3-786 **United States Government Printing Office:** United States (Access via **Georgia On-Line Library Information System**)

3-787 **Universidad Catolica Andres Bello:** Venezuela (Access via **Biblioteca Nacional de Venezuela**)

3-788 **Universidad Central de Venezuela:** Venezuela (Access via **Biblioteca Nacional de Venezuela**)

3-789 **Universidad Complutense de Madrid:** Spain *LIBERTAS*
   Access: `eucmvx.sim.ucm.es` ◗ at the first prompt enter `biblioteca`

3-790 **Universidad de Alcala:** Spain *LIBERTAS*
   Access: `130.206.82.2` ◗ at the first prompt enter `biblos`

3-791 **Universidad de Concepcion:** Chile *DYNIX*
   Access: `cisne.bib.udec.cl` ◗ at the first prompt enter `opac`

3-792 **Universidad de Guadalajara:** Mexico *custom*
   Access: `udgserv.cencar.udg.mx` ◗ at the first prompt enter `tequilla`
   ◗ wait for the prompt `password:` ◗ enter `informa`

3-793 **Universidad de las Americas, Pueblas:** Mexico *custom*
   Access: `bibes.pue.udlap.mx` ◗ at the first prompt enter `library`

3-794 **Universidad Nacional Experimental de Guayana:** Venezuela (Access via **Biblioteca Nacional de Venezuela**)

3-795 **Universidad Nacional Experimental de Tachira:** Venezuela (Access via **Biblioteca Nacional de Venezuela**)

3-796 **Universidad Politecnica de Valencia:** Spain *custom*
   Access: `vega.cc.upv.es` ◗ at the first prompt enter `libros`

3-797 **Universidad Pompeu i Fabra:** Spain *VTLS*
   Access: `sahara.upf.es` ◗ at the first prompt enter `biblio`

3-798 **Universidade de Sao Paulo:** Brazil *custom*
   Access: `bee08.cce.usp.br` ◗ at the first prompt enter `dedalus`

3-799 **Universitaet des Saarlandes:** Germany *custom*
   Access: `unisb.rz.uni-sb.de` ◗ at the first prompt enter `.a logon ub,ub`

3-800 **Universitaet für Bildungswissenschaften, Klagenfurt:** Austria (Access via **Austrian Academic Library Network**)

3-801 **Universitaet für Bodenkultur:** Austria (Access via **Austrian Academic Library Network**)

3-802 **Universitaet Heidelberg:** Germany *custom*
   Access: `TN3270 vm.urz.uni-heidelberg.de.` ◗ at the first prompt enter ™

3-803 **Universitaetsbibliothek Erlangen-Nuernberg:** Germany *custom*
   Access: `faui43.informatik.uni-erlangen.de` ◗ at the first prompt enter `gi`

3-804 **Universitaire Fakulteiten St. Ignatius Antwerpen:** Belgium (Access via **University of Antwerp**)

3-805   **Universitat Autonoma de Barcelona:** Spain *VTLS*

> **Access:** `babel.uab.es` ❯ at the first prompt enter `hello uab.bib` ❯ wait for the prompt that ends in `continuar...` ❯ press ↵ ❯ wait for the prompt that ends in `TERMINAL TYPE` ❯ enter `10` ❯ wait for the prompt that ends in `cerca assistida` ❯ enter `/lang 1`

3-806   **Universitat de Valencia:** Spain *DOBIS/LIBIS*

> **Access:** TN3270 `mvs.ci.uv.es` ❯ at the first prompt enter ™❯ wait for the prompt `Application` ❯ enter `bluv` ❯ press ↵ ❯ enter PF1

3-807   **Universitat Jaume I:** Spain *VTLS*

> **Access:** `violant-telnet.uji.es` ❯ at the first prompt enter `hello yourname,user.clas01`

3-808   **Universitat Politecnica de Catalunya:** Spain *VTLS*

> **Access:** `tahat.upc.es` ❯ at the first prompt enter `biblioteca` ❯ press ↵ ❯ press ↵ ❯ wait for the prompt that ends in `LEIBNIZ.BIB` ❯ enter `hello leibniz.bib` ❯ you will see a terminal-type menu ❯ enter `10` ❯ wait for the prompt that ends in `entreu 100` ❯ enter `100`

3-809   **Universite de Caen:** France *custom*

> **Access:** `192.33.163.200` ❯ at the first prompt enter `busciences`

3-810   **Universite de Moncton—Bibliotheque Champlain:** Canada *GEAC*

> **Access:** `139.103.2.2` ❯ at the first prompt enter `champ`

3-811   **Universite de Sainte-Etienne:** France *GEAC*

> **Access:** `stroph.univ-st-etienne.fr` ❯ at the first prompt enter `brise`

3-812   **Universite de Sherbrooke:** Canada *MultiLIS*

> **Access:** `catalo.biblio.usherb.ca` ❯ at the first prompt enter `biblio`

3-813   **University Center—Tulsa:** United States *DRA*

> **Access:** `192.234.12.3` ❯ at the first prompt enter `library`

3-814   **University College, Cork:** Ireland *DOBIS/LIBIS*

> **Access:** `vax1.ucc.ie` ❯ at the first prompt enter `library`

3-815   **University College, Dublin:** Ireland *custom*

> **Access:** `pacx.ucd.ie` ❯ at the first prompt enter `library` ❯ press ↵

3-816   **University College of Cape Breton:** Canada *GEAC*

> **Access:** `novanet.dal.ca` ❯ press ↵

3-817   **University College of North Wales, Bangor:** United Kingdom *GEAC*

> **Access:** `sun.nsf.ac.uk` ❯ at the first prompt enter `janet` ❯ wait for the prompt `Password:` ❯ press ↵ ❯ wait for the prompt `Hostname:` ❯ enter `uk.ac.bangor.lib`

3-818 **University College, London:** United Kingdom *LIBERTAS*
    Access: `lib.ucl.ac.uk`
    Access: `sun.nsf.ac.uk` ▶ press ↵ ▶ enter `janet` ▶ wait for the prompt `Password:`
    ▶ press ↵ ▶ wait for the prompt `Hostname:` ▶ enter `uk.ac.lon.consull`
    ▶ wait for the prompt `Username:` ▶ enter `library`

3-819 **University Library of Limburg:** Belgium (Access via **University of Antwerp**)

3-820 **University of Adelaide:** Australia *DYNIX*
    Access: `library.adelaide.edu.au` ▶ at the first prompt enter `bslnet`

3-821 **University of Akron:** United States *VTLS*
    Access: `library.uakron.edu`

3-822 **University of Alabama—Birmingham Lister Hill Health Sciences Library:** United States *DYNIX*
    Access: `lhhost2.lhl.uab.edu` ▶ at the first prompt enter `lpub`

3-823 **University of Alabama—Huntsville:** United States *PALS*
    Access: `library.uah.edu` ▶ at the first prompt enter `he`

3-824 **University of Alabama:** United States *NOTIS*
    Access: TN3270 `ua2mvs.ua.edu` ▶ at the first prompt enter `library` ▶ press ↵

3-825 **University of Alaska:** United States *VTLS*
    Access: `gnosis.alaska.edu` ▶ at the first prompt enter `hello, user.gnosis`

3-826 **University of Antwerp:** Belgium *custom*
    Access: `main.bib.uia.ac.be`

3-827 **University of Arizona:** United States *INNOPAC*
    Access: `sabio.arizona.edu`

3-828 **University of Arkansas Medical Sciences Library:** United States *custom*
    Access: `uamslib.uams.edu` ▶ at the first prompt enter `uams`

3-829 **University of Aukland:** New Zealand *NOTIS*
    Access: `ccvcom.aukuni.ac.nz` ▶ at the first prompt enter `aucat`

3-830 **University of Baltimore Law:** United States (Access via **University of Maryland Library System**)

3-831 **University of Baltimore:** United States (Access via **University of Maryland Library System**)

3-832 **University of Brighton:** United Kingdom *BLCMP*
    Access: `sun.nsf.ac.uk` ▶ at the first prompt enter `janet` ▶ wait for the prompt
    `Password:` ▶ press ↵ ▶ wait for the prompt `Hostname:` ▶ enter `uk.ac.bton.lib`

3-833 **University of Bristol:** United Kingdom *LIBERTAS*
    Access: `lib.bris.ac.uk`

3-834 **University of British Columbia:** Canada *custom*
    Access: `library.ubc.ca` ◗ press ↵

3-835 **University of Buffalo:** United States *NOTIS*
    Access: `bison.cc.buffalo.edu`

3-836 **University of Calgary:** Canada *custom*
    Access: `develnet.ucalgary.ca` ◗ at the first prompt enter `library`

3-837 **University of California and California State:** United States *(*See **MELVYL***)*

3-838 **University of California Northern Regional Library Facility:** United States *INNOPAC*
    Access: `128.48.48.14` ◗ at the first prompt enter `library`

3-839 **University of California—Berkeley:** United States *custom*
    Access: `gopac.berkeley.edu`

3-840 **University of California—San Diego ROGER System:** United States *INNOPAC*
    Access: `sdacs.ucsd.edu 7000`

3-841 **University of California—San Diego:** United States *INNOPAC*
    Access: `library.ucsd.edu` ◗ at the first prompt enter `library`

3-842 **University of California—San Francisco:** United States *INNOPAC*
    Access: `128.218.15.5`

3-843 **University of California—Santa Barbara:** United States *NOTIS*
    Access: `TN3270 ccnh.ucsb.edu`

3-844 **University of Canberra:** Australia *URICA*
    Access: `library.canberra.edu.au`

3-845 **University of Canterbury:** New Zealand *URICA*
    Access: `cantva.canterbury.ac.nz` ◗ at the first prompt enter `opac`
    ◗ wait for the prompt CONNTECTED ◗ press ↵

3-846 **University of Central Florida:** United States (Access via **Florida State University**)

3-847 **University of Central Oklahoma:** United States *NOTIS*
    Access: `aix0.ucok.edu` ◗ at the first prompt enter `,,,library` ◗ the screen will
    clear ◗ press ↵

3-848 **University of Chicago:** United States *custom*
    Access: `olorin.uchicago.edu` ◗ at the first prompt enter `lib48`
    Access: `illinet.aiss.uiuc.edu`

3-849 **University of Cincinnati:** United States *INNOPAC*
    Access: `ucolk3.olk.uc.edu` ◗ at the first prompt enter `uclid`
    Access: `cat.ohiolink.edu`

3-850 **University of Colorado—Boulder:** United States (Access via **CARL**)

3-851 **University of Colorado—Colorado Springs:** United States *custom*
 Access: `arlo.colorado.edu` ◗ at the first prompt enter ARLO ◗ you will see a logo screen ◗ press ↵

3-852 **University of Copenhagen:** Denmark *custom*
 Access: `129.142.161.005` ◗ at the first prompt enter press the ESC key ◗ wait for the prompt `att` ◗ enter `rex` ◗ wait for the prompt `password:` ◗ enter `kb rex` ◗ press ↵ ◗ enter `dia eng`

3-853 **University of Dayton:** United States *DYNIX*
 Access: `udaprl.oca.udayton.edu` ◗ at the first prompt enter `public`

3-854 **University of Delaware:** United States *NOTIS*
 Access: `delcat.udel.edu`

3-855 **University of Dundee:** United Kingdom *DYNIX*
 Access: `libb.dundee.ac.uk` ◗ at the first prompt enter `library`

3-856 **University of East Anglia:** United Kingdom *CATS*
 Access: `info.uea.ac.uk` ◗ at the first prompt enter `info`

3-857 **University of Essex:** United Kingdom *OCLC*
 Access: `sersun1.essex.ac.uk` ◗ at the first prompt enter `library`

3-858 **University of Exeter:** United Kingdom *LIBERTAS*
 Access: `sun.nsf.ac.uk` ◗ at the first prompt enter `janet` ◗ wait for the prompt `Password:` ◗ press ↵ ◗ wait for the prompt `Hostname:` ◗ enter `uk.ac.ex.lab` ◗ wait for the prompt `Username:` ◗ enter `library`

3-859 **University of Florida:** United States (Access via **Florida State University**)

3-860 **University of Georgia and Georgia College:** United States *custom*
 Access: TN3270 `uga.cc.uga.edu` ◗ tab to COMMAND: ◗ enter `dial vtam` ◗ press ↵ ◗ enter LIBRARY
 Access: `gsvms2.cc.gasou.edu` ◗ at the first prompt enter INFO ◗ press ↵ ◗ enter 3 ◗ press ↵ ◗ enter LIBRARY

3-861 **University of Georgia—Athens:** United States (Access via **Georgia On-Line Library Information System**)

3-862 **University of Gothenburg:** Sweden *VTLS*
 Access: `gunda.ub.gu.se` ◗ press ↵

3-863 **University of Groningen:** Netherlands *custom*
 Access: `129.125.19.10` ◗ at the first prompt enter OPC

3-864 **University of Hawaii—Honolulu:** United States *custom*
 Access: `starmaster.uhcc.hawaii.edu` ◗ at the first prompt enter `lib`

Access: pac.carl.org ▶ at the first prompt enter PAC ▶ press ↵ ▶ enter 4

Access: victor.umd.edu ▶ at the first prompt enter pac ▶ press ↵ ▶ press ↵

3-865 **University of Hawaii—Manoa:** United States *custom*

Access: starmaster.uhcc.hawaii.edu ▶ at the first prompt enter lib

3-866 **University of Hong Kong:** Hong Kong *DRA*

Access: hkulbr.hku.hk ▶ at the first prompt enter hkulopac

3-867 **University of Houston:** United States *GEAC*

Access: uhopac.lib.uh.edu

3-868 **University of Iceland:** Iceland *LIBERTAS*

Access: saga.rhi.hi.is

3-869 **University of Idaho Libraries:** United States *custom*

Access: ida.lib.uidaho.edu ▶ press ↵

3-870 **University of Illinois—Champaign/Urbana:** United States *custom*

Access: illinet.aiss.uiuc.edu

3-871 **University of Illinois—Chicago:** United States *NOTIS*

Access: TN3270 uicvm.uic.edu ▶ at the first prompt enter luis

3-872 **University of Illinois—Medical:** United States (Access via **ILLINET On-line Catalog**)

3-873 **University of Illinois—Urbana:** United States (Access via **ILLINET On-line Catalog**)

3-874 **University of Iowa:** United States *NOTIS*

Access: oasis.uiowa.edu ▶ at the first prompt enter 1

3-875 **University of Kansas:** United States *custom*

Access: kuhub.cc.ukans.edu

3-876 **University of Kentucky:** United States *custom*

Access: TN3270 ukcc.uky.edu ▶ tab to COMMAND: ▶ enter dial vtam ▶ press ↵ ▶ enter L

3-877 **University of Kings College:** Canada *GEAC*

Access: novanet.dal.ca ▶ press ↵

3-878 **University of Konstanz:** Germany *custom*

Access: polydos.uni-konstanz.de 775 ▶ at the first prompt enter boddb ▶ wait for the prompt *info ▶ enter suche

3-879 **University of Lethbridge:** Canada *INNOPAC*

Access: darius.uleth.ca ▶ at the first prompt enter library

3-880 **University of London Central Libertas Consortium:** United Kingdom *LIBERTAS*
    Access: `sun.nsf.ac.uk` ◗ at the first prompt enter `janet` ◗ wait for the prompt
    `Password:` ◗ press ↵ ◗ wait for the prompt `Hostname:` ◗ enter
    `uk.ac.lon.consull` ◗ wait for the prompt `Username:` ◗ enter `library`

3-881 **University of London Serials Database:** United Kingdom *LIBERTAS*
    Access: `sun.nsf.ac.uk` ◗ at the first prompt enter `janet` ◗ wait for the prompt
    `Password:` ◗ press ↵ ◗ wait for the prompt `Hostname:` ◗ enter `uk.ac.lon.flcs`
    ◗ wait for the prompt `Username:` ◗ enter `library`

3-882 **University Of Lowell:** United States *DRA*
    Access: `libvax.ulowell.edu` ◗ at the first prompt enter `library`

3-883 **University of Luton:** United Kingdom *LIBERTAS*
    Access: `sun.nsf.ac.uk` ◗ at the first prompt enter `janet` ◗ wait for the prompt
    `Password:` ◗ press ↵ ◗ wait for the prompt `hostname:` ◗ enter
    `uk.ac.luton.lib`

3-884 **University of Maine Library System:** United States *INNOPAC*
    Access: `ursus.maine.edu`

3-885 **University of Maine School of Law:** United States (Access via **University of Maine Library System**)

3-886 **University of Maine—Augusta:** United States (Access via **University of Maine Library System**)

3-887 **University of Maine—Farmington:** United States (Access via **University of Maine Library System**)

3-888 **University of Maine—Fort Kent:** United States (Access via **University of Maine Library System**)

3-889 **University of Maine—Machias:** United States (Access via **University of Maine Library System**)

3-890 **University of Maine—Presque Isle:** United States (Access via **University of Maine Library System**)

3-891 **University of Manitoba Libraries:** Canada *PALS*
    Access: `umopac.umanitoba.ca`

3-892 **University of Maryland Baltimore County:** United States (Access via **University of Maryland Library System**)

3-893 **University of Maryland College Park:** United States (Access via **University of Maryland Library System**)

3-894 **University of Maryland Eastern Shore:** United States (Access via **University of Maryland Library System**)

3-895 **University of Maryland Health Sciences Library:** United States *LS/2000*
    Access: `annex.ab.umd.edu` ◗ press ↵ ◗ wait for the prompt `select` ◗ enter
    `hsl4800` ◗ press ↵

3-896 **University of Maryland Law Library:** United States (Access via **University of Maryland Library System**)

3-897 **University of Maryland Library System:** United States *custom*
   Access: `victor.umd.edu` ▶ at the first prompt enter `pac` ▶ press ↵ ▶ press ↵

3-898 **University of Maryland University College:** United States (Access via **University of Maryland Library System**)

3-899 **University of Massachusetts Medical Center Library:** United States (Access via **CARL**)

3-900 **University of Massachusetts—Amherst:** United States (Access via **Boston Library Consortium**)

3-901 **University of Massachusetts—Boston:** United States *custom*
   Access: `libra.cc.umb.edu` ▶ at the first prompt enter `catalog`
   Access: `blc.lrc.northeastern.edu`

3-902 **University of Massachusetts—Dartmouth:** United States *MultiLIS*
   Access: `library.umassd.edu` ▶ at the first prompt enter `library`

3-903 **University of Medicine and Dentistry of New Jersey:** United States *custom*
   Access: `library.umdnj.edu` ▶ at the first prompt enter `library` ▶ wait for the prompt that ends in `last name` ▶ enter any character

3-904 **University of Melbourne:** Australia *custom*
   Access: `library.unimelb.edu.au`

3-905 **University of Miami Medical Library:** United States *INNOPAC*
   Access: `callcat.med.miami.edu` ▶ at the first prompt enter `library`

3-906 **University of Miami:** United States *INNOPAC*
   Access: `stacks.library.miami.edu` ▶ at the first prompt enter `library`

3-907 **University of Michigan Business School:** United States *INNOPAC*
   Access: `lib.bus.umich.edu` ▶ at the first prompt enter `mentor`

3-908 **University of Michigan Law Library:** United States *INNOPAC*
   Access: `lexcalibur.lib.law.umich.edu` ▶ at the first prompt enter `um-lex`

3-909 **University of Michigan—Dearborn:** United States *INNOPAC*
   Access: `141.215.16.4`

3-910 **University of Michigan:** United States *NOTIS*
   Access: `hermes.merit.edu` ▶ at the first prompt enter `mirlyn`
   Access: TN3270 `lib.cc.purdue.edu`
   Access: `thorplus.lib.purdue.edu` ▶ at the first prompt enter `catnet`

3-911 **University of Minnesota:** United States *NOTIS*
   Access: `pubinfo.ais.umn.edu`

       Access: TN3270 `pubinfo.ais.umn.edu`
       Access: `thorplus.lib.purdue.edu` ▶ at the first prompt enter `catnet`
       Access: `lib.cc.purdue.edu (tn3270`

3-912   **University of Mississippi:** United States *CLSI*
       Access: `lib1.lib.olemiss.edu` ▶ at the first prompt enter `olemiss`

3-913   **University of Missouri—Columbia:** United States *custom*
       Access: TN3270 `umcvmb.missouri.edu` ▶ tab to COMMAND:
       ▶ enter `dial vtam` ▶ wait for the prompt VTAM LOGON: ▶ enter `libcics`

3-914   **University of Missouri—Rolla:** United States *custom*
       Access: TN3270 `umrvmb.umr.edu` ▶ tab to COMMAND: ▶ enter `dial vtam`
       ▶ press ↵ ▶ enter `lumin`

3-915   **University of Missouri—St. Louis:** United States *custom*
       Access: TN3270 `umslvma.umsl.edu` ▶ tab to COMMAND: ▶ enter `dial vtam`
       ▶ wait for the prompt VTAM LOGON: ▶ enter `libcics`

3-916   **University of Montana:** United States *DYNIX*
       Access: `lib.umt.edu`

3-917   **University of Natal—Durban:** South Africa *URICA*
       Access: `library.und.ac.za` ▶ press ↵ ▶ press ↵ .

3-918   **University of Nebraska Medical Center:** United States *custom*
       Access: `library.unmc.edu`

3-919   **University of Nebraska—Kearney:** United States *INNOPAC*
       Access: `144.216.1.5` ▶ at the first prompt enter `library`

3-920   **University of Nebraska—Omaha:** United States *INNOPAC*
       Access: `genisys.unomaha.edu` ▶ at the first prompt enter `genisys`

3-921   **University of Nebraska:** United States *INNOPAC*
       Access: `unllib.unl.edu`

3-922   **University of Nevada—Las Vegas:** United States (Access via **Nevada Academic Libraries Information System**)

3-923   **University of Nevada—Reno Library:** United States (Access via **Nevada Academic Libraries Information System**)

3-924   **University of New Brunswick:** Canada *custom*
       Access: TN3270 `unbmvs1.csd.unb.ca`

3-925   **University of New England Orange Agricultural Coll:** Australia (Access via **New South Wales Libraries**)

3-926 **University of New England—Northern Rivers:** Australia *GEAC*
   Access: `pac.une.edu.au`
   Access: `opac.clann.edu.au` ◗ press ↵ ◗ enter UNE<space><space><space>L120
   (Note: all capitals)
   Access: `unilinc.edu.au`

3-927 **University of New England:** Australia *VTLS*
   Access: `opac.une.oz.au` ◗ press ↵ ◗ enter `pac`

3-928 **University of New Mexico General Library:** United States *INNOPAC*
   Access: `library.unm.edu`

3-929 **University of New Mexico Law School Library:** United States *INNOPAC*
   Access: `libros2.unm.edu` ◗ at the first prompt enter `library` ◗ wait for the
   prompt `Password:` ◗ enter `library`

3-930 **University of New Mexico Medical Center Library:** United States *INNOPAC*
   Access: `biblio.unm.edu` ◗ at the first prompt enter `library`

3-931 **University of New Mexico:** United States *custom*
   Access: `tome.unm.edu`

3-932 **University of New South Wales College of Fine Arts:** Australia (Access via **New South Wales Libraries**)

3-933 **University of New South Wales:** Australia *custom*
   Access: `libprime.libsys.unsw.oz.au` ◗ press ↵ ◗ enter `libcat`
   Access: `unilinc.edu.au` ◗ at the first prompt enter `liblink`

3-934 **University of Newcastle:** Australia *INNOPAC*
   Access: `bliss.newcastle edu.au (134.148.192.2)` ◗ at the first prompt
   enter `library`

3-935 **University of North Carolina Library:** United States (Access via **Triangle Research Libraries**)

3-936 **University of North Carolina—Asheville:** United States *GvB*
   Access: `uncavx.unca.edu` ◗ at the first prompt enter `dhramsey`

3-937 **University of North Carolina—Greensboro:** United States *DRA*
   Access: `steffi.uncg.edu` ◗ at the first prompt enter `jaclin`

3-938 **University of North Carolina—Wilmington:** United States *LS/2000*
   Access: `152.4.1.202` ◗ press ↵

3-939 **University of North Florida:** United States (Access via **Florida State University**)

3-940 **University of North Texas:** United States *VTLS*
   Access: `library.unt.edu` ◗ at the first prompt enter `hello user.lib`

3-941 **University of Northern Colorado:** United States (Access via **CARL**)

3-942 **University of Northern Iowa:** United States *INNOPAC*
    Access: `starmaster.uni.edu` ▶ at the first prompt enter 1

3-943 **University of Notre Dame:** United States *NOTIS*
    Access: `irishmvs.cc.nd.edu` ▶ at the first prompt enter `library`
    Access: TN3270 `lib.cc.purdue.edu`
    Access: `thorplus.lib.purdue.edu` ▶ at the first prompt enter `catnet`

3-944 **University of Odense:** Denmark *custom*
    Access: `odin.bib.dk` ▶ at the first prompt enter `odin` ▶ wait for the prompt that ends in `oub9000` ▶ enter press the ESC key ▶ wait for the prompt `att` ▶ enter `odin` ▶ wait for the prompt > ▶ enter `odin`

3-945 **University of Oklahoma:** United States *NOTIS*
    Access: TN3270 `uokmvsa.backbone.uoknor.edu` ▶ tab to APPLICATION: ▶ enter `olin`

3-946 **University of Oregon:** United States *INNOPAC*
    Access: `janus.uoregon.edu` ▶ at the first prompt enter `janus`

3-947 **University of Otago:** New Zealand *DYNIX*
    Access: `libcat.otago.ac.nz` ▶ at the first prompt enter `libcat`

3-948 **University of Ottawa:** Canada *DYNIX*
    Access: `lib.uottawa.ca 3001`

3-949 **University of Pennsylvania Law School Library:** United States *INNOPAC*
    Access: `lola.law.upenn.edu` ▶ at the first prompt enter `lola`

3-950 **University of Pennsylvania:** United States *NOTIS*
    Access: `pennlib.upenn.edu` ▶ press ↵ ▶ press ↵

3-951 **University of Pittsburgh:** United States *NOTIS*
    Access: `gate.cis.pitt.edu` ▶ at the first prompt enter `pittcat`

3-952 **University of Plymouth:** United Kingdom *LIBERTAS*
    Access: `sun.nsf.ac.uk` ▶ at the first prompt enter `janet` ▶ wait for the prompt `Password:` ▶ press ↵ ▶ wait for the prompt `Hostname:` ▶ enter `uk.ac.plym.lib` ▶ wait for the prompt `Username:` ▶ enter `library`

3-953 **University of Pretoria:** South Africa *DOBIS/LIBIS*
    Access: `prefect.ee.up.ac.za` ▶ at the first prompt enter `libis`

3-954 **University of Prince Edward Island:** Canada *DRA*
    Access: TN3270 `lib.cs.upei.ca` or `lib.cs.upei.ca` ▶ at the first prompt enter `bobcat`

3-955 **University of Puerto Rico:** United States *custom*
    Access: `136.145.2.10` ◗ tab to COMMAND: ◗ enter `dial vtam` ◗ press ↵ ◗ press ↵ ◗ you will see a blank screen ◗ enter `luup`

3-956 **University of Puget Sound:** United States *INNOPAC*
    Access: `192.124.98.2` ◗ at the first prompt enter `library`

3-957 **University of Queensland:** Australia *PALS*
    Access: `libsys.campus.uq.oz.au`

3-958 **University of Rhode Island:** United States (Access via **Rhode Island Higher Education Library Information Network**)

3-959 **University of Rochester:** United States *GEAC*
    Access: `128.151.226.71` ◗ press ↵ ◗ wait for the prompt that ends in NOT RECOGNIZED BY THE SYSTEM ◗ press ↵

3-960 **University of San Diego:** United States *INNOPAC*
    Access: `sally.acusd.edu` ◗ at the first prompt enter `library`

3-961 **University of San Francisco:** United States *INNOPAC*
    Access: `138.202.29.1` ◗ at the first prompt enter `library`

3-962 **University of Saskatchewan:** Canada *GEAC*
    Access: `sklib.usask.ca` ◗ at the first prompt enter `sonia`

3-963 **University of South Australia:** Australia *DYNIX*
    Access: `library.unisa.edu.au`

3-964 **University of South Florida:** United States (Access via **Florida State University**)

3-965 **University of Southern Colorado:** United States *DYNIX*
    Access: `starburst.uscolo.edu` ◗ at the first prompt enter `publ` ◗ wait for the prompt `Password?` ◗ enter `usc`

3-966 **University of Southern Indiana:** United States *NOTIS*
    Access: TN3270 `lib.cc.purdue.edu` ◗ at the first prompt enter `remote` ◗ press ↵ ◗ enter `usicat`

3-967 **University of Southern Maine:** United States (Access via **University of Maine Library System**)

3-968 **University of Southern Mississippi:** United States *CLSI*
    Access: `library.lib.usm.edu` ◗ at the first prompt enter `oscar`

3-969 **University of Southern Queensland:** Australia *VTLS*
    Access: `library.usq.edu.au` ◗ at the first prompt enter `hello libbie.vtls`

3-970 **University of St. Thomas—Chaska Center:** United States *DYNIX*
    Access: `host.clic.edu` ◗ at the first prompt enter `tpac`

3-971 **University of St. Thomas—O'Shaughnessy-Frey Library:** United States *DYNIX*
    Access: `host.clic.edu` ⏵ at the first prompt enter `tpac`

3-972 **University of Sunderland:** United Kingdom *LS/2000*
    Access: `sun.nsf.ac.uk` ⏵ at the first prompt enter `janet` ⏵ wait for the prompt
    `Password:` ⏵ press ↵ ⏵ wait for the prompt `Hostname:` ⏵ enter
    `uk.ac.sundp.span` ⏵ wait for the prompt `SERVICE?` ⏵ enter `library` ⏵ wait for
    the prompt `Username:` ⏵ enter `library` ⏵ wait for the prompt `Password:`
    ⏵ enter `library`

3-973 **University of Surrey:** United Kingdom *custom*
    Access: `info-server.surrey.ac.uk` ⏵ at the first prompt enter `library`
    Access: `sun.nsf.ac.uk` ⏵ at the first prompt enter `janet` ⏵ wait for the prompt
    `Password:` ⏵ press ↵ ⏵ wait for the prompt `Hostname:` ⏵ enter `uk.ac.surr`
    ⏵ press ↵ ⏵ enter `library`

3-974 **University of Sussex:** United Kingdom *GEAC*
    Access: `sun.nsf.ac.uk` ⏵ at the first prompt enter `janet` ⏵ wait for the prompt
    `Password:` ⏵ press ↵ ⏵ wait for the prompt `Hostname:` ⏵ enter `uk.ac.susx.lib`

3-975 **University of Sydney Conservatorium of Music:** Australia (Access via **New South Wales Libraries**)

3-976 **University of Sydney:** Australia *custom*
    Access: `lib2.fisher.su.oz.au` ⏵ at the first prompt enter `library`

3-977 **University of Tasmania:** Australia *custom*
    Access: `library.utas.edu.au` ⏵ press ↵

3-978 **University of Technology—Sydney:** Australia (Access via **New South Wales Libraries**)

3-979 **University of Technology:** Australia *GEAC*
    Access: `opac.clann.edu.au` ⏵ press ↵ ⏵ enter in UTS   L119 Note: all caps three
    spaces

3-980 **University of Teesside:** United Kingdom *custom*
    Access: `sun.nsf.ac.uk` ⏵ at the first prompt enter `janet` ⏵ wait for the prompt
    `Password:` ⏵ press ↵ ⏵ wait for the prompt `Hostname:` ⏵ enter `uk.ac.tees.lib`
    ⏵ wait for the prompt `Login:` ⏵ enter `library` ⏵ wait for the prompt `Password?`
    ⏵ enter `library`

3-981 **University of Tennessee—Chatanooga:** United States *custom*
    Access: `library.utc.edu`

3-982 **University of Tennessee—Knoxville:** United States *GEAC*
    Access: `txh101.lib.utk.edu`

3-983 **University of Tennessee—Memphis Health Science Library:** United States *custom*
    Access: `utmem1.utmem.edu` ⏵ at the first prompt enter `harvey`

3-984 **University of Texas—Arlington:** United States *NOTIS*

> **Access:** `admin.uta.edu` ▶ press ↵ ▶ wait for the prompt `TERMINAL TYPE:` ▶ enter `vt100` ▶ you will see a VTAM menu ▶ enter `notis` ▶ you will see a CICS logo ▶ press ↵

3-985 **University of Texas—Austin:** United States *UTCAT*

> **Access:** `utcat.utexas.edu` ▶ press ↵ ▶ wait for the prompt `GO` ▶ press ↵
>
> **Access:** `panam2.panam.edu` ▶ at the first prompt enter `packey` ▶ pick `Other Library Catalogs` from the Texas-Pan American Library main menu

3-986 **University of Texas Health Center—Tyler:** United States *custom*

> **Access:** `athena.uthscsa.edu` ▶ at the first prompt enter `lis`

3-987 **University of Texas Health Science Center—San Antonio:** United States *custom*

> **Access:** `athena.uthscsa.edu` ▶ at the first prompt enter `lis`

3-988 **University of Texas Medical Branch—Galveston Moody Medical Library Automated Catalog:** United States *custom*

> **Access:** `ibm.gal.utexas.edu`
>
> **Access:** `panam2.panam.edu` ▶ at the first prompt enter `packey` ▶ pick `Other Library Catalogs` from the Texas-Pan American Library main menu

3-989 **University of Texas Southwestern Medical Center:** United States *UNICORN*

> **Access:** `library.swmed.edu` ▶ at the first prompt enter `tlntutsw` ▶ wait for the prompt `Password:` ▶ enter `library`

3-990 **University of Texas—Austin Tarlton Law Library (TALLONS):** United States *INNOPAC*

> **Access:** `tallons.law.utexas.edu` ▶ at the first prompt enter `library`

3-991 **University of Texas—Dallas:** United States *NOTIS*

> **Access:** `ibm.utdallas.edu` ▶ at the first prompt enter `VT10X` ▶ press ↵ ▶ enter `library` ▶ clear the screen
>
> **Access:** `TN3270 vm.utdallas.edu` ▶ press ↵ ▶ enter `library` ▶ clear the screen

3-992 **University of Texas—San Antonio:** United States *custom*

> **Access:** `utsaibm.utsa.edu` ▶ press ↵ ▶ you will see a UTSA screen ▶ enter `library`

3-993 **University of Texas—Pan American Library:** United States *DRA*

> **Access:** `panam2.panam.edu` ▶ at the first prompt enter `packey`

3-994 **University of Texas—Permian Basin Library:** United States *DRA*

> **Access:** `panam2.panam.edu` ▶ at the first prompt enter `packey` ▶ pick `Other Library Catalogs` from the Texas-Pan American Library main menu

3-995 **University of the District of Columbia:** United States (Access via **Washington Research Library Consortium**)

3-996 **University of the Pacific:** United States *INNOPAC*
    Access: `pacificat.lib.uop.edu` ▶ at the first prompt enter `library`

3-997 **University of the West of England:** United Kingdom *LIBERTAS*
    Access: `sun.nsf.ac.uk` ▶ at the first prompt enter `janet` ▶ wait for the prompt
    `Password:` ▶ press ↵ ▶ wait for the prompt `Hostname:` ▶ enter `uk.ac.uwe.lib`

3-998 **University of Toledo:** United States *NOTIS*
    Access: `TN3270 uoft01.utoledo.edu` ▶ You will see a UT logo screen ▶ press ↵
    ▶ wait for the prompt that ends in `commands...` ▶ enter `dial mvs` ▶ wait for the
    prompt that ends in `mvs ####` ▶ enter `utmost`

3-999 **University of Toronto:** Canada *DRA*
    Access: `vax.library.utoronto.ca` ▶ at the first prompt enter `utlink`

3-1000 **University of Tulsa:** United States *custom*
    Access: `vax2.utulsa.edu` ▶ at the first prompt enter `lias`

3-1001 **University of Umea:** Sweden *custom*
    Access: `TN3270 libum.umu.se` ▶ press ↵ ▶ you will see the top menu; select 4 to
    change language

3-1002 **University of Utah:** United States *NOTIS*
    Access: `TN3270 lib.utah.edu` ▶ tab to `COMMAND:` ▶ press ↵

3-1003 **University of Vermont:** United States *NOTIS*
    Access: `luis.uvm.edu` ▶ wait for the prompt `Terminal Type:` ▶ enter `VT100`

3-1004 **University of Victoria:** Canada *NOTIS*
    Access: `mpg.uvic.ca`

3-1005 **University of Virginia Health Sciences Library:** United States *custom*
    Access: `ublan.acc.virginia.edu` ▶ press ↵ ▶ wait for the prompt > ▶ enter
    `connect health`

3-1006 **University of Virginia Law Library:** United States *INNOPAC*
    Access: `ublan.virginia.edu` ▶ press ↵ ▶ press ↵ ▶ wait for the prompt > ▶ enter
    `connect law`

3-1007 **University of Virginia:** United States *NOTIS*
    Access: `ublan.acc.virginia.edu` ▶ press ↵ ▶ wait for the prompt >
    ▶ enter `c virgo` ▶ wait for the prompt `ENTER TERMINAL TYPE:` ▶ enter `VT100`

3-1008 **University of Wales—Aberystwyth:** United Kingdom *LIBERTAS*
    Access: `sun.nsf.ac.uk` ▶ at the first prompt enter `janet` ▶ wait for the prompt
    `Password:` ▶ press ↵ ▶ wait for the prompt `Hostname:` ▶ enter `uk.ac.aber.lib`
    ▶ wait for the prompt `Username:` ▶ enter `library`

3-1009 **University of Warwick:** United Kingdom *BLCMP*
    Access: `opac.warwick.ac.uk`

3-1010 University of Washington—Gallagher Law Library: United States *custom*
      Access: uwin.u.washington.edu

3-1011 University of Washington: United States *custom*
      Access: uwin.u.washington.edu

3-1012 University of Waterloo: Canada *GEAC*
      Access: watcat.uwaterloo.ca

3-1013 University of West Florida: United States (Access via **Florida State University**)

3-1014 University of Western Australia: Australia *URICA*
      Access: library.uwa.oz.au ▶ at the first prompt enter library

3-1015 University of Western Ontario: Canada *GEAC*
      Access: geac.lib.uwo.ca

3-1016 University of Western Sydney Libraries: Australia (Access via **New South Wales Libraries**)

3-1017 University of Westminster: United Kingdom *LIBERTAS*
      Access: sun.nsf.ac.uk ▶ at the first prompt enter janet ▶ wait for the prompt
      Password: ▶ press ↵ ▶ wait for the prompt Hostname: ▶ enter uk.ac.wmin.lib
      ▶ wait for the prompt Username: ▶ enter library

3-1018 University of Windsor: Canada *NOTIS*
      Access: library.uwindsor.ca

3-1019 University of Wisconsin—Superior: United States *LS/2000*
      Access: sail.uwsuper.edu ▶ press ↵

3-1020 University of Wisconsin—Eau Claire: United States *LS/2000*
      Access: lib.uwec.edu ▶ press ↵

3-1021 University of Wisconsin—Green Bay: United States *LS/2000*
      Access: gbls2k.uwgb.edu ▶ press ↵

3-1022 University of Wisconsin—La Crosse: United States *LS/2000*
      Access: library.acs.uwlax.edu

3-1023 University of Wisconsin—Madison: United States *custom*
      Access: lego.adp.wisc.edu
      Access: TN3270 lib.cc.purdue.edu
      Access: thorplus.lib.purdue.edu ▶ at the first prompt enter catnet

3-1024 University of Wisconsin—Milwaukee: United States *custom*
      Access: nls.lib.uwm.edu

3-1025 University of Wisconsin—Oshkosh: United States *LS/2000*
      Access: polk.cis.uwosh.edu ▶ press ↵

3-1026 **University of Wisconsin—Parkside:** United States *LS/2000*
    Access: `library.uwp.edu` ▸ press ↵

3-1027 **University of Wisconsin—River Falls:** United States *LS2000*
    Access: `davee.dl.uwrf.edu`

3-1028 **University of Wisconsin—Stevens Point:** United States *LS2000*
    Access: `lib.uwsp.edu` ▸ at the first prompt enter `lib`

3-1029 **University of Wisconsin—Whitewater:** United States *LS/2000*
    Access: `lib.uww.edu`

3-1030 **University of Wollongong:** Australia (Access via **New South Wales Libraries**)

3-1031 **University of Wolverhampton:** United Kingdom *custom*
    Access: `library.wlv.ac.uk`

3-1032 **University of Wyoming:** United States (Access via **CARL**)

3-1033 **University of York:** United Kingdom *DYNIX*
    Access: `sun.nsf.ac.uk` ▸ at the first prompt enter `janet` ▸ wait for the prompt
    `Password:` ▸ press ↵ ▸ wait for the prompt `Hostname:` ▸ enter
    `uk.ac.york.library`

3-1034 **University System of Georgia On-Line Library Information System:** United States (Access via **Georgia On-Line Library Information System**)

3-1035 **Utrecht University:** Netherlands *GEAC*
    Access: `ruut.cc.ruu.nl` ▸ at the first prompt enter `brunet` ▸ press ↵

3-1036 **Vaasan University:** Finland *VTLS*
    Access: `kustaa.uwasa.fi` ▸ at the first prompt enter `hello`
    yourname,`user.clas01` ▸ you will see a terminal-type menu ▸ enter   ▸ wait for the
    prompt that ends in `tai?` ▸ enter `100` ▸ wait for the prompt that ends in `komento`
    ▸ enter `/lang 1` ▸ press ↵ ▸ enter ?

3-1037 **Vail Public Library:** United States (Access via **MARMOT Library Network**)

3-1038 **Valdosta State College Odum Library:** United States *DRA*
    Access: `131.144.8.233` ▸ at the first prompt enter `library`
    Access: `grits.valdosta.peachnet.edu` ▸ at the first prompt enter `guest`
    ▸ wait for the prompt `Password:` ▸ enter `dragon` ▸ arrow to `<DRAGON>`

3-1039 **Valencia Community College—Florida:** United States *NOTIS*
    Access: `luis.nerdc.ufl.edu` ▸ at the first prompt enter `luis` ▸ select LINCC
    (`Florida Community Colleges`) from the menu

3-1040 **Vanderbilt University:** United States *NOTIS*
    Access: `ctrvax.vanderbilt.edu` ▸ at the first prompt enter `acorn`

3-1041 Vermont College: United States *custom*

    Access: `lib.middlebury.edu` ◗ at the first prompt enter `lib` ◗ you will see the Middlebury College Library system menu ◗ enter 1 ◗ you will see a `Library resource` menu ◗ enter 1 ◗ press ↵ until you get to the main catalog menu, where you will see a branch library selection menu ◗ press ↵

3-1042 Vermont Regional Libraries: United States (Access via **Middlebury College**)

3-1043 Vermont State Colleges: United States *custom*

    Access: `lib.middlebury.edu` ◗ at the first prompt enter `lib` ◗ you will see the Middlebury College Library system menu ◗ enter 1 ◗ you will see a `Library resource` menu ◗ enter 1 ◗ press ↵ until you get to the main catalog menu, where you will see a branch library selection menu ◗ press ↵

3-1044 Vermont State Library—Montpelier: United States (Access via **Middlebury College**)

3-1045 Vermont State—Department of Libraries: United States *custom*

    Access: `lib.middlebury.edu`

3-1046 Vermont Technical College: United States (Access via **Middlebury College**)

3-1047 Veterinaermedizinischen Universitaet Wien: Austria (Access via **Austrian Academic Library Network**)

3-1048 Vicksburg Community Library: United States (Access via **KELLY**)

3-1049 Vicksburg Community Schools: United States (Access via **KELLY**)

3-1050 Victoria University of Technology: Australia *INNOPAC*

    Access: `zebra.vut.edu.au` ◗ at the first prompt enter `library`

3-1051 Victoria University of Wellington: New Zealand *DYNIX*

    Access: `library.vuw.ac.nz` ◗ press ↵ ◗ wait for the prompt `logon:` ◗ enter `opac`

3-1052 Vincennes University: United States *NOTIS*

    Access: TN3270 `lib.cc.purdue.edu` ◗ at the first prompt enter `remote` ◗ press ↵ ◗ enter `vucat`

3-1053 Virginia Commonwealth University: United States *NOTIS*

    Access: TN3270 `vcuvm1.ucc.vcu.edu` ◗ tab to COMMAND: ◗ enter `dial vtam`

3-1054 Virginia Military Institute: United States *DRA*

    Access: `vax.vmi.edu` ◗ at the first prompt enter `library`

3-1055 Virginia Tech: United States *VTLS*

    Access: `vtls.vt.edu` ◗ press ↵ ◗ press ↵

3-1056 Vrije Universiteit Brussels: Belgium *custom*

    Access: `rc1.vub.ac.be` ◗ at the first prompt enter `vubis`

3-1057 **Vrije Universiteit:** Netherlands *CLSI*
  Access: `ubvucat.vu.nl`

3-1058 **Wake Forest University:** United States *DYNIX*
  Access: `lib.wfunet.wfu.edu` ▶ at the first prompt enter `wake`

3-1059 **Washburn University:** United States *INNOPAC*
  Access: `lib.wuacc.edu` ▶ at the first prompt enter `lib`

3-1060 **Washington and Lee University:** United States *INNOPAC*
  Access: `iii.library.wlu.edu` ▶ at the first prompt enter `library`

3-1061 **Washington College:** United States *INNOPAC*
  Access: `library.washcoll.edu` ▶ at the first prompt enter `library`

3-1062 **Washington Research Library Consortium:** United States *custom*
  Access: TN3270 `gmuibm.gmu.edu`

3-1063 **Washington State University and Eastern Washington University:** United States *custom*
  Access: `jaguar.csc.wsu.edu` ▶ at the first prompt enter `cougalog`
  Access: TN3270 `wsuvm1.csc.wsu.edu` ▶ tab to COMMAND: ▶ enter `dial vtam`

3-1064 **Washington University of St. Louis Medical Library:** United States *custom*
  Access: `mcftcp.wustl.edu` ▶ at the first prompt enter `catalog`

3-1065 **Washington University of St. Louis:** United States *NOTIS*
  Access: `library.wustl.edu`

3-1066 **Watervliet District Library:** United States (Access via **KELLY**)

3-1067 **Wayne County Community College:** United States (Access via **Detroit Area Library Network**)

3-1068 **Wayne State College:** United States *INNOPAC*
  Access: `nscs.unl.edu` ▶ at the first prompt enter `library`

3-1069 **Wayne State University:** United States *NOTIS*
  Access: `hme4.merit.edu` ▶ at the first prompt enter `wsunet`
  Access: TN3270 `cms.cc.wayne.edu` ▶ tab to COMMAND: ▶ enter `dial vtam`
   ▶ press ↵ ▶ enter `luis`

3-1070 **Weber State University:** United States *DYNIX*
  Access: `lib.weber.edu` ▶ at the first prompt enter `pac`

3-1071 **Webster, Colorado, Library:** United States (Access via **CARL**)

3-1072 **Weizmann Institute of Science:** Israel (Access via **Hebrew University**)

3-1073 **Wellesley College:** United States *custom*
  Access: `blc.lrc.northeastern.edu`
  Access: `luna.wellesley.edu`

3-1074 **Wentworth Institute:** United States (Access via **Fenway Libraries Online, Inc.**)

3-1075 **Wesleyan University, Connecticut College, and Trinity College:** United States *NOTIS*
Access: `library.wesleyan.edu` ▶ press ↵

3-1076 **West Boylston, Colorado, Library:** United States (Access via **CARL**)

3-1077 **West Georgia College—Carrollton:** United States (Access via **Georgia On-Line Library Information System**)

3-1078 **West Georgia College:** United States *UNICORN*
Access: `library.isil.westga.edu` ▶ at the first prompt enter `public`
▶ wait for the prompt `Password:` ▶ enter `public`

3-1079 **West Michigan Information Network (WESTNET):** United States (See **KELLY**)

3-1080 **West Springfield Public Library:** United States (Access via **CARL**)

3-1081 **West Virginia University:** United States *NOTIS*
Access: `e3270.wvnet.edu` ▶ enter terminal type ▶ press ↵ ▶ enter 5

3-1082 **Westborough Public Library:** United States (Access via **CARL**)

3-1083 **Western Illinois Library System:** United States (Access via **ILLINET On-line Catalog**)

3-1084 **Western Illinois University:** United States (Access via **ILLINET On-line Catalog**)

3-1085 **Western Mass Regional Library:** United States (Access via **CARL**)

3-1086 **Western Michigan Regional Online Catalog:** United States (See **KELLY**)

3-1087 **Western Michigan University:** United States *NOTIS*
Access: `TN3270 library.wmich.edu`
Access: `hme4.merit.edu` ▶ at the first prompt enter `wmu-finder` ▶ press ↵
▶ enter w

3-1088 **Western Nevada Community College:** United States (Access via **Nevada Academic Libraries Information System**)

3-1089 **Western New England College:** United States (Access via **CARL**)

3-1090 **Western Oregon State College:** United States *INNOPAC*
Access: `140.211.118.20`

3-1091 **Western State College Library:** United States (Access via **MARMOT Library Network**)

3-1092 **Westfield State College:** United States (Access via **CARL**)

3-1093 **Westminster College:** United States *DYNIX*
Access: `libr.wcslc.edu` ▶ at the first prompt enter `pac`

3-1094 **Westmont College:** United States *DYNIX*
Access: `westmx.westmont.edu` ▶ at the first prompt enter `public`

3-1095 **Wheelock College:** United States (Access via **Fenway Libraries Online, Inc.**)

3-1096 **Whitinsville Social Library:** United States (Access via **CARL**)

3-1097 **Wichita State University:** United States *NOTIS*
    Access: TN3270 twsuvm.uc.twsu.edu   ▶ press ↵ ▶ enter dial menu

3-1098 **Widener University School of Law:** United States *INNOPAC*
    Access: lawcat.widener.edu ▶ at the first prompt enter library

3-1099 **Wien, Universitaetsbibliothek:** Austria (Access via **Austrian Academic Library Network**)

3-1100 **Wilbraham, Colorado, Public Library:** United States (Access via **CARL**)

3-1101 **Wilfred Laurier University:** Canada *custom*
    Access: mach1.wlu.ca ▶ at the first prompt enter public

3-1102 **Willamette University:** United States *INNOPAC*
    Access: library.willamette.edu

3-1103 **Williams College:** United States *INNOPAC*
    Access: library.williams.edu

3-1104 **Williamstown Public Library:** United States (Access via **CARL**)

3-1105 **Winchendon, Colorado, Library:** United States (Access via **CARL**)

3-1106 **Wirtschaftsuniversitaet Wien:** Austria (Access via **Austrian Academic Library Network**)

3-1107 **Worcester Polytechnic Institute:** United States (Access via **CARL**)

3-1108 **Worcester Public Library:** United States (Access via **CARL**)

3-1109 **Worcester State College:** United States (Access via **CARL**)

3-1110 **Wright State University:** United States *INNOPAC*
    Access: wsuol2.wright.edu ▶ at the first prompt enter library
    Access: cat.ohiolink.edu

3-1111 **Wye College:** United Kingdom (Access via **University of London Central Libertas Consortium**)

3-1112 **Xavier University:** United States *INNOPAC*
    Access: xulas.xu.edu ▶ at the first prompt enter library

3-1113 **Yale University:** United States *NOTIS*
    Access: umpg.ycc.yale.edu 6520

3-1114 **York University:** Canada *NOTIS*
    Access: yorkline.yorku.ca

3-1115 **Youngstown State University:** United States *VTLS*
    Access: library.ysu.edu ▶ at the first prompt enter library

3-1116 **Zentralbibliothek für Physik in Wien:** Austria (Access via **Austrian Academic Library Network**)

3-1117 **Zentralbibliothek Zurich:** Switzerland *GEAC*

   Access: nuz.unizh.ch ▶ press ↵ ▶ wait for the prompt enter: ▶ enter call e100 ▶ press ↵

4. ARCHIE SERVERS

The host addresses listed below are the addresses of the Archie servers, which maintain searchable indexes of the contents of anonymous-FTP sites. These hosts also provide public Archie clients which you can access using telnet. Simply log in as `archie`. Note that these public Archie clients are overused; if at all possible, use a client running on your local host. Archie client software is available via FTP from `ftp.ans.net` in the `/pub/archie/clients/` directory and documentation for it is in `/pub/archie/doc/`. For more information on clients and servers, please see "An Internet Refresher" in the introduction. Below is a list of important public Archie client commands:

- `about`   a blurb about Archie
- `bugs`   known bugs and undesirable features
- `email`   how to contact the Archie e-mail interface
- `help`   this message
- `list`   list the sites in the Archie database
- `mail`   mail output to a user
- `prog`   search the database for a file
- `site`   list the files at an archive site
- `whatis`   search for keyword in the software description database
- `quit`   exit Archie

Entry Format:

Item
Number

5-n   **Country:** `server address`   Name of server or hosting institution
        i `contact address`

Where to Find It: When you log into the Archie at SURA, the current most up-to-date list of other Archie servers is displayed.

Netiquette: To decrease traffic on international network connections, Archie servers have been set up in many countries. Be considerate and don't use an international server unless you have no other option.

Entries:

4-1 **USA:** `ds.internic.net`   AT&T InterNIC Directory and Databaserver
   i `admin@ds.internic.net`

4-2 **USA (MD):** `archie.sura.net`   Server at SURAnet
   i `archie-admin@sura.net`

4-3 **USA (NE):** `archie.unl.edu`   University of Nebraska, Lincoln
   i `archie-admin@unl.edu`

4-4 **USA (NJ):** `archie.rutgers.edu`   Rutgers University Archie server
   i `archie-l@archie.rutgers.edu`

4-5 **USA (NY):** `archie.ans.net`   Advanced Network & Services, Inc
   i `archie-admin@ans.net`

4-6 **Australia:** `archie.au`   Melbourne
   i `ccw@archie.au`

4-7 **Austria:** `archie.univie.ac.at`   Austrian Archie server

4-8 **Austria:** `archie.edvz.uni-linz.ac.at`   Johannes Kepler University, Linz

4-9 **Canada:** `quiche.cs.mcgill.ca`   McGill School of Computer Science Archie server
   i `archie-l@cs.mcgill.ca`

4-10 **Canada:** `archie.uqam.ca`   University of Quebec

4-11 **England:** `archie.doc.ic.ac.uk`   Imperial College, London
   i `ukuug-soft@doc.ic.ac.uk`

4-12 **Finland:** `archie.funet.fi`   Finnish University and Research Network server

4-13 **Germany:** `archie.th-darmstadt.de`   Technische Hochschule Darmstadt
   i `archie-admin@archie.th-darmstadt.de`

4-14 **Israel:** `archie.ac.il`   Hebrew University of Jerusalem
   i `archie-admin@archie.ac.il`

4-15 **Italy:** `archie.unipi.it`   Italian Archie server

4-16 **Japan:** `archie.wide.ad.jp`   Japanese Archie server
   i `jp-archie-admin@wide.ad.jp`

4-17 **Korea:** `archie.sogang.ac.kr`   Sogang University

4-18 **Korea:** `archie.kr`   Telecom Research Center
   i `archie-admin@archie.kr`

4-19 **New Zealand:** `archie.nz`   Victoria University, Wellington

4-20   **Spain:** `archie.rediris.es`   RedIRIS
         i `infoiris@rediris.es`

4-21   **Sweden:** `archie.luth.se`   University of Lulea
         i `archie-workers@dc.luth.se`

4-22   **Switzerland:** `archie.switch.ch`   SWITCH Archie server
         i `switchinfo@switch.ch`

4-23   **Taiwan:** `archie.ncu.edu.tw`   National Central University, Chung-li
         i `archie-l@sparc5.src.ncu.edu.tw`

5. ANONYMOUS FTP ARCHIVES

Implementations of the File Transfer Protocol (FTP) exist for practically all computer platforms, though it was originally designed for use on Unix machines. When using FTP there are a few things you should be aware of. Unlike host and e-mail addresses, file names on many archive systems are case-sensitive; you must type in the file and directory name exactly as you see them listed. When you retrieve a file that is not plain text—for example, a compressed file, which might end in `.zip` or `.Z`—you must put FTP in binary mode, or the file will not be retrieved correctly. What follows is a quick reference list of FTP commands:

- `cd [dir]` change directory on remote machine
- `ls` list contents of remote directory.
- `get [file]` transfer the remote file.
- `mget [files]` transfer many remote files (you can use patterns, e.g., `*.txt`)
- `binary` set file-transfer mode to binary (for compressed files, programs, etc.)
- `ascii` set file-transfer mode to text
- `help` get a list of commands

Entry Format:

Item
Number

5-n   **FTP Archive name:** `host address`
      i `contact address`
         Description of FTP archive provided by hosting institution.
      Contents: list of what's unique to the archive
      Mirrors: `host address` of mirror archives

Where to Find It: There are a number of lists of FTP archives floating around on the net, and there are also some gophers that provide access to FTP archives. Please see Chapter 11 (Online Resource Lists) for their addresses. The first step in creating the entries in this chapter was to gather information from those sources. I knew that a large number of the FTP sites listed would no longer be in service, or would be too small to take the load that wide publicity would entail, so I needed to both verify the existence of the sites and get permission to list them. These two things were done, and the "contents" information that I have listed was provided by the maintainer of the archive.

Netiquette: Most anonymous FTP archives exist purely by the goodwill of their hosting institutions. Usually they are maintained by volunteers and are run on computers that are used for "real work." So if use of the archives begins to affect the performance of the host computers, the archives will be discontinued. This means you should follow some simple rules:

- Keep connection times short!
- Search for what you want with Archie first, then go and get it directly, so that you don't have to spend lots of time browsing.
- If you do need to browse, then download the index file, disconnect from the FTP archive, and reconnect later once you have found what you want in the index.
- Do your downloading after hours (and remember to take into account time-zone changes).
- Download files from a mirror archive close to you. Mirrors are almost always less busy than the source archives. Use them and you'll be less likely to have your connection refused!

Entries:

5-1   **a2i Subscriber Archive:** `ftp.rahul.net`

   i `support@rahul.net`

   A service to a2i subscribers who wish to make files available to others on the Internet. Individual subscribers maintain their own subdirectories.

   Contents: Check archive for details.

   Comments: Subscribers come and go, and their archives may or may not have any long-term permanence.

5-2   **Ada Joint Program Office (AJPO) FTP server:** `ajpo.sei.cmu.edu`

   i `postmaster@ajpo.sei.cmu.edu`

   DoD's Ada Joint Program Office (AJPO)-sponsored host archives a wide range of information on the Ada programming language and the Ada community. The host is supported by the Ada Information Clearinghouse (AdaIC).

   Contents: look in `/public`

   `/acvc-current/` Ada Compiler Validation Capability (ACVC) test suite
   `/acvc-9x/` Pointer file to ACVC 9X-Basic compiler-validation test suite
   `/ada-adoption-hbk/` Ada Adoption Handbook, A Program Manager's Guide
   `/ada-comment/` complete list of Ada Commentaries
   `/ada-info/` AdaIC files, general info for Ada community
   `/ada-lsn/` Ada Language Study Notes (Ada 9X)
   `/ada-ui/` ISO WG9 Ada Uniformity Issues (UIs) and meeting minutes
   `/ada9x/` Ada 9X Project Office reports and announcements
   `/adanews/` Issues of AdaIC newsletter
   `/adasage/` Draft plan for evolving AdaSAGE application-development

`/adastyle/` suggested Ada Style Guide

`/artdata/` Ada Runtime Environment Working Group (ARTEWG) info files

`/asis/` Ada Semantic Interface Specification (ASIS) CASE tool interface

`/atip/` AJPO's Ada Technology Insertion Program (ATIP) (source code)

`/atip/1553` General Avionics Data Bus Tool Kit

`/atip/adar/` Ada Decimal Arithmetic and Representations

`/atip/samedl/` SQL Ada Module Description Language Development Environment

`/bindings/` AdaIC report, "Available Ada Bindings"

`/comp-lang-ada/` FAQ files and archived digests from Usenet newsgroup `comp.lang.ada`

`/crease/` AdaIC report, list of universities who offer Ada courses

`/ev-info/` APSE Evaluation & Validation Team info files

`/infoada/` info-ada mailing list archived digests & other info files

`/irds draft/` Ada binding to draft IRDS Standard

`/kitdata/` Kernel Ada Programming Support Environment (KAPSE) Interface Team info files

`/lrm/` Ada Language Reference Manual, ANSI/MIL-STD-1815A (1983)

`/misc/` miscellaneous reports

`/pcis/` Portable Common Interface Set (PCIS) Programme info files

`/piwg/` SIGAda Performance Issues Working Group (PIWG) benchmark test suite

`/rationale/` "The Rationale for the Design of the Ada Programming Language"(1986)

`/RRG/` ISO/JTC1/SC22/WG9 Real-Time Rapporteur Group (RRG) documents

`/tools/` Customized searches from AdaIC Products and Tools database

Mirrors: `ftp.cnam.fr` (European FTP server); Ada information is partially mirrored at `wuarchive.wustl.edu`

5-3 **Andrew User Interface System:** `emsworth.andrew.cmu.edu`

i `info-andrew-request@andrew.cmu.edu`

Source and other information related to the Andrew User Interface System.

Contents: AUIS is a suite of integrated applications—word processor, help browser, electronic mail and bulletin boards, and so on—together with a collection of embeddable objects/editors such as text, drawings, images, table/spreadsheet, equations, and rasters. Source code and tools are provided in the archive (see the `README`) so it is easy to add new object/editors and applications. The archive contains the source code and also past contents of the Usenet newsgroup `comp.soft-sys.andrew`.

Comments: This archive may move to `ftp.cs.cmu.edu`

Mirrors: With each X Windows release there is an Andrew release included. This is mirrored to all the FTP sites that mirror the X tape.

5-4 **ANU Bioinformatics:** `life.anu.edu.au`

i `david.green@anu.edu.au` or `ftp-manager@life.anu.edu.au`

Biological FTP service of the Australian National University's Bioinformatics Facility.

Contents: Range of software, images, databases, bibliographies, and documents organized under (mainly) biological themes:

`/pub/complex_systems` artificial life, chaos, fractals, genetic algorithms, etc.

`/pub/biodiversity` Conservation and taxonomy

`/pub/molecular_biology` Essential software, bibliographies, etc.

`/pub/weather` Current weather images for Australia, North America, and Europe/Africa

`/pub/landscape_ecology` Landscapes, biogeography, GIS, etc.

`/pub/landscape_ecology/firenet` information service on landscape fires

`/pub/landscape_ecology/pollen` paleobiology

`/pub/netkit` Essential software for using online services: gopher, WWW, etc.

`/pub/viruses` Virus groups and plant viruses—-NOT computer viruses

`/pub/bioinformation` Standards, FAQs, etc., on bioinformatics

Comments: See the file `/pub/policy.txt` for procedures and conditions.

5-5 **ANU News Archive:** `kuhub.cc.ukans.edu`

i `sloane@kuhub.cc.ukans.edu`

Distribution of ANU News, a Usenet News package for VMS.

Contents: ANU News is a Usenet News package which provides both NNTP client and local database support and runs under the VMS system operating on both VAX and ALPHA AXP hardware.

5-6 **Arabidopsis Research Companion Archive:** `weeds.mgh.harvard.edu`

i `curator@weeds.mgh.harvard.edu`

Archive of software, update files, and general information provided for the worldwide Arabidopsis research community.

Contents:

`/aatdb/` Software and Updates for AAtDB

`/aatdb-info/` Information about AAtDB

`/acedb_dev/` Development archives for the ACEDB software

`/acedb_doc/` Documentation for the ACEDB software

`/arab-gen/` Archive of the BioSci Arabidopsis Genome group

`/compleat_guide` Compleat Guide by Caroline Dean and David Flanders

`/images/` Arabidopsis strain, RFLP and restriction digest Images

`/maps/` Tables and Maps on Arabidopsis genetics

`/nottingham` The Nottingham Arabidopsis Stock Centre Catalog

Comments: The Compleat Guide is available as an archive of WriteNow 3.0 Macintosh documents. The Nottingham Seed list is available as an archive of Microsoft Word Macintosh documents. The source and update files for AAtDB and the ACEDB development archives are compressed tar files; remember to transfer these in binary mode.

5-7 **Astronomy and Earth Sciences Archive at Stanford:** `hanauma.stanford.edu`

i `joe@sep.stanford.edu`

Astronomy/Earth Science-oriented material.

Contents:

`Earth_Topo/` A USGS Earth Topography database, decimated to make it smaller

`SuperiorMorse4Unix/` A generic morse-code practice program for Unix workstations

`Temperature_Monitor/` Source code and hardware specifications for a program to monitor computer-room temperature. Warns if things go wrong, and shuts down the computer if nobody heeds the warnings

`World_Map/` The vector information from the CIA World Database II, in compressed format

`astro/` Various astronomy stuff: programs to calculate moon phase, sunrise and sunset times, satellite tracking, etc.

`graphics/` The vplot graphics system, a device-independent Unix plotting package. Only contains the bottom-level routines that support the virtual graphics device on a variety of workstations

`tp_snoqualmie/` Some "Twin Peaks" stuff

`zhongwen/` Chinese-language X fonts

`Hershey_Fonts.tar.Z/` The Hershey Fonts distributed several years ago. Includes vectors defining several English, Russian, Greek, Math, Symbol, and Japanese fonts. The English fonts are now widely used in vector graphics packages, but the Japanese vector font information may not be available anywhere else

Comments: All the programs at this site are for Unix computers, NOT PCs or Macs. They are all source, not binaries. Other sites should grab copies of everything on `hanauma.stanford.edu` they find useful, because this archive may soon be defunct.

5-8 **AUC FTP Archive:** `ftp.iesd.auc.dk`

i `ftp@iesd.auc.dk`

University of Aalborg, Denmark Mathematics and Computer Science Archive.

Contents:

`/pub/emacs-lisp/` AUC TeX

`/pub/ObjC/` GNU Objective C

`/pub/CoCo/` Tandy Color Computer Archives

`/pub/lpmud/` Deeper Trouble MUD

`/pub/Tav`

5-9 **Automated Reasoning Programme FTP Archive:** `arp.anu.edu.au`

i `postmaster@arp.anu.edu.au`

The archive maintained by the Automated Reasoning Programme Research Group, Centre for Information Science Research, The Australian National University.

Contents: Programs and papers written by researchers associated with the Automated Reasoning Programme, and an archive of e-news groups related to automated reasoning, artificial intelligence, and parallel computing.

5-10　**BayLISA Archive:** `ftp.baylisa.org`

i `bigmac@baylisa.org`

An archive for BayLISA, the Bay Area Large Installation System Adminitrators user group.

Contents: BayLISA main archive.

Comments: Most files are compressed, and must be transferred in binary mode.

5-11　**Brown University Public Archive:** `ftp.brown.edu`

i `postmaster@brown.edu` (best) or `Peter_DiCamillo@brown.edu` (alternate)

This archive is maintained by Computing and Information Services at Brown University in Providence, Rhode Island. Its main purpose is the distribution of software developed or modified at Brown University.

Contents: See README file

5-12　**California State University Sacramento:** `ftp.csus.edu`

i `archives@csus.edu`

Various software made available by University Computing and Communications Services, CSU Sacramento.

Contents:

- Banyan/VINES archive
- Vectrex (circa 1982 game system) archive
- Backup site for CMU/OpenVMS (TCP/IP for VMS)
- Miscellaneous tidbits

Comments: 24-hour, 7-day open access.

5-13　**Caltech Physics of Computation Laboratory Archive:** `hobiecat.pcmp.caltech.edu`

i `root@hobiecat.pcmp.caltech.edu`

Primarily analog VLSI stuff, maintained by Carver Mead's laboratory at Caltech.

Contents:

`/pub/chipmunk/` Caltech VLSI design tools (analog, wol, until, view)

`/pub/scanners/` Analog VLSI scanners

`/pub/aer/` Archive of Address-Event protocol/layout/tools

`/pub/anaprose/` Papers about analog VLSI

5-14　**Carnegie-Mellon University Artificial Intelligence Repository:** `ftp.cs.cmu.edu`

i `ai.repository@cs.cmu.edu.`

Collection of nearly all materials of interest to AI researchers, educators, practitioners and students.

Contents: Look in the `/user/ai` directory.

5-15　**Carnegie-Mellon University Networking Archive:** `ftp.net.cmu.edu`

i `dc0m+@andrew.cmu.edu`

This FTP archive is informally maintained by the Network Development (NetDev) staff at Carnegie-Mellon University in Pittsburgh, PA, USA. The site's primary purpose is to distribute free networking software and related materials written by the NetDev group.

Contents: SNMP tools, sample SNMP code, some MIBs, SNMP-related protocol documents, Unix BOOTP server, BIND 4.8.1 + TTL fixes, and other miscellaneous TCP/IP networking software.

Comments: This is not a large general archive site for CMU, but rather a small casually-maintained site for the NetDev group (a small specific group of programmers). Everything is subject to change without notice including the site's very existence. Most files are in Unix tar format and should be transferred using binary representation.

5-16 **Carnegie-Mellon University Software Engineering Institute:** `ftp.sei.cmu.edu`

i `info-manage@sei.cmu.edu`

The Software Engineering Institute is a federally funded research and development center sponsored by the Department of Defense under contract to Carnegie-Mellon University.

Contents: Check archive for contents.

5-17 **Case Western Reserve University GNU bash distribution:** `slc2.ins.cwru.edu`

i `chet@po.CWRU.Edu`

The CWRU Bash (Bourne-Again SHell) distribution and related files.

5-18 **Casti Collection:** `vector.intercon.com`

i `disc@vector.intercon.com`

The Casti Collection is a privately owned and maintained FTP site.

Contents:

`BBS/` All known BBS lists in the world. There is a submissions directory for you to add lists to this repository

`QRD/` The Queer Resource Directory. More than 20M of files on topics and issues of interest to gay folk

`RFCs/` Some frequently accessed RFCs. The contents of this directory will change from time to time

`gifs/` Some miscellaneous GIFs that are on their way to other systems on the network. Sorry, nothing pornographic

`info/` Obscure knowledge. The contents of this directory will change from time to time

`mac/` Files of interest to Mac users

`next/` Binaries of selected programs which will run on NeXT '040 hardware

`soc.motss/` Bios of people from soc.motss

`tech/` InterCon Public Tech Notes

`unix/` Selected source code for use with Unix machines

Mirrors: The Queer Resources Directory is mirrored actively on `nifty.andrew.cmu.edu`

5-19 **Cayman Systems FTP server:** `ftp.cayman.com`

i `atierney@cayman.com` or `support@cayman.com`

Cayman Systems, Inc., based in Cambridge, Mass., is the leading provider of internetworking solutions designed to integrate Appletalk workgroups with enterprise networks.

Contents: Current software releases for Cayman products. These are typically upgrades (for which Cayman charges and which are therefore password protected), free network diagnostic tools such as Watch, GatorTools, and NetCapture Ethernet/Localtalk (by Neon Software), which will allow users to capture packets without the ability to look at them unless they own a licensed copy of NetMinder software.

Comments: FTP to `ftp.cayman.com` (not just `cayman.com`) and always cd to the `/pub` directory. When FTPing a file to the incoming directory, please send mail to `support@cayman.com` to let the support department know that the file is there.

5-20   **CCIC (Chinese Community Information Center):** `ifcss.org`

i `ftp-admin@ifcsss.org`

The CCIC FTP site is the Chinese Community Information Center set up by IFCSS (Independent Federation of Chinese Students and Scholars in the US) to serve its community and its friends.

Contents:

`/cnd/` China News Digest archive, daily news

`/hxwz/` HXWZ Chinese weekly archive

`/6.4pictures/` 1989 student movement pictures

`/ifcss/` IFCSS archive

`/immigration/` Immigration information regarding Chinese nationals

`/job/` Job announcements

`/tax/` Tax information regarding Chinese nationals

`/org/` Magazines, newsletters and files from Chinese Students and Scholars' organizations

`/software/` Chinese computer software. The world's largest site of its kind

`/china-studies/compute/` Computer use involving Chinese language, CCNET archive

`/china-studies/directories/` Phone numbers, addresses, and network drmains of some institutes in China; telephone area code of Chinese cities

`/china-studies/hz/` Chinese text archive in "hz" format

`/china-studies/language/`

`/china-studies/literature/`

`/china-studies/misc/`

`/china-studies/net-resources/` Introduction to resources and discussion groups

Comments: Software uploaded must be accompanied by a description. To upload other data, please write to `ftp-admin@ifcss.org`

Mirrors: `cnd.org` and `ftp.edu.tw` (`NCTUCCCA.EDU.TW`)

5-21   **CEPH and GENETHON Archives:** `ftp.genethon.fr`

i `info-ftp@genethon.fr` or `pat@genethon.genethon.fr`

Data from the Fondation Jean-Dausset CEPH and Human Research Genome Centre GENETHON research projects.

Contents: This site contains gene sequences, marker data, a PostScript version of genetic maps, and the CEPH database.

5-22 **Chalmers Original LPmud Archive:** `ftp.cd.chalmers.se`

i `ltt@cd.chalmers.se`

The LPmud and ZyXEL archives maintained by Chalmers Computer Society at Chalmers University of Technology, Gothenburg, Sweden.

Contents:

`/pub/8051/` Freeware for the 8051 microprocessor

`/pub/cdlib/` LPmud mudlib

`/pub/lpmud/` LPmud gamedriver

`/pub/lpmudr/` The LPmud client

`/pub/zyxel/` ROMs and software for ZyXEL modems, especially voicemail

Mirrors: `/pub/zyxel` at `ftp.rz.uni-karlsruhe.de`

5-23 **CICNet:** `ftp.cic.net`

i `holbrook@cic.net` (J. Paul Holbrook)

Archives of CICNet, an Internet access provider.

Contents:

`/pub/resourceguide/` The June 1992 CICNet Resource Guide

`/pub/newsletter/` On-line copies of the CICNet newsletter "The Circuit"

`/pub/nircomm/` Files relating to the CICNet NIRCOMM (Network Information Resources Committee)

`/pub/policies/` CICNet policies, including CICNet fees, an acceptable use policy, and the CICNet policy on "backdoor" connections

`/pub/maps/` IP and geographical maps of CICNet and netILLINOIS (which CICNet manages)

`/pub/reports/` Reports and projects within CICNet.

`/pub/security/` Useful security information. Includes a copy of RFC1244, the Site Security Handbook, which was co-edited by Paul Holbrook of CICNet

`/pub/netsoftware/` Several useful software packages taken from other locations. Includes FTPD-sirius, the logging FTP package running on `ftp.cic.net`

`/pub/great-lakes/` Data on the Great Lakes Information Network (GLIN), a cooperative information service from a variety of agencies and organizations having special concern for the Great Lakes economy, environment, and culture

`/pub/e-serials/` An archive of Electronic Serials. Maintained by Paul Southworth for CICNet

`/pub/talk-radio/` An archive of Internet Talk Radio shows

`/pub/pdf/` An archive of samples of Adobe's Portable Document Format (PDF) files, created with the Adobe Acrobat software. Only usable by folks with the Acrobat software

5-24 **Columbia University Center for Telecommunications Research Archive:** `ftp.ctr.colum-`

bia.edu

i archivist@ctr.columbia.edu

> *The CUCTR archive is tasked with distributing the research produced by the CTR and the packages developed by the System Managers.*

Contents:

/pub/ Misc. programs and packages

/pub/DA/ Disney Afternoon pictures, sounds, and related material

/Xkernel/ Packge to turn Suns into X terminals

/CTR-Research/ CTR research related information (tech reports, etc.)

5-25 **Computer Aided Engineering Center at UW-MADISON anonymous HP-UX FTP archive:**
ftp.cae.wisc.edu

i ftp@cae.wisc.edu

> *An archive for software that has been compiled and tested under HP-UX, maintained by the Computer Aided Engineering Center in the College of Engineering at the University of Wisconsin-Madison, Madison, Wisconsin, USA.*

Contents: A list of all available software on the archive can be found in /ls-lR.Z or /ls-lR.gz or /ls-lRt.gz . Also available: /README /Conventions

/hpux8/ software tested and installed under hp-ux 8.07

/hpux9/ software tested and installed under hp-ux 9.01

/Rfc/ Requests for Comments

Comments: Please read /Conventions and /README before you get/compile X11R4, X11R5 packages.

Mirrors: There are four identical sites: in the USA (this site), UK, France, and Germany. Consistency is maintained daily between these sites via mirroring.

5-26 **Concurrency Modeling:** boole.stanford.edu

i pratt@cs.stanford.edu

> *Papers (Latex source and dvi) on modeling concurrent behavior written by members of the Boole Group, c/o Prof. Vaughan Pratt, Computer Science Department, Stanford University.*

Contents: Paper titles as follows. Get the README (linked to ABSTRACTS) for their abstracts.

gates.tex Gates Accept Concurrent Behavior

branch.tex What is branching time and why use it

scbr.tex The Second Calculus of Binary Relations

spectrum.ps The linear time-branching time spectrum II

complete.tex A complete ax'n for branching bisim. cong. of fin. state behaviors

ql.tex Linear Logic for Generalized Quantum Mechanics

dti.tex The Duality of Time and Information

ldomain.tex Disjunctive Systems and L-Domains

monoidal.tex Some Monoidal Closed Categories of Stable Domains & Event Structures

twod.tex A Roadmap of Some Two-Dimensional Logics

`ocbr.tex` Origins of the Calculus of Binary Relations

`dalg.tex` Dynamic Algebras: Examples, Constructions, Applications

`algecon.tex` Arithmetic + Logic + Geometry = Concurrency

`esrs.tex` Event Spaces and Related Structures

`crewthes.tex` Metric Process Models

`atch.tex` Interleaving Semantics and Action Refinement with Atomic Choice

`casthes.tex` On the Specification of Concurrent Systems

`es.tex` Event Spaces and their Linear Logic

`cg.tex` Modeling Concurrency with Geometry

`jelia.tex` Action Logic and Pure Induction

`man.tex` Temporal Structures

`pp2.tex` Teams Can See Pomsets

`am4.tex` Enriched Categories and the Floyd-Warshall Connection

`iowatr.tex` Dynamic Algebras as a well-behaved fragment of Relation Algebras

`ijpp.tex` Modelling Concurrency with Partial Orders

Comments: DVI files are all in the `/pub/DVI` subdirectory, for which binary mode must be used. ASCII mode should be used for the .tex files in `/pub`. Boole's FTP daemon is configured so that when you log in as `anonymous` your home directory is `/pub` rather than `/`.

5-27 **Convex User Group Software Library:** `pemrac.space.swri.edu`

i `info-convex-request@pemrac.space.swri.edu`

The Convex User Group Software Library of public domain software built and/or patched for Convex computers.

Contents: The file `INDEX` contains the list of software available.

5-28 **Cryptographic Software Archive:** `ripem.msu.edu`

i `mrr@ripem.msu.edu`

RIPEM and other cryptographic software.

Comments: Most of the software requires an FTP account, which will be given to US and Canadian citizens who agree to some fairly simple terms.

5-29 **CSIRO Archive:** `ftp.mel.dit.csiro.au`

i `hostmaster@mel.dit.csiro.au`

At this laboratory, Commonwealth Scientific and Industrial Research Organisation, the Division of Information Technology performs research into open systems, supercomputing, and high-performance computers.

Contents: (See `README`.) Pacific Rim distribution point for ISODE and PP, Solaris 2 software. Archive for Systems Administrators Guild of Australia

5-30 **Dartmouth College Archives:** `ftp.dartmouth.edu`

i `ftp@ftp.dartmouth.edu`

Archives of Dartmouth College.

Contents:

- Dartmouth Information
- GNUPLOT Archive
- International Computer Music Assn. Software
- Intl. Assn. of Learning Labs
- Job Openings in the Federal Government
- Libernet Archive
- Dartmouth Macintosh Software
- Sense of Place (Environmental Journal)

Comments: Files may be retrieved via e-mail. Send mail to `ftpmail@ftp.dartmouth.edu` with the word "help" in the body of the message.

5-31 **DCG FTP Archive:** `audrey.levels.unisa.edu.au`

i `ftp@audrey.levels.unisa.edu.au`

> *This archive is maintained by the Digital Communications Group, a research group within the University of South Australia, located in Adelaide, Australia.*

Contents:

`/twin-peaks/` Information and pictures from the TV series "Twin Peaks"

`/space/` Manifests, information on various rocket launches and news from the Ausroc amateur rocketry group

`/src/lemacs/` Lucid emacs mirrored from `lucid.com`

5-32 **Digital Equipment Corporation FTP Archive:** `gatekeeper.dec.com`

i `gw-archives@pa.dec.com`

> *Archive of information on DEC products maintained by Digital Corporate Research. The server resides at Digital's Network Systems Laboratory, Palo Alto, California, USA.*

Contents: `gatekeeper.dec.com` contains over 7 Gigabytes of public domain software and information from the Internet and Digital Equipment Corporation. Our archive is organized into the following hierarchy:

`/DEC/` Digital-related files

`/DEC/DECinfo/` Digital hardware and software product descriptions

`/GNU/` Software from the GNU project

`/ISO/` Drafts of proposals for ISO standards

`/Mach/` Documentation and updates for the Mach operating system

`/TriAdd/` Digital's TriAdd documentation

`/UCB/` Berkeley Unix software and documentation

`/VMS/` Software of particular interest to VMS users

`/X11/` Lots of X11 related software

`/athena/` Athena documentation and software, such as kerberos

`/binaries/` Software in binary form (very little here)

`/bsd-sources/` Sources for Berkeley Unix and applications

`/case/` Software development tools

`/comm/` Communication software, such as kermit and zmodem

`/comp.sources.games/` Game software (archive of a Unix newsgroup)

`/comp.sources.misc/` Misc. software (archive of a Unix newsgroup)

`/comp.sources.reviewed/` Reviewed software (archive of a Unix newsgroup)

`/comp.sources.sun/` software for Suns (archive of a Unix newsgroup)

`/comp.sources.unix/` Unix software (archive of a Unix newsgroup)

`/comp.sources.x/` X related software (archive of a Unix newsgroup)

`/db/` Database software, such as Postgres

`/doc/` Documentation, papers, and reports

`/editors/` Text editors

`/games/` Game software

`/graphics/` Graphics software (khoros, rayshade, urt, etc.)

`/humor/` Jokes

`/idrafts-old/` Old versions of Internet documents

`/internet-drafts/` Internet documents

`/lwall/` Software contributed by Larry Wall, such as perl and rn

`/macintosh/` Various Macintosh-related stuff

`/mail/` Mail software (mail11, sendmail, mh, etc.)

`/maps/` PostScript maps of the Usenet network

`/micro/` Various software for micros (Amiga, Macintosh, MSDOS, etc.)

`/misc/` Miscellaneous stuff (example: Bible, orange-book, misc. software)

`/net/` Network-related software

`/news/` Software related to the Usenet newsgroups

`/plan/` Programming languages (Modula-2, oberon, scheme, etc.)

`/recipes/` An on-line cookbook, one file per recipe

`/recipes.tar.Z` All the recipes gathered into one file

`/sysadm/` Programs of use to Unix system administrators

`/text/` Typesetting programs (TeX, roff, etc.)

`/comp.sources.unix/` Mirrored from `ftp.vix.com` in
  `/pub/usenet/comp.sources.unix`

`/BSD/386bsd/0.1-ports/` Mirrored from `XFree86.cdrom.com`

`/net/info/rfc/` Mirrored list of RFCs from `ds.internic.net`

`/net/infosys/gopher/` Gopher information mirrored from
  `boombox.micro.umn.edu`

`/net/infosys/wais/` WAIS sources mirrored from `ftp.think.com`

`/net/infosys/archie/` Mirrored from `ftp.sura.net` (excludes sites)

`/net/infosys/mosaic/` Mirrored from `ftp.ncsa.uiuc.edu` (excludes xmosaic-old)

`/net/infosys/www/` World Wide Web files mirrored from `info.cern.ch`

`/forums/dmtf/` Mirrored from `aurora.intel.com`

`/pub/GNU/` Mirrored from `prep.ai.mit.edu`

5-33 **Electronic Frontier Foundation FTP Archive Service:** `ftp.eff.org`

i `ftphelp@eff.org`

A set of archive collections hosted by the Electronic Frontier Foundation, a 501(c)3 non-profit organization dedicated to "civilizing the electronic frontier."

Contents:

`/pub/EFF/` EFF information, articles, papers, newsletters, and so forth

`/pub/cud/` The Computer underground Digest archive

`/pub/academic/` The Computers & Academic Freedom archive

5-34 **EMBL Anonymous FTP Server:** `ftp.embl-heidelberg.de`

i `Nethelp@EMBL-Heidelberg.DE`

Molecular Biology FTP archive maintained by the EMBL Data Library.

Contents:

`/pub/databases/` Molecular biology databases repository, including complete releases of EMBL nucleotide sequence database, SWISS-PROT protein sequence database, and weekly updates

`/pub/software/` Free molecular biology software for Unix, VMS, Macintosh and MS-DOS computers

`/pub/doc/` General information and documentation for molecular biologists

`/pub/avs_mirror/` Files mirrored from `avs.ncsc.org`

`/INDEX` Complete listing of all files in the archive

`/NEWFILES` Listing of all files new or modified within the last two weeks

Comments: Automatic file compression/decompression during downloading is supported.

Mirrors: `sunbcd.weizmann.ac.il`

5-35 **EUnet Germany Software & Information Archive:** `ftp.Germany.EU.net`

i `archive-admin@Germany.EU.net`

The public archive maintained by EUnet Germany, a network services provider.

Contents:

`/pub/EUnet/` Information on EUnet

`/pub/X11/` X11 distribution & contributions

`/pub/applications/` Applications software

`/pub/comp/` Software for different platforms

`/pub/documents/` Network-related documents

`/pub/network/` Network-related software

`/pub/news/` Software for the NetNews system

`/pub/newsarchive/` Archived newsgroups

`/pub/packages/` Popular software packages

`/pub/programming/` Programming tools

`/pub/utils/` Utility programs (+other directories)

• X11R5 software and documents mirrored from `ftp.x.org`

• xmosaic mirrored from `ftp.ncsa.uiuc.edu`

- InterViews mirrored from `interviews.stanford.edu`
- Point editor mirrored from `ftp.cs.unm.edu`
- SVLIB mirrored from `iti.gov.sg`
- GNU mirrored from `prep.ai.mit.edu`
- Cygnus GNU implementation mirrored from `ftp.uu.net`
- Lucid Emacs mirrored from `lucid.com`
- NetBSD mirrored from `agate.berkeley.edu`
- 386BSD ports mirrored from `agate.berkeley.edu`
- 386BSD mirrored from `agate.berkeley.edu`
- Linux mirrored from `sunsite.unc.edu`
- SUN fixes mirrored from `metten.fenk.wau.nl`
- SUN patch mailing list mirrored from `sasun1.epfl.ch`
- MIME mirrored from `thumper.bellcore.com`
- NetBSD-Amiga mirrored from `ftp.eunet.ch`
- World Wide Web mirrored from `info.cern.ch`
- IESG/IETF/ISOC/CCR documents mirrored from `nnsc.nsf.net`

Comments: wuarchive FTPD extensions (tar, compress). E-mail access: `archive-server@Germany.EU.net`

5-36 **Finnish University and Research Network (FUNET) archive:** `ftp.funet.fi`

i `managers@ftp.funet.fi`. Note that each subdirectory has a different contact address; see online top-level README file for up-to-date list.

FUNET archive for freely distributable material.

Contents: For questions about each directory, send e-mail to listed address.

`/pub/archive/` Selected Usenet newsgroups *i* `managers@ftp.funet.fi`

`/pub/amiga/` Amiga software *i* `amiga-adm@ftp.funet.fi`

`/pub/atari/` Atari software *i* `atari-adm@ftp.funet.fi`

`/pub/astro/` Amateur astronomy *i* `astro-adm@ftp.funet.fi`

`/pub/cae/` Electronics CAE sw+data *i* `cae-adm@ftp.funet.fi`

`/pub/cbm/` Micros: VIC20, C64. *i* `cbm-adm@ftp.funet.fi`

`/pub/csc/` Centre for Scientific Computing *i* `csc-adm@ftp.funet.fi`

`/pub/culture/music/` Theory, samples, lyrics *i* `music-adm@ftp.funet.fi`

`/pub/culture/` Misc culture related sw/info *i* `culture-adm@ftp.funet.fi`

`/pub/crypt/` Cryptographical sw, DES, PGP *i* `unix-adm@ftp.funet.fi`

`/pub/doc/etext/` E-Text (Proj. Guttenberg) *i* `etext-adm@ftp.funet.fi`

`/pub/doc/` Misc documentation from the net *i* `managers@ftp.funet.fi`

`/pub/dx/` DX-listeners interests *i* `dx-adm@ftp.funet.fi`

`/pub/gnu/` GNU software *i* `gnu-adm@ftp.funet.fi`

`/pub/graphics/` Graphics algorithms, etc. *i* `graphics-adm@ftp.funet.fi`

`/pub/ham/` Radio-amateur sw/data *i* `ham-adm@ftp.funet.fi`

`/pub/ic/` ISODE-consortium *i* `icadm@ftp.funet.fi`

/pub/kermit/ Kermit programs *i* kermit-adm@ftp.funet.fi

/pub/languages/ Programming languages *i*
languages-adm@ftp.funet.fi

/pub/mac/ Apple Macintosh *i* mac-adm@ftp.funet.fi

/pub/mach/ CMU Mach microkernel *i* mach-adm@ftp.funet.fi

/pub/microprocs/ Misc. microprocessor tools *i*
microprocs-adm@ftp.funet.fi

/pub/minix/ MINIX sw+comp.os.minix archives *i* minix-adm@ftp.funet.fi

/pub/misc/hp/* HP calculators *i* calculators-adm@ftp.funet.fi

/pub/misc/ poorly/not at all classified *i* managers@ftp.funet.fi

/pub/msdos/ MSDOS *i* msdos-adm@ftp.funet.fi

/pub/netinfo/ Networking information *i* netinfo-adm@ftp.funet.fi

/pub/networking/ Networking software *i* netinfo-adm@ftp.funet.fi

/pub/NeXT/ NeXT computer software *i* next-adm@ftp.funet.fi

/pub/OS/Linux/ The Linux operating system *i* linux-adm@ftp.funet.fi

/pub/os2 OS/2 interests *i* os2-adm@ftp.funet.fi

/pub/pics/ A lot of pictures, GIF, JPEG *i* gif-adm@ftp.funet.fi

/pub/sci/molbio/ Molecular Biology software+info *i*
molbio-adm@ftp.funet.fi

/pub/sci/neural/ Neural networking theory/sw *i*
neural-adm@ftp.funet.fi

/pub/sci/papers/ "Research Papers" -project *i* papers-adm@ftp.funet.fi

/pub/sci/ "Serious Science" material *i* sci-adm@ftp.funet.fi

/pub/standards/ Various networking standards *i* managers@ftp.funet.fi

/pub/TeX/ The TeX typesetting system *i* tex-adm@ftp.funet.fi

/pub/unix/ General Unix area *i* unix-adm@ftp.funet.fi

/pub/unix/386ix/ Various 386/486 Unixes *i* 386ix-adm@ftp.funet.fi

/pub/vms/ Some VMS software *i* vms-adm@ftp.funet.fi

/pub/X11/ MIT X-Window software *i* xwindow-adm@ftp.funet.fi

/pub/win-nt/ MS-Windows NT software *i* win-nt-adm@ftp.funet.fi

5-37 **GNU Software Archive:** prep.ai.mit.edu

i gnu@prep.ai.mit.edu

> *The archive of the Free Software Foundation's GNU project. GNU is a free, user-modifiable and -distributable Unix-compatible software system designed to eliminate user dependence on commercial software distributors.*

Contents:

/pub/gnu/ FSF GNU Software distribution (emacs, gcc)

Mirrors: wuarchive.wustl.edu and ftp.uu.net

5-38 **Grind Filesystem:** grind.isca.uiowa.edu

i macpd@icaen.uiowa.edu

5,000 Mb of files for all systems types. The Grind Filesystem is a project of the Iowa Student Computer Association, at the University of Iowa in Iowa City, Iowa, USA.

Contents:
- Macintosh files (1420 Mb)
- IBM & MS-DOS Systems (960 Mb)
- Amiga (520 Mb)
- Apple2 (130 Mb)
- NeXT (60 Mb)
- Pictures and images (190 Mb)
- Articles and magazines (220 Mb)
- Sound files (70 Mb)
- Unix source code (160 Mb)

Comments: The Grind Filesystem is also searchable via a telnet interface (telnet `grind.isca.uiowa.edu` [login = `iscabbs`]) and files are downloadable using kermit, zmodem, and xmodem.

5-39 **Gustavus Adolphus College FTP server:** `ftp.gac.edu`

i `ftp@ftp.gac.edu`

This is the anonymous FTP server run by Gustavus Adolphus College, a private liberal arts college in St. Peter, MN, USA.

Contents:

`/pub/chem/` Materials for Gustavus chemistry department's challenge lab

`/pub/E-mail-archives/fam-med/` e-mail archives for `fam-med` mailing list

`/pub/E-mail-archives/family-l/` e-mail archives of `family-l` mailing list

`/pub/E-mail-archives/t-and-f/` e-mail archives of the `t-and-f` mailing list

`/pub/GACnet/` Gustavus campus network information

`/pub/Mathematica/` Interesting Mathematica files

`/pub/NeXT/` Programs and files for NeXT(tm) computers

`/pub/SICP/` Materials for the Gustavus course "Structure and Interpretation of Computer Programs"

`/pub/prob/` programs and files for "prob," a CAI program. Prob is a package of computer programs designed to stimulate individual student effort on numerical calculations by assigning each student a unique set of data

`/pub/unix/` programs and files for Unix

`/pub/vms/` programs and files for VMS

Comments: Gustavus Adolphus College and this system's administrator have provided this service with the intent that it can be a benefit to others. Please keep your file transfers to non-prime hours (1800 - 0700 GMT-6)

5-40 **Hamburg University Computer Science Archive:** `ftp.informatik.uni-hamburg.de`

i `zierke@informatik.uni-hamburg.de` or
`bontchev@informatik.uni-hamburg.de` for `/pub/virus`,
`dfncert@informatik.uni-hamburg.de` for `/pub/security`

Information and software archive maintained by the Hamburg University Computer Science Department.

Contents:

/pub/security/ Computer-security related documents collected from the Internet by the DFN-CERT

/pub/virus/ Computer virus related informations, maintained by the Virus Test Center VTC Hamburg

/pub/usenet/ Automatically archived sources from comp.sources.* newsgroups

/pub/o-reilly/ Mirror of the O'Reilly FTP site ora.com

/pub/gnu GNU software

/pub/lang languages (Modula3, Scheme, perl, etc.)

/pub/linux Linux software (SLS, slackware, documentation)

/doc/news.answers/ Automatically archived FAQs from the news.answers newsgroup

/doc/DECnews/ DEC newsletters

/doc/rfc Internet documents

5-41 **HANA Net Freeware Archive:** ftp.hana.nm.kr

i postmaster@hana.nm.kr

The Freeware Software Archive maintained by HANA Net in Seoul, Korea.

Contents:

/pub/pc/ Freeware for IBM PC compatibles

/pub/hangul/ Freeware for using Hangul (Korean language) with Unix

/hana-info/ information about HANA Net

5-42 **Hebrew University Institute of Computer Science Anonymous FTP Archive:** ftp.huji.ac.il

i system@cs.huji.ac.il

Copies of various files and programs used at the Hebrew University.

Contents:

/pub/X11/R5/ Official copy of X11R5

/pub/local/xhterm/ Xterm with Hebrew support

/pub/misc/transis/ The Transis System Papers

/pub/msdos/fprot/ The Fprot anti-virus programme

/pub/msdos/network/sntp/xmib1.0b.tar.gz/ An X interface for handling SNMP MIBs

/pub/network/snoop Various network (mainly Ethernet) "snooping" programmes

/pub/network/snoop/NNStat network usage statistics programme (the most updated version)

/pub/postgres/xpg an X interface for the Postgres database system

/pub/security security-related programmes and libraries

/pub/sgi various SGI goodies

`/pub/yval` many local netBSD patches

Comments: This is a wuarchive-based FTP daemon with all the conveniences, in particular practically all files are compressed with GNU gzip, but on-the-fly conversion is available.

5-43 **Helsinki University of Technology Computer Science Lab:** `cs.hut.fi`

i `root@cs.hut.fi`

A small archive maintained by the HUT CS lab for mostly local use.

Contents: Mostly local stuff.

`/pub/drinking_games/` A large archive of drinking games.

Mirrors: `ftp.funet.fi`

5-44 **HUJIvms anonymous archive:** `vms.huji.ac.il`

i `yehavi@vms.huji.ac.il`

The Hebrew University computation center.

Contents: HUJI-written software put into the public domain.

5-45 **Informatics, University of Oslo:** `ftp.ifi.uio.no`

i `drift@ifi.uio.no`

The Informatics archive at the University of Oslo, Norway.

Contents: Information on SGML (Standard Generalized Markup Language), the Simula computer language, image processing, SCI, and VLSI.

5-46 **Informatikarchiv:** `neptune.ethz.ch`

i `dias@inf.ethz.ch`

Software and Documentation published by the Department of Computer Science, ETH Zurich, Switzerland.

Contents:

`/Oberon` Compiler and Operating System for Macintosh, SPARC, PC/DOS, DECstation, Silicon Graphics, and IBM RS6000 platforms with documentation

`/VIS/` Verein Informatik Studenten Information

`/XYZ/` Educational software for teaching geometry

`/macmeth/` Modula2 Language Compiler for Macintosh, including source and documentation

`/maple/` Info and updates to the mathematics package "Maple"

`/dbs/` Info and reports of the Data Base group of the Dept. Informatik

`/dinfk/` Info of the Dept. Informatik

5-47 **Iowa State University Department of Computer Science FTP Archive:**
`ftp.cs.iastate.edu`

i `postmaster@cs.iastate.edu`

The FTP Archive is maintained by the Department of Computer Science at Iowa State University, providing access to a small number of technical reports and software made available by the department. This FTP service is provided for backward compatibility for those who do not yet have access to gopher or WWW.

Contents:

```
/pub/larchc++/
/pub/ox/
/pub/techreports/
```

5-48 **James Cook University Anonymous FTP Archive:** `ftp.jcu.edu.au`

   i `helpdesk@jcu.edu.au`

   This archive is maintained by various departmental representatives at James Cook University of North Queensland.

   Contents:

   `/JCUMetSat/` Contains weather-satellite pictures received by the JCUMetSat Weather Satellite Receiving System operated by Professor C. J. Kikkert in the Department of Electrical and Computer Systems Engineering

   `/pub/ibmpc/` Freeware for IBM PC compatibles

   `/pub/SCO/` Freeware for SCO Unix

   `/pub/X11R5/` X11R5 sources

   `/pub/alpha/` Freeware for Alpha OSF/1

   `/pub/novell/` Freeware for NOVELL

   `/pub/progress/` Information for PROGRESS DBMS

   `/pub/ultrix/` Freeware for Unix (Ultrix flavour)

   Comments: Most files are gzip'ed.

5-49 **Jyvaskyla University FTP Archive:** `ftp.jyu.fi`

   i `ftp@jyu.fi`

   General-purpose FTP archive maintained by the Computing Center at Jyvaskyla University, Finland.

   Contents: Macintosh software mirrored from `sumex-aim.stanford.edu`

   Comments: The same archive is also available through FSP.

5-50 **Kaiserslautern University FTP Archive:** `ftp.uni-kl.de`

   i `ftpadm@uni-kl.de`

   Central software and information archive of Kaiserslautern University, Germany.

   Contents:

   `/pub/` `[acorn amiga apple2 atari mac novell pc]/` Software for various personal computers

   `/pub/` `[packages X11R5 bsd-sources ...]/` GNU software and more software for Unix

   `/pub/` `[docs+papers game-solutions ham-radio humor linux lists reports_uni-kl security sun-patches ...]/` Many other interesting or even useful things

   Mirrors: `ftp.uu.net` or `ftp.uni-oldenburg.de` or `ftp.uni-paderborn.de` or `ftp.uni-passau.de` or `ftp.rz.uni-wuerzburg.de` or `ftp.cs.tu-berlin.de`

   Comments: Please note policy/usage information at login.

5-51 **Kansas State University Department of Computing and Information Sciences FTP archive:**
 `ftp.cis.ksu.edu`

 i `ftp@cis.ksu.edu`

> *This FTP server is maintained by the Department of Computing and Information Sciences at Kansas State University, Manhattan, Kansas, USA.*

Contents:

 `/pub/CIS/` Faculty technical reports

 `/pub/386BSD/` 386 BSD files

 `/pub/FUN/` Framemaker User's Group files

 `/pub/alt.startrek.creative/` Star Trek creative fiction from Usenet news-group `alt.startrek.creative`

Comments: A mailserver is also available; for more information, send e-mail to `mailserver@cis.ksu.edu` with `help` in the body of the message.

5-52 **Laboratoire de Biometrie, Genetique et Biologie des Populations Archive:**
 `biom3.univ-lyon1.fr`

 i `postmaster@biom3.univ-lyon1.fr`

> *Archives of the Biometrics, Genetics, and Population Biology Laboratory URA CNRS 243, Universite Lyon 1, 69622 Villeurbanne, CEDEX, France.*

Contents: see README files in `/pub/acnuc` and `/pub/macmulti`

 `/pub/acnuc/` ACNUC is a retrieval system for the nucleotide sequence databases GenBank or EMBL and for the protein sequence data base NBRF/PIR (contact: `mgouy@biomserv.univ-lyon1.fr`)

 `/pub/macmulti/` Multivariate analysis software for Macintosh (contact: `thioulou@biomserv.univ-lyon1.fr`)

 `/pub/theses/` PhD dissertations—Microsoft Word files, Macintosh format (contact: `gonidec@biomserv.univ-lyon1.fr`)

 `/pub/images/` Collection of anime pictures—GIF and JPEG format (contact: `perriere@biomserv.univ-lyon1.fr`)

Comments: The number of simultaneous connections is limited to 10 during working hours. Please note that this site is in France.

5-53 **LLNL VMS GNU Emacs Distribution:** `addvax.llnl.gov`

 i `brand@addvax.llnl.gov`

> *GNU Emacs for VMS binary distribution site maintained by Lawrence Livermore National Lab.*

Contents: Primarily VMS BACKUP savesets of GNU Emacs for VMS; some other PD VMS software.

Comments: VMS site running MultiNet TCP/IP.

5-54 **Lund Institute of Technology, Sweden:** `ftp.lth.se`

 i `jh@lth.se`

> *This archive is mainly for automatic archiving of the* `*.sources` *Usenet newsgroup, as well as other useful software.*

Contents:

`/pub/X11/R5/` X11R5 distribution

`/pub/athena/` Different packages from MIT's Athena project

`/pub/netnews/` From `alt.sources`, `comp.sources.*`, `news.answers`

`/pub/mac/` Mirror of `info-mac` at `sumex-aim.stanford.edu`

Comments: Compressed with gzip.

5-55 **Lysator ACS Anonymous FTP Software Archive:** `ftp.lysator.liu.se`

i `ftp@lysator.liu.se`

The Anonymous FTP Software Archive maintained by the Lysator Academic Computer Society at the Linkoping University in Linkoping, Sweden.

Contents:

`/pub/asl/` Advanced Squad Leader archive

`/pub/aviation/` Info about aircraft

`/pub/blake7/` Blake's 7 mailing list archive

`/pub/comics/` Info about comics

`/pub/emacs/` Contains the following packages: pcl-cvs (Frontend to CVS) elib (Lib. of Emacs Lisp utils & ADTs) kiwi (IRC client)

`/pub/gardening/` Info about gardening

`/pub/geography/` Maps, CIA World Factbook; not up to date

`/pub/ident/` RFC1413 "IDENT" source & doc

`/pub/lyskom/` Free Client/Server "BBS" system

`/pub/magick/` Info about magick

`/pub/marine_mammals/` Info about marine mammals

`/pub/primos/` Prime/PRIMOS software

`/pub/runeberg/` Free e-texts in Scandinavian languages

`/pub/sf-texts/` Archive of interesting SF and Fantasy related texts from Usenet since 86-87

`/pub/svenskmud/` Documentation for the wizards of the Swedish-language MUD "SvenskMUD"

`/pub/solutions/` Hints for adventure games

Mirrors: `pub/ident` on `ftp.uu.net` in `pub/networking/ident`

5-56 **MacMaster University Archives:** `maccs.dcss.mcmaster.ca`

Contents: See `/pub/README` file for details.

5-57 **Math Sciences Archive of the University of Kentucky:** `ftp.ms.uky.edu`

i `chaney@ms.uky.edu` (Dan Chaney)

The Math Sciences Archive is maintained by the Math Sciences Department of the University of Kentucky in Lexington, KY, USA.

Contents:

`/pub3/gnu/` The GNU Project packages

`/pub2/rfc/` A frequently updated list of RFCs

`/pub3/linux/` Files related to the Linux operating system

`/pub/bsd/` Files for the BSD operating system

`/pub2/386BSD/` Files associated with the 386BSD Operating System

`/pub2/NetBSD/` Files associated with the NetBSD Operating System

`/pub4/next/` Files related to the NeXT family of computers

`/pub3/X11R5-dist/` X11R5 distribution and files

`/pub3/Xwindows/` Various XWindows files

`/pub3/calculus/` Files associated with the Calculus Reform Movement

`/pub3/mailing.lists/` Various mailing lists run from Math Sciences

`/pub/tech-reports/` Various technical reports and papers of UK

`/pub/NSF/` Files associated with various NSF grants

`/pub/amiga/` Files for the Amiga family of computers

`/pub/appleII/` Files for the Apple II family of computers

`/pub2/atari/` Files for the Atari family of computers

`/pub4/msdos/` Files for the DOS operating system

`/pub/mac/` Files related to the Macintosh family of computers

`/pub/games/` Various games

`/pub/graphics/` Various graphics files, programs, etc.

`/pub/irc/` Files related to the IRC chat system

`/pub/misc/` Files Chaney can't think of a better place for

`/pub/primos/` Files related to the Primos (Prime) Operating System

`/pub/unix/` Files associated with the Unix operating system

`/pub/7300/` Files for the AT&T 7300 PC

5-58   **Memorial University Earth Sciences Archive:** `sparky2.esd.mun.ca`

   i `daryl@sparky2.esd.mun.ca` or `daryl@cs.mun.ca`

   Archive of MS-DOS and Windows-based geochemical software maintained by the Earth Sciences Department.

   Contents:

   `/pub/geoprogs`

   Mirrors: COGS, geological BBS's

5-59   **Michigan State Engineering Archive:** `ftp.egr.msu.edu` or `archive.egr.msu.edu`

   i `ftp@egr.msu.edu`

   A collection of files of interest to the MSU engineering students and faculty.

   Contents: X11 for the NeXT, antivirus software, and Society for Creative Anachronism information

   Comments: Submissions must be approved.

5-60   **Minnesota Regional Network FTP archive:** `ftp.mr.net`

   i `info@mr.net`

   The Minnesota Regional Network provides Internet access in the state of Minnesota. The FTP archive is maintained for the use of its attached member organizations as a central information repository.

Contents: Information on the Internet in general and on MRNet in particular.

5-61   **Minnie 386BSD Archive:** `minnie.cs.adfa.oz.au`

i `wkt@csadfa.cs.adfa.oz.au`

Minnie is run and owned by Warren Toomey, `wkt@csadfa.cs.adfa.oz.au`, with basic network connection support from the Australian Defence Force Academy, Canberra, Australia.

Contents:

`/386bsd-0.1/` 386BSD 0.1 binaries and the latest patchkit

`/apple2/` Apple][programs, emulator

`/bsdnews/` 386BSD news (comp.unix.bsd, comp.os.386bsd.*)

`/hamradio/` Amateur radio files, including NOS src and exe's

`/minix/` The Minix archive

`/misc/` Miscellaneous

`/postcript/` PostScript stuff, e.g., Type 1 -> Metafont converters

`/spice/` Circuit models for Spice and variants

5-62   **MIT Media Lab Music & Cognition Group 'Cecelia' FTP Site:**
`cecelia.media.mit.edu`

i `dpwe@media.mit.edu` (Dan Ellis)

FTP site for the distribution of papers and programs written by the members of the MIT Media Lab, Learning & Common Sense, and Perceptual Computing sections.

Contents: A variety of papers and programs produced by past and current students of the associated sections of the MIT Media Lab, including:

- In `pub/`: PostScript of theses and papers; various audio processing tools, including Csound (Barry Vercoe's Mac/Unix software audio synthesis system), mood (C++ music composition language), machine rhythm (Lisp automatic rhythm tracking), and reverb (real-time reverb designer for Mac/Audiomedia); various knowledge-representation and understanding systems including arlotje (Ken Haase's representation-language language) and cyrano

`/framer/` Persistent, portable knowledge representation system.

Comments: There is very little documentation with most of these programs. In general, they are provided as backup to published papers, rather than as stand-alone, plug-and-play packages.

5-63   **MIT SIPB Usenet FAQ archive:** `Rtfm.mit.edu.`

i `Rtfm-maintainers@athena.mit.edu.`

An archive of Usenet periodic informational postings (FAQ postings), maintained by the Student Information Processing Board at the Massachusetts Institute of Technology.

Contents: See `/pub/index` for details

Comments: Usenet periodic postings are archived automatically on `rtfm.mit.edu` if they are listed in the "List of Periodic Informational Postings" FAQ posting or if they are cross-posted to the `*.answers` newsgroups. For more information about these options, see the files `/pub/usenet/news.answers/periodic-postings/part1` and `/pub/usenet/news.answers/news-answers/guidelines` in the archive.

5-64 **MIT/Athena software archive:** `athena-dist.mit.edu`

i `root@athena-dist.mit.edu`

Archives of MIT's Athena Project.

Contents:

`/pub/discuss/` The distributed message system developed by the MIT Student Information Processing Board (SIPB) and used by Project Athena

`/pub/kerberos/` A network authentication system for open networks

`/pub/usenix/` Various papers that Athena has presented at UseNIX conferences

`/pub/virus/` Various papers about the Internet Worm/Virus

`/pub/zephyr/` A network notification service for real-time high-throughput user notification of events

Mirrors: `wuarchive.wustl.edu`

Comments: See also GNU Software archive.

5-65 **Monash University (Australia) anonymous FTP archives:** `ftp.cc.monash.edu.au`

i `steve@cc.monash.edu.au` (Steve Balogh)

Anonymous FTP Archive maintained by the Computer Centre at Monash University in Melbourne, Australia.

Contents:

`/pub/graphics.formats/` A description of various graphics formats

`/pub/msj/` Microsoft Systems Journal source files

`/pub/nihongo/` Japanese language and culture archives (e-mail to `jwb@capek.rdt.monash.edu.au` (Jim Breen))

`/pub/vietnam/` Vietnamese language and culture archives

`/pub/wddj/` Windows/DOS Developers Journal source files

`/pub/win3/` Microsoft Windows archives mirrored from `ftp.cica.indiana.edu`

`/pub/wordperfect/` Macros and other information relating to Wordperfect

`/pub/vi/` vi editor archives mirrored from the archive at `alf.uib.no`

Comments: Most of the files are in the ZIP format and must be downloaded in binary. The latest copy of pkunzip is usually available in `/pub/pc`.

5-66 **National Center for Supercomputing Applications Software Archive:** `ftp.ncsa.uiuc.edu`

i `sdgadmin@ncsa.uiuc.edu` for technical problems with the server; `softdev@ncsa.uiuc.edu` for inquiries regarding software packages.

Dedicated to high performance computing and communications resources for the national research community. The archive contains many software packages as well as general information produced at NCSA.

Contents:

`/Telnet NCSA/` Telnet for the Macintosh, PC, and Microsoft Windows

/PC/ NCSA's software for the IBM PC

/Web/ NCSA's Mosaic and HTTP server

/Mac/ NCSA software for the Macintosh

/HDF/ NCSA's HDF library for high-performance scientific file formatting

/UNIX/ NCSA's Unix and XWindows software

/SGI/ NCSA's software for the Silicon Graphics, Inc. workstations

5-67 **National Institutes of Health Computer Utility:** `ftp.cu.nih.gov`

i `postmaster@cu.nih.gov`

> *Contains whatever the users of cu.nih.gov wish to make available to the net*

Contents: Various items related to medical research, grants, and other government agencies.

5-68 **NCAR/UARS VMS archive:** `uars.acd.ucar.edu`

i `pack@ncar.ucar.edu`

> *Upper Atmosphere Research Satellite project at NCAR.*

Contents: Various VMS sources, e.g. nethack in `/SRC.NETHACK`

Comments: Running Multinet, which supports VMS transfer mode.

Mirrors: VMS nethack at `hamlet.caltech.edu`

5-69 **Netrek Information Archive:** `gs69.sp.cs.cmu.edu`

i `jch@cs.cmu.edu`

> *Rules, information, hints, and tips for the multiplayer game Netrek.*

Contents: Get these files before using this archive: `netrek-faq.Z`, `server-list.Z` and `ftp-list.Z`

Comments: Also available via WAIS (`gourd.srv.cs.cmu.edu`, port 6000, name `netrek-ftp`) and AFS (`/afs/cs.cmu.edu/user/jch/netrek`). Host machine may change in the near future.

5-70 **NIST MEL Archive:** `ftp.cme.nist.gov`

i `ftp-admin@ftp.cme.nist.gov`

> *National Institute of Standards and Technology (NIST) Manufacturing Engineering Laboratory (MEL) performs research and service to improve U.S. manufacturing. NIST is part of the U.S. Department of Commerce.*

Contents:

`expect/` Expect papers and distribution. Includes Tcl and Tk

`express-users.mai.Z` EXPRESS User's Group mailing list archive

`pptb/` NIST pubs, data, etc. related to process planning research

`step/` Documents and source code for STEP—Standard for The Exchange of Product model data

5-71 **North Dakota State University VM1 Archive:** `vm1.nodak.edu`

i `postmaster@vm1.nodak.edu`

> *Mainly archives of e-mail lists hosted by `listserv@vm1.nodak.edu`. The NDSU VM1 FTP archive is maintained by the Computer Center and others.*

Contents: Most of the files in the VM1 archive are related to list archives or are file repositories related to e-mail lists hosted by `listserv@vm1.nodak.edu`. Some of the larger or more popular lists and file collections are NEW-LIST (new list announcements), ROOTS-L (genealogy), L-HCAP and ADA-LAW (handicap or disability information), and KIDLink (project for 10-15-year-olds). Most of the public e-mail lists hosted on VM1 make their files available via anonymous FTP as well as through LISTSERV.

Comments: For a complete list of public lists at vm1, send e-mail to `listserv@vm1.nodak.edu` with the text containing the command `list`. To receive a detailed list of files for a specific list include index listname (e.g., `index roots-l`). Usually the result of the index command will indicate if the files are available via anonymous FTP. Our file system is NOT hierarchical. In general you use `cd listname` (e.g., `cd roots-l`) to get to the files you want. To go back to the root, use `cd anonymous`. Within FTP we suggest you first try the `DIR` command with the list name. For example `dir kidlink.*`. Some of the lists share common disk areas and there may be a lot of files.

5-72 **OCF Archive:** `ocf.berkeley.edu`

     i `ftp@ocf.berkeley.edu`

         Archives of Open Computing Facility (OCF) at the University of California at Berkeley.

     Contents:

         `/pub/Apollo/` Software for Apollo computers

         `/pub/Cal_Graphics/` Picture files of places at UCB

         `/pub/Comics/` Kid Dynamo and gunkldunk

         `/pub/Library/` The OCF On-Line Library, a large number of e-texts arranged by subject

         `/pub/Usenet_Olympics/` Parodies of Usenet and its inhabitants

         `/pub/netrek/` Many files, including source code, for the networking game NetTrek

         `/pub/purity/` The computerist's purity test

5-73 **Ohio State University Math Department Usenet archive:** `math.ohio-state.edu`

     i `postmaster@math.ohio-state.edu`

         Archive of nntplink software. Also contains most of the Usenet sources archive.

     Contents:

         `/pub/nntplink/` nntplink archive

         `/pub/archives/` Usenet sources archives

5-74 **Oxford University and the Oxford Text Archives:** `black.ox.ac.uk`

     i `pcl@ox.ac.uk` or `archive@ox.ac.uk` (OTA personnel)

         The Oxford University and Oxford Text Archives, maintained by Oxford University Computing Services, Oxford, UK.

     Contents: Please get `/README` from `black.ox.ac.uk`

5-75 **PBM Archive:** `ftp.erg.sri.com`

     i `bigmac@erg.sri.com`

An archive of the PBEM Fanzine and rule sets for play-by-e-mail games.

Contents:

/pub/pbm/PBEM-Fanzine/ Editions of Greg Lindahl's fanzine

/pub/pbm/Game-Rules/ Collection of rule sets from rec.games.pbm

Comments: Most files are compressed and must be transferred in binary mode.

5-76 **Penguin Public Archive:** penguin.gatech.edu

i mike@penguin.gatech.edu or root@penguin.gatech.edu

Usenet Movie Ratings List and local caving info.

Contents:

- Usenet Movie Ratings List and shell and LaTeX scripts
- local Outdoor Recreational Georgia Tech caving info
- Also see the README files

Mirrors: pyramind.com (coming soon). e-mail pc@pyramid.com (Pat Conner) for details.

Comments: Please access during off hours only, which are any time other than 7am-7pm Eastern time.

5-77 **POPmail and Gopher software distribution:** boombox.micro.umn.edu

i root@boombox.micro.umn.edu

This site is run by the Computer and Information Systems Department of the University of Minnesota—Minneapolis, USA.

Contents:

/pub/gopher/ Internet gopher client and server software

/pub/POPmail/ POPmail client software

5-78 **Portland State University Computer Science Department Archive:** ftp.cs.pdx.edu

i trent@cs.pdx.edu

Archives of the Portland State University Computer Science Department.

Contents:

/pub/frp/ Fantasy role-playing game archive (Including AD&D, Navero UCR, Guildman, Champions, Tekumel, and more)

/pub/perl/ Archive of locally written Perl tools

/pub/flamingos/ "Parker Lewis Can't Lose" (TV show) archive

Comments: Some files are compressed; use binary mode.

5-79 **Prentice Centre Freeware Archive:** brolga.cc.uq.oz.au

i Marek.Krawus@brolga.cc.uq.oz.au

The Freeware Software Archive maintained by The Prentice Centre at The University of Queensland, Brisbane, Australia.

Contents:

/comp.sources.sun/ Freeware from Usenet newsgroup comp.sources.sun

/comp.sources.misc/ Freeware from Usenet newsgroup comp.sources.misc

/comp.sources.unix/ Freeware from Usenet newsgroup comp.sources.unix

/comp.sources.games/ Freeware from Usenet newsgroup
comp.sources.games

/comp.sources.x/ Freeware from Usenet newsgroup comp.sources.x

/comp.sources.reviewed/ Freeware from Usenet newsgroup
comp.sources.reviewed

/postscript/ Many PostScript goodies

/TeXbits/ TeX tools

/rfc/ RFC documents

Comments: This machine has real work to do, so please try to retrieve things only outside of normal business hours, i.e., 0900-1700 EST.

5-80   **Purdue University Department of Computer Sciences FTP server:** ftp.cs.purdue.edu

i postmaster@cs.purdue.edu

The FTP archive maintained by the Department of Computer Sciences at Purdue University, West Lafayette, Indiana.

Contents:

/pub/RCS/ Current release of RCS

/pub/X11/ Current release of X11

/pub/grad-info/ Information for prospective graduate students

/pub/pcert/ Security documentation and tools

/pub/reports/ Some technical reports and other miscellaneous things

5-81   **Qiclab/SCN Research Archive:** qiclab.scn.rain.com

i neighorn@qiclab.scn.rain.com

The Qiclab/SCN Research Archive is maintained by SCN Research located in Tigard, Oregon, USA.

Contents:

/pub/NeWS/ Files for Sun's NeWS windowing system

/pub/X11/ Files for MIT's X11 system

/pub/astronomy/ Files relating to astronomy

/pub/bench/ Files for benchmarking computers and peripherals

/pub/calculators/ Various calculator programs

/pub/cdrom/ Files relating to CD/ROM

/pub/cisco/ Files relating to cisco routers

/pub/cygnus/ Cygnus's GNU tools for Solaris

/pub/database/ Various database programs

/pub/docs/ Various general interest documents

/pub/games/ Various game and entertainment programs

/pub/gnu/ The GNU project distribution

/pub/graphics/ Various graphics software programs

/pub/mail/ Files relating to e-mail usage and processing

/pub/math/ Various mathematics programs

/pub/misc/ Miscellaneous programs

/pub/multimedia/ Files relating to multimedia systems

/pub/music/ Various music related programs

/pub/network/ Files relating to networks, networking, and modems

/pub/news/ Files relating to reading and processing Usenet news

/pub/postscript/ Various PostScript utilities and programs

/pub/programming/ Files relating to programming and debugging

/pub/rfc/ Collection of the RFCs and related files

/pub/security/ Files relating to Unix security and testing

/pub/shells/ Source for various unix shells

/pub/simulation/ Various computer simulations

/pub/solaris/ Files relating to Sun's Solaris OS

/pub/sun/ Various Sun related files specific to Sun workstations

/pub/sunos-patches/ Many patches to Sun's SunOS and Solaris OS releases

/pub/sysadmin/ Various programs for system administrators

/pub/text/ Various text processing programs

/pub/ucb/ Source code to various Berkeley utilities

/pub/xview/ Source and code examples for Sun's XVIEW toolkit

Comments: most files are either in compressed (.Z) form or GNU zip form (.gz).

5-82 **Rensselaer Polytechnic Institute FTP Archive:** ftp.rpi.edu

i ftp-maint@rpi.edu

Rensselaer Polytechnic Institute FTP Archive is maintained by the campus computing center (Information Technology Services) in Troy, NY, USA.

Contents: Files for RPI faculty, staff, and students.

Comments: If you put a file in incoming, you MUST send a message to ftp-maint@rpi.edu explaining what the file is, when it can be deleted, and how it can be categorized.

5-83 **RIPE Network Coordination Centre Archive:** ftp.ripe.net

i ncc@ripe.net

RIPE is a collaborative forum for IP service providers and operators in Europe. Information is stored relevant to the operation of the Internet in Europe.

Contents:

/ripe/ The RIPE archive subtree

/earn/ EARN Documents

/ebone/ EBONE documents

/fyi/ FYI documents

/iesg/ Internet Engineering Steering Group docs

/ietf/ Internet Engineering Task Force docs

/internet-drafts/ Internet Drafts

/internet-society/ Internet Society docs

/nsf/ NSFnet related docs

/rare/ RARE documents

/rfc/ RFC documents

/tools/ WAIS, gopher, WWW, DNS

Mirrors: ftp.funet.fi and ftp.germany.eu.net and others

5-84 **Rutgers University Combined FTP server:** ftp.rutgers.edu

i mcgrew@ftp.rutgers.edu

Maintained by the Laboratory for Computer Science Research, Rutgers University.

Contents:

/pub/Info/ Software for our Info system

/pub/maps/ Maps of Rutgers campuses, in various formats

/pub/msdos/ Wuarchive's msdos directory (nfs-mounted to lower load on that server)

/pub/rfcs/ Collected Internet Requests for Comment documents

/pub/src/ Much publicly available source (Unix)

/pub/src2/ More more more!

/pub/ufo/ Collected documents of interest to UFO buffs

/pub/wuarchive/ Wuarchive FTP files (nfs-mounted)

/pub/wwii/ Collected "50 years ago" USAAF history files

• Information and catalogs for Rutgers-Camden, Rutgers-Newark, and Rutgers-New Bruswick campuses and departments; information about Rutgers computing services; class schedule and registration information; online library card-catalog and information on library hours and services; current Rutgers news; faculty research information, and student services, including career services, financial aid, grants, off-campus housing, recreational facilities, campus buses, etc.

5-85 **Sam Houston State University main FTP archive:** ftp.shsu.edu

i file-mgr@shsu.edu

Home of the Comprehensive TeX Archive Network (CTAN), and authoritative host for North America, as well as serving as a mirroring host for a number of files for the Sam Houston State University Network Access Initiative project.

Contents:

/tex-archive/ Files of the Comprehensive TeX Archive Network (CTAN)

Mirrors:

ftp.tex.ac.uk (authoritative CTAN host, UK)

ftp.uni-stuttgart.de (authoritative CTAN host, Germany)

wuarchive.wustl.edu in /packages/TeX (North American CTAN mirror)

nic.switch.ch in /mirror/tex/ (Swedish CTAN mirror)

ftp.uni-bielefeld.de in /pub/tex (German CTAN mirror)

kth.se (partial, in development)

src.doc.ic.ac.uk in /packages/tex/uk-tex/

5-86 **Sam Houston State University VMS FTP archive:** `Niord.shsu.edu`

    i `file-mgr@shsu.edu`

      Prior preferred archive for SHSU, now evolving into a VMS-specific archive for files.

    Contents: A variety of VMS files.

5-87 **San Diego State University FTP archive:** `ucssun1.sdsu.edu`

    i `ftp@ucssun1.sdsu.edu` or `root@ucssun1.sdsu.edu` or
      `caasi@ucssun1.sdsu.edu`

      The San Diego State University FTP Archive is maintained by SDSU University Computing
      Services at San Diego State University, San Diego, CA, USA.

    Contents:

      `/pub/acm/` Local chapter of SDSU ACM

      `/pub/doc/` Computer guides

      `/pub/equestrian/` Equestrian archive

      `/pub/ibm/` IBM PC software, includes networking

      `/pub/ibm/netware/` Novell software

      `/pub/mac/` Macintosh networking software

      `/pub/sdscinfo/` San Diego Supercomputing Center guides

      `pub/sun-fixes/` Sun software patches

      `/pub/unix/` Unix software

      `/pub/vax/` VAX software

5-88 **Scholarly Communications Project Archive:** `borg.lib.vt.edu`

    i `jpowell@borg.lib.vt.edu`

      The Scholarly Communications Project of Virginia Tech was started to help publish scholarly
      journals as electronic journals.

    Contents: Archives of the VPIEJ-L journal, as well as many electronic texts and electronic
    publishing utilities.

5-89 **Stanford University Genomic Information Archive:** `genome-ftp.stanford.edu`

    i `ftp-curator@genome.stanford.edu`

      The Yeast Genome Database Project and Stanford University Genomic Sequencing Project at
      the Department of Genetics, Stanford University, La Jolla, CA, USA.

    Contents: This archive is new and expanding (created in the summer of 1993). The interest-
    ing directories are located under `/pub`. However, this will be changing as the archive's
    information increases to include more of the public information. Types of information
    currently available include but are not limited to DNA and protein sequences, genetic
    maps, physical (cosmid, YAC and lambda clone) maps, bibliographic citations, analysis
    software, database client software, and a list of yeast researchers' contact and research
    information.

    Comments: Files for Unix and Macintosh will be included in separately labeled directories.
    The Unix files are generally compressed, ending in `.Z`, while the Macintosh files are
    BinHex encoded, ending in `.hex`. The StuffIt application is used for large sets of
    Macintosh files.

5-90 **StarFleet Project Public Release:** `ftp.cs.cmu.edu`

i `starfleet-request@andrew.cmu.edu`

Publicly available sources to build clients, servers, and maintainance utilities for the distributable portion of the StarFleet project.

Contents:

`/afs/andrew/scs/cs/StarFleet2/dist/CONTENTS` Simple contents file

`/afs/andrew/scs/cs/StarFleet2/dist/sf_latest.tar.Z/` Current version of the StarFleet distribution

`/afs/andrew/scs/cs/StarFleet2/dist/contrib/` Contributed code, configurations, etc.

Comments: To get things, you must first log in as `anonymous` (please leave an e-mail id as a password), then type `cd /afs/andrew/scs/cs/StarFleet2/dist` all at once; cd-ing partway there will fail.

5-91 **StatLib:** `lib.stat.cmu.edu` Login: `statlib`

i `mikem@stat.cmu.edu` (Mike Meyer)

Carnegie-Mellon University statistical software archives.

Contents: StatLib is an archive of statistical software, datasets, and general information. The archive contains macros for statistical packages, complete statistical systems, subroutine libraries, and a large collection of useful datasets

5-92 **Sumex-AIM:** `sumex-aim.stanford.edu`

Sumex-AIM info-mac Archives at Stanford University.

Contents: This archive contains the largest collection of Macintosh software on the Internet. Look in `/info-mac/` for lots of freeware, shareware, sounds, pictures, movies, Hypertext files, desk accessories, utilities, anti-virus software, and much, much more.

Mirrors: `ftp.jyu.fi`, INFO-MAC archives at `wuarchive.wustl.edu`

5-93 **SUNET:** `sunic.sunet.se`

i `postmaster@sunet.se`

Swedish University Network Archive.

Contents:

`/comp/sources/` Alt.sources, comp.sources

`/pub/gnu/` Some GNU stuff

`/pub/misc/` Various popular packages

`/pub/network/` Mail and networking

`/pub/news/` Netnews software

5-94 **SunSITE Archives:** `sunsite.unc.edu`

i `ftpkeeper@sunsite.unc.edu`

Sun Microsystems' anonymous FTP archive, operated by the Office of Information Technology at the University of North Carolina at Chapel Hill.

Contents: This archive contains a huge variety of information. Look in the `/pub` directory:

`UNC-info/` Information about and pertaining to the University of North Carolina

X11/ Interesting packages that run under X-Windows

academic/ Software written by researchers in different disciplines including agriculture (scientific farming, horticulture, and gardening), astronomy (astronomical, astrophysics, telescope programs), biology (evolutionary biology, artificial-life, etc.), chemistry and molecular modeling, computer science, engineering, data analysis, Earth science (geography, geology, geophysics, seismology), library and information science, medicine, mathematics, physics and political science (presidential press conferences, press briefings, etc.)

docs/ a large selection of documents, books, speeches, papers, and tutorials

gnu/ Unix Software written by the Free Software Foundation

languages/ Compilers and interpreters for many computer languages

Linux/ A free Unix-like Operating system for 386 and 486 machines

micro/ software for microcomputers

multimedia/ software for manipulation of sound and video with computers including a large collection of Chinese music

pictures/ Graphic images in various formats (GIFs, JPEG)

sun-info/ Information, patches, and fixes from and about Sun Computers

sun-sounds/ sounds that you can play on SUNs

talk-radio/ archives of the Internet Talk Radio shows

wais/ wais clients for accessing archived databases on this host

Z39.50/ documents and software for the Z39.50 (WAIS) standard of information transfer

Comments: Please see the file /how.to.submit if there is information that you would like to deposit on the SunSITE archive.

Mirrors: Linux files mirrored at ftp.rz.uni-karlsruhe.de

5-95 **SWITCHinfo Anonymous FTP Archive:** nic.switch.ch

i switchinfo@switch.ch (X.400: S=switchinfo; O=switch; P=switch; A=arcom; C=CH;)

SWITCH is a foundation whose goal is to install and operate a Swiss Academic and Research Network. All universities and supercomputing centers as well as many libraries and engineering schools are connected to the network.

Contents: This is a fairly large FTP site (>7 Gigabytes) with many mirrors in the /mirror directory. The most important mirrors are: Atari, DECinfo, EMB, GNU, Gopher, Internet Drafts and Standards, Kermit, Linux, Macintosh, MS-DOS, Novell, Oberon, OS/2, RARE, TeX, VMS, Windows 3, WWW, X11

Comments: An up-to-date list of the mirrors can be found in the file /mirror/README

Mirrors: Several European sites mirror parts of this archive.

5-96 **Technion Archive:** ftp.technion.ac.il

i ftp-admin@ftp.technion.ac.il

Archive of the Technion University in Israel.

Contents: Check archive for contents.

5-97 **Texas Internet Consulting and MIDS Archive:** `ftp.tic.com`

i `ftp.tic.com`

Texas Internet Consulting is a network consulting firm, specializing in TCP/IP, Unix systems, and standards. MIDS (Matrix Information and Directory Services) publishes Matrix News and Matrix Maps Quarterly.

Contents: See `README` file.

5-98 **The Archive:** `src.doc.ic.ac.uk`

i `ukuug-soft@doc.ic.ac.uk`

An archive maintained by the Department of Computing, Imperial College, London, UK.

Contents:

`computing/` The hierarchy of computing related material: archiving, ccitt, communications, compilers, databases, design, document, general, gnu, graphics, hardware, information-systems, Internet, mail, networks, neural, news, operating-systems, programming, security, systems, telecoms, tie-ins, usenet, vendor gnu, the GNU collection of useful Un*x utilities

`media/` Area relating to printed media literary authors, collections, magazines, newsletters, published audio ITR

`politics/` Area relating to politics

`weather/` Area relating to weather (gif maps and similar)

`packages/` A central place to find "major packages"

`info/` Useful information about this archive (in progress)

`JIPS/` Janet IP Services information

Comments: This archive is very large. It currently mirrors over 300 other sites (maintainer is the author of the Mirror package in perl) and currently has over 15 gigabytes of gzipped and compressed material. The FTP daemon can automatically ungzip or uncompress files and has special support for remote Mac and PC clients. Site has recently upgraded to a 20Gigabyte disk, half Gig memory, 6 processor machine as part of its becoming a Sun sponsored "Sunsite." Apart from FTP, the archive is also available under the ISO FTAM system, Internet FSP, JANET NiFTP, and interactively. It is on the Internet as well as JANET and the European IXI network. It also supports interactive accesses via telnet, ISO VT, and dialup. There is also `ftpmail@doc.ic.ac.uk` to allow access for mail-only users.

5-99 **The World's FTP Archive:** `world.std.com`

i `info@world.std.com`

The World's FTP archive is maintained by the staff of Software Tool and Die, a company located in Brookline, Massachusetts, that offers a professionally managed Internet host providing network access for businesses and individuals.

Contents:

• OBI—The Online Book Initiative was formed to make available freely redistributable collections of information. There exists a collection of books, conference proceedings, reference material, catalogues, etc., which can be freely shared.

• Vendor Archive—access to software and information from commercial customers of

World. Among the available vendors are bookstores, commercial software, and computer supplies.

- Membership Organizations—access to information about professional and membership organizations including the Boston Computer Society, the Boston BMUG, Women in Technology International, the New England Chapter for the ACM SIGGRAPH, and the Boston Amateur Radio Club.
- Publications—a collection of materials from magazines and newspapers including Sun Expert, Network World, and The Middlesex News.

Comments: The World welcomes the addition of materials for the FTP archive. In particular, commercial businesses are encouraged to participate in distributing information about their products and services via the World's FTP archive.

5-100 **Thinking Machines Archive:** `ftp.think.com`

i `postmaster@think.com`

Software and documents produced by Thinking Machines and its employees.

Contents:

`/cm/` Connection Machine software

`/cm/starlisp/` Includes portable *Lisp simulator

`/pub/` Includes subdirectories containing archives of some public mailing lists

`/think/` Some PD utilities from TMC

`/think/lisp/` Includes Scheme and Lisp FAQs

`/think/trs/` TMC Technical Reports

`/users/` Maintained by individual employees

`/wais/` WAIS software and documents

5-101 **U.S. Radiance Distribution Site:** `hobbes.lbl.gov`

i `greg@hobbes.lbl.gov`

The U.S. Radiance Distribution Site is maintained by the Building Systems Research Group and the Lawrence Berkeley Laboratory.

Contents:

`Radiance2R1.tar.Z` Radiance source and documentation

`meta1R0.tar.Z` 2-d plotting software

`/pub/digest/` Digest of questions and answers

`/pub/generators/` Object generator programs

`/pub/iesdata/` IES luminaire data

`/pub/libraries/` Patterns, textures, etc.

`/pub/mac/` Macintosh applications related to Radiance

`/pub/models/` Contributed models (complete)

`/pub/objects/` Contributed objects (individual)

`/pub/patch/` Patches to this release of Radiance

`/pub/pics/` Radiance renderings

`/pub/ports/` Radiance ports to non-Unix systems

`/pub/programs/` Miscellaneous programs linked to Radiance

/pub/tests/ Global illumination solutions for comparison

/pub/translators/ Object and image translators to/from Radiance

Mirrors: dasun2.epfl.ch

Comments: Radiance is a suite of programs for the analysis and visualization of lighting in design.

5-102 **UC—San Francisco, Pharm/Chem. Cohen Group archives:** babar.ucsf.edu

i srp@cgl.ucsf.edu

Software for protein structure research; misc. software and patches for SGI IRIX applications.

Comments: Some software requires licensing.

5-103 **UCI-ICS anonymous FTP:** ftp.ics.uci.edu

i support@ics.uci.edu

University of California—Irvine Department of Information and Computer Science.

Contents:

/pub/mh MH Mail Handler

/pub/machine-learning-databases/ Machine Learning Databases and Domain Theories

Mirrors: /pub/mh is mirrored at many major FTP sites (uunet, etc.).

5-104 **University of Colorado Computer Science Department:** ftp.cs.colorado.edu

i trouble@ftp.cs.colorado.edu

Research results and system administration tools.

Contents:

/pub/cs/distribs/ Distributions of several packages including SeeTeX, Netfind, Essence, etc.

/pub/cs/sysadmin/ System administration tools, incl. Queue MH

/pub/cs/HPSC/ Instructional materials for the high-performance supercomputing course

• Many other miscellaneous items

Comments: The data on this FTP server can be searched and accessed via WAIS, using our Essence semantic indexing system. Users can pick up a copy of the WAIS .src file for accessing this service by anonymous FTP from ftp.cs.colorado.edu, in pub/cs/distribs/essence/aftp-cs-colorado-edu.src. This file also describes where to get the prototype source code and a paper about this system.

5-105 **University of Delaware FTP archive:** ftp.udel.edu

i staff@udel.edu

FTP archive for the University of Delaware.

Contents: See /README file list in /FIND-LS.Z

/pub/ntp/ main site for the Network Timekeeping Protocol programs

/pub/midi/ collection of MIDI music stuff

5-106 **University of Hawaii Meteorology & Geophysics Archive:** `satftp.soest.hawaii.edu`:
Meteorological/geophysical information for the Pacific.

Contents: Weather satellite photos, sea surface temperature datasets, etc.

`avhrr/` Data from the hrpt receiving system

`gms/` Data from the gms receiving system

`jgofs/` Data from the Pacific Joint Global Ocean Flux Study experiment

`outgoing/` Personal directories for our staff

`catalogs/` Catalogs of our raw data holdings on 8mm tapes

`papers/` Text and figures of papers published by this group

`tiwe/` Data from the Tropical Instability Wave Experiment

`seawifs/` Data from the NASA/OSC SeaWifs satellite. Restricted

`spectacular/` Special data and plots of particular interest

`tools/` Miscellaneous software tools

5-107 **University of Houston Gene-Server FTP:** `ftp.bchs.uh.edu`

i `davison@uh.edu`

Home of molecular biological software and data for many different platforms (Unix, VMS, DOS, Mac). Everything available via anonymous FTP is also available via electronic mail. Send mail consisting of the word "help" to `gene-server@evolution.bchs.uh.edu` *for more information.*

Contents:

`/pub/gene-server/dos/` DOS software for molecular biology

`/pub/gene-server/mac/` Mac software for molecular biology

`/pub/gene-server/unix/` Unix software for molecular biology

`/pub/gene-server/vms/` VAX/VMS software for molecular biology

`/pub/gene-server/pir/` Protein Information Resource (latest release)

`/pub/gene-server/Alpha/` Software for DEC's ALPHA

`/pub/gene-server/pdb/` Protein data-bank (latest release)

5-108 **University of Illinois's Smalltalk Archive:** `st.cs.uiuc.edu`

i `ftp@st.cs.uiuc.edu`

An archive devoted to the Smalltalk programming language.

Contents: See file `pub/Index` for a current overview of the archive.

Comments: Also available via e-mail. Send the message `help` to `goodies-lib@st.cs.uiuc.edu`

Mirrors: `mushroom.cs.man.ac.uk`

5-109 **University of Karlsruhe, CC, FTP Archive:** `ftp.rz.uni-karlsruhe.de`

i `ftp@rz.uni-karlsruhe.de`

FTP Archive at the Computing Center of the University of Karlsruhe, Germany.

Contents:

`/pub/bsd-sources/` Berkeley Networking Distribution II

`/pub/cert/` Archive of the German CERT at the University of Karlsruhe

/pub/doc/ Miscellaneous documentation (FTP, isode)

/pub/emacs/ Emacs (for HP-UX)

/pub/gopher/ Sources and binaries for various gopher clients/servers

/pub/hp-ux/ Software for HP-UX

/pub/lapack/ Linear Algebra Package

/pub/linux/ Linux files mirrored from tsx-11.mit.edu and sunsite.unc.edu

/pub/net/irc/ Sources for IRC clients/servers

/pub/net/news/ Sources for News clients/servers

/pub/net/packetdriver/ Sources and binaries for MS-DOS network packet drivers

/pub/news/ Archive of Usenet news postings (alt.security, comp.archives, comp.security.misc, comp.sys.hp, comp.unix.ultrix)

/pub/pctex/ MS-DOS TeX software (EmTeX)

/pub/pvm/ PVM package (distributed computing)

/pub/zyxel/ Roms, voice/FAX-software for ZyXEL 1496 modems mirrored from ftp.cd.chalmers.se

5-110 **University of Michigan/Merit Software Archives:** archive.umich.edu

i archive-admin@archive.umich.edu.

Collections of public domain, freeware, shareware, and licensed software. Contacts for each archive portion are listed below. Please note that most of the work on the archives is being done by volunteers..

Contents:

/mac Mac software (445Mb) *i* mac-archivist@archive.umich.edu
Alternate host name: mac.archive.umich.edu

/msdos IBM PC and compatible software (350Mb) *i* msdos-archivist@archive.umich.edu Alternate host name: msdos.archive.umich.edu

/atari Atari software (325Mb) *i* atari-archivist@archive.umich.edu
Alternate host name: atari.archive.umich.edu

/apple2 Apple 2 software (45Mb) *i* apple2-archivist@archive.umich.edu Alternate host name: apple2.archive.umich.edu

/linguistics linguistics software (16Mb) *i* linguistics-archivist@archive.umich.edu Alternate host name: linguistics.archive.umich.edu

/amiga Amiga software (16Mb) *i* amiga-archivist@archive.umich.edu
Alternate host name: amiga.archive.umich.edu

/apollo Apollo software (4Mb) *i* apollo-archivist@archive.umich.edu

/physics physics software (5Mb) *i* physics-archivist@archive.umich.edu

/economics economics software and data

Mirrors:

```
wuarchive.wustl.edu in /mirrors/archive.umich.edu/
src.doc.ic.ac.uk in /packages/mac/umich
archie.au in /micros/mac/umich
```

Comments: You may request that files be mailed to you from the Atari or Mac archives (see the Help file in those archives for details). This service will be expanded to include other archives in the future. For help via e-mail, send the command `help` in the body (not in the subject line) to either `mac@mac.archive.umich.edu` or `atari@atari.archive.umich.edu`.

5-111 **University of Passau Lehrstuhl fur Mathematik Archive:** `alice.fmi.uni-passau.de`

i `ftp@alice.fmi.uni-passau.de`

The FTP-server of the "Lehrstuhl für Mathematik, Universität Passau." The main purpose of this server is to make computer-algebra software (e.g. the MAS Modula-Algebra-System) developed here available.

Contents: Some software for RS/6000, NeXT, Atari-ST and others.

`/pub/ComputerAlgebraSystems/masMAS` Modula-Algebra-System

5-112 **University of Pennsylvania CIS Department FTP server:** `ftp.cis.upenn.edu`

i `manager@ftp.cis.upenn.edu` unless explicitly specified otherwise for individual packages.

The Penn CIS Department FTP Server is provided by the Computer and Information Science Department at the University of Pennsylvania in Philadelphia, Pennsylvania, USA. It is intended for public distribution and receipt of packages that are of interest to those cooperating with CIS-affiliated research activities.

Contents:

`/pub/Lolli/` Prolog-like language based on intuitionistic linear logic

`/pub/NH3.1/` NetHack 3.1 release

`/pub/dsl/` CIS Department—Distributed Systems Lab publications & code

`/pub/graphics/` CIS Department—Graphics Lab publications & code; includes Jack

`/pub/grasp/` CIS Department—GRASP Lab publications & code

`/pub/ircs/` Institute for Research in Cognitive Science publications

`/pub/ircs/tr/` IRCS Technical Reports

`/pub/ldc/` Linguistics Data Consortium publications & code

`/pub/linc/` CIS Department—LINC Lab publications & code

`/pub/lprolog/` Lambda Prolog publications & notes

`/pub/meetings/` Collection of announcements and proceedings of selected events

`/pub/papers/` Selected papers and publications of CIS faculty/researchers

`/pub/screamer.tar.Z` Extension of Common Lisp for nondeterministic programming

`/pub/theory/` CIS Department—Theory Group publications & code

`/pub/tr/` Selected Technical Reports not found in papers or Lab directories

`/pub/xtag/` A Graphical Workbench for Developing Tree-Adjoining Grammars

/pub/xv/ John Bradley's image viewer/manipulator

Comments: Consult the README files in individual directories for more information on contents. Large transfers should be done outside local time business hours (9AM-6PM). The FTP server we run supports automatic tar and compress/uncompress features when retrieving files.

5-113 **University of Toronto Computer Systems Research Institute:** `ftp.csri.toronto.edu`

i `ftp@csri.toronto.edu`

CSRI FTP Archive.

Contents: CSRI Technical reports

5-114 **University of Vaasa, Finland, Computer Center:** `ftp.uwasa.fi`

i `ftp@uwasa.fi`

Archive of the University of Computer Center at Vaasa, Finland.

Contents: A wide selection of useful, tested PC and Mac software, and some of the major Unix packages.

5-115 **University of Waterloo Computer Engineering Archive:** `sunee.uwaterloo.ca`

i `broehl@sunee.uwaterloo.ca`

The U of W Computer Engineering Archive is maintained by the Department of Electrical and Computer Engineering, University of Waterloo, Waterloo, Ontario, Canada.

Contents:

/pub/rend386/ Dave Stampe and Bernie Roehl's fast screen renderer

/pub/vr/ Miscellaneous files related to Virtual Reality

/pub/wattcp/ Erick Engelke's implementation of a TCP/IP library

/pub/jpeg/ Eric Praetzel's JPEG viewer

/pub/bicycle/ Information about bicycling

/pub/glove/ Files related to the PowerGlove

/pub/netgame/ Early ideas related to networked games and shared VRs

/pub/radio/ Files related to amateur radio

/pub/shadows/ Files related to the TV series "Dark Shadows"

5-116 **University of Wollongong Department of Computer Science:** `ftp.cs.uow.edu.au`

i `postmaster@cs.uow.edu.au`

Publicly available files offered by the Computer Science Department at the University of Wollongong, Australia.

Contents: Netlib and miscellaneous files.

Comments: FTP mail gateway via `ftpmail@cs.uow.edu.au`

5-117 **USENIX SAGE Archive (SAGE = SysAdmin Guild):** `ftp.sage.uxenix.org`

i `sage-archivist@usenix.org` (soon) or `verber@parc.xerox.com` (current)

Archives of material related to SAGE, and materials that are deemed useful to SAGE members.

Contents:

• Papers presented at SAGE conferences

- Material generated by various SAGE working groups
- Material which the SAGE board wishes to be distributed to the general public
- Material to aid system & network administrators in carrying out their jobs

5-118 **UUNET Archive:** `ftp.uu.net`

i `archive@uunet.uu.net`

This site contains a large general-purpose archive of sources and documentation for Unix-ish systems and popular micros. The largest area of concentration is Unix-ish systems software and documentation (including networking).

Contents: Look in `/info/layout`

Comments: The password given for anonymous FTP should be the user's e-mail address. The archive is also available via 900 dialup anonymous UUCP; see `/uunet-info/900`

5-119 **UWO Engineering FTP site:** `ftp.engrg.uwo.ca`

i `ftp-owner@engrg.uwo.ca`

Mainted by the DA&MR Lab, Mechanical Engineering, University of Western Ontario, London, Ontario, Canada.

Contents:

- FrameMaker (Desktop publishing) FTP site
- TML (Traveller Mailing List) archives
- Convergence-Zone (Harpoon) archives

5-120 **Washington University of St. Louis FTP Archive:** `wuarchive.wustl.edu`

i `archives@wugate.wustl.edu.`

Largest archive in the US, maintained by Washington University of St. Louis.

Contents: Retrieve `files.lst` for a complete listing of all files in the archive. Please be careful retrieving this file as it is currently over 7 Mb long. If you have access to the Unix uncompress program, you can retrieve `files.lst.Z`, which is only about 1 Mb.

`/ls-lR` Output of a recursive directory listing of the archive

`/files.list` Like above but with full pathnames shown for each file

`/bin/` System support programs

`/etc/` System support information

`/pub/` Public access directory—leave contributions here

`/decus/` The latest DECUS Symposia tapes and other new DECUS releases, including tools and info useful for extracting software from DECUS tapes; a catalog of other DECUS software

`/doc/` General interest information and standards documents, including the OnLine Bible; specifications for some graphics formats; Internet Engineering Task Force documents; interest-group mailing lists for Internet users; the Internet Draft documents; Amateur Computerist Newsletter, ShareDebate International, and other electronic publications; The Internet Resource Guide; RFCs; and NSFnew usage statistics

`/graphics/` Graphics programs and files, including line-printer art, images from the Magellan mission, and lots of source code related to 3D graphics and user interaction

/network_info/ (Local Interest) Information about the Washington U. network

/packages/ Various packages runnable on multiple systems, including X11R5, source and results for various benchmarks, source code to various compression programs, source and patches to ELM version 2.3, source to the Ferret image processing program (assembly lang), source to a public domain math library, source to various news transport and reading programs, source to the news transmission manager, source to the Postgres database system, and source to the top system monitor package, with Ultrix patches

/systems/ System-specific programs for various PCs and workstations, including Sun, Apple II, IBM PC, Hewlett-Packard, Macintosh, Atari, Amiga, and Unix

/usenet/ Archived files from various comp.* Usenet newsgroups and digests from rec.food.recipes

• This site mirrors a large number of archives from around the world.

5-121 **Wisconsin Primate Center Software Archive:** ftp.primate.wisc.edu

i software@primate.wisc.edu

Wisconsin Regional Primate Research Center (University of Wisconsin–Madison). The archive's purpose is to provide a distribution point for software developed at WRPRC.

Contents:

/pub/imake-stuff/ Miscellaneous papers and software related to imake

/pub/imake-book/ Archives for O'Reilly & Associates book "Software Portability with imake"

/pub/RTF/ RTF translator tools (e.g., rtf2troff, rtf2text)

/pub/troffcvt/ Troff translator tools (e.g., troff2rtf, unroff)

/pub/mac/ Macintosh software (e.g., TransSkel, Blob Manager)

Mirrors: ftp.ora.com and ftp.uu.net mirror the imake-book directory.

6. GOPHER SERVERS

The gopher protocol was designed at the University of Minnesota's Microcomputer and Workstation Networks Center to provide distributed document search and retrieval on the Internet. Gopher works on the client-server model (for more information on the client-server model, please see "An Internet Refresher" at the beginning of the book). When you ask your local gopher client to search "gopherspace" for the files you want, it takes care of connecting to gopher servers all over the Internet and then builds you a menu of the options returned by your search. You then choose items from the menu, and the gopher client retrieves the files for you.

Entry Format:

Item
Number

6-n   **Gopher name:** `gopher address` [Port # if other than 70]
       i `contact address`
            Description of the gopher provided by hosting institution.
       Services: list of what's unique to the gopher

Public Gopher Clients: Although it is preferable that you run gopher from a local client, there are some publicly available clients that you can telnet to. These are listed below, along with the login name you should use to access each client (if login is other than `gopher`) and the country in which the host computer is located. Please use clients in your area only.

North America:
`consultant.micro.umn.edu`
`ux1.cso.uiuc.edu`
`panda.uiowa.edu` login as `panda`
`gopher.msu.edu`
`infoslug.ucsc.edu`

Europe: `gopher.ebone.net`
Australia: `info.anu.edu.au` login as `info`
Sweden: `gopher.chalmers.se`
South America: `tolten.puc.cl`
Ecuador: `ecnet.ec`
Japan: `gan.ncc.go.jp`

Where to Find It: This list was built by sending a request for information to every gopher maintainer for whom I could find an address. The "Services:" information was provided by the maintainers themselves. New gophers are being created all the time, so if you use Veronica or browse through gopherspace on your own you will find everything that's listed here, and more.

Comments: If you are interested in new gopher servers and client software, you can subscribe to the Gopher-News mailing list by sending a piece of e-mail to the following address: `gopher-news-request@boombox.micro.umn.edu`. Gopher client software for many computer platforms is available via anonymous FTP from `boombox.micro.umn.edu` in the `/pub/gopher/` directory. Gopher is also discussed on the `comp.infosystems.gopher` Usenet newsgroup.

Entries:

6-1   **Academic Position Network:** `wcni.cis.umn.edu port 1111`

i `apn@staff.tc.umn.edu`

> *This is a worldwide listing of announcements of academic positions. Institutions pay a fee to place a position announcement on the gopher; users (other than commercial) may browse and search at no charge.*

Services: The Academic Position Network (APN) is an online service accessible worldwide through Internet. It provides notice of academic position announcements, including faculty, staff, and administrative positions. Included are notices of announcements for postdoctoral positions and graduate fellowships and assistantships.

6-2   **Academy of Sciences Slovakia:** `savba.savba.cs`

i `vystavil@savba.cs`

> *This is the CWIS of the Slovak Academy of Sciences, Bratislava, Slovakia.*

Services:
- Campus directory
- Information on Institutes of Slovak Academy of Sciences
- Information on conferences organized by Slovak Academy of Sciences
- Gateway to a telnet/FTP resource

6-3   **ACCD CWIS:** `accd.edu`

i `syswork1@accd.edu`

> *This is the CWIS at the Alamo Community Colleges in San Antonio, Texas.*

Services:
- Campus directory
- Local weather forecast
- Pointers to other CWISs and telnet/FTP resources
- Local sports scores, etc.

6-4   **ACTLab (University of Texas at Austin, RTF Department):** `actlab.rtf.utexas.edu`

i `gopher@actlab.rtf.utexas.edu`

The ACTLab gopher is maintained by the Advanced Communications Technologies Laboratory (ACTLab) in the Radio, Television, and Film (RTF) Department of the Communications College at the University of Texas at Austin (USA). The purpose of this gopher is to make available information related to the issues of interfaces, interaction, and agency.

Services:

- Information and services pertaining to MUDs (multi-user dungeons), also known as text-based virtual realities. Includes access to research papers and gateways organized by type of MUD
- Pointers to other notable MUD sites
- Conferences: information on upcoming and past conferences on topics related to the purposes of the gopher (including 3CyberConf and INET '93)
- Information on the Internet (articles, services, etc.)
- Archive of papers presented at the Third International Conference on Cyberspace
- Japanese Animation Infospace Project

6-5 **AGINFO:** `bluehen.ags.udel.edu`

i `betsy@bluehen.ags.udel.edu`

A tool to distribute information on the teaching, research, and extension mission of the College of Agricultural Sciences, University of Delaware, Newark, Delaware.

Services:

- College publications such as newsletters, fact sheets, extension bulletins, research abstracts, teaching and curriculum information, etc.
- Pointers to several other agriculture-related gophers such as Perdue, Penn State, and Illinois

6-6 **Anesthesiology Gopher:** `eja.anes.hscsyr.edu`

i `gopher@eja.anes.hscsyr.edu`

This gopher covers topics of interest to those interested in the fields of anesthesiology and critical care and is maintained by the Department of Anesthesiology at the State University of New York Health Science Center at Syracuse.

Services:

- Archive of the Anesthesiology Bitnet/Internet mailing list
- Boards, keywords, book reviews
- Clinical tidbits
- M & M case conference reports
- Faculty positions
- Lecture notes
- Research abstracts

6-7 **ANU Bioinformatics:** `life.anu.edu.au`

i `david.green@anu.edu.au` or `gopher-manager@life.anu.edu.au`

Biological gopher service of the Bioinformatics Facility at the Australian National University, Canberra.

Services: Comprehensive range of services (databases, software, etc.) and links to important resources organized under (mainly) biological themes, including the following:

- Complex systems, e.g., artificial life, chaos, fractals, genetic algorithms
- Molecular biology (links to all major databases)
- Weather and global monitoring
- Biodiversity
- Biomathematics and biocomputing
- "FireNet," an information service on landscape fires
- Landscape ecology
- Medical databases and services
- Paleobiology
- Viruses (real ones, NOT computer viruses!)

6-8 **Apple Computer Higher Education Gopher Server:** `info.hed.apple.com`

i `feedback@info.hed.apple.com`

> *Information provided by Apple Computer Higher Education Marketing for maintaining on-going communication with the higher-ed community. It also allows interaction to share the use of technology within (currently) seven different academic disciplines.*

Services:

- Apple Computer product information
- Dialog forum for business, computer science and engineering, foreign language, library and information systems, mechanical engineering, medical and health sciences, and schools of education
- Intellimation software catalog
- Public relations and marketing information
- Query publications
- Syllabus publications
- U.S. regional news
- U.S. service, support, and training

6-9 **Arabidopsis Research Companion:** `weeds.mgh.harvard.edu`

i `curator@frodo.mgh.harvard.edu`

> *Information server for the AAtDB Project from the Department of Molecular Biology, Massachusetts General Hospital, Boston, Massachusetts.*

Services: This server provides access to the information contained in the brassica genomic database: AAtDB (An *Arabidopsis thaliana* Database), the nematode genomic database: ACeDB (A *Caenorhabditis elegans* Database), as well as information from the faculty of the Department of Molecular Biology at MGH.

- Arabidopsis information and indexes
- Caenorhabditis information as a searchable WAIS index
- Department of Molecular Biology, MGH

6-10 **Arizona East Asian Gopher:** `enuxva.eas.asu.edu` port 9000, or enuxhb.eas.asu.edu port 9000

i sridhar@enuxha.eas.asu.edu

> *This gopher is intended to serve Asian Indians.*

Services:

- Topics related to Asian Indians, including music, food, etc.

6-11 **Armadillo, the Texas Studies Gopher:** chico.rice.edu port 1170

i armadillo@chico.rice.edu

> *This is an Internet gopher server designed to provide instructional resources and information about Texas natural and cultural history and the Texas environment. Armadillo has been created to support teachers and students who are interested in enriching their instruction and study with multimedia material and Internet resources.*

Services:

- Primary source documents on the natural and cultural history of Texas
- Internet resources

6-12 **ASK-Gopher:** gopher.ask.uni-karlsruhe.de

i boden@ask.uni-karlsruhe.de

> *This is the gopher service of the Akademische Software Kooperation, University of Karlsruhe, Germany Please note: half of the information is in German.*

Services:

- Software server for public-accessible teaching software for higher education
- Collection of more than 3,200 descriptions of software for higher education, which can be investigated through a WAIS index or through a telnet dialog to ASK-SISY, the software information system of ASK
- Information about ASK itself

6-13 **Association for Computing Machinery (ACM):** gopher.acm.org

i helpdesk@acm.org

> *This gopher server provides access to online information services available from the Association for Computing Machinery (ACM). ACM, founded in 1947, is the largest and oldest international educational and scientific computer society in the industry.*

Services: Information services for the following ACM activities are available:

- Conferences
- Publications
- Thirty-four special-interest groups
- Local activities: ACM International Collegiate Programming Contest, Technology Outreach Program, and chapters

6-14 **Austin Hospital, Melbourne, Australia:** pet1.austin.unimelb.edu.au

i danny@austin.unimelb.edu.au (Daniel O'Callaghan)

> *Gopher of the PET Centre, Austin Hospital, Melbourne, Victoria, Australia.*

Services: Provides medically oriented information, including links to other medically oriented gopher sites and annotated sample Positron Emission Tomography.

6-15 **Australian Environmental Resources Information Network (ERIN):** `kaos.erin.gov.au`

i `gopher@erin.gov.au`

Australian environmental information

Services: The environmental information accessible through the ERIN gopher includes the following:

- Biodiversity: lists, locations, and statistics on Australian species, including over 800,000 individual specimens or observations
- Protected areas: information on Australian nature conservation reserves, their management, history, vegetation, etc.
- Terrestrial/marine environments: information on environmental regionalizations and ecosystems of Australia
- Environment protection: information on the status and management of feral animals and pest plants in Australia
- Legislation: information on Australian environmental legislation
- International agreements: information on international environmental agreements and conventions
- ERIN information systems overview: information on the ERIN program, projects, data, and systems
- General Information: ERIN newsletter, associates, collaborators, etc.

6-16 **Automated Reasoning Program (ARP):** `arp.anu.edu.au`

i `postmaster@arp.anu.edu.au`

This service is provided on top of the FTP anonymous area, which is the primary mode of distributing information within this system. Some items of relevance to parallel and symbolic computing are provided.

Services:

- Software developed at the ARP
- Other software of interest to the ARP
- Papers written by the ARP researchers
- Archive of some mailing lists related to automated reasoning
- Archive of selected newsgroups related to automated reasoning and parallel computing
- Archive of SunOS patches

6-17 **Ball State University Gopher Server:** `gopher.bsu.edu`

i `gopher@bsu.edu`

This is the CWIS of Ball State University in Muncie, Indiana.

Services: Campus directory

- Campus host help systems
- Campus newsletters; college, department, and faculty publications
- Usenet newsgroups; locally accessible AP wire feed
- Interface to campus hosts

6-18 **Banach Space Theory Bulletin Board Index:** `hardy.math.okstate.edu`
i `alspach@math.okstate.edu`

> *This is an index to the archive of papers in Banach Space Theory maintained by the Department of Mathematics at Oklahoma State University, Stillwater, Oklahoma.*

Services: This gopher provides a keyword search of the archive.

6-19 **Bar-Ilan University Campus Wide Information System:** `vm.biu.ac.il`
i `hank@vm.biu.ac.il`

> *This is the CWIS for Bar-Ilan University in Israel.*

Services:

- Campus directory
- Local bus lines
- Israeli network information

6-20 **Base de Dados Tropical (Campinas, SP, Brazil):** `bdt.ftpt.br` port 70
i `manager@bdt.ftpt.br`

> *The Tropical Data Base (Base de Dados Tropical-BDT) is an information center housed at the Fundacao Tropical de Pesquisas e Tecnologia "Andre Tosello," a not-for-profit, private foundation. BDT is involved with the collection, analysis, and dissemination of data relevant to biodiversity and biotechnology, and with the development of software for data management.*

Services:

- BDTNet tropical database network (extensive collections of information are available through this link)
- BDTNet database searches
- BDTNet discussion list
- BDTNet electronic publications
- LeishNet-Leishmaniasis network

6-21 **Baylor College of Medicine Biogopher:** `mbcr.bcm.tmc.edu`
i `steffen@bcm.tmc.edu`

> *This gopher is run by Baylor College of Medicine's Molecular Biology Computing Resource (MBCR) for the purposes of (1) making databases of biological and biomedical data developed at Baylor College of Medicine available to the scientific and medical communities, and (2) making the worldwide collection of such databases available to the MBCR user community via links to other gophers.*

Services:

- Tumor gene database: a database of genes involved in cancer, including oncogenes, proto-oncogenes, and tumor supressor genes
- Transcription factor database

6-22 **Bilkent University Gopher:** `gopher.bilkent.edu.tr`
i `akgul@bilkent.edu.tr`

> *Part of the CWIS of Bilkent University, Turkey.*

Services:

- Campus directory
- Pointers to other Internet services in Turkey
- Pointers to specialized pointers for TeX, math, and optimization
- Access to Bilkent archives which includes locally developed software on Computational Linguistics (Prof. Oflazer and his coworkers) and locally developed software on Machine Learning and other areas
- TeX archives for Unix, PC
- GNU and X11-contrib archives
- Optimization archive

6-23 **Bioinformatics (Weizmann Institute of Science, Israel):**
 `bioinformatics.weizmann.ac.il`
 i `lsprilus@weizmann.weizmann.ac.il`
> *This is the main source for data and software related to bioinformatics and molecular biology on this side of the world. This is a gopher+ server.*

Services:
- Public-domain software for biology
- Mirror storage for the main databases of the Human Genome Project and Molecular Biology
- Anonymous FTP server

6-24 **Biological Sciences Administrative Gopher Server (University of Chicago):**
 `bsd-gopher.bsd.uchicago.edu`
 i `gopher@delphi.bsd.uchicago.edu` or `rich@delphi.bsd.uchicago.edu`
> *This is the Biological Sciences administrative gopher server of the University of Chicago in Chicago, Illinois. The gopher is in its infancy, and plans to expand are in the works.*

Services:
- NIH Guide (National Institutes of Health)

6-25 **Bloomfield Hills Model High School:**
 i `gopher@mhs-server.bloomfield.k12.mi.us`
> *This gopher is run by students at the Model High School in Bloomfield Hills, Michigan.*

6-26 **Board of Governors of State Colleges and Universities Gopher:** `gopher.bgu.edu`
> *This is an Information Service of the Board of Governors of State Colleges and Universities Chancellor's Office which is made up of Chicago State University, Eastern Illinois University, Governors State University, Northeastern Illinois University, and Western Illinois University.*

Services: This service contains information from the Board of Governors of State Colleges and Universities Chancellor's Office to the five campuses.

6-27 **Boston University CWIS:** `gopher.bu.edu`
 i `cwis@bu.edu`
> *This is the CWIS serving Boston University. The purpose of this system is to provide students, faculty, and staff at Boston University with convenient access to useful information.*

Services: The system provides a wide range of information about topics of general and specific interest. These include schedules of events; announcements; descriptions of campus facilities; financial aid options; campus safety issues; listing and descriptions of student organizations; housing and employment opportunities; policy statements; university publications, including an electronic phone book; the university library's card catalog and circulation system; weather reports; and access to hundreds of information systems around the world.

6-28 **Bowling Green State University CWIS Gopher:** `gopher.bgsu.edu`

i `hasley@bgsu.edu`

This is the CWIS of Bowling Green State University, Bowling Green, Ohio.

6-29 **Brussels Free Universities Computing Centre:** `gopher.vub.ac.be`

i `gopher@vub.ac.be`

This is the gopher server of the Computing Centre of the Brussels Free Universities VUB/ULB.

Services:

- National entry point for EMBnet in Belgium
- Links to university library systems and EMBnet databases

6-30 **Building Technology Gopher (Technion–Israel Institute of Technology):**
`ari.technion.ac.il` port 1070

i `kargon@ari.technion.ac.il`

A nascent collection of material related to architecture and construction technologies. This server is intended to form the hub of a national (and international) online resource for professional architectural practice.

Services:

- Project material
- Architecture in a marine environment
- Intelligent buildings slide library
- Links to other architecture gopher collections
- Links to online art/architecture journals

6-31 **Calvin Knightline Gopher:** `gopher.calvin.edu`

i `gopher-admin@calvin.edu`

This is the CWIS for Calvin College and Seminary in Grand Rapids, Michigan.

Services:

- Campus directory
- Campus library catalog

6-32 **Camosun College CWIS:** `gopher.camosun.bc.ca`

i `postmaster@camosun.bc.ca`

This is the CWIS of Camosun College in Victoria, British Columbia, Canada.

Services:

- Campus directory
- Online committee minutes

- Current job postings
- Departmental newsletters
- Community education course descriptions
- Access to the college's online library
- Access to other CWIS services and Victoria Freenet

6-33 **CAN:** `canb.can.nl`

i `can@can.nl`

Expertise Centre CAN (Computer Algebra Netherlands), Amsterdam, the Netherlands.

Services:
- Information on the Expertise Centre CAN
- Information on the CA (Computer Algebra) packages running on CAN computers
- Information on distribution of CA packages by CAN

6-34 **CAOS/CAMM Center:** `camms1.caos.kun.nl`

i `schaft@caos.kun.nl`

This is the Dutch EMBnet node.

Services:
- Course information
- Pointers to databases of biological interest
- Pointers to Dutch services

6-35 **Case Western Reserve University Campus Root Gopher:** `gopher.cwru.edu`

i `gopher@gopher.cwru.edu`

This is the central gopher server at Case Western Reserve University, Cleveland, Ohio.

Services:
- Lists all other gophers at CWRU
- University information
- Class information
- Collections of pointers to off-campus information
- Various gateways to other services. This is the only published entry point to gopherspace at CWRU. All other CWRU gophers are linked transparently into this one to provide a single consistent view of everything in gopher at CWRU

6-36 **Catholic University of Eichstaett—Gopher Information Service:**
`gopher.ku-eichstaett.de`

i `gopher@ku-eichstaett.de`

This gopher provides information for students and staff of the Catholic University of Eichstaett, Germany.

6-37 **Center for Advanced Medical Informatics at Stanford (CAMIS):** `camis.stanford.edu`

i `torsten_heycke@med.stanford.edu`

CAMIS is a shared computing resource supporting research activities in biomedical informatics at the Stanford University School of Medicine.

Services:

- Pointers to other gopher sources that include medical schools, medical publications, genetic engineering, computational biology, etc.
- Technical report abstracts since 1982

6-38 **Centre for Experimental and Constructive Mathematics Gopher Server:**
gopher.cecm.sfu.ca

i gopher@cecm.sfu.ca or cecm@cecm.sfu.ca

This is the Canadian Mathematics Network Information Service of Simon Fraser University, Burnaby, British Columbia.

Services:

- Access to CECM materials and information
- Electronic publications documents
- Mathematical journal abstracts
- Pointers and summaries of mathematical resources on the Internet
- Archived information, software, and libraries for a variety of popular mathematical tools
- Canadian Mathematical Society information and services

6-39 **CERRO (Central European Regional Research Organization):** gopher.wu-wien.ac.at

i gunther.maier@wu-wien.ac.at

This gopher provides information about the economic restructuring of Central Europe.

Services:

- Electronic discussion list and archive devoted to regional economic aspects of Central European restructuring
- Papers about Central Europe, economic restructuring, regional development, etc.
- Information about research institutes and individuals active in this field
- News summaries
- Pointers to other gophers in Central Europe

6-40 **CESNET Root Gopher Server:** gopher.cesnet.cz

i gopheradm@cuni.cz

The authoritative national entry point for the Czech Republic, referencing all other gopher servers.

Services: Provides information about CESNET (Czech Educational and Scientific Network), as well as access to other resources of this academical network.

6-41 **Chance Database:** chance.dartmouth.edu

i dart.chance.edu

This is a database of materials relating to current events that rely on probability and statistical concepts. It is maintained by Dartmouth College.

Services:

- Archive for Chance News, a biweekly report that provides abstracts of articles in current newspapers and journals that might be of interest to anyone teaching a statistics or probability course

- Information about the Chance course, which is an introductory course designed to make students more informed readers of current chance events as reported in the media
- Information about topics found particularly successful in teaching a Chance course. Examples: the use of DNA fingerprinting in the courts, gender issues with SAT tests, clinical trials, and streaks in sports
- Teaching aids: items such as computer programs, articles on teaching statistical concepts, etc.; information on videotapes, etc., that might be useful in teaching an introductory course in probability or statistics

6-42 **Charles University Computer Center Gopher Server:** `gopher.cuni.cz`

i `gopheradm@cuni.cz`

This gopher maintains information about the Charles University in Prague, Czech Republic.

Services:

- Charles University information (its structure, directions of education and research, addresses, profiles of faculties)
- Information about the Pasnet network (Pasnet stands for "Prague Academical Network")

6-43 **Chicago State University Gopher:** `gopher.csu.bgu.edu`

This is a CWIS of Chicago State University.

Services: Campus undergraduate and graduate catalogs.

6-44 **Children, Youth, and Family Consortium Electronic Clearinghouse:**
`tinman.mes.umn.edu` port 80

i `cyfce@staff.tc.umn.edu`

The CYF Consortium is a collaborative effort of the University of Minnesota and public and private organizations and agencies throughout Minnesota, USA, addressing child, youth, and family issues. The Clearinghouse provides research-based information and practical resources on children, youth, and families to agencies and individuals.

Services:

- CYF research summaries, especially research conducted in Minnesota
- MN statistical and demographic information on CYF
- Activities, advice columns, brochures
- CYF experts, coursework, programs, bibliographies
- Selections reprinted from "Daily Report Card"
- Gateway/telnet to LUMINA (University of Minnesota card catalog), ERIC, PENPages and QUERRI (ES-USDA databases and resources)
- Information on CYF Consortium and its collaborative work

6-45 **CICNet:** `gopher.cic.net`

i `holbrook@cic.net`

Gopher of the CICNet Internet Access Provider.

Services:

- CICNet Resource Guide
- Conferences and events

- Electronic serials
- Great Lakes Information Network
- Access to other CICNet gopher servers
- The Circuit, the CICNet Newsletter

6-46 **CILEA:** `imicilea.cilea.it`

i `guglielm@imicilea.cilea.it`

This is the gopher for the CILEA (Consorzio Interuniversitario Lombardo per la Elaborazione Automatica) InterUniversity Computer Center in Milan, Italy.

Services:

- Network Information retrieval (by anonymous FTP)
- Access to CILEA hosts
- Access to databases in Europe
- Access to CERN services such as WWW and ALICE
- Access to CBCUP (Collective Bibliographic Catalogue of Po Universities)
- Access to Usenet newsgroups
- PostScript documentation on various items
- Access to Italian research network information
- Local information for CILEA users

6-47 **CIUWInfo:** `plearn.edu.pl`

i `chomac@plearn.edu.pl` or `chomac@plearn.bitnet`

This is the Informatics Center information service of Warsaw University, Poland.

Services:

- Logistic database LOGBANK
- Archives of the discussion lists CIUW-L and NASK
- Local information

6-48 **Cleveland State University Law Library Gopher:** `gopher.law.csuohio.edu`

i `root@trans.csuohio.edu`

This gopher services the CSU and Law School community, including local attorneys. The gopher has been configured to assist these groups in accessing legal information or Internet-legal information with easy search and retrieval tools. Suggestions to better the resources are welcome.

Services:

- Law sources to the public
- FTP/Archie/finding combinations ("one of the finest in the world")
- Alex gateway to enhance Internet file sharing

6-49 **College for Applied Technical, Economic, and Social Sciences Zittau/Goerlitz Gopher:** `gopher.htw-zittau.de`

i `hubein@hermes.informatik.htw-zittau.de` or `gopheradmin@gopher.htw-zittau.de`

Campus Wide Information System (CWIS).

Services: Information about study in Zittau/Goerlitz (only in German).

6-50 **College of Engineering Gopher:** `lenz.engr.utk.edu`

i `kanthraj@sun1.engr.utk.edu`

This is the Engineering gopher server of the University of Tennessee, Knoxville, Tennessee.

Services:
- Engineering School materials
- Pointers to subject-based servers
- Collection of papers
- Faculty listing and course details

6-51 **Colorado K–12 Internet Gopher Server:** `k12.colostate.edu`

i `redder@k12.colostate.edu`

This is the Colorado K–12 gopher server at Colorado State University, Fort Collins, Colorado.

Services: This gopher server is intended to support K–12 Internet networking in Colorado and beyond. Currently it is just being brought up, but will maintain archives of programs and material useful for K–12 Internet sites (or wanna-be Internet sites), along with Internet curriculum material.

6-52 **Colorado State University CWIS:** `gopher.colostate.edu`

i `dave@lamar.colostate.edu`

CSUgopher is the CWIS for Colorado State University, Fort Collins, Colorado.

Services:
- Campus student/staff phone book
- Student information, campus bulletin board
- Colorado Water Resources Institute
- Agriculture extension office bulletins
- National Association of Foreign Student Advisors (NAFSA)

6-53 **ComNet-Gopher, RWTH-Aachen:** `balrog.dfv.rwth-aachen`

i `broe@dfv.rwth-aachen.de`

Services:
- Short Unix manuals in German
- Synthesizer archive
- Information about the local soccer team, Alemannia Aachen
- Internal information of the institute

6-54 **Computational Economics Gopher:** `gopher.sara.nl`

i `amman@sara.nl`

This gopher is intended to support activities in the field of Computational Economics.

Services:
- Software
- Working papers
- Conference information

- Handbook information

6-55 **Computer Professionals for Social Responsibility Gopher:** `gopher.cpsr.org`

i `cpsr@cpsr.org`

CPSR Internet Library

Services: CPSR is a national, public-interest organization with offices in Palo Alto, California, Washington, D.C., and twenty-two chapters across the country. `cpsr.org` is a public electronic resource with information on the impact of technology on society, including political and social problems.

6-56 **CONICIT—VENEZUELA:** `dino.conicit.ve`

i `jrivas@conicit.ve`

Gopher of the National Council on Science and Technology Investigation (CONICIT).

Services:

- Information on CONICIT
- News and events in science and technology in Venezuela

6-57 **COOMBSQUEST Social Science and Humanities Information Facility (ANU):**
`coombs.anu.edu.au` or `cheops.anu.edu.au`

i `tmciolek@coombs.anu.edu.au`

This is the worldwide Social Sciences and Humanities Information Service of the Coombs Computing Unit, Research Schools of Social Sciences and Pacific Studies, Australian National University, Canberra, Australia.

Services:

- Direct access to the Coombspapers Social Sciences Research Data Bank [The Coombspapers were established in December 1991 to act as the world's major electronic repository of the social science and humanities papers, documents, bibliographies, directories, theses abstracts, and other high-grade research material dealing with Australia, the Pacific region, and Southeast and Northeast Asia, as well as Buddhism, Taoism, Shamanism, and other oriental religions.]
- Access to FTP archive on `coombs.anu.edu.au` and to its major mirrors in USA and other countries
- Online searching of the ANU-xxx-xxx series of WAIS databases: ANU-Aboriginal-Studies, ANU-Asian-Computing, ANU-Asian-Religions, ANU-Australian-Economics, ANU-CAUT-Academics, ANU-CAUT-Projects, ANU-Coombspapers-Index, ANU-French-Databanks, ANU-Local-Waiservers, ANU-Pacific-Linguistics, ANU-Pacific-Manuscripts, ANU-Pacific-Relations, ANU-SocSci-Netlore, ANU-Strategic-Studies, ANU-SSDA-Catalogues, ANU-Taoism-Listserv, ANU-Thai-Yunnan, ANU-Theses-Abstracts, ANU-ZenBuddhism-Calendar, ANU-ZenBuddhism-Listserv
- Pointers to the world's leading social science and humanities gophers
- Pointers to the world's leading electronic archives, databases, and information facilities dealing with (a) Aboriginal Studies, (b) Asian Studies (esp. China, Indonesia, Philippines, Thailand, Tibet), (c) Buddhist Studies (esp. Zen and Tibetan Buddhism). (d) Linguistics (esp. Australia and Pacific region), (e) Prehistory and Archaeology (especially Australia and the Pacific region)

- Pointer to the East Asia/Pacific Wireless Files (U.S. Information Service/ANU)
- Pointer to the ELISA (Electronic Library Information System (ANU)) gopher

6-58 **Cornucopia of Disability Information:** `val-dor.cc.buffalo.edu`

i `leavitt@ubvms.cc.buffalo.edu`

> *CODI is a gopher intended to serve as a community resource for consumers and professionals by providing, via the Internet, disability-related information in a wide variety of areas. The information addresses university, local, state, national, and international audiences. Its contents are determined by these communities; their submissions and suggestions are welcome.*

Services:

- N.Y. state and local services
- The WNY Independent Living Center service directory
- County and state services
- Pupils with disabilities provided special education (demographics)
- College services and resources: University at Buffalo
- National information sources on disabilities
- Directory of Organizations
- List of directories organized by category; cross-index of organizations by function/service
- Directory of databases
- Digest of data on persons with disabilities, 1992
- "Coming to Terms with Disabilities": a product of the N.Y. Senate Select Committee on the Disabled
- WNY TDD directory: a collection of local, state, and national TDD phone numbers
- Government documents
- Computers for the disabled
- Network resources: FTP sites, bulletin boards, etc.

6-59 **CREN Gopher Server:** `info.cren.net`

i `hernandez@cren.net`

> *This gopher provides access to network, research, and educational information provided by CREN (the Corporation for Research and Educational Networking) for use by its members and the whole networking community. (Access to some resources is restricted to CREN member organizations.)*

Services:

- Information about resources available through the Internet and Bitnet
- Information about CREN and its services
- Connection to other gopher services, and to Archie, Veronica, X.500, WAIS, and other servers

6-60 **CS Gopher, University of Trento:** `mambo.cs.unitn.it`

i `zorat@cs.unitn.it`

> *This is a gopher server that is maintained by the Department of Computer and Management Science of the University of Trento, Italy.*

Services:
- Campus directory
- Pointers to other gophers of interest to students in economics
- Pointers to the gopher server of the University of Padova for the "RECORD project": an experiment on remote-access university education
- Lecture notes of Professor Zorat's course "Calcolo Automatico" (in Italian): an introductory course in computer science for economics students
- References (bibliography) for authors in computer science, VLSI design, neural networks

6-61 **CSUINFO—California State University Network (CSUnet) Gopher:** `eis.calstate.edu`

i `nethelp@calstate.edu`

> *This is a central gopher of the Chancellor's Office of the California State University located in Long Beach, California. CSUnet is the system-wide network connecting the 20 CSU campuses. The Chancellor's Office is the coordinating body for the 20 campuses.*

Services:
- Archives of newsletters from Academic Affairs, Information Resources and Technology
- Biographies of CSU executives
- Fact sheets on the 20 California State University campuses
- Library Links provides pointers to other CSU library catalogs and a library catalog browsing program called LIBS with more than 400 other libraries
- Pointers to other CSU directories and gophers
- CSU faculty employment opportunities
- Telnet connections to various CSU campus and central resources
- Admissions information to the 20 CSU campuses
- CSUPERnet
- CSU International Studies programs
- Distance Learning project reports (DELTA)

6-62 **CUINFO Gopher at Cornell University.:** `gopher.cit.cornell.edu`

i `cuinfo-admin@cornell.edu`

> *The CUINFO gopher is the CWIS of Cornell University in Ithaca, New York, providing information about Cornell and the Ithaca area.*

Services: This gopher offers a huge variety of services, including campus directories, course and textbook information, weekly dining hall menus, vast computing resources, intramural and varsity athletics schedules/results, a wide array of information about the Ithaca area, entertainment listings (movies, concerts, radio), archives of many campus publications and all Cornell press releases, and the world's first CWIS-based "dialogue," "Dear Uncle Ezra," which is still going strong alongside its newer companions, "Letters from Eunice" and "Conversations with Mr. Chips." The scope of the CUINFO gopher is simply too great to do justice to its contents here. Also, as is common, the gopher offers standard pointers to the University of Minnesota's collection of "All the Gopher Servers in the World," FTP resources, and WAIS resources.

6-63 **CUNY Graduate School and University Center Gopher:** `timessqr.gc.cuny.edu`

i `anil.khullar@mailhub.gc.cuny.edu`

Services:

- Information about the graduate school, library, library handbook, student handbook
- Information about the Environmental Psychology program and a bibliography on Environmental Psychology
- General information about New York City (museums, bars, clubs, sports schedules)

6-64 **CYFER-NET/ES-USDA Gopher:** `cyfer.esusda.gov`

i `gopher-admin@cyfer.esusda.gov`

This gopher provides information on Children, Youth, Family Development programs. It is managed as a joint project of the Youth Development Information Center (YDIC) of the National Agricultural Library (NAL), USDA, Extension Service (ES)/4-H and Youth Development, ES/Home Economics and Human Nutrition (HEHN), and ES/Communications and Information Technology (CIT).

Services: Research resources for child, youth, and family development programs

6-65 **Daniel: Science and Technology Server:** `daniel.conicyt.cl`

i `daniel@daniel.conicyt.cl`

Information server of the Chilean National Commision for Investigation of Science and Technology (CONICYT).

Services:

- Information and forms on grants offered by CONICYT to promote development in science and technology
- Access to WAIS resources of information on current grants
- Articles and publications generated by the grant projects
- Press releases, articles, and other publications on science and technology in Chile
- Statistcis on science and technology in Chile
- Information on legislation relating to science and technology in Chile
- Documents of the Chilean University Network (REUNA)
- Information on scientists in Chile

6-66 **Danish Internet Libraries:** `gopher.denet.dk`

6-67 **Dartmouth College Gopher:** `gopher.dartmouth.edu`

i `gopher@dartmouth.edu`

This is the primary gopher server for Dartmouth College.

Services:

- Dartmouth information
- GNUPLOT archive
- International Computer Music Association
- Software International Association of Learning Labs
- Job openings in the federal government
- Libernet archive

- Dartmouth Macintosh software
- Sense of Place (environmental journal)

6-68 **Delft University of Technology CWIS:** `gopher.tudelft.nl`

i `info@rc.tudelft.nl`

This is the CWIS of the Delft University of Technology in Delft, the Netherlands.

Services:

- General campus information
- Library services

6-69 **Delft University of Technology—Electronic Engineering:** `olt.et.tudelft.nl`

i `patrick@donau.et.tudelft.nl`

This is the information system of the Electronic Engineering group at Delft University of Technology in Delft, the Netherlands.

Services:

- Group directory, activity information
- Archive and distribution of the OCEAN sea-of-gates design system
- Information on research topics in electronic engineering
- Digital picture archive
- Online lists of words in various languages; Dutch spelling dictionary
- Online Bible
- Archive of various Unix sources
- Collection of pointers to online services in and around Delft University

6-70 **DENet Information Server:** `gopher.denet.dk`

i `steen.linden@uni-c.dk`

This is the information service of the Danish national academic network, DENet. It is located at UNI-C, the Danish Computer Centre for Research and Education.

Services:

- DENet information and statistics
- DENet file archive
- Current DENet status
- UNI-C information
- Directory services and phone books
- Pointers to Danish electronic libraries
- Pointers to all Danish gopher information servers
- Index of the contents of major Danish FTP archives
- News in Danish

6-71 **Dresden University of Technology/ Department of Computer Science:**
`gopher.inf.tu-dresden.de`

i `gopher@gopher.inf.tu-dresden.de`

This is the information service of the Department of Computer Science, Dresden University of

Technology, Germany.

Services: The only requirement for using the dictionary and zip-code service, and also the information given in English and German, is a real gopher+ client, otherwise the user may be disappointed.

- Department of Computer Science information, including scripts
- German–English dictionary
- New Zip Codes for Germany
- Usenet news gateway
- Department of Computer Science FTP archive
- Dresden city information
- Satellite weather images

6-72 **e-MATH Gopher:** `e-math.ams.com`

i `support@e-math.ams.com`

The American Mathematical Society's e-MATH gopher provides professional and research information of interest to the mathematics community.

Services:

- Access to information about archived, peer-reviewed, electronic journals in the mathematical sciences
- Access to information about electronic preprint services in the mathematical sciences
- A listing of mathematical discussion lists and bulletin boards, including the discussion list devoted to Andrew Wiles's announced proof for Fermat's Last Theorem
- An online version of the combined membership list, the membership directory of the AMS, the Mathematical Association of America, and the Society for Industrial and Applied Mathematicians
- An online version of the 1991 Mathematics Subject Classification scheme
- Links to other mathematics-related gophers

6-73 **Eindhoven University of Technology Department of Math and Computer Science:** `gopher.win.tue.nl`

This is part of the CWIS of Eindhoven University of Technology in Eindhoven, the Netherlands.

Services:

- Newsgroup archives (local groups, `comp.sys.acorn`, FAQs from `news.answers`)
- Gateway to `ftp.win.tue.nl` and other FTP archives
- Information on various local groups and associations

6-74 **Electronic Frontier Foundation Gopher Service:** `gopher.eff.org`

i `gopher@eff.org`

The Electronic Frontier Foundation is a 501(c)3 non-profit organization dedicated to "civilizing the electronic frontier."

Services: The EFF's gopher archive includes a number of papers, articles, and other items related to the social aspects of computer networking, ranging from John Barlow's "Crime and Puzzlement" to issues of their biweekly newsletter, EFFector Online.

6-75 **Electronic Library Information System at the Australian National University (Elisa):**
info.anu.edu.au

i tony@info.anu.edu.au

This is an information delivery service of the Library of the Australian National University.

Services:

- Australian mirrors of a number of major gopher directories (e.g. the Minnesota world menus and the Yale library access menus)
- National entry point for Australian electronic services available via gopher (CWIS systems, library catalogs, FTP sites, etc.)
- Subject bases approach to the Internet based on the Library of Congress classification
- Consolidated menu of all Australian e-mail and phone directories
- Links to the major databases maintained at ANU in biocomplexity, Asian studies, Aboriginal studies, data archives, supercomputing, bioinformatics, etc.

6-76 **EMBnet Bioinformation Resource EMBL (EMBL BioGopher):**
ftp.embl-heidelberg.de

i nethelp@embl-heidelberg.de

This is the molecular biological Internet gopher maintained by the EMBL data library.

Services:

- Large repository of molecular biological databases, including complete releases and updates of the EMBL nucleotide sequence database and the SWISS-PROT protein sequence database
- Large archive of molecular biological free software for Unix, VMS, Macintosh and MS-DOS computers
- General information and documentation for molecular biologists
- Pointers to other biogophers and gophers in the EMBnet gopher network

6-77 **EnviroGopher, The EnviroLink Network:** envirolink.org

i env-link+@cmu.edu

This is the archive site of the EnviroLink Network and provides "the most comprehensive compilation of environmental information available online."

Services:

- About EnviroLink: information on other EnviroLink Network services
- EnviroInfo: on almost every relevant topic
- EnviroNetworks: archives of every major environmental network
- EnviroActions: action alerts from all over the earth
- EnviroOrgs: archived information from many environmental organizations
- EnviroIssues: specific and detailed information on many environmental issues
- General network pointers (FTP, telnet, WWW, IRC, etc.)

6-78 **ETH Zurich (Swiss Federal Institute of Technology), Switzerland:**

i karrer@ks.id.ethz.ch

This is the information service of ETH Zurich, Switzerland.

Services:
- ETHZ phone book
- Link to ETHZ main library

6-79 **EUnet Czechia:** `gopher.eunet.cz`

i `gopher-admin@czechia.eunet.cz`

This is the information service of EUnet Czechia, the network service provider in the Czech Republic. This gopher also contains information about top-level domain `.cz`

Services:
- Information about EUet Czechia services
- Information about top-level domain `cz`
- All the information necessary for registration of second-level domains under `.cz`
- All the information necessary for registration of IP network numbers in the Czech Republic
- Pointers to other CWISs

6-80 **EUnet Germany Information Service:** `gopher.germany.eu.net`

i `info-admin@germany.eu.net`

This is the information service of EUnet Germany, a network services provider.

Services:
- Server for new German zip codes
- Gateway to the EUnet Germany FTP archive
- Document retrieval by keyword search
- Directory with links to all other gopher servers
- Http/WWW server (port 80 of `www.Germany.EU.net`)

6-81 **Euromath Center Gopher Server:** `gopher.euromath.dk`

i `emc@euromath.dk`

This gopher server provides information about the Euromath Center, the Euromath Project, and related activities.

Services: This gopher also serves as the root gopher server for the Mathematics chapter of the Gopher Subject Tree.

6-82 **European Root Gopher:** `sunic.sunet.se`

i `gopher@ebone.net` or `gopher-info@sunet.se`

The Swedish University Network is running root gopher server and registry for European gophers as a service for the European user community.

6-83 **Fachhochschule Lippe CWIS:** `gopher.fh-lippe.de`

i `hegger@noc.fh-lippe.de`

This is the CWIS of the Fachhochschule Lippe, Lippe, Germany.

Services: Information about the province of Lippe. Currently with a 9600-bps connection; connectivity only in Germany.

6-84 **Fairfield University Gopher:** `funrsc.fairfield.edu`

i `gordon@funrsc.fairfield.edu`

This gopher not only provides an easy way for the university to access the Internet but also provides information about Fairfield University.

6-85 **Finland Root Gopher:** `gopher.funet.fi`

i `gopher-admin@gopher.funet.fi`

Gopher of the Finnish University and Research Network, FUNET.

Services:

- FUNET information
- Pointers to all Finnish gophers
- Gopher/FTP gateway to `ftp.funet.fi` archive
- Finnish X.400 gateway address converter
- Finnish gopher in English

6-86 **FU Gopher:** `gopher.fu-berlin.de`

i `gopher@gopher.fu-berlin.de`

This is the gopher for the Freien Universitaet Berlin, Germany.

Services:

- Local (Berlin) weather forecast in directory "Das Wetter in und um Berlin"

6-87 **Genethon-Human Research Genome Center:** `gopher.genethon.fr`

i `info-ftp@genethon.fr` or `pat@genethon.genethon.fr`

This gopher accesses public data from CEPH and Genethon research projects.

Services:

- Sequences
- Marker data
- PostScript versions of genetic maps
- Genethon publication list
- TOCs of journals (mainly biology)

6-88 **GeoGopher, UT El Paso, Department of Geological Sciences:**
`dillon.geo.ep.utexas.edu`

i `roberts@dillon.geo.ep.utexas.edu`

Hosted by the UTEP Department of Geological Sciences to provide an index of pointers to earth science resources on the Internet.

Services: Gateway to earth science resources available on the Internet

6-89 **Georgetown University Academic Computer Center Gopher:** `guvax.georgetown.edu`

i `pmangiafico@guvax.georgetown.edu`

This is an information service for the Georgetown University community and all scholars on the Internet.

Services:

- Information on Georgetown University Academic Computer Center policy and services

- Information on the 1993 Joint International Conference of the Association for Computers and the Humanities and the Association for Literary and Linguistic Computing (ACH-ALLC93)
- The Georgetown University Catalog of Projects in Electronic Text (CPET)
- Information from the Georgetown University Office of Student Programs
- Pointers to other gophers of general interest

6-90 **Georgia Southern University:** `gopher.gasou.edu`

i `ken_williams@gasou.edu` (administrative) or `feffwms@gasou.edu` (technical)

This is the CWIS of Georgia Southern University, Statesboro, Georgia.

Services:

- Campus directory
- General institutional information
- Information about the Internet
- Collection of pointers to other CWISs and Internet resources

6-91 **German Climate Computer Center (DKRZ):** `gopher.dkrz.de`

This is the DKRZ information service, which mainly includes links to other services.

Services:

- Pointers to Meteosat weather pictures
- Link to FTP server `ftp.dkrz.de`

6-92 **Gettysburg College:** `jupiter.cc.gettysburg.edu`

i `gopherm@gettysburg.edu`

This is the CWIS and Internet source locator for Gettysburg College, Gettysburg, Pennsylvania, built and maintained by Computing Services.

Services:

- Campus phone book
- Faculty information sheets
- Campus event information
- Student schedules
- Faculty reports
- Pointers to many academic gophers

6-93 **GMD Gopher:** `gopher.gmd.de`

i `horch@vm.gmd.de`

German National Research Center for Computer Science (GMD) in St. Augustin, Germany

Services:

- Access to BITEARN nodes, Internet database (rare), and X.400 database (German)
- Archives of lists located at `listserv@dearn.bitnet`
- RFCs
- New German zip codes

6-94   **Go M-Link:** `vienna.hh.lib.umich.edu`

     i `davidsen@umich.edu`

       Go M-Link is an online information server for Michigan libraries.

     Services:

- Resources for the professional development of librarians and library workers
- Electronic journals in library science
- Legislation affecting libraries and other materials
- Access to gophers and library catalogs around the world

6-95   **Gothenburg Universities' Computing Centre (GD) Information Service:**
   `gopher.gd.chalmers.se`

     i `matz.engstrom@gd.chalmers.se`

       This is the information service of the computing center jointly owned by the general University of Gothenburg (Goteborg) and Chalmers University of Technology in Gothenburg, Sweden.

     Services: Telephone and e-mail directory (WHOIS link) of employees; information about the campus stores for personal computers and workstations; and information about the services provided by the computing center.

6-96   **Governors State University Gopher:** `gopher.gsu.bgu.edu`

       This is a CWIS of Governors State University.

     Services: Campus undergraduate and graduate catalogs

6-97   **GrainGenes, the Triticeae Genome Gopher:** `greengenes.cit.cornell.edu`

     i `matthews@greengenes.cit.cornell.edu` or `oandersn@wheat.usda.gov`

       This is the gopher version of the USDA Plant Genome Research Program's genome database for wheat, barley, oats, and related species.

     Services:

- Genetic maps of wheat, barley, oat, and sugarcane
- 1,500 DNA probes
- 2,800 Triticum aestivum accessions
- 600 Oat pedigrees
- 500 Triticeae scientists
- K.D. Kephart's "Commercial Wheat Cultivars of the United States"
- R.A. McIntosh's "Catalogue of Gene Symbols for Wheat," 1988-Annual Wheat Newsletter, Vol. 37

6-98   **Gustavus Gopher:** `gopher.gac.edu`

     i `gopher@gac.edu`

       This is the CWIS of Gustavus Adolphus College, a private liberal arts college in St. Peter, Minnesota.

     Services:

- Campus information
- Campus calendar
- Campus directory

- Collection of documentation
- Collection of pointers to other CWISs
- Gateway to Gustavus Library catalog
- Gateway to `ftp.gac.edu`, Gustavus's anonymous FTP site
- Medical references
- Archive of `fam-med`, `family-l`, and `t-and-f` mailing lists

6-99 **Heidelberg University Information Server:** `gopher.urz.uni-heidelberg.de`
  i `x02@sun3.urz.uni-heidelberg.de`

   This is the CWIS of University of Heidelberg, Germany. It consists of several gopher servers; the main entrance is the central gopher server at the University Computing Center (URZ).

Services:
- Telnet to other Computing Center machines
- Collection of subject trees
- Complete inventory of the Greek papyri of Egypt

6-100 **Hood College CWIS (HoodInfo):** `merlin.hood.edu` port `9999`
  i `egallagher@nimue.hood.edu`

   This is a CWIS for Hood College, Frederick, Maryland.

Services: This system was the product of a donation to the Career Center. It is a very good site for federal employment information, example resumes, and the like. The site also carries unique information local to the city of Frederick, Maryland, and a wide variety of telnet links to libraries around the world.

6-101 **Hungarian Gopher (HIX):** `andrea.stanford.edu`
  i `hollosi@andrea.stanford.edu`

   This is the main Hungarian gopher of the world, courtesy of Stanford University.

Services:
- Full archives of the Hungarian mailing lists (TIPP, SZALON, FORUM) and Hungarian daily news services (HIRMONDO, KEP)
- Hollosi Information eXchange (HIX)
- Collection of Hungarian and related documents
- Directory of registered Hungarian net-people
- List of all gophers in Hungary

6-102 **Hyper-G Server, Graz University of Technology:** `finfo.tu-graz.ac.at`
  i `fkappe@iicm.tu-graz.ac.at`

   This is the CWIS of the Graz University of Technology, Graz, Austria. Not just a gopher server, it is a gopher gateway to the local Hyper-G server.

Services:
- Information about Hyper-G
- General information about Graz University of Technology and Graz, Austria (including events database, street directory, etc.)
- Research activities of all institutes of the university.

- Courses offered by the faculty of Mechanical Engineering in a format compatible with the European Credit Transfer System (ECTS).
- Phone numbers on campus
- Access to the library OPAC
- Gateway to selected entry points in the Austrian Videotex system (e.g., the Austrian phone book, train schedule, weather information)
- ACM SIGGRAPH bibliography (15,000 references) in searchable form
- Pointers to (all) other Austrian information servers and (most) other information systems worldwide
- Fun stuff (e.g., the famous "Hacker Jargon")

6-103 **ICGEBnet:** `icgeb.trieste.it`

i `pongor@icgeb.trieste.it`

This is the information server of the International Centre for Genetic Engineering and Biotechnology, Trieste, Italy. It carries molecular biology and biotechnology-related information.

Services:
- ICGEB directory
- ICGEB information
- ICGEBnet user manual
- Molecular biology software documentation
- Collection of pointers to search (all) biological databanks and pointers to other biological gophers
- The SBASE protein domain library

6-104 **ICTP—International Centre for Theoretical Physics, Trieste, Italy:**
`gopher.ictp.trieste.it`

i `bordin@ictp.trieste.it` or `canessae@ictp.trieste.it`

ICTP's gopher purpose is to spread out online information regarding the many scientific activites carried out at ICTP throughout the year, as well as information on the in-house scientific publications, courses, and alternative services offered by the ICS (International Centre for Science and High Technology) and the TWAS (Third World Academy of Sciences) located at Trieste.

Services:
- Presentation of ICTP
- ICTP computer resources
- Administrative information: phone book, scientists present at ICTP scientific courses
- Publications
- Activities research groups
- Pointers for computational sciences (computational algebra, biology, economics, and physics)

6-105 **IDS World Network Gopher:** `gopher.ids.net`

i `asysadmin@ids.net`

The IDS World Network is an Internet access provider for the Eastern and Southeastern United States.

Services: Gateway contains special information relating to the State of Rhode Island. It also serves as a gateway for beginners who are just starting with the Internet. Some of the more popular databases on the Internet are lumped together here into a simple, easy-to-understand menu tree. The dialup service also serves beginners.

6-106 **Imperial College Department of Computing:** `src.doc.ic.ac.uk`

i `ukuug-soft@src.doc.ic.ac.uk`

This is the Department of Computing, Imperial College, United Kingdom, home of the UKUUG Archive and the DoC Information service.

Services:

- One of the worlds largest archives (15Gigabytes plus) of software, media related, politics, weather, etc.
- Departmental directory
- Access to campus library
- Pointers to other DoC CWISs
- Janet host database (NRS)

6-107 **Information Services in Germany:** `gopher.tu-clausthal.de`

i `lange@rz.tu-clausthal.de` or `foest@dfn.dbp.de`

This gopher is an informal entry point for Germany together with some hints to specialities in German information systems.

Services: Access to other gophers throughout Germany

6-108 **InfoSlug:** `scilibx.ucsc.edu`

i `watkins@scilibx.ucsc.edu`

InfoSlug is an excellent gopher site put together by the UC Santa Cruz University Library.

Services:

- Information on the InfoSlug and the Internet Gopher software
- UCSC information (course offerings, departmental information files, phone books, calendars, class schedules, etc.)
- An extensive virtual library, which includes access to UCSC's online library catalog and information on books and reference sources; research guides, bibliographies and brochures; course reserve lists; circulation status of books; UCSC faculty publications lists; video and media services as well as an extensive collection of electronic journals, newspapers, reference books, and pointers to many other libraries
- A large directory tree of links to other gopher servers, organized by subject matter. This is an excellent tool for doing research on the Internet
- Directory of links to other gophers by location

6-109 **International Federation for Information Processing:** `ietf.cnri.reston.va.us`

i `jstewart@cnri.reston.va.us`

Services:
- Information for the International Federation for Information Processing
- Information for the Internet Society (includes IETF)
- Information for the Corporation for National Research Initiatives

6-110 **InterNIC:** `internic.net`

i `info@is.internic.net` or `admin@ds.internic.net`

The InterNIC gopher is a high-level menu linking all three InterNIC partners' gophers into a seamless gopher interface. The InterNIC is a project of the National Science Foundation (NSF), and is comprised of three partners each of which provides different services: General Atomics (CERFNet) provides information services; AT&T provides directory and database services, and Network Solutions, Inc. (NSI) provides registration services. The InterNIC Information Services part of this trio is known as the InfoSource, a specialized gopher/database of networking and Internet resource information.

Services: Below is a sample of the services and information available on the InterNIC gophers, but you should really check each of them out carefully for yourself.
- Network and networking information
- Service provider information
- Discipline-specific information
- Templates for IP addresses and class addresses
- A WHOIS databases
- A searchable directory of directories, containing lists of FTP sites, lists of various types of servers available on the Internet, lists of white and yellow page directories, library catalogs and data archives. AT&T also provides white- and yellow-pages directory services.
- Information on Internet organizations
- Links to virtually all the treasures of the Internet
- Books and documents to assist organizations and individuals in getting connected
- Lots of helpful getting started and getting connected information for new and intermediate users

6-111 **IRIS Explorer Center Information Server Gopher Description:** `nags2.iec.co.uk`

i `caroline@nag.co.uk`

This gopher provides information on the IRIS Explorer data visualization system.

Services:
- Availability information
- User group information
- Technical reports

6-112 **IST BioGopher:** `istge.ist.unige.it`

i `gophman@istge.ist.unige.it`

This is the gopher server of the National Institute for Cancer Research and of the Advanced Biotechnology Center of Genoa, Italy.

Services:

- Cell line database (human and animal cell lines available in Europe)
- B line database (HLA typed B lymphoblastoid cell lines)
- Molecular probe database (tested synthetic oligonucleotides)
- Italian biotechnology mailing list
- Pointers to other BioGophers
- Collection of sources of WAIS databases devoted to biology
- Pointers to FTP sites relevant for biology

6-113 **ITESM Gopher:** `academ01.mty.itesm.mx`

i `jpadres@mtecv2.mty.itesm.mx`

This is the campus gopher of the ITESM (Instituto Tecnologico y de Estudios Superiores de Monterrey), in Monterrey, Mexico.

Services:

- Various campus services (phone directories, etc.)
- Images from Mexico
- Architectural images
- Hints and tips from various systems, like Informix, AFS, SAS, SWB, Lotus, CAEDS, Unix, etc.
- FTP gateway

6-114 **IUBio Archive:** `ftp.bio.indiana.edu`

IUBIO Archive for Biology is an archive of biology data and software. The archive includes items to browse, search, and fetch molecular data, software, biology news and documents, as well as links to remote information sources in biology and elsewhere.

Services:

- Archive for Usenet newsgroups `sci.bio` and `info.gcg`
- Drosophila research data
- Software for many operating systems
- Pointers to other biogophers
- Access to GenBank,the databank of all gene sequences
- Access to BIOSCI network news, Prosite database, the Genome of Drosophila book, and other biology data (indexed for keyword searching)

6-115 **IUPUI CWIS:** `gopher.iupui.edu`

i `comments@iupui.edu`

This is the main CWIS of Indiana University–Purdue University, Indianapolis, Indianapolis, Indiana.

Services:

- Campus directory
- Pointers to other Indiana gophers

6-116 **IVIC Gopher:** `kanojo.ivic.ve`

    i `eguinand@ivic.ivic.ve`

        Gopher of the Venezulan Institue of Scientific Investigation (IVIC).

    Services:

- Information on IVIC
- Information on scientists and current projects
- Access to various Internet services (Netfind, Libs, Archie, etc)

6-117 **James Cook University CWIS:** `gopher.jcu.edu.au`

    i `gopher@jcu.edu.au`

        This is the CWIS of James Cook University in Townsville, Queensland, Australia.

    Services:

- CLIONET: The Australian Electronic Journal Of History
- JCU MetSat and JCU WeatherView Project
- Campus library access
- Campus directory

6-118 **JKU Info Service:** `gopher.edvz.uni-linz.ac.at`

    i `netadmin@edvz.uni-linz.ac.at`

        This is the Campus Information Service of the Johannes Kepler University of Linz, Austria.

    Services:

- Campus phone book, information, and other campus gophers
- Netnews Gateway
- Gateway to the Austrian library system

6-119 **Jyvaskyla University Gopher:** `gopher.jyu.fi`

    i `houghton@jyu.fi`

        This gopher is the campus information server.

    Services:

- Faculty and department information
- Main computer information and local help

6-120 **K.U.Leuven gopher server:** `gopher.kuleuven.ac.be`

    i `systhvu@cc1.kuleuven.ac.be`

        K.U.Leuven gopher server

    Services:

- List of all EARN/Bitnet nodes, by country
- Usenet FAQs
- Documents about computer-based education in higher education

6-121 **Keio University, Science and Technology campus gopher:** `gopher.st.keio.ac.jp`

    i `gopher@cc.keio.ac.jp`

        This is the CWIS for the Faculty of Science and Technology, Keio University, Yokohama,

Japan.

Services:

- Campus directory
- Documentation and software for using computer networks (in Japanese)
- Collection of pointers to other gophers in Keio University
- A section on regional areas nearby
- Technical reports published by members of the faculty
- List of papers published by professors in the faculty
- Admissions information for Keio University

6-122 **KIDLINK Gopher:** `kids.ccit.duq.edu`

i `mark@kids.ccit.duq.edu`

This gopher is primarily dedicated to serving the needs of those involved with or interested in KIDLINK: global networking for youth ages 10–15.

Services:

- Menu-driven access to the KIDLINK archives
- Documentation on research into KIDLINK and related projects
- Gopher pointers to resource materials for KIDFORUM activities
- Some links to documents that would be of interest to KIDLINK people. Note: To help create a safe environment for youth, this gopher does not contain any major links to global gopherspace.

6-123 **Kutztown University CWIS:** `acad.csv.kutztown.edu`

i `frye@acad.csv.kutztown.edu`

This is the CWIS of Kutztown University, Kutztown, Pennsylvania.

Services:

- Campus directory including staff, faculty, and students
- Administration directory
- Information about the State System of Higher Education (SSHE) for Pennsylvania
- Information about most of the universities in SSHE
- Easy access to Usenet newsgroups

6-124 **La Trobe University (Victoria, Australia):** `gopher.latrobe.edu.au`

i `p.nankervis@latrobe.edu.au`

This is the CWIS of La Trobe University in Melbourne, Australia.

Services:

- University administrative information
- Campus/transport maps
- DECUS program extracts
- Gateway to La Trobe University Library catalog

6-125 **Lake Forest College, Math/Computer Science Gopher:** `davinci.lfc.edu`

i `boardman@davinci.lfc.edu`

Services:
- Faculty and course lists
- Math-related items
- Contacts to other mathematics gophers
- Searchable `sci.math.faq` (local database)
- Searchable AMS combined membership list
- Telnet access to libraries
- Pointer to weather forecasts
- Pointers to interesting gophers (such as NSD, Library of Congress, Census data, UN, etc.)
- Fun
- All the known smileys
- Search Usenet Cookbook (local files)
- Contact Internet hunt

6-126 **Liverpool University, Computer Science, United Kingdom:** `gopher.csc.liv.ac.uk`

i `gophermaster@csc.liv.ac.uk`

This is the Computer Service departmental gopher at the University of Liverpool, United Kingdom.

Services:
- Access to an extensive archive of software ported and tested on HP-UX systems
- CTI Centre for Biology information
- Access to the HP-UX Software Porting and Archive Centre
- Links to other UK gopher servers

6-127 **Loesje Information System:** `gopher.loesje.org`

i `gophermaster@loesje.org`

This is the information service of the Loesje Organization in Arnhem, The Netherlands.

Services:
- General information
- The latest posters generated by Loesje
- Announcements

6-128 **Los Alamos National Laboratory Gopher Server:** `gopher.lanl.gov`

i `gopher@lanl.gov`

This is the central information server for the Los Alamos National Laboratory, located in Los Alamos, New Mexico. The major purpose of this server is to provide timely information to employees of the laboratory, and to link to other useful information services in the laboratory and on the Internet.

Services: LANL directory, daily news bulletin, calendar of events, current and back issues of the Computing Division News, links to other LANL information services, access to LANL library.

6-129   **Lund University Electronic Library, Sweden, UB2 Gopher:** `munin.ub2.lu.se`

    i `anders@munin.ub2.lu.se` (technical) or `traugott@munin.ub2.lu.se` (contents)

The gopher is managed by Lund University Library, UB2 (main library for technology, science, and medicine) electronic library service for Lund University, Lund, Sweden, and the "rest of the world."

Services:

- Acting as an intelligent gateway to electronic information resources on Internet by providing a huge subject structure
- Building a local information server that collects and organizes electronic documents
- Publishing research projects and publications from Lund University
- About "Lund University Electronic Library Service: WAIS" at UB2
- Collection of papers about our electronic library project
- WAIS databases, published at UB2
- More than 20 WAIS databases published at Lund University in the subject areas of library automation and computer network information
- Environment information
- Computer Science
- Experiment with automatic classification of WAIS databases, UB2
- Effort to automate the detection and classification of all WAIS databases into a subject structure based on a standard library classification system (UDC
- Research projects and publications of Lund University
- Descriptions of research projects and lists of publications partly including abstracts and full text papers
- Subject trees, other information systems, Internet resource classification
- Extensive subject structure based on a standard library classification system (UDC) organizing all the different types of Internet resources

6-130   **Lysator's Gopher service:** `gopher.lysator.liu.se`

    i `gopher@lysator.liu.se`

Lysator is the name of an Academic Computer Society at Linkoping University in Linkoping, Sweden. Since Lysator is built on the voluntary efforts by students in their spare time, any service or activity runs as long as they think it is fun, and the content will always reflect their personal interests.

Services:

- The files of "Project Runeberg," a collection of free electronic texts in Scandinavian languages
- Science Fiction archive, which is quite an international collection of reviews and abstracts of SF texts
- Information on MUD and other games that run at Lysator and are available over the Internet
- Information about Sweden, Linkoping, and Linkoping University

6-131   **Management Archive:** `chimera.sph.umn.edu`

    i `ma@chimera.sph.umn.edu.`

      This gopher is an entirely free, state-of-the-art electronic forum for management ideas of all varieties.

    Services:

- Access to current working papers in management
- Recent paper calls
- Conference announcements
- Connections to other relevant Internet resources

6-132   **Massachusetts Institute of Technology:** `gopher.mit.edu`

    i `gopher@mit.edu`

      The MIT gopher coordinates a set of campus services.

    Services: The MIT gopher is still evolving. At this time, one of its main purposes is to provide a gateway to MIT's public information system, e.g., online directory; MIT public information (TechInfo, a service that allows MIT community members to contribute information about MIT); and library services.

6-133   **Mathematics Department, University of Oviedo:** `telva.ccu.uniovi.es`

    i `nuevos@hp400.ccu.uniovi.es`

      This is the gopher of the University of Oviedo located in the LabCAD, Mathematics Department.

    Services:

- Local university information
- Gateway to FTP resources
- Gateway to Usenet news
- Pointers to libraries and news/information areas

6-134   **MECCA (Memphis Educational Computer Connectivity Alliance):** `physio1.utmem.edu` (scheduled to change)

    i `ltague@physio1.utmem.edu`

      An alliance of academic institutions in Memphis, Tennessee, with the purpose of enhancing Internet connectivity and programmed application of that connectivity for local schools.

    Services:

- Integration of CWIS for Memphis academic campuses
- A Memphis Freenet-type service
- Planned services include World Wide Web and Newsnet servers
- U.T. Memphis/College of Medicine/Division of Gastroenterology endoscopic images
- U.T. Memphis/College of Medicine/Anatomy and Neurobiology dictionary of the mouse genome

6-135   **MegaGopher—DNA Sequencing and Organellar Genome Research:** `megasun.bch.umontreal.ca`

    i `tim@bch.umontreal.ca`

The MegaGopher supports the information requirements for the MegaSequencing project, centered at the University of Montreal, Canada.

Services:

- Computational molecular biology
- Computer applications with an emphasis on DNA sequencing, molecular evolution, and organellar genomes
- Data for research into organellar genomes (mitochondria and chloroplasts)
- Biogopher news and administration information
- Internet resources with an emphasis on biology and the "Internet Radio"
- Listings of current biology seminars in Montreal
- Latest information on Sun Microsystems Computers, including computer security and software patches as well as links to archives of postings to Usenet groups dedicated to Sun Microsystems Computers
- "Australiana": the expatriated Australians information site, including the latest news from Australian newspapers (updated weekly), sports, films, etc., and links to other Australian gopher holes

6-136 **MeritNIC Gopher:** `nic.merit.net`

i `userhelp@nic.merit.edu`

This gopher is maintained by the Merit Network Information Center Services staff. In it you can find the answers to many questions about NSFNET, MichNet, and the Internet.

Services:

- Access to `nic.merit.edu` and `archive.umich.edu` Anonymous FTP archives
- Large listing of Internet Access Providers
- Collection of many good introductions to the Internet
- Current LinkLetter Newsletter
- Information on NREN and NSFNet
- Conference proceedings from the Harvard University conference on Public Access to the Internet

6-137 **Meta Network Gopher:** `tmn.com`

i `info@tmn.com`

This is the public information space for organizations hosted by The Meta Network.

Services:

- Archive of the Electronic Networking Association's newsletter, NETWEAVER
- Iris Online Network for Teachers' Newsletter
- Arts Wire resources for artists and arts organizations
- Northern Exposure episode plots and list of music used in the TV show

6-138 **Minnesota Extension Service:** `tinman.mes.umn.edu`

i `dmadison@mes.umn.edu`

This gopher is the official electronic information service for the Minnesota Extension Service, which is located on the St. Paul campus of the University of Minnesota.

Services:

- Information on agriculture and agricultural related issues
- Natural resources
- Community economic development
- Home economics
- 4-H and youth issues
- Gateways to other cooperative extension system electronic services and gophers

6-139 **Mississippi State University gopher:** `gopher.msstate.edu`

i `gopher@ra.msstate.edu`

> *This gopher provides academic and administrative information relating to Mississippi State University and its departments.*

Services:

- Faculty/staff online directory
- University information administrative database
- Course catalog
- History archive (including NCHE newsletter)
- Mitchell Memorial Library card catalog database
- National Center for Technology Planning archives
- FineArt Online newsletter archives

6-140 **MRNet—Minnesota Regional Network:** `gopher.mr.net`

i `gopher@mr.net`

> *This is the gopher server for the MRNet, an Internet network service provider in Minnesota.*

Services:

- Information on MRNet and the Internet

6-141 **NAG Information Server:** `nags2.nag.co.uk`

i `caroline@nag.co.uk`

> *This gopher provides information on products and services from The Numerical Algorithms Group Ltd. (No prices or other commercial information provided)*

Services:

- Product information
- Availability information
- User group information
- Technical reports

6-142 **NASA Goddard Space Flight Center gopher:** `gopher.gsfc.nasa.gov`

i `gopher@gopher.gsfc.nasa.gov`

Services:

- NASA, GSFC, and science information
- Images

- Internetworking information
- Gateways to NASA and GSFC FTP archives.

6-143 **NASA Mid-Continent Technology Transfer Center information Services Gopher:**
technology.com

i info@technology.com

The purpose of this gopher is to provide information to technology transfer organizations and their clients in the mid-continent service region. While the primary emphasis is on NASA technology, other federal technology sources can be used. This gopher server is part of a larger bulletin board system intended to provide "one stop shopping" for technology transfer services.

Services:

- Access to a regional federal lab directory
- Access to other specialized databases
- Pointers to other gopher servers that provide information on specific technologies (Boolean searches are supported)

6-144 **National Cancer Center, Tokyo, Japan:** gopher.ncc.go.jp

i gophermaster@gan.ncc.go.jp

Information service for the National Cancer Center in Tokyo, Japan.

Services:

- National Cancer Center information (seminars, phone book, activities, etc.)
- Japan information
- Cancer information
- Cell and gene bank information
- Network trouble information
- Weather information
- Link to anonymous-ftp at ftp.ncc.go.jp
- Daily mirror of UMN-othergophers link directories

6-145 **National Center for Atmospheric Research:** gopher.ucar.edu

This gopher accesses information made available by the National Center for Atmospheric Research and its parent organization, the University Corporation for Atmospheric Research.

Services:

- Phone and e-mail directory of NCAR/UCAR employees and scientific collaborators
- NCAR online library catalog
- NCAR/UCAR news and information
- Miscellaneous scientific information provided by divisions of NCAR

6-146 **National Center on Adult Literacy (cross-listed as Literacy Research Center/University of Pennsylvania):** litserver.literacy.upenn.edu

i mailbox@literacy.upenn.edu (general),
rethemeyer@literacy.upenn.edu (gopher) or
russell@literacy.upenn.edu (administrative)

This server distributes the National Center on Adult Literacy's publications and points to gopher resources relevant to researchers, policymakers, and practitioners in adult literacy.

Services:

- Archive of the National Center on Adult Literacy's publications
- List of adult literacy-related conferences and events
- Databases of information on adult literacy software and adult literacy software publishers
- Pointers to libraries card catalogs, ERIC resources, electronic journals, Usenet news-groups, and shareware/freeware relevant to adult literacy
- Archive of demonstration versions of adult literacy software

6-147 **National Institutes of Allergy and Infectious Disease (NIAID):** `gopher.niaid.nih.gov`
i `dwhite@nih.gov`

Services: The NIAID gopher server contains unique HIV/AIDS resources, as well as pointers to other sites with a similar focus. It maintains the following unique items:

- CDC's AIDS daily summaries
- CDC's morbidity and mortality weekly report
- NIAID HIV study recruitment information
- NIAID press releases
- NIH job vacancies
- Selected National AIDS Information Clearinghouse information

6-148 **National Institutes of Health (NIH) Gopher:** `gopher.nih.gov`
i `gopher@gopher.nih.gov`

The NIH Gopher server provides health and biomedical information useful to the NIH intramural research community in Bethesda, Maryland, and biomedical researchers around the world.

Services:

- Health and clinical information including CancerNet and NIH
- Consensus development conference statements
- Molecular biology databases including Genbank, PIR, SWISS-PROT, PDB, Prosite, TFD, and Limb
- NIH guide to grants and contracts
- NIH Office of Education program guide
- Access to NIH and NLM library online catalogs
- Information about events on the NIH campus in Bethesda, Maryland
- NIH phone and e-mail directories
- Information about computer and network resources at NIH

6-149 **NCSU Libraries Gopher Server:** `dewey.lib.ncsu.edu`
i `eric_morgan@ncsu.edu`

This gopher server's purpose is to maintain information and pointers to information for the needs of the faculty, staff, and students of the North Carolina State University.

6-150 **NEXUS—National Network of Physics Societies:** `alpha.qmw.ac.uk`

i `p.k.Guinnessy@qmw.ac.uk`

This is the information service for the students and societies connected to the Institute of Physics.

Services:

- Job information, events, Ph.D. and M.Sc. positions, society programs, and contact addresses
- Past copies of NEXUS News

6-151 **NIST Gopher Server:** `gopher-server.nist.gov`

i `gopher_info@nist.gov`

Informations about NIST programs, products, and activities.

Services:

- GAMS: Guide to Available Mathematical Software
- Open systems engineering
- Computer security bulletin board
- Standard reference data program
- NIST phone book and e-mail directory

6-152 **NORDUnet region Root Gopher:** `nic.nordu.net`

i `gopher-info@nic.nordu.net`

Nordic University and Research Network, NORDUnet

Services:

- NORDUnet information
- Pointers to all Nordic countries' gopher roots (countries: Denmark, Finland, Iceland, Norway, Sweden)
- nic.nordu.net FTP

6-153 **North Carolina Cooperative Extension Gopher:**

i `gopher_admin@gopher.ces.ncsu.edu`

This is the NC Cooperative Extension Gopher server located at North Carolina State University, Raleigh, North Carolina.

Services:

- Sustainable agriculture information
- Horticulture leaflets (some specific to NC)
- Other cooperative extension databases and information servers

6-154 **North Dakota Higher Education Computing Network Gopher:**
`chiphead.cc.ndsu.nodak.edu`

i `puklich@plains.nodak.edu`

This gopher is a root for several gophers within the state. Some of these include the North Dakota State University CWIS, the University of North Dakota School of Medicine, and the SENDIT gopher.

Services:

- Campus directory
- North Dakota State Legislative information
- Internet Resource Guide (searchable)

6-155 **Northeastern Illinois University Gopher:** `gopher.neiu.bgu.edu`

This is a CWIS at Northeastern Illinois University.

Services: Campus undergraduate and graduate catalogs.

6-156 **Northwestern University, CTDNet:** `ctdnet.acns.nwu.edu`

i `ctd@nwu.edu`

This is the gopher server of the Center for Talent Development, Northwestern University.

Services:

- A variety of information of interest to academically talented students in grades 5–9, and their parents, teachers, and counselors
- Information about Center for Talent Development summer, correspondence, and Saturday programs for children aged 4 to 16
- Information about the Midwest Talent Search and Midwest Talent Search for Young Students out-of-level testing programs for students in grades 5–8
- Book reviews, articles, and research reports on the education of academically talented students
- Information about contests and competitions in areas such as chess, mathematics, and science
- College Guide magazine

6-157 **Norwegian vocational education gopher:** `samson.ypedhs.no`

i `geir@pedagog.ypedhs.no`

Statens yrkespedagogiske hogskole (National College for the Education of Vocational and Technical Teachers) is teaching, on the undergraduate and graduate levels, students who have their background as mechanics, electricians, home-economics teachers, etc., and we are specializing in vocational pedagogy and vocational didactics. This gopher is intended as an information system for students, would-be students, and collegues in the teaching trade.

Services:

- Campus directory
- Oslo information
- Gateway to the `pedagog.ypedhs.no` FTP server with an excellent collection of public-domain, freeware, and shareware software

6-158 **NUInfo—Northwestern University:** `nuinfo.nwu.edu`

i `nuinfo@nwu.edu`

NUInfo is dedicated to serving the Northwestern community and those interested in learning about Northwestern. Therefore it does not point out to any resources that are without boundaries.

Services:

- Course catalogs for undergraduate studies and the graduate school

- Admissions information
- Financial aid information
- Housing information
- Open positions listings
- Local recreation, food, and entertainment

6-159 **OCF Archive:** `ocf.berkeley.edu`

i `gopher@ocf.berkeley.edu`

Archives of Open Computing Facility (OCF) at the University of California

Services:

- Information on University of California at Berkeley
- Bylaws, meeting minutes, etc. of the Open Computing Facility
- OCF Online Library: access to huge variety of e-texts organized by subject
- OCF Online Help: A number of good reference files for help on using the Internet
- Access to the `ocf.berkeley.edu` Anonymous FTP Archive

6-160 **Ogpher (the SunSITE gopher):** `sunsite.unc.edu`

i `ftpkeeper@sunsite.unc.edu`

Ogpher is the gopher server for Sun Microsystems' SunSITE archives operated by the Office of Information Technology at the University of North Carolina at Chapel Hill.

Services:

- Surf the Net!—Archie, libraries, gophers, FTP sites
- Access to the Sunsite archives by topic
- SUN Microsystems Newsgroups and archives
- Access to LaUNChpad—UNC's Internet services facility
- Access to other gophers, including entertainment, news, weather, and sports
- UNC-CH information and facilities
- Search of interest groups list
- Collection of pointers to Internet electronic references and books
- Access to the UNC Library
- Pointers to other gophers at UNC
- Access and searching of National Performance Review (Reinventing Government), National Information Infrastructure Information and National Health Security Plan

6-161 **Ohio Northern University CWIS:** `gopher.onu.edu`

i `gopher@onu.edu`

This is the CWIS of Ohio Northern University in Ada, Ohio.

Services:

- Campus Directory
- Other gopher and information servers

6-162 **Ohio Supercomputer Center:** `gopher.osc.edu`

i `gopher@osc.edu`

This is the document server for OSC.

Services:

- A list of current and planned activities at OSC
- Online journals (Superbits, OSC Bits, Alloc, user publications, Visions)
- OSC program book
- Software list for the Cray
- OVL guide
- Grant applications

6-163 **Ohio University Gopher Server:** `gopher.ohiou.edu.`

i `tysko@boss.cs.ohiou.edu.`

This is the gopher server for general information about Ohio University, Athens, Ohio.

Services:

- General university administrative/academic information
- Southeast Asia Council Services data files

6-164 **ONENET—Oklahoma Networking NIC:** `nic.onenet.net`

i `info@nic.onenet.net`

This is the Oklahoma Network for the Enrichment of Education and Telecommunication information gopher.

Services:

- Networking information and software
- Provides information on how to connect to ONENET and the Internet.

6-165 **Optical Computing Laboratory at Colorado State University:**
`sylvia.lance.colostate.edu`

i `root@sylvia.lance.colostate.edu` or `l.irakliotis@ieee.org`

This gopher is a database server with information on Digital Optical Computing.

Services:

- Archive of lab's publications and technical reports on optical computing GIFs from optical computing experiments

6-166 **OWLScoop:** `kscsuna1.kennesaw.edu`

i `nhumphri@kscmail.kennesaw.edu` (maintainer) or `lparris@kscmail.kennesaw.edu` (tech support)

CWIS connecting/linking to the "rest of the World". Maintained by Administrative Computer Services of of Kennesaw State College, Marietta, Georgia.

Services:

- Campus directory, CWIS, campus library (TEL)
- Unique gopher pointers (federal servers) for Federal Register (subscription required); economic bulletin board; extension service, USDA; National Science Foundation (STIS); Library of Congress records; information from the U.S. government
- (general servers) for U.S. geographic names database; resources by subject; GC EduNet (TEL); news, weather, and travel advisories; phone books at other institutions

6-167 **Oxford Brookes University central gopher:** `cs3.brookes.ac.uk`

i `gophermaster@brookes.ac.uk`

This gopher provides course details and various information related to Oxford Brookes University, as well as some useful jumping-off points to other gophers.

Services:
- Online electronic mail (staff and students)
- Telephone directory (all telephone extensions)
- Local city information

6-168 **Oxford University Libraries Board OLIS Gopher:** `gopher.lib.ox.ac.uk`

i `jose@olis.lib.ox.ac.uk`

Services:
- Oxford University e-mail and telephone directories in an easily searchable format
- Search menus and links to all Oxford University gopher servers
- OLIS (Oxford University Library Information System) information
- Links to other gopher servers and telnet-based services
- Section for users and administrators of IBMs VM/ESA operating system. This includes about 32Mb of utilities from the 1993 VM workshop tape plus links to other VM-related Gopher servers

6-169 **Panix:** `gopher.panix.com`

i `gopher@panix.com`

Gopher of the New York City Internet access provider Panix (Public Access Unix/Internet).

Services: Contains the archives of the Society for Electronic Access, the Del Rey Internet newsletter, the Tor Books online newsletter, and a photography database.

6-170 **Physics and Astronomy Department, University of Oklahoma:** `phyast.nhn.uoknor.edu`

i `feldt@phyast.nhn.uoknor.edu`

This gopher provides information useful to the Department of Physics and Astronomy at the University of Oklahoma.

Services: Departmental colloquium schedule
- OU holidays

6-171 **PIR Archive:** `ftp.bchs.uh.edu`

i `Davison@uh.edu`

Distribution site for the Protein Information Resource database via Gopher

Services: Full searches of the PIR database on any keyword, in any field of the protein entry

6-172 **Poudre R-1 School District Gopher Server:** `lobo.rmh.pr1.k12.co.us`

i `redder@k12.colostate.edu`

This is the CWIS of the Poudre R-1 School District in Fort Collins, Colorado.

Services: Maintains information for a K–12 school district. Will soon provide information about all district schools via gopher, and is beginning to maintain information for the district's media centers. Gopher server geared toward the K–12 environment.

6-173 **Prague University of Economics Gopher Service:** `pub.vse.cz`
i `marta@vse.cz`

Information, archive and news service of the Prague University of Economics, Czech Republic.

Services:

- Czech coding page selection
- Campus information in Czech
- General university information, in English
- News, reduced, with local news and some listserv lists added
- Public-domain software
- CESNET resources
- Pointers to other gophers

6-174 **Presbyterian College Gopher Server:** `cs1.presby.edu`
i `gopher-admin@presby.edu`

This is the CWIS of Presbyterian College, Clinton, South Carolina.

Services:

- A collection of religious documents (Bible, Koran, etc.) on which full-text searches can be performed.
- "Introduction to Usenet News and the 'trn' Newsreader," in various formats (plain text, PostScript, etc.)
- Other informational documents about the Internet.

6-175 **Princeton Regional Schools:** `gopher.prs.k12.nj.us`
i `gopher@prs.k12.nj.us`

This is a student-and-staff-run gopher server provided to distribute information of potential interest to K–12 students and their teachers.

Services:

- Pointers to various K–12-oriented gopher, FTP, and other sources
- Archive of "From Now On" technology newsletters

6-176 **Princeton University Information Service:** `gopher.princeton.edu`
i `gopher@princeton.edu`

This is the CWIS of Princeton University, Princeton, New Jersey.

6-177 **PSGnet/RAINet low-cost and international networking:** `gopher.psg.com`
i `lowcost-net@psg.com`

This gopher is supported and maintained by PSGnet and RAINet, and concerns itself mostly with networking in the developing world, low-cost networking tools, and computer networking in general.

Services:

- Low-cost networking technology and tools
- Network connectivity from/to the developing countries

- Metronets: metropolitan IP networking
- Use and resources on the various networks
- K12net (FidoNet's K–12 group) archive
- Information about Oregon networking

6-178 **Purdue CS Gopher Information Service:** `gopher.cs.purdue.edu`

i `gopher@cs.purdue.edu`

> *This is the gopher information service for the Purdue University Department of Computer Sciences, West Lafayette, Indiana.*

Services:

- Information on graduate programs
- WAIS indexes of selected technical reports
- Resources from various research projects
- Purdue Computer Emergency Response Team (PCERT) archives
- Pictures of the faculty and staff

6-179 **Queen's University at Kingston:** `gopher.queensu.ca`

i `gopher-admin@post.queensu.ca`

> *This is the campus and community information service of Queen's University, Kingston, Ontario, Canada.*

Services:

- Academic information, including calendars and scholarships
- Campus information such as services, facilities, library, research, policies, and other information
- Campus telephone and e-mail directory
- Campus publications (Queen's Gazette, Queen's Journal student newspaper)
- FTP gateway to TCrunchers archive (Consortium for Computing in the Humanities COCH-COSH)
- Eastern Ontario and southern Quebec weather forecasts
- X.500 "White Pages" pilot directory gateway
- Pointers to other information sources (gopher and WAIS)

6-180 **Queensland University of Technology, Brisbane:** `gopher.qut.edu.au`

i `w.fisher@qut.edu.au`

> *The QUT Gopher is a general-purpose gopher, both to direct the university's staff and students to outside gophers and to provide people outside the university with information about QUT.*

Services:

- Information about QUT and its faculties, schools, and services.
- Pointers to the library via telnet
- Pointers to other gophers in subject lists for some of our schools.

6-181 **RedIRIS, FUNDESCO, (ES):** `gopher.rediris.es` or `gopher.rediris.es`

(port 71 for gopher+)

i `infoiris@rediris.es`

> *This is the RedIRIS gopher server. RedIRIS is the Spanish Academic and Research Network.*

Services:

- RedIRIS information
- Local city information
- Pointers to other Spanish CWIS-FUNDESCO information
- Spanish online libraries catalog
- X.400/RFC822 e-mail addresses
- Gateway to X.500 directory services (Spanish entry point)
- Online access to RedIRIS archie server
- Gateway to Spanish anonymous FTP sites
- Gateway to Spanish Rare

6-182 **Ribosomal Database Project:** `rdpgopher@uiuc.edu`

i `mrmike@geta.life.uiuc.edu`

> *This is the Ribosomal Database Project server at the University of Illinois at Urbana-Champaign, Urbana, Illinois.*

Services: The Ribosomal Database Project offers microbiologists unique access to a database of rRNA sequence data, alignments, phylogenetic trees and associated sequence manipulation programs.

6-183 **Rice University CMS Gopher Server:** `ricevm1.rice.edu`

i `troth@rice.edu`

> *This is the VM/CMS (mainframe) server for RiceInfo, the Rice University CWIS.*

Services: Serves CMS Help files (local access only), problem-tracking system records (local access only), various CMS software packages, listserv logs for RICEVM1 (local access only), and various informational items about the campus mainframe.

6-184 **RiceInfo: Rice University CWIS:** `riceinfo.rice.edu`

i `riceinfo@rice.edu`

> *This is the CWIS of William Marsh Rice University in Houston, Texas.*

Services:

- An extensive "Information by Subject Area" tree, created by merging lists of resources maintained at other gopher sites
- Rice University campus directory
- Rice University course schedules
- "Graduate Students Association Yellow Pages," a guide to graduate student life at Rice University
- The usual CWIS material (campus calendars, policies, library services, etc.)
- A number of other resources accessible only from within Rice University, notably several large bibliographic databases (Current Contents, the MLA Bibliography, Compendex, Expanded Academic Index)

6-185 **RIPE Network Coordination Centre Gopher:** `gopher.ripe.net`

i `ncc@ripe.net`

> *The RIPE Network Coordination Centre is an organization that provides support services to Internet service providers in Europe.*

Services: The gopher server is useful to network service providers, NICs, and NOCs alike. The documents stored relate to a wide variety of networking and technical topics. For example, EBONE, the Internet Engineering Task Force (IETF), the Internet Engineering Steering Group (IESG), RARE, RFCs, FYIs, and documents relating to the work of RIPE.

6-186 **Rowan College of New Jersey Gopher Server:** `gboro.rowan.edu` port 150

i `klein@rowan.edu`

> *This is the Rowan College of New Jersey Gopher Server, run by the Department of Academic Computing at Rowan College of New Jersey (formerly Glassboro State College) in Glassboro, New Jersey.*

Services:

- Campus calendar

6-187 **Royal Postgraduate Medical School Gopher:** `mpcc2.rpms.ac.uk`

i `d.abrams@rpms.ac.uk`

> *This facility is provided by the Department of Medical Physics, Royal Postgraduate Medical School, Hammersmith Hospital, London, England, and provides an information retrieval system for the RPMS.*

Services:

- Campus directory
- Timetables for courses
- Campus information

6-188 **RPI CS Lab Gopher Server:** `cs.rpi.edu`

i `weltyc@cs.rpi.edu`

> *This is the gopher of the Rensselaer Polytechnic Institute, Computer Science Department.*

Services: This gopher provides access to information, software, and technical reports from the RPI Computer Science Department.

6-189 **SISSA–ISAS Gopher:** `babbage.sissa.it`

i "none for the moment"

> *This is the gopher for a postgraduate school in mathematics and physics, located in Trieste, Italy.*

Services:

- Electronic archive of physics and math preprints in the following areas: condensed matter, high energy, astrophysics, functional analysis, mathematical physics, nuclear physics, algebraic geometry, general relativity, and quantum cosmology, etc.
- Local information (e.g., SISSA phone book)
- Pointers to other gopher sites

6-190 **Saint Louis University CWIS:** `sluava.slu.edu`

   i `postmaster@sluvca.slu.edu`

    This is the CWIS of Saint Louis University in St. Louis, Missouri.

   Services:
- Law library and health sciences (medical campus)

6-191 **Salk Genome Center:** `rangersmith.sdsc.edu` port 210

   i `romberg@molly.sdsc.edu`

    This is the WAIS server for the Salk Institute for Biological Studies and San Diego Genome Center, in San Diego, California.

   Services: This database contains the results of physical mapping of human chromosome 11, and other chromosomes, from the San Diego Genome Center at the Salk Institute.

6-192 **Sam Houston State University (VMS Gopher):** `niord.shsu.edu`

   i `gopher-mgr@shsu.edu`

    This gopher serves as the "front door" to GopherSpace from Sam Houston State University, Huntsville, Texas.

   Services: Access or reference to all known resources on the network related to the field of economics:
- Links to economics-oriented gophers
- Directory of economists (by name)
- Calls for papers and manuscripts
- Meeting announcements and notices
- CERRO: the Central European Regional Research Organization
- CIA World Factbook (1991, 1992)
- Other government information (US and UN)
- EconBib (LaTeX/BibTeX style archives for economics)
- EconData (economic data and analysis package)
- Economic bulletin board (U.S. Department of Commerce)
- Economic and Social Research Council RAPID (UK) Economics Working Paper archive
- Gross state product tables
- U.S. Bureau of Economic Analysis Internet Business Journal
- Investment data collection
- Selected Usenet newsgroups
- The Cyberchronicle of Political Economy (COPE)
- United States Commerce Business Daily
- U.S. Supreme Court decisions
- White House information
- FTP gateways to other economics information
- Access to the world's largest collection of TeX-related files
- Access to VMS-related gopher files, including software, and access to related informa-

tion, utilities, and a complete links list of all known VMS-based gopher servers
- Anonymous FTP archives

6-193 **San Diego State University, College of Sciences:** `gopher.sdsu.edu`

This gopher provides various campus information and centralized access to other campus resources.

Services:
- Class schedule
- Campus phone directory
- Software distribution
- SDSU library access
- Access to other gopher servers

6-194 **San Diego Supercomputer Center Online Information Services:** `gopher.sdsc.edu`

i `consult@sdsc.edu`

This is a public interface to SDSC's online documentation, available software, and the National Science Foundation MetaCenter Project.

Services:
- SDSC online documentation
- More than 800 anonymous FTP sites
- NSF Metacenter Project

6-195 **Scientists On Disk (JHU History of Science and Medicine):** `gopher.hs.jhu.edu`

i `editors@gopher.hs.jhu.edu`

Scientists On Disk is a pilot project to assess new electronic media tools for their use in education and research in the study of the history of science and medicine. Scientists On Disk has also worked with material relevant to architecture and visual culture studies.

Services:
- Aerospace oral history project
- Oppenheimer manuscript collection (WAIS gateway)
- Class material and syllabuses
- Visual culture studies
- Architectural building images

6-196 **Seneca Information Service:** `info.senecac.on.ca`

i `paul@mars.cenecac.on.ca`

This is the CWIS of Seneca College of Applied Arts and Technology, Toronto, Canada.

Services:
- Information about the college
- Description of academic programs from the college calendars
- E-mail directory of Seneca and links to e-mail directories at other Ontario colleges

6-197 **SIGART Electronic Information Service:** `sigart.acm.org`

i `infodir@sigart.acm.org`

A public service to the AI community sponsored by ACM SIGART, the Special Interest Group on Artificial Intelligence.

Services:
- Information about ACM SIGART
- Announcements relating to AI (such as conference programs and CFPs, job openings, journal announcements and CFPs, software availability, etc.)
- AI-related news
- SIGART sponsored conference information
- Back issues of the SIGART Bulletin

6-198 **SIGDA Gopher Server:** `kona@ee.pitt.edu`

i `gopher@ee.pitt.edu`

This gopher server provides access to online information services available from the ACM's Special Interest Group on Design Automation (SIGDA).

Services: FAQs for `comp.lsi` and `comp.lsi.cad`
- Technical papers in PostScript
- CAD research from various academic institutions
- Conferences
- Information on academic and industrial software
- Pointers to other SIGDA resources (SIGDA benchmark library)

6-199 **Silesian University Computer Center Gopher:** `usctoux1.cto.us.edu.pl`

i `muhlig@usctoux1.cto.us.edu.pl`

This is the Information Service of Computer Center, Silesian University, Katowice, Poland.

Services: Local information for Internet users.

6-200 **Skidmore College Gopher:** `gopher.skidmore.edu`

i `ldg@skidmore.edu`

This gopher offers campus information and access to diverse network resources at Skidmore College, an undergraduate liberal-arts college in upstate New York.

Services:
- Campus information including catalog, faculty handbook, academic information guide
- Home of EDUCOM Project Jericho to develop an index of curricular uses of technology

6-201 **Society for Industrial and Applied Mathematics (SIAM) Gopher Server:**
`gopher.siam.org`

i `gopher@siam.org`

An electronic magazine and information service of the Society for Industrial and Applied Mathematics.

Services:
- Book reviews from SIAM Review
- Complete listing of all SIAM books with complete tables of contents and ordering information
- Conference calls-for-papers and advance programs

- Membership information
- Professional opportunities
- Selected articles and commentaries from SIAM News
- Visiting Lecturer Program: description of program and list of participating speakers
- Journal descriptions, editorial policies, and macros

6-202 **Sonoma State University CIS Department Gopher:** `zippy.sonoma.edu`

i `gopher@zippy.sonoma.edu`

> *This is the gopher server for the Computer and Information Science Department at Sonoma State University, Rohnert Park, California.*

Services:

- Information for computer science majors at Sonoma State
- Information on human-powered vehicles, including archives of the HPV mailing list, articles, reviews, and JPEG images of HPVs
- Project Censored (a media research project on censorship) "Top Ten Censored Stories" lists

6-203 **South African Bibliographic and Information Network:** `info2.sabinet.co.za`

i `sabinet@info1.sabinet.co.za`

> *The gopher is hosted by SABINET.*

Services: This gopher provides information about the kind of databases that SABINET hosts and how to access them.

6-204 **Spanish EMBnet Node Gopher Server:** `gopher.cnb.uam.es`

i `lpezzi@cnbvx3.cnb.uam.es`

> *This gopher holds data of interest to biologists working in sequence analysis.*

Services:

- Description of the Centro Nacional de Biotecnologia
- Description of the EMBnet project
- Pointers to other gophers of interest to biologists
- Frequently Asked Questions about sequence analysis software
- Courses
- Job opportunities

6-205 **SpiGopher at Iowa State University:** `isumvs.iastate.edu`

i `ga.jas@isumvs.iastate.edu` or `jastruss@vincent.iastate.edu`

> *This is the Computation Center gopher server at Iowa State. The server itself is located on the ISUMVS system (WYLBUR) at Iowa State and primarily uses the SPIRES database facility.*

Services:

- Iowa State University schedule of classes
- Faculty/staff research profiles
- Fisher scientific material safety data sheets database
- Iowa State Computation Center newsletter

- Directory of e-mail addresses at Iowa State
- SPIRES Guide to Restaurants
- Access to Iowa State library catalog
- Video and movie review database (allows data entry)

6-206 **Sprintlink:** `ftp.sprintlink.net`

i `con@icm1.icp.net`

This is an experimental gopher intended to provide users with information relating to a wide variety of internetworking activities in addition to those with which Sprint is involved. Additionally, this Gopher will provide Sprint information considered of interest and relevence to the Internet community.

Services:

- NSFNET ICM statistics and monthly reports
- Usage statistics and implementation progress reports

6-207 **St. John's University Internet Gopher:** `sjuvm.stjohns.edu`

i `$sju@sjumusic.stjohns.edu`

The SJU gopher serves as the university's CWIS, as well as hosting the SJU Electronic Rehabilitation Resource Center and the SJU Learning Styles Network..

Services:

- St. John's University CWIS Electronic Rehabilitation Resource Center: an extensive collection of software, papers, and resources related to disabilities and rehabilitation
- Learning Styles Network: papers and resources devoted to learning styles and individual differences education and teaching resources
- Resources for K–12 teachers
- EASI (Equal Access to Software and Information): a unit of Educom chartered to serve the higher education community by providing information and guidance in the area of access-to-information technologies by persons with disabilities

6-208 **St. Olaf College Gopher:** `gopher.stolaf.edu`

i `gopher@stolaf.edu`

This is the CWIS for St. Olaf College, Northfield, Minnesota.

Services:

- Official archive site of the U.S. State Department travel warnings and consular information sheets
- Official archive site of the MacPsych mailing list, the NeXT-Managers mailing list, and the MuTeX (MusicTeX) mailing list
- Official archive site of the Omni-Cultural-Academic-Resource campus directory
- Course descriptions and class schedule

6-209 **Stanford University Genomic Information Service:** `genome-gopher.stanford.edu`

i `gopher-curator@genome.stanford.edu`

Information from the genome projects at Stanford University. The current information is provided by the Yeast Sequencing and Yeast Genome Database projects.

Services:

- List of gopher and FTP services for molecular biology
- Information from the nascent Yeast Genome Database project
- Searchable WAIS index of the budding yeast (Saccharomyces cerevisiae)
- Saccharomyces Genome
- BioSci electronic conference on yeast is provided as a searchable WAIS index. This includes all articles ever posted to the `bionet.molbio.yeast` Usenet newsgroup and the YEAST mailing list provided by `net.bio.net`.
- Yeast BioSci Electronic Conference

6-210 **StatLib:** `lib.stat.cmu.edu`

i `mikem@stat.cmu.edu`

StatLib is an archive of statistical software, datasets, and general information. The archive contains macros for statistical packages, complete statistical systems, subroutine libraries, and a large collection of useful datasets.

Services: Archive of statistical software.

6-211 **Student Union of HUT Gopher System:** `gopher.tky.hut.fi`

i `gopher@tky.hut.fi`

The machine is owned and maintained by the Student Union of Helsinki University of Technology to publish information relevant to activities somehow connected to HUT or the campus area.

Services:

- Campus phone/e-mail directory
- An open network information library where all HUT Student Union machine users can install information (other users possible in future)
- Information on exams and lectures for HUT students
- Where and what to eat at HUT student cafeterias
- Directory of Finnish gophers by location

6-212 **SURFnet-KB Infoserver:** `gopher.nic.surfnet.nl`

i `infoservices@surfnet.nl`

SURFnet is the National Research Network Organisation of the Netherlands. The SURFnet information server contains documents and publications from SURFnet and affiliate organizations. The gopher server also provides access to all Dutch network resources accessible through SURFnet and subject access to Internet resources. The gopher is maintained by an editorial board staffed by the National Library of the Netherlands: the Koninklijke Bibliotheek.

Services:

- SURFnet information and publications
- RARE information and publications
- Pointers to Dutch resources
- Pointers to worldwide Internet resources
- Classification scheme

6-213 **Swarthmore College Gopher Server:** `gopher.cc.swarthmore.edu`

i `postmaster@cc.swarthmore.edu`

> *This is the main gopher server for the Swarthmore College campus community. Swarthmore College is a small liberal-arts college in Swarthmore, Pennsylvania, a suburb of Philadelphia.*

Services: Most of the college publications such as the college catalog and student handbook are online. College calendars, Swarthmore e-mail lookups, and almost anything pertaining to the college are there.

6-214 **Swiss Main Gopher:** `gopher.switch.ch`

i `gopher@switch.ch`

> *This is the main gopher server for Switzerland.*

Services:

- Directory of all known Swiss gopher servers
- Directory with Swiss libraries (access information and telnet gateways)
- "SWITCH" directory with services provided by the Swiss organization
- FAQ (Frequently Asked Questions) lists: The staff extracts the FAQs from Netnews, and the archive probably has some features that other archives don't have: several indexes (subject, keyword, newsgroup); FAQs are WAIS-indexed, so they can be searched; FAQs can be listed; updated FAQs are marked.

6-215 **Swiss Scientific Supercomputing Center (CSCS) Info Server:** `pobox.cscs.ch`

i `mgay@cscs.ch`

> *This is the information server of the Swiss scientific supercomputing center.*

Services: This gopher server provides interesting (and also useful) information about the CSCS supercomputing center, its organization, its supercomputing and support equipment, its services, and so on.

6-216 **SyraCWIS: Syracuse University CWIS:** `cwis.syr.edu`

i `bbalakri@syr.edu`

> *This is the CWIS of Syracuse University, Syracuse, New York.*

Services:

- General campus information about Syracuse University
- [CSO] E-mail address directory (voluntary enrollment)
- Link to SUMMIT, Syracuse University Library online catalog
- ERIC (Educational Resources Information Clearinghouse) abstracts

6-217 **Tampere University of Technology (TUT) Information Service:** `gopher.cc.tut.fi`

i `mika.uusitalo@cc.tut.fi`

> *CWIS at Tampere University of Technology, Finland.*

Services: Information about TUT and services available on campus, phone, and e-mail addresses, pictures.

6-218 **Technet, Singapore:** `gopher.technet.sg`

i `milton@solomon.technet.sg`

> *This gopher is the main gopher of Singapore. It also serves as a registration of all the gopher*

servers within Singapore.

Services:
- Local city information
- Siflash: "a news bulletin, twice weekly"
- BC: "British council courses in Singapore"
- NSTB: "National Technology Plan"
- A registry for main gopher servers in Singapore

6-219 **Technical University of Nova Scotia Gopher Server:** `newton.ccs.tuns.ca`

i `gopher@tuns.ca`

This is the CWIS of the Technical University of Nova Scotia, Halifax, Nova Scotia, Canada.

Services: "The usual array of pointers as well as a CSO nameserver."

6-220 **Telerama Neighborhood Gopher:** `telerama.pgh.pa.us`

i `info@telerama.pgh.pa.us`

This is the Telerama public-access Internet gopher.

Services:
- Information about Telerama (policies and rates)
- Online catalogs and service listings
- Manuals, documents, and Telerama School tutorials
- Pointers to e-text, card catalogs, Internet periodicals
- Gateway to other gophers
- Information on how to get an account; overview of services

6-221 **Texas A&M University Gopher:** `gopher.tamu.edu`

i `gopher@tamu.edu`

The Texas A&M gopher provides information about Texas A&M University and the surrounding Bryan/College Station area.

Services:
- Information from the White House (press briefings, speeches, nominations, budget, etc.)
- Browse information by subject (from agriculture to political science to weather)
- Pointer to all on-campus departmental gophers
- Soviet archives
- Copy of pointers from Minnesota's "Gophers Worldwide"
- Campus directory
- Local restaurant guide
- Information on departments
- Local information for students, staff, and faculty
- Texas A&M University's Evans Library online card catalog
- Texas A&M central calendar of events

6-222   **Texas Department of Commerce Gopher:** `gopher.tdoc.texas.gov`

    i `gofer@tourism.tdoc.texas.gov`

Services:

- Community profiles: data on 541 Texas communities
- County time series: Demographic and econometric time series reports on all 254 Texas counties
- TDOC services and publications: list of services and publications offered by TDOC
- Telnet gateway to Texas Marketplace: Texas Marketplace is a BBS with comprehensive demographic data for the State of Texas. Population, financial, economic, and business statistics are among the reports offered by Texas Marketplace. Texas Marketplace also offers product matching services for businesses wishing to buy Texas products and for Texas companies wishing to find new markets for their products

6-223   **Texas Internet Consulting and MIDS Gopher:** `gopher.tic.com`

    i `gopher@tic.com`

Texas Internet Consulting is a network consulting firm, specializing in TCP/IP, Unix systems, and standards. MIDS (Matrix Information and Directory Services) publishes Matrix News and Matrix Maps Quarterly.

Services:

- The Online Book Store: electronic books at a fair price
- MIDS information
- Bruce Sterling's agitprop
- EFF-Austin information

6-224   **Texas Metronet, Inc.:** `gopher.metronet.com`

    i `gopher@metronet.com`

Internet for the individual. Extensive PERL archive and various other topics of interest.

Services: Extensive PERL archive, scripts, info, and distribution source. Internet services and information. Many other helpful sources and links. Entire archive boolean WAIS indexed for easy searching and retrieval.

6-225   **TLG Gopher:** `gopher-server.cwis.uci.edu`

    i `tlg@uci.bitnet`

The Thesaurus Linguae Graecae information server offers information about the TLG.

Services:

- Listings of the contents of TLG CD-ROMs
- Information about the sources of TLG CD-ROM-compatible software
- Addenda and corrigenda to the printed Thesaurus Linguae Graecae Canon of Greek Authors
- Works, samples of TLG license agreements
- Instructions on how to order TLG products and resources
- Special announcements, and other items of potential interest to the TLG user and to the field at large.

6-226 **Trent University Information Service:** `blaze.trentu.ca`

i `kbrown@trentu.ca` or `ccksb@blaze.trentu.ca`

This is the CWIS for Trent University, Peterborough, Ontario, Canada.

Services:

- Departmental information (academic and administration)
- Listing of current events
- Description of computing resources
- Links to FTP tree for software distribution
- Help files for general, VMS, and Ultrix users
- Pointers to other Internet resources (other gophers, CWISs, libraries, etc., of interest to Trent)
- Campus telephone and e-mail directory (CCSO's NS-server)
- Extensive descriptions of the library's services
- Trent University archives
- Distribution of faculty work/publications, notably D. Theall's work on James Joyce and Sarah Keefer's work on Old English

6-227 **Trenton State College Gopher:** `gopher.trenton.edu`

i `ssivy@trenton.edu`

Services:

- Various Mac, DOS, Windows, OS/2, and Unix FTP archives including Dr. Norm Neff's own version of Prolog
- TSC Information Management Newsletter Online
- TSC Mac and IBM resale information
- TSC Computer Lab biographies (hours, managers, etc.)
- Course syllabuses and projects/homework (just Unix and C classes right now)
- Records and registration information (classes, important dates, final exams, etc.)
- Campus phone book
- Campus library card catalog
- Pointers to WAIS sources
- Weather information

6-228 **TU Magdeburg Gopher:** `gopher.tu-magdeburg.de`

i `emmerich@urz.tu-magdeburg.de`

This is the CWIS of the Technical University of Magdeburg, Germany.

Services:

- Information about the university, its departments, institutions, and central services
- Pointers to other CWISs

6-229 **TU Munich Electrotechnical Gopher Server:** `gopher.e-technik.tu-muenchen.de`

i `gopher@e-technik.tu-muenchen.de`

This is the information service of the Electrotechnical Department of the Technical University, Munich, Germany.

Services: Information of the Electrotechnical Department of the Technical University, Munich, Germany.

6-230 **Turku School of Economics:** `gopher.tukkk.fi`

i `skarvinen@abo.fi`

Information service of the Turku School of Economics and Business Administration, Turku, Finland.

Services:
- General information about the school, in English
- E-mail list of school's personnel
- Internal information services of the school, in Finnish

6-231 **U-Discover!:** `gopher.udel.edu`

i `gopher@mvs.udel.edu.`

University of Delaware's gopher server provides institutional data.

Services:
- University of Delaware policies, newsletters, agenda, minutes
- "Campus Collage" (images of campus scenes, people, activites)
- "Tour de Delaware" (pictorial tour of campus)
- Faculty/staff/student e-mail address and phone lookup
- Bulletin board info: classified, employment info, etc.

6-232 **U.C. Berkeley Museum of Paleontology:** `ucmp1.berkeley.edu`

i `robg@fossil.berkeley.edu`

This gopher provides information concerning the events, activities, and collections of the museum, as well as other sources of information of interest for biologists and geologists. The gopher includes a great white shark exhibit.

Services:
- Searchable museum type specimen catalogs
- Images of sharks taken from VCR footage

6-233 **UB Wings:** `wings.buffalo.edu`

i `gerland@ubvms.cc.buffalo.edu`

This is the CWIS of the State University of New York at Buffalo.

Services:
- Campus information
- Faculty and staff phone directories
- Libraries
- Western New York information
- Access to the Internet

6-234 **UHINFO:** `gopher.hawaii.edu`

i `gopher.hawaii.edu`

This is the CWIS for the University of Hawaii System, which includes UH Manoa, UH Hilo,

UH West Oahu, Hawaii CC, Honolulu CC, Kapiolani CC, Kauai CC, Leeward CC, Maui CC, and Windward CC.

Services:
- 1993-95 UH Manoa general and graduate information catalog
- Faculty/staff phone directory (system-wide)
- Student phone directory (UH Manoa campus only)
- Weekly UH bulletins and online calendar of events
- Athletic and academic calendars
- Schedule of classes and registration information
- Computer price lists
- Large collection of user documentation from the Computing Center
- Links to other gopher or information servers supported by various university campuses or departments
- Administrative policies, procedures, and plans.
- Various other university services

6-235 **UIC/ADN Gopher:** `uicvm.uic.edu`
i `gopher@uicvm.cc.uic.edu`
> *This is the CWIS of the University of Illinois at Chicago.*

Services:
- Campus events
- Computer center's INFORM document library
- College of Dentistry document collection
- College of Business Administration newsletter
- Faculty/staff directory and university yellow pages
- National Institute for the Environment (NIE) document collection
- The Paleontological Society document collection
- Timetable course section information server
- UICNews: UIC's administration newspaper (articles and full-text search)
- Vice Chancellor for Research document collection

6-236 **ULibrary:** `gopher.lib.umich.edu`
i `ulibrary@um.cc.umich.edu`
> *This is the University of Michigan Library's gopher system.*

Services:
- Connections to online library catalogs worldwide
- U.S. Census data for Michigan
- U.S. Commerce Department's Economic Bulletin Board data
- UPI Newswire data (available only to University of Michigan faculty, staff, and students)
- Electronic journals, including the Bryn Mawr Classical Review, Current Cites, PACS-L Review, Postmodern Culture, and Psycoloquy

6-237 **UNC-ECS (UNC System) Gopher Server:** `uncecs.edu`

   i `dgm@uncecs.edu`

This server provides information services primarily to the 16 constituent institutions of the University of North Carolina.

Services:

- Centralized access to UNC library catalogs
- Pointers to other UNC CWISs
- Information of interest to computing and library personnel at institutions of higher learning
- Internet resource guides

6-238 **Uni-Passau gopher:** `gopher.uni-passau.de`

   i `thomas.eiler@rz.uni-passau.de`

All articles are writen in German and deal with "Uni Passau"-specific items.

6-239 **United Nations Development Programme Information System:** `gopher.undp.org`

   i `gopher@undp.org`

This gopher contains information related to the United Nations Development Programme and other United Nations agencies.

Services:

- The United Nations, what it is and what it does
- United Nations Conference on Environment and Development (UNCED)
- United Nations press releases
- United Nations Development Programme (UNDP) documents
- United Nations system directories
- United Nations system telecommunications catalog
- Other United Nations and related gophers
- Environment-related Information

6-240 **Universitaet Regensburg Gopher:** `gopher.uni-regensburg.de`

   i `ulrich.krauss@rrzc1.rz.uni-regensburg.de`

Computer information system at the University of Regensburg, Germany.

Services:

- Documentation of computer software and hardware available on campus
- General campus information (phone directory, course schedule, currently mostly limited to the Physics department)
- cultural information

6-241 **University at Stony Brook CWIS:** `ccvm.sunysb.edu`

   i `sbnews@ccvm.sunysb.edu`

This is the CWIS of State University of New York at Stony Brook, New York.

Services:

- University news service

- General information about the university
- Campus directory
- Access to the library catalog

6-242 **University CWIS:** `gopher.chalmers.se`

i `wall@adm.chalmers.se`

This is the CWIS of Chalmers University of Technology in Gothenburg (Goteborg), Sweden.

Services: WHOIS directory of campus; administrative information; information about the campus library, research, and education; time tables for public transportation relevant to the campus; menus for restaurants; and computing information.

6-243 **University of Maryland Information Server:** `inform.umd.edu`

i `inform-editor@umail.umd.edu`

CWIS of the University of Maryland at College Park.

Services:

- Faculty/staff directory
- Economic time series data (These series include various national accounts, labor information, price indices, current business indicators and industrial production, information over state and regions, and international data.)
- Womens' studies repository
- Academic information
- On-campus job listings
- Campus calendar of events

6-244 **University of Amsterdam Campus Information System:** `gopher.uva.nl`

i `gopher@uva.nl`

This is the CWIS of University of Amsterdam, the Netherlands.

Services:

- Campus directory

6-245 **University of Bergen:** `gopher.uib.no`

i `vagar.aabrek@edb.uib.no`

This is the CWIS of the University of Bergen, Norway.

Services:

- Campus directory
- Directory of pointers to various dictionaries
- Norwegian Social Science Data Services (NSD) Information Service

6-246 **University of Canberra CWIS:** `services.canberra.edu.au`

i `cwis@services.canberra.edu.au`

This is the CWIS of the University of Canberra, ACT, Australia.

Services:

- University committees
- Course information; directories; faculty information

- News and events
- Profile and research information
- Services on campus
- Timetables

6-247 **University of Chicago (UCInfo):** `gopher.uchicago.edu`

i `gopher-team@midway.uchicago.edu`

This a primary entry point to UCInfo, the CWIS of the University of Chicago.

Services: UCInfo provides access to a campus directory, job openings, course offerings and other student information, and links to numerous on-campus specialized gopher servers (Library, Law, Biological Sciences, etc.)

6-248 **University of Cologne / RRZK-Gopher:** `gopher.rrz.uni-koeln.de`

i `gophermgr@rrz.uni-koeln.de`

This is the Regional Computing Centre of the University of Cologne (RRZK), Germany.

Services:

- Computing Center (RRZK) information
- Information on other institutions of the university
- WAIS for this gopher
- Access to RRZK+s anonymous FTP server
- Access to OPAC service at the University of Cologne

6-249 **University of Connecticut Health Center—Neuroscience/Research Group:**
`gopher.uchc.edu`

i `postmaster@neuron.uchc.edu`

Experimental VMS gopher at the University of Connecticut Health Center in Farmington, Connecticut. Main focus is campus research and academic topics.

Services:

- General campus information
- Sample publications
- Pointers to other campus bulletin boards
- Library access info

6-250 **University of Constance:** `gopher.uni-konstanz.de`

i `dierk@gopher.rz.uni-konstanz.de`

This is the CWIS of the University of Constance, Germany. The resources are almost all in German.

6-251 **University of Economics and Business Administration, Vienna, Austria (Wirtschaftsuniversitaet Wien):** `gopher.wu-wien.ac.at`

i `gopher-adm@wu-wien.ac.at` (server administration) or
`gopher-chat@wu-wien.ac.at` (general gopher service discussion)

This is the gopher service of the University of Economics and Business Administration, Vienna, Austria.

Services:

- This server lists all gopher servers and related systems in Austria and provides entry points
- Archive for mailing lists (discussion log files and related material): `earlym-l` and `rec.music.early` (medieval, Renaissance, and baroque music and earlier); `cerro-l` (Central European Regional Research Organization); `wafe` (widget Athena front end, X Windows development package); `netzbuch` (mailing list for the book "Maier, Wildberg: In 8 Sekunden um die Welt")
- Material about the international MBA program and list of gophers of participating universities
- Pointers to other economics-oriented services
- Access to VieGopher source (VM/CMS server and client)

6-252 **University of Economics, Poznan, Poland:** `gopher.ae.poz.edu.pl`

i `wlat@novci1.ae.poz.edu.pl`

Hosted by the computer center, the gopher serves as a campus info server, a quick reference to Internet resources, and a contact target for anyone trying to reach Poznan and its universities.

Services:

- Directory of campus information, including phones and contacts
- Pointers to Internet services (telnet)
- Pointers to games like chess or backgammon, including a huge collection of pointers to muds, mushes, tinymucks, lpmuds, and so on.

6-253 **University of Edinburgh gopher:** `gopher.ed.ac.uk`

i `gophermaster@ed.ac.uk`

This is a gopher server provided by the Computing Services Department of the University of Edinburgh, providing an index to public-domain XWindow application sources and access to the university's campus information service.

Services:

- Link to the universty's CWIS
- Link to Meteorology Department METEOSAT satellite weather images
- Index of public-domain X sources

6-254 **University of Goettingen—Medical Informatics Gopher:** `serversun.mdv.gwdg.de`

i `gopher@serversun.mdv.gwdg.de`

This is an information system by the Department of Medical Informatics at the Medical Center of the University of Goettingen, Germany.

Services:

- Research report of medicine at the University of Goettingen
- Fields of research
- Medical superintendents and heads of the departments (listing and the possibility of contact)
- General Information about the Medical Center (events, meetings, etc.)
- Syllabi of lectures

- General information about the university
- Local informations for students
- Exchange Projekt for students (build up)
- Links to medical gophers around the world
- Library access (national and international)
- Listings of medical resources on the Internet
- Link to organizations (for example, the World Health Organization)
- Links to databases (DNA, protein, medical software, etc.)
- Pointers to CWISs (Germany, Europe, world)

6-255 **University of Goteborg:** `gopher.gu.se`

i `stoltz@adm.gu.se`

Information about the university and campus (Goteborg, Sweden).

Services:

- University WHOIS directory
- Campus administrative, library, research, and education information
- Facts and figures about the university, the city of Goteborg, and the summer academy
- Seminar and conference information for visiting students and researchers
- Course and project information

6-256 **University of Idaho Gopher Server:** `gopher.uidaho.edu`

i `postmast@uidaho.edu` or `gopher@uidaho.edu`

This is the central information server for the University of Idaho, Moscow, Idaho.

Services:

- CSO directory of faculty/staff (e-mail, office, phone, etc.) with student directory to be added soon
- Online services from UI library (card catalog, local newspapers, and copies of Environmental News Network newsletter) and College of Agriculture (IDEX BBS)
- Local weather data
- Student services information
- Pointers to other gopher servers in the Pacific Northwest
- Gateway to UI FTP server and other popular anonymous FTP sites around the world.

6-257 **University of Illinois Weather Machine Gopher Server:** `wx.atmos.uiuc.edu`

i `gopher@wx.atmos.uiuc.edu`

The purpose of the Weather Machine is to provide easy access to weather information to members of the University of Illinois at Urbana/Champaign community. Access is also provided to the rest of the Internet, time and resources permitting. The Weather Machine is run by the Department of Atmospheric Sciences at the University of Illinois at Urbana/Champaign.

Services:

- Weather-related documents
- Weather images (satellite, surface, forecast, etc.)
- Current National Weather Service reports

6-258 **University of Joensuu CWIS:** `gopher.joensuu.fi`

    i `gophermaster@gopher.joensuu.fi`

      This is the CWIS of University of Joensuu, Finland.

    Services:

- Education offered in the university
- Access to local library system (VTLS)

6-259 **University of Kansas TISL Gopher:** `gopher.tisl.ukans.edu`

    i `gopher@tisl.ukans.edu`

      Information service for the Telecommunications and Information Sciences Laboratory at the University of Kansas.

    Services:

- Directories for affiliated University of Kansas departments
- Pointers to other University of Kansas CWISs
- Archive for TISL technical reports in networking, DSP, communications, etc.
- Archive for information on the MAGIC gigabit (information superhighway) test bed
- Pointer to the UNITE Explorer K-12 educational resource server at University of Kansas
- Gateway to the TISL FTP archives

6-260 **University of Karlsruhe:** `gopher.rz.uni-karlsruhe.de`

    i `scheller@rz.uni-karlsruhe.de`

      This gopher is still being developed as a CWIS for the University of Karlsruhe (Germany).

    Services:

- Local information about the computing center and some faculties
- FTP servers of the university
- Telnet to B.I.S (information system of our ibm3090), the servers of the academic software cooperation (ASK), and online service of the library of the university
- Pointers to some other databases
- Gateways to X.500, WAIS, Archie

6-261 **University of Kentucky:** `ukcc.uky.edu`

    Services: Information for and about the UK community. It provides campus news and announcements, class schedules, administrative manuals, weather, access to the campus library catalog, campus job openings, and links to other information services.

6-262 **University of Mining and Metallurgy, Cracow:** `gopher.uci.agh.edu.pl`

    i `js@uci.agh.edu.pl`

      This is the CWIS of the University of Mining and Metallurgy, Cracow, Poland.

    Services:

- Campus phone book (with e-mail addresses, if any)
- Student bulletin
- Rector's bulletin
- University regulations, etc.

- Local city information
- Text of local newspaper "Gazeta Wyborcza w Krakowie"
- Archive of Polish Internet magazines (Donosy, Spojrzenia, etc.)
- Index of all Polish network resources
- Archive of some discussion lists
- RFC archive
- interesting programs, files, gifs, etc.
- SIMTEL and CICA archives available on CD-ROMs mounted non-stop
- Links to all Polish gophers
- Links to many gophers worldwide
- Telnet links to about 600 library infosystems
- Gateways to more than 1000 anonymous FTP systems

6-263 **University of Minnesota Gopher:** `gopher.tc.umn.edu`

i `gopher@boombox.micro.umn.edu`

This is where it all started. The one, the original Gopher Server. Now doing double duty as the CWIS for the University of Minnesota and providing many other interesting services.

Services:

- Canonical listing of all the gopher servers in the world.
- Weather for the U.S.A.
- Gopher news archive
- Recipes
- Movie reviews
- Campus phone book
- College and departmental information
- Computer Q&A
- WAIS and FTP gateways
- Events on campus

6-264 **University of Natal (Durban) Gopher and CIS:** `gopher.und.ac.za`

i `gopher@und.ac.za`

This is the gopher and Campus Information System for the University of Natal (Durban), South Africa.

Services:

- Campus information system
- Campus directory
- "Offical" collection of pointers to other South African gophers

6-265 **University of Natal, Pietermaritzburg, Gopher Server:** `gopher.unp.ac.za`

i `gopher@gopher.unp.ac.za`

This is a gopher server operating as the CIS for the University of Natal, Pietermaritzburg, Republic of South Africa.

Services:

- Campus information
- Links to other sites, including several South African FTP sites

6-266 **University of North Texas CWIS:** `gopher.unt.edu`

i `gopher@unt.edu`

> *This is part of the CWIS for the University of North Texas, Denton, Texas.*

Services:

- Employement opportunities
- National Science Foundation grant information
- National Institute of Health guide
- North Texas Research periodical
- Local campus phone book with e-mail addresses
- Departmental information from various UNT schools and colleges
- UNT events and activities
- Online library catalog access
- Computing documentation and articles
- Registration and admissions information
- Meeting notes and newsletters from various campus organizations (including a local Novell users group)
- Telnet links to statewide library online catalog systems
- Localized documentation for PCs, Macs, Apple II's, Unix, X windows, Windows
- Our anonymous FTP site, `ftp.unt.edu`, via a gateway

6-267 **University of Notre Dame:** `gopher.nd.edu`

i `gopher@gopher.nd.edu`

> *This is Notre Dame's campus information system, repository of publicly available academic and research data, and electronic archive.*

Services:

- Campus information. Information supplied by both academic and administrative units of the University of Notre Dame
- NABS (North American Benthic Society) database in WAIS-searchable format. The WAIS software supports boolean searches.
- Collection of worldwide electronic directory services. Notre Dame's gopher is the root site for the worldwide list of directory services running at various institutions around the global Internet. The collection consists of a unified listing of CSO nameservers, whois sites, WAIS databases, and telnet-based services. The collection is broken down alphabetically and geographically. There is also a simple search feature that allows single keyword searching for a particular site.

6-268 **University of Oregon:** `gopher.uoregon.edu`

i `gopher@gopher.uoregon.edu`

> *This is the top-level gopher server for the University of Oregon, in Eugene, Oregon. It provides*

access to a variety of information, including DuckScoop, the UO CWIS.

Services:

- DuckScoop, UO CWIS, including campus directory, etc.
- State of Oregon purchasing agreements
- LaneNet: Lane County K–12 public schools gopher service
- Links to all other gopher servers at the University of Oregon

6-269 **University of Pennsylvania Psychology Department:** `psych.upenn.edu`

> *This gopher accesses information about the Psychology Department and papers by staff members.*

6-270 **University of Pretoria Gopher Server:** `prefect.ee.up.ac.za.`

i `gopher@ee.up.ac.za` or `gopherd@ee.up.ac.za`

> *This is the primary gopher server for the University of Pretoria campus, as well as certain research groupings in and arround Pretoria, Republic of South Africa.*

- Campus telephone directory
- Collection of pointers to other CWISs
- Gateway to university library catalog
- Cricket scores
- Information about the university and its departments

6-271 **University of Redlands:** `ultrix.uor.edu`

i `gopher@ultrix.uor.edu`

> *This is the CWIS for the University of Redlands.*

6-272 **University of Rhode Island Gopher System:** `gopher.uri.edu`

i `jms@uriacc.uri.edu`

> *This is the CWIS for the University of Rhode Island in Kingston, Rhode Island.*

Services:

- Pointers to URI departmental gophers
- Pointer to URI library online catalog

6-273 **University of Saarbruecken Campus Information System:**
`pfsparc02.phil.uni-sb.de`, reachable thru `solaris.rz.tu-clausthal.de` port 89

i `gopher@phil.uni-sb.de`

> *A voluntary group of students maintains this gopher to provide a modern means of information to the students and other interested persons.*

Services:

- Campus information (common information, lectures, phone numbers, foreign-language information about the University of Saarland and the region, etc.)
- Local information (cities, regional)
- Local cultural events (cinemas, theater, etc.)
- Archive against Xenophobia (lots of gophers have a link on it)
- Compilation of resources for Information Science

- German-language travel reports
- Links to neighbor gophers in Germany, France, and Luxembourg
- Several links to worldwide resources in several topics

6-274 **University of Saarbruecken Gopher Project:** `134.96.82.13`

i `sigel@phil15.uni-sb.de`

Services:

- "Archiv gegen AuslaenderInnenfeindlichkeit": a collection of articles reporting hostility against foreigners and actions taken against it

6-275 **University of Sao Paulo—Institute of Physics:** `uspif.if.usp.br`

i `becherini@uspif.if.usp.br`

This is the gopher server of the Institute of Physics, at the University of Sao Paulo, Sao Paulo, Brazil.

Services:

- Informations about USP and IFUSP
- Available Services in the Brazilian Network
- List of Brazilian nodes
- Information about BRAS-NET
- News from Brazilian newspapers

6-276 **University of Saskatchewan Gopher:** `gopher.usask.ca`

i `earl.fogel@usask.ca`

This is the CWIS of the University of Saskatchewan, Canada.

Services:

- Campus phone book
- Gardening information
- Local weather forecasts and satellite images
- Archive of U. of S. Computing Services Newsletter

6-277 **University of Southampton Faculty of Mathematical Studies:** `mir.maths.soton.ac.uk`

i `jhr@uk.ac.soton.maths`

This gopher is designed to provide a resource for the Faculty of Mathematical Studies at Southampton University.

Services:

- Information about members of staff and faculty/departmental activities
- Pointers to lots of other mathematical gophers/information servers on the Internet
- Collection of newletters/discussion lists of mathematical interest

6-278 **University of Sunderland:** `gopher.sunderland.ac.uk`

i `gophermaster@gopher.sunderland.ac.uk`

This is the central campus information service of the University of Sunderland.

Services:

- Pointers to other gophers

- Internet resources for the convenience of people at Sunderland
- University telephone directory
- Hardware and software pricing

6-279 **University of Sydney Faculty of Law:**

i nelsonv@sulaw.law.su.oz.au

This is the faculty's information service for external and internal users.

Services:

- List of e-mail faculty addresses; List of academic and general staff; phone book
- Library online catalog
- New South Wales libraries
- Discussion lists
- List of law-related resources worldwide
- Link to law resources sites
- Gateway for gopher sources; archie, FTP, finger, etc.
- Faculty's departments and centers information
- Faculty news and conferences lists.

6-280 **University of Tampere Gopher:** gopher.uta.fi

i gopher@uta.fi

This is the gopher server for University of Tampere in Tampere, Finland.

Services:

- University of Tampere information
- Administration, departments, faculties, computer center, the library, etc.
- Information for students from student organizations, students' union, etc.
- Calendar system for current information and events.
- Interface for reading local Internet news. Information is mainly in Finnish, but the English-language part of the gopher is continuously supported.

6-281 **University of Tasmania Campus Information Service:** info.utas.edu.au

i postmaster@utas.edu.au

This is the CWIS for the University of Tasmania, Hobart, Tasmania, Australia.

Services:

- Electronic Antiquity: Communicating The Classics (an electronic periodical)
- General CWIS information for the University of Tasmania

6-282 **University of Tennessee–Knoxville Libraries:** gopher.lib.utk.edu

i kanthraj@utklib.utk.edu

This is the Knoxville Libraries gopher server.

Services:

- Online catalog
- Smoky Mountains database
- Manuscripts

- Internet resources
- Next indexing
- CWIS info

6-283 **University of Texas at Austin Fusion Studies Gopher:** `hagar.ph.utexas.edu`

i `gopher@hagar.ph.utexas.edu`

This is the gopher server of the Institute for Fusion Studies and Fusion Research Center at the University of Texas at Austin. This Gopher was created to further communication between worldwide laboratories engaged in fusion research in an attempt to develop a clean and nearly limitless source of electric power for future generations.

Services:
- Repository of physics and fusion newsletters and Washington science funding status reports
- Largest? collection of pointers to physics-related gophers
- Collection of white pages directories for fusion labs
- Information of interest to employees of the University of Texas
- Technical reports from the Institute for Fusion Studies and Fusion Research Center
- Description and drawings of TEXT-U Tokamak and diagnostics (a tokamak is a research device used to heat a gas to more than 10 million degrees to simulate the center of the sun and eventually produce fusion reactions)
- Software and documentation pertaining to fusion research

6-284 **University of Texas at Austin, Economics Department:** `gopher.eco.utexas.edu`

i `gopher@mundo.eco.utexas.edu`

This gopher provides information for and about the department.

Services:
- Departmental news
- General help system
- Departmental seminar schedule
- System announcements

6-285 **University of Texas Austin Computation Center:** `gopherhost.cc.utexas.edu`

i `gopher@gopherhost.cc.utexas.edu`

This gopher provides information for and about UT Austin.

Services:
- Computation Center documents and newsletter
- Computer class schedules
- Daily Texan, the student newspaper
- Information from the Texas Union, the student center, including movie schedules, and special events calendar
- Information from UT Austin academic departments
- Microlib, a software archive for Mac, DOS, and Windows software
- Price lists from the Texas Union MicroCenter, the campus computer store

- Student, faculty, staff directory
- Skywatch astronomy news
- Texas natural history collection

6-286 **University of Texas Austin Fusion Studies:** `hagar.ph.utexas.edu`

i `gopher@hagar.ph.utexas.edu`

This gopher provides information for and about the Institute for Fusion Studies (IFS) and Fusion Research Center (FRC) at UT Austin.

Services:

- Archive of technical reports and publications of the FRC and IFS
- Information on the TEXT-U Tokamak, a plasma-containment device
- Information for FRC and IFS employees

6-287 **University of Texas Austin General Libraries:** `gopherhost.cc.utexas.edu`

i `j.kupersmith@utxvm.cc.utexas.edu`

This gopher provides convenient access to UT Austin library catalogs and other finding aids, and to other local and remote information resources.

Services:

- UTCAT PLUS: general libraries, library catalog, and database system including UT Austin faculty/staff/student directory and current listing of jobs available.
- TALLONS: Tarlton Law Library catalog
- Finding aids for some manuscript collections in the Harry Ransom Humanities Research Center
- Selected library guides and bibliographies
- Pointers to fact sources, indexes and abstracts, electronic texts, and subject-specific servers

6-288 **University of Texas Austin, Computer Sciences Department:** `gopher.cs.utexas.edu`

i `unix@cs.utexas.edu`

This gopher provides information for and about the department.

Services:

- Archive of Computer Science Department technical reports
- Departmental academic information
- Departmental directory
- Departmental policies

6-289 **University of Texas Austin, Physics Department:** `utmama.ph.utexas.edu`

i `gopher-adm@gopherhost.ph.utexas.edu`

This gopher provides information for and about the department

Services:

- Departmental calendar of events
- Departmental computer facilities

6-290 **University of Texas M. D. Anderson Cancer Center Gopher:** `utmdacc.uth.tmc.edu`

i `gopher-admin@utmdacc.uth.tmc.edu`

This is the gopher serving as an online information service for the University of Texas M. D. Anderson Cancer Center.

Services:
- Campus telephone directory
- Collection of pointers to biomedical gophers
- Gateway to UTMDACC Research Medical Library

6-291 **University of Texas Medical Branch Medical CWIS:** `phil.utmb.edu`

i `perry@phil.utmb.edu`

This is the Campus Wide Medical Information Service of the University of Texas Medical Branch at Galveston, Texas.

Services:
- Pointers to various medical databases and services as well as local medical information
- Links to the antiviral archives localed on `phil.utmb.edu`

6-292 **University of Texas—Latin American Network Information Center:** `lanic.utexas.edu`

i `info@lanic.utexas.edu`

The objective is to provide Latin American users with access to academic databases and information services worldwide, and to provide Latin Americanists around the world with access to the information on and from Latin America.

Services:
- Libraries worldwide, especially in Latin America (Spanish and Portuguese menus)
- Subject access to academic databases and information services
- Latin America information
- PROFMEXIS information
- Information resource access tools, including UT-LANIC database evaluation project

6-293 **University of Toronto, Computer Systems Research Institute (CSRI) Gopher Information Service:** `gopher.csri.toronto.edu`

i `gopher@csri.toronto.edu`

This is the CSRI Information Service.

Services:
- University of Toronto CSRI technical reports

6-294 **University of Turku Campus-Wide Information:** `gopher.utu.fi`

i `gopher@gopher.utu.fi`

University of Turku, Turku, Finland

Services:
- Lookup of local people (under "General Information")
- Internal information and user guides (in Finnish)

6-295 **University of Utah:** `gopher.cc.utah.edu`

    i `jonzy@cc.utah.ed` or `kenhulme@cc.utah.edu`

This gopher server at the University of Utah is its top-level gopher server, and is the service used to distribute campus and state information.

Services:

- Directory pointing to all known gopher servers
- Directory pointing to all known ph servers
- Online campus phone book
- Schedules of the campus shuttle and classes
- Campus events
- Campus newsletters
- Jobs
- Research opportunities
- Information about the Internet
- Directory pointing to some anonymous FTP sites
- Information about the State of Utah

6-296 **University of Vaasa:** `gopher.uwasa.fi`

    i `gopher@uwasa.fi`

This is the gopher for the University of Vaasa, Finland.

Services:

- Campus information, in Finnish and also in English
- Some scientific material

6-297 **University of Valencia (Spain):** `gopher.uv.es`

    i `gopher@uva.ci.uv.es`

This gopher is open to academic and research information and also is part of the CWIS of the Universitat de Valencia.

Services:

- University directory
- Gateway to local FTP and Hytelnet service
- WAIS (Research in Surgery Database location)
- Gateway X.500 service
- University services announcements

6-298 **University of Victoria Faculty of Fine Arts:** `kafka.uvic.ca`

    i `ejordan@nero.uvic.ca`

This is a CWIS for the Faculty of Fine Arts, University of Victoria, Canada, with a special focus on fine arts.

Services:

- Archive of mail from the gopher newsgroup
- Archive of Fine Art Forum and Leonardo Electronic News (fine arts journals)

- Collection of photographs from UVic theater productions
- Collection of Egyptian images
- Course calender, newspapers, information, etc.
- Visual Arts Health and Safety Manual
- Recipes from University of Victoria (one of our more popular items)
- Unix fortune

6-299 **University of Vienna Department of Medical Cybernetics and Artificial Intelligence:**

```
gopher.ai.univie.ac.at
```

i `gopheradmin@ai.univie.ac.at`

> *This is the information service of the Department for Medical Cybernetics and Artificial Intelligence, University of Vienna, and the Austrian Research Institute for Artificial Intelligence, Vienna, Austria.*

Services:

- Publications in the field of artificial intelligence
- Searchable calendar of international artificial-intelligence-related events
- Various searchable archives of mailing lists
- Collection of pointers to artificial intelligence Internet sites

6-300 **University of Virginia GWIS:**

i `gwis@virginia.edu`

> *This is the Grounds-Wide Information System for the University of Virginia.*

Services:

- Online journals, reference works, news and announcements, and connections to the worldwide Internet
- Specialized resources related to ecology
- Departmental and school information
- Collections of 1990 Census information
- Electronic journals and books from traditional publishers
- Collections of images from the Vatican Library exhibit at the Library of Congress
- Sound recordings from the 1992 Presidential debates
- Connection to the Library of Congress's online system
- Academic American Encyclopedia and the United Press International (UPI) wire service.
- Bryn Mawr Classical Review

6-301 **University of Washington, Pathology Department:**

```
larry.pathology.washington.edu
```

i `dadler@u.washington.edu`

> *The Department of Pathology at the University of Washington, Seattle, Washington, is experimenting with providing graphic images of interest to biologists. The initial focus is cytogenetics and chromosome images, and then a gallery of photomicrographs of pathology sections.*

Services: Human and mouse chromosome idiograms in various file formats are available.

The PostScript-formatted files can be manipulated band-by-band with common graphics software. Scanned photomicrograph images of chromosomes and pathology sections are available experimentally.

6-302 **University of Western Ontario Gopher:** `gopher.uwo.ca`
i `gopher@julian.uwo.ca`

This is the CWIS of University of Western Ontario, London, Ontario, Canada.

Services:

- Campus directory of faculty and staff
- Introductory and orientation information about the university
- University course calendar (course descriptions)
- University policies and procedures
- Campus computing newsletters
- UWO library system catalog, services, and resources
- Index to journalism periodicals
- Index to the local stories in the London Free Press (newspaper)
- Pointers to various network sources organized by departments in social science

6-303 **University of Wisconsin–Parkside:** `gopher.uwp.edu`
i `gopher@gopher.uwp.edu`

This is the gopher version of the Music FTP Archive.

Services: Discographies for over 350 artists; lyrics to over 15,000 songs; `rec.music.info` archives; "sounds and pictures"; Usenet mailing lists for many popular recording artists and styles.

6-304 **University of Wollongong Campus Information System:** `gopher.uow.edu.au`
i `gopher@uow.edu.au`

This is the CWIS provided by the Information Technology Services Department of the University of Wollongong.

Services:

- University of Wollongong undergraduate and postgraduate handbooks/calendars
- University-specific information
- Australian weather information and satellite images
- University management documents

6-305 **University of Zurich Computing Center (RZU):** `gopher.unizh.ch` port 1500
i `gopher@rzu.unizh.ch`

This gopher is maintained by the computing center of the University of Zurich Irchel

Services:

- General information about the Computing Center at the University of Zurich (software, hardware)
- Campus directory
- Phone books (including the Swiss Federal Institute of Technology)

- Telnet access to rzubiz (service for connecting to some libraries)
- Gateway to the FTP server at the University of Zurich

6-306 **USC-Math Gopher Service:** `bigcheese.math.scarolina.edu`

i `gopher@bigcheese.math.scarolina.edu`

A multitopic information service hosted at the University of South Carolina Department of Mathematics in Columbia, South Carolina.

Services:

- Archives and dynamic links to wavelet-related mathematical materials
- Archives of the locally originated "Wavelet Digest"
- Site-independent organizations of computer-related and multitopic informational resources

6-307 **USDA Extension Service:** `esusda.gov`

i `gopher-admin@esusda.gov`

This server is set up to provide access to information from the USDA Extension Service, other USDA agencies, and other federal agencies as it relates to the Cooperative Extension System.

Services:

- USDA Extension Service related information
- USDA Extension Service National Initiatives information
- USDA Extension Service educational base programming
- Links to other Cooperative Extension Service gophers

6-308 **USDinfo:** `teetot.acusd.edu`

USDinfo is the name given a suite of tools used to provide campus-wide access to local and off-campus information and computer resources.

Services:

- Campus directories, schedules, and information
- Resource pointers grouped by discipline
- The Privacy Rights Clearinghouse, a free bulletin board providing information about rights to privacy in telecommunications, mail, etc.

6-309 **USGS Atlantic Marine Geology gopher:** `bramble.er.usgs.gov`

i `gopher@bramble.er.usgs.gov`

An experimental Internet service of the U.S. Geological Survey, Branch of Atlantic Marine Geology, Woods Hole, Massachusetts.

Services: Scientific data and mapping information, primarily of marine geology and geophysics, for the geological, geophysical, and oceanographic reseach community.

6-310 **UT-Austin Mathematics:** `henri.ma.utexas.edu`

i `chari@math.utexas.edu`

This gopher provides information for and about the department.

Services:

- Mathematical physics preprint archive

- Math FTP archive
- Math system information

6-311   **UVicINFO:** `gopher.uvic.ca`

> *This is the gopher service of the University of Victoria, British Columbia, Canada.*

Services: All other public UVic gopher servers are available via this server.

6-312   **UWSAinfo—University of Wisconsin System Administration Information:** `gopher1.uwsa.edu`

i `mgopher@gopher1.uwsa.edu`

> *This is the system-wide information service of the University of Wisconsin in Madison, Wisconsin.*

Services:

- Board of Regents minutes
- Travel information, contracts, expense maximums
- State of Wisconsin classified civil service listings
- Purchasing contracts

6-313   **VCRIS—Virginia Coast Reserve Information System:** `atlantic.evsc.virginia.edu`

i `jporter@lternet.edu`

> *This server is operated by the Virginia Coast Reserve Long-Term Ecological Research Project (VCR/LTER).*

Services:

- Selected weather and ecological data for Virginia coast sites
- Bibliography for VCR/LTER
- Selected GIF images of the Virginia coast

6-314   **Venezuela's Gopher Server:** `figment.mit.edu` port 9999

i `hb@mit.edu` or `hbriceno@mit.edu`

> *This is the place where one can get a lot of information and news about Venezuela.*

Services:

- Venezuelan News (updated daily from many sources)
- A forum about Venezuela
- Tourist information, including some anecdotal stories in English from tourists
- A list of some events and conventions to happen in Venezuela
- A Jesuit magazine in electronic form (updated monthly)
- Important information about Venezuelan resources (telephone numbers of the consulates, airline information, etc.)
- Pointers to gopher servers in Venezuela

6-315   **Victoria University of New Zealand gopher:** `gopher.vuw.ac.nz`

i `gopher-admin@vuw.ac.nz`

> *This contains a pointer to the CWIS and the staff directory of Victoria University of Wellington.*

Services:
- X.500 directory
- Link to our library

6-316 **Vienna University Medical School Department of Cardiology:**
`gopher.kardio.akh-wien.ac.at`

i `porenta@awiimc12.bitnet` or `paolo@ai.univie.ac.at` (for technical issues)

This is the gopher of the Department of Cardiology at the Vienna University Medical School, offering data from the fields of cardiology and related research areas with emphasis on clinical issues.

Services:
- Searchable archives of abstracts of leading publications
- Review articles and position papers as published by professional societies
- Results of literature searches on specific topics with clinical relevance
- Personal summaries of major international meetings
- Drug database of cardiac medications (under construction)
- Sample images of cardiovascular imaging modalities (under construction)

6-317 **Villanova Center for Information Law and Policy:** `ming.law.vill.edu`

i `gopher@ming.law.vill.edu`

This gopher is affiliated with the Villanova Law School and the Villanova Law School graduate tax program.

Services: Mostly tax and employment law materials.
- Pointers to other law-related gophers

6-318 **Virology gopher of the University of Western Australia:** `virus.microbiol.uwa.edu.au`

i `robert@arbo.microbiol.uwa.edu.au`

This gopher, maintained by the Department of Microbiology, contains information of interest to virologists.

Services:
- Database of monoclonal antibodies against viruses
- Pointers to other biologically oriented gophers

6-319 **Vortex Technology:** `gopher.vortex.com`

i `gopher@vortex.com`

This is the gopher information service of Vortex Technology, Woodland Hills, California.

Services:
- Internet Privacy forum archive
- Television and film information
- Miscellaneous other services and information

6-320 **Wake Forest University "Deacons On-Line":** `gopher.wfu.edu`

i `gopher@wfu.edu`

This is the CWIS of Wake Forest University in Winston-Salem, North Carolina.

Services:

- Wake Forest campus directory
- Campus events
- University publications
- Data Services Newsletter archives
- Archive of American Founding documents

6-321 **Warsaw University Physics Department:** `gopher.fuw.edu.pl`

i `michalj@fuw.edu.pl`

> *This gopher is an information service of the Physics Department of Warsaw University, Warsaw, Poland.*

Services:

- Local physics department information
- Department e-mail and phone directory
- Some Poland (esp. Warsaw) travel and tourist information (including pictures and timetables)
- Pointers to other Polish gophers

6-322 **Washington and Lee University Gopher:** `liberty.uc.wlu.edu`

Services:

- Searchable database of the high-level menus
- Searchable database of the Hytelnet data (telnet logins to public Internet sites)
- A port of the Hytelnet hypertext structure to gopher format
- Comprehensive and up-to-date listing of worldwide gopher sites.

6-323 **WebNet Information Service:** `gopher.zcu.cz`

i `wimmer@zcu.cz`

> *This is the information service of the University of West Bohemia, Pilsen, Czech Republic.*

Services:

- University introduction
- Local city information
- Pointers to other information systems
- Gateway to an FTP resource containing Simtel, GNU, X11, Win3, and more

6-324 **Western Illinois University Gopher:** `gopher.wiu.bgu.edu`

> *This is a CWIS of Western Illinois University.*

Services:

- Campus undergraduate and graduate catalogs.

6-325 **WINFO (Warwick Information Service):** `gopher.csv.warwick.ac.uk`

i `gopher@warwick.ac.uk` or `d.m.anthony@warwick.ac.uk`

> *This is the CWIS of Warwick University, Coventry CV4 7AL, Great Britain.*

Services:

- Library system

- Local documents
- General documents
- Documents about information servers
- Course information (actual text of courses in many cases)
- Pointer to the Law Technology Centre

6-326 Wisconsin Primate Center Gopher: `gopher.primate.wisc.edu`

i `software@primate.wisc.edu`

Gopher of the Wisconsin Regional Primate Research Center, University of Wisconsin–Madison.

Services:

- Software developed at WRPRC
- Access point for the Primate Info-Net, an archive of information for primatological materials

6-327 World Health Organization (WHO) Gopher Server: `gopher.who.ch`

i `akazawa@who.ch`

This is the root gopher server for the World Health Organization (WHO) for provision of public health and other WHO-related information.

Services:

- WHO official press releases

6-328 ZIB (Konrad-Zuse-Zentrum fuer Informations-Technik Berlin): `ufer@zib-berlin.de`

i `malesse@zib-berlin.de` (technical) or `stech@zib-berlin.de` (contents)

This is the documentation service "DOC" of ZIB, a non-university research institute of the State of Berlin. It operates in the field of research and development on application-oriented algorithmic mathematics in close interdisciplinary cooperation with the universities and scientific institutes in Berlin, and it offers access to high-performance computers.

Services:

- Documentation service for the use of ZIB's Cray X-MP/216 and Cray Y-MP/264 and the software-packages
- Gateway to the elib (electronic library) of ZIB
- Links to the cooperating universities within the NVV (Norddeutscher Vektorrechner-Verbund: North-German supercomputer network): Technische Universitaet Berlin, Freie Universitaet Berlin, Humboldt-Universitaet, Universitaet Kiel, Universitaet Hannover

7. WIDE AREA INFORMATION SERVERS (WAIS)

WAIS is Thinking Machines Corporation's implementation of the Z39.50 information-indexing, search, and retrieval protocol. This protocol uses the client-server model to provide query services to indexes of databases, as well as retrieval of located items. (For more information on the client-server model, please see "An Internet Refresher" in the Introduction.) WAIS clients vary substantially in their interfaces, but the concept behind them is the same. First you select the resources you want to search through, and then you provide a query containing the information you want to search for. The client sends this information to the servers of the selected resources, which return any matches to the query. The client displays a list of these matches, and then you can select any of them for retrieval. A public WAIS client is available via telnet on the host `quake.think.com`. Log in using the name `wais`.

Entry Format:

Item
Number

7-n   **Resource Name:** `server address   port number` (if other than 210)
        `database name`
            Description of the resource.
        i `contact address`

Where to Find It: The entries in this chapter were compiled by editing and verifying the contents of the master WAIS source file available via FTP from `quake.think.com` in the `/wais/` directory. This chapter contains many fewer entries than the master list because all of the master list's entries could not be verified by the time this book was printed. Watch this space in the next edition for many more WAIS resources or—even better—retrieve the list yourself and browse it.

Entries:

7-1   **aarnet-resource-guide.src:** `archie.au`
    `aarnet-resource-guide`

This server holds a copy of the AARNet Resource Guide, which includes listings on archives, computer resources, directories, libraries, gateways, and network members of AARNet, the Australian Academic and Research Network.

i `wais@archie.au`

7-2   **academic_email_conf.src:** `munin.ub2.lu.se`
    `academic_email_conf`

This resource contains information on newsgroups and other electronic conferences. Included are the Directory of Scholarly Electronic Conferences (ACADLIST) collected by Diane K. Kovacs and a list of Usenet newsgroups with one line of information about each group.

i `anders@munin.ub2.lu.se`

7-3   **acronyms.src:** `wraith.cs.uow.edu.au`
    `acronyms`

A public domain database of acronyms and abbreviations.

i `steve@wraith.cs.uow.edu.au`

7-4   **agricultural-market-news.src:** `nostromo.oes.orst.edu`
    `agricultural-market-news`

Archive of the agricultural commodity market reports compiled by the Agricultural Market News Service of the United States Department of Agriculture. There are approximately 1,200 reports from all over the United States. Most of these reports are updated daily. Try searching for `portland grain`*.*

i `wais@oes.orst.edu`

7-5   **alt.sys.sun.src:** `sun-wais.oit.unc.edu`
    `alt-sys-sun`

Archived news articles from Usenet newsgroup `alt.sys.sun`

i `wais@sunsite.oit.unc.edu`

7-6   **amiga_fish_contents.src:** `nic.funet.fi`
    `amiga_fish_contents`

An index of the contents of Fred Fish's disks #1—current with a freely distributable AMIGA software library containing an extensive collection of PD, shareware, and demo programs. Search for `disknr` *to see the current (latest) disk number. Search for* `ftp` *to see some FTP sites where you can get the disks.*

i `hakan@hera.dit.lth.se`

7-7   **ANU-Aboriginal-EconPolicies.src:** `coombs.anu.edu.au`
    `ANU-Aboriginal-EconPolicies`

Abstracts of discussion papers produced at the Centre for Aboriginal Economic Policy Research (CAEPR), Faculty of Arts, The Australian National University, Canberra.

i `wais@coombs.anu.edu.au`

7-8   **ANU-Aboriginal-Studies.src:** `coombs.anu.edu.au`
    `ANU-Aboriginal-Studies`

A loose collection (100Kb) of catalog records of the Aboriginal Studies Electronic Data Archive (ASEDA) at The Australian Institute of Aboriginal and Torres Strait Islander Studies (AIATSIS), Canberra, and of an index to the 14 volumes (1977-1990) of the Aboriginal History Journal, Research School of Pacific Studies, The Australian National University, Canberra.

i wais@coombs.anu.edu.au

7-9 **ANU-Asian-Computing.src:** coombs.anu.edu.au
ANU-Asian-Computing

A loose and continuously growing collection of research information, archives, publications, software, fonts, supplier addresses, notes, solutions, and practical hints pertaining to the effective use of Asian and other non-Latin scripts and fonts in academic computing and text-processing.

i wais@coombs.anu.edu.au

7-10 **ANU-Asian-Religions.src:** coombs.anu.edu.au
ANU-Asian-Religions

A loose collection (590Kb) of bibliographic references to selected (mainly Buddhist) Asian religions, including Zen Buddhism, Taoism, Chinese Buddhism, Tibetan Buddhism, and shamanism.

i wais@coombs.anu.edu.au

7-11 **ANU-Australian-Economics.src:** coombs.anu.edu.au
ANU-Australian-Economics

A bibliographic database with details of Discussion Papers 1980–1990 and Conference Publications 1980–1991 prepared at the Centre for Economic Policy Research, Research School of Social Sciences, Australian National University, Canberra. This database also comprises information about Working Papers in Economic History prepared at the Department of Economic History, RSSS.

i wais@coombs.anu.edu.au

7-12 **ANU-CAUT-Academics.src:** coombs.anu.edu.au
ANU-CAUT-Academics

April 1993 register kept by the Committee for the Advancement of University Teaching with details of 325 Australian academics working on the teaching development projects.

i wais@coombs.anu.edu.au

7-13 **ANU-CAUT-Projects.src:** coombs.anu.edu.au
ANU-CAUT-Projects

March 1993 register of 1993 Australian national teaching development projects funded by the Committee for the Advancement of University Teaching.

i wais@coombs.anu.edu.au

7-14 **ANU-Coombspapers-Index.src:** coombs.anu.edu.au
ANU-Coombspapers-Index

The annotated index to the Coombspapers Social Sciences Research Data Bank built at the Australian National University, Canberra. This index is updated at regular intervals, roughly twice a month.

i wais@coombs.anu.edu.au

7-15 **ANU-French-Databanks.src**: coombs.anu.edu.au
ANU-French-Databanks

A catalog (140Kb) of recent French-language publications, people, commercial servers (providers), research projects, and online as well as stand-alone databases available in France that are of relevance to humanities, arts, and social-sciences research.

i wais@coombs.anu.edu.au

7-16 **ANU-Local-Waiservers.src**: coombs.anu.edu.au
ANU-Local-Waiservers

The central (and authoritative) register of sources of the WAIS servers built at the Australian National University, Canberra.

i wais@coombs.anu.edu.au

7-17 **ANU-Pacific-Archaeology.src**: coombs.anu.edu.au
ANU-Pacific-Archaeology

Selected references to Australian and Pacific archaeology and prehistory research based on the publications of the Dept. of Prehistory, Research School of Pacific Studies, Australian National University, Canberra.

i wais@coombs.anu.edu.au

7-18 **ANU-Pacific-Linguistics.src**: coombs.anu.edu.au
ANU-Pacific-Linguistics

A complete catalog (130Kb) of publications within the PACIFIC LINGUISTICS series published by the Department of Linguistics, Research School of Pacific Studies, Australian National University. Canberra.

i wais@coombs.anu.edu.au

7-19 **ANU-Pacific-Manuscripts.src**: coombs.anu.edu.au
ANU-Pacific-Manuscripts

Complete annotated catalog of the microfilm collection of the Pacific Manuscripts Bureau (PAMBU), Research School of Pacific Studies, Australian National University, Canberra.

i wais@coombs.anu.edu.au

7-20 **ANU-Pacific-Relations.src**: coombs.anu.edu.au
ANU-Pacific-Relations

Excerpts from select working papers, publication lists, and other documents dealing with Australian foreign policies, her neighbors, and the Pacific Ocean region, produced by the Department of International Relations and the Peace Research Centre at the Research School of Pacific Studies, Australian National University, Canberra.

i wais@coombs.anu.edu.au

7-21 **ANU-Philippine-Studies.src**: coombs.anu.edu.au
ANU-Philippine-Studies

Abstracts of 95 papers delivered at the 4th International Philippine Studies Conference held July 1992 on the campus of the Australian National University, Canberra.

i wais@coombs.anu.edu.au

7-22 **ANU-Radiocarbon-Abstracts.src**: coombs.anu.edu.au
ANU-Radiocarbon-Abstracts

This database is an electronic publication of a book by Dilette Polach entitled "Radiocarbon Dating Literature: The Next 12 Years, 1969–1980 Annotated Bibliography." This is the second part (5,300+ references) of a bibliography by Dilette Polach, whose first part (2,800+ references) entitled "Radiocarbon Dating Literature, the First 21 Years, 1947–1968" was published in 1988 by the Academic Press (Harcourt Brace Jovanovich, London–New York–Sydney).

i wais@coombs.anu.edu.au

7-23 **ANU-SocSci-Netlore.src:** coombs.anu.edu.au
ANU-SocSci-Netlore

A loose collection (1,030Kb strong) of documents, notes, hints, solutions, addresses, and other net-lore dealing with the information resources, e-mail and networking procedures of significance to academic researchers in the fields of the social sciences, the arts and the humanities. The database is continuosly updated with new materials being added approximately every two weeks.

i wais@coombs.anu.edu.au

7-24 **ANU-Strategic-Studies.src:** coombs.anu.edu.au
ANU-Strategic-Studies

A bibliography of publications and working papers produced by the Strategic and Defence Studies Centre, Research School of Pacific Studies, Australian National University, Canberra.

i wais@coombs.anu.edu.au

7-25 **ANU-Taoism-Listserv.src:** coombs.anu.edu.au
ANU-Taoism-Listserv

A collection of communications and exchanges submitted to the TAOISM-L mailing list.

i wais@coombs.anu.edu.au

7-26 **ANU-Thai-Yunnan.src:** coombs.anu.edu.au
ANU-Thai-Yunnan

Annotated bibliography and the late Dr. Richard Davis's research notes collection of the Thai-Yunnan Project, Department of Anthropology, Research School of Pacific Studies, Australian National University, Canberra

i wais@coombs.anu.edu.au

7-27 **ANU-Theses-Abstracts.src:** coombs.anu.edu.au
ANU-Theses-Abstracts

The ANU-Theses-Abstracts is a database of abstracts of the graduate and post-graduate theses produced at the Australian National University.

i wais@coombs.anu.edu.au

7-28 **ANU-Tropical-Archaeobotany.src:** coombs.anu.edu.au
ANU-Tropical-Archaeobotany

Selected references to tropical paleo- and archaeobotany research based on the publications of the Department of Prehistory, Research School of Pacific Studies, Australian National University, Canberra.

i wais@coombs.anu.edu.au

7-29 **ANU-ZenBuddhism-Calendar.src:** coombs.anu.edu.au
ANU-ZenBuddhism-Calendar

A database of dates, anniversaries, and festivals of Zen Buddhism. It has been prepared on the basis of materials collected by Dr. T. M. Ciolek for his planned book on the history of contemporary Zen Buddhism. This database is continuously expanded and improved on. Please e-mail any additions and/or corrections to this calendar to `tmciolek@coombs.anu.edu.au`

i `wais@coombs.anu.edu.au`

7-30 **ANU-ZenBuddhism-Listserv.src:** `coombs.anu.edu.au`
`ANU-ZenBuddhism-Listserv`

A collection of communications and exchanges submitted to the ZenBuddhism-L mailing list.

i `wais@coombs.anu.edu.au`

7-31 **archie.au-amiga-readmes.src:** `archie.au`
`archie.au-amiga-readmes`

This is an index of the Readme, Index, *and* Contents *files for the archive at* `archie.au` *in* `/micros/amiga`

i `wais@archie.au`

7-32 **archie.au-ls-lRt.src:** `archie.au`
`archie.au-ls-lRt`

This is an index of the ls-lRt *file for the archive site* `archie.au`.

i `wais@archie.au`

7-33 **archie.au-mac-readmes.src:** `archie.au`
`archie.au-mac-readmes`

This is an index of the Readme, Index, *and* Contents *files for the FTP Macintosh archive at* `archie.au` *in* `/micros/mac`

i `wais@archie.au`

7-34 **archie.au-pc-readmes.src:** `archie.au`
`archie.au-pc-readmes`

This is an index of the Readme, Index, *and* Contents *files for the FTP PC archive at* `archie.au` *in* `/micros/mac`

i `wais@archie.au`

7-35 **ASK-SISY-Software-Information.src:** `askhp.ask.uni-karlsruhe.de`
`ASK-SISY-Software-Information`

ASK-SISY is the software information system of the "Akademische Software Kooperation," which resides at the University of Karlsruhe, Germany. It operates a database containing more than 2,000 software descriptions for different fields. Most of this software has been developed at colleges and universities and is used in teaching. ASK-SISY also contains some commercial products of special interest for universities. Moreover SISY offers information about software from CIP pools and from scientific institutions and research centers.

i `boden@askhp.ask.uni-karlsruhe.de`

7-36 **astropersons.src:** `ndadsb.gsfc.nasa.gov`
`astropersons`

This database is made available by the STELAR Project, part of the Astrophysics Data Facility (ADF) at Goddard Space Flight Center in Greenbelt, Maryland. It contains a list of the names, institutional affiliations, and e-mail addresses of approximately 9,000 astronomers and was compiled by Chris Benn at LaPalma Observatory.

i stelar-info@Hypatia.gsfc.nasa.gov

7-37 **au-directory-of-servers.src:** archie.au
au-directory-of-servers

> *This is a backup copy of the directory-of-servers which is maintained by* brewster@think.com. *It is located in Australia and may provide pointers to local (Australian) copies of international databases, if available. For a list of all available sources, search for* source. *This may be limited by the maximum number of results allowed by a client.*

i wais@archie.au

7-38 **AVS_TXT_FILES.src:** doppler.ncsc.org
/usr1/avs/wais-sources/AVS_TXT_FILES

> *All of the* .txt *files for Application Visualization System (AVS) modules freely available on the International AVS Center's anonymous FTP site have been indexed, as well as informational files such as AVS_README and FAQ. The anonymous FTP site can be accessed at* avs.ncsc.org. *Please send e-mail to* avsemail@ncsc.org *for an automated reply with information about the International AVS Center and how you can make use of it.*

i avs@ncsc.org

7-39 **BGRASS-L.src:** ndadsb.gsfc.nasa.gov
BGRASS-L

> *Contains the archives of the BGRASS-L mailing list, which is dedicated to sharing an interest in bluegrass music.*

i warnock@Hypatia.gsfc.nasa.gov

7-40 **bib-appia.src:** wais.fct.unl.pt
bib-appia

> *Contains entries for bibliographic references of conferences and advanced schools sponsored by APPIA, the Portuguese association for artificial intelligence. In the near future, it will also contain references published by its members.*

i archive@fct.unl.pt

7-41 **bib-ens-lyon.src:** wais-server.ens-lyon.fr
bib-ens-lyon

> *The card catalog (including books, conference proceedings, and periodicals on computer science, mathematics, physics, and chemistry) of the library of the Ecole Normale Superieure de Lyon, France.*

i moisy@ens.ens-lyon.fr

7-42 **biologists-addresses.src:** net.bio.net
biologists-addresses

> *This is an address directory of biologists who use the BIOSCI/bionet newsgroups dedicated to research in biology/biological sciences.*

i biosci@net.bio.net

7-43 **biology-journal-contents.src:** net.bio.net
biology-journal-contents

> *This server contains periodical references to journals in the area of biology. Examples of such journals are NAR, J. Biol. Chem., Mol. Cell. Biol., J. Bact., and CABIOS. Original postings*

come for the BIOSCI / bionet newsgroup `bionet.journals.contents`. *This database is updated daily.*

i `biosci@net.bio.net`

7-44 **biosci.src:** `net.bio.net`
    `biosci`
    Contains a WAIS-indexed version of newsgroups of the bionet hierarchy (except for `bionet.molbio.genbank.updates`) *using the master set of files kept on* `net.bio.net`

i `biosci@net.bio.net`

7-45 **bit-listserv-novell.src:** `cyberdyne.ece.uiuc.edu`
    `bit-listserv-novell`
    This database contains archives of the discussions found in the `bit.listserv.novell` *newsgroup.*

i `rjoyner@ece.uiuc.edu`

7-46 **bit.listserv.cdromlan.src:** `munin.ub2.lu.se`
    `bit.listserv.cdromlan`
    An index of the files in the newsgroup `bit.listserv.cdromlan`

i `anders@munin.ub2.lu.se`

7-47 **bit.listserv.cwis-l.src:** `wais.cic.net`
    `usenet/bit.listserv.cwis-l`
    Index of the CWIS-L mailing list, a good source of information about campus-wide information systems, including gopher, PNN, WAIS, WWW, and any number of others.

i `holbrook@cic.net` (J. Paul Holbrook)

7-48 **bit.listserv.pacs-l.src:** `munin.ub2.lu.se`
    `bit.listserv.pacs-l`
    Index of the PACS-L mailing list.

i `anders@munin.ub2.lu.se`

7-49 **bitearn.nodes.src:** `wais.cic.net`
    `bitnet/bitearn.nodes`
    Bitnet nodes database.

i `holbrook@cic.net` (J. Paul Holbrook)

7-50 **bryn-mawr-clasical-review.src:** `orion.lib.Virginia.EDU`
    `/gopher-data/pub/.indexes/bmcr`
    The Bryn Mawr Classical Review archives.

i `jpw@orion.lib.Virginia.EDU`

7-51 **bush-speeches.src:** `SunSite.unc.edu`
    `bush-speeches`
    Not so much speeches as sound bites originating from the ex-president of the USA, George Herbert Walker Bush.

i `waiskeeper@sunsite.unc.edu`

7-52 **cacm.src:** `quake.think.com`
    `cacm`

Communications of the ACM, April 1988 to the present.

i `wais@quake.think.com`

7-53 **CCINFO.src:** `fragrans.riken.go.jp`
CCINFO

The World Directory of Culture Collection, maintained by The World Data Center of Microorganisms (WDC), RIKEN, Japan.

i `sugawara@viola.riken.go.jp`

7-54 **cdbase.src:** `cs.uwp.edu`
cdbase

A WAIS database of compact discs.

i `datta@cs.uwp.edu`

7-55 **cicg.bibliotheque.src:** `cicg-communication.grenet.fr`
cicg.bibliotheque

This database contains bibliographic references for the library of CICG (Centre Interuniversitaire de Calcul de Grenoble, France). It is a small database covering mainly books about computer science.

i `cherhal@cicg-communication.grenet.fr`

7-56 **cicnet-directory-of-servers.src:** `wais.cic.net`
cicnet-directory-of-servers

Directory of servers at CICnet. Mirrors the directory at `quake.think.com`, *plus adds information about CICnet servers and also the things running at* `wais.funet.fi`

i `holbrook@cic.net` (J. Paul Holbrook)

7-57 **cicnet-resource-guide.src:** `wais.cic.net`
cicnet-resource-guide

The CICNet Resource Guide, released in June 1992, is a guide to some of the resources available on the Internet, with particular emphasis on the resources available from CICNet members, which include most of the Big Ten universities in the U.S. Midwest.

i `holbrook@cic.net` (J. Paul Holbrook)

7-58 **cicnet-wais-servers.src:** `wais.cic.net`
INFO

Index of all the WAIS resources available at the CICnet network information center in Ann Arbor, Michigan. These include:

    • *tools for finding people:*

usenet–addresses	*e-mail addresses of people who post to Usenet*
college–email	*how to find e-mail addresses at universities*
uumap	*UUCP mapping project maps (*`comp.mail.maps`*)*
bitearn.nodes	*Bitnet, CREN, EARN, NETNORTH site contacts*
domain–contacts	*whois information for* `nic.ddn.mil`
disi–catalog	*Available X.500 client and server software*

    • *archives of discussions, and how to find them:*

lists	*descriptions of mailing lists and newsgroups*
bit.listserv.cwis-l	*Campus-Wide Information Systems*

fj.sources	*Japanese sources (index only)*
comp.dcom.fax	*Fax hardware, software, and protocols*

• *anonymous FTP site information:*

ftp-list	*annotated list of many FTP sites*
wuarchive	*index of* `wuarchive.wustl.edu`
uunet	*index of* `uunet.uu.net`
uxc.cso.uiuc.edu	*index of* `uxc.cso.uiuc.edu`
utsun.s.u-tokyo.ac.jp	*index of* `utsun.s.u-tokyo.ac.jp`

• *internetworking information:*

rfc-index	*index (and abstracts where available) to RFCs*
nren-bill	*High Performance Computing Act of 1991*

• *electronic texts:*

roget-thesaurus	*Roget's 1911 Thesaurus from Project Gutenberg*

Please see the Usenet newsgroup `alt.wais` *for periodic announcements and updates. A current set of CICnet .src files can always be FTP'd from* `nic.cic.net` *in* `/pub/nir-comm/wais/*.src`

i `holbrook@cic.net` (J. Paul Holbrook)

7-59 **`cirm-books.src.src`**: `cirm5.univ-mrs.fr`
`/bases/bibli-cirm/cirm-books.src`

Catalog of books and conferences proceedings on mathematics in the library of the Centre International de Rencontres Mathematiques (France).

i `jlm@cirm5.univ-mrs.fr`

7-60 **`cissites.src`**: `wais.cic.net`
`cissites`

A list of contacts for most known organizations in the former Soviet Union who either have or plan to have e-mail connections. It is available via FTP from `impaqt.drexel.edu` *in* `/pub/suearn/misc/cissites.txt`

i `holbrook@cic.net` (J. Paul Holbrook)

7-61 **`clinton-speeches.src`**: `sunsite.unc.edu`
`clinton-speeches`

Speeches given by Bill Clinton as Governor of Arkansas.

i `waiskeeper@sunsite.unc.edu`

7-62 **`CM-applications.src`**: `quake.think.com`
`CM-applications`

Connection Machine applications done at Thinking Machines and elsewhere. The author, status, and restrictions are stated along with descriptions of what the application does. Everything from fluid flow to artificial life codes are briefly described. To submit a new entry, please send a note to `ottavia@think.com`

i `wais@quake.think.com`

7-63 **`cm-zenon-inria-fr.src`**: `zenon.inria.fr`
`cm-zenon-inria-fr`

This source contains all the administrative information needed to use The Connection Machine located at INRIA Sophia Antipolis. The files are in DVI format.

i `wais-admin@zenon.inria.fr`

7-64 **cold-fusion.src:** `SunSite.unc.edu`
`cold-fusion`

This is an annotated bibliography of published materials related to Cold Fusion (the Pons and Fleischmann effect).

i `cfh@sunsite.unc.edu`

7-65 **college-email.src:** `wais.cic.net`
`college-email`

How to find e-mail addresses for undergraduate and graduate students

i `holbrook@cic.net` (J. Paul Holbrook)

7-66 **comp-acad-freedom.src:** `wais.eff.org`
`comp-acad-freedom`

Files relating to the Computers and Academic Freedom lists. Includes computer usage policies, bibliographies, archives of old discussions, and much more.

i `wais@eff.org`

7-67 **comp.dcom.fax.src:** `wais.cic.net`
`usenet/comp.dcom.fax`

Index of the `comp.dcom.fax` *newsgroup, from the archives on* `nisca.ircc.ohio-state.edu` *in* `/pub/fax/fax-archives/fax.*` *For discussion of facsimile hardware, software, and protocols.*

i `holbrook@cic.net` (J. Paul Holbrook)

7-68 **comp.doc.techreports.src:** `munin.ub2.lu.se`
`comp_techreports`

i `anders@munin.ub2.lu.se`

7-69 **comp.internet.library.src:** `munin.ub2.lu.se`
`comp.internet.library`

Index of the newsgroup `comp.internet.library` *(discussion of electronic libraries).*

i `anders@munin.ub2.lu.se`

7-70 **comp.robotics.src:** `wilma.cs.brown.edu` 8000
`comp.robotics`

This WAIS server contains all articles posted to the `comp.robotics` *newsgroup. It will be updated daily, at about 6 AM EST.*

i `mlm@cs.brown.edu`

7-71 **comp.software-eng.src:** `ftp.qucis.queensu.ca`
`software-eng`

This database is the archives of newsgroup `comp.software-eng`*. It consists of files announced periodically in the FAQ for the group.*

i `dalamb@qucis.queensu.ca`

7-72 **comp.sys.mips.src:** `rangersmith.sdsc.edu`
`comp.sys.mips`

This database is composed of the back-postings of the `comp.sys.mips` *newsgroup, updated about bi-monthly.*

i mangalam@uci.edujik@security.ov.com or hjm@salk-sgi.sdsc.edu

7-73 **comp.sys.sgi.admin.src:** rangersmith.sdsc.edu
comp.sys.sgi.admin
This database is composed of the back-postings of the comp.sys.sgi.admin *newsgroup, updated about bi-monthly.*

i mangalam@uci.edujik@security.ov.com or hjm@salk-sgi.sdsc.edu

7-74 **comp.sys.sgi.announce.src:** rangersmith.sdsc.edu
comp.sys.sgi.announce
This database is composed of the back-postings of the comp.sys.sgi.announce *newsgroup, updated about bi-monthly.*

i mangalam@uci.edu or hjm@salk-sgi.sdsc.edu

7-75 **comp.sys.sgi.apps.src:** rangersmith.sdsc.edu
comp.sys.sgi.apps
This database is composed of the back-postings of the comp.sys.sgi.apps *newsgroup, updated about bi-monthly.*

i mangalam@uci.edu or hjm@salk-sgi.sdsc.edu

7-76 **comp.sys.sgi.bugs.src:** rangersmith.sdsc.edu
comp.sys.sgi.bugs
This database is composed of the back-postings of the comp.sys.sgi.bugs *newsgroup, updated about bi-monthly.*

i mangalam@uci.edu or hjm@salk-sgi.sdsc.edu

7-77 **comp.sys.sgi.graphics.src:** rangersmith.sdsc.edu
comp.sys.sgi.graphics
This database is composed of the back-postings of the comp.sys.sgi.graphics *newsgroup, updated about bi-monthly.*

i mangalam@uci.edujik@security.ov.com or hjm@salk-sgi.sdsc.edu

7-78 **comp.sys.sgi.hardware.src:** rangersmith.sdsc.edu
comp.sys.sgi.hardware
This database is composed of the back-postings of the comp.sys.sgi.hardware *newsgroup, updated about bi-monthly.*

i mangalam@uci.edujik@security.ov.com or hjm@salk-sgi.sdsc.edu

7-79 **comp.sys.sgi.misc.src:** rangersmith.sdsc.edu
comp.sys.sgi.misc
This database is composed of the back-postings of the comp.sys.sgi.misc *newsgroup, updated about bi-monthly.*

i mangalam@uci.edujik@security.ov.com or hjm@salk-sgi.sdsc.edu

7-80 **comp.sys.sgi.src:** rangersmith.sdsc.edu
comp.sys.sgi
This database is composed of the back-postings of the comp.sys.sgi *newsgroup, updated about bi-monthly.*

i mangalam@uci.edujik@security.ov.com or hjm@salk-sgi.sdsc.edu

7-81 **comp.text.sgml.src:** `ifi.uio.no`
`comp.text.sgml`

> *Archive of the* `comp.text.sgml` *newsgroup. SGML is an abbreviation for the Standard Generalized Markup Language. SGML is defined in an International Standard published by the International Organization for Standardization (ISO), with reference number ISO 8879:1986, bearing the full name "Information processing—Text and office systems— Standard Generalized Markup Language (SGML)."*

i `anders@ifi.uio.no`

7-82 **comp.windows.x.motif.src:** `services.canberra.edu.au`
`comp.windows.x.motif`

> *This is an archive of the Usenet newsgroup* `comp.windows.x.motif`

i `jan@pandonia.canberra.edu.au`

7-83 **computers-freedom-and-privacy.src:** `quake.think.com`
`/proj/wais/db/sources/computers-freedom-and-privacy`

> *This database contains the ASCII text of the proceedings from the Conference on Computers, Freedom, and Privacy II.*

i `wais@quake.think.com`

7-84 **cool-cdr.src:** `aldus.stanford.edu`
`cool-cdr`

> *Contains a directory of people professionally involved with the conservation and preservation of library, archives, and museum materials (conservators, preservation administrators, conservation scientists, archivists, curators, bibliographers, librarians, etc.).*

i `waiscool@aldus.stanford.edu`

7-85 **cool-cfl.src:** `aldus.stanford.edu`
`cool-cfl`

> *Contains files concerning the conservation of library, archive, and museum materials. Topics include: CD-ROMs (compact disks, optical disks); Civil War materials at NARA; copyright and fair use; cradles; digital imaging; scanning and digitization of electronic media; flood and disaster preparedness; historical costume; image standards and implications for preservation; insects, mold, and fumigation; job descriptions for preservation positions; library binding; library preservation; microfilming and reformatting; oils; permanent papers; preservation and condition surveys, random sampling; reprographics; Requests For Proposals (RFPs) for preservation services; standards; textiles; and videotape.*

i `waiscool@aldus.stanford.edu`

7-86 **cool-directory-of-servers.src:** `aldus.stanford.edu`
`cool-directory-of-servers`

> *A top-level directory of the WAIS sources of Conservation OnLine (CoOL), a project of the Preservation Department of Stanford University Libraries. These sources contain information of interest to people involved with the conservation of library, archive, and museum materials. To determine which CoOL database will best meet your needs, query* `cool-directory-of-servers`*. To see a list of all the CoOL databases, use the word* `source` *as your search term. New databases will be added to CoOL, so it will be a good idea to search* `cool-directory-of-servers` *regularly. The existing databases are* `cool` *(archives of the Conservation DistList);* `cool-cdr` *(conservation directory)* `cool-cfl` *(files about conser-*

vation issues); `cool-ref` *(bibliographic citations);* `cool-bib` *(complete bibliographies);* `cool-lex` *(lexical and classification material pertaining to conservation);* `cool-net` *(files about networking, mailing list, etc.); and* `cool-waac` *(The Western Association for Art Conservation Newsletter).*

i `waiscool@aldus.stanford.edu`

7-87 **cool-lex.src:** `aldus.stanford.edu`
`cool-lex`

Contains lexical and classification material pertaining to conservation and preservation, including thesauri (or microthesauri), glossaries, classification schemes, authority lists (descriptors, subject headings), etc. These items are segregated from other CoOL databases in order to avoid false hits in the other databases.

i `waiscool@aldus.stanford.edu`

7-88 **cool-net.src:** `aldus.stanford.edu`
`cool-net`

Information on networks, networking, mailing lists, computers, etc. from the Conservation OnLine (cool) project of the Preservation Department of Stanford University Libraries.

i `waiscool@aldus.stanford.edu` (Walter Henry)

7-89 **cool-ref.src:** `aldus.stanford.edu`
`cool-ref`

Contains complete bibliographies on topics pertaining the conservation of library, archives, and museum materials.

i `waiscool@aldus.stanford.edu` (Walter Henry)

7-90 **cool-waac.src:** `aldus.stanford.edu`
`cool-waac`

Contains articles from the WAAC Newsletter (ISSN 1052-0066), a publication of the Western Association for Art Conservation, a nonprofit organization founded in 1974. Published since 1979, WAAC Newsletter publishes ideas, information, news, and other material pertaining to the conservation of cultural property, especially matters of interest to conservators in the western United States.

i `waiscool@aldus.stanford.edu`

7-91 **cool.src:** `aldus.stanford.edu`
`cool`

Contains the archives of the Conservation DistList. Searches will return individual messages (i.e., undigestified DistList postings). The DistList, a moderated digest, is an electronic forum for discussion of technical and administrative issues of concern to people conservation professionals.

i `waiscool@aldus.stanford.edu`

7-92 **cpsr.src:** `wais.cpsr.org`
`cpsr`

This database was created from the Computer Professionals for Social Responsibility Internet Library.

i `listserv-owner@cpsr.org` or `banisar@washofc.cpsr.org` or `phyland@gwuvm.gwu.edu`

7-93 **cs-journal-titles.src:** daneel.rdt.monash.edu.au
cs-journal-titles

This database contains a list of journal article titles and authors from approximately 600 computing journals, conference proceedings, books, and seminars.

i rik.harris@fcit.monash.edu.au

7-94 **cs-techreport-abstracts.src:** daneel.rdt.monash.edu.au
cs-techreport-abstracts

This is a database of titles and authors of approximately 10,000 techreports, preprints, reprints, technical notes, and papers from universities and research institutes from around the world. Now contains over 2,300 abstracts from technical reports. This data is available by anonymous FTP [login = anonymous password = e-mail-address] from daneel.rdt.monash.edu.au *in* pub/techreports. *Any queries, questions, etc. to* rik.harris@fcit.monash.edu.au, *or* wais@rdt.monash.edu.au

i rik.harris@fcit.monash.edu.au

7-95 **cs-techreport-archives.src:** daneel.rdt.monash.edu.au
cs-techreport-archives

This is a list of about 210 archive sites that maintain computer science (and similar) technical reports for public access: usually for FTP, or by e-mail server. On some sites there is a small description of the research area covered. This list is posted in comp.doc.techreports *and* news.answers *on a regular basis.*

i rik.harris@fcit.monash.edu.au

7-96 **cscwbib.src:** wais.cpsc.ucalgary.ca
cscwbib

This is a comprehensive bibliography of Computer Supported Cooperative Work in reference format. It contains many of the relevant papers from proceedings such as CSCW, ECSCW, CHI; from HCI and related journals; from CSCW-related books; and from technical reports.

i hernadi@cpsc.ucalgary.ca

7-97 **current.cites.src:** wais.cic.net
current.cites

Database of the Current Cities Journal.

i holbrook@cic.net (J. Paul Holbrook)

7-98 **cwis_list.src:** munin.ub2.lu.se
cwis_list

Judy Hallman's list of Campus-Wide Information Systems (CWIS).

i anders@munin.ub2.lu.se

7-99 **ddbs-info.src:** ds.internic.net
ddbs-info

Information about InterNIC services.

i admin@ds.internic.net

7-100 **directory-of-servers.src:** quake.think.com
directory-of-servers

This is a White Pages listing of WAIS servers. To server makers: Please make new servers of

text, pictures, music, whatever. We will try to list all servers in the directory that get sent in to:
`directory-of-servers@quake.think.com`

i `wais-directory-of-servers@quake.think.com`

7-101 **directory-zenon-inria-fr.src:** `zenon.inria.fr`
`/1/wais/index/directory-zenon-inria-fr`

> *This source is a directory for the WAIS sources located at INRIA (Institut de Recherche en Informatique et Automatique, France) and in some research labs located in France.*

i `wais-admin@zenon.inria.fr`

7-102 **disco-mm-zenon-inria-fr.src:** `zenon.inria.fr`
`disco-mm-zenon-inria-fr`

> *Multimedia database of various compact disks. Each CD has a description (in ASCII format), an image of the cover (in GIF format), and an audio sample about 20 seconds long.*

i `djossou@charly.inria.fr`

7-103 **disi-catalog or x.500.working-group.src:** `wais.cic.net`
`disi-catalog`

> *Information about availability and capability of X.500 implementations. Note: the RFC for this has come out, so this index is out of date.*

i `holbrook@cic.net` (J. Paul Holbrook)

7-104 **dit-library.src:** `munin.ub2.lu.se`
`dit-library`

> *Library catalog for Department of Computer Engineering, University of Lund, Lund, Sweden.*

i `anders@munin.ub2.lu.se`

7-105 **domain-contacts.src:** `wais.cic.net`
`netinfo/domain-contacts`

> *Index of the file on* `nic.ddn.mil` *in* `/netinfo/domain-contacts.txt`*, which contains Internet domains and the listed phone numbers to contact the responsible parties.*

i `holbrook@cic.net` (J. Paul Holbrook)

7-106 **domain-organizations.src:** `wais.cic.net`
`domain-organizations`

> *A WAIS index of the July 15, 1992, seed database for Netfind. It matches domain names and the acronyms they are based on with the full names of the organizations they belong to.*

i `holbrook@cic.net` (J. Paul Holbrook)

7-107 **dynamic-archie.src:** `ftp.cs.colorado.edu   8000`
`DYNAMIC archie`

> *This WAIS server performs Archie searches. It uses the WAIS server from the Dynamic WAIS prototype at the University of Colorado in Boulder. To use this WAIS server, supply a keyword for an Archie search. A list of Archie servers will be returned as relevant documents. Choose one of the Archie servers to retrieve the results from an Archie query. Typically, Archie queries take more than 5 minutes due to the load on the Archie servers. Dynamic WAIS uses the Archie-Prospero client to query Archie servers.*

i `hardy@cs.colorado.edu`

7-108 **edis.src:** `kumr.lns.com`
      `edis`

        EDIS, the State of California's "Emergency Digital Information System," is a developing protocol and transport service for the broadcast of emergency public information from authorized official agencies to the news media. Current EDIS communications are test messages to show continuity in fire and earthquake information.

      i `pozar@kumr.lns.com`

7-109 **eff-documents.src:** `wais.eff.org`
      `eff-documents`

        WAIS archive of EFF documents and newsletters. Should generally mirror the EFF FTP archives on `ftp.eff.org`*. Contact* `wais@eff.org` *if you have problems. Should be available 24 hours a day, 7 days a week.*

      i `wais@eff.org`

7-110 **eff-talk.src:** `wais.eff.org`
      `eff-talk`

        WAIS-accessible archive of the `comp.org.eff.talk` *newsgroup.*

      i `wais@eff.org`

7-111 **EIA-Petroleum-Supply-Monthly.src:** `quake.think.com`
      `/proj/wais/db/EIA-petroleum-supply-monthly/EIA-psm`

        This source contains Postscript versions of the tables and figures from the Department of Energy, Energy Information Agency's "Petroleum Supply Monthly."

      i `wais@quake.think.com`

7-112 **elec_journ_newslett.src:** `munin.ub2.lu.se`
      `elec_journ_newslett`

        Information about electronic journals and newsletters. The main source is Michael Strangelove's Directory of Electronic Journals and Newsletters.

      i `anders@munin.ub2.lu.se`

7-113 **environment-newsgroups.src:** `munin.ub2.lu.se`
      `environment-newsgroups`

        This source contains a number of enivironment-related newsgroups, mainly bionet groups. Topics include software, agroforestry, neuroscience, journals, evolution, the environment, genetics, and population biology.

      i `anders@munin.ub2.lu.se`

7-114 **ERIC-archive.src:** `nic.sura.net`
      `/export/software/nic/wais/databases/ERIC-archive`

        ERIC (Educational Resources Information Center) Digests: short reports (1,000–1,500 words or one or two pages) on topics of prime current interest in education targeted specifically at teachers and administrators.

      i `info@sura.net`

7-115 **eric-digests.src:** `sunSITE.unc.edu`
      `eric-digests`

        ERIC (Educational Resources Information Center) Digests: 1 to 2-page reports on education, targeted specifically for teachers and administrators but generally useful to the broad educational community. These provide an overview of information, plus references to more detailed information, and are reviewed by specialists in the field. Funded by the Office of Educational Research and Improvement (OERI) of the U.S. Department of Education (ED).

i paul_jones@unc.edu

7-116 **eshic.src:** romana.crystal.pnl.gov
eshic

ESHIC is an acronym for Environmental Safety and Health Information Center. The ESHIC is a central repository for the Department of Energy (DOE) Tiger Team Assessment documents, Corrective Action Plans, Progress Assessments; DOE site-specific information such as maps, site fact sheets, and site profiles; and other relevant DOE documents concerning compliance, regulations, policy, training, and long-term planning. The information in ESHIC is also available through WWW.

i eshic@romana.dc.pnl.gov

7-117 **falcon3.src:** urbino.mcc.com 8000
falcon3

A collection of most of the mail and news traffic about Falcon 3 since February 1992.

i knutson@urbino.mcc.com

7-118 **Fascism.src:** sunsite.unc.edu
/home3/wais/Fascism

An index of files on fascism.

i ses@tipper.oit.unc.edu

7-119 **fidonet-nodelist.src:** kumr.lns.com
nodelist

Database of all the systems within FidoNet.

i pozar@kumr.lns.com

7-120 **file-archive-uunet.src:** wais.cic.net
uunet

The directory listing of uunet.uu.net (updated nightly).

i holbrook@cic.net (J. Paul Holbrook)

7-121 **finding-sources.src:** wais.cic.net
faq/finding-sources

Jonathan Kamens document on how to find sources on the net. Includes information about prospero, Archie, comp.archives, the charlie server, and mail-based archive servers.

i holbrook@cic.net (J. Paul Holbrook)

7-122 **fj.sources.src:** wais.cic.net
usenet/fj.sources

Index to the Japanese source group fj.sources (the actual files can be found at utsun.s.u-tokyo.ac.jp in /fj/fj.sources/* and other archive sites; see Archie for likely locations).

i holbrook@cic.net (J. Paul Holbrook)

7-123   **flight_sim.src:** urbino.mcc.com   8000
         flight_sim

> *A collection of postings on various flight simulators.*

i knutson@urbino.mcc.com

7-124   **ftp-list.src:** wais.cic.net
         ftp-list

> *This source has Jon Granrose's anonymous FTP list, available on* pilot.njin.net *in* /pub/ftp-list/

i holbrook@cic.net (J. Paul Holbrook)

7-125   **Func-Prog-Abstracts.src:** coral.cs.jcu.edu.au   8000
         Func-Prog-Abstracts

> *This is a small collection of computer-science technical reports, abstracts, and papers gathered from FTP sites, etc., all over the world. Due to space considerations, it is limited to functional programming, the maintainer's area of interest, and papers produced by the department (which may or may not be related to functional programming).*

7-126   **fusion-digest.src:** sunsite.unc.edu
         fusion-digest

> *This is an indexed version of the* sci.physics.fusion *mail digests. These digests cover the period from April 1989 to the present.*

i cfh@sunsite.unc.edu

7-127   **fyis.src:** ds.internic.net
         fyis

> *RFCs that are informational in nature.*

i admin@ds.internic.net

7-128   **gdb-citation.src:** wais.gdb.org
         gdb-citation

> *Citation manager information from the Genome Data Base (GDB).*

i help@gdb.org

7-129   **gdb-contact.src:** wais.gdb.org
         gdb-contact

> *Contact manager information from the Genome Data Base (GDB).*

i help@gdb.org

7-130   **gdb-locus.src:** wais.gdb.org
         gdb-locus

> *Locus manager information from the Genome Data Base (GDB).*

i help@gdb.org

7-131   **gdb-map.src:** wais.gdb.org
         gdb-map

> *Map manager information from the Genome Data Base (GDB).*

i help@gdb.org

7-132   **gdb-mutation.src:** wais.gdb.org
         gdb-mutation

Mutation manager information from the Genome Data Base (GDB).

i help@gdb.org

7-133 **gdb-polym.src:** wais.gdb.org
gdb-polym
Polymorphism manager information from the Genome Data Base (GDB).

i help@gdb.org

7-134 **gdb-probe.src:** wais.gdb.org
gdb-probe
Probe manager information from the Genome Data Base (GDB).

i help@gdb.org

7-135 **gdb.src:** wais.gdb.org
gdb
WAIS index to the Genome Data Base (GDB).

i help@gdb.org

7-136 **genpept.src:** nusunix2.nus.sg
genpept
This is the WAIS-indexed version of the GenPept database, a database of protein sequences translated from genes deposited with GenBank.

i bchtantw@nuscc.nus.sg

7-137 **great-lakes-factsheets.src:** wais.cic.net
great-lakes-factsheets
Fact sheets on a variety of issues and subjects relevant to the Great Lakes/St. Lawrence River region and ecosystem maintained by The Center for the Great Lakes.

i holbrook@cic.net (J. Paul Holbrook)

7-138 **HDB.src:** fragrans.riken.go.jp
HDB
HYBRIDOMA DATABANK (HDB) contains a catalog of hybridoma cell lines/monoclonal antibodies available throughout the world. It has been developed by Amerian Type Culture Collection in USA and WDC (World Data Center), RIKEN (The Institute of Physical and Chemical Research) in Japan. The current HDB contains around 26,000 records. For details on how to use the database, please consult the WDC BioGopher at fragrans.riken.go.jp *or e-mail Dr. H. Sugawara at* sugawara@viola.riken.go.jp

i sugawara@viola.riken.go.jp

7-139 **higher-education-software.src:** info.curtin.edu.au
higher-education-software
The Software and Courseware On-line Reviews (SCOR) database provides information on software suitable for use in educational institutions of all levels.

i scor@info.curtin.edu.au

7-140 **hst-aec-catalog.src:** stsci.edu
hst-aec-catalog
The Archived Exposures Catalog (AEC) is an archive of viewing events (exposures) of the Hubble Space Telescope. Information includes target name, position, scientific instrument con-

figuration and mode, spectral elements, exposure time, date of observation, program ID number, DMF root name, and proprietary release date for the data.

i reppert@stsci.edu

7-141 **hst-status.src:** stsci.edu
/var/spool/uucppublic/.waisindex/hst-status

Daily Activity / Instrument Status Reports for Hubble Space Telescope (HST). The following acronyms may appear in the files: AST: Astrometry Team. DF224: Onboard computer on HST. ERO: Early Release Observations. ESA: European Space Agency. FGS: Fine Guidance Sensors. FHST: Fixed-Head Star Tracker. FOC: Faint Object Camera. FOS: Faint Object Spectrograph. GHRS: Goddard High Resolution Spectrograph. GS: Guide Star(s). GSC: Guide Star Catalog. GSFC: Goddard Space Flight Center. H&S: Health and Safety. HGA: High-Gain Antenna. HSP: High Speed Photometer. HST: Hubble Space Telescope. HV: High Voltage. LV: Low Voltage. MOC: Mission Operations Control. MSFC: Marshall Space Flight Center. NSSC-1: NASA Standard Spacecraft Computer. OSS: Observation Support System. OTA: Optical Telescope Assembly. OV: Orbital Verification. PASS: POCC Application Software Support. PC: Planetary Camera. PCS: Pointing Control System. PMT: Photomultiplier Tube. POCC: Payload Operations Control Center. PODPS: Post-Observation Data Processing System. RGA: Rate Gyro Assembly. SAA: South Atlantic Anomaly. SAO: Science Assessment Observations. SI: Scientific Instrument. SMS: Science Mission Specifications. SPA: Solar Panel Assembly. SPSS: Science Planning and Scheduling System. STOAT: Space Telescope Operations Advisory Team. STR: Science Tape Recorder. SSC: Science Support Center. STOCC: Space Telescope Operations Control Center. STScI: Space Telescope Science Institute. TDRSS: Tracking and Data-Relay Satellite System. UT: Universal Time. WF/PC: Wide Field/Planetary Camera.

i reppert@stsci.edu

7-142 **hst-weekly-summary.src:** stsci.edu
/var/spool/uucppublic/.waisindex/hst-weekly-summary

Weekly Summary of Hubble Space Telescope (HST) completed observations.

i reppert@stsci.edu

7-143 **hst-weekly-timeline.src:** stsci.edu
/var/spool/uucppublic/.waisindex/hst-weekly-timeline

Weekly Timeline files for current year's Hubble Space Telescope (HST) observations.

i reppert@stsci.edu

7-144 **hyperbole-ml.src:** wilma.cs.brown.edu 8000
hyperbole

This WAIS server contains all messages sent to the Hyperbole mailing list. Hyperbole is a flexible information manager built on top of GNU Emacs. It is available for anonymous FTP at wilma.cs.brown.edu *in* /pub/hyperbole. *See the README file there for details.*

i mlm@cs.brown.edu

7-145 **IAT-Documents.src:** sunsite.unc.edu
/home3/wais/IAT-Documents

Contains articles from the UNC-CH Institute for Academic Technology newsletter ("Briefings"), copies of papers from the IAT Technology Primers and Technical Papers series, and source lists and bibliographies from the Information Resource Guides series. These files are also available via anonymous FTP from sunsite.unc.edu

i kotlas@sunsite.unc.edu

7-146 **iesg.src:** ds.internic.net

iesg

IESG information, working group charters, and meeting minutes.

i admin@ds.internic.net

7-147 **ietf.src:** ds.internic.net

ietf

IETF information, meeting announcements, working group charters, and minutes.

i admin@ds.internic.net

7-148 **indian-classical-music.src:** enuxva.eas.asu.edu 8000

music

Database of CDs of Indian classical music. You can search using keywords containing Ragas or musician's name or anything that is present as a word in the database. Try Ali *or* Khan *or* Ravi *or* Shankar *or* Krishnan *as a first search to see what format the database is in.*

i sridhar@enuxha.eas.asu.edu

7-149 **inet-libraries.src:** munin.ub2.lu.se

inet-libraries

Information on Internet-accessible libraries collected from various places: UNT's Accessing On-Line Bibliographic Databases, JANET-OPACs, Internet Libraries compiled by Dana Noonan, and a few smaller lists are also included.

i anders@munin.ub2.lu.se

7-150 **info-afs.src:** cmsun.cmf.nrl.navy.mil

info-afs

Index of archives of the mailing list info-afs.

i wais-maint@cmf.nrl.navy.mil

7-151 **INFO.src:** quake.think.com

INFO

This source is exactly the same as the directory-of-servers source.

i wais-directory-of-servers@quake.think.com

7-152 **internet-mail.src:** sunsite.unc.edu

internet-mail

Scott Yanoffs inter-network mail guide, which provides information on how to address e-mail to networks gatewayed on to the Internet.

i jem@sunsite.unc.edu

7-153 **internet-rfcs-europe.src:** wais.cnam.fr

RFC

Request For Comments (RFC) of the Internet community. Updated automatically from nic.ddn.mil

i bortzmeyer@cnam.cnam.fr

7-154 **internet-standards.src:** ds.internic.net

stds

The subset of all the RFCs that have been declared standards by the IETF.

i `admin@ds.internic.net`

7-155 **internet_info.src:** `munin.ub2.lu.se`
`internet_info`

Various introduction texts, guides, help texts, and general information on Internet use and etiquette.

i `anders@munin.ub2.lu.se`

7-156 **internet_services.src:** `munin.ub2.lu.se`
`internet_services`

Various documents describing services available on the Internet, including Internet Databases by Billy Barron; Internet mailservers; The Internet Resources Guide, compiled by the NSF Network Service Center; and Not Just Cows—A Guide to Internet/Bitnet Resources in Agriculture and Related Sciences, written and compiled by Wilfred Drew.

i `anders@munin.ub2.lu.se`

7-157 **internic-internet-drafts.src:** `ds.internic.net`
`internet-drafts`

IETF Internet Draft Documents—these documents describe work in progress in IETF Working Groups.

i `admin@ds.internic.net`

7-158 **internic-whois.src:** `rs.internic.net`
`whois`

WAIS index to the whois database on `rs.internic.net`. *Whois is comprised of root level domains, networks, DNS servers, autonomous system numbers, organizations, and POCs of the domains, networks, servers, and autonomous system numbers. This information is updated daily from the whois database maintained at* `rs.internic.net` *by InterNIC Registration Services. InterNIC Registration services is run by Network Solutions, Inc. of Herndon, Virginia.*

i `markk@internic.net`

7-159 **InvertPaleoDatabase.src:** `ucmp1.berkeley.edu`
`/home/ucmp1/gopher-data/mustypes/invert/.waisindex/paleoiv`

This database provides information about all the invertebrate type specimens available in the Museum of Paleontology at the University of California at Berkeley. Provides three subsets of information: taxonomic, locality, and citation. Taxonomic information includes genus, species, subspecies, original author, and type number. Locality information includes continent/ocean, country, state, county, system/period, and epoch, as well as museum locality number. The citation information includes first author, second author, date, and citation. The database contains over 11,000 entries. The full database and index are also available via gopher at `ucmp1.berkeley.edu`

i `davidp@ucmp1.berkeley.edu`

7-160 **irtf-rd.src:** `wais.cic.net`
`irtf-rd`

An archive of the IRTF Resource Discovery mailing list.

i `holbrook@cic.net` (J. Paul Holbrook)

7-161 **isoc.src:** `ds.internic.net`
    `isoc`

Internet Society documents.

i `admin@ds.internic.net`

7-162 **Jainist-texts.src:** `sunsite.unc.edu`
    `/home3/wais/Jainist-texts`

A collection concerning the beliefs and practices of Jainism, a religion originating in India. These files are also available via anonymous FTP from `SunSITE.unc.edu`

i `Paul_Jones@unc.edu`

7-163 **JFCC-Bacteria.src:** `fragrans.riken.go.jp`
    `/data/waisguy/src/JFCC-Bacteria`

The Japan Federation for Culture Collections (JFCC) Catalog of Cultures for bacteria.

i `sugawara@viola.riken.go.jp`

7-164 **JFCC-Bacteriophages.src:** `fragrans.riken.go.jp`
    `/data/waisguy/src/JFCC-Bacteriophages`

The Japan Federation for Culture Collections (JFCC) Catalog of Cultures for bacteriophages.

i `sugawara@viola.riken.go.jp`

7-165 **JFCC-Fungi.src:** `fragrans.riken.go.jp`
    `/data/waisguy/src/JFCC-Fungi`

The Japan Federation for Culture Collections (JFCC) Catalog of Cultures for fungi.

i `sugawara@viola.riken.go.jp`

7-166 **JFCC-Invertebrate_virus.src:** `fragrans.riken.go.jp`
    `/data/waisguy/src/JFCC-Invertebrate_virus`

The Japan Federation for Culture Collections (JFCC) Catalog of Cultures for viruses of invertebrates.

i `sugawara@viola.riken.go.jp`

7-167 **JFCC-Microalgae.src:** `fragrans.riken.go.jp`
    `/data/waisguy/src/JFCC-Microalgae`

The Japan Federation for Culture Collections (JFCC) Catalog of Cultures for microalgae.

i `sugawara@viola.riken.go.jp`

7-168 **JFCC-Plant_virus.src:** `fragrans.riken.go.jp`
    `/data/waisguy/src/JFCC-Plant_virus`

The Japan Federation for Culture Collections (JFCC) Catalog of Cultures for plant viruses.

i `sugawara@viola.riken.go.jp`

7-169 **JFCC-Proto.src:** `fragrans.riken.go.jp`
    `/data/waisguy/src/JFCC-Proto`

The Japan Federation for Culture Collections (JFCC) Catalog of Cultures for protozoa.

i `sugawara@viola.riken.go.jp`

7-170 **JFCC-Vertebrate_virus.src:** `fragrans.riken.go.jp`
    `/data/waisguy/src/JFCC-Vertebrate_virus`

The Japan Federation for Culture Collections (JFCC) Catalog of Cultures for viruses of verte-

brates.

i sugawara@viola.riken.go.jp

7-171 **journalism.periodicals.src:** gopher.uwo.ca 3041
journalism.periodicals

Archive of the Index to Journalism Periodicals, which contains almost 20,000 citations to articles from about forty trade, professional, and academic journals related to journalism and mass communication. The index is maintained by the Graduate School of Journalism at the University of Western Ontario.

i peter@julian.uwo.ca

7-172 **JTCA_cat.src:** fragrans.riken.go.jp
/data/waisguy/src/JTCA_cat

JTCA Cell Line Database is compiled by the Cell Bank Committee of Japan Tissue Culture Association. It contains a catalog of cell lines. See also related bibliographic references in
JTCA_ref.src

i sugawara@viola.riken.go.jp

7-173 **JTCA_ref.src:** fragrans.riken.go.jp
/data/waisguy/src/JTCA_ref

JTCA Cell Line Database is compiled by the Cell Bank Committee of Japan Tissue Culture Association. It contains a list of bibliographic references pertaining to the catalog of cell lines (see
JTCA_ref.src).

i sugawara@viola.riken.go.jp

7-174 **k-12-software.src:** info.curtin.edu.au
k-12-software

The Software and Courseware On-line Reviews (SCOR) database provides information on software suitable for use in all levels of educational institutions.

i scor@info.curtin.edu.au

7-175 **kidsnet.src:** wais.cic.net
kidsnet

Archive of the kidsnet mailing lists.

i holbrook@cic.net (J. Paul Holbrook)

7-176 **lawrence-obrien-interview.src:** sunsite.unc.edu
lawrence-obrien-interview

Interviews with former Democratic Party head Lawrence O'Brien concerning his life in politics with special interest in his work with the Johnson and Kennedy administrations.

i jem@sunsite.unc.edu

7-177 **linux-addresses.src:** sunsite.unc.edu
linux-addresses

Address of many people associated with the Linux (free Unix) project.

i jem@sunsite.unc.edu

7-178 **linux-faq.src:** sunSITE.unc.edu
linux-faq

This is the Frequently Asked Questions (FAQ) list for the Linux operating system and comp.os.linux newsgroup. Linux is a Unix-like operating system for the 386, 486, and 586 available under the terms of the GNU public license.

i ewt@sunSITE.unc.edu

7-179 **linux-gcc-faq.src:** sunSITE.unc.edu

linux-gcc-faq

This is the Linux FAQ for the Gnu C compiler; it contains answers to frequently asked questions about using GCC under the Linux operating system.

i ewt@sunSITE.unc.edu

7-180 **linux-mail-faq.src:** sunSITE.unc.edu

linux-mail-faq

These are answers to Frequently Asked Questions about setting up Usenet news and e-mail under the Linux operating system, using UUCP and SMTP.

i ewt@sunSITE.unc.edu

7-181 **linux-net-faq.src:** sunSITE.unc.edu

linux-net-faq

This is information on how to set up a computer running Linux operating system on a TCP/IP network.

i ewt@sunSITE.unc.edu

7-182 **linux-software-map.src:** sunSITE.unc.edu

linux-software-map

The LSM (Linux Software Map) project is an attempt to document all software and other materials for the Linux operating system using a format based upon that proposed by the IAFA working group of the IETF. The LSM contains the following information about each documented package: name, title, version, description, author, maintained by, maintained at, platforms, copying policy, keywords, approximate size, last 3 releases, comments, and last checked.

i ewt@sunSITE.unc.edu

7-183 **livestock.src:** hermes.ecn.purdue.edu 6001

/home/hermes/cems/livestock/wais-sources/livestock

Educational materials for livestock production and management. Text of many documents from the popular "Pork Industry Handbook" are included.

i cems@ecn.purdue.edu

7-184 **lolita-dator.src:** munin.ub2.lu.se

lolita-dator

From the Lund University library catalog, a selection of computer-related literature. Some texts are in Swedish.

i anders@munin.ub2.lu.se

7-185 **lolita-miljo.src:** munin.ub2.lu.se

lolita-miljo

From the Lund University library catalog, a selection of environmental-related literature. Some texts are in Swedish.

i anders@munin.ub2.lu.se

7-186 **london-free-press-regional-index.src:** `gopher.uwo.ca` 3041
`london-free-press-regional-index`

This is an index of local and regional stories in the London Free Press (London, Canada), including birth notices and obituaries, editorials, and letters to the editor on regional issues. The sports section is not indexed (although a few sports stories are included). The index is maintained by the Graduate School of Journalism at the University of Western Ontario.

i `peter@julian.uwo.ca`

7-187 **lp-bibtex-zenon-inria-fr.src:** `zenon.inria.fr`
`lp-bibtex-zenon-inria-fr`

This source, due to the courtesy of `rscheidhauer@dfki.uni-sb.de`*, contains references to most of the proceedings of the last ICLP (International Conference on Logic Programming), SLP (Symposium on Logic Programming), and NACLP (North American Conference on Logic Programming).*

i `wais-admin@zenon.inria.fr`

7-188 **lp-proceedings.src:** `wais.fct.unl.pt`
`lp-proceedings`

This resource indexes the BibTeX references of Logic Programming Conferences collected by `scheidhr@dfki.uni-sb.de` *(Ralf Scheidhauer).*

i `archive@fct.unl.pt`

7-189 **lyrics.src:** `cs.uwp.edu`
`lyrics`

The lyrics archives consist of complete lyrics to over 5,000 songs by over 1,100 artists. All lyrics are gracefully donated by Usenet readers and archive users. Search for the word `index` *to get the index file.*

i `datta@cs.uwp.edu`

7-190 **MacPsych.src:** `gopher.stolaf.edu` 8001
`MacPsych`

Software archive for the discussion list MacPsych. Also the software archive for Macintosh-related articles published in the journal "Behavior Research Methods, Instruments, and Computers."

i `macpsych-request@stolaf.edu`

7-191 **mailing-lists.src:** `wais.cic.net`
`lists`

This source has several long lists of Usenet newsgroups, Internet and Bitnet mailing lists, and electronic serials and journals. There is a fair amount of overlap between the various components used to build this list.

i `holbrook@cic.net` (J. Paul Holbrook)

7-192 **matrix_news.src:** `ftp.tic.com`
`matrix_news`

This directory contains articles, columns, and other information from Matrix News, the monthly newsletter of Matrix Information and Directory Services, Inc. (MIDS). Each item contains copyright information.

i `jsq@ftp.tic.com`

7-193 **meval-bibtex-zenon-inria-fr.src:** `zenon.inria.fr`
    `meval-bibtex-zenon-inria-fr`
      This source contains the bibtex bibliography of the MEVAL project at INRIA Sophia Antipolis, France
    i `wais-admin@zenon.inria.fr`

7-194 **midwest-weather.src:** `wais.cic.net`
    `midwest-weather`
      National Weather Service forecasts for the states of Michigan, Ohio, Indiana, Illinois, Wisconsin, Iowa, and Minnesota. Updated hourly from the gopher weather server at the University of Minnesota.
    i `holbrook@cic.net` (J. Paul Holbrook)

7-195 **miljodatabas.src:** `munin.ub2.lu.se`
    `miljodatabas`
      A local database on environment-related research projects at Lund University, Sweden. In Swedish.
    i `anders@munin.ub2.lu.se`

7-196 **music-surveys.src:** `cs.uwp.edu`
    `music-surveys`
      This server contains the results of the `rec.music.*` *eclectic music surveys.*
    i `datta@cs.uwp.edu`

7-197 **MuTeX.src:** `gopher.stolaf.edu` `8003`
    `MuTeX`
      Archive of the MuTeX mailing list. MuTeX allows you to use TeX to typeset single-staff music and lyrics. This list also discusses MusicTeX, another powerful package which allows the typesetting of orchestral and polifonic music.
    i `mutex-request@stolaf.edu`

7-198 **nafta.src:** `sunsite.unc.edu`
    `nafta`
      The full text of the North American Free Trade Agreement, which would eliminate most restrictions on trade, export, and import among the North American countries of Canada, the United States, and Mexico.
    i `jem@sunsite.unc.edu`

7-199 **NASA-directory-of-servers.src:** `ndadsb.gsfc.nasa.gov`
    `NASA-directory-of-servers`
      This database contains WAIS source files of interest to the NASA community. Some, but not all, are run by the STELAR project at the National Space Science Data Center. Others are here purely as a service to the astronomy, astrophysics, planetary, and space-physics communities. Queries about specific databases should go to the maintainers listed in the individual source files.
    i `stelar-info@Hypatia.gsfc.nasa.gov`

7-200 **nasa-larc-abs.src:** `techreports.larc.nasa.gov`
    `nasa-larc-abs`
      NASA Langley Research Center Technical Reports, also available in compressed PostScript for-

mat via anonymous FTP from `techreports.larc.nasa.gov`

i `M.L.Nelson@LaRC.NASA.GOV`

7-201 **National-Performance-Review.src:** `sunsite.unc.edu`
National-Performance-Review

This is the report of the United States "National Performance Review" (NPR), created by a committee headed by Vice President Albert Gore. It is a series of recommendations for improving the efficiency of government and reducing waste.

i `jem@sunsite.unc.edu`

7-202 **nc-supreme-court.src:** `sunsite.unc.edu`
nc-supreme-court

Test selection of opinions of the Supreme Court of North Carolina. These Advance Sheets represent information from 332 NC No.4, pages 487-672, dated January 4, 1993. Please send comments on the usefulness of this experiment to `gopher@sunsite.unc.edu`

i `jem@sunsite.unc.edu`

7-203 **netlib-index.src:** `wraith.cs.uow.edu.au`
netlib-index

This server contains the netlib indexes as they exists on the Australian netlib server (wraith).

i `steve@cs.uow.edu.au`

7-204 **netpolicy.src:** `ds.internic.net`
netpolicy

Network policies and procedures.

i `admin@ds.internic.net`

7-205 **netrek-ftp.src:** `gourd.srv.cs.cmu.edu` 6000
netrek-ftp

This is an archive for information of interest to the Netrek community. The original source was the `andrew.games.xtrek` *board at CMU; later items came from the* `alt.games.xtrek` *newsgroup, and now the* `rec.games.netrek` *newsgroup. Netrek is a real-time space battle game. There is a Netrek FTP archive at* `gs69.sp.cs.cmu.edu` *maintained by* `jch@cs.cmu.edu`

i `spot@cs.cmu.edu`

7-206 **network-bibliography.src:** `munin.ub2.lu.se`
network-bibliography

Network-related bibliographies.

i `anders@munin.ub2.lu.se`

7-207 **neuroprose.src:** `wais.cic.net`
neuroprose

WAIS index of the neuroprose index at `archive.cis.ohio-state.edu` *in* `/pub/neuroprose/INDEX`

i `holbrook@cic.net` (J. Paul Holbrook)

7-208 **NeXT-Managers.src:** `gopher.stolaf.edu` 8004
NeXT-Managers

Archive of all messages posted to the NeXT-Managers mailing list.

i `next-managers-request@stolaf.edu`

7-209 **nren-bill.src:** `wais.cic.net`
    `nrenbill`
> *The High-Performance Computing Act of 1991, otherwise known as the NREN bill.*

i `holbrook@cic.net` (J. Paul Holbrook)

7-210 **nsf-awards.src:** `stis.nsf.gov`
    `nsf-awards`
> *This WAIS database contains award abstracts for awards made by the National Science Foundation. The database covers from the beginning of 1990 to the present.*

i `stis@nsf.gov`

7-211 **nsf-pubs.src:** `stis.nsf.gov`
    `nsf-pubs`
> *Contains the publications of the National Science Foundation.*

i `stis@nsf.gov`

7-212 **Omni-Cultural-Academic-Resource.src:** `gopher.stolaf.edu` 8002
    `Omni-Cultural-Academic-Resource`
> *A collection of material with an international or intercultural bent. The contents of OCAR is constantly changing. Items within are collected from various network newsgroups, databases, and mailing lists.*

i `ocar@stolaf.edu`

7-213 **online-mendelian-inheritance-in-man.src:** `wais.gdb.org`
    `omim`
> *Archive of online Mendelian inheritance in man. Catalogs of autosomal dominant, autosomal recessive, and X-linked phenotypes.*

i `help@gdb.org`

7-214 **online@uunet.ca.src:** `wais.cic.net`
    `online`
> *Archive of the* `online@uunet.ca` *mailing list, which is for information brokers and other people who search online databases. Good coverage of commercial, pay-per-use systems like Dialog, LEXIS, NEXIS, etc.)*

i `holbrook@cic.net` (J. Paul Holbrook)

7-215 **ota.src:** `quake.think.com`
    `/proj/wais/db/ota/ota`
> *Archive of some of the reports from the Congressional Office of Technology Assessment (OTA).*

i `wais@quake.think.com`

7-216 **oz-postcodes.src:** `pet1.austin.unimelb.edu.au`
    `oz-postcodes`
> *This source is an index of Australian postcodes. Search by place name or by postcode.*

i `danny@austin.unimelb.edu.au`

7-217 **pegasus-mail-disc.src:** `cyberdyne.ece.uiuc.edu`
    `pegasus-mail-disc`
> *This database consists of mail sent to all Pegasus Mail administrators throughout the world.*

The mail is a discussion of features/bugs in Pegasus Mail and Charon. Pegasus Mail is a sophisticated IBM-PC based e-mail program that runs either stand-alone or on Novell networks. Charon is a SMTP gateway program written specifically to interface with Pegasus Mail. It serves as the Internet transport and provides some other useful functions, like Unix to Netware printing, etc.

i `rjoyner@cyberdyne.ece.uiuc.edu`

7-218 **POETRY-index.src:** `sunsite.unc.edu`
`/home3/wais/POETRY-index`

This is an index of all the poems and reviews published since volume 151 (October 1987) in POETRY magazine of Chicago. POETRY was founded in 1912 by Harriet Monroe and quickly became a major publication venue for poets worldwide.

i `paul_jones@unc.edu`

7-219 **Preprints-alg-geom.src:** `enslapp.ens-lyon.fr`
`/usr/local/wais-sources/Preprints-alg-geom`

This server contains all titles and abstracts that have been submitted to the algebra and geometry preprint server in SISSA.

i `degio@difool.ens-lyon.fr`

7-220 **Preprints-cond-mat.src:** `enslapp.ens-lyon.fr`
`/usr/local/wais-sources/Preprints-cond-mat`

This server gives all titles/abstracts on the SISSA preprint server for condensed matter.

i `degio@difool.ens-lyon.src`

7-221 **Preprints-gr-qc.src:** `enslapp.ens-lyon.fr`
`/usr/local/wais-sources/Preprints-gr-qc`

This server contains all titles/abstracts of papers submitted to the gr-qc server in Los Alamos.

i `degio@difool.ens-lyon.fr`

7-222 **Preprints-hep-ph.src:** `enslapp.ens-lyon.fr`
`Preprints-hep-ph`

This server contains all titles/abstracts emitted by the hep-ph server at `babbage.sissa.it`. *They are all about high energy phenomenology.*

i `degio@difool.ens-lyon.fr`

7-223 **Preprints-hep-th.src:** `enslapp.ens-lyon.fr`
`/usr/local/wais-sources/Preprints-hep-th`

This server gives all titles/abstracts on the Los Alamos preprint server for theoretical physics.

i `degio@difool.ens-lyon.fr`

7-224 **prosite.src:** `solomon.technet.sg`
`prosite`

WAIS index of the PROSITE database, a compilation of sites and patterns found in protein sequences. Newcomers are advised to use the keywords PROSITE or `help` *or* `documentation` *to find out more about the PROSITE dictionary.*

i `waisguy@solomon.technet.sg`

7-225 **quake.think.com-ftp.src:** `quake.think.com  211`
`anonymous-ftp`

This is a prototype WAIS FTP server. This server searches README files throughout the entire FTP directory tree at `quake.think.com`. *When an interesting file is found, it is used as a relevancy feedback document. When the search is redone, the user will get a listing of the FTP directory in which the README file resides. The user can then retrieve files from that directory. Text files are returned as type TEXT, all other files are returned as type FTP.*

i `wais@quake.think.com`

7-226 **Queer-Resources.src:** `vector.intercon.com`
`/wais/qrd`

The Queer Resources Directory, files of interest to the queer community. AIDS TREATMENT NEWS; the GLAAD/LA newsletter; contact information for activist and support groups; lists of films with gay/lesbian/bisexual characters; lists of organizations and companies with domestic partnership benefits; anti-discrimination ordinances; and the Gay Rights Laws of Vermont, New Jersey, California, and Minnesota.

i `buckmr@vector.intercon.com`

7-227 **queuing-literature-database.src:** `lurker.dfv.rwth-aachen.de`
`queuing-literature-database`

WAIS index of the Queuing Literature Database (QLD), a database of documents on performance analysis of telecommunication systems.

i `broe@rantanplan.dfv.rwth-aachen.de` or `cg@dfv.rwth-aachen.de` or `le@pki-nbg.philips.de`

7-228 **rec.gardens.src:** `munin.ub2.lu.se`
`rec.gardens`

Index of articles in the newsgroup `rec.gardens`

i `anders@munin.ub2.lu.se`

7-229 **reports-abstracts.src:** `bloch.informatik.uni-kl.de`
`reports-abstracts`

References to technical reports of various origins.

i `reitherm@informatik.uni-kl.de` (Steffen Reithermann)

7-230 **rfc-index.src:** `wais.cic.net`
`rfc-index`

Index to the RFCs. The original source, indexed one paragraph at a time, is at `ftp.nisc.sri.com` *in* `/rfc/rfc-index.txt`

i `holbrook@cic.net` (J. Paul Holbrook)

7-231 **rfcs.src:** `ds.internic.net`
`rfcs`

Request For Comment documents—Internet standards and information.

i `admin@ds.internic.net`

7-232 **roget-thesaurus.src:** `wais.cic.net`
`roget-thesaurus`

Roget's Thesaurus as provided by Project Gutenberg.

i `holbrook@cic.net` (J. Paul Holbrook)

7-233 **Salk_Genome_Center.src:** rangersmith.sdsc.edu
Salk_Genome_Center

> *This database contains the results of physical mapping of human chromosome 11, and other chromosomes, from the San Diego Genome Center and Molecular Genetics Lab at the Salk Institute.*

i romberg@molly.sdsc.edu

7-234 **sample-books.src:** quake.think.com
sample-books

> *Archive of some online e-texts, including Alice in Wonderland, the Declaration of Independence, The Hunting of the Snark, The Night Before Christmas, Through the Looking Glass, and The U.S. Constitution.*

i wais@quake.think.com

7-235 **sci.astro.hubble.src:** wfpc3.la.asu.edu
/disk1/wais/wais-sources/sci.astro.hubble

> *Archive of materials posted to the* sci.astro.hubble *newsgroup.*

i sah@wfpc3.la.asu.edu

7-236 **sci.astro.hubble.src:** tycho.la.asu.edu
/mnt/wais/wais-sources/sci.astro.hubble

> *Archive of materials posted to* sci.astro.hubble *newsgroup.*

i sah@tycho.la.asu.edu

7-237 **sf-reviews.src:** net.bio.net
sf-reviews

> *This database is an archive of the Usenet newsgroup* rec.arts.sf.reviews, *which is a forum for reviews of works of interest to fans of science fiction/speculative fiction/fantasy/horror (and sometimes comics).*

i rasfr-comments@presto.ig.com

7-238 **sfsu-phones.src:** sfsuvax1.sfsu.edu
phones

> *San Francisco State University telephone book.*

i wais@sfsuvax1.sfsu.edu

7-239 **SGML.src:** ifi.uio.no
SGML

> *Standard Generalized Markup Language information.*

i anders@ifi.uio.no

7-240 **Sheet_Music_Index.src:** iliad.lib.duke.edu
Sheet_Music_Index

> *Index of the sheet music in the Duke University Libraries' collection. The collection chiefly consists of popular music (e.g., songs, dance music for piano, etc.) from the 19th and 20th centuries and includes items published in the United States, United Kingdom, France, Germany, Italy, and Austria. Of particular note are items from the Justin Herman collection of "tin-pan alley" publications and illustrated material from the Alexander Weinmann collection of Viennese publications.*

i lois@iliad.lib.duke.edu

7-241 **SIGHyper.src:** ifi.uio.no
SIGHyper

> *These documents are from the SGML Users' Group's (SGML-UG) Special Interest Group on Hypertext and Multimedia (SIGhyper).*

i anders@ifi.uio.no

7-242 **smf-annuaire.src.src:** cirm5.univ-mrs.fr
/bases/bibli-cirm/smf-annuaire.src

> *Directory of the Centre International de Rencontres Mathematiques (France).*

i jlm@cirm5.univ-mrs.fr

7-243 **statfaqs.src:** bongo.cc.utexas.edu
/home/ccix/u13/cc/ssg/wais/statfaqs

> *List of Frequently Asked Questions and their answers on topics concerning statistics and statistical computing. This list is compiled monthly by the Statistical Services Group, University of Texas at Austin Computation Center.*

i ssg@bongo.cc.utexas.edu

7-244 **STRAINS-bact.src:** fragrans.riken.go.jp
STRAINS-bact

> *The STRAIN databases, comprising the bacterial, fungi, and yeast databases, were developed by the World Data Center for Microorganisms (WDC), sponsored by UNEP and UNESCO. STRAINS-bact contains a list of bacterial strains preserved in the collections registered in the CCINFO database.*

i sugawara@viola.riken.go.jp

7-245 **STRAINS-fungi.src:** fragrans.riken.go.jp
STRAINS-fungi

> *The STRAIN databases, comprising the bacterial, fungi, and yeast databases, were developed by the World Data Center for Microorganisms (WDC), sponsored by UNEP and UNESCO. STRAINS-fungi contains a list of fungal strains preserved in the collections registered in the CCINFO database.*

i sugawara@viola.riken.go.jp

7-246 **STRAINS-yeast.src:** fragrans.riken.go.jp
STRAINS-yeast

> *The STRAIN databases, comprising the bacterial, fungi, and yeast databases, were developed by the World Data Center for Microorganisms (WDC), sponsored by UNEP and UNESCO. STRAINS-yeast contains a list of yeast strains preserved in the collections registered in the CCINFO database.*

i sugawara@viola.riken.go.jp

7-247 **stsci-docs.src:** stsci.edu
/var/spool/uucppublic/.waisindex/stsci-docs

> *User manuals produced by the Space Telescope Science Institute for use by Hubble Space Telescope (HST) proposers and observers.*

i reppert@stsci.edu

7-248 **stsci-preprint-db.src:** stsci.edu
    stsci-preprint-db

      STScI-STEP is a bibliographic listing of astronomy and astrophysics preprints received at the Space Telescope Science Institute Library.

    i reppert@stsci.edu

7-249 **sun-admin.src:** sunsite.unc.edu
    sun-admin

      This server maintains postings to the comp.sys.sun.admin *newsgroup.*

    i wais@sunsite.unc.edu

7-250 **sun-announce.src:** sun-wais.oit.unc.edu
    sun-announce

      Archive of comp.sys.sun.announce *newsgroup.*

    i wais@sunsite.unc.edu

7-251 **sun-apps.src:** sun-wais.oit.unc.edu
    sun-apps

      Archive of comp.sys.sun.apps *newsgroup.*

    i wais@sunsite.unc.edu

7-252 **sun-fixes.src:** wais.vifp.monash.edu.au
    sun-fixes

      This is a list of most Sun Microsystems bug patches. It does not include the patches themselves, just the README files, so there is enough information to find, for example, all bug reports on the error "Panic: sdlc_rexmit", then get the full patch, given the Sun ID number. Actual fixes are available from (among others) ftp.uu.net *in* /systems/sun/sun-dist

    i rik.harris@fcit.monash.edu.au

7-253 **sun-hardware.src:** sun-wais.oit.unc.edu
    sun-hardware

      On Sun hardware.

    i wais@sunsite.unc.edu

7-254 **sun-managers-summary.src:** info.latech.edu
    sun-managers-summary

      Index of summaries of the Sun-managers mailing list.

    i dan@engr.latech.edu

7-255 **sun-misc.src:** sun-wais.oit.unc.edu
    sun-misc

      Archive of comp.sys.sun.misc *newsgroup.*

    i wais@sunsite.unc.edu

7-256 **sun-openlook.src:** sun-wais.oit.unc.edu
    sun-openlook

      Archive of the Sun OpenLook comp.windows.open-look *newsgroup.*

    i wais@sun-wais.oit.unc.edu

7-257 **sun-sounds.src:** sunsite.unc.edu
/home3/wais/sun-sounds
Sounds for the Sun.
i wais@sunsite.unc.edu

7-258 **sun-wanted.src:** sun-wais.oit.unc.edu
sun-wanted
Archive of comp.sys.sun.wanted *newsgroup.*
i wais@sunsite.oit.unc.edu

7-259 **sun-whitepapers.src:** sunsite.unc.edu
sun-whitepapers
Technical white papers from Sun Microsystems.

7-260 **sunflash-1989.src:** sunsite.unc.edu
/home3/wais/sunflash-1989
1989 Issues of the Florida Sunflash, Sun Microsystems' Sunflash Journal.
i wais@sunsite.unc.edu

7-261 **sunflash-1990.src:** sun-wais.oit.unc.edu
sunflash-1990
1990 issues of The Florida Sunflash, Sun Microsystems' Sunflash Journal.
i wais@sun-wais.oit.unc.edu

7-262 **sunflash-1991.src:** sun-wais.oit.unc.edu
sunflash-1991
1991 Issues of the Florida Sunflash, Sun Microsystems' Sunflash Journal.
i wais@sun-wais.oit.unc.edu

7-263 **sunflash-1992.src:** sun-wais.oit.unc.edu
sunflash-1992
1992 Issues of the Florida Sunflash, Sun Microsystems' Sunflash Journal.
i wais@sun-wais.oit.unc.edu

7-264 **sunflash-1993.src:** sunsite.unc.edu 210
/home3/wais/sunflash-1993
1993 Issues of the Florida Sunflash, Sun Microsystems' Sunflash Journal.
i wais@sunsite.unc.edu

7-265 **SunSITE-ftp.src:** sunsite.unc.edu
SunSITE-ftp
This is an index of all the index and README files found in the anonymous FTP directory of SunSITE. This source can be used by the FTP's WAIS client and any other client capable of relevancy feedback to search and retrieve files of all sorts including pictures, sounds, programs, and documents. For more on FTP and WAIS, see the file ftp.wais.readme *in this index or via anonymous FTP to* sunsite.unc.edu *in* /pub/wais
i root@sunsite.unc.edu

7-266 **sustainable-agriculture.src:** sunSITE.unc.edu
/home3/wais/sustainable-agriculture

Files having to do with sustainable agriculture, appropriate technology, rural living, organic farming, gardening, bulbs, seeds, bees, and the like.

i root@sunsite.unc.edu

7-267 **Tantric-News.src:** sunsite.unc.edu
/home3/wais/Tantric-News

Information from the Society for Tantric Studies.

i wais@sunsite.unc.edu

7-268 **the-scientist.src:** ds.internic.net
the-scientist

The Scientist—A biweekly newspaper for research scientists and managers in industry, academia, and government. Focuses on life sciences and biotechology.

i root@ds.internic.net

7-269 **thesaurus.src:** wais.cic.net
roget-thesaurus

Roget's Thesaurus as provided by Project Gutenberg.

i holbrook@cic.net (J. Paul Holbrook)

7-270 **UC-motif-FAQ.src:** services.canberra.edu.au
UC-motif-FAQ

Frequently asked questions file on UC motif.

i root@services.canberra.edu.au

7-271 **unced-agenda.src:** quake.think.com
/proj/wais/db/sources/unced-agenda

This is the agenda for the United Nations Rio Summit on the environment.

i wais@quake.think.com

7-272 **unix-manual.src:** quake.think.com
unix-manual

WAIS index of the entire set of man pages (online manual) of the Unix operating sytem.

i wais@quake.think.com

7-273 **unl-di-reports.src:** wais.fct.unl.pt
unl-di-reports

This index contains reference entries for the technical reports of the Computer Science Department, Universidade Nova de Lisboa, Portugal.

i archive@fct.unl.pt

7-274 **US-Budget-1993.src:** sunsite.unc.edu
US-Budget-1993

This is a copy of the Proposed United States of America's federal budget for 1993.

i wais@sunsite.unc.edu

7-275 **US-Congress-Phone-Fax.src:** sunsite.unc.edu
/home3/wais/US-Congress-Phone-Fax

Telephone numbers and fax numbers for members of the U.S. Senate and House of Representatives.

i `jem@sunsite.unc.edu`

7-276 **US-State-Department-Travel-Advisories.src:** `gopher.stolaf.edu`
`8000`
`US-State-Department-Travel-Advisories`

> *Archive of the travel -advisories mailing list which distributes U.S. State Department Consular Information Sheets and travel warnings.*

i `travel-advisories-request@stolaf.edu`

7-277 **usda-csrs-pwd.src:** `eos.esusda.gov`
`usda-csrs-pwd`

> *Directory of professional workers in State Agricultural Experiment Stations and other cooperating institutions from the U.S. Department of Agriculture Cooperative State Research Service.*

i `sconn@esusda.gov`

7-278 **usda-rrdb.src:** `es-cit.esusda.gov`
`rrdb`

> *The U.S. Department of Agriculture Extension Service Research Results Database (RRDB). Contains short summaries of recent research results from the USDA's Agricultural Research Service (ARS) and Economic Research Service (ERS).*

i `wais@esusda.gov`

7-279 **ut-research-expertise.src:** `oac.hsc.uth.tmc.edu`
`ut_core`

> *The UT_CORE source catalogs the research interests and expertise of the faculty of the University of Texas Health Science Center at Houston. CORE profiles include information relevant to the investigator's research interests: academic and administrative appointments, educational background, intramural and extramural professional activities, keywords of research interests and disciplines, selected journal publication citations, and, when provided, a short abstract of current research.*

i `root@oac.hsc.uth.tmc.edu`

7-280 **utsun.s.u-tokyo.ac.jp.src:** `wais.cic.net`
`archives/utsun.s.u-tokyo.ac.jp`

> *Archives of* `utsun.s.u-tokyo.ac.jp` *(a major Japanese anonymous FTP site). Includes archives of the* `fj.*` `newsgroups`*, information about networks in Japan, and other useful things.*

i `holbrook@cic.net` (J. Paul Holbrook)

7-281 **uumap.src:** `wais.cic.net`
`uumap`

> *The UUCP mapping project keeps track of UUCP and Usenet sites around the world. This source has the full set of maps. It is not a complete index to every computer on the Internet, but it does have particularly good coverage of otherwise difficult-to-locate sites in South America and Asia, as well as information about Fidonet. Some countries with particularly good coverage in these maps include Canada (all domains), Japan (commercial only, not academic), and Russia (all domains).*

i `holbrook@cic.net` (J. Paul Holbrook)

7-282 **uunet.src:** `wais.cic.net`
      `uunet`

         The directory listing of the FTP archive at `uunet.uu.net` *(updated nightly).*

     i `holbrook@cic.net` (J. Paul Holbrook)

7-283 **uxc.cso.uiuc.edu.src:** `wais.cic.net`
      `archives/uxc.cso.uiuc.edu`

         Recursive directory listing of the FTP archive at `uxc.cso.uiuc.edu`

     i `holbrook@cic.net` (J. Paul Holbrook)

7-284 **vpiej-l.src:** `borg.lib.vt.edu`
      `/LocalLibrary/WAIS/vpiej-l/vpiej-l`

         Archive of the VPIEJ-L mailing list.

     i `jpowell@borg.lib.vt.edu`

7-285 **wais-discussion-archives.src:** `quake.think.com`
      `wais-discussion-archives`

         This source provides access to the WAIS-discussion mailing list's archives. The files have been indexed as mail digests to give access on a per-message basis, and also as complete files so you may retrieve an entire issue (titles will be called `issue-##.text`*).*

     i `wais@quake.think.com`

7-286 **wais-docs.src:** `quake.think.com`
      `wais-docs`

         This is a database containing the text of all the current documentation provided in the WAIS distribution.

     i `wais@quake.think.com`

7-287 **wais-talk-archives.src:** `quake.think.com`
      `wais-talk-archives`

         Archive of the WAIS-talk mailing list and `alt.wais` *newsgroup.*

     i `wais@quake.think.com`

7-288 **water-quality.src:** `hermes.ecn.purdue.edu   6001`
      `/home/hermes/cems/water_quality/wais-sources/water-quality`

         Educational materials on water-quality assessment, maintenance, and improvement in the United States, prepared by the Cooperative Extension System.

     i `cems@ecn.purdue.edu`

7-289 **weather.src:** `quake.think.com`
      `weather`

         This is the WEATHER server, brought to you courtesy of the WAIS folks from Thinking Machines and the weather folks at `vnd.cso.uiuc.edu` *and the University of Michigan. Currently you'll get the best results by asking this server for* `weather`*. The returned list of files should include this file, as well as the day's satellite weather maps. Include* `gif` *if you want the maps and* `txt` *if you want the textual weather forecasts.*

     i `weather-server@quake.think.com`

7-290 **Welsh.src:** `sunsite.unc.edu`
      `/home3/wais/Welsh`

> *This is a WAIS database of the Welsh–L mailing list, which deals with questions concerning Wales and the Welsh language. Much of the discussion is in Welsh.*

i `paul_jones@unc.edu`

7-291 **White-House-Papers.src:** `sunsite.unc.edu`
`/home3/wais/White-House-Papers`

> *These are the White House press briefings and other postings dealing with William Jefferson Clinton and Albert Gore as well as members of the President's cabinet and the First Lady Hillary Rodham Clinton, Chelsea, Socks, and others in Washington, D.C.*

i `wais@sunsite.unc.edu`

7-292 **windows-nt-knowledge-base.src:** `sunsite.unc.edu`
`windows-nt-knowledge-base`

> *Information on Microsoft's new operating system Windows NT.*

i `wais@sunsite.unc.edu`

7-293 **winsock.src:** `sunsite.unc.edu`
`winsock`

> *This database contains the complete archives of the windows sockets (winsock) mailing list. You can also access this archive via FTP to* `sunsite.unc.edu` *in* `/pub/micro/pc-stuff/ms-windows/winsock`

i `ses@sunsite.unc.edu`

7-294 **world-factbook92.src:** `gopher.uwo.ca`
`world-factbook92`

> *The CIA World Factbook 1992 (published January 1993) slightly modified from Project Gutenberg sources for WAIS indexing by Peter Marshall at the University of Western Ontario (*`peter@julian.uwo.ca`*). Search by country or international organization name. Also includes a long section on abbreviations and one on weights and measures. Returns all sorts of geographic, political, economic, communications, and defense information.*

i `peter@julian.uwo.ca`

7-295 **world91a.src:** `quake.think.com`
`/proj/wais/db/sources/world91a`

> *The CIA World Factbook 1991.*

i `wais@quake.think.com`

7-296 **wuarchive.src:** `wais.cic.net`
`wuarchive`

> *The directory listing of the FTP archive* `wuarchive.wustl.edu` *(updated nightly).*

i `holbrook@cic.net` (J. Paul Holbrook)

7-297 **zipcodes.src:** `quake.think.com`
`/proj/wais/db/sources/zipcodes`

> *WAIS index of USA zip code database.*

i `wais@quake.think.com`

8. WORLD WIDE WEB (WWW) PUBLIC CLIENTS

This chapter lists hosts where public WWW clients are available. WWW, or W3, was developed in Switzerland at the European Laboratory for Particle Physics (known as CERN). To access a WWW client, simply telnet to the host address and login as www. Once you are connected you will see that WWW clients are very easy to use. Usually what appears is a page of text, with numbers in square brackets sprinkled throughout. To find out more about a given item, simply type in the number associated with that item and a new page with more information will be displayed. As you navigate through the web you will be connecting to many types of servers all over the globe, but WWW gives you uniform and easy access to all these diverse resources. Try it out and you'll see the power of a hypertext interface to information.

Entry Format:

Item
Number

8-n   **Name of hosting institution:** host address
            Services: Description of special services available.

Where To Find It: This list of public WWW clients was taken from the Hytelnet database. (For more information on Hytelnet, please see the introduction to Chapter 3.) For information on the WWW project, including a text-based WWW client and more, you can FTP to info.cern.ch and look in the directory /pub/www/. The University of Kansas has also developed a very nice WWW client called Lynx, which is available by FTP to ftp2.cc.ukans.edu in the directory /pub/lynx. There is also a mailing list that distributes information and announcements about WWW; to subscribe, send e-mail with add www-announce in the body of your message to listserv@info.cern.ch.

Netiquette: These are *public* clients, and as such they receive heavy use. Please use them sparingly, as you should use all other public resources on the Internet. Also, use the clients that are close to you. If at all possible, don't use them at all! Instead, get local client software installed on your system. Not only will that be a better use of bandwidth, but most local clients are more powerful and easier to use than these public clients.

Entries:

8-1 **European Particle Physics Laboratory (CERN), Geneva, Switzerland:** `info.cern.ch`
   Services: On-line help for the text-based WWW client, information on the World Wide Web project, CERN phone book, CERN newsgroups, connections to many other sites organized by subject, access to a number of High Energy Physics resources, and more.

8-2 **Finnish University and Research Network (FUNET):** `info.funet.fi`
   Services: Information from and on FUNET, the Finnish University and Research networks and their services.

8-3 **Hebrew University of Jerusalem:** `vms.huji.ac.il`
   Services: CWIS of the Hebrew University of Jerusalem, Israeli libraries, and information on Jerusalem.

8-4 **New Jersey Institute of Technology:** `www.njit.edu`
   Services: Access to the NJIT library and other campus information.

8-5 **Legal Information Institute, Cornell Law School:** `www.law.cornell.edu`
   Services: Information on U.S. Statutes regarding intellectual property, copyrights, patents, and trademarks.

8-6 **University of Arizona Center for Computing and Information Technology:**
   `lanka.ccit.arizona.edu`
   Services: Local information.

8-7 **Academy of Sciences, Slovakia:** `sun.uakom.cs`
   Services: Generic WWW access.

8-8 **University of Kansas:** `ukanaix.cc.ukans.edu`
   Services: Information on Lynx (a WWW client), the University of Kansas CWIS, History Net Archives, and gopher sources.

8-9 **KFKI/RMKI Computer Network Center, Budapest, Hungary:** `fserv.kfki.hu`
   Services: Generic WWW access.

9. ELECTRONIC SERIALS

A large number of serial publications are available on the Internet. Most are only published electronically, but there are a growing number of electronic versions of hardcopy serials. Online serials come in an astonishing variety. This list includes anything I could find that is published at least semi-regularly. This ranges from scholarly journals to newsletters distributed by science-fiction publishers to counterculture magazines known as "zines."

Entry Format:

Item
Number

9-n   **Publication name:** Description of what the publication is about and of the organization or individual(s) who publish it. *Frequency of publication*

    i contact address

    ±subscription address (if applicable)

    Archive: Method of access and archive address

Where to Find It: Because they share the same method of distribution, the listserv, I ran across many of the serials in this chapter while searching for Bitnet mailing lists. Another portion of the entries was found while I was examining FTP sites. But the majority of the entries are reprinted, by permission, from the Association of Research Libraries (ARL) publication *Directory of Electronic Journals, Newsletters and Academic Discussion Lists.* ARL's book provides much more extensive information on each of the serials listed and is a valuable tool for the serious Internet user. ARL can be reached at (202) 296-2296 or by e-mail at osap@cni.org. The serials published in the ARL book are taken from Professor Michael Strangelove's EJOURNAL list (see Chapter 11 for details on how to find it on the Internet).

Entries:

9-1   **A & G Information Services:** Information about Russia and St. Petersburg, divided into sections: St. Petersburg News, Privatization, Legislation, Financial News, Markets, Company News, Politics, Business Review. This newsletter is not free; for more information send e-mail to the contact address. *One to two times weekly*

    i ± spbeac@sovamsu.sovusa.com or esa@cfea.ecc.spb.su (Elena Artemova)

9-2 **A Byte Of Torah (and) A MegaByte Of Torah:** A Byte of Torah is a weekly newsletter on the Torah portion of the week. A MegaByte Of Torah is a monthly newsletter that deals with topics somehow related to the current Jewish month. *Weekly and monthly*

i bytetorah@israel.nysernet.org (Zev S. Itzkowitz)

± listserv@israel.nysernet.org [body = SUBSCRIBE BYTETORAH]

Archive: FTP israel.nysernet.org in /israel/tanach/commentary/bytetorah/

9-3 **Acquisitions Librarians Electronic Network (ACQNET):** A newsletter/bulletin board for library professionals in acquisitions, serials management, collection development, and administration. *Irregular*

i cri@cornellc.cit.cornell.edu (Bitnet: CRI@CORNELLC) (Christian M. Boissonnas)

Archive: FTP library.cornell.edu in /pub/ACQNET/

9-4 **AI Medicine Digest:** A newsletter on the use of Artificial Intelligence in medicine. *Once or twice a month*

i ± ai-medicine-REQUEST@med.stanford.edu

Archive: FTP lhc.nlm.nih.gov in /pub/ai-medicine/; gopher CAMIS in ai-medicine/Biblio/Digest

9-5 **AIDS Book Review Journal:** Reviews books, videos, journal titles, and other materials covering AIDS, safer sex, and sexually transmitted diseases. *Two to three issues per month*

i u50095@uicvm.uic.edu (Bitnet: U50095@UICVM) (H. Robert Malinowsky)

± listserv@uicvm.uic.edu (Bitnet: LISTSERV@UICVM) [body = SUBSCRIBE AIDSBKRV]

Archive: listserv@uicvm.uic.edu (Bitnet: LISTSERV@UICVM) [body = INDEX AIDSBKRV]

9-6 **AIDS Treatment News:** Electronic version of a print publication which reports on experimental and standard treatments, especially those available now. Also includes interviews with physicians, scientists, and other health professionals, and persons with AIDS or HIV, as well as information from meetings and conferences, medical journals, and computer databases. *Twice a month*

i aidsnews@igc.apc.org

± Usenet newsgroup sci.med.aids

9-7 **ALAWON, the American Library Association Washington Office Newsline:** Covers a wide range of United States federal government activities of interest to librarians. *Irregular*

i alawash@alawash.org

± listserv@uicvm.uic.edu (Bitnet: LISTSERV@UICVM) [body = SUBSCRIBE ALA-WO first-name last-name]

Archive: listserv@uicvm.uic.edu (Bitnet: LISTSERV@UICVM) [body = INDEX ALA-WO]

9-8 **ALCTS Network News (AN2):** Items of concern to librarians in collection management, acquisitions, cataloging, serials, preservation, and the reproduction of library materials. Advance copies of articles and features from the ALCTS Newsletter. *Irregular*

    i u19466@uicvm.bitnet (Bitnet: U19466@UICVM) (Karen Muller)

    ± listserv@uicvm.bitnet (Bitnet: LISTSERV@UICVM) [body = SUBSCRIBE ALCTS]

9-9 **AM/FM Online Edition:** Reports on current events and news on BBC national and local radio, independent national and local radio, and satellite radio services. *Monthly*

    i steveh@orbital.demon.co.uk (Stephen Hebditch)

    ± listserv@orbital.demon.co.uk [body = SUBSCRIBE AMFM

    Archive: listserv@orbital.demon.co.uk [body = INDEX AMFM]

9-10 **Amateur Computerist:** Articles on labor issues and computer and networking history and achievements. *Quarterly*

    i ± au329@cleveland.freenet.edu or hauben@columbia.edu (Ronda Hauben)

    Archive: FTP wuarchive.wustl.edu in /doc/misc/acn

9-11 **Amazons International:** Digest-newsletter for and about physically and psychologically strong women who are not afraid to break free from traditional ideas about gender roles, femininity, and the female physique. *Monthly, on average*

    i ± thomas@smaug.uio.no (Thomas Gramstad)

    Archive: FTP ftp.css.itd.umich.edu in /poli/Amazons.Intl/; e-mail thomas@smaug.uio.no

9-12 **American Arab Scientific Society Newsletter:** Society news and articles related to development of Arab communities. *Quarterly*

    i amass-request@cs.bu.edu (Abdelsalam Heddaya)

    Archive: FTP cs.bu.edu in /amass/newsletters/

9-13 **American Psychological Association's Research Funding Bulletin:** An index of funding announcements from federal and private funding agencies. *Twice a month, on average*

    i apasdcf@gwuvm.bitnet (Cheri Fullerton)

    ± listserv@vtvm2.bitnet (Bitnet: LISTSERV@VTVM2) [body = SUBSCRIBE APASD-L]

9-14 **Andrew View:** Update on the activities of the Andrew Consortium, which maintains and enhances the Andrew User Interface System, including the Andrew User Environment, the Andrew Toolkit, and the Andrew Message System. *Four times a year*

    i wilfred.hansen@cs.cmu.edu or wjh+@cmu.edu (Fred Hansen)

    ± info-andrew-request@andrew.cmu.edu [body = SUBSCRIBE ANDREW]

    Archive: FTP emsworth.andrew.cmu.edu in /newsletters/; e-mail info-andrew-request@andrew.cmu.edu

9-15 **Arachnet Electronic Journal on Virtual Culture:** Encourages, advances, and communicates scholarly analysis, evaluation, and research in multiple disciplines about virtual culture. *Monthly*

   i dkovacs@kentvm.kent.edu (Bitnet: DKOVACS@KENTVM) (Diane Kovacs)

   ± listserv@acadvm1.uottawa.ca (Bitnet: LISTSERV@UOTTAWA) [body = SUBSCRIBE ARACHNET]

   Archive: FTP ksuvxa.kent.edu in /library/; listserv@kentvm.kent.edu (Bitnet: listserv@kentvm); gopher (contact editor for access details)

9-16 **Architronic—The Electronic Journal of Architecture:** Gathers and disseminates scholarly and critical articles about architecture. Presents and reviews research. *Three times per year, with irregular supplements*

   i arcitron@kentvm.kent.edu (Bitnet: ARCITRON@KENTVM)

   ± listserv@kentvm.kent.edu (Bitnet: LISTSERV@KENTVM) [body = SUBSCRIBE ARCITRON]

   Archive: FTP ksuvxa.kent.edu in v1n1.txt [login = ARCHITECTURE password = ARCHIVES]

9-17 **Arm The Spirit:** An autonomist/anti-imperialist collective disseminating information and discussion about liberation struggles in advanced capitalist countries and in the so-called "Third World." Topics include political prisoners, the struggles of native peoples in the Americas, and guerrilla groups. *Bi-monthly*

   i aforum@moose.uvm.edu

   ± aforum@moose.uvm.edu [extra line in header = ATS: e-mail request]

   Archive: FTP 141.211.182.91 in /poli/Arm.the.Spirit/

9-18 **Armadillo Culture—The Journal of Modern Dasypodidae:** A fanzine about concerts and events in the DC area, with a focus on the underground/indie/punk scene as well as articles and general info on cyberculture. *Quarterly, on average*

   i ± sokay@cyclone.mitre.org (Steve Okay)

   Archive: FTP etext.archive.umich.edu in /pub/zines/armadillo.culture

9-19 **ARTCOM Magazine:** Interface of contemporary art and new communication technologies.

   i cel@andrew.cmu.edu (Carl Loeffler) or fjt@well.sf.ca.us (Fred Truck)

   ± Usenet newsgroup alt.artcom

9-20 **Automatome:** Newsletter of the American Association of Law Libraries, Automation and Scientific-Development Special Interest Section.

   i leiserab@ctrvax.vanderbilt.edu (Anna Belle Leiserson)

   ± listserv@ucdavis.edu [body = SUBSCRIBE LAW-LIB]

9-21 **AXE, Revue Electronique de la Litterature Québeçoise et Francophone:** Publication on contemporary French language and literature (incl. Quebec, Africa, Switzerland, Caribbean). Mainly in French. Access provided to individual articles, not entire issues. *Three times a year*

   i cxzn@musica.mcgill.ca (Janusz Przychodzen)

± `listserv@vm1.mcgill.ca` [body = SUBSCRIBE AXE-LIST]

Archive: `listserv@vm1.mcgill.ca` [body = INDEX AXE-LIST]

9-22 **Bean Bag:** Communication among research scientists concerned with legume systematics. Columns include news of meetings, major events, announcements, etc.; Latin American Legume Report; and Nodulation and Nitrogen Fixation (new nodulation records). *May and November of each year*

i `jkirkbride@asrr.arsusda.gov` (Joseph H. Kirkbride, Jr.)

± gopher `huh.harvard.edu`; e-mail `kirkbride@asrr.arsusda.gov` (include name, address, telephone numbers, and e-mail address)

Archive: FTP `huh.harvard.edu` in `/pub/newsletters/beanbag/` [login = FTP password = FTP]; e-mail `jkirkbride@asrr.arsusda.gov` (for some hard-copy back issues)

9-23 **BEN (Botanical Electronic News):** News related to botany, plant ecology, plant distributions, plant protection, conferences, botanical techniques, etc., preferably related to British Columbia and the Pacific Northwest of North America. *Once or twice a month*

i ± `aceska@cue.bc.ca` (Dr. Adolf Ceska)

9-24 **Between the Lines:** A digest about pop singer Debbie Gibson and her music. *Monthly*

i ± `mkwong@freedom.nmsu.edu` (Myra Wong)

9-25 **Biomedical Library Acquisitions Bulletin (BLAB):** News and opinions contributed by readers concerning biomedical library acquisitions. *Monthly, on average*

i ± `dmorse@hsc.usc.edu` (David H. Morse)

9-26 **Blind News Digest:** Digest of articles on visual disabilities, taken from the Usenet newsgroup `misc.handicap` and the Fidonet conference BlinkTalk. The first 700 issues were distributed as issues of the Handicap Digest. *Irregular*

i `wtm@bunker.afd.olivetti.com` (Bill McGarry)

± `listserv@vm1.nodak.edu` (Bitnet: LISTSERV@NDSUVM1) [body = SUBSCRIBE BLINDNWS]

Archive: `listserv@vm1.nodak.edu` (Bitnet: LISTSERV@NDSUVM1) [body = INDEX BLINDNWS]

9-27 **Braille Forum:** Newsletter from the American Council of the Blind. *Bimonthly*

Archive: FTP `handicap.shel.isc-br.com` in `/pub/forum/`

9-28 **Bryn Mawr Classical Review:** Reviews of current work in Greek and Roman studies. *Irregular*

i `jod@ccat.sas.upenn.edu` (James J. O'Donnell)

± `listserv@cc.brynmawr.edu` [body = SUBSCRIBE BMCR-L]

Archive: FTP `orion.lib.virginia.edu` in `/pub/journals/bmcr/`; WAIS `bmcr.src` on `orion.lib.virginia.edu`; gopher `orion.lib.virginia.edu` in `Journals/Bryn Mawr Classical Review/` or `gopher.cic.net`

9-29 **Buffer:** News-journal of computing at the University of Denver. *Monthly* *i* ±buffer@du.edu (Bitnet: BUFFER@DUCAIR) (Rebecca Rowe)

Archive: telnet du.edu [login = atdu select buffer]

9-30 **Bulletin of the General Theological Library of Bangor:** Reviews and annotations of recent acquisitions to the Seminary's libraries, plus occasional scholarly articles on current theological or religious topics. *Quarterly*

i mark@btsgatep.caps.maine.edu (Mark Stoffan)

± FTP panda1.uottawa.ca in /pub/religion/

9-31 **Burma Focus:** Newsletter on Burma from the All Burma Students' Democratic Front (ABSDF). *Bi-monthly*

i ± absdf@pns.apc.org (Aye Chan Naing, Representative)

9-32 **Cache Update:** Newsletter about the Andrew File System(AFS).

Archive: FTP grand.cantral.org in /pub/cache.update

9-33 **CACTUS Newsletter:** Newsletter for members and sponsors of the Capital Area Central Texas Unix Society. *Monthly*

i ± newsletter@cactus.org or officers@cactus.org

9-34 **Carolina:** Electronic news from the Czech Republic in the Czech language. *Weekly*

i carolina@n.fsv.cuni.cs (Bitnet: TROJAN@CSEARN) (Vaclav Trojan)

± listserv@csearn.bitnet (Bitnet: LISTSERV@CSEARN) [body = SUBSCRIBE CAR-CS]

9-35 **Catalyst:** The Community Services Catalyst: Refereed print journal serving community-college educators. Features practitioner-oriented articles on practices in continuing and community education. *Quarterly*

i savage@vtvm1.cc.vt.edu (Bitnet: SAVAGE@VTVM1) (Lon Savage)

± listserv@vtvm1.cc.vt.edu (Bitnet: LISTSERV@VTVM1) [body = SUBSCRIBE CATALYST]

Archive: FTP borg.lib.vt.edu in /pub/CATALYST/; WAIS catalyst.src (access is provided to individual articles)

9-36 **CCNEWS—Campus Computing Newsletter:** Electronic forum for campus-computing newsletter editors and other publications specialists. Focuses on writing, editing, design, and production of campus-computing publications.

i ccnews@bitnic.bitnet (Wendy Rickard Bollentin)

± listserv@bitnic.bitnet (Bitnet: LISTSERV@BITNIC) [body = SUBSCRIBE CCNEWS first-name last-name]

9-37 **CERFNet NEWS:** Newsletter of CERFnet, a mid-level network linking academic, government, and industrial research facilities throughout California, the United States, and internationally. *Bi-monthly*

i help@cerf.net

± listserv@cerf.net [body = SUBSCRIBE CERF-NEWS]

Archive: FTP nic.cerf.net in /cerfnet/cerfnet_info/cernet_news/

9-38 **Chalisti:** Hackers' newsletter, in German. *Every 8 weeks*
    i `terra@sol.ccc.de`
    ± Usenet newsgroup `de.mag.chalisti`
    Archive: FTP `ftp.ccc.de` in `public/ccc/chalisti/`

9-39 **Chaos Corner:** A small newsletter that mentions things the author has found in the process of wandering across the network. *Irregular*
    i `rdc@cornella.cit.cornell.edu` (Bob Cowles)
    Archive: FTP `pelican.cit.cornell.edu` in `/pub/`

9-40 **Chaos Digest (ChaosD):** Shares French information among computerists. Readers are encouraged to submit reasoned articles relating to computer culture and telecommunications (in French, English, or German). *Weekly*
    i ± `jbcondat@attmail.com` (Jean-Bernard Condat)
    Archive: FTP `ftp.eff.org` in `/pub/cud/misc/` or `etext.archive.umich.edu` in `/cud/` or `halcyon.com` in `/pub/mirror/cud/` or `ftp.ee.mu.oz.au` in `/pub/text/CuD/` or `nic.funet.fi` in `/pub/doc/cud/`

9-41 **ChE Electronic Newsletter:** Information of interest and relevance to chemical engineers. *Every two weeks*
    i ± `trayms@cc.curtin.edu.au` (Dr. Martyn S. Ray)
    Archive: FTP `cc.curtin.edu.au` in `/chemeng/`

9-42 **China News Digest:** News digest service about China and Chinese. *Daily and weekly*
    i `cnd-editor@sdsc.edu` (Zuofeng Li) or `cnd-manager@sdsc.edu` (Wei Lin)
    ± `listserv@asuacad.bitnet` (Bitnet: `LISTSERV@ASUACAD`) [body = SUBSCRIBE CHINA-NN] or `listserv@kentvm.bitnet` [body = SUBSCRIBE CHINA-ND] (US readers) or `listserv@uvvm.bitnet` [body = SUBSCRIBE CNC-L] (Canadian readers) or `listserv@iubvm.bitnet` [body = SUBSCRIBE CND-EP] (Europe & Pacific readers)
    Archive: FTP `ifcss.org` in `/cnd/`

9-43 **CHIP—Political, Environmental, Economic and Human Rights News Chile Information Project:** News summaries on human rights and democratization developments in Chile. Also covers environmental and economic development trends in Chile. Not free. *Daily*
    i `anderson@chip.mic.cl` (Steve Anderson)

9-44 **Christian LIFE in the Computer Era:** Intended to help Christians grow. Includes personal testimonies, encouraging articles, book reviews, and a calendar of events. *Monthly*
    i `tony.mcgregor@rdt.monash.edu.au` (Tony McGregor)

9-45 **Chronic Fatigue Syndrome Electronic Newsletter (CFS-NEWS):** Newsletter about Chronic Fatigue Syndrome, with an emphasis on news of recent medical research. (See also CFS-L and CFS-MED in Chapter 1.) *1-4 issues per month*
    i `cfs-news@list.nih.gov` (Roger Burns)
    ± `listserv@list.nih.gov` (Bitnet: `LISTSERV@NIHLIST`) [body = SUBSCRIBE CFS-NEWS]

Archive: `listserv@list.nih.gov` (Bitnet: `LISTSERV@NIHLIST`) [body = INDEX CFS-NEWS]

9-46 **Citations for Serial Literature:** Disseminates literature related to the serial information chain and creates an electronically searchable index. Publishes tables of contents and abstracts for a variety of journals that address issues of concern to serials librarians, vendors, and publishers. *Irregular*

i `mgeller@athena.mit.edu` (Marilyn Geller)

± `listserv@mitvma.mit.edu` (Bitnet: `LISTSERV@MITVMA`) [body = SUBSCRIBE SERCITES]

Archive: Gopher `gopher.cic.net` or `dewey.lib.ncsu.edu`; `listserv@mitvma.mit.edu` (Bitnet: `LISTSERV@MITVMA`) [body = INDEX SERCITES]

9-47 **Class Four Relay Magazine:** A magazine by Relay Ops for the relay community.

i ± `stjs@vm.marist.edu` (Bitnet: `STJS@MARIST`) (Joey J. Stanford)

9-48 **CLIONET—An Electronic Journal of History:** An electronic journal/network providing FTP and gopher sites for documents of interest to historians of Australasia, South Asia, and Melanesia. Publishes new work in Australian and related historical fields. *Monthly*

i ± `hipgt@marlin.jcu.edu.au` (Paul Turnbull)

9-49 **Community Services CATALYST:** Published by the Scholarly Communications Project of Virginia Polytechnic Institute and State University. *Quarterly*

i `savage@vtvm1.cc.vt.edu` (Lon Savage) or `powell@borg.lib.vt.edu` (James Powell)

± `catalyst@vtvm1.cc.vt.edu`

Archive: FTP `borg.lib.vt.edu` in `/pub/CATALYST/`; gopher `borg.lib.vt.edu`; WAIS `catalyst.src`; WWW `http://borg.lib.vt.edu/`

9-50 **Computer Science Center Link:** Issues in academic computing at the University of Maryland with articles about networking, new trends in computing, and innovative uses of computing. *Five times a year*

± Link Editor, Computer Science Center, University of Maryland, College Park, MD 20742

9-51 **Computer Underground Digest (CuD or Cu-Digest):** Discussion of legal, ethical, social, and other issues regarding computerized information and communications. *Weekly*

i `tk0jut2@mvs.cso.niu.edu` (Jim Thomas and Gordon Meyer)

± `tk0jut2@mvs.cso.niu.edu` [subject = SUB CuD body = SUB CuD first-name last-name e-mail-address]

Archive: FTP `ftp.eff.org` in `/pub/cud/` or `etext.archive.umich.edu` in `/cud/` or `halcyon.com` in `/pub/mirror/cud/` or `ftp.ee.mu.oz.au` in `/pub/text/CuD/` or `nic.funet.fi` in `/pub/doc/cud/`; Usenet newsgroup `comp.society.cu-digest`; `mailserv@batpad.lgb.ca.us`

9-52 **Computing and Network News:** Published for the Kansas State University community. *Monthly*

> *i* betsy@ksuvm.ksu.edu (Bitnet: BETSY@KSUVM) (Betsy Edwards)
>
> ± editor@ksuvm.ksu.edu (Bitnet: EDITOR@KSUVM)
>
> **Archive:** Only accessible from within the KSUVM system.

9-53 **Computists' Communique:** A career-oriented newsletter serving professionals in artificial intelligence, information science, and computer science. Available to members of Computists International, a networking group for computer and information scientists. This newsletter is not free; for more information send e-mail to the contact address. *Weekly*

> *i* ± laws@ai.sri.com (Dr. Kenneth I. Laws)

9-54 **Connect!:** Connect! Communications Company newsletter. *Monthly*

> *i* ± david.wachenschwanz@atomiccafe.com (Fidonet: David Wachenschwanz@f235.n106.z1.fidonet.org) (David Wachenschwanz)

9-55 **Consortium Update:** An informal newsletter about happenings in the SPIRES Consortium. *Quarterly*

> *i* ± consortium@forsythe.stanford.edu (Bitnet: CONSORTIUM@STANFORD)

9-56 **Copt-Net Newsletter:** News, activities, and services of the Coptic Orthodox Churches and Coptic communities outside Egypt. Topics include history of the Coptic Orthodox Church, biographies of key Church figures, tradition, art, and archaeology. *Quarterly, on average*

> *i* ± bassili@cs.arizona.edu (Amgad Bassili)
>
> **Archive:** FTP cs.bu.edu in /CN/newsletters/; gopher gopher.cic.net

9-57 **CORE:** An electronic journal of poetry, fiction, essays, and criticism. *Monthly*

> *i* ± rita@etext.archive.umich.edu (Rita Rouvalis). Please specify if you are subscribing to CORE.
>
> **Archive:** FTP etext.archive.umich.edu in /pub/Zines/Literary/CORE-Zine

9-58 **Cosmic Update:** Identifies new computer software from the National Aeronautics and Space Administration (NASA) made available for international use. *Monthly*

> *i* ± service@cossack.cosmic.uga.edu

9-59 **CPSR/PDX Newsletter:** On-line newsletter of the Portland, Oregon, chapter of Computer Professionals for Social Responsibility. *Monthly*

> *i* ± erikn@boa.mitron.tek.com (Erik Nilsson)
>
> **Archive:** erikn@boa.mitron.tek.com (Erik Nilsson)

9-60 **CRTNet—Communication Research and Theory Network:** On all topics related to human communications.

> *i* t3b@psuvm.psu.edu (Bitnet: T3B@PSUVM) (Tom Benson)
>
> ± listserv@psuvm.psu.edu (Bitnet: LISTSERV@PSUVM) [body = SUBSCRIBE CRTNET first-name last-name]
>
> **Archive:** listserv@psuvm.psu.edu [body = INDEX CRTNET]

9-61 **ctt-Digest—The comp.text.tex Newsgroup Digest:** Digest of posts appearing on the Usenet newsgroup comp.text.tex that do not originate on INFO-TeX. Combined with INFO-

TeX and TeX-Pubs, it completes the triangle of major network-based communications on TeX-related topics. *Daily*

i `bed_gdg@shsu.edu` (Bitnet: `BED_GDG@SHSU`) (George D. Greenwade)

± `listserv@shsu.edu` (Bitnet: `LISTSERV@SHSU`) [body = `SUBSCRIBE CTT-DIGEST`]

Archive: FTP `niord.shsu.edu` in [`FILESERV.COMP-TEXT-TEX`]

9-62 **Cult of the Dead Cow:** Topics and form vary wildly, covering religion, defecation, cows, simulated and real capture files from BBSs, politics, very occasional hack/phreak articles, poetry, short stories, interviews, and mindless raving. Common themes: dead cows and extreme wackiness. *2–4 new files per month, on average*

i `obscure@mindvox.phantom.com` (Paul Leonard)

± Carried on various computer bulletin boards, including Demon Roach Underground (806) 794-4362

Archive: FTP `ftp.eff.org` in `/pub/cud/cdc/`

9-63 **Current Cites:** Articles on the use of technology in libraries, covering optical disk technologies, computer networks and networking, information transfer, expert systems and artificial intelligence, and hypermedia and multimedia. *Monthly*

i ± `cites@library.berkeley.edu`

Archive: FTP `ftp.lib.berkeley.edu` in `pub/Current.Cites` or `ftp.cni.org` in `current.cites`

9-64 **Cyberspace Vanguard:** News, interviews, reviews, and articles on science fiction and fantasy media, comics, and animation, published in electronic form (free) and hard copy (for a nominal charge). *Every two months*

i `cn577@Cleveland.Freenet.Edu` or `tlg4@po.cwru.edu` (TJ Goldstein)

± `cn577@Cleveland.Freenet.edu`

Archive: FTP `quartz.rutgers.edu` or `etext.archive.umich.edu` in `/pub/Zines/Sci_Fi/Cyberspace.Vanguard`

9-65 **Dargonzine—The Magazine of the Dargon Project:** Publishes stories written for the Dargon Project, a shared-world sword-and-sorcery anthology. *Irregular*

i ± `white@duvm.bitnet` (To subscribe or unsubscribe, include user id, full name, and the preferred file transfer format: DISK DUMP, PUNCH/MAIL, or SENDFILE/NETDATA. Non-Bitnet subscribers have only one option: mail)

Archive: FTP `etext.archive.umich.edu` in `/pub/Zines/Sci-fi/DargonZine`

9-66 **DATA ENTRIES:** Covers events at the Mary Evelyn Blagg-Huey Library in Denton, Texas, as well as developments in public services and the Woman's Collection. *Irregular*

i `s_natale@twu.edu` (Bitnet: `S_NATALE@TWU`) (Joe Natale)

± `s_natale@twu` (Bitnet: `S_NATALE@TWU.EDU`)

Archive: e-mail to *i* specifying specific issues

9-67 **Dateline—Starfleet:** Fanzine providing news and analysis of the various Star Trek television series and motion pictures. Accessible from the Star Trek: The Club forum software library on the America Online network. Distributed informally to other sites around the country. No subscription or mailing list. *Monthly*

i data1701d@aol.com (Bill Mason)

Archive: FTP sumex-aim.stanford.edu

9-68 **DDN Management Bulletin:** Communicates official policy, procedures, and other information of concern to management personnel at Defense Data Network facilities. *Irregular*

i nic@nic.ddn.mil

Archive: FTP nic.ddn.mil in /ddn-news/

9-69 **DECNEWS for Education and Research:** Information on new Digital Equipment Corporation products and services, customer implementations, and various Internet and Digital resources available. *Monthly*

i decnews@akocoa.enet.dec.com (Anne Marie McDonald)

± listserv@ubvm.cc.buffalo.edu (Bitnet: LISTSERV@UBVM) [body = SUBSCRIBE DECNEWS]

Archive: FTP gatekeeper.dec.com in /pub/DEC/DECinfo/; listserv@ubvm.cc.buffalo.edu (Bitnet: LISTSERV@UBVM) [body = INDEX DECNEWS]

9-70 **DECnews for Unix:** Electronic newsletter from Digital Equipment Corporation containing product and service information of interest to the Digital Unix community. *Every three weeks*

i ± decnews-unix-request@pa.dec.com (Russ Jones)

Archive: FTP gatekeeper.dec.com in /pub/DEC/DECinfo/DECnews-UNIX

9-71 **Del Rey Internet Newsletter:** Publication data, news, and informative articles from the editors at Del Rey Books, the science-fiction and fantasy publisher. *Monthly*

i ± ekh@panix.com (Ellen Key Harris); Usenet newsgroup rec.arts.sf.written

Archive: gopher gopher.panix.com; fileserver: delrey@tachyon.com [body= help]

9-72 **Delaware Valley Rail Passenger:** Newsletter of the Delaware Valley Association of Railroad Passengers. Includes news about rail and transit services in the greater Philadelphia area and analysis of transportation issues, budgets, politics, planning, and management. (Hard copy available with photographs and special material.) *Monthly*

i iekp898@tjuvm.tju.edu (Bitnet: IEKP898@TJUVM) (Matthew Mitchell)

± listserv@cunyvm.bitnet [body = RINDEX RAILROADS]

9-73 **DevelopNet News:** On technology transfer in international development. (See also DEVEL-L in Chapter 1.) *Monthly*

i ± vita@gmuvax.gmu.edu (Bitnet: VITA@GMUVAX) (R.R. Ronkin)

Archive: e-mail to *i*.

9-74   **Disaster Research:** Newsletter dealing with hazards and disasters. Includes articles on recent events and policy developments, ongoing research, and upcoming meetings. *Every two to three weeks*

    i `hazards@vaxf.colorado.edu` (Bitnet: `HAZARDS@COLORADO`) (David Butler)

    ± `mailserv@vaxf.colorado.edu` (Bitnet: `MAILSERV@COLORADO`) [body = `SUBSCRIBE HAZARDS`]

    Archive: `mailserv@vaxf.colorado.edu` (Bitnet: `MAILSERV@COLORADO`) [body = `INDEX HAZARDS`]

9-75   **Distance Education Online Symposium (DEOSNEWS):** Consists of DEOSNEWS, a biweekly, international, electronic journal about distance education, and DEOS-L, an international discussion forum about distance education. *Biweekly*

    i `morten@nki.no` (Morten Flate Paulsen)

    ± `listserv@psuvm.psu.edu` [body = `SUBSCRIBE DEOSNEWS`]

    Archive: `listserv@psuvm.psu.edu` [body = `INDEX DEOSNEWS`]

9-76   **Donosy:** Daily news on Polish and related topics, in Polish. English translation is available from `przemek@ndcvx.cc.nd.edu` *Daily*

    i `Donosy@fuw.edu.pl`

    ± `przemek@ndcvx.cc.nd.edu` (US & Canadian subscribers); `donosy@plearn.bitnet` (all others)

    Archive: e-mail to *i*

9-77   **Drosophila Information Newsletter:** An offshoot of DIS, the Drosophila Information Service. *Quarterly*

    i `matthewk@ucs.indiana.edu` (Bitnet: `MATTHEWK@IUBACS`) (Kathy Matthews)

    ± `listserv@iubvm.ucs.indiana.edu` (Bitnet: `LISTSERV@IUBVM`) [body = `SUBSCRIBE DIS-L`]

    Archive: FTP `ftp.bio.indiana.edu` in `/flybase/news/`

9-78   **DYRDYMALKI:** News digest derived from the Polish press. (See also POLAND-L in Chapter 1.) *Bi-weekly*

    i `zbigniew@engin.umich.edu` (Zbigniew J. Pasek)

    ± `zbigniew@engin.umich.edu`

    Archive: FTP `tirana.berkeley.edu` in `/pub/VARIA/polish/dir_dyrdymalki` or `galaxy.uci.agh.edu.pl` in `/pub/e-press/dyrdymalki` or `laserspark.anu.edu.au` in `/pub/polish/dyrdymalki`; gopher `tirana.berkeley.edu`

9-79   **EARNEST:** The European Advanced Research Network Newsletter

    i `grange@frors12` (Nadine Grange) or `a79@taunivm` (David Sitman)

    ± `listserv@frors12.bitnet` (Bitnet: `LISTSERV@FRORS12`) [body = `SUBSCRIBE EARNEST first-name last-name`]

9-80   **Education Policy Analysis Archives:** Articles and reviews dealing with education policy at all levels and in many nations. *Irregular* *i* atgvg@asuvm.inre.asu.edu (Bitnet: ATGVG@ASUACAD) (Gene V. Glass)

± listserv@asuvm.inre.asu.edu (Bitnet: LISTSERV@ASUACAD) [body = SUBSCRIBE EDPOLYAR]

Archive: listserv@asuvm.inre.asu.edu (Bitnet: LISTSERV@ASUACAD) [body = GET EDPOLYAR FILELIST]

9-81 **EDUPAGE:** A summary of some of the week's news items on information technology, provided by EDUCOM. *Weekly*

i ± edupage@educom.edu (to subscribe, include name, institution name, and e-mail address)

9-82 **EFFector Online—The Electronic Frontier Foundation, Inc:** News, information, and discussion about the world of computer-based communications media that constitute the electronic frontier. Covers freedom of speech in digital media, privacy rights, censorship, standards of responsibility, policy issues such as the development of a national information infrastructure, and intellectual property. *Every two weeks*

i editors@eff.org

± eff-request@eff.org; Usenet newsgroup comp.org.eff.news

Archive: FTP ftp.eff.org in /pub/EFF/newsletters/; gopher gopher.eff.org; WAIS at wais.eff.org

9-83 **EJASA:** The Electronic Journal of the Astronomical Society of the Atlantic, dedicated to amateur and professional astronomy and space exploration, and to the social and educational needs of ASA members. *Monthly*

i klaes@verga.enet.dec.com (Larry Klaes)

± The EJASA is currently available only through the Usenet newsgroups sci.astro and sci.space and the ASA BBS, (404) 985-0408, 300/1200 baud

Archive: FTP chara.gsu.edu in /pub/ejasa/; gopher gopher.cic.net

9-84 **EJOURNAL:** Covers implications of electronic documents and networks and the theory and praxis surrounding the creation, transmission, storage, interpretation, alteration, and replication of electronic text. Also covers broader implications of computer-mediated networks. *Irregular*

i ejournal@rachel.albany.edu (Bitnet: EJOURNAL@ALBNYVMS) (Ted Jennings)

± listserv@albany.edu (Bitnet: LISTSERV@ALBANY) [body = SUSCRIBE EJRNL]

Archive: listserv@albany.bitnet [body = GET EJRNL CONTENTS]

9-85 **Electronic AIR:** Newsletter for institutional researchers and college and university planners. Reports on news, publications, position openings, requests for help, etc. *Bi-weekly*

i nelson_l@plu (Larry Nelson)

± listserv@vtvm1 [body = SUSCRIBE AIR-L]

Archive: e-mail to *i*

9-86 **Electronic Hebrew Users Newsletter (E-Hug):** Covers all things relating to the use of Hebrew, Yiddish, Judesmo, and Aramaic on computers. Addresses questions on use of the Hebrew alphabet on computers, and on software or Hebrew-related resources. *Every 1-2 weeks, on average*

i well!ari@apple.com (Ari Davidow)

± listserv@dartcms1.bitnet (Bitnet: LISTSERV@DARTCMS1) [body = SUSCRIBE E-HUG]

Archive: listserv@dartcms1 (Bitnet: LISTSERV@DARTCMS1) [body = INDEX E-HUG]

9-87 **Electronic Journal of Communication/La Revue Electronique de Communication (EJC/REC):** Bilingual English/French academic journal devoted to the study of communication theory, research, practice, and policy. *Twice a year*

i winter@ucc.uwindsor.ca (Jim Winter) or support@vm.its.rpi.edu (Bitnet: SUPPORT@RPITSVM)

± comserve@vm.its.rpi.edu (Bitnet: COMSERVE@RPITSVM) [body = JOIN EJCREC]

Archive: comserve@vm.its.rpi.edu (Bitnet: COMSERVE@RPITSVM) [body = SEND EJCREC DIRECTRY]; gopher gopher.cic.net

9-88 **End Process:** Magazine of visuals and impact. GIFs available monthly. Mainly a print publication, but offers a variety of image files for distribution. *Quarterly*

i ± ed@cwis.unomaha.edu (Ed Stastny)

9-89 **Energy Ideas:** Articles and case studies on the use of energy-efficient and renewable-energy technologies in public-sector facilities. *Monthly*

i ei@igc.apc.org (Jonathan Kleinman)

± ei@igc.apc.org; EcoNet conference climate.news

Archive: All back issues remain posted on EcoNet's conference climate.news

9-90 **Energy Research in Israel Newsletter:** Disseminates local and international information on energy research. *Irregular*

i wolff@ilncrd.bitnet (Bitnet: WOLFF@ILNCRD) (Dr. Michael Wolff)

± listserv@taunivm.bitnet (Bitnet: LISTSERV@TAUNIVM) [body = SUBSCRIBE ENERGY-L]

9-91 **ENEWS—An International Newsletter on Energy Efficiency Issues in the Developing Countries:** Informs people in developing countries of ongoing projects, shares brief analyses of important energy-related issues, and disseminates information on potential sources of funding and interesting publications. *Three issues per year*

i enews@fem.unicamp.br (Gilberto Jannuzzi)

± listserv@fem.unicamp.br [body = SUBSCRIBE L-ENEWS]

9-92 **Erofile:** Provides reviews of the latest books on French and Italian studies, including literary criticism, cultural studies, film studies, pedagogy, and software.

i ± erofile@ucsbuxa.ucsb.edu (Bitnet: EROFILE@UCSBUXA)

9-93 **Ethnomusicology Research Digest:** For teachers, researchers, librarians, and students interested in ethnomusicology. News, discussion, queries, bibliographies, and archives. *Irregular* *i* signell@umdd.umd.edu (Bitnet: SIGNELL@UMDD) (Dr. Karl Signell)

± listserv@umdd.umd.edu (Bitnet: LISTSERV@UMDD) [body = SUBSCRIBE ETHMUS-L]

Archive: FTP info.umd.edu in /info/ReadingRoom/Newsletters/EthnoMusicology; telnet info.umd.edu

9-94 **EUVE Electronic Newsletter:** Newsletter issued by the Center for Extreme Ultraviolet Astrophysics, University of California at Berkeley. Contains information useful for guest observers of the EUVE science mission. *Every two weeks, on average*

i ceanews@cea.berkeley.edu or archive@cea.berkeley.edu

± ceanews@cea.berkeley.edu

Archive: FTP cea-ftp.cea.berkeley.edu in /pub/archive/newsletters/; archive@cea.berkeley.edu [body = help]

9-95 **FACE:** Central Ohio Fathers and Children for Equality Newsletter. Contains articles on visitation, custody, child support, poverty, parenting, propaganda, feminism, justice, equality, etc. (See also FREE-L in Chapter 1.) *Monthly*

i tr@cbnea.att.com (Aaron L. Hoffmeyer)

± Available via subscription to FREE-L mailing list

Archive: FTP cwgk4.chem.cwru.edu in /face

9-96 **Factsheet Five—Electric:** The electronic version of Factsheet Five, a compilation of small press magazines (or zines) with ordering information, subject matter, and reviews of the contents. *Quarterly, plus updates*

i ± jerod23@well.sf.ca.us (Jerod Pore)

Archive: FTP etext.archive.umich.edu; gopher gopher.well.sf.ca.us; BBSs around the world

9-97 **FARNET Gazette:** Newsletter for network service providers with research and education focus. *Irregular*

i breeden@farnet.org (Laura Breeden) or roblesc@farnet.org (Carlos Robles)

± gazette-request@farnet.org

Archive: FTP farnet.org in /farnet/farnet_docs/

9-98 **Federal Information News Syndicate:** News column focused on the emerging philosophy of the Information Age and issued on a subscription basis, for re-publication in all electronic and print formats. Priced at $30.00 per year for 24 issues. *Biweekly*

i ± fins@access.digex.com

9-99 **Fineart Forum:** A moderated electronic newsletter published by ISAST on behalf of ASTN, covering all applications of science and technology to the contemporary arts and music. *Monthly*

i ± fast@garnet.berkeley.edu (Bitnet: FAST@UCBGARNE) To subscribe [body = SUBSCRIBE FINE-ART]

9-100 **Flora Online:** Systematic botany, including original data-intensive studies and original programs dealing with botanical topics. *Irregular* *i* visbms@ubvms.cc.buffalo.edu (Bitnet: VISBMS@UBVMS) (Richard H. Zander)

± FTP huh.harvard.edu in /pub/newsletters/flora.online/; gopher gopher.cic.net

9-101 **Florida Extension Beekeeping Newsletter:** Covers bees, beekeeping, apiculture, and associated issues. (See also BEE-L in Chapter 1.) *Monthly*

i mts@gnv.ifas.ufl.edu (Bitnet: MTS@IFASGNV) (Dr. Malcolm T. Sanford)

± Subscribe to BEE-L or e-mail to *i*

Archive: e-mail to *i*

9-102 **Florida SunFlash:** A moderated, e-mail-based news service from the Sun Microsystems office in Ft. Lauderdale, FL. Provides relevant technical and marketing information about Sun Microsystems, its technology, and its products. *Irregular; 25-35 articles per month, posted several times per week*

i flash@sun.com or info-sunflash@sun.com (John McLaughlin)

± sunflash-request@sun.com or direct requests to local Sun office

Archive: FTP sunsite.unc.edu in /pub/sun-info/sunflash/ or sunsite.unc.edu in /pub/sun-info/sunflash/ or solar.nova.edu in /pub/sunflash/ or src.doc.ic.ac.uk in /sun/sunflash/ or ftp.uu.net in /systems/sun/sunflash/ or ftp.adelaide.edu.au in /pub/sun/sunflash/; e-mail sunflash info@sun.com or info-sunflash@sun.com for automatic reply describing SunFlash in detail

9-103 **FOREFRONTS:** Newsletter highlighting scientific research being conducted using the Cornell Theory Center's supercomputing resources, and related scientific visualization. For hardcopy subscription information, e-mail herzog@tc.cornell.edu (Michael Herzog). *Quarterly*

i allison@tc.cornell.edu (Allison Loperfido)

± gopher gopher.tc.cornell.edu

Archive: e-mail to *i*

9-104 **French Language Press Review:** Covers the press and the French Ministry of Foreign Affairs.

Archive: Gopher gopher.cic.net

9-105 **Fulbright Educational Advising Newsletter (FULBNEWS):** For advisers in Brazil under the sponsorship of the Fulbright Commission of Brazil. Geared to professionals involved in educational advising and international education exchange. *Three times a year: March, July, and November*

i fulb@brlncc (Rita Monteiro)

± listserv@brlncc.bitnet (Bitnet: LISTSERV@BRLNCC) [body = SUBSCRIBE FULBNEWS]

Archive: listserv@brlncc.bitnet (Bitnet: LISTSERV@BRLNCC) [body = INDEX FULBNEWS]

9-106 **Funhouse:** Newsletter of alternative fun. Includes articles on offbeat films, music, literature, and experiences. *3-4 times a year*

i ± jeffdove@well.sf.ca.us

Archive: FTP etext.archive.umich.edu in /pub/Zines/Funhouse/ or
ftp.cic.net; gopher gopher.well.sf.ca.us

9-107   **FutureCulture FAQ:** Guide to resources and information on technoculture, new edge, cyberpunk, and cyberculture. Covers a wide variety of on- and offline resources and media. A document that is regularly revised, rather than a true e-serial. *Quarterly*

i ahawks@nyx.cs.du.edu

± future-request@nyx.cs.du.edu [body = SEND FAQ or SEND INFO];

Archive: FTP ftp.eff.org in /pub/cud/papers/future or
ftp.css.sitd.umich.edu in /poli/future.culture.d or
ftp.u.washington.edu in /public/alt.cyberpunk/; gopher
gopher.cic.net

9-108   **GLOSAS News (GLObal Systems Analysis and Simulating):** Newsletter divided into two
parts, dedicated to global electronic education (GN/Global Education) and to the use of simulation for the promotion of peace and the care of the natural environment (GN/Gobal Peace
Gaming). (See also GLOSAS-L in Chapter 1.) *GN/Global Education—quarterly; GN/Gobal
Peace Gaming—7–8 times a year*

i anton@vax2.concordia.ca (Anton Ljutic)

± listserv@vm1.mcgill.ca [body = SUBSCRIBE GLOSAS first-name last-name]

9-109   **GNET—Global Networking:** An archive/journal for documents pertaining to the effort to bring
the Net to lesser-developed nations and the poorer parts of developed nations. *Monthly, on
average*

i lpress@dhvx20.csudh.edu (Larry Press)

± gnet_request@dhvx20.csudh.edu

Archive: FTP dhvx20.csudh.edu in /global_net/

9-110   **GNU's Bulletin:** Newsletter of the Free Software Foundation, with news about the GNU
Project. *Semi-annual (January and June)*

i gnu@prep.ai.mit.edu

± info-gnu-request@prep.ai.mit.edu

9-111   **Grochz Kapusta:** News summaries on political, social, and cultural life in Poland, with humorous
commentary. (See also POLAND-L in Chapter 1.) *Weekly*

i eikuras@plkrcy11.bitnet (Marian Kuras)

± bielewcz@uwpg02.uwinnipeg.ca

Archive: FTP tirana.berkeley.edu in /pub/VARIA/polish/dir_groch/

9-112   **Handicap Digest:** Digest of articles about issues affecting the handicapped, taken from the
Usenet newsgroup misc.handicap and various Fidonet conferences. Articles dealing with
visual disabilities are now distributed separately in the Blind News Digest.

i wtm@bunker.afd.olivetti.com (Bill McGarry)

± listserv@vm1.nodak.edu (Bitnet: LISTSERV@NDSUVM1) [body = SUBSCRIBE
L-HCAP]

Archive: `listserv@vm1.nodak.edu` (Bitnet: `LISTSERV@NDSUVM1`) [body = `INDEX L-HCAP`]

9-113 **HICNet Newsletter (MEDNEWS—The Health InfoCo Newsletter):** A medical newsletter (large; broken up into sections to facilitate network movement). *Weekly*

i `david@stat.com` (David Dodell)

± `listserv@asuacad.bitnet` (Bitnet: `LISTSERV@ASUACAD`) [body = `SUBSCRIBE MEDNEWS`]

Archive: `listserv@asuacad.bitnet` (Bitnet: `LISTSERV@ASUACAD`) [body = `INDEX MEDNEWS`]; FTP `vm1.nodak.edu` in `/hicnews/`; e-mail `david@stat.com` or `hicn-notify-request@stat.com` to subscribe to a notification list (which alerts subscribers to new releases available via FTP)

9-114 **High Weirdness by Email:** A publication of bizarre literature. Note: this document is updated regularly. *Irregular*

i `mporter@nyx.cs.du.edu`

Archive: FTP `etext.archive.umich.edu` in `/zines/weirdness/` or `slopoke.mlb.semi.harris.com` in `/pub/weirdness/`; Usenet newsgroups `alt.slack` and `alt.discordia` (back issues are superseded by each subsequent edition)

9-115 **Holy Temple of Mass Consumption:** Rantings, ravings, news, and latest adventures of the newest affiliate organization of the Church of the SubGenius. *Monthly*

i ± `slack@ncsu.edu` (Pope John Paul George Ringo)

Archive: FTP `quartz.rutgers.edu` in `/pub/journals/HToMC/`

9-116 **HORT-L:** Newsletter from Virginia Tech Horticulture Department. *Monthly*

i `pdrelf@vtvm1.cc.vt.edu` (Bitnet: `PDRELF@VTVM1`) (Diane Relf)

± `listserv@vtvm1.cc.vt.edu` (Bitnet: `LISTSERV@VTVM1`) [body = `SUBSCRIBE HORT-L first-name last-name`]

9-117 **Hot Off the Tree (HOTT):** UCSD Library's Technology Watch Information Group newsletter. Contains excerpts and abstracts of articles from trade journals, popular periodicals, and online sources on developments and issues in computer technology, networking, information transfer, and retrieval. *Weekly*

i `sjurist@ucsd.edu` (Bitnet: `SJURIST@UCSD`) (Susan Jurist)

± `listserv@ucsd.edu` (Bitnet: `LISTSERV@UCSD`) [body = `SUBSCRIBE HOTT-LIST`]

Archive: e-mail to *i* , specify ASCII or MicroSoft Word format

9-118 **Hungarian Electronic Exchange (Magyar Elektronikus Tozsde):** News about the Hungarian stock and commodity exchange. *Weekly*

i ± `h4458orc@ella.hu` (Bitnet: `H4458ORC@HUELLA`) (Csaba Orczan)

9-119 **I.S.P.O.B. Bulletin YSSTI:** YSSTI is the Yugoslav System for Scientific and Technology Information. The Bulletin contains news about the functioning and development of YSSTI. *Quarterly*

i `sostaric@uni-mb.ac.mail.yu` or `sostaric@ean.uni-mb.ac.mail.yu`
(Bitnet: DAVOR%RCUM@YUBGEF51) (Davor Sostaric)

± `POB@UNI-MB.AC.MAIL.YU` (Bitnet: `POB%RCUM@YUBGEF51`) [body = SUBSCRIBE
P.O.B.]

Archive: `POB@UNI-MB.AC.MAIL.YU` (Bitnet: `POB%RCUM@YUBGEF51`) [body = GET
number volnumber]

9-120 **ICS Electrozine—Information, Control, Supply:** An e-zine containing stories, articles, editorials, letters, etc. on topics including the unknown, the Internet, society, philosophy, music, role-playing games, and science. *Every two weeks*

i ± `org_zine@wsc.colorado.edu`

9-121 **IHOUSE-L International Voice Newsletter Prototype List:** Electronic version of publication of the International Office of Washington University. Contains articles of interest to international students and scholars, professors, administrators, and others interested in and involved with our international visitors. *Twice a semester plus ongoing Listserv version*

i `c73221dc@wuvmd` (Doyle Cozadd)

± `listserv@wuvmd.bitnet` (Bitnet: `listserv@wuvmd`) [body = SUBSCRIBE
IHOUSE-L]

9-122 **In-Fur-Nation:** Electronic version of In-Fur-Nation, the news and information resource for anthropomorphic animal fandom (furry fandom), including the ConFurence Progress Report. *Quarterly, on average*

i ± `john@ontek.com` (John Alan Stanley)

9-123 **Information Networking News:** Presents case studies from worldwide library sites that will help other institutions thinking of implementing a network. Also highlights new developments in the market, with evaluations. *Quarterly*

i `gartner@vax.ox.ac.uk` (Richard Gartner)

± `listserv@idbsu.bitnet` [body = SUBSCRIBE CDROMLAN]; gopher
`bubl.bath.ac.uk`

Archive: FTP `hydra.uwo.ca` in `/libsoft/`

9-124 **Instant Math Preprints (IMP):** Database of abstracts of math preprints, searchable by author, title words, abstract words, and other words. Also the full text of preprints, in electronic form, accessible via anonymous FTP.

i `katherine_branch@quickmail.cis.yale.edu` (Katherine Branch)

Archive: To use IMP via Internet, you need a copy of a communications program called
TN3270. Using TN3270, connect to `yalevm.ycc.yale.edu` user id = Math1 (or
Math2, Math3, Math4, or Math5), password = Math1 (or Math2, Math3, Math4,
or Math5), operator ID = Math1 (or Math2, Math3, Math4, or Math5)

9-125 **Information Technology Times:** Covers information-technology services, facilities, and activities at University of California, Davis. *Quarterly*

i `isbalkits@ucdavis.edu` (Ivars Balkits)

Archive: FTP `silo.ucdavis.edu` in `/it-newsletter/`; gopher
`gopher.ucdavis.edu`

9-126 **Internet Business Journal—Commercial Opportunities in the Networking Age:** For businesses interested in staying informed about commercial opportunities on the Internet. News of successful business ventures on or related to the Internet, Bitnet, and affiliated networks; details of legislation changes affecting commercial activity on the Internet. Not free. *Six times a year, with six special supplements*

    i `441495@acadvm1.uottawa.ca` (Michael Strangelove)

9-127 **Internet Monthly Report:** A status report from the NSFNET operations groups, the regional networks, the Information Centers, The Internet Activities Board (IAB), the Internet Engineering Task Force (IETF), the Internet Research Task Force (IRTF), other organizations and network research groups. *Monthly*

    i `cooper@isi.edu`

    ± `imr-request@isi.edu`

    Archive: FTP `venera.isi.edu` in `/in-notes/` or `nic.merit.edu` in `/internet/newsletters/internet.monthly.report/`; mailserver `rfc-info@isi.edu` [body = `help: ways_to_get_imrs`]

9-128 **Internet Radio Journal:** Information and discussion pertaining to domestic broadcast radio (radio broadcasting that is primarily for reception within the same country from which it originates).

    i `wdp@airwaves.chi.il.us` (William Pfeiffer)

    ± `journal@airwaves.chi.il.us`; Usenet newsgroup `rec.radio.broadcasting`

    Archive: FTP `deja-vu.aiss.uiuc.edu` in `/misc/rec.radio.b-cast` (for archive help, e-mail `rrb@deja-vu.aiss.uiuc.edu` [subject = `HELP FILE`]

9-129 **Interpersonal Computing and Technology Journal—An Electronic Journal for the 21st Century:** IPCT addresses concerns about the use of electronic journals as outlets for scholarly research, including copyright, coordination with print publication, and the electronic journal as an outlet for dissemination of scholarly studies suitable for credit toward promotion and tenure. *Quarterly or semi-annually, depending on submissions*

    i `berge@guvax.georgetown.edu` (Zane L. Berge)

    ± `listserv@guvm.georgetown.edu` [body = `SUBSCRIBE IPCT-L`]

    Archive: `listserv@guvm.georgetown.edu` [body = `INDEX IPCT-L`]

9-130 **Intertext—An Electronic Fiction Magazine:** Contains all kinds of material, including mainstream stories, fantasy, horror, science fiction, and humor. *Bimonthly*

    i ± `jsnell@ocf.berkeley.edu` or `intertxt@network.ucsd.edu` (Jason Snell) (For subscription, specify ASCII, PostScript, or FTP notification)

    Archive: FTP `network.ucsd.edu` in `/intertext/`

9-131 **IOUDAIOS Review:** A review journal of the international electronic forum for scholarship on Early Judaism and Christian Origins. *Irregular*

    i `dreimer4@mach1.wlu.ca` (David Reimer)

    ± `listserv@vm1.yorku.ca` (Bitnet: `LISTSERV@YORKVM1`) [body = `SUBSCRIBE IOUDAIOS`]

Archive: `listserv@vml.yorku.ca` (Bitnet: `LISTSERV@YORKVM1`) [body = `INDEX IOUDAIOS`]

9-132 **IR-LIST Digest (IR-L Digest):** Papers, meeting announcements, information searches, job listings, conference proceedings, bibliographies, dissertation abstracts, and other material about information retrieval. *Weekly*

i ± `ncgur@uccmvsa.ucop.edu` (Bitnet: `NCGUR@UCCMVSA`) (Nancy Gusack)

Archive: `listserv@uccmvsa.ucop.edu` (Bitnet: `LISTSERV@UCCMVSA`) [body = `INDEX IR-L`]

9-133 **Issues In Science and Technology Librarianship:** Provides short, substantial articles on timely and important topics in science and technology librarianship, as well as conference and workshop reports. *March, May, August, October; ALA Meeting Updates in January and June; special bulletins irregularly*

i ± `acrlsts@hal.unm.edu` (Harry Llull)

Archive: e-mail to *i*

9-134 **Jonathan's Space Report:** Summary of spaceflight activity. *Irregular*

i ± `mcdowell@urania.harvard.edu` (Jonathan McDowell)

9-135 **Journal of Computing in Higher Education:** Scholarly essays, reviews, reports, and research articles about the issues, problems, and research associated with instructional technology. Articles representing all aspects of academic computing are encouraged. *Biannual, soon to be quarterly*

i ± `cmacknight@ucs.umass.edu` (Carol B. MacKnight)

Archive: e-mail to *i*

9-136 **Journal of Extension:** Expands and updates the research and knowledge base for extension professionals and other adult educators, sharing successful educational applications, original and applied research findings, scholarly opinions, educational resources, and challenges. *Quarterly*

i `hoymand@joe.uwex.edu` (Dirk Herr-Hoyman)

± `almanac@joe.uwex.edu` [body = `SUBSCRIBE JOE`]; FTP `joe.uwex.edu`; gopher `joe.uwex.edu`; WAIS `joe.src` on `joe.uwex.edu`; e-mail `almanac@joe.uwex.edu` with the single line `send joe announcement` for summary of current issue

9-137 **Journal of Fluids Engineering:** Contains only the raw research data, not the entire journal.

i `telionis@vtvml.cc.vt.edu` (Dr. Demetri Telionis)

Archive: FTP `borg.lib.vt.edu` in `/pub/JFE/`

9-138 **Journal of Technology Education:** Scholarly discussion on topics relating to technology education (a subject area in the public schools formerly known as "industrial arts"). *Two issues per year (fall and spring)*

i `msanders@vtvml.cc.vt.edu` (Mark Sanders)

± `listserv@vtvml.cc.vt.edu` [body = `SUBSCRIBE JTE-L`]

Archive: FTP `borg.lib.vt.edu` in `/pub/JTE/`; `listserv@vtvml.cc.vt.edu` [body =`INDEX JTE-L`]; WAIS `jte.src`; gopher `gopher.cic.net`

9-139 **Journal of the International Academy of Hospitality Research:** Covers basic and applied research in all aspects of hospitality and tourism. This journal is not free; for more information send e-mail to the contact address. *Irregular*

  i `jiahred@vtvm1.cc.vt.edu`

  ± `listserv@vtvm1.cc.vt.edu` [body = SUBSCRIBE JIAHR-L]

  Archive: `listserv@vtvm1.cc.vt.edu` [body = SUBSCRIBE JIAHR-L] INDEX JIAHR-L]; FTP `borg.lib.vt.edu` in `/pub/JIAHR`; WAIS `jiahr.src`

9-140 **Journal of Undergraduate Research:** Original undergraduate research, including all liberal art and humanities subjects. *Semi-annual*

  i `fox@csf.colorado.edu`

  Archive: FTP `spot.colorado.edu` in `/spot/usr/ftp/eforum/honors/journal_ugr/`; gopher `csf.colorado.edu`

9-141 **Kanji of the Day:** Introduction to the Japanese Writing System. Each issue contains the derivation of a Japanese character, its etymology, meaning, pronunciation, and a short list of compound words using this character. *Weekly, on average*

  i `stueber@vax.mpiz-koeln.mpg.dbp.de`

  ± `LISTSERV@MITVMA.BITNET` [body = SUB NIHONGO]; Usenet newsgroup `sci.lang.japan`

  Archive: Gopher `gopher.cic.net`; FTP `uesama.tjp.washington.edu` in `/pub/Japanese/KanjiOfTheDay` or `ftp.uwtc.washington.edu` in `/pub/Japanese/KanjiOfTheDay`

9-142 **KIDLINK Newsletter:** KIDLINK is a grassroots initiative aimed at getting children 10-15 involved in global dialog, organized into one-year projects called KIDS-92, KIDS-93, etc. The Newsletter is an information bulletin for teachers, participants, sponsors, mediators, promoters, and others. *Approximately every second month*

  i ± `opresno@extern.uio.no` (Odd de Presno)

  Archive: `listserv@vm1.nodak.edu` (Bitnet: LISTSERV@NDSUVM1) [body = GET KIDLINK MASTER]

9-143 **Laboratory Primate Newsletter:** Information about nonhuman primates and related matters, for scientists who use these animals in their research and those whose work supports such research. Information on care and breeding for laboratory research, general information and news, requests for research material or information related to specific research problems, etc. *Quarterly*

  i `primate@brownvm.brown.edu` (Bitnet: PRIMATE@BROWNVM) (Judith E. Schrier)

  ± `listserv@brownvm.brown.edu` [body = SUBSCRIBE LPN-L]

9-144 **Law and Politics Book Review:** Seeks to comprehensively review books of interest to political scientists studying law, the courts, and the judicial process. *Irregular, although generally once a week*

  i `mzltov@nwu.edu` (Herbert Jacob)

  ± `listserv@mizzou1.missouri.edu` [body = SUBSCRIBE PSRT-L]

Archive: `listserv@mizzou1.missouri.edu` [body = `GET LPBR PACKAGE`]; gopher `gopher.nwu.edu`

9-145 **LC Cataloging Newsline:** Cataloging activities at the Library of Congress, including new or revised policy decisions, technological developments, new publications, and employment opportunities in cataloging. *At least quarterly (January, April, July, October)*

i `hiatt@mail.loc.gov` (Robert M. Hiatt)

± `listserv@sun7.loc.gov` [body = `SUBSCRIBE LCCN`]

Archive: `listserv@sun7.loc.gov` [body = `INDEX LCCN`]

9-146 **Leonardo Electronic News:** Distributed by ISAST, this newsletter carries items linked to the journal Leonardo such as Words on Works, member news, Leonardo calls for papers, product evaluations, book reviews, and a calendar. *Monthly*

i `malloy@well.sf.ca.us` or `fast@garnet.berkeley.edu` (Judy Malloy)

± `fast@garnet.berkeley.edu` [body = `SUB LEN`, your name, email address and postal address.]

9-147 **LIBRES:** Library and Information Science Research Electronic Conference, designed to foster library and information science research and support the development of the library and information science researcher knowledge base. *Monthly*

i `dkovacs@kentvm.kent.edu` (Bitnet: `DKOVACS@KENTVM`) (Diane Kovacs)

± `listserv@kentvm.kent.edu` (Bitnet: `LISTSERV@KENTVMD`) [body = `SUBSCRIBE LIBRES`];

Archive: `listserv@kentvm.kent.edu` (Bitnet: `LISTSERV@KENTVMD`) [body = `INDEX LIBRES`]; gopher `ksuvxa.kent.edu`

9-148 **Liminal:** An alternative scholarly culture studies magazine. *3 issues a year*

i ± `swilbur@andy.bgsu.edu`

Archive: FTP `etext.archive.umich.edu` in `/pub/Zines/Liminal/`

9-149 **Link Letter:** The Merit/NSFNET newsletter. *Irregular*

i `nsfnet-info@merit.edu` (Patricia Smith)

± `nsfnet-linkletter-request@merit.edu`

Archive: FTP `nic.merit.edu` in `/newsletters/linkletter/`

9-150 **List Review Service:** Brief reviews of e-mail distribution lists, primarily Bitnet Listserv, with usage statistics. *Irregular*

i `srcmuns@umslvma.umsl.edu` (Raleigh C. Muns)

± `listserv@kentvm.kent.edu` (Bitnet: `LISTSERV@KENTVM`) [body = `SUBSCRIBE LIBREF-L`]

Archive: `listserv@kentvm.kent.edu` (Bitnet: `LISTSERV@KENTVM`) [body = `INDEX LIBREF-L`]

9-151 **LymeNet Newsletter:** Issues pertaining to the prevention and treatment of Lyme Disease. *2 issues per month*

i `mcg2@lehigh.edu` (Marc Gabriel)

± `listserv@lehigh.edu` [body = SUBSCRIBE LYMENET-L]

Archive: `listserv@lehigh.edu` [body = INDEX LYMENET-L]

9-152 **MAB Northern Sciences Network Newsletter:** Information Newsletter for MAB Northern Sciences Network members and other interested persons. *Twice yearly*

i `sippola@finfun.bitnet` (Anna-Liisa Sippola)

± `listserv@finhutc.bitnet` (Bitnet: LISTSERV@FINHUTC) [body = SUBSCRIBE NSNNEWS]

Archive: Available upon subscription.

9-153 **Material Science in Israel Newsletter:** Local (Israel) and international information on Material Sciences. *Irregular*

i `wolff@ilncrd.bitnet` (Michael Wolff)

± `listserv@taunivm.bitnet` (Bitnet: LISTSERV@TAUNIVM) [body = SUBSCRIBE MATERI-L]

9-154 **Matrix News:** A newsletter on cross-network issues. This newsletter is not free; for more information send e-mail to the contact address. *Monthly*

i ± `mids@tic.com` (For 12 monthly issues, online: $25 or $15 student, ASCII or PostScript, or $30 for both online and paper).

9-155 **MC Journal—Journal of Academic Media Librarianship:** Encompasses all aspects of academic media librarianship. *Irregular*

i `hslljw@ubvm.cc.buffalo.edu` (Bitnet: HSLLJW@UBVM) (Lori Widzinski)

± `listserv@ubvm.cc.buffalo.edu` (Bitnet: LISTSERV@UBVM) [body = SUBSCRIBE MCJRNL first-name last-name]

9-156 **MeckJournal:** An electronic service offered through Meckler's Electronic Publishing Division. Issues include an editorial, late-breaking news, a feature article reprinted from one of Meckler's periodicals, and other features. *Monthly*

i `meckler@jvnc.net` (Tony Abbott)

± `meckler@jvnc.net` [body = SUBSCRIBE MECKJOURNAL]

Archive: gopher `gopher.cic.net`; telnet `nicol.jvnc.net` [login = `nicol` select MC]

9-157 **Media Relations Network News (MRN News):** News and developments in college and university public relations and media placement. *Monthly*

i ± `daniel.forbush@sunysb.edu` (Dan Forbush)

9-158 **MichNet News:** The free newsletter of MichNet, Michigan's regional computer network. *Quarterly*

i `patmcg@merit.edu` (Bitnet: USERW02V@UMICHUM) (Pat McGregor)

± `mnn-request@merit.edu`

Archive: FTP `nic.merit.edu` in `michnet/michnet.news`

9-159 **MICnews:** Microcomputer and advanced-workstation computing news relevant to the computing populace at the University of California, Los Angeles.

± listserv@uclacn1.ucla.edu [body = SUBSCRIBE MICNEWS]

9-160   **Modal Analysis:** The International Journal of Analytical and Experimental Modal Analysis: Free distribution of the abstracts of papers appearing in Modal Analysis, prior to their print publication. Abstracts are sent to subscribers electronically as each paper is accepted for publication in the print journal. *Quarterly*

   i savage@vtvm1.cc.vt.edu (Bitnet: SAVAGE@VTVM1) (Lon Savage)

   ± listserv@vtvm1.cc.vt.edu [body = SUBSCRIBE MODAL or INDEX MODAL]; FTP borg.lib.vt.edu in /pub/MODAL/; WAIS ijaema_a.src

   Archive: No back issues available electronically. For print copies e-mail to *i*

9-161   **Mudlist:** The Totally Unofficial List of Internet MUDs. *Weekly, on average*

   i scott@glia.biostr.washington.edu

   ± mudlist@glia.biostr.washington.edu or pjc@computer-science.manchester.ac.uk

   Archive: FTP caisr2.caisr.cwru.edu in /pub/mud

9-162   **Music Theory Online (MTO):** Each issue contains a lead article on a music-theoretical topic; commentaries on past lead articles (discussion threads); plus book reviews, announcements, and new dissertation registry. *Bimonthly*

   i rothfarb@husc.harvard.edu (Bitnet: ROTHFARB@HUSC) (Lee Rothfarb)

   ± listserv@husc.harvard.edu [body = SUBSCRIBE MTO-J]

   Archive: FTP husc4.harvard.edu in /pub/smt/mto/

9-163   **Navy News Service (NAVNEWS):** Official news and information about fleet operations and exercises, personnel policies, budget actions, and more. *Weekly*

   i navnews@nctamslant.navy.mil (CDR Tim Taylor, USN)

   ± navnews@nctamslant.navy.mil [body = e-mail address]

   Archive: FTP nctamslant.navy.mil in /misc/; e-mail to *i*

9-164   **NEAR FUTURES:** Science-fiction and fantasy publishing news from Tor Books. *Irregular*

   i ± pnh@panix.com (Patrick Nielsen-Hayden)

   Archive: gopher gopher.panix.com

9-165   **NEARnet Newsletter:** For users of NEARnet and others interested in academic and research networking. *Quarterly*

   i ± nearnet-staff@nic.near.net

   Archive: FTP nic.near.net in /newsletters/

9-166   **NEARnet this Month:** Published by NEARnet User Services staff; encourages input from information liaisons at member organizations. *Monthly*

   i ± nearnet-us@nic.near.net

   Archive: FTP nic.near.net in /newsletters/

9-167   **Nekuda E-Journal:** An Israeli journal of academic articles on the Jewish settlements in Judea, Samaria, the West Bank, and Gaza and the Arab-Israeli conflict. *Monthly* *i* ± `lando@brachot.jct.ac.il` (Zvi Lando) (A small intro about yourself and/or where you are from is requested though not required of subscribers.)

9-168 **netlib-news:** Reports on the netlib software. *Quarterly*

i `ehg@research.att.com`

Archive: FTP `research.att.com` in `/netlib/news/`

9-169 **Network News:** Focuses on library and information resources on the Internet. Updates the information found in A Guide to Internet/Bitnet. *Irregular*

i `noonan@msus1.msus.edu` (Dana Noonan)

± `listserv@vm1.nodak.edu` (Bitnet: `LISTSERV@NDSUVM1`) [body = `SUBSCRIBE NNEWS first-name last-name`]

Archive: FTP `vm1.nodak.edu` in `nnews`; `listserv@vm1.nodak.edu` (Bitnet: `LISTSERV@NDSUVM1`) [body = `INDEX NNEWS`]

9-170 **Network-Audio-Bits:** Reviews of and information about current rock, pop, new age, jazz, funk, folk, and other musical genres. *Bi-monthly*

i ± `murph@maine.maine.edu` (Bitnet: `MURPH@MAINE`) (Michael A. Murphy)

Archive: FTP `dg-rtp.dg.com` in `/pub/AudioBits/`; e-mail to *i*

9-171 **Network—Nova Scotia's Industrial Technology Newsletter:** Produced by the Technology Associations Secretariat, an office-support and marketing service managed by the Nova Scotia Advanced Technology Collegium (NSATC), and shared with many Nova Scotia organizations. Includes articles submitted by participating societies as well as paid advertisements. *Bi-monthly*

i ± `vroma@nsatc.ns.ca` (Valerie Roma)

9-172 **New Horizons in Adult Education:** Current thinking and research in adult education and related fields. *3 times a year*

i `horizons@suvm.acs.syr.edu` (Bitnet: `HORIZONS@SUVM`)

± `listserv@suvm.acs.syr.edu` (Bitnet: `LISTSERV@SUVM`) [body = `SUBSCRIBE AEDNET`]

Archive: `listserv@suvm.acs.syr.edu` (Bitnet: `LISTSERV@SUVM`) [body = `INDEX AEDNET`]

9-173 **Newsbrief:** Provides a variety of information and feature articles for an audience composed primarily of UNC-Chapel Hill computer users. Class listings, meetings, demonstrations, announcements, and articles on communications developments. *Biweekly*

i `romine@uncvx1.oit.unc.edu` (Scott Romine)

± `listserv@uncvm1.bitnet` [body = `SUBSCRIBE OIT-NEWS`]

Archive: `listserv@uncvm1.bitnet` [body = `INDEX OIT-NEWS`]

9-174 **Newsletter on Serials Pricing Issues:** For librarians; covers problems of and strategies for dealing with serials pricing, as well as serial pricing news. *Irregular*

i `tuttle@gibbs.oit.unc.edu` (Marcia Tuttle)

± `listserv@gibbs.oit.unc.edu` [body = `SUBSCRIBE PRICES`]

Archive: `istserv@gibbs.oit.unc.edu` [body = `INDEX PRICES`]

9-175 **Newsline:** Newsletter describing additions to or changes in Comserve, the electronic information and discussion service for communication faculty and students. *Irregular*

i support@vm.its.rpi.edu (Bitnet: SUPPORT@RPITSVM) (Timothy Stephen or Teresa Harrison)

± comserve@vm.its.rpi.edu (Bitnet: COMSERVE@RPITSVM) [body = SUBSCRIBE NEWSLINE]

Archive: comserve@vm.its.rpi.edu (Bitnet: COMSERVE@RPITSVM) [body = SEND NEWS DIRECTRY]

9-176 **NIBNews:** Newsletter on Medical Informatics from the State University of Campinas, Brazil. Covers Latin-American activities, people, news, scientific events, publications, software, etc., in the area of computer applications in health care, medicine and biology. *Monthly*

i ± sabbatini@ccvax.unicamp.br (Bitnet: SABBATINI@BRUC) (Renato M.E. Sabbatini)

Archive: FTP ccsun.unicamp.br in /pub/medicine/documents/

9-177 **NLSNews Newsletter:** Supported by the Bureau of Labor Statistics, U.S. Department of Labor. Information of interest to the NLS research community, including status and availability of data, errors in data, summaries of research. *Quarterly*

i mcclaskie@ohsthr.bitnet (Steve McClaskie)

± nlserve@ohsthr [body = SEND SUBSCRIBE.INFO]

Archive: nlserve@ohsthr [body = SEND NLSDIR.LIS]

9-178 **Non Serviam:** Discussions on the philosophy of Max Stirner and other rebellious spirits.

i ± solan@math.uio.no (Svein Olav Nyberg)

9-179 **NorthWestNet NodeNews:** Produced by the NorthWestNet staff for distribution to its member organizations. Covers national and regional news pertinent to the growth and development of NorthWestNet services, and includes information on enhancements and new editions of NorthWestNet's "The Internet Passport." *Quarterly*

i eveleth@nwnet.net (Jan Eveleth)

± info@nwnet.net

Archive: FTP ftphost.nwnet.net in /nwnet/newsletter/

9-180 **Notes From The Edge:** Newsletter on the Yes rock group, Anderson-Bruford-Wakeman-Howe, and band-member related news. Includes interviews. *Every two weeks, on average*

i ± hunnicutt@vxc.uncwil.edu (Jeff Hunnicutt)

Archive: mail-serve yes-archive@meiko.com [body = help]

9-181 **Obscure Electric:** Electronic version of the hardcopy newsletter of profiles the people in the zine publishing subculture. *Irregular*

i Obscure@csd4.csd.uwm.edu

Archive: FTP etext.archive.umich.edu in /pub/Zines/Obscure.Electric/; gopher gopher.well.sf.ca.us

9-182 **OFFLINE:** Covers the actual and potential use of computers in religious studies in general. *Quarterly* *i* `kraft@ccat.sas.upenn.edu` (Robert A. Kraft)

± FTP `ccat.sas.upenn.edu` in `/pub/offline/`; gopher `ccat.sas.upenn.edu`

Archive: `listserv@brownvm.bitnet` (Bitnet: `LISTSERV@BROWNVM`) [body = `GET HUMANIST FILELIST`]

9-183 **Oingo Boingo:** Official monthly newsletter of the Oingo Boingo Secret Society (the fan club of the rock group). With information on Danny Elfman and Food for Feet.

i ± `eln4204@ritvax.isc.rit.edu` (Eric L. Neumann)

9-184 **Old English Computer-Assisted Language Learning Newsletter (OE-CALL):** For persons interested in computer-assisted language-learning methods for teaching Old English. *Irregular; suspended while new editors sought*

i ± `lees@fordmurh.bitnet` or `u47c2@wvnvm.bitnet`

9-185 **Online Chronicle of Distance Education and Communication:** Covers distance education; communications that fall outside the domain of formal learning; telecommunications in education; and overcoming cultural barriers through the use of electronic communication.

i `jfjbo@acad1.alaska.edu` (Bitnet: `JFJBO@ALASKA`) (Jason B. Ohler)

± `listserv@uwavm.bitnet` (Bitnet: `LISTSERV@UWAVM`) [body = `SUBSCRIBE DISTED`]

9-186 **Online Journal of Current Clinical Trials:** The latest in primary medical research, including full text and graphics. Includes research reports, reviews, meta-analyses, methodological papers, editorials, information on trials or therapies, procedures, and other interventions relevant to all areas of medical care. This journal is not free. *Continuous*

i `jbarnes@aaas.org` (Jennifer Barnes)

± Subscriptions are available from AAAS (202) 326-6446.

Archive: All articles remain in the journal database and are available to subscribers to the journal.

9-187 **Organized Thoughts:** Articles about libertarian socialism or industrial democracy. Emphasis is on: syndicalist or industrial union models; Daniel De Leon's interpretation of Marxism; related social issues (environmentalism, militarism, etc.). Reprints of historical documents and the position papers of organizations. *Irregular, but approximately 6 issues per year*

i `mlepore@mcimail.com` or `M.LEPORE@genie.geis.com` (Mike Lepore)

± `listserv@uvmvm.uvm.edu` (Bitnet: `LISTSERV@UVMVM`) [body = `SUBSCRIBE L-UNION`]

Archive: FTP `etext.archive.umich.edu` in `/pub/Politics/Organized.Thoughts/`

9-188 **Parthenogenesis:** Short fiction. *Irregular*

i ± `dherrick@nyx.cs.du.edu` (Dan Herrick)

Archive: FTP `etext.archive.umich.edu` in `/pub/Zines/Parthenogenesis/`

9-189 **People's Tribune (Online Edition):** Devoted to the proposition that an economic system which can't or won't feed, clothe, and house its people ought to be changed.

i ± `jdav@igc.org`

Archive: gopher `gopher.cic.net`

9-190 **PIGULKI:** Occasional magazine of news and humor relating to Poland and Polish issues, especially democratic evolution and computer networking. Written in English. *Irregular*

i `davep@acsu.buffalo.edu` (Dave Phillips)

± North America: `davep@acsu.buffalo.edu` (Dave Phillips); Oceania: `mjs111@phys.anu.edu.au` (Marek Samoc); Europe, Africa: `zielinski@acfcluster.nyu.edu` (Marek Zielinski)

Archive: FTP `mthvax.cs.miami.edu` or `lfa.camk.edu.pl` or `galaxy.uci.agh.edu.pl` or `info.in2p3.fr` or `laserspark.anu.edu.au` or `tirana.berkeley.edu` or `zsku.p.lod.edu.pl` in `/poland/`; gopher `galaxy.uci.agh.edu.pl` or `tirana.berkeley.edu`

9-191 **Pirradazish:** Bulletin of Achaemenian Studies: Information, primarily bibliographical, on the study of the Achaemenian empire and the periods immediately preceding and following it. *Semi-annual*

i `ce-jones@uchicago.edu` (Charles E. Jones)

± `listserv@emuvm1.bitnet` [body = `GET PERSIA BIB`]

9-192 **Postmodern Culture:** Discussion of postmodernism, including analytical essays and reviews, video scripts, and other new literary forms. *Three times per year (September, January, May)*

i `pmc@ncsuvm.cc.ncsu.edu` (Bitnet: `PMC@NCSUVM`)

± `listserv@ncsuvm.cc.ncsu.edu` (Bitnet: `LISTSERV@NCSUVM`) [body = `SUBSCRIBE PMC-LIST`]

Archive: `listserv@ncsuvm.cc.ncsu.edu` (Bitnet: `LISTSERV@NCSUVM`) [body = `INDEX PMC-LIST`]

9-193 **Postmodern Jewish Philosophy BITNETWORK:** Dedicated to a philosophic review of the variety of postmodern Jewish discourses and to postmodern reflections on Jewish philosophies and Jewish philosophic theologies. *Irregular*

i ± `pochs@drew.drew.edu` (Bitnet: `POCHS@DREW`) (Peter Ochs)

Archive: hardcopies for $10/volume, request to *i*

9-194 **PowderKeg:** Literary electronic magazine with stories, poetry, and reviews.

i `ifirla@epas.utoronto.ca`

Archive: FTP `nebula.lib.vt.edu`

9-195 **Power to the People Mover:** E-zine on mass transit, also published in a hard copy version designed to look like a bus schedule and free with a SASE. Covers the cultural aspects of bus riding. *Monthly*

i ± `knut@wendy.ucsd.edu` (Erik Knutzen)

Archive: FTP `etext.archive.umich.edu` in `/pub/Zines/People.Mover/`

9-196 **Practical Anarchy Online:** International anarchist news and analysis, e-zine reviews, updates on anarchist projects, and suggestions for practical anarchy. *Bimonthly*

i `ctmunson@macc.wisc.edu` (Chuck Munson)

± `cardell@lysator.liu.se` or `ctmunson@macc.wisc.edu`

Archive: FTP `etext.archive.umich.edu` in
`/pub/Politics/Spunk/Practical.Anarchy.*`

9-197 **Principia Cybernetica Newsletter:** Newsletter about the Principia Cybernetica Project (PCP), a computer-supported collaborative attempt to develop an integrated evolutionary-systemic philosophy or world view. *Once a year*

i `fheyligh@vnet3.vub.ac.be` (Dr. Francis Heylighen)

± `fheyligh@vnet3.vub.ac.be` (include address, affiliations, and your interest in the Project)

Archive: available on request from the editor

9-198 **Programming Freedom:** The Electronic Newsletter of The League for Programming Freedom. Action and commentary on patents and copyrights as a limitation on freedom of expression. *Bi-monthly*

i ± `spiker@prep.ai.mit.edu` or `league@prep.ai.mit.edu`

Archive: FTP `prep.ai.mit.edu` in `/pub/lpf`

9-199 **Project Gutenberg Newsletter:** Project Gutenberg encourages creation and distribution of English language electronic texts. Its goal is to provide a collection of 10,000 of the most-used books by the year 2001 (See also Chapter 10). *Monthly*

i `dircompg@ux1.cso.uiuc.edu` (Project Gutenberg Communications Director)

± `listserv@vmd.cso.uiuc.edu` (Bitnet: `LISTSERV@UIUCVMD`) [body = `SUBSCRIBE GUTNBERG`]

Archive: FTP `mrcnext.cso.uiuc.edu` in `/etext/`

9-200 **Prompt:** News tips and briefs for the North Carolina State University campus community. Timely, up-to-date information about all computing platforms. *Every two to three weeks to campus mail addresses*

i `sarah_noell@ncsu.edu` (Sarah Noell)

± `listserv@ncsuvm.cc.ncsu.edu` [body = `SUBSCRIBE PROMPT-L`]

Archive: `listserv@ncsuvm.cc.ncsu.edu` [body = `INDEX PROMPT`]

9-201 **PSYCHE:** An Interdisciplinary Journal of Research on Consciousness: Exploration of the nature of consciousness and its relation to the brain, from the perspectives of cognitive science, philosophy, psychology, neuroscience, artificial intelligence, and anthropology. (See also PSYCHE-D in Chapter 1.) *Quarterly*

i `x91007@phillip.edu.au` (Patrick Wilken)

± `listserv@nki.bitnet` (Bitnet: `LISTSERV@NKI`) [body = `SUBSCRIBE PSYCHE-L`]

9-202 **Psychology Graduate Student Journal:** The PSYCGRAD Journal (PSYGRD-J): Publishes professional-level papers in the field of psychology from the graduate student perspective. (See also PSYCGRAD and PSYGRD-D in Chapter 1.) *Irregular*

i `054340@acadvm1.uottawa.ca` (Bitnet: `054340@UOTTAWA`) (Matthew Simpson)

± `listserv@acadvm1.uottawa.ca` (Bitnet: `LISTSERV@UOTTAWA`) [body = `SUBSCRIBE PSYGRD-J`]

9-203 **PSYCOLOQUY:** A Refereed Journal of Peer Commentary in Psychology, Neuroscience and Cognitive Science: Brief reports of new ideas and findings, in all areas of psychology and its related fields, on which the author wishes to solicit rapid peer feedback. Multiple reviews of books in psychology and related fields. *Irregular (items posted upon acceptance)*

   i `harnad@princeton.edu` (Stevan Harnad)

   ± `listserv@pucc.princeton.edu` (Bitnet: `LISTSERV@PUCC`) [body = `SUBSCRIBE PSYC`]; Usenet newsgroup `sci.psychology.digest`

   Archive: FTP `princeton.edu` in `/pub/harnad/`; gopher: `gopher.cic.net`; listserv `listserv@pucc.bitnet` [body = `GET PSYC FILELIST`]

9-204 **Public-Access Computer Systems News:** Brief news items about end-user computer systems in libraries. *Irregular*

   i `libpacs@uhupvm1.bitnet` (Dana Rooks)

   ± `listserv@uhupvm1.hh.edu` (Bitnet: `LISTSERV@UHUPVM1`) [body = `SUBSCRIBE PACS-L`]

   Archive: `listserv@uhupvm1.hh.edu` (Bitnet: `LISTSERV@UHUPVM1`) [body = `INDEX PACSNEWS`]

9-205 **Public-Access Computer Systems Review:** Papers on topics such as campus-wide information systems, CD-ROM LANs, document delivery systems, electronic publishing, expert systems, hypermedia and multimedia systems, locally-mounted databases, microcomputer labs, network-based information resources, and online catalogs. (See also PACS-L and PACS-P in Chapter 1.) *Irregular*

   i `lib3@uhupvm1.uh.edu` (Bitnet: `LIB3@UHUPVM1`) (Charles W. Bailey, Jr.)

   ± `listserv@uhupvm1.uh.edu` (Bitnet: `LISTSERV@UHUPVM1`) [body = `SUBSCRIBE PACS-L`]; gopher `gopher.lib.umich.edu` or `gopher.unt.edu` or `gopher.cic.net`

   Archive: `listserv@uhupvm1.uh.edu` (Bitnet `LISTSERV@UHUPVM1`) [body = `GET INDEX PRV1 F=MAIL`]

9-206 **PUBS-IAT:** Current schedule of information-technology courses and satellite broadcasts offered by the Institute for Academic Technology, as well as articles on innovative uses of information technology in institutions of higher learning.

   i `jonp.iat@mhs.unc.edu` (Jonathan Pishney)

   ± `listserv@gibbs.oit.unc.edu` [body = `SUBSCRIBE PUBS-IAT` first-name last-name]

9-207 **Purple Thunderbolt of Spode (PURPS):** Official e-mail news/literary magazine of the OTISian faith (a small but growing cult worshiping Otis, the ancient Sumerian God[dess] of life). *Irregular (monthly or more often)*

   i `jstevens@world.std.com` or `scott@plearn.bitnet` or `mal@socpsy.sci.fau.edu`

   ± `HailOtis@socpsy.sci.fau.edu` (preferred) or `barker@acc.fau.edu`

   Archive: FTP `etext.archive.umich.edu` in `/pub/Zines/Purps/` or `quartz.rutgers.edu` in `/pub/journals/Purps/`

9-208 **QUANTA—Science, Fact, and Fiction:** Magazine of science-fiction and fantasy by amateur and professional authors. *Irregular*

i dan@visix.com (Daniel Appelquist)

± quanta+requests-postscript@andrew.cmu.edu or quanta+requests-ascii@andrew.cmu.edu

Archive: FTP export.acs.cmu.edu in /pub/quanta/ or ftp.eff.org in /journals/Quanta/ or lth.se in /documents/Quanta/; gopher gopher-srv.acs.cmu.edu

9-209 **Radio Havana Cuba Newscast:** A selection of the top stories in the Radio Havana Cuba newscast, datelined mainly from Cuba, Latin America, the Caribbean, and Africa. *Daily, Monday through Friday*

i radiohc@tinored.cu

± support@igc.apc.org for information (access through the "carnet.cubanews" conference of Peacenet)

9-210 **RAH:** Random Access Humor magazine. *10/year (September–June)*

i ± dbealer@clark.net

Archive: FTP etext.archive.umich.edu in /pub/Zines/RAH/

9-211 **RD:** Graduate Research in the Arts: Publishes the work of graduate scholars in the arts, providing an appropriate forum for their scholarly work and a collective voice for their issues and interests. *Twice yearly*

i rd@writer.yorku.ca or engl5105@nexus.yorku.ca (Stephen N. Matsuba)

± rd@writer.yorku.ca

9-212 **REACH—Research and Educational Applications of Computers in the Humanities:** Newsletter of the Humanities Computing Facility, University of California—Santa Barbara. *Quarterly*

i hcf1dahl@ucsbuxa.ucsb.edu (Bitnet: HCF1DAHL@UCSBUXA) (Eric Dahlin)

± listserv@ucsbvm.bitnet (Bitnet: LISTSERV@UCSBVM) [body = SUBSCRIBE REACH]

Archive: FTP ucsbuxa.ucsb.edu in /hcf/; listserv@ucsbvm.bitnet [body = INDEX REACH]

9-213 **Religious Studies Publications Journal—CONTENTS:** Publishes theses and dissertations, subject bibliographies, glossaries, course syllabi, and other research materials such as prepublication papers and dissertation abstracts in the field of Religious Studies. *Irregular*

i 441495@acadvm1.uottawa.ca (Bitnet: 441495@UOTTAWA) (Michael Strangelove)

± listserv@acadvm1.uottawa.ca (Bitnet: LISTSERV@UOTTAWA) [body = SUBSCRIBE CONTENTS]; gopher gopher.cic.net

Archive: listserv@acadvm1.uottawa.ca (Bitnet: LISTSERV@UOTTAWA) [body = INDEX CONTENTS]; FTP panda1.uottawa.ca in /pub/religion/

9-214 **ReNews (RELCOM NEWS):** Magazine covering informatic problems, the computer and software market in Russia and CIS, and current events in the economy of Russia. *English published monthly, Russian published weekly* *i* ± nev@renews.relcom.msk.su (Vladimir Shliemin)

Archive: e-mail to *i*

9-215 **Rezo, bulletin irregulomadaire du RQSS:** Newsletter of Regroupment Quebecois des Sciences Sociales (Quebec, Canada). *Irregular*

i hamelpj@inrs-urb.uquebec.ca (Pierre J. Hamel)

± listserv@uquebec.bitnet (Bitnet: LISTSERV@UQUEBEC) [body = SUBSCRIBE RQSS]

Archive: listserv@uquebec [body = INDEX RQSS]

9-216 **RFE/RL Research Institute Daily Report:** A digest of the latest developments in Russia, Transcaucasia and Central Asia, and Central and Eastern Europe. (See also E-EUROPE in Chapter 1.) *Daily, Monday to Friday*

i mannd@rferl.org (Dawn Mann)

± listserv@ubvm.cc.buffalo.edu (Bitnet: LISTSERV@UBVM) [body = SUBSCRIBE RFERL-L first-name last-name]; Usenet newsgroup misc.news.east-europe.rferl

Archive: Listserv LISTSERV@UBVM.cc.buffalo.edu

9-217 **Risks-Forum Digest:** A moderated newsgroup on the topic of problems with computer security, privacy, integrity, reliability, availability, human safety, financial fraud, etc. *Two to three per week*

i neumann@csl.sri.com (Peter G. Neumann)

± risks-request@csl.sri.com

Archive: FTP crvax.sri.com in RISKS:

9-218 **RSInetwork:** Newsletter for people concerned about tendonitis, Carpal Tunnel Syndrome (CTS), and other Repetitive Strain Injuries. Covers resources, products, and discussion. *Bimonthly*

i ± dadadata@world.std.com (Craig O'Donnell)

Archive: FTP world.std.com in /pub/rsi; gopher world.std.com

9-219 **SCHOLAR:** Natural Language Processing: Covers all aspects of natural language processing in such fields as literary studies, linguistics, history and lexicography. *Irregular*

i jqrqc@cunyvm.cuny.edu (Joseph Raben)

± listserv@cunyvm.cuny.edu [body = SUBSCRIBE SCHOLAR]

Archive: FTP jhuvm.hcf.jhu.edu [logon = scholar password = anonymous]

9-220 **Scientist:** News articles, features, departments, and opinion pieces targeted at science professionals in all disciplines, especially the biotechnology marketplace. Covers funding legislation, new grants and areas of study, ethical debates, etc. *Biweekly except in August and December.*

i garfield@aurora.cis.upenn.edu (Eugene Garfield)

Archive: FTP nnsc.nsf.net in /the-scientist/; mail server info-server@nnsc.nsf.net [body = HELP or INDEX the-scientist]

9-221 **Scope News:** Newsletter of the SUNY—Albany School of Information Science and Policy Student Association. *Monthly, eight times per calendar year* *i* ± `mt0296@albnyvms.bitnet` (Maryhope Tobin) or `rp0358@albnyvms.bitnet` (Richard Pugh)

9-222 **Scratch:** Articles and reviews of other zines. *Irregular*

i ± `spingo@echonyc.com`

Archive: FTP `etext.archive.umich.edu` in `/pub/Zines/Scratch/`

9-223 **Scream Baby:** E-zine on the subculture of cyberpunk cyberspace. Articles, interviews, satire, editorials, and reviews of music, film, literature, zines, etc. *Once every two or three months*

i `bladex@wixer.bga.com`

± No listserv subscription; send editor an essay question from any issue or back issue to subscribe

Archive: FTP `etext.archive.umich.edu` in `/pub/Zines/ScreamBaby`

9-224 **SCUP e-mail News:** A service of the Society for College and University Planning. Covers notices of national and regional SCUP and other relevant meetings; pertinent news items; useful articles, books, or other materials; requests from the members for information, and job postings. *Biweekly*

i ± `budlao@uccvma.ucop.edu` (Bitnet: `BUDLAO@UCCVMA`) (Joanne Cate)

9-225 **Sense of Place:** Environmentalist magazine produced in HyperCard that presents information about environmental concerns significant to the Dartmouth College community and others. *Twice monthly*

i ± `sop@dartmouth.edu`

Archive: FTP `dartmouth.edu` in `/pub/SOP/`

9-226 **Simulation Digest:** Digest for Usenet's comp.simulation and all topics of computer simulation. *Weekly*

i `fishwick@cis.ufl.edu` (Paul A. Fishwick)

± `simulation-request@cis.ufl.edu`; gopher `gopher.cis.ufl.edu`

9-227 **Simulations Online:** Devoted to the hobby of board war-gaming and conflict simulation. *Irregular*

i `xorg@cup.portal.com` or `72637.2272@compuserve.com` (Peter T. Szymonik)

± Available on Usenet, CompuServe, GEnie, and America Online (Mac and PC versions) in the respective Gaming sections.

9-228 **Soae:** E-zine on Christian heavy metal and thrash music. By the publisher of Screams of Abel, a Christian thrash magazine. *Weekly*

i `Phil.Powell@launchpad.unc.edu` or `Phil.Powell@lambada.oit.unc.edu` (Phil Powell)

± Usenet `alt.zines`

Archive: FTP `etext.archive.umich.edu` in `/pub/Zines/Screams.of.Abel/`

9-229 **Socjety Journal:** For alumni of the Technical University of Wroclaw, Poland.

i `lewanowi@plwrtu11.bitnet` (Ala Lewanowicz) or `misiak@plwrtu11.bitnet` (Pawel Misiak)

± `listserv@plearn.bitnet` (Bitnet: `LISTSERV@PLEARN`) [body = `SUBSCRIBE WROCLAW`]

9-230 **SOLSTICE:** An Electronic Journal of Geography and Mathematics: About solstices and related matter. *Twice annually, on the astronomical solstices*

i ± `sandy.arlinghaus@um.cc.umich.edu` (Bitnet: `SOLSTICE@UMICHUM`) (Dr. Sandra L. Arlinghaus)

Archive: hard copy only; inquire for prices.

9-231 **Somalia News Update:** Analysis and comments on the political developments in Somalia, entirely independent and not linked to any organization or faction. *Irregular, but at least biweekly*

i ± `bernhard.helander@antro.uu.se` (Bernhard Helander)

Archive: FTP `ftp.cic.net` in `/pub/nircomm/gopher/`; gopher `gopher.cic.net`

9-232 **Sonic Verse (TM) Music Magazine:** (Formerly Update Music Newsletter.) On current music. Inlcudes record reviews and edtiorials. *Monthly*

i `uicd%maris@vm.marist.edu`

± `sonic-l@vm.marist.edu` (Bitnet: `SONIC-L@MARIST`)

Archive: `LISTSERV@VM.MARIST.EDU` (Bitnet: `LISTSERV@MARIST`); FTP `cs.uwp.edu`

9-233 **SOUND News and Arts:** Text of the Omaha-based, advertiser-supported, free newspaper focusing on artists, issues, news, music, creative writing, art, and events in the Omaha and Lincoln area. *Monthly*

i ± `ed@cwis.unomaha.edu` (Ed Stastny)

Archive: FTP `quartz.rutgers.edu` in `/pub/journals/Sound/`

9-234 **Sound Newsletter:** Electronic serial about sound cards, sound programs, and multimedia demos for the PC/Mac/Amiga/Sun. *Approximately 6 times a year*

i `sound@ccb.ucsf.edu` (Dave Komatsu)

Archive: FTP `safffron.inset.com` in `/pub/sound/Newsletters/`

9-235 **South Florida Environmental Reader:** Newsletter distributing information on the South Florida environment. *Irregular; suspended until further notice*

i `aem@mthvax.cs.miami.edu` (Bitnet: `AEM@UMIAMI`) (Andrew Mossberg)

± `sfer-request@mthvax.cs.miami.edu`

9-236 **South Scanner Satellite Services Chart:** A satellite services guide listing the North American television satellites and their audio/video services. *Monthly, on average*

i `roberts@triton.unm.edu` (Robert Smathers)

± Posted to rec.video.satellite at release date; e-mail version can be sent to those who request it (request to `roberts@triton.unm.edu`).

Archive: FTP `oak.oakland.edu` in `/pub/msdos/satellite`; e-mail to *i*

9-237 **SpaceNews:** News of the Amateur Space Program. *Weekly (Mondays)*

i `kd2bd@ka2qhd.de.com`

± Usenet sci.space.news

9-238 **SpaceViews:** International news related to outer space, recent and planned launches, commercial development and eventual settlement of space, published by the Boston Chapter of the National Space Society. *Monthly*

i brucem@ptltd.com (Bruce Mackenzie)

± brucem@ptltd.com or tombaker@world.std.com

9-239 **Spojrzenia:** Devoted to Polish culture, history, politics, etc., in Polish. *Weekly*

i ± krzystek@u.washington.edu (Jerzy Krzystek)

Archive: FTP poniecki.berkeley.edu in /pub/polish/publications/Spojrzenia; gopher poniecki.berkeley.edu

9-240 **STARNET:** Lists scientists' interests, meetings, classifieds, jobs, etc. for echinoderm biologists. Sister publication of the Echinoderm Newsletter, a 200-page yearly publication. *Quarterly*

i ± whide@matrix.bchs.uh.edu (Winston Hide)

9-241 **Surfaces:** Interdisciplinary journal in the humanities and social sciences. Published in English and French. *Irregular*

i ± guedon@ere.umontreal.ca

Archive: FTP harfang.cc.umontreal.ca in /Surfaces/

9-242 **SURFPUNK Technical Journal:** A multinational hacker e-zine sampling the leading edge of the net. *Daily*

i strick@osc.versant.com

± surfpunk-request@osc.versant.com

Archive: e-mail to ±

9-243 **TapRoot Reviews Electronic Edition:** Quarterly review of independent, underground, and experimental language-centered arts (micropresses). Mostly short, descriptive blurb-reviews. *Quarterly*

i au462@cleveland.freenet.edu (Luigi-Bob Drake)

± au462@cleveland.freenet.edu This is not an automated server, so please say something human.

Archive: Available on request.

9-244 **Taylorology:** A newsletter focusing on the life and murder of William Desmond Taylor, a top Paramount film director in early Hollywood. *Monthly*

i bruce@asu.edu (Bruce Long)

± Usenet newsgroup alt.true-crime

Archive: FTP etext.archive.umich.edu in /pub/Zines/Taylorology

9-245 **Teiresias:** Bibliography (boiotian studies). *Irregular*

i ± czas@musica.mcgill.ca (A. Schachter)

9-246 **TELECOM Digest:** Telecommunications news and commentary, generally but not exclusively in the field of voice telephony. *Daily*

   i `telecom@eecs.nwu.edu` (Patrick Townson)

   ± `telecom-request@eecs.nwu.edu` (include e-mail address and the workds `subscribe to digest`)

   Archive: FTP `lcs.mit.edu` in `telecom-archives`

9-247 **Teleputing Hotline and Field Computing Source Letter:** Covers telephone connections and field-computing developments worldwide. *Weekly*

   i ± `76200.3025@compuserve.com` (Dana Blankenhorn)

   Archive: available on request from the editor

   Other: Japanese and Russian language versions available.

9-248 **Temple ov Psychick Youth On-Line Transmission:** Relevant Ratio-ZER0 information about thee Temple Ov Psychick Youth. Subjects: Magick, Shamanism, poetry, Modern Occultism, Neuromancy, and Discordianism. *Monthly*

   i `alamut@netcom.com`

   ± `vajra@u.washington.edu`

   Archive: FTP `netcom.com` in `/pub/alamut/`

9-249 **Temptation of Saint Anthony:** Weirdness, humor, fiction, and observation. *Monthly*

   i ± `mbcs@gradient.cis.upenn.edu`.

9-250 **TeX Publication Distribution List:** Redistribution list for TeX-related electronic periodicals. Includes TeX hax Digest, UK TeX, TeX MaG, the TeX Users Group's TeX and TUG News, and the "Frequently Asked Questions" and "Supplementary TeX Information" posts from the comp.text.tex newsgroup. *Irregular*

   i `bed_gdg@shsu.edu` (Bitnet: `BED_GDG@SHSU`) (George D. Greenwade)

   ± `listserv@shsu.edu` (Bitnet: `LISTSERV@SHSU`) [body = `SUBSCRIBE TEX-PUBS`]

9-251 **Texas Technology Newsletter:** News from the Texas Department of Commerce Office of Advanced Technology. *Monthly*

   i `parish@tpis.cactus.org`

   ± `TexasTechnology-requests@tpis.cactus.org`

   Archive: Turning Point Information Services BBS. Dialup access only Go to LIBRARY. No charge for downloading back issues.

9-252 **TeXMaG:** E-journal on the TeX typesetting software. *Monthly*

   i `nabtexm@rigel.tamu.edu` (Bitnet: `NABTEXM@TAMVENUS`) (Neil Burleson)

   ± `listserv@uicvm.uic.edu` (Bitnet: `LISTSERV@UICVM`) [body = `SUBSCRIBE TEXMAG-L`]

   Archive: FTP `ymir.claremont.edu` in `[ANONYMOUS.TEX.PERIODICALS.TEXMAG]`

9-253   **The Observer:** Newsletter on Humberto Maturana's and Francisco Varela's theories of autopoiesis and "enactive cognitive science," and their linkages to systems theory, cognitive science, phenomenology, artificial life, etc. Digest format.

    i ± rwhitaker@falcon.aamrl.wpafb.af.mil (Randall Whitaker)

9-254   **THINKNET:** Newsletter on philosophy, systems theory, interdisciplinary studies, and thoughtful conversation in cyberspace. *Irregular*

    i thinknet@world.std.com or palmer@world.std.com (Kent D. Palmer)

    ± palmer@world.std.com [body = SUBSCRIBE THINKNET address]

    Archive: by request to editor

9-255   **TidBITS:** Covers interesting products and events in the computer industry, with an emphasis on the world of the Macintosh. *Weekly*

    i ace@tidbits.com or info@tidbits.com (Adam C. Engst)

    ± listserv@ricevm1.rice.edu (Bitnet: LISTSERV@RICEVM1) [body = SUBSCRIBE TIDBITS]; Usenet newsgroup comp.sys.mac.digest

    Archive: FTP sumex-aim.stanford.edu in /info-mac/digest/tb/

9-256   **TitNet—Titnews—Titnotes:** The electronic mail network of the International Tit Society. TITNET: listing of e-mail subscribers and their interests; TITNEWS: forum for exchange on academic activities; TITNOTES: information about tits and other hole-nesting birds. *Irregular*

    i jhailman@macc.wisc.edu (Bitnet: JHAILMAN@WISCMACC) (Jack P. Hailman)

    ± jhailman@vms.macc.wisc.edu. (Bitnet: HAILMAN@WISCMACC) (Include full name, e-mail address, institutional affiliation, species studied, and topics studied.) e-mail subscribers automatically become members of TITS.

    Archive: e-mail to *i*

9-257   **TREK-REVIEW-L:** Critical opinion on all things pertaining to Star Trek of any generation and in any medium. *Irregular*

    i mss1@cornell.edu (Michael Shappe)

    ± listserv@cornell.edu [body = SUBSCRIBE TREK-REVIEW-L]

9-258   **Tunisian Scientific Society Newsletter:** On technology transfer to Tunisia. *Quarterly*

    i bnj@ecl.psu.edu (Bitnet: JOMAA@UTKVX) (Bilel N. Jamoussi)

    ± tssnews@athena.mit.edu

9-259   **UKUUG Newsletter:** Newsletter of the United Kingdom Unix User Group. *Bi-monthly*

    i sue@dcs.bbk.ac.uk

    ± ukuug@uknet.ac.uk

    Archive: FTP src.doc.ic.ac.uk

9-260   **Ulam Quarterly:** Publishes original research and open problems in all areas of mathematics. Dedicated to the universal character of Stanislaw Ulam's scientific interests, which led him to make contributions in many mathematical fields. *Quarterly*

    i ± blass@goliath.pbac.edu

Archive: FTP `math.ufl.edu` in `/pub/ulam/`

9-261 **Undiscovered Country:** E-zine on life, art, philosophy, etc. *Irregular*

i `cblanc@pomona.claremont.edu` or `rm09216@nyssa.swt.edu`

± `cblanc@pomona.claremont.edu`

Archive: FTP `ftp.eff.org` in `/pub/journals/The_Undiscovered_Country/` or `etext.archive.umich.edu` in `/pub/Zines/Undiscovered.Country/` or `cs.uwp.edu` in `/pub/music/listuc` or `pa.claemont.edu` in `po_19:[cblanc.tuc]`

9-262 **Unplastic News:** Newsletter of strange quotes, weird news, and odd humorous snippets. *Bi-monthly, on average*

i ± `tt1@netcom.com` (Todd Tibbetts)

Archive: FTP `ftp.eff.org` in `/pub/journals/Unplastic_News` or `quartz.rutgers.edu`

9-263 **Virginia Tech Spectrum:** Weekly bulletin of Virginia Polytechnic Institute and State University. *Weekly during the academic year*

i `savage@vtvm1.cc.vt.edu` (Lon Savage) or `powell@borg.lib.vt.edu` (James Powell)

± `JPOWELL@VTVM1.CC.VT.EDU`

Archive: gopher `borg.lib.vt.edu`; FTP `borg.lib.vt.edu` in `/pub/spec/archives/spectrum`; WWW `http://borg.lib.vt.edu/`

9-264 **Voices From The Net:** Discussion and exploration of the philosophical and sociological issues inherent in the nascent on-line community. *9/year + supplements*

i `swilbur@andy.bgsu.edu` or `mgardbe@andy.bgsu.edu`

± `Voices-request@andy.bgsu.edu`

Archive: FTP `etext.archive.umich.edu` in `pub/Zines/Voices/` or `aql.gatech.edu` in `pub/Zines/Voices_from_the_Net/` or `wiretap.spies.com` in `pub/Library/Zines/`

9-265 **Vreme News Digest:** Vreme News Digest (VND) is an English-language newsletter published by the Vreme News Digest Agency (VNDA) from Belgrade.

i ± `dimitrije@buenga.bu.edu` (Dimitrije Stamenovic)

9-266 **WAAC Newsletter:** Electronic archive of the hardcopy publication (ISSN 1052-0066) of the Western Association for Art Conservation. Ideas, information, news, etc. on conservation of cultural property, especially matters of interest to conservators in the western United States. *Three times per year*

i `waiscool@aldus.stanford.edu`

± Not available.

Archive: WAIS `aldus.stanford.edu` in `cool-waac.src`

9-267 **WAC NEWS—The World Archaeological Congress Newsletter:** Provides members information about the activities of WAC, including reports from regional representatives, comments about current archaeological issues, etc. *Irregular*

i ± moly@charlie.usd.edu (Brian L. Molyneaux)
Archive: FTP sunfish.usd.edu in /pub/WAC/

9-268 **We_Magazine:** E-Zine of poetry. *Irregular.*
    i cf2785@albnyvms.bitnet (Bitnet CF2785@ALBNYVMS)
    ± We Press, Postoffice Box 1503, Santa Cruz, CA 95061. $15/3 issues.
    Archive: FTP ftp.eff.org in /pub/journals/We_Magazine

9-269 **Wind Energy Weekly:** Covers news of the wind-energy industry worldwide, including energy policy, wind energy technology, global climate change, sustainable development. *Weekly*
    i tgray@igc.apc.org (Tom Gray)
    ± tgray@igc.apc.org (Include name, address, organization, and reason for interest)

9-270 **Windows Online Review:** Distributed as a Windows 3.1 help file (extension .HLP). A hypertext publication that can be viewed on screen with Windows software.
    ± FTP ftp.cica.indiana.edu in /pub/pc/win3/uploads/WOLR69.ZIP

9-271 **World View Magazine:** Covers politics, editorials, global computing issues, computer security, and legal issues. *Bi-monthly*
    i dfox@fennec.com or dfox@wixer.cactus.org (Scott A. Davis)
    ± wv-sub@fennec.com
    Archive: FTP ftp.eff.org in /pub/cud/wview/; e-mail to ±

10. ELECTRONIC TEXT RESOURCES

The number of texts available online is growing phenomenally, as is the breadth of the topics of these texts. This chapter lists some of the more important organizations and archives that store such texts.

Entry Format:

Item
Number

10-n   **Resource Name**

Description of the resource

i `contact address`

Access: type of resource (FTP, gopher) and `host address`

Mirrors: additional `host addresses` of sites that mirror the resource.

Includes: samples of what appears in the resource.

Where to Find It: This list was built simply by scanning the Internet. I used Archie and Veronica to discover the different resources (I searched on words like text, book, e-text). After examining each resource, I verified the information gathered with the contact addresses I had found. To find individual e-texts see Chapter 11 (Online Resource Lists), which lists a number of gophers with particularly good e-text menus.

Netiquette: Please remember that the archives where these texts are stored are heavily used. Download from a mirror site when possible.

Entries:

10-1   **Center for Computer Analysis of Texts (CCAT)**

The University of Pennsylvania's Center for Computer Analysis of Texts provides gopher and FTP access to a number of locally archived texts as well as pointers to other texts on the Internet. It also provides an index to all the texts available at CCAT, some of which, due to copyright restrictions, are not available on the Internet.

i `jacka@ccat.sas.upenn.edu`

Access: gopher `ccat.sas.upenn.edu` in `/CCAT's Archival Holdings/Text Libraries`

10-2 ## Center for Electronic Texts in the Humanities (CETH)

CETH is a collaboration between Rutgers and Princeton Universities. It maintains a large body of electronic texts, works toward making high quality e-texts available via the Internet, and provides educational programs for humanities computing and methodologies for research and instruction using electronic texts.

Access: listserv `listserv@pucc.princeton.edu` (Bitnet: LISTSERV@PUCC) [body = SUBSCRIBE CETH first-name last-name]

10-3 ## The Coombspapers Social Sciences Research Data Bank (ANU)

An electronic repository of the Australian National University's social-science and humanities papers, bibliographies, directories, thesis abstracts, and other high-grade research material. Selected Coombspapers data are used to form the ANU series of the WAIS specialist databases.

i coombspapers@coombs.anu.edu.au

Access: FTP `coombs.anu.edu.au` in `/coombspapers/`
gopher `coombs.anu.edu.au` or `cheops.anu.edu.au`

Mirrors: FTP `wuarchive.wustl.edu` in `/doc/coombspapers/`
or `knot.queensu.ca` in `/wuarchive/doc/coombspapers/`
or `ftp.uu.net` in `/doc/papers/coombspapers/`
or `uceng.uc.edu` in `/pub/wuarchive/doc/coombspapers/`
or `unix.hensa.ac.uk` in `/pub/uunet/doc/papers/coombspapers/`

Includes: ANU's research materials on Australian, Pacific, Southeast and Northeast Asian anthropology, demography, development studies, economic history, economics, history, international relations, linguistics, political science, prehistory, and sociology. Also on aboriginal studies and on Buddhism, Taoism, and other Asian religions.

10-4 ## Catalogue of Projects in Electronic Text (CPET)

CPET is a database compiled by the Center for Text and Technology (CTT) at Georgetown University. The database provides references to more than 350 projects worldwide that compile electronic texts in the humanities. The Ingres-based version of the database is available via telnet to guvax3.georgetown.edu *login as CPET, or you can access a digest version—organized by discipline or language of the electronic texts—via FTP or gopher.*

i pmangiafico@guvax.georgetown.edu (Paul Mangiafico, CPET Project Assistant) or neuman@guvax.georgetown.edu (Dr. Michael Neuman, Director, Center for Text & Technology)

Access: FTP `guvax.georgetown.edu` in
`/cpet_projects_in_electronic_text/`
gopher `gopher.georgetown.edu`

Includes: digests on archaeology, fine arts, information services, rhetoric, the natural sciences; African studies, American studies, classical studies, Indian studies, medieval studies, Mesopotamian studies, Native American studies, Renaissance studies; philosophy, Buddhist studies, Christian theology, Hindu studies, Islamic studies; and the literature and linguistics of more than 40 language groups.

10-5 The Online Book Initiative (OBI)

The Online Book Initiative is a collection of publicly distributable texts. It mirrors the Gutenberg texts and includes many others.

i bzs@world.std.com (Barry Shein)

Access: FTP world.std.com in /obi/
gopher world.std.com

Includes: Edwin Abbott, James Allen, antarctica, Jane Austen, William Blake, Emily Bronte, book reviews, Canticles from the Catholic Mass, Lewis Carroll, census information, conspiracy, Desert Storm, economics, Esperanto, Martin Luther King, Karl Marx, H.H Munro, Ezra Pound, fairy tales, George Bush, the Brothers Grimm, Hippocrates, Hiroshima survivors, Abbie Hoffmann, the Holocaust, the Hugo Awards, The Irish Emigrant, John F. Kennedy, Tracy LaQuey's *The Internet Companion*), Katherine Mansfield, Spooner, nerd humor, OtherRealms, patents, Shakespeare, Percy Bysshe Shelley, Soviet archives, Star Trek parodies, Star Trek stories, stocks, Supreme Court, U.S. Congress, the Usenet Cookbook, the Vatican, Virgil, William Butler Yeats, Roget's Thesaurus, Paul Tsongas, and weather maps.

10-6 The Oxford Text Archive (OTA)

As of July 1993, the Oxford Text Archive contained 1,336 titles in 28 languages. Most of these are scholarly articles; this is an important resource for the humanities. A complete index of the texts, as well as a few of the texts themselves, is available by anonymous FTP. The others are available by written agreement on magnetic tape, floppy disks, or over the Internet.

i archive@ox.ac.uk

Access: FTP black.ox.ac.uk in /ota/

Includes: Marvell, Edgar Rice Burroughs, James Conrad, Darwin, Dickens, Arthur Conan Doyle, Henry James, London, Melville, Milton, Orczy, Bram Stoker, Trollope, Mark Twain, H.G. Wells, and more, as well as dictionaries and a number of U.S. historical documents.

10-7 Project Gutenberg

Founded and led by Michael Hart at Illinois Benedictine College, Project Gutenberg released its first e-text, the U.S. Declaration of Independence, in 1971. This was followed by the Bill of Rights, the Constitution, the Gettysberg address, etc., and the Bible. Starting in 1988 it began releasing more "family-oriented" literature. Please note that texts are stored in the archive by the year of addition.

i hart@vmd.cso.uiuc.edu

Access: FTP mrcnext.cso.uiuc.edu in /etext/

Mirrors: FTP quake.think.com in /pub/etext/
or world.std.com in /obi/obi2/Gutenberg/
or sunsite.unc.edu in /pub/docs/books/gutenberg

Includes: a wide and eclectic assortment of classic and entertainment literature including Aesop's fables, Edgar Rice Burroughs, Descartes, Thoreau, Mark Twain, Milton's *Paradise Lost* and *Paradise Regained*, various mathematical constants calculated to a huge number of decimal places, the Bible, and a number of introductions to the Internet. You really have to check Project Gutenberg out for yourself.

10-8 ## Project Runeberg

Project Runeberg is an effort by the Lysator students' computer club at Linkoping University in Linkoping, Sweden to make public-domain works in Scandinavian languages available online.

i `aronsson@lysator.liu.se`

Access: gopher `gopher.lysator.liu.se`
FTP `ftp.lysator.liu.se` in `/pub/texts`

Includes: a Swedish translation of the Bible, Swedish copyright law, various classic and medieval Swedish texts, a dictionary, poetry, and a GIF file of the face of Johan Ludvig Runeberg!

10-9 ## Wiretap Online Library

The Internet Wiretap Online Library contains a broad range of texts and articles.

i `archive@wiretap.spies.com`

Access: gopher `wiretap.spies.com`
FTP `wiretap.spies.com`

Includes: civic and historical documents, classics texts (e.g., a Vulgate Bible), articles on cyberspace, texts on the "fringes of reason," humor, mass media, music, religion texts, lots of technical information, archives of many e-serials, and a large number of miscellaneous but very interesting articles. All good net citizens should browse this library at least once!

11. ONLINE RESOURCE LISTS

Many thousands of resources on the Internet are cataloged in a great many directories, gopher menus, FTP archives, newsgroup FAQ (Frequently Asked Question) postings, and so on. Knowing where to find these resource lists increases your Internet knowledge exponentially. A number of lists of these lists also exist, and there are even a few lists that are compilations of those lists of lists!

This chapter contains a variety of resource compilations. It is not complete, merely enough to get you started.

Entry Format:

Item
Number
11-n   **List name:** description of the compilation.

      (FTP, e-mail, gopher): address or instructions necessary to access the compilation.

      ....

Where to Find It: Sort of contradictory, isn't it? :-) The entries in this chapter were all found while I was searching for other things, mostly while cruising gopherspace. Some of them were pointed out to me by people on the net; others I found hidden deep in FTP archives. Many can't be avoided online because they are so ubiquitous.

Netiquette: Some of the compilations listed in this chapter are copyrighted. Please be sure to check for copyright notices.

Lists of Resource Lists: These lists are all compilations of pointers to other resources, just like this chapter.

11-1   **Information Sources—the Internet and Computer-Mediated Communication:** Organized by topic and easy to use. This list is maintained and copyrighted by John December.
      FTP: `ftp.rpi.edu` in `pub/communications/internet-cmc`

11-2   **MaasInfo.TopIndex:** This list is a compilation of compilations similar to this chapter. It lists over 80 resource lists available on the Internet. The list is copyrighted by Robert Elton Maas.
      E-mail: `fileserv@shsu.edu` [body = SENDME MAASINFO.TOPINDEX*]
      FTP: `niord.shsu.edu` in `maasinfo`

11-3 **University of Michigan Clearinghouse of Resource Guides:** A compilation of many Internet resource guides available via gopher.

Gopher: `una.hh.lib.umich.edu` in `/inetdirs`

Resource Lists:

11-4 **AARNET Resource Guide:** A guide to internet resources in Australia, including computer resources, archives, libraries, etc.

FTP: `aarnet.edu.au` in `/pub/resource-guide`

11-5 **List of Periodic Informational Usenet Postings:** This compilation lists the Usenet postings that are updated and posted periodically to various groups, itself being a prime example! It is a very useful source of information for discovering what's available on Usenet and the Internet in general. The periodic postings include:

1. How-to articles explaining some of the basics and fine points of network usage, etiquette, standards, etc.
2. Introductory notes about one or more newsgroups, covering policies (if any) for submissions to that group, usage, etc. Common questions and answers pertinent to a newsgroup(s).
3. Indexes of archives or pointers to archives for various groups. Periodic newsletters, calendars, and pointers to publications.
4. Statistical information and reports about Usenet, tables of Usenet hosts, links, etc.
5. Miscellany, including small useful sources, "fun" lists, and so on.

Usenet newsgroup: `news.announce.newusers`

11-6 **MaasInfo.DocIndex:** A bibliography of online tutorials and other documents that describe how to use many Internet resources. This list is copyrighted by Robert Elton Maas.

E-mail: `fileserv@shsu.edu` [body = SENDME MAASINFO.DOCINDEX]
FTP: `niord.shsu.edu` in `maasinfo`

11-7 **NSF Internet Resource Guide:** Compiled by the NSF, this list covers a broad range of resources available on the Internet, including information on computer resources (supercomputers), library catalogs, archives, network information centers, white-pages directory services, and more.

FTP: `ds.internic.net` in `/resource-guide/` or `ftp.uu.net` in `/inet/resource-guide/`

11-8 **NYSERNet Resource Guide:** This list accurately describes itself as a "New User's Guide To Useful and Unique Resources on the Internet."

FTP: `nysernet.org` in `/pub/resource/guide/`

11-9 **Special Internet Connections (Yanoff List):** A collection of many hard-to-categorize but interesting and useful Internet resources.

E-mail: `bbslist@aug3.augsburg.edu`
Usenet newsgroup: `alt.internet.services`
FTP: `csd4.csd.uwm.edu` in `/pub/inet.services.txt`
Gopher: `csd4.csd.uwmn.edu`

Interest Group Resources:

11-10 **Academic Discussion Lists and Interest Groups (ACADLIST):** List of mailing lists of particular interest to academics, maintained by Diane Kovacs and The Directory Team of the Kent State University Libraries. This list is also available in hardcopy (see Bibliography for citation). ·

E-mail: listserv@kentvm.kent.edu [body = GET ACADLIST README]

FTP: ksuvxa.kent.edu in library

Gopher: gopher.usask.ca in /Computing/Internet Information/ Directory of Scholarly Electronic Conference

11-11 **Bitnet Global List:** A list of worldwide mailing lists distributed by Bitnet Listserv software.

E-mail: listserv@bitnic.educom.edu [body = global list]

11-12 **Dartmouth Interest Groups List:** Dartmouth maintains a merged list of the Listserv and manually maintained lists on Bitnet and the Interest Group lists on the Internet. This list contains more than 3,500 entries, and is also available in electronically searchable form from the sources below.

E-mail: listserv@dartcms1.dartmouth.edu [body = SEND READ.ME]

FTP: dartcms1.dartmouth.edu in SIGLISTS

11-13 **Publicly Accessible Mailing Lists (PAML):** List of e-mail mailing lists originating mostly on the Internet. This list is maintained and copyrighted by Stephanie da Silva and is updated monthly.

Usenet newsgroup: news.announce.newusers

11-14 **Usenet Newsgroups:** One-line descriptions of all Usenet newsgroups. This list is maintained by David Lawrence and is updated monthly.

Usenet newsgroup: news.announce.newusers or news.groups

FTP: ftp.uu.net in /news/config/newsgroups.Z

Lists of FTP Archives:

11-15 **Mac FTP list:** A list of FTP archives with Macintosh software and information. This list was originally created and copyrighted by Mike Gleason. It is currently maintained by Bruce Grubb.

Usenet newsgroup: comp.sys.mac.misc

FTP: sumex-aim.stanford.edu in /info-mac/info-mac/comm/info

11-16 **PC FTP list:** A list of FTP archives with PC software and information. This list is copyrighted and jointly maintained by Rhys Weatherley and Timo Salmi.

FTP: oak.oakland.edu in /pub/msdos/info/moder*.zip

FTP: garbo.uwasa.fi in /pc/pd2/moder*.zip

11-17 **University of San Diego Gopher FTP Gateway:** This gopher provides access to many FTP sites across the Internet.

Gopher: gopher.sdsc.edu in Gopher Gateways to Other Network Services/

Topical Resources:

11-18   **The Legal List:** A compilation of law-related resources on the Internet and elsewhere. This list is copyrighted by Erik J. Heels.

FTP: `ftp.midnight.com` in `/pub/LegalList/legallist.txt`

11-19   **Medical Resources List:** This is an extensive list of mailing lists, FTP sites, WAIS sources, telnet-accessible databases, and other resources of interest to those in the medical profession. This list is maintained and copyrighted by Lee Hancock.

FTP: `ftp.sura.net` in `/pub/nic/medical.resources`

11-20   **Not Just Cows:** Listings of agriculture and related science resources available via the Internet.

FTP: `nysernet.org` in `/pub/resource/guide/agguide.dos`

Lists of Library Resources:

11-21   **Accessing On-Line Bibliographic Databases:** A list of library catalogs and how to access them, maintained by Billy Barron and Marie-Christine Mahe.

FTP: `ftp.unt.edu` in `/library/`

Gopher: `yaleinfo.yale.edu port 7000`

11-22   **Hytelnet:** A program and a database that provide hypertext access to OPACs and other resources reachable by telnet. Versions exist for Macintosh, PC, Unix, VMS, etc.

Telnet: `access.usask.ca` login as `hytelnet`

FTP: `ftp.usask.ca` in `/pub/hytelnet/`

E-publication Resource Lists:

11-23   **EJOURNAL:** A list of e-serials compiled and maintained by Professor Michael Strangelove. A mid-1993 version of this list appears in the Association of Research Libraries (ARL) publication *Directory of Electronic Journals, Newsletters and Academic Discussion Lists* (see Bibliography for full citation).

E-mail: `listserv@acadvm1.uottawa.ca` [body = GET EJOURNL1 DIRECTRY <return> GET EJOURNL2 DIRECTRY] (Note the abbreviated spelling of EJOURNAL and that the two "get" commands should be on different lines.)

FTP: `cadvm1.uottawa.ca` in `/pub/religion/electronic-serials-directory.txt`

Gopher: `info.umd.edu`

11-24   **E-serial and e-text lists in gophers:** Here are a few gophers that contain organized and comprehensive lists of e-texts, e-serials, and other documents:

`gopher.unt.edu` (University of North Texas)

`gopher.cic.net` (CICNet)

`gopher.eff.org` in `Instant Karma Zine Stand/` (Electronic Frontier Foundation)

`ocf.berkeley.edu` in `Library/` (Berkeley OCF Online Library)

`gopher.carleton.edu` (Carleton College)

`library.cpl.org` (Cleveland Public Library)

`gopher.law.cornell.edu` (Cornell Law School Gopher)

`scilibx.ucsc.edu` (The Infoslug—UCSC Library)

`ns3.cc.lehigh.edu` in `LIBRARY` (Electronic Journals and Texts at Lehigh)

`ucsbuxa.ucsb.edu` 3001 (Government Publications and the Law Library at UCSB)

`gopher.loc.gov` (Library of Congress LC MARVEL)

`riceinfo.rice.edu` in `Information by Subject Area/` (Riceinfo Gopher)

`grace.skidmore.edu` in `The Electronic Reading Room/` (Skidmore Electronic Reading Room)

`dewey.lib.ncsu.edu` in `NCSU's "Library Without Walls"/` (North Carolina State University)

`sparcwood.princeton.edu` 9321 (Text Data Archives)

`gopher.netsys.com` 2001 (United States Federal Register)

`gopher.netsys.com` in `The Electronic Newsstand(tm)/` (The Internet Company's The Electronic Newsstand™)

`gopher.lib.virginia.edu` (University of Virginia Library)

`gopher.well.sf.ca.us` (Whole Earth 'Lectronic Link—The Well)

Lists of Internet Access Providers:

11-25 **Nixpub:** A list of public-access Unix providers maintained by Phil Eschallier.

FTP: `vfl.paramax.com` in `/pub/pubnet/`

Mailserv: `mail-server@bts.com` [body = `get PUB nixpub.long` or `get PUB nixpub.short`]

Mailing list: `mail-server@bts.com` [body = `subscribe NIXPUB-LIST` first-name last-name]

Usenet newsgroup: `comp.misc` or `comp.bbs.misc` or `alt.bbs`

11-26 **Pdial:** A list of public-dialup access providers maintained by Peter Kaminski. These sites do not neccessarily provide Unix access to the Internet.

Mailserv: `info-deli-server@netcom.com` [body = `Send PDIAL`]

Mailing list: `info-deli-server@netcom.com` [body = `subscribe PDIAL`]

Usenet newsgroup: `alt.internet.access.wanted` or `alt.bbs.lists` or `alt.on-line-service`

FTP: `ftp.netcom.com` in `/pub/info-deli/public-access/pdial` or `nic.merit.edu` in `/internet/pdial`

11-27 **Other Internet access provider lists:**

FTP: `vfl.paramax.com` in `/pub/pubnet/`

FTP: `liberty.uc.wlu.edu` in `/pub/lawlib/internet.access`

Gopher: `internic.net` in `InterNIC Information Services (General Atomics)/Getting Connected to the Internet/`

12. INTERNET ACCESS PROVIDERS

The services you can buy from providers are generally of two sorts: interactive services and protocol services. The former are the services you would use with standard telecommunications software, in which your home computer acts like a terminal to some interface program such as a menu system or a Unix shell. Protocol services, on the other hand, simply provide data transport to and from the Internet. To use protocol services you must have special software (and, in the case of high-speed leased-line links, specialized hardware as well). Protocol services include e-mail and Usenet news in the case of UUCP, POP, SMTP, and NNTP, as well as direct access to the Internet (in which your computer becomes an actual host) in the case of SLIP, PPP, and TCP/IP.

Entry Format:

Item
Number

12-n   **System/Service Name (**`domain name`**):** Organization Name

> **Area:** area serviced
>
> *i* phone number (voice and FAX); e-mail address; online help if available; FTP if available
>
> **Dialup Information:** phone numbers
>> Area Codes: list of local-access area codes
>> Modem Information: speed range   special modem protocols available
>
> **Interactive Services:** interfaces available
>> Service: pricing
>>
>> ...
>>
>> Internet service goodies: services offered with Internet access, other than FTP and telnet
>> *comments*
>
> **Protocol Services:**
>> Service: pricing
>>
>> ...
>>
>> *comments*
>
> **Special Services:** any unique or special services provided
>
> **online Registration:** phone number (modem), login instructions
>
> **Other:** further information

Where to Find It: This list was composed from many source listings on the Internet and then verified with the access providers. Most of the entries can be found in the following lists:

Nixpub: A list of public-access Unix providers maintained by Phil Eschallier.

FTP `vfl.paramax.com` in `/pub/pubnet/`

Mailserv `mail-server@bts.com`
> [body = `get PUB nixpub.long` or `get PUB nixpub.short`]

mailing list `mail-server@bts.com`
> [body = `subscribe NIXPUB-LIST` first-name last-name]

Usenet newsgroups `comp.misc` or `comp.bbs.misc` or `alt.bbs`

Pdial: A list of public-dialup access providers maintained by Peter Kaminski

Mailserv `info-deli-server@netcom.com` [body = `Send PDIAL`]

Mailing list `info-deli-server@netcom.com` [body = `subscribe PDIAL`]

Usenet newsgroups `alt.internet.access.wanted` or `alt.bbs.lists`
> or `alt.on-line-service`

FTP `ftp.netcom.com` in `/pub/info-deli/public-access/pdial`
> or `nic.merit.edu` in `/internet/pdial`

Other access provider lists:

FTP `vfl.paramax.com` in `/pub/pubnet/`

FTP `liberty.uc.wlu.edu` in `/pub/lawlib/internet.access`

Gopher `internic.net` in
> `InterNIC Information Services (General Atomics)/`
> `/Getting Connected to the Internet/`

Comments: Access providers offer a variety of interactive services that are all subtly different. To make things easier, I have grouped them into four categories: BBS, Limited, Basic, and Internet. BBS service means access to local e-mail and conferencing only. Limited service means access to either e-mail or Usenet newsgroups, but not both. Basic service means access to e-mail and Usenet newsgroups. Internet means access to TCP/IP-based information services, the bare bones of which are FTP and telnet. If "Internet" access is provided, any extras that are offered are listed under "Internet service goodies." Remember, this classification is for interactive services, which are accessed by logging into an account on the provider's computer using terminal-emulation software or telnet.

Please note also that Internet access providers are growing and changing all the time. The information provided here should by no means be taken as the final word. Almost all providers are upgrading and adding new services frequently, and prices change just as quickly. Always check with the contact address (*i*) for the latest information.

INTERNET ACCESS PROVIDERS

Entries By Area Code: On the following pages you will find an index to access providers, sorted by the area code in which dialup access is a local call. This should make it easier to find a provider in your area. Again, remember that providers are starting up or expanding their services all the time, and this list, though accurate at press time (October 1993), will rapidly become out of date. If your area code is not listed here, check with a provider in a nearby area code to see if it has expanded or is planning to expand into your area.

201
JVNCnet
Panix

202
CAPCON Connect
Express Access
tnc

203
JVNCnet

206
netcom

212
mindVOX
Panix

213
CERFnet
netcom

214
zgnews

215
JVNCnet
cellar
jabber

216
OARnet
wariat

301
CAPCON Connect
Express Access
decode
tnc

303
bohemia
cns
csn
nyx

310
CERFnet
Express Access
netcom

312
MCSNet
gagme
vpnet
CICNet

313
MSen

314
sugar

401
JVNCnet

403
debug

404
crl
netcom

407
GatorNet

408
a2i network
deepthought
gorn
netcom
quack
szebra

409
pro-haven

410
CAPCON Connect
Express Access
decode

414

Milwaukee Internet
Xchange
edsi
solaria

415
CERFnet
IGC
crl
netcom
well

416
Web
uunorth

419
OARnet

502
OARnet
WinNET

503
agora
bucket
m2xenix
netcom
techbook

504
sugar

508
NEARnet
NovaLink
genesis
northshore

510
CERFnet
bdt
crl
netcom
well

512
Illuminati Online

513
OARnet

516
JVNCnet
kilowatt

517
MSen

518
sixhub

519
uunorth

602
coyote
crl

603
NEARnet
mv

604
Web

606
lunatix

608
fullfeed
madnix

609
JVNCnet

612
skypoint

613
Web
uunorth

614

OARnet

616
MSen
wybbs

617
NEARnet
delphi
genesis
netcom
northshore
world

619
CERFnet
cg57
crash
netcom

703
Access <=> Internet
BBS
CAPCON Connect
Express Access
tnc
uunet

707
crl

708
MCSNet
gagme
sandv
vpnet

713
blkbox
sugar

714
CERFnet
Express Access
conexch
netcom

718
mindVOX
Panix

719
cns
csn

800
ANS CO+RE Services
IGC
JVNCnet
MSen
NovaLink
OARnet
WinNET
cns
crl
csn
uunet

804
wyvern

815
MCSNet
vpnet

816
delphi

818
CERFnet
abode
netcom

900
uunet

904
amaranth

906
Great White North
BBS

908
Express Access
JVNCnet

914
Panix

916
netcom

PDN
HoloNet
IGC
MSen
NovaLink
Delphi
psi

well
world

Australia
connect
Kralizec
uunet

New Zealand
actrix

United Kingdom
ANS CO+RE Services
DEMON
ExNet
GreenNet
infocom
Pegasus
uunet
WinNET

South America
AlterNex
ANS CO+RE Services
Chasque
Ecuanex
Nicarao
uunet

Russia & CIS
GlasNet

Italy
nervous

Scandinavia
NordNet

Germany
ANS CO+RE Services
isys-hh
rhein-main
scuzzy
uunet

Canada
ANS CO+RE Services
debug
uunet
uunorth
Web
WinNET

Switzerland
ANS CO+RE Services

Entries:

12-1 **a2i network** (`rahul.net`): a2i communications

Area: CA: Campbell, Los Altos, Los Gatos, Moutain View, San Jose, Santa Clara, Saratoga, Sunnyvale, Half Moon Bay, La Honda, Redwood City, San Carlos, Belmont, San Mateo, Woodside, Foster City.

i (408) 293-8078; info server: `info@rahul.net`; login as `guest`; FTP `ftp.rahul.net` in `/pub/BLURB`

Dialup: (408) 293-9010, (408) 293-9020 (PEP)

    Area Codes: 408

    Modem Information: 1200-14.4k   PEP

Interactive Services: Unix shell, custom menu system

    Basic + Internet: $12-20/month

    Online MS-DOS from within SunOS, Multiple virtual terminals

Protocol Services:

    UUCP + Domain name registration: $20-55/month

    Domain name registration: $40

12-2 **abode** (`abode.ttank.com`): **Abode Computer Services**

Area: El Monte, CA

i `eric@abode.ttank.com` (UUCP: `cerritos.edu!ttank!abode!eric`)

Dialup: (818) 287-5115

    Area Codes: 818

    Modem Information: 2400-9600 (9600 PEP only)   PEP

Interactive Services: Unix shell

    Basic: $40/year

Protocol Services: None

Special Services: games, C compiler

Other: PC Pursuit accessible

12-3 **Access <=> Internet BBS** (`sytex.com`): **Sytex Communications, Inc.**

Area: Arlington, VA

i (703) 358-9139; `info@sytex.com`

Dialup: (703) 528-4380

    Area Codes: 703

    Modem Information: 300-14.4k   PEP

Interactive Services: Waffle BBS

    BBS: Free

    Limited (e-mail only): $5/month

    Basic: $10/month

    Basic + Files from the Internet: $15/month

Protocol Services:

    UUCP: $5/month + 2/mb

Special Services: Electronic publishing, FTP by request, UUCP from UUNET Archives

Online Registration: Login as `bbs` password: `4internet`

12-4 **actrix** (`actrix.gen.nz`): Actrix Networks Ltd

Area: Wellington, New Zealand

i John Vorstermans +64-4-389-6316

Dialup: +64-4-389-5478

Modem Information: 300-14.4k   PEP, X.25

Interactive Services: Unix shell, Teamate BBS

Basic + Internet: NZ$72/year

Internet service goodies: gopher, etc

All services include volume charge

Protocol Services:

UUCP: NZ$25 setup fee + NZ$72/year for individuals and NZ$144/year for businesses

PPP, IP: NZ$1000 per year plus usage costs

ISND: Contact for charges

Anonymous UUCP: Free

All services include volume charge

Special Services: ClariNet, Planet (APC node) newsfeed, online CD-ROM

Online Registration: Login as `BBS` and fill out questionnaire

Other: One-week free trial of Usenet for all users

12-5 **agora** (`agora.rain.com`): RainDrop Laboratories

Area: Portland, Oregon

i `batie@agora.rain.com` (Alan Batie); info server: `info@agora.rain.com`; FTP `agora.rain.com` in `/pub/gopher-data/agora/fees`

Dialup: number available on request.

Area Codes: 503

Modem Information: 1200-14.4k

Interactive Services: Unix shell

Basic + Internet: $2 for 15 min/day, $6 for 1 hr/day, $16 unlimited

Internet service goodies: IRC, gopher, Archie

Protocol Services:

Contact for details

Online Registration: Login as `apply`

Other: PC Pursuit accessible

12-6 **AlterNex** (`ax.apc.org`): IBASE (The Instituto Brasilero de Analises Socias e Economicas) in cooperation with the Association of Progressive Communications (APC).

Area: Brazil

i +55(21)286-0348, Fax: +55(21)286-0541; `suporte@ax.apc.org` or `cafonso@ax.apc.org` (Carlos Afonso); PO: Rua Vicente de Souza 29, 22251-070

Rio de Janeiro, Brazil
Dialup: +55 (21) 286 0024 NUA: 7241 2150479

12-7 **amaranth** (`amaranth.com`): Amaranth Communications
Area: Pensacola, FL
i (904) 456-1993 (Jon Spelbring); `jsspelb@amaranth.com` (Jon Spelbring)
Dialup: (904) 456-2003
Area Codes: 904
Modem Information: 1200-14.4k   Telebit
Interactive Services: GDX-BBS, Unix Shell
BBS: Free
BBS + e-mail + Usenet: $3/month
Basic: $5/month + $5 setup fee
Protocol Services:
UUCP e-mail only to Unix/DOS/Mac: $8/month + $10 setup fee
UUCP + e-mail: $10/month + $10 setup fee
Special Services: 300+Mb Unix software (sources) online, including XWindows and SVR4
Online Registration: Login as `bbs` and send mail to Jon Spelbring or sysop
Other: Partial newsfeeds only—new groups added on request

12-8 **ANS CO+RE Services** (`ans.net`): ANS CO+RE Systems, Inc.
Area: Elmsford, NY
i 800-456-8267 or 914-789-5300, FAX 914-789-5310; `info@ans.net`
Dialup: Contact for number
Area Codes: 800
Modem Information: 1200-14.4k
Interactive Services: Custom menu
Internet (telnet only): $25-45/month + $8.50/hour
Protocol Services:
UUCP: $45/month + $8.50/hour
SLIP, PPP: $35/month + $8.50/hour
Leased Line: (56k): $15,500
Leased Line: (T1): $32,000-36,000
Domain name registration
Protocol services are available in Canada, Germany, Mexico, Switzerland, and the UK
Special Services: Security services; gateway services for others who wish to become service providers; LiteSpeed: a high-bandwidth, occasional-use service

12-9 **bdt** (`bdt.com`): Beckemeyer Development
Area: Oakland, CA
i `david@bdt.com` (David Beckemeyer)
Dialup: (510) 530-9682
Area Codes: 510

Modem Information: 1200-14.4k   PEP

Interactive Services: Custom menu system
Basic: $35/year

Protocol Services:
UUCP: Free—Limited Availability

Other: 30-day free trial

12-10   **blkbox** (`blkbox.com`): The Black Box
Area: Houston, TX
i `mknewman@blkbox.com` (Marc Newman)
Dialup: (713) 480-2686 (5+ lines)
Area Codes: 713
Modem Information: 300-14.4k

Interactive Services: Unix shell
Basic + Internet: $21.65/month or $108.25/6 months
Internet service goodies: Archie, gopher, NCFTP, IRC, WAIS, WWW, whois, etc.

Protocol Services:
SLIP, PPP: $108.25/month (14,400-baud modems)

Special Services: 25+ online adventure games

Other: PC Pursuit accessible

12-11   **bohemia** (`metronet.org`): bohemia public access Unix
Area: Denver, CO
i (303) 657-0128 (Jason Taubman); `jason@metronet.org` (Jason Taubman)
Dialup: (303) 429-9110, (303) 429-9205
Area Codes: 303
Modem Information: 300-14.4k

Interactive Services: Custom menu system, Unix Shell
Basic: contact for information

Protocol Services:
UUCP: $5/month

Online Registration: Login as new

12-12   **bucket** (`bucket.rain.com`): none provided
Area: Portland, OR
i `rickb@pail.rain.com`
Dialup: (503) 632-7891
Area Codes: 503
Modem Information: 300-2400   PEP

Interactive Services: Unix shell
Basic: $30/year
Basic + Internet: $50/year

Protocol Services:
UUCP: Free
Other: PC Pursuit accessible

12-13 CAPCON Connect (`capcon.net`): CAPCON Library Network

Area: District of Columbia, Suburban Maryland, Northern Virginia; access available nation-wide

i (202) 331-5771 FAX (202) 797-7719; `capcon@capcon.net`

Dialup: Contact for number
Area Codes: 202, 301, 410, 703
Modem Information: 300-14.4k

Interactive Services: Custom menu system
Basic + Internet: $19-37/month + $35 setup fee
Internet Access Training (one day): $75
Internet service goodies: Archie, gopher, WAIS, whois

Protocol Services:
FTP Archive Space: $15 setup fee + $25.00/month for up to 2Mb
SLIP/PPP (in development)

Special Services: Free customer support by telephone, fax, and e-mail 8:30-5:30, Monday through Friday. Full-day training and CAPCON Connect User Manual

Other: "At CAPCON Connect we attempt to maximize the use of and contribution to information resources on the Internet through training and technical support of librarians, researchers and other information professionals."

12-14 cellar (`cellar.org`): The Cellar

Area: Trooper/Oaks, PA (Philadelphia metro area)

i `toad@cellar.org` (Tony Shepps)

Dialup: (215) 539-3043
Area Codes: 215 (changing to 610 after January 1995)
Modem Information: 300-14.4k HST

Interactive Services: Waffle with many friendly modifications
BBS: free
Basic: $10/month, $55/6 months, or $90/year

Protocol Services: none

Special Services: The Cellar is an electronic coffeehouse of sorts. It provides an active set of local message sections and a diverse community of users. Has a wide collection of e-texts, and fairly current releases of Linux for download

Other: PC Pursuit accessible

12-15 CERFnet (`cerf.net`): California Education and Research Federation Network

Area: CA: Los Angeles, Oakland, San Diego, Irvine, Pasadena, Palo Alto

i 800-876-2373 or 619-455-3900, `help@cerf.net`, FTP `nic.cerf.net` in `/cerfnet/dial-n-cerf/`

Dialup: Contact for numbers

Area Codes: 213, 310, 415, 510, 619, 714, 818
Interactive Services: Unix shell, menu
Basic + Internet: $10/hour ($8/hour on weekend) + $20/month
Internet service goodies: IRC, hytelnet, gopher, WAIS, WWW
Protocol Services:
SLIP, PPP: Contact for details
Leased Line: (56k, T1): Contact for details

12-16 **cg57 (**`cg57.cts.com`**): E & S Systems Public Access Unix**
Area: San Diego, CA
i (619) 278-4641 (Steve Froeschke); `steve@cg57.cts.com` (Steve Froeschke)
Dialup: (619) 278-3905,8267,9837
Area Codes: 619
Modem Information: 300-14.4k   PEP & TurboPep, HST
Interactive Services: Custom menu system, XWindows, Waffle
BBS: Free
Basic: $30/3 months, $50/6 months, $80/9 months, $100/year
Basic + Internet: coming soon
Protocol Services:
UUCP: $10/month
ANON UUCP: Free
Special Services: Fidonet Echomail conferences, Nethack, Moria, Abermud, and
DikuMUD available from BBS
Online Registration: Login as `bbs`, no password

12-17 **Chasque (**`chasque.apc.org`**): ITeM (Instituto del Tercer Mundo) in coopera-
tion with the Association of Progressive Communications (APC)**
Area: Uruguay, Argentina, Paraguay
i +598(2)496192, FAX +598(2)419222; `apoyo@chasque.apc.org` or
`rbissio@chasque.apc.org` (Roberto Bissio)
Dialup: +598 2 499147 (3 lines) NUA: 748250029

12-18 **CICNet (**`cic.net`**): CICNet, Inc (Committee for Institutional Cooperation)**
Area: Michigan, Illinois, Indiana, Ohio, Wisconsin, Minnesota, and Iowa
i (313) 998-6102 or (313) 998-6104, FAX (313) 998-6105 or (313) 998-6105;
`hankins@cic.net` or `shaffer@cic.net`
Dialup: Contact for numbers
Area Codes: 312
Modem Information: 2400-14.4
Interactive Services:
Telnet only: $10-30/month for first 10 hours, thereafter at $1.25-2.50/hour
Protocol Services:
SLIP (dialup): $175-300 startup fee + $15-40/month for first 10 hours, therafter at
$2.00-3.50/hour

SLIP (dedicated): $735-1150 startup fee + $250-350/month for first 10 hours, thereafter at $2-3.50/hour

Leased Line (56k, T1, all protocols): Contact for pricing

Special Services: Dial-up service

12-19 **cns** (`cscns.com`): Community News Service

Area: Colorado Spring, CO

i (800) 748-1200 or (719) 592-1240; `service@cscns.com`

Dialup: (719) 520-1700 or (303) 758-2656

Area Codes: 303, 719, 800

Modem Information: 300-14.4k

Interactive Services: Unix shell

Basic + Internet: $2.75/hour ($250/month cap) for Colorado Springs/Denver, $8/hour for 800 access

Internet service goodies: gopher, IRC, WAIS

Protocol Services:

UUCP:

Internet Routing:

SLIP, PPP: $75 startup fee + $2.75/hour ($250/month cap) or $8/hour for 800 service

Leased Line (56k, T1) SLIP, PPP: Contact for pricing

Special Services: ClariNet, USA Today, easy-to-use menus, full customer support

Online Registration: Login as `new`; password: `newuser`

12-20 **ComLink** (`oln.comlink.apc.org`): ComLink e.V. in cooperation with the Association of Progressive Communications (APC).

Area: Germany, (and in parts: Austria, Switzerland, Zagred, Beograd, Northern Italy)

i +49(511)350-1573; `support@oln.comlink.apc.org` or `udo@oln.comlink.apc.org` (Udo Schacht-Wiegand); PO: Casilla Correo 1539, Montevideo, Uruguay, PO: Moorkamp 46, D-W3000 Hannover 1, Germany

Dialup: 546661

12-21 **conexch** (`conexch.uucp`): Dighera Data Services; The Consultants' Exchange BBS

Area: Santa Ana, CA

i (714) 842-2862; `sysop@conexch.uucp` (UUCP: ...!`uunet!{wilbur|stanton}!conexch!sysop`)

Dialup: (714) 842-5851 (714) 842-6348

Area Codes: 714

Modem Information: 300-9600

Interactive Services: Unix shell, BBS, guest

BBS: Free

Limited (Unix shell, Usenet: read only): Free

Basic: $25.00/quarter minimum donation

Protocol Services:
> Anon UUCP: Login as `nuucp`, no password

Other: PC Pursuit accessible

12-22 **connect** (`connect.com.au`): connect.com.au pty ltd

> **Area:** Australia: Adelaide, Brisbane, Canberra, Melbourne, Perth, Sydney
>
> *i* +61 3 5282239, FAX +61 3 5285887; `connect@connect.com.au`; FTP `ftp.connect.com.au`
>
> **Dialup:** Contact for number
>> Area Codes: +61 8, +61 7, +61 6, +61 3, +61 9, +61 2
>> Modem Information: 2400-14.4k   PEP in Melbourne and Sydney
>
> **Interactive Services:** None
>
> **Protocol Services:**
>> UUCP: A$2,000 for 90 minutes connect time per day per year
>> A$400 per additional hour per day per year
>> A$5,000 permanent per year (plus setup cost)
>> ISDN: A$2,000 for 60 minutes connect time per day per year
>> A$400 per additional half hour per day per year
>> A$10,000 permanent per year (plus setup cost)
>> SLIP, PPP: A$2,000 for 90 minutes connect time per day per year
>> A$400 per additional hour per day per year
>> A$5000 permanent per year (plus setup cost)

12-23 **coyote:** Datalog Consulting

> **Area:** Tucson, AZ
>
> *i* `ejm@datalog.com` (E.J. McKernan)
>
> **Dialup:** (602) 744-7586
>> Area Codes: 602
>> Modem Information: 300-14.4k   PEP
>
> **Interactive Services:** Waffle BBS
>> BBS (Login as `bbs`, no password): Free
>
> **Protocol Services:**
>> Anon-UUCP (Login as `nuucp`, no password)
>> UUCP conections for mail use available

12-24 **crash** (`crash.cts.com` or `ctsnet.cts.com`): CTS Network Services (CTSNET)

> **Area:** San Diego, CA
>
> *i* (619) 593-9597, FAX (619) 444-9247; `bblue@crash.cts.com` or `support@crash.cts.com`; info server: `info@crash.cts.com` (server), (human)
>
> **Dialup:** (619) 593-6400, 7300, 9500
>> Area Codes: 619
>> Modem Information: HST, PEP

Interactive Services: Unix shell
- Basic: $18-35/month
- Basic + Internet: $18-35/month
- Internet service goodies: IRC, Gopher, Archie, WAIS, POP, SMTP, NNTP
- Domain name registration: Free
- UMDSS (Apple ProLine Gateway): included
- *Internet interface T1; wide variety of services of all types*

Protocol Services:
- UUCP: included (basic service)
- NNTP: $10-25
- SLIP, PPP, POP: $23-150/month (depends on time, dedication, number of IP addresses, etc.)
- Leased Line 56k (TCP/IP, SLIP, PPP): $865/month, dedicated
- DNS, MX Forwarding, Routing: from $10

Special Services: Reuters, ClariNet, 3000+ newsgroups

Other: PC Pursuit accessible. POPs in various San Diego County areas. Telnetable, FTPable

12-25 **crl** (`crl.com`): CR Laboratories Dialup Internet Access

Area: CA: San Francisco Bay area + Concord, San Rafael, Santa Rosa; AZ: Phoenix, Scottsdale, Mesa, Tempe, and Glendale; GA: Greater Atlanta Metro Area

i (415) 381-2800; `info@crl.com`

Dialup: 415-389-UNIX
- Area Codes: 404, 415, 510, 602, 707, 800
- Modem Information: 300-14400   PEP, TurboPEP

Interactive Services: Unix shell
- Basic + Internet: $17.50/month + $19.50 signup fee
- Internet service goodies: Dedicated MUD server running several simulations

Protocol Services:
- SLIP + NNTP: $150/month
- UUCP: $45/month
- Leased Line 56k: $400/month + local loop charge

Special Services: Extensive software archives, FTP mirrors

12-26 **csn** (`csn.org`): Colorado SuperNet, Inc.

Area: CO: Golden, Alamosa, Boulder/Denver, Colorado Springs, Durango and more

i (303) 273-3471, FAX (303) 273-3475; info server: `info@csn.org`; FTP `csn.org` in `/CSN/reports/DialinInfo.txt`

Dialup: Contact for numbers
- Area Codes: 303, 719, 800
- Modem Information: 1200-14.4k

Interactive Services: Unix shell or custom menu
- Basic + Internet: $20 startup fee + $1-3/hour up to $250/month and $15/month minimum
- Internet service goodies: IRC, gopher, WAIS, Archie, WWW, talk

Remote Internet Only: $1/hour up to $250/month maximum
$15/month min or 8$/hour on 800 number

Protocol Services:
UUCP: $40 startup fee + $1-3/hour up to $250/month and $15/month minimum
SLIP, PPP: $100 startup fee + $1-3/hour up to $250/month and $15/month minimum
XRemote: $20 + $1-3/hour up to $250/month and $15/month minimum
Leased Line 56k (all protocols): $10,000 + line costs
Leased Line T1 (all protocols): $15,000 + line costs
Domain name registration: $20 setup fee

Special Services: On-site training, consulting, FTP archive space, online games, software archives, access to Colorado libraries

12-27 **debug** (`debug.cuc.ab.ca`): Debug Computer Services, The Magic BBS

Area: Calgary, Alberta, Canada
i (403) 248-5798 (Rob Franke); `root@debug.cuc.ab.ca`
Dialup: (403) 569-2882
Area Codes: 403
Modem Information: 300-14.4k   PEP, HST
Interactive Services: Unix shell, BBS System
BBS: $10/month
Unix Shell: $25/month
Internet service goodies: FTP-server access, MUD
Domain name registration: $60/year
Protocol Services:
UUCP e-mail only: $10/month
UUCP Usenet (Partial feed) + e-mail - $20/month
UUCP Usenet (Full feed) + e-mail - $25/month
ANON UUCP: Free but only used for site information.
SLIP, PPP, POP: Coming soon
Special Services: NYSE stock quotes, legal forms, menuized world facts, multi-user games
Online Registration: Follow instructions given at connect
Other: Debug is a multi-line service, currently with 7 lines, but expanding all the time. Platform is currently SCO Unix, and SCO Xenix, on Intel-based systems

12-28 **decode** (`decode.uucp`): American Cryptogram Association

Area: Columbia, MD
i `postmaster@decode.uucp`
Dialup: (410) 730-6734
Area Codes: 301, 410
Modem Information: 300-9600   HST
Interactive Services: Waffle
Basic: Free
File downloads: Free

Protocol Services:
UUCP: Free

Special Services: Specializes in cryptography and security. Home of the American Cryptogram Association

Online Registration: Login as new for a short questionnaire; validation within 24 hours. Level of access granted based on interest and group affiliation

12-29 deepthought (deepthought.armory.com): The Armory

Area: Santa Cruz, CA

i (408) 458-9347 (John DuBois); root@armory.com

Dialup: 423-4810, 423-1767
Area Codes: 408
Modem Information: 300-14.4k   ZyXEL

Interactive Services: Unix shells, scosh, XWindows
Basic + Internet: Free

Protocol Services:
Anonymous UUCP: Free
Login as uuanon, no password; get /usr/spool/uucppublic/pub/index
Dialup SLIP & PPP for interactive access: Free

Special Services: UUNET source archives, C/Pascal/Fortran/BASIC compilers, TinyMud, rn/trn

Online Registration: Login as request, no password

12-30 Delphi (delphi.com): DELPHI Internet Services

Area: MA: Boston; KS: Kansas City

i (800) 695-4005; walthowe@delphi.com

Dialup: 800-365-4636
Area Codes: 617, 816, PDN (Sprintnet, Tymnet, DATAPAC)
Modem Information: 2400 (9600 where available on Sprintnet and Tymnet)

Interactive Services: Menu system
Basic: $10/month for 4 hours or $20/month for 20 hours
Basic + Internet: $13/month for 4 hours or $23/month for 20 hours
Internet service goodies: gopher, WAIS, Archie, netfind, finger, Hytelnet, IRC, MUD, whois

Special Services: wire services (UPI and Reuters), member conferencing, encyclopedia, financial services, stock quotes, travel services, multi-player games, DIALOG, shopping, large databases

Online Registration: (800) 695-4002 by modem, login as JOINDELPHI password: INTERNETSIG

12-31 DEMON INTERNET (demon.co.uk): Demon Internet Limited

Area: London and Warrington, England; Edinburgh, Scotland

i +44 (0)81 349 0063; internet@demon.co.uk

Dialup: +44 81 343 4848, +44 925 411383, +44 31 552 8883

Area Codes: +44 81, +44 925 (local to +44 61 and +44 51), +44 31
Modem Information: 2400-14.4k

Interactive Services:
Basic + Internet: £10/month or £120/year + £12.50 startup fee

Protocol Services:
PPP & SLIP: £10/month or £120/year + £12.50 startup fee

12-32 **Ecuanex** (`ecuanex.apc.org`): INTERCOM (Corporacion Interinstitucional de Comunicacion Electronica) in cooperation with the Association of Progressive Communications (APC)

Area: Ecuador

i +593(2) 528-716, FAX +593(2) 505-073; `intercom@ecuanex.apc.org` (Sally Burch), PO: 12 de Octubre 622, Oficina 504, Casilla 1712566, Quito, Ecuador

Dialup: Contact for numbers

Interactive Services: none

Protocol Services:
Contact for details

12-33 **edsi:** Enterprise Data Systems Incorporated

Area: Appleton, WI

i (414)-734-3462 (Chuck Tomasi); `chuck@appleton.wi.us` (Chuck Tomasi); login as `help`

Dialup: (414) 734-2499 (other lines available to system members)
Area Codes: 414
Modem Information: 300-14.4k   Telebit

Interactive Services: BBS (menus and command line), Unix shell
BBS (Single line, local mail): Free
Basic: $15/year

Protocol Services:
UUCP: $15/year

Special Services: Full-featured bulletin board with command-line-driven interface as well as menu interface. Uploads and downloads available. Multi-user chat and multi-user games also available.

Online Registration: Login as `new` or `newuser`

12-34 **ExNet** (`exnet.com`): ExNet Systems Ltd

Area: London, England, UK

i +44 81 755 0077 (GMT 1300-2300); `HelpEx@exnet.co.uk`

Dialup: Contact for numbers
Area Codes: +44
Modem Information: 300-14.4k

Interactive Services: Unix shell, custom menu
Basic: £5 + VAT

Protocol Services:
UUCP: £100/year

Special Services: Fully Qualified Domain Name unlimited data transfer for £300/year

12-35 **Express Access (**`digex.net`**): Digital Express Group, Inc.**

Area: Greenbelt, MD; Serves Washington, DC/Baltimore, MD/Northern VA/New Brunswick, NJ /Orange County, CA

i (800) 969-9090 or (301) 220-2020, FAX (301) 220-0477; info server: `info@digex.net`

Dialup: (301) 220-0258, (410) 768-8774, (908) 937-9481, (714) 377-9784

Area Codes: 202, 301, 310, 410, 703, 714, 908

Modem Information: 300-14.4k

Interactive Services: Unix shell

Basic: $15/month or $150/year

Basic + Internet: $25/month or $250/year

Internet service goodies: all included with Internet service

Remote Internet Only: $8.95/month

Protocol Services:

SLIP, PPP: $35/month "Personal IP" (includes POP and NNTP)

SLIP, PPP: $45/month "Business IP" (includes custom domain name)

Leased Line: 56k through T3: Contact for pricing

Domain name registration

Special Services: ClariNet, archive space accessible via anonymous FTP for businesses or organizations

Online Registration: Login as `new`

Other: PC Pursuit accessible. T1 connection to domestic backbone.

12-36 **fullfeed (**`fullfeed.com` or `fullfeed.uucp`**): FullFeed Communications**

Area: Madison, Wisconsin, USA, serving the Madison local-calling area

i (608) 246-4239; `sysop@fullfeed.com`

Dialup: (608) 246-2701 (multiple data lines on rollover)

Area Codes: 608

Modem Information: 300-14.4k   SuperPEP

Interactive Services: Unix shell

Basic + Internet: $16/month

Protocol Services:

UUCP: $24/month (low volume) and $32/month (high volume)

SLIP, PPP, POP: Contact for pricing

Leased Line 56k (TCP/IP, SLIP, PPP): Contact for pricing

Domain name registration

UUCP map registrations

Special Services: Green Bay Packers mailing list, mailing list services, nano-technology archive, UUCP smart-host mail addressing, UUCP map database

Online Registration: Login as `newuser` read docs, then send e-mail to `SYSop`

12-37 **gagme (**`gagme.chi.il.us`**): GAGME Public Access Unix**
    Area: Chicago, IL
    i `info@gagme.chi.il.us`
    Dialup: (312) 282-8606
        Area Codes: 312, 708
        Modem Information: 300-14.4k   PEP
    Interactive Services: Unix shell
        Limited (e-mail only): Free
        Limited (Usenet only): Free
        Basic: $60/year ($40/year for full-time students)
    Protocol Services:
        UUCP: Free with Basic
    Other: PC Pursuit accessible

12-38 **GatorNet (**`gator.oau.org`**): Gator Communications**
    Area: Orlando, Florida
    i (407) 324-9033; `larry@gator.oau.org`
    Dialup: Yes
        Area Codes: 407
        Modem Information: 300-14.4k   PEP, HST, v.fast, v.terbo
    Interactive Services:
        Basic: $7/month
        Basic + Internet: $29/month
        Internet service goodies: complete with all available services
    Protocol Services:
        UUCP: $20/month
        NNTP: $1/month
        SLIP, PPP, POP: $100/month
        Leased Line: 56k (all protocols): $600/month
        Frame Relay: $5/month
        Internet Routing: $20/month
        Domain name registration: $40
    Online Registration: available in 1994

12-39 **genesis (**`genesis.nred.ma.us`**): Genesis Public Access Unix**
    Area: North Reading, MA
    i `steve1@genesis.nred.ma.us` (Steve Belczyk); info server:
        `info@genesis.nred.ma.us`
    Dialup: (508) 664-0149
        Area Codes: 508, 617
        Modem Information: 300-14.4k   HST
    Interactive Services: Unix shell, menu
        Basic: Free

Protocol Services:
   UUCP: Free

12-40 **GlasNet** (`glas.apc.org`): in cooperation with the Association of Progressive Communications (APC)

   Area: Russia, Commonwealth of Independent States

   i +7(095)207-0704 or +7(095)207-0889, FAX +7(095)207-0889;
      `support@glas.apc.org` or `avoronov@glas.apc.org` (Anatoly A. Voronov);
      P.O.: Ulitsa Yaroslavaskaya 8, Korpus 3, Komnata 111, 129164 Moscow, Russia, CIS

   Dialup: +7-095-262-4857, 262-0209

12-41 **gorn** (`gorn.echo.com`): none provided

   Area: Santa Cruz, CA

   i `falcon@gorn.echo.com`

   Dialup: (408) 458-2289
      Area Codes: 408
      Modem Information: 300-14.4k   PEP

   Interactive Services: Unix shell
      Basic: Donation

   Protocol Services:
      UUCP: Free

   Special Services: games

12-42 **Great White North BBS** (`lopez.marquette.mi.us`): Great White North UPlink, Inc.

   Area: Marquette, Michigan; Michigan's Upper Peninsula

   i (906) 228-3275 (Gary Bourgois), FAX (906) 228-7477;
      `flash@lopez.marquette.mi.us`

   Dialup: (906) 228-4399
      Area Codes: 906
      Modem Information: 1200-9600

   Interactive Services: Menu, custom BBS shell (Starbase III), Unix shell, nn newsreader
      BBS: 90 days free access, $15/year
      Basic: $30/year

   Protocol Services: None

   Special Services: Free in-home tutoring for members; BBS specializes in communications topics, including ham and shortwave radio, TVRO Satellite (it puts on a national two-way talk show every Friday heard over Spacenet 3, Channel 21 5.8 audio); several online games; and software archives for many popular platforms, including DOS, Amiga, and old 8-bit machines

   Online Registration: Login as new

12-43 **GreenNet** (`gn.apc.org`): GreenNet in cooperation with the Association of Progressive Communications (APC)

Area: Great Britain, Western Europe, Africa, Asia

i +44(71)608-3040, FAX +44(71)253-0801; `support@gn.apc.org` or `viv@gn.apc.org` (Viv Kendon); 23 Bevenden Street, London N1 6BH, England

Dialup: +44 (71) 608-2622, +44 (71) 608-2911 NUA: 2342 12301371

Modem Information: 1200-14.4k

12-44 **HoloNet** (`holonet.net`)**:** Information Access Technologies Inc.

Area: Berkeley, CA

i (510) 704-0160; `support@holonet.net`; info server: `info@holonet.net`

Dialup: national dial-up numbers (call 1-800-NET-HOLO with your modem at 8-N-1 to find a local number)

Area Codes: nationwide

Modem Information: 1200-14.4k

Interactive Services: Menu-driven

Basic: $6/month or $60/year plus hourly connect charges

Basic + Internet: $2/hour off-peak, $4/hour peak + volume charges of $1-2/Mb after the first Mb

Internet service goodies: IRC, games, offline reader support, Archie, gopher, WAIS, WWW, etc.

Protocol Services:

UUCP: $50 setup fee (must be a HoloNet member)

Special Services: USA Today Descisionline, games, HoloQM Service (for Quick Mail users), and HoloDNS Service (domain name registration)

Online Registration: Call (510) 704-1058 with modem at 8-N-1, and follow prompts (use all lower-case letters)

12-45 **IGC** (`igc.apc.org`) **PeaceNet, EcoNet, ConflictNet, LaborNet:** Institute for Global Communications/IGC Networks

Area: CA: Palo Alto, San Francisco

i (415) 442-0220; `support@igc.apc.org`; FTP `igc.apc.org` in `/pub`

Dialup: 415-322-0284

Area Codes: 415, 800, PDN (SprintNet), 617 (via `world.std.com`)

Modem Information: 300-14.4k

Interactive Services: Custom menu system

Basic + telnet: $15 startup + $10/month + $3/hour after first hour

FAX gateway

Telex gateway

Protocol Services:

Contact for details

Special Services: Local forums on environmental, peace, and social-justice issues. Low-cost Internet access provider for non-profit organizations

Online Registration: Login as `new`

12-46 **Illuminati Online a.k.a Freegate (**`illuminati.io.com`**): Steve Jackson Games Incorporated**
Area: Austin, TX
i (512) 447-7866, FAX (512) 447-1144; `admin@io.com`
Dialup: (512) 448-8950
    Area Codes: 512
    Modem Information: 300-14.4k
Interactive Services:
    Basic+Internet: Cheap plan: $10/month for 20 hours, thereafter at $0.80/hour. Or
        $28/month for 80 hours, thereafter at $0.80/hour
    Internet service goodies: IRC, gopher, MUD, WWW, and more
    Internet Remote Only (io.com): $10/month for 80 hours, thereafter at $0.80/hour
Protocol Services: None
Special Services: Online games (both single-player and multi-user), conferencing service, uncensored Usenet news, shell accounts.
Online Registration: Login as NEW
Other: 1-year advance signup gets you a 15% discount. Two-week free trial

12-47 **infocom (**`infocom.co.uk`**): DGI-INFOCOM**
Area: Berkshire, UK
i +44 734 344000, FAX +44 734 32 09 88; `sysop@infocom.co.uk`; info server:
    `info@infocom.co.uk`
Dialup: +44-734-34-00-55 +44
    Modem Information: 300-14.4k
Interactive Services: BBS
    Basic: £50/year or £5/month
Protocol Services:
    UUCP: included with Basic
Special Services: Sofware archives and Teletext pages
Online Registration: Login as new

12-48 **isys-hh (**`isys-hh.hanse.de` or `isys-hh.hanse.sub.org`**): iSYS Infosystems & loth systemtechnik**
Area: Hamburg, DE
i +49-40-40192182; `mike@isys-hh.hanse.de` (Michael "Mike" Loth)
Dialup: +49-40-404866 +49-40-494867 +49-40-4905801
    Modem Information: 300-14.4k   ZyXEL, ISDN
Interactive Services: Unix shell, GEONET menu system
    Basic: $10/month
Protocol Services:
    UUCP: $10/month
    ANON UUCP: Free (UUCP only, no rnews/rmail, get `~/nuucp.help`, for index get
        `~/ls-lgR.[z|Z|F]` or `~/index.[zip|lzh|txt]`

NNTP: $10/month
SLIP/PPP: $10/month

Special Services: Mailserver `mailserver@isys-hh.hanse.de`; Listserver `isys-request@isys-hh.hanse.de`; Net Directory Service `netdir@isys-hh.hanse.de`

Online Registration: Login as `guest`, no password

12-49 **jabber** (`bts.com`): Bux Technical Services

Area: Doylestown, PA

i (215) 348-9721, FAX (215) 348-2567; `phil@bts.com` (Phil Eschallier)

Dialup: (215) 348-9727
Area Codes: 215
Modem Information: 300-14.4k   PEP, TurboPEP

Interactive Services: "*NIX Depot" BBS
BBS: Free

Protocol Services:
UUCP: $20-205/month depending on volume

Other: BTS is a consulting and contracting firm—computer & network admin., software engineering, hardware sales, and publishing services are all available

12-50 **JvNCnet** (`jvnc.net`): Global Enterprise Services, Inc.

Area: Princeton, New Jersey; national and international access

i (609) 897-7300, FAX (609) 897-7310; `info@jvnc.net`; FTP `jvnc.net` in `/pub/jvnc.net-info`

Dialup: Contact for numbers
Area Codes: 800, 201, 203, 212, 215, 401, 516, 609
Modem Information: 300-14.4k

Interactive Services: none

Protocol Services:
Telnet only: $19/month + $10/hour + $36 setup fee
SLIP (various levels of access): $19-120/month + $36-99 setup fee
SLIP (dedicated port:): $300/month + $1,000 setup fee
Leased Line: 19.2k to T1 (all protocols): contact for charges
Domain name registration: included
SLIP software interface included for Mac and PC platforms, discount for Unix platforms

12-51 **kilowatt** (`kilowatt.linet.org`): Kilowatt Computers of Deer Park, NY

Area: Deer Park, NY

i (516) 253-2805 (Arthur Krewat); `krewat@kilowatt.linet.org` or `krewat@kilowatt.uucp`

Dialup: (516) 586-4743, (516) 667-6142, (516) 595-2405
Area Codes: 516
Modem Information: 300-14.4k   PEP Turbo-PEP

Interactive Services: BBS

    Basic: Free

Protocol Services:

    UUCP: Free

    SLIP: Free (for development only)

Special Services: XWindows—full source distribution for X11R5PL25

12-52 **Kralizec Dialup Unix System (`kralizec.zeta.org.au`):** Zeta Microcomputer Software

Area: Sydney, Australia

i +61-2-837-1397; `nick@kralizec.zeta.org.au`

Dialup: +61-2-837-1183, 1868, 2349, 1933

    Modem Information: 300-14.4k

Interactive Services: Unix shell

    Basic + Internet: AU$10/month (provides up to 10 hours connect time)

Protocol Services:

    SLIP, PPP - Planned

Special Services: Voice hotline, quick service with committed service levels, large software library

Online Registration: Login as `guest`, no password

12-53 **lunatix (`lunatix.lex.ky.us`):** Lexington Public Access Unix

Area: Lexington, KY

i (606) 233-2051; `robert@lunatix.lex.ky.us`

Dialup: (606) 255-9121, (606) 255-9312

    Area Codes: 606

    Modem Information: 300-14.4k   WorldBlazer

Interactive Services: Unix shell, BBS

    BBS: Free

    Basic: Free

Protocol Services:

    UUCP: $0-10/month

Special Services: Multiuser games

12-54 **m2xenix (`m2xenix.psg.com`):** PSGnet

Area: Portland, OR

i (503) 297-9145; `randy@psg.com`

Dialup: (503) 297-3211, (503) 297-0935

    Area Codes: 503

    Modem Information: 300-14.4k   PEP on 3211

Interactive Services: Unix shell

    Basic+Internet: Free

    Internet service goodies: gopher and more

Protocol Services:
    Domain name registration: Free
    UUCP: Free
    NNTP, PPP, SLIP, POP, IMAP: Free

Special Services: Network operations center for RAINet, Portland's metro IP network

Other: PC Pursuit accessible

12-55   **madnix** (`madnix.uucp`): ARP Software

Area: Madison, WI

i `ray@madnix.uucp` (Ray Hill)

Dialup: (608) 273-2657
    Area Codes: 608
    Modem Information: 300-14.4k

Interactive Services: Unix shell, BBS
    BBS + e-mail + news: Free
    Basic: $0.50-2/month

Protocol Services:
    UUCP: $2/month

Special Services: Online archives of: Atari software, games, laserdisc information, lynx, movies, MUDs, music, PC shareware, source code from Usenet, mirror of Star Wars archives, misc text files, and Unix-related FAQs and archives

Online Registration: Login as `bbs`

12-56   **MCSNet** (`mcs.com`): Macro Computer Solutions

Area: Chicago, IL

i (312) 248-8649; `karl@ddsw1.mcs.com` (Karl Denninger); info server: `info@genesis.mcs.com`

Dialup: (312) 248-0900
    Area Codes: 312, 708, 815
    Modem Information: 300-14.4k   PEP
    ISDN "B" channel (56k) supported

Interactive Services: Unix shell, AKCS BBS
    BBS: Free for 1 hour/day
    Basic: $20/quarter or $60/year
    Basic + Internet: $10-25/month
    Internet service goodies: IRC, gopher, Hytelnet
    Internet Remote Only: $6.60-15/month

Protocol Services:
    anonymous UUCP (NUUCP) from 12 AM to 6 AM (~/DIRECTORY/README for info on anon uucp)
    SLIP: $1/hour
    Leased Line: 56k: Contact for pricing

12-57 **Milwaukee Internet Xchange (`mixcom.com`): MIX Communications**

Area: Milwaukee, WI

i (414) 962-8172 (Dean Roth); `sysop@mixcom.com`

Dialup: (414) 241-5469

Area Codes: 414

Modem Information: 1200-14.4k

Interactive Services: Unix shell, menu

Basic: $9/month

Basic + Internet: $14/month

Protocol Services: None

Online Registration: Login as `newuser`; password `newuser`

Other: PC Pursuit accessible

12-58 **mindVOX (`phantom.com`): Phantom Access Technologies, Inc.**

Area: New York City, NY

i (800) 646-3869 or (212) 989-2418, FAX (212) 989-8648; `info@phantom.com`

Dialup: (212) 989-4141, (212) 989-1550

Area Codes: 212, 718

Modem Information: 300-14.4k   PEP

Interactive Services: Custom shell, Unix access

Limited (local conferencing, games, and chat + e-mail): $10/month

Basic (no local conferencing, no access to local archives): $10/month

Basic + Internet: $15/month

Internet service goodies: IRC, gopher, hytelnet, fsp, WWW, WAIS, talk, Archie

Protocol Services:

UUCP: Contact for pricing

PPP, SLIP, POP: Contact for pricing

Leased Lines (56k, T1 fractional, all protocols): Contact for pricing

Domain name registration

Special Services: Wide range of online forums and conferencing, archives, multi-user games, and business and commercial setup services

Online Registration: Login as `mindvox`; password `guest`

Other: PC Pursuit accessible

12-59 **MSen (`msen.com`): MSen, Inc.**

Area: Ann Arbor, Michigan, serving Michigan, Ohio, Indiana and Illinois

i (313) 998-4562, FAX (313) 998-4563; info server: `info@msen.com`; FTP `ftp.msen.com` in `/pub/vendor/msen`; gopher gopher.msen.com

Dialup: Contact for numbers

Area Codes: 800, 313, 517, 616, PDN (PSI network)

Modem Information: 1200-14.4k   PEP, ISDN (contact for details)

Interactive Services: Unix shell

Basic + Internet: $20 startup, + $20/month + $2/hour or $160/month

Internet service goodies: WAIS, gopher, IRC, WWW, talk, Archie, NNTP, POP, IMAP

Protocol Services:

UUCP: $35 startup fee, + $30/month + 1$/hour or $175/month

SLIP, PPP (single host dialup): $20 startup, + $20/month + $2/hour or $175/month

SLIP, PPP (multi host dialup): $100 startup, + $50/month + $2/hour or $250/month

SLIP, PPP (multi host dialup dedicated port): $500 startup + $350/month

Leased Line (56k to T1, all protocols): Contact for pricing

Domain name registration

Special Services: Home of the online carrier center, ClariNet, Reuters News Service and Feed, proxy domain registration and delivery, archive service, hardware and software sales, consulting

Other: PC Pursuit accessible

12-60 **mv** (`mv.com`): MV Communications Inc

Area: Litchfield, NH

i (603) 429-2223; `info@mv.com`; login as `info`; FTP `ftp.mv.com` in `/pub/mv`

Dialup: (603) 424-7428 PDN (InfoPath X.25 access in New Hampshire)

Area Codes: 603

Modem Information: 1200-14.4k   PEP, TurboPEP, ZyXEL

Interactive Services: Unix shell, customized gopher menu

Basic + Internet: $5/month minimum; $2/hour first 5 hrs, $1.50/hour next 5, $1.00/hour next 10, $0.75/hour thereafter

Internet service goodies: gopher, IRC, news, ClariNet, etc.

Domain name registration: $20/month

Protocol Services:

SLIP: $150/month dedicated phone line or $25/month shared pool access, includes 15 hours/month + $2/hour thereafter.

UUCP: $7/month "casual" (1 hour/month), $20/month "basic" (3 hours/month), $2/hr after basic, with $20/30-hour block bulk rates.

Special Services: archives, ClariNet

12-61 **NEARnet** (`nic.near.net`): New England Academic and Research Network

Area: Boston, MA; Nashua, NH

i (617) 873-8730; `nearnet-join@nic.near.net`; FTP `nic.near.net` in `/docs`

Dialup: Contact for numbers

Area Codes: 508, 603, 617

Modem Information: 1200-14.4k

Interactive Services:

Basic: $250/month

Protocol Services:

UUCP: Contact for pricing

SLIP: $1,000-4,000 startup fee + $2,980-4,740/year

Leased Line (all protocols & speeds) $7,450-13,500 startup fee + $7,600-54,100/year

Domain name registration

Special Services: Full customer support, turnkey installation, consulting services

12-62   **nervous** (`nervous.com`): The Nervous XTC unix BBS

Area: Rimini (Fo), Italy

i `pizzi@nervous.com`

Dialup: +39-541-27135 +39-541-23111

Modem Information: 1200-14.4k   ZyXEL, PEP, HST

Interactive Services: BBS

Basic: Contact for pricing

Protocol Services:

UUCP accounts for private sites (not for BBSs)

Special Services: Unix sources, Fidonet conferences, erotic images

12-63   **netcom** (`netcom.com`): Netcom Online Communication Services, Inc.

Area: CA: San Jose

i (800) 501-8649, (408) 554-8649; info server: `info@netcom.com`; login as `guest`, no password

Dialup: call (800) 488-2558 for listing of local numbers

Area Codes: 206, 213, 310, 404, 408, 415, 503, 510, 619, 617, 714, 818, 916

Modem Information: 1200-14.4k

Interactive Services: Unix shell, custom menu

Basic + Internet: $20 startup fee + $19.50/month ($17.50 when autobilled to credit card)

Internet service goodies: IRC, WAIS, gopher, Archie, MUDs

Protocol Services:

UUCP: $25 (for low-volume e-mail) $45 for news/mail feed

SLIP, PPP, POP: $19.50/month + $2/hour

SLIP, PPP, POP with dedicated port: $750 startup fee + $160/month

Leased Line: 9600-14.4, SLIP: $750 startup fee + $180/month

Leased Line: 56k, SLIP: $1,200 startup fee + $400/month

Leased Line: T1: $3,200 startup fee + $1000/month

DNS Registration: Free

Special Services: user guide, online FAQ program, ClariNet, UPI news, stock reports, anonymous FTP, 5 Mb of disk space free

Other: PC Pursuit accessible

12-64   **Nicarao** (`nicarao.apc.org`): CRIES (Coordinadora Regional de Investigaciones Economicas y Sociales) in cooperation with the Association of Progressive Communications (APC)

Area: Nicaragua, Central America and Panama

i +505(2)621312, FAX +505(2)621244; `support@nicarao.apc.org` or `cvasconi@nicarao.apc.org` (Cristina Vasconi); P.O.: Apartado 3516, Iglesia Carmen, 1 cuadra al lago, Managua, Nicaragua

Dialup: +505(2)623188 NUA: 712 237020003

12-65 **NordNet** (`pns.apc.org`): Swedish Peace and Arbitration Society, SPAS Swedish Fellowship of Reconciliation, IFOR Swedish Peace Council, in cooperation with the Association of Progressive Communications (APC)

    Area: The Nordic, Baltic, and St Petersburg region

    i +46(8)600-0331, FAX +46(8)600-0443; `support@pns.apc.org` or `cilla@pns.apc.org` (Cilla Lundstroem); P.O.: Huvudskaersvaegen 13 nb., S-12154 Johanneshov, Sweden

    Dialup: +46(8)6000422, +46(8)6000371 NUA: 24037131034 (Datapak from within Sweden)

      Modem Information: 1200-9600k

    Other: FidoNet node `2:201/313`

12-66 **northshore** (`northshore.ecosoft.com`): North Shore Access

    Area: MA: Wakefield, Lynnfield, Lynn, Saugus, Revere, Peabody, Salem, Marblehead, Swampscott

    i (617) 593-3110; `info@northshore.ecosoft.com`; FTP `northshore.ecosoft.com` in `/pub/flyer`

    Dialup: (617) 593-4557

      Area Codes: 617, 508

      Modem Information: 300-14.4k   PEP, TurboPEP

    Interactive Services: Unix shell

      Basic + Internet: $9/month up to 10 hrs+3Mb quota, thereafter $1/hour $1/Mb/month

      Internet service goodies: Archie, gopher, WAIS, and more

    Protocol Services:

      UUCP: Free

    Online Registration: Login as `new`

12-67 **NovaLink** (`novalink.com`): NovaLink Information Service, a service of Inner Circle Technologies, Inc.

    Area: International

    i (800) 274-2814; `info@novalink.com`; login as `info`

    Dialup: (800) 937-7644 , (508) 754-4009

      Area Codes: 508, 800, PDN (SprintNet and CompuServe Packet Network)

      Modem Information: 1200-14.4k

    Interactive Services: Custom menu interface, XWindows, Unix shell, custom "easy" shell

      Basic + Internet: $12.95 startup fee + $9.95/month for five hours, thereafter $1.80/hour

      Internet service goodies: gopher, IRC, Archie, WAIS, whois, finger

      FAX gateway: $1.50/first page, $0.75/additional pages

    Protocol Services:

      UUCP: $35-75/month depending on traffic

      Domain name registration + name server: $30 setup fee

    Special Services: Home of Legends of Future Past (a multi-player fantasy game) and the Virtual Cafe (a social teleconferencing system); large library of shareware, freeware, graphics, music, and science files; moderated/hosted bulletin boards (also known as forums or conferences)

Online Registration: Login as new

Other: "NovaLink is as much a gateway to the Internet as a virtual environment where many relationships and online communities have developed."

12-68 **nyx** (`nyx.cs.du.edu`): University of Denver, Department of Mathematics and Computer Science

Area: Denver, CO

i `aburt@nyx.cs.du.edu` (Prof. Andrew Burt)

Dialup: (303) 871-3324

Area Codes: 303

Modem Information: 300-14.4k   HST, PEP

Interactive Services: Custom menu or Unix shell

Basic + Internet: Free; donations accepted but not required

Internet service goodies: gopher, IRC

Special Services: Many games, semi-anonymous usernames (e.g., anon0001), local download area, large user-accessible temporary disk space

Online Registration: Login as new

Other: PC Pursuit accessible

12-69 **OARnet** (`oar.net`): OARnet

Area: OH: Columbus, Cincinnati, Cleveland, Dayton, Akron; KY: Louisville

i (614) 292-8100, FAX (614) 292-7168; `info@oar.net`

Dialup: send e-mail to `nic@oar.net`

Area Codes: 614, 513, 419, 216, 502, 800

Modem Information: 9600-14.4k

Interactive Services:

Basic + Internet: $4/hour to $330/month

Internet service goodies: gopher, WAIS, WWW, Hytelnet, POP, SMTP, NNTP

Domain name registration: Free

Protocol Services:

NNTP: no additional charges

SLIP, PPP, POP: $4/hour to $330/month

Leased Line: 56k, T1 (all protocols): $11,500 to $32,000/year

Internet Routing: Free

Special Services: IP Consulting, information services (contact for details)

12-70 **Panix** (`panix.com`): Public Access Unix and Internet

Area: New York area: New York City, Long Island, White Plains; New Jersey

i 212-787-6160; `staff@panix.com` (Alexis Rosen and Jim Baumbach); info server/finger `info@panix.com`

Dialup: 212-787-3100

Area Codes: 212, 718, 914, 201
Modem Information: 1200-14.4k   ZyXEL

Interactive Services: Unix shell, custom menu system
Basic: $10/month or $100/year
Basic + Internet: $19/month
Internet service goodies: gopher, Hytelnet, WWW, WAIS, & IRC, Archie, talk

Protocol Services:
UUCP: $15/month
SLIP, PPP (dialup): $2/hour
SLIP, PPP (dedicated).: .$300/month
Leased Line: (56k, T1, SLIP, TCP/IP): Contact for pricing

Special Services: Archives, gopher server, FTP server

Other: PC Pursuit accessible

Online Registration: Login as newuser

12-71 **Pegasus (**`peg.apc.org`**): Pegasus Networks Communications Pty Ltd in cooperation with the Association of Progressive Communications (APC)**

Area: Australia, Pacific Islands, Southeast Asia

i +61(7) 257-1111, FAX +61(7) 257-1087; `support@peg.apc.org` or `ianp@peg.apc.org` (Ian Peter); P.O.: Box 284, Broadway 4006, Queensland, Australia

NUA: 505 272523000

Dialup: +61 7 257 1097

12-72 **pro-haven (**`pro-haven.cts.com`**): Pariahs' Haven BBS**

Area: Bryan, TX

i (409) 845-1411 (days); `tye@pro-haven.cts.com` or `botting@leper.tamu.edu`

Dialup: (409) 846-5534
Area Codes: 409
Modem Information: 300-9600

Interactive Services: BBS, Interactive menu, Unix-style shell
BBS: free
Basic: free

Protocol Services:
UUCP: Free, in the form of UMDSS or MDSS

Special Services: Batch FTP by arrangement; discussion and files for the Apple //(+,e,c,gs), Atari ST, Amiga, and Mac, as well as discussion areas for the PC; various ProLine discussion groups; various online games available.

Online Registration: Login as new

12-73 **psi (**`psi.com`**): PSI, Inc.**

Area: Reston, VA; Provides services world wide

i (800) 827-7482 or (703) 620-6651, FAX (703) 620-4586; `info@psi.com`; info server all-info@psi.com or world-dial-info@psi.com; FTP ftp.psi.com

Dialup: for numbers send e-mail to numbers-info@psi.com

Area Codes: PDN (PSINet)

Interactive Services:

Basic + Internet: $1.25/hour and up

PSI provides a compete range of interactive services. Please call for more information

Protocol Services:

UUCP: Contact for pricing

SLIP, PPP: Contact for pricing

Leased Line: (all speeds, all protocols): Contact for pricing

Domain name registration

Special Services: ClariNet feeds, hardware and software sales, turnkey installation for commercial sites

12-74 **quack** (quack.kfu.com): none provided

Area: Santa Clara, CA

i postmaster@quack.kfu.com

Dialup: (408) 249-9630

Area Codes: 408

Modem Information: 300-14.4k   PEP

Interactive Services: Unix shell

Basic + Internet: $10-15/month

Internet service goodies: gopher, IRC

Protocol Services:

Contact for details

Other: PC Pursuit accessible

Online Registration: Login as guest

12-75 **rhein-main** (rhein-main.de): Individual Network, Rhein-Main Area

Area: Frankfurt/Main, Germany

i +49-69-39048413 (Oliver Boehmer) or +49-69-6312083 (Michaela Merz); info@rhein-main.de or oli@rhein-main.de (Oliver Boehmer) or misch@rhein-main.de (Michaela Merz)

Dialup: +49-69-308265

Modem Information: 300-14.4k   PEP, TurboPEP

Interactive Services: Unix shell, BBS

Basic: 5 DM/month, + 3 DM/Mb in Europe and 4 DM/Mb worldwide

Basic + Internet: 15 DM/month, + 3 DM/Mb in Europe and 4 DM/Mb worldwide

Internet service goodies: gopher, Archie, IRC, and more

Protocol Services:

UUCP: 15 DM/month, + 3 DM/Mb in Europe and 4 DM/Mb worldwide

Anon-UUCP: 3 DM/Mb in Europe and 4 DM/Mb worldwide

SLIP/PPP/ISDN: 40 DM/month, + 3 DM/Mb in Europe and 4 DM/Mb worldwide

Other: This service is only available to non-commercial sites

12-76 **sandv** (`sandv.chi.il.us`): SandV—Chicago Area OS-9 User Group (CAOS-9 UG) support BBS

Area: LaGrange Park, IL

i (708) 579-1314; `sysop@sandv.chi.il.us`

Dialup: (708) 352-0948

Area Codes: 708

Modem Information: 300-9600

Interactive Services: StG Net V4 BBS

Basic: Free

Protocol Services: None

Special Services: There is a large OS-9/6809, OS-9/68K and a growing OS-9000 file section available to all users. File sections will be provided for other systems as needed. Large collection of GIF pictures, FLI animations, and IFF and MOD sound files are also available. Online games also available to all users

Online Registration: Login as `guest` and leave e-mail

12-77 **scuzzy** (`uropax.contrib.de`): Contributed Software GbR

Area: 10967 Berlin, Germany

i +49 30 694 6907; `info@contrib.de` or `src@contrib.de` (Heiko Blume) or `thomax@contrib.de` (Thomas Kaulmann) or `funghi@contrib.de` (Michael Pilz) or `sascha@contrib.de` (Sascha Zumbusch)

Dialup: +49 30 694 {6749, 6182, 6055, 6056, 6057, 6058, 6059}

Modem Information: 2400-14.4k   HST

Interactive Services: Menu, Unix shell, IP-Clients

Basic: ~$15 for private persons, ~$55 for companies

Basic + Internet: ~$30 for private persons, ~$110 for companies

Internet service goodies: IRC, gopher, WWW, WAIS, LP-MUD, and more

Protocol Services:

UUCP: Free

ANON UUCP: Free

SLIP, PPP - ~$1.50 per hour + ~$30 for private persons, ~$3 per hour + ~$110 for companies

Internet Routing: Free

Special Services: Free access account for our 4Mb Unix source archive

Online Registration: Login as `guest`, no password

12-78 **sixhub** (`sixhub.uucp`): Upstate NY Unix User's Group

Area: Albany NY

i `davidsen@sixhub.uucp`

Dialup: (518) 346-8033

Area Codes: 518

Modem Information: 300-14.4k   PEP

Interactive Services: MBS BBS
    BBS: Free
    Basic: Free
Protocol Services:
    UUCP: Free

12-79   **skypoint** (`skypoint.com`)**:** Sky Point Communications, Inc.
    Area: Newport, MN
    i (612) 459-7554; `info@skypoint.com`
    Dialup: (612) 458-3889
        Area Codes: 612
        Modem Information: 300-14.4k
    Interactive Services: Unix shell, Sentience BBS
        E-mail only: $25/year for up to 13 hours a month
        Basic: $45-130/year
    Protocol Services:
        UUCP: Contact for pricing
    Special Services: ClariNet, USA Today, Board Watch, News Bytes, binary archives on
        CD-ROMs

12-80   **solaria** (`solaria.mil.wi.us`)**:** Solaria Public Access Unix
    Area: Milwaukee, WI
    i `jgreco@solaria.mil.wi.us` (Joe Greco); login as `help`
    Dialup: (414) 342-4847
        Area Codes: 414
        Modem Information: 300-14.4k
    Interactive Services: Unix shell
        Basic: Free
    Protocol Services:
        UUCP: Free

12-81   **sugar** (`NeoSoft.com`)**:** NeoSoft's Sugar Land Unix
    Area: Houston, TX; St. Louis, MO; New Orleans, LA
    i (713) 684-5969; `info@NeoSoft.com`
    Dialup: (713) 684-5900
        Area Codes: 713, 314, 504
        Modem Information: 300-14.4k   PEP, TurboPEP
    Interactive Services: Unix shell, BBS
        BBS: $9.95/month
        Basic + Internet: $29.95/month
        Internet service goodies: IRC, MUD, gopher, WWW
    Protocol Services:
        UUCP: $4.95/month

SLIP (dedicated): $1/hour or $130/month

56k, ISDN, fractional and full T1 services are available

Special Services: ClariNet, complete `*.sources` and `*.binaries` archives

Other: PC Pursuit accessible

12-82 **szebra** (`szebra.saigon.com`): TL Consulting

Area: Sunnyvale, CA

i `tin@szebra.saigon.com` (UUCP: `{claris,zorch,sonyusa}!szebra!tin`);
login as `bbs`

Dialup: (408) 739-1092

Area Codes: 408

Modem Information: 300-14.4k   PEP

Interactive Services: BBS, Unix shell

BBS + e-mail + Usenet: Free

Basic + Internet: $40/3 months, $60 /6 months, $100/year

Internet service goodies: gopher, WAIS, WWW

Protocol Services:

Anonymous UUCP: Free

Special Services: GNU, X11R4 and R5 source archives, viet-net/SCV and VNese
files/software archives, online CD-ROM archives, archive site for
`comp.binaries.ms-windows`

Other: PC Pursuit accessible

12-83 **techbook** (`techbook.com`): TECHbooks

Area: Portland, OR

i (503) 223-4245; `info@techbook.com`

Dialup: (503) 220-0636

Area Codes: 503

Modem Information: 300-14.4k   PEP

Interactive Services: Unix shell, custom menu system

Basic: $60/year

Basic + Internet: $10/month, $90/year

Internet service goodies: IRC, MUD, gopher, WAIS, WWW, POP, NNTP

Internet Remote only: $30/year

Domain name registration: Free

FAX Gateway: Free in Portland

Protocol Services:

UUCP - Free with any account

NNTP - Free with any account

SLIP, PPP, POP - $25/month, $250/year

Internet Routing: Free for multi-host access

Special Services: ClariNet & Reuters newswires available

Online Registration: Login as `new`

Other: PC Pursuit accessible

12-84 **tnc** (`tnc.uucp`): The Next Challenge

Area: Fairfax Station, VA

i `tom@tnc.uucp` or (UUCP: `uunet!tnc!tom`) (Tom Buchsbaum)

Dialup: (703) 803-0391

Area Codes: 703, 301, 202 (Washington, D.C. Metro Area)

Modem Information: 300-14.4k   PEP

Interactive Services: BBS

BBS + Usenet: Free

Basic: $25/year for light e-mail use

Protocol Services:

UUCP: Contact for pricing

Special Services: Multi-user space game

Other: PC Pursuit accessible

12-85 **uunet** (`uunet.uu.net`): UUNET Technologies, Inc.

Area: Falls Church, VA / Global network

i (800) 488-6385 or (703) 204-8000; `info@uunet.uu.net` or `alternet-info@uunet.uu.net`

Dialup: (900) 468-7727 for anonymous UUCP, PDN (CompuServe Packet Network)

Area Codes: 900, 800, 703

Modem Information: 300-14.4k   PEP

Interactive Services: None

Protocol Services:

Anonymous UUCP: Login as `uucp`, no password; get `uunet!~/help` for more information

UUCP: Contact for pricing

SLIP, PPP: Contact for pricing

Leased Line (all speeds, all protocols): Contact for pricing

UUNET provides a very wide range of access services. Please contact them directly for more information

Special Services: Large software archives (available via anonymous UUCP Anonymous dialup), discounts on networking books, software, hardware, and more

12-86 **uunorth** (`uunorth.north.net`): UUnorth

Area: Toronto, Ontario, Canada

i (416) 225-8649, FAX (416) 225-0525; `uunorth@uunorth.north.net`; telnet to `accesspt.north.net` and login as `new`

Dialup: Contact for numbers

Area Codes: 416, 519, 613

Modem Information: 2400-14.4k

Interactive Services: Custom menu system

Basic + Internet: C$1.25-3/hour

Internet service goodies: gopher, IRC, and more

Protocol Services:

SLIP, PPP: C$5.00/hour or C$600/month for a dedicated line

UUCP: C$2.50/hour or C$12-50/month

Leased Line (56k, frame relay): Contact for details

Special Services: As well as providing Internet access, UUnorth offers extensive customer support services and consulting services for organizations that are establishing their connection to the Internet

12-87 **vpnet** (`vpnet.chi.il.us`): GPS Microdata

Area: Villa Park, IL—Serves greater Chicagoland

i (708) 833-8122 (Gerry Swetsky); `lisbon@vpnet.chi.il.us` (Gerry Swetsky)

Dialup: (708) 833-8126

Area Codes: 708, 312, 815

Modem Information: 2400-14.4k   PEP, HST

Interactive Services:

Unix shell, AKCS BBS

BBS + e-mail + limited Usenet: Free

Basic: Minimum acceptable contribution $30-60/year

Internet Remote: Contribution

Protocol Services:

UUCP: Contribution

Online Registration: Login as `new`

Other: PC Pursuit accessible

12-88 **wariat** (`wariat.org`): APK- Public Access UNI* Site

Area: Cleveland, OH

i (216) 481-9428; `zbig@wariat.org` (Zbigniew Tyrlik)

Dialup: (216) 481-9445, (216) 481-9425 (V.32bis, SuperPEP)

Area Codes: 216

Modem Information: 2400-14.4k   PEP, TurboPEP

Interactive Services: Unix shell, Uniboard BBS

BBS + e-mail: Free

Basic: Donation

Basic + Internet: $20 setup fee + $35/month

Internet service goodies: IRC, gopher, TF, WAIS, WWW, Archie, whois, finger, net-stat, Hytelnet, ytalk

Comment: Students vacation special—$50/2 months.

Protocol Services:

UUCP: Donation

Anonymous UUCP (file transfer only): login as `nuucp`, no password; request `/x/files/ls-lR.Z`

12-89 **Web** (`web.apc.org`): Nirv Community Resource Centre in cooperation with the Association of Progressive Communications (APC)

Area: Toronto, Ottawa, Vancouver Canada

i (416) 596-0212, FAX (416) 596-1374; `support@web.apc.org` or `kirk@web.apc.org` (Kirk Roberts); P.O.: 401 Richmond Street West, Suite 104, Toronto, Ontario, M5V 3A8, Canada

Dialup: (416) 348 9388, (613) 238-1912 (604) 732-4450 NUA: 3020 95400842
Area Codes: 416, 613, 604

12-90 **well** (`well.sf.ca.us`): The Whole Earth 'Lectronic Link

Area: Sausalito, CA

i (415) 332-4335; `info@well.sf.ca.us`; login as `guest`; gopher gopher.well.sf.ca.us

Dialup: (415) 332-6106 (415) 332-8410 (if 8-N-1 doesn't work, use 7-E-1)
Area Codes: 415, 510, PDN (Compuserve Packet Network)
Modem Information: 1200-14.4k

Interactive Services: Unix shell, PicoSpan BBS
Basic + Internet: $15/month + $2/hour
Internet service goodies: rlogin, gopher, IRC, Archie, Hytelnet, TF, etc.

Protocol Services:
UUCP: $35/month + $1/hour

Special Services: The WELL is primarily a conferencing system—though all accounts have Internet access for e-mail, FTP, telnet, etc., the main reason most people join the Well is for the conferencing. There are over 200 public discussion areas (conferences) and about the same number of private conferences. Anyone may start a private conference to which they control access.

Other: PC Pursuit accessible

12-91 **WinNET** (`win.net`): Computer Witchcraft

Area: Louisville, Kentucky

i (502) 589-6800, FAX (502) 589-7300; `help@win.net`; info server: `request@win.net` [subject = `info` or `WinNET` for a copy of WinNet software]

Dialup: (502) 589-4131, (800) 800-1482 US, (800) 284-6599 Canada
Area Codes: 502, 800 and Canada, UK, others (call for details)
Modem Information: 2400, 14.4k

Interactive Services: none

Protocol Services:
UUCP: $8/hour
Use of 800 number incurs a per-minute charge of $0.11–0.40 depending on time of day and location
Domain name registration

Special Services: Computer Witchcraft provides a free, very easy to use Windows front end for e-mail and news that automatically handles all aspects of your UUCP connection, including subscribing and unsubscribing to news and batch sending and receiving of your e-mail

Online Registration: Automatic with custom software

12-92 **world (**`world.std.com`**):** Software Tool & Die
   Area: Brookline, MA
   i (617) 739-0202; `geb@world.std.com` or `office@world.std.com`; FTP
      `world.std.com` in `/world-info/description`
   Dialup: (617) 739-9753
      Area Codes: 617, PDN (CompuServ Packet Network)
      Modem Information: 300-14.4k
   Interactive Services: Unix shell
      Basic + Internet: $5/month + $2/hr or $20/month for 20 hours
      Internet service goodies: IRC
   Protocol Services:
      Contact for details
   Special Services: Full-time customer support via phone and e-mail; home of the Open
      Book Initiative (e-text project); electronic newswire services from Reuters and ClariNet
   Online Registration: Login as `new`
   Other: PC Pursuit accessible; gopher and FTP provided to businesses for commercial use

12-93 **wybbs (**`wyn386.mi.org`**):** Consultants Connection
   Area: Grand Rapids, MI
   i `danielw@wyn386.mi.org`
   Dialup: (616) 363-6680, (616) 363-6128
      Area Codes: 616
      Modem Information: 300-14.4k   Telebit TB+
   Interactive Services: Unix shell
      BBS: Free
      Basic: Free
   Protocol Services:
      Anonymous UUCP

12-94 **wyvern (**`wyvern.wyvern.com`**):** Wyvern Technologies, Inc.
   Area: Norfolk, VA
   i (804) 622-4289; `system@wyvern.wyvern.com` or (UUCP: `uunet!wyvern!sys-`
      `tem`)
   Dialup: (804) 627-1828 Norfolk, (804) 886-0662 (Peninsula)
      Area Codes: 804
      Modem Information: 1200-14.4k   PEP
   Interactive Services: Unix shell, custom menu system
      Basic + Internet: $20/month for up to 30 hours
      Internet service goodies: gopher, IRC, Archie
      Domain name registration: $50, including nameserver/MX record setup

Protocol Services:
> UUCP: Private user $30/month + $2/hour; corporate e-mail $100/month; e-mail + news $250/month

Special Services: UPI News

Online Registration: Login as guest, no password

12-95 **zgnews** (zgnews.lonestar.org): Zeitgeist Bulletin Board

Area: Plano, TX

i postmaster@zgnews.lonestar.org

Dialup: (214) 596-3720
> Area Codes: 214
> Modem Information: 300-14.4k   HST & ZyXEL

Interactive Services: Waffle
> Basic: $20/year for 90 minutes daily connect time

Protocol Services:
> UUCP: Free

Special Services: Over 27,000 files, including Walnut Creek's SIMTEL, CICA, and Hobbes CD-ROMs, updated quarterly.

13. E-MAIL ADDRESSING FOR CONNECTED NETWORKS

This chapter provides instructions on how to send e-mail to and from many of the networks connected to the Internet. Networks *connected* to the Internet, but not *on* the Internet, are networks that use an e-mail addressing style other than the Internet's domain-name style (user@host). Therefore, to send e-mail between connected networks and the Internet, you must translate the e-mail address.

Entry Format: Each entry in this chapter has two subentries. The first explains how to send e-mail from the Internet to an address on the connected network; the second explains how to send e-mail from the connected network to an address on the Internet. All entries use the sample address of Mr. Anansi The Spider, a well-connected fellow who has accounts on all of the networks. I have tried to use the most common form of address on each network (for example, `anansi.t.spider` instead of `anansi`). Each entry has the following form:

Item
number

13-n   **Name of connected network:** Organizational affiliation   *network type*
　　　　From the Internet to **address on connected network:**
　　　　　　`Internet address`
　　　　　　Comments.
　　　　　　i where to get information on the connected network (usually an Internet address)
　　　　From connected network to **anansi@jungle.com:**
　　　　　　`connected-network address`
　　　　　　Comments.
　　　　　　i where to get information on Internet addressing (usually a network address)

Where to Find It: This list was adapted by permission from the Inter-Network Mail Guide, first compiled by John J. Chew and currently maintained by Scott A. Yanoff, which is posted regularly to the `alt.internet.services` newsgroup. Some entries were also found in Scott Hoppe's list (send him e-mail at `71641.2400@compuserve.com` for a copy).

Netiquette: Keep in mind that some of the gateways connecting other networks to the Internet can handle only limited amounts of traffic, and that some networks charge users for mail received. Any such conditions are mentioned in the comments section.

Entries:

13-1 **America Online (AOL):** America Online, Inc.   *commercial*

    From the Internet to AOL user **Anansi Spider**:

        `aspider@aol.com`

        Messages are truncated to 32K (8K for PCs); all characters except newline and printable ASCII characters are mapped to spaces; users are limited to 75 pieces of Internet mail in their mailbox at a time.

        i postmaster@aol.com

    From AOL to Internet address **anansi@jungle.com**:

        `anansi@jungle.com`

        i `Internet`

13-2 **AppleLink:** Apple Computer, Inc.   *in-house*

    From the Internet to AppleLink user **anansi**:

        `anansi@applelink.apple.com`

    From AppleLink to Internet address **anansi@jungle.com**:

        `anansi@jungle.com@internet#`

    Address must be less than 35 characters.

13-3 **AT&T Mail:** AT&T   *commercial*

    From the Internet to AT&T Mail user **anansi**:

        `anansi@attmail.com`

    From AT&T Mail to Internet address **anansi@jungle.com**:

        `internet!jungle!com!anansi`

13-4 **BITNET:** none   *academic*

    From the Internet to Bitnet address **anansi@jungle**:

        `anansi@jungle.bitnet`

        Mail to Bitnet sites gets sent to a gateway computer that is on both Bitnet and the Internet. Usually your site will translate addresses of the above form to the nearest such gateway. In some cases you will have to do this by hand, in which case the address would be `anansi%jungle.bitnet@gateway` *where* `gateway` *is a gateway domain name. Some examples of gateways are:* `cunyvm.cuny.edu` *and* `mitvma.mit.edu`.

    From Bitnet to Internet address **anansi@jungle.com**:

        `anansi@jungle.com` (usually—see comment)

        Methods for sending mail from Bitnet to the Internet vary depending on what mail software is running at the Bitnet site in question. In the best case, users should simply be able to send mail that looks like this: `anansi@jungle.com`. *If this doesn't work, try sending mail in this form:* `anansi%jungle.com@gateway` *where* `gateway` *is a Bitnet-Internet gateway site nearby. Finally, if neither of these works, you may have to try hand-coding an SMTP envelope for your mail.*

13-5 **Byte Information eXchange (bix):** Byte magazine   *commercial*

From the Internet to bix user **anansi**:

```
anansi@dcibix.das.net
```

Reaches only paying users registered through the DASNet gateway.

13-6 **CompuServe:** CompuServe Inc.   *commercial*

From the Internet to CompuServe user **Anansi Spider (71234,567)**:

```
71234.567@compuserve.com
```

Ordinary CompuServe account IDs are pairs of octal numbers.

From the Internet to CompuServe address **organization:department:anansi**:

```
anansi@department.organization.compuserve.com
```

This syntax is for e-mail to members of organizations that have a private CompuServe mail area. The department *section may not always be present.*

From CompuServe to Internet address **anansi@jungle.com**:

```
>INTERNET:anansi@jungle.com
```

13-7 **Easynet:** DEC   *in-house*

From the Internet to Easynet address **Jungle::ANANSI**:

```
anansi%Jungle.enet@decwrl.dec.com
```

i admin@decwrl.dec.com

From the Internet to Easynet user **Anansi Spider @JUNGLE**:

```
Anansi.Spider@JUNGLE.MTS.DEC.COM
```

This syntax is for sending mail to ALL-IN-1 users.

i admin@decwrl.dec.com

From Easynet to Internet address **anansi@jungle.com**:

nm%DECWRL::"anansi@jungle.com" from VMS using NMAIL or
anansi@jungle.com from Ultrix, or
anansi%jungle.com@decwrl.dec.com from Ultrix via IP, or
DECWRL::"anansi@jungle.com" from Ultrix via DECnet, or
anansi@jungle.com @Internet when using ALL-IN-1

i DECWRL::ADMIN

13-8 **Envoy-100:** Telecom Canada   *commercial (X.400)*

From the Internet to Envoy-100 user **Anansi Spider (ID=123)**:

/C=CA/ADMD=TELECOM.CANADA/DD.ID=123/PN=Anansi_Spider/
    @Sprint.COM or uunet.uu.net!att!attmail!mhs!envoy!123

From Envoy-100 to Internet address **anansi@jungle.com**:

```
[RFC-822="anansi(a)jungle.com"]INTERNET/TELEMAIL/US
```

Special characters must be converted: @ → (a) ! → (b) _ → (u)

13-9 **FidoNet:** none   *bbs*

From the Internet to FidoNet address **anansi spider at 1:2/3.4**:

```
anansi.spider@p4.f3.n2.z1.fidonet.org
```

From FidoNet to Internet address **anansi@jungle.com**:

```
anansi@jungle.com ON 1:1/31
```

13-10 **GEnie:** General Electric Information Services   *commercial*

From the Internet to GEnie user **Anansi.Spider123**:
```
Anansi.Spider123@genie.geis.com
```
From GEnie to Internet address **anansi@jungle.com**:
```
anansi@jungle.com@INET#
```

13-11 **GNS Gold 400 (Gold-400):** British Telecom   *commercial (X.400)*

From the Internet to Gold-400 user **(G:Anansi, I:T, S:Spider, OU:House, O:Jungle, PRMD:co.uk):**
```
anansi.t.spider@org_unit.org.prmd.gold-400.gb or
"/G=Anansi/I=T/S=Spider/OU=House/O=Jungle/PRMD=co.uk/
    ADMD=gold 400/C=GB/"@mhs-relay.ac.uk
```
From Gold-400 to Internet address **anansi@jungle.com**:
```
/DD.RFC-822=anansi(a)jungle.com/O=uknet/PRMD=uk.ac/
    ADMD=gold 400/C=GB/
```
Special characters must be converted: @ ➡ (a)   % ➡ (p)   ! ➡ (b)   " ➡ (q)

13-12 **GreenNet:** Soft Solutions Ltd   *commercial*

From the Internet to GreenNet user **anansi**:
```
anansi@gn.co.uk
```
i `support@gn.co.uk`

From GreenNet to Internet address **anansi@jungle.com**:
```
anansi@jungle.com
```

13-13 **GSFCmail:** NASA/Goddard Space Flight Center   *in-house (X.400)*

From the Internet to GSFCmail user **anansi**:
```
anansi@gsfcmail.nasa.gov
```
i (800) 858-9947 `naic@nasa.gov`

From GSFCmail to Internet address **anansi@jungle.com**:
Using the COMPOSE command, send a message to
(UN:POSTMAN,O:NASA,PRMD:NASAMAIL,ADMD:TELEMAIL,C:USA) and set
the first line of message to TO: anansi@jungle.com

13-14 **KeyLink:** Telecom Australia   *commercial (X.400)*

From the Internet to KeyLink address **(G:Anansi, S:Spider, O:House, P:AusGov, A:Telememo, C:au):**
```
Anansi.Spider@House.AusGov.telememo.au
```
i `aarnet@aarnet.edu.au`

From the Internet to KeyLink address **(G:Anansi, I:T, S:Spider, O:Jungle, A:Telememo, C:au):**
```
Anansi.T.Spider@Jungle.telememo.au
```
i `aarnet@aarnet.edu.au`

From KeyLink to Internet address **Anansi Spider <anansi@jungle.com>**:
```
(C:au, A:telememo, P:oz.au, "RFC-822":"Anansi Spider
    <anansi(a)jungle.com>")
```
Special characters must be mapped: @ ➡ (a)   % ➡ (p)   ! ➡ (b)   " ➡ (q)

i (G:CUSTOMER, S:SERVICE, O:CUST.SERVICE, P:telememo, C:au)

13-15 **MCIMail:** MCI, Inc. *commercial*

From the Internet to MCIMail user **Anansi Spider (123-4567)**:

1234567@mcimail.com or
ASpider@mcimail.com or
Anansi_Spider@mcimail.com or
Anansi_Spider/1234567@mcimail.com

Abbreviated forms may only be used if they are unique. So if there is an Albert Spider on MCI mail, you would have to use a form other than ASpider@mcimail.com

From MCIMail to Internet address **Anansi Spider <anansi@jungle.com>**:

At the To: prompt type Anansi Spider (EMS) at the EMS: prompt type INTERNET at the Mbx: prompt type anansi@jungle.com

i 267-1163 (MCI Help)

13-16 **NASAMail:** NASA *in-house*

From the Internet to NASAMail user **anansi**:

anansi@nasamail.nasa.gov

i (800) 858-9947 naic@nasa.gov

From NASAMail to Internet address **anansi@jungle.com**:

POSTMAN with TO: anansi@jungle.com as the first line of the text of the message

i (800) 858-9947; naic@nasa.gov

13-17 **NASA Science Internet (nsi):** NASA *government*

From the Internet to NSI-DECnet address **jungle::anansi**:

anansi@jungle.dnet.nasa.gov

These instructions pertain only to NSI-DECnet addresses. NSI-TCP/IP addresses are in standard domain-name style format.

i (800) 858-9947; niac@nasa.gov

From NSI-DECnet to Internet address **anansi@jungle.com**:

EAST::"anansi@jungle.com"

i (800) 858-9947 EAST::"naic@nasa.gov"

13-18 **OMNET:** OMNET *commercial*

From the Internet to OMNET user **a.spider**:

/DD.UN=a.spider/O=OMNET/ADMD=TELEMAIL/C=US/@sprint.com

i (617) 244 4333; /DD.UN=omnet.service/O=OMNET/ADMD=TELEMAIL/
    C=US/@sprint.com

From OMNET to Internet address **anansi@jungle.com**:

Enter compose manual at the command prompt. Choose the Internet address option from the menu that appears, and enter anansi@jungle.com

Note that this gateway service charges based on the number of 1000-character blocks sent.

i (617) 244 4333; omnet.service

13-19 **PeaceNet:** Institute for Global Communications *non-profit*

From the Internet to PeaceNet user **anansi**:

```
anansi@cdp.igc.org
```
i support@igc.org

From PeaceNet to Internet address **anansi@jungle.com**:
```
anansi@jungle.com
```

13-20 **SprintMail:** Sprint *commercial*

From the Internet to SprintMail user **Anansi Spider at Jungle**:
```
/G=Anansi/S=Spider/O=Jungle/ADMD=TELEMAIL/C=US/@sprint.com
```
i (800) 827-4685 or (703) 318-7740

From SprintMail to Internet address **anansi@jungle.com**:
```
(C:USA,A:TELEMAIL,P:INTERNET,"RFC-822":
    <anansi(a)jungle.com>) DEL
```
i (800) 827-4685 or (703) 318-7740

13-21 **Texas Higher Education Network (thenet):** University of Texas *academic*

From the Internet to thenet user **anansi@jungle**:
```
anansi%jungle.decnet@utadnx.cc.utexas.edu
```

From thenet to Internet address **anansi@jungle.com**:
```
UTADNX::WINS%" anansi@jungle.com "
```

13-22 **UUNET:** UUNET Technologies, Inc. *commercial*

From the Internet to UUNET user **jungle!anansi**:
```
jungle!anansi@uunet.uu.com or
anansi@jungle.uucp
```
To e-mail to hosts connected to the Internet via UUCP, you may have to specify a more lengthy path through which the mail travels. For example, if Anansi is on the host "house" which is connected to "Jungle" then to send mail to Anansi, you would address your mail to `jungle!house!anansi@uunet.uu.net`

From UUNET to Internet address **anansi@jungle.com**:
```
uunet!anansi@jungle.com
```

14. FOR YOUR INFORMATION (FYI) TEXTS

FYIs are best explained by a quote from FYI #1:

> The FYI series of notes is designed to provide Internet users with a central repository of information about any topics which relate to the Internet. FYI topics may range from historical memos on "Why it was done this way" to answers to commonly asked operational questions.

If you have never read FYIs #4 and #7, I urge you to do so, because they answer a number of basic questions about the Internet.

Entry Format: The For Your Information (FYI) list is in reverse chronological order. Next to each description is the date the FYI was written.

Item Number		
14-n	FYI title. Date	#FYI number

Where to Find It: An index of all FYIs as well as the text of individual FYIs is available via FTP from `nic.ddn.mil` in `/fyi/fyi/`.

Entries:

15. REQUEST FOR COMMENT (RFC) TEXTS

Taken as a whole, the RFC documents perhaps provide the best definition of what the Internet is. Internet protocols are described in the RFCs, as are answers to questions frequently asked by beginners on the net. Many of them are quite technical, but don't ignore them all because of that! An RFC is pretty much the last word on any Internet subject.

Entry Format: The Request For Comment (RFC) list is in inverse chronological order. Next to each description is the date the RFC was written.

Item
Number
15-n   RFC title. Date   #RFC number

Where to Find It: An index of all RFCs and the texts of many of them are available via FTP from `nic.ddn.mil` in the `/rfc/rfc/` directory.

Comments: This list is an edited version of the complete index of RFCs. A large number of the RFCs have become obsolete, and those, as well as some that are not available online because they are so old, have not been included in the list.

Entries:

15-1	Encoding Header Field for Internet Messages. 8/93	#1505
15-2	Appletalk Update-Based Routing Protocol: Enhanced Appletalk Routing. 8/93	#1504
15-3	Algorithms for Automating Administration in SNMPv2 Managers. 8/93	#1503
15-4	X.400 Use of Extended Character Sets. 8/93	#1502
15-5	OS/2 User Group. 8/93	#1501
15-6	INTERNET OFFICIAL PROTOCOL STANDARDS. 8/93	#1500
15-7	On the Naming and Binding of Network Destinations. 8/93	#1498
15-8	BOOTP Vendor Information Extensions (Updates RFC 951). 8/93	#1497
15-9	Rules for Downgrading Messages from X.400/88 to X.400/84 when MIME Content-Types are Present in the Messages (Updates RFC 1328). 8/93	#1496
15-10	Mapping between X.400 and RFC-822 Message Bodies. 8/93	#1495

APPENDIX: LANDWEBER'S INTERNATIONAL CONNECTIVITY LIST

This list is created and maintained by Larry Landweber at the University of Wisconsin-Madison. It describes the level of connectivity to the Internet of all of the countries in the world. Obviously this list will become out of date very quickly, but it will give you a good idea of current worldwide connectivity.

Entry Format: The connectivity list has three columns. The first column contains the connectivity summary, the second contains the ISO 3166 country code (note that this code isn't always the same as the top level domain name code), and the third column contains the full name of the country.

The connectivity summary in the first column is a 5-character code, each character of which is a hyphen if there is no connectivity of the given type. If there is connectivity, the codes are as shown.

BITNET (b = minimal, B = widespread)
UUCP (u = minimal, U = widespread)
OSI (o = minimal, O = widespread)

BIUFO   US   **United States (United States of America)**

FIDONET (f = minimal, F = widespread)
IP INTERNET (i = operational, I = on NSF backbone)

Where To Find It: To find the latest version of this international connectivity list, FTP to ftp.cs.wisc.edu in the /connectivity_table/ directory.

Comments: Note that in this list BITNET is used generically to refer to Bitnet plus similar networks around the world (e.g., EARN, NETNORTH, GULFNET, etc.).

This is the August 1st, 1993 version of the connectivity list. Please send corrections, information, or comments to Larry Landweber, lhl@cs.wisc.edu

Entries:

----- AF	Afghanistan (Democratic Republic of)	----- CX	Christmas Island (Indian Ocean)
----- AL	Albania (Republic of)	----- CC	Cocos (Keeling) Islands
----- DZ	Algeria (People's Democratic Republic of)	B-u-- CO	Colombia (Republic of)
----- AS	American Samoa	----- KM	Comoros (Islamic Federal Republic of the)
----- AD	Andorra (Principality of)	--u-- CG	Congo (Republic of the)
----- AO	Angola (People's Republic of)	----- CK	Cook Islands
----- AI	Anguilla	bIuf- CR	Costa Rica (Republic of)
-I--- AQ	Antarctica	--uf- CI	Cote d'Ivoire (Republic of)
----- AG	Antigua and Barbuda	-IuFo HR	Croatia
BIUF- AR	Argentina (Argentine Republic)	--U-- CU	Cuba (Republic of)
--u-- AM	Armenia	bI--- CY	Cyprus (Republic of)
---f- AW	Aruba	BIUF- CZ	Czech Republic
-IUFo AU	Australia	bIUFO DK	Denmark (Kingdom of)
BIUFO AT	Austria (Republic of)	----- DJ	Djibouti (Republic of)
--U-- AZ	Azerbaijan	----- DM	Dominica (Commonwealth of)
----- BS	Bahamas (Commonwealth of the)	--Uf- DO	Dominican Republic
b---- BH	Bahrain (State of)	----- TP	East Timor
----- BD	Bangladesh (People's Republic of)	bIu-- EC	Ecuador (Republic of)
--u-- BB	Barbados	b-U-- EG	Egypt (Arab Republic of)
--UF- BY	Belarus	----- SV	El Salvador (Republic of)
BIUFO BE	Belgium (Kingdom of)	----- GQ	Equatorial Guinea (Republic of)
----- BZ	Belize	-IUF- EE	Estonia (Republic of)
----- BJ	Benin (People's Republic of)	---f- ET	Ethiopia (People's Democratic Republic of)
--uf- BM	Bermuda		
----- BT	Bhutan (Kingdom of)	----- FK	Falkland Islands (Malvinas)
--U-- BO	Bolivia (Republic of)	----- FO	Faroe Islands
----- BA	Bosnia-Herzegovina	-Iu-- FJ	Fiji (Republic of)
--uf- BW	Botswana (Republic of)	BIUFO FI	Finland (Republic of)
----- BV	Bouvet Island	BIUFO FR	France (French Republic)
BIUFO BR	Brazil (Federative Republic of)	--u-- GF	French Guiana
----- IO	British Indian Ocean Territory	--u-- PF	French Polynesia
----- BN	Brunei Darussalam	----- TF	French Southern Territories
bIUF- BG	Bulgaria (Republic of)	----- GA	Gabon (Gabonese Republic)
--u-- BF	Burkina Faso (formerly Upper Volta)	----- GM	Gambia (Republic of the)
----- BI	Burundi (Republic of)	--UF- GE	Georgia (Republic of)
----- KH	Cambodia	BIUFO DE	Germany (Federal Republic of)
--u-- CM	Cameroon (Republic of)	---F- GH	Ghana (Republic of)
BIUFO CA	Canada	----- GI	Gibraltar
----- CV	Cape Verde (Republic of)	BIUFO GR	Greece (Hellenic Republic)
----- KY	Cayman Islands	-I-f- GL	Greenland
----- CF	Central African Republic	--u-- GD	Grenada
----- TD	Chad (Republic of)	b-uf- GP	Guadeloupe (French Department of)
BIUF- CL	Chile (Republic of)	---F- GU	Guam
--u-O CN	China (People's Republic of)		

B/b = **Bitnet**   I/i = **TCP/IP Internet**   U/u = **UUCP**   F/f = **Fidonet**   O/o = **OSI (X.400)**

--u--	GT	Guatemala (Republic of)	----- MQ	Martinique (French Department of)
-----	GN	Guinea (Republic of)	----- MR	Mauritania (Islamic Republic of)
-----	GW	Guinea-Bissau (Republic of)	--uf- MU	Mauritius
-----	GY	Guyana (Republic of)	BIuF- MX	Mexico (United Mexican States)
-----	HT	Haiti (Republic of)	----- FM	Micronesia (Federated States of)
-----	HM	Heard and McDonald Islands	--UF- MD	Moldova (Republic of)
-----	HN	Honduras (Republic of)	----- MC	Monaco (Principality of)
BI-F-	HK	Hong Kong	----- MN	Mongolia (Mongolian People's Republic)
BIUFo	HU	Hungary (Republic of)	----- MS	Montserrat
-IUFo	IS	Iceland (Republic of)	----- MA	Morocco (Kingdom of)
bIUfO	IN	India (Republic of)	--u-- MZ	Mozambique (People's Republic of)
--u--	ID	Indonesia (Republic of)	----- MM	Myanmar (Union of)
b----	IR	Iran (Islamic Republic of)	--u-- NA	Namibia (Republic of)
-----	IQ	Iraq (Republic of)	----- NR	Nauru (Republic of)
BIUFO	IE	Ireland	----- NP	Nepal (Kingdom of)
BIUFO	IL	Israel (State of)	BIUFO NL	Netherlands (Kingdom of the)
BIUFO	IT	Italy (Italian Republic)	----- AN	Netherlands Antilles
--u--	JM	Jamaica	----- NT	Neutral Zone (between Saudi Arabia and
BIUF-	JP	Japan		Iraq)
-----	JO	Jordan (Hashemite Kingdom of)	--U-- NC	New Caledonia
--Uf-	KZ	Kazakhstan	-IUF- NZ	New Zealand
---f-	KE	Kenya (Republic of)	--u-- NI	Nicaragua (Republic of)
--u--	KI	Kiribati (Republic of)	--u-- NE	Niger (Republic of the)
-----	KP	Korea (Democratic People's Republic of)	----- NG	Nigeria (Federal Republic of)
BIUFO	KR	Korea (Republic of)	----- NU	Niue
-I---	KW	Kuwait (State of)	----- NF	Norfolk Island
--U--	KG	Kyrgyzstan	----- MP	Northern Mariana Islands
-----	LA	Lao People's Democratic Republic		(Commonwealth of the)
-IUF-	LV	Latvia (Republic of)	BIUFO NO	Norway (Kingdom of)
-----	LB	Lebanon (Lebanese Republic)	----- OM	Oman (Sultanate of)
--u--	LS	Lesotho (Kingdom of)	--U-- PK	Pakistan (Islamic Republic of)
-----	LR	Liberia (Republic of)	----- PW	Palau (Republic of)
-----	LY	Libyan Arab Jamahiriya	b-uF- PA	Panama (Republic of)
---f-	LI	Liechtenstein (Principality of)	--u-- PG	Papua New Guinea
--UFo	LT	Lithuania	--u-- PY	Paraguay (Republic of)
bIUFo	LU	Luxembourg (Grand Duchy of)	--Uf- PE	Peru (Republic of)
---F-	MO	Macau (Ao-me'n)	--uF- PH	Philippines (Republic of the)
-----	??	Macedonia (Former Yugoslav Republic of)	----- PN	Pitcairn
-----	MG	Madagascar (Democratic Republic of)	BIUF- PL	Poland (Republic of)
--u--	MW	Malawi (Republic of)	bIUFo PT	Portugal (Portuguese Republic)
bIUF-	MY	Malaysia	bIUF- PR	Puerto Rico
-----	MV	Maldives (Republic of)	----- QA	Qatar (State of)
--u--	ML	Mali (Republic of)	--u-- RE	Réunion (French Department of)
--u--	MT	Malta (Republic of)	BI-f- RO	Romania
-----	MH	Marshall Islands (Republic of the)	BiUF- RU	Russian Federation

B/b = **Bitnet**   I/i = **TCP/IP Internet**   U/u = **UUCP**   F/f = **Fidonet**   O/o = **OSI (X.400)**

----- RW	Rwanda (Rwandese Republic)	
----- SH	Saint Helena	
----- KN	Saint Kitts and Nevis	
--u-- LC	Saint Lucia	
----- PM	Saint Pierre and Miquelon (French Department of)	
----- VC	Saint Vincent and the Grenadines	
--u-- WS	Samoa (Independent State of)	
----- SM	San Marino (Republic of)	
----- ST	Sao Tome and Principe (Democratic Republic of)	
B---- SA	Saudi Arabia (Kingdom of)	
--Uf- SN	Senegal (Republic of)	
--u-- SC	Seychelles (Republic of)	
----- SL	Sierra Leone (Republic of)	
bIuF- SG	Singapore (Republic of)	
bIUF- SK	Slovakia	
-IUFO SI	Slovenia	
--u-- SB	Solomon Islands	
----- SO	Somalia (Somali Democratic Republic)	
-IUFO ZA	South Africa (Republic of)	
BIUFO ES	Spain (Kingdom of)	
--U-- LK	Sri Lanka (Democratic Socialist Republic of)	
----- SD	Sudan (Democratic Republic of the)	
--u-- SR	Suriname (Republic of)	
----- SJ	Svalbard and Jan Mayen Islands	
--u-- SZ	Swaziland (Kingdom of)	
BIUFo SE	Sweden (Kingdom of)	
BIUFO CH	Switzerland (Swiss Confederation)	
----- SY	Syria (Syrian Arab Republic)	
BIuF- TW	Taiwan, Province of China	
--uf- TJ	Tajikistan	
---f- TZ	Tanzania (United Republic of)	
-IUF- TH	Thailand (Kingdom of)	
--u-- TG	Togo (Togolese Republic)	
----- TK	Tokelau	
--u-- TO	Tonga (Kingdom of)	
--u-- TT	Trinidad and Tobago (Republic of)	
bIUfo TN	Tunisia	
BI-F- TR	Turkey (Republic of)	
--U-- TM	Turkmenistan	
----- TC	Turks and Caicos Islands	
--u-- TV	Tuvalu	
---f- UG	Uganda (Republic of)	
-iUF- UA	Ukraine	

----- AE	United Arab Emirates
bIUFO GB	United Kingdom (United Kingdom of Great Britain and Northern Ireland)
BIUFO US	United States (United States of America)
----- UM	United States Minor Outlying Islands
--UF- UY	Uruguay (Eastern Republic of)
--UF- UZ	Uzbekistan
--u-- VU	Vanuatu (Republic of, formerly New Hebrides)
----- VA	Vatican City State (Holy See)
-IU-- VE	Venezuela (Republic of)
----- VN	Vietnam (Socialist Republic of)
----- VG	Virgin Islands (British)
---f- VI	Virgin Islands (U.S.)
----- WF	Wallis and Futuna Islands
----- EH	Western Sahara
----- YE	Yemen (Republic of)
---f- YU	Yugoslavia (Socialist Federal Republic of)
----- ZR	Zaire (Republic of)
--uf- ZM	Zambia (Republic of)
--uf- ZW	Zimbabwe (Republic of)

B/b = **Bitnet**   I/i = **TCP/IP Internet**   U/u = **UUCP**   F/f = **Fidonet**   O/o = **OSI (X.400)**

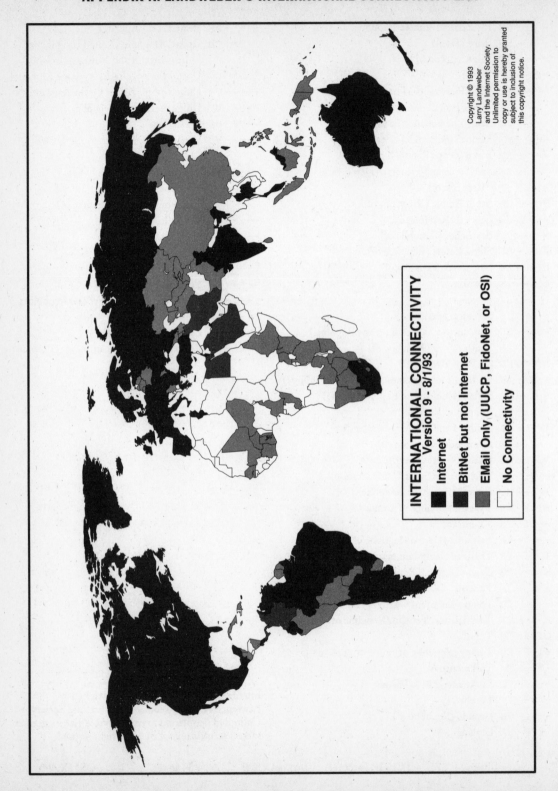

INTERNATIONAL CONNECTIVITY
Version 9 - 8/1/93

- Internet
- BitNet but not Internet
- EMail Only (UUCP, FidoNet, or OSI)
- No Connectivity

BIBLIOGRAPHY

This is in no way a complete bibliography of books on the Internet. Instead, it is meant to serve as a pointer to some of the more easily available user's guides and introductions, as well as a few detailed sources that explain in more depth various aspects of the Internet. For more background and information on the Internet's organization, structure, and development, see the Request For Comment (RFC) texts listed in Chapter 15 and the For Your Information (FYI) texts listed in Chapter 14. For up-to-date lists of the resources available on the Internet, make use of the online lists in Chapter 11 (Online Resource Lists).

Books and Articles:

B-1   Anderson, Bart, Barry Costales, and Harry Henderson. *The Waite Group's Unix Communications*. Carmel, IN: SAMS, 1991. More than most people will ever need to know, told well and thoroughly. Extensive sections on newsreaders, UUCP, etc.

B-2   Fisher, Sharon. *Riding the Internet Highway*. Carmel, IN: New Riders Publishing, 1993.

B-3   Gibbs, Mark, and Richard Smith. *Navigating the Internet*. Carmel, IN: SAMS, 1993. A good general introduction to the Internet and its resources, with detailed explanations and instructions for each type of resource; lists many resources by topic.

B-4   Kehoe, Brendan. *Zen and the Art of the Internet: A Beginner's Guide*. Englewood Cliffs, NJ: Prentice-Hall, 1993. A version of this well-known introductory guide is widely (and legally) available on many FTP servers. The first edition is available in zipped format at `cs.widener.edu` in the `/pub/zen/` directory, or in ASCII format from `quake.think.com` in the `/pub/etext/1992` directory, file `Zen10.txt`.

B-5   Kochmer, Jonathan. *NorthWestNet User Services Internet Resource Guide (NUSIRG)*. Bellevue, WA: Northwest Academic Computer Consortium, Inc., 1991. Available online via FTP from `ftphost.nwnet.net` in the `/nic/nwnet/user.guide/` directory.

B-6   Krol, Ed. *The Whole Internet User's Guide & Catalog.* Sebastopol, CA: O'Reilly & Associates, 1992. A thorough and excellent general introduction to all facets of using the Internet. Catalogs a basic sampling of online resources, arranged by topic.

B-7   LaQuey, Tracy, with Jeanne C. Ryer. *The Internet Companion: A Beginner's Guide to Global Networking.* New York, NY: Addison Wesley, 1993.

B-8   LaQuey, Tracy L., ed. *The User's Directory of Computer Networks.* Bedford, MA: Digital Press, 1990. An exhaustive list and description of Bitnet, DECnet, the Internet, Janet, Usenet, UUCP, domains, X.500, and e-mail.

B-9   Nielsen, Brian. "Finding it on the Internet: the Next Challenge for Librarianship." *Database*, Vol. 13, October 1990, pp. 105-107.

B-10 Perry, Andrew. *New User's Guide to Useful and Unique Resources on the Internet.* Syracuse, NY: NYSERNET, Inc. Available from NYSERNET, Inc., 111 College Place, Syracuse, NY 13244-4100.

B-11 Rittner, Don. *Whole Earth Online Almanac: Info from A to Z.* New York, NY: Brady Publishing (a division of Prentice-Hall), 1993. Good coverage of Usenet newsgroups and adequate coverage of Bitnet mailing lists, plus introductions to and listings from the Internet access provider The Well and the commercial computer networks America Online, CompuServe, and GEnie.

B-12 Quarterman, John S. *The Matrix: Computer Networks and Conferencing Systems Worldwide.* Bedford, MA: Digital Press, 1990.

B-13 Strangelove, Michael, Diane Kovacs, and The Directory Team (Ann Okerson, ed.). *Directory of Electronic Journals, Newsletters and Academic Discussion Lists*, Third Edition. Washington, DC: Association of Research Libraries, 1993. Detailed lists of electronic serials, organized by type (journals and newsletters) or subject area (academic discussion lists and interest groups).

Journals:

B-14 *Computers in Libraries.* Westport, CT: Meckler, 1989–

B-15 *Internet World.* Westport, CT: Meckler, 1992–

B-16 *Electronic Networking: Research, Applications and Policy.* Westport, CT: Meckler, 1991–

INDEX

character sets, multibyte-coded, 1-735

charge, 1-1039

chargeback of computer resources, 2-845

chasque [access provider], 12-17

chatback [mailing list], 1-252

chatback planning group, 1-252

chatsubo, 2-162

che electronic newsletter, [e-serial], 9-41

chem-eng [mailing list], 1-253

chemcord [mailing list], 1-254

cheme-l [mailing list], 1-255

chemed-l [mailing list], 1-256

chemic-l [mailing list], 1-257

chemical engineering, 1-255, 1-773, 2-2479, 9-41

chemical information, sources, 1-266

chemical sensitivities, 1-685

chemistry, 2-2464, 5-94

    and chemical engineering, 1-773

    card catalog, 7-41

    education (all grades) , 1-256

    organometalic, 2-2465

chemists & radiochemistry, etc., 1-1156

chemometrics, 1-665

cheops, 10-3

chess, 1-258, 2-2178

    chess-l [mailing list], 1-258

    chessnews [mailing list], 1-259

    server, 2-103

chia pets, 2-469

chicago area showslist [mailing list], 1-260

chicago cubs, 2-643

chicago state university, cwis, 6-43

chicano literature & culture, 1-261

chicle [mailing list], 1-261

chief information officers (higher education), 1-272

child custody, 1-536

child support, 1-536, 2-104

child-centered learning, 1-1366

children & parenting, news of, clarinet, 2-1199

children in project chatback, 1-1347

children youth & family consortium, 6-44

children's & teens' rights, 1-1519

children's rights, [e-serial], 9-95

children, 2-2022, 2-2023, 6-44

    computers and, 2-2023

    youth, family development programs, 6-64

chile

    mathematical society, 1-1294

    news, 1-163, 9-43

    science & technology in, 6-65

xxi magazine, 1-1518

chile-l [mailing list], 1-262

chilehoy [mailing list], 1-263

china [mailing list], 1-264

china news digest

    archive, 5-20

    [e-serial], 9-42

china news-canada, 1-291

china, 1-264, 2-2566, 2-2645

    academic exchanges, 1-38

    computing networks in, 1-228

    early medieval, 1-465

    language, 2-106, 2-107, 2-108

    mainland, area codes, 5-20

    music research, 1-22

    overseas-chinese student organizations, 1-265

china-nt [mailing list], 1-265

chinchillas, farming, 2-105

chinese communication scholars, 1-666

chinese community

    employment/immigration issues, 1-229

    information center, 5-20

chinese friendship association, queen's, 1-833

chinese graduate student association, 1-248

chinese

    geographic information system, 1-325

    language, 5-7, 5-20

        software, 5-20

    music, 5-94

    nationals, immigration information, 5-20

    student movement, 1989, 5-20

    studies, 1-264

    text archive, 5-20

chip, [e-serial], 9-43

chlamydomonas, the green alga, 2-781

chloroplasts, 6-135

chminf-l [mailing list], 1-266

chorus [mailing list], 1-267

christia [mailing list], 1-268

christian life in the computer era, [e-serial], 9-44

christian origins & early judaism, [e-serial], 9-131

christian

    computer graphics, 1-574

    living, 1-268

    studies, 10-4

    theology, 10-4

    visions, prophecies, spiritual gifts, 1-1458

christianity, 2-2626, 2-2627

    eastern orthodox, 1-473

evangelical, 1-613

chromosome idiograms, human & mouse, 6-301

chromosomes, photomicrographs, 6-301

chronic fatigue syndrome electronic newsletter (cfs-news), [e-serial], 9-45

chronic fatigue syndrome, 1-220, 1-244, 1-685, 2-395

    general discussion, 1-243

    medical database, 1-242

    newsletter, 1-245, 2-857

church of the subgenius, [e-serial], 9-115

cia world factbook, 1991, 7-295

    1992, 7-294

cicnet [access provider], 12-18

cicnet resource guide, 7-57

cicnet wais resources, index, 7-58

cics discussion list, 2-859

cics users, 1-170

cics, transaction-oriented system, 1-269

cics-l [mailing list], 1-269

cicsug [mailing list], 1-270

cidr deployment in the internet [rfc], 15-38

cilea, italy, 6-46

cincinnati reds, 2-644

cineca (ital.esearch organization) & its networks, 1-292

cinema, 1-271, 2-2074

    all forms, 2-860

    cinema-l [mailing list], 1-271

    managers and/or projectionists, etc., 1-489

cio-l [mailing list], 1-272

circplus [mailing list], 1-273

circuit

    newsletter

        archive, 5-23

        gopher access, 6-45

circulation reserve & related library issues, 2-861

cis, email sites existing or planned, 7-60

cisco [mailing list], 1-274

cisco routers & bridges, 2-1383

cisco systems, inc., network products, 1-274

cisdn-l [mailing list], 1-275

citation & bibliography software, 1-159

citations for serial literature, [e-serial], 9-46, 1-1250

citizens band radio, 2-2306

city university of new york graduate school information, 6-63

planetary science, 2-561
plant biology, 2-813
plant ecology, 9-23
plant viruses, 5-4
plants, 5-4
pli, 2-1454
pmdf, 2-958
pnwmla-l [mailing list], 1-1095
poet [mailing list], 1-1096
poetry index, poetry magazine, 7-218
poetry, 1-1096, 2-2093, 9-268
pofp-j [mailing list], 1-1097
point to point protocol (internet ppp),
    2-1574
point-to-point protocol (ppp) exten-
    sions for bridging [rfc],
    15-261
point-to-point protocol, 2-1574
    appletalk control protocol (atcp)
        [rfc], 15-123
    authentication protocols [rfc],
        15-163
    decnet phase iv control protocol
        (dncp) [rfc], 15-125
    initial configuration options [rfc],
        15-303
    internet protocol control protocol
        (ipcp) [rfc], 15-165
    link quality monitoring [rfc],
        15-164
    osi network layer control protocol
        (osinlcp) [rfc], 15-124
    ppp [mailing list], 1-1112
    ppp [rfc], 15-166
    transmission of multi-protocol
        datagrams [rfc], 15-304
poisoning, dental amalgam & mer-
    cury, 1-65
poker, san franciso bay area, 1-135
poland, 2-2598, 6-47
    alumni of technical university of
        wroclaw, 9-229
    cracow, city information, 6-262
    culture, 1-1098
        history, politics (in polish),
            9-239
    gophers in, 6-321
    network resources, 6-262
    news bulletin from, 1-417
    news
        and humor [e-serial] (in english),
            9-190
        and internet magazines (in pol-
            ish), 6-262
        digest, 9-78
        in polish 9-76
        summaries, [e-serial], 9-111
    poland-l [mailing list], 1-1098
    theoretical computer science

researchers in, 1-1383
    warsaw, travel and tourist informa-
        tion, 6-321
polar-l [mailing list], 1-1099
poles, of the earth, 1-1099
police & its members, 1-1100
police [mailing list], 1-1100
police, 2-426
policy based routing [rfc], 15-354
political issues, serious discussion,
    1-1101
political science and the judicial sys-
    tem, [e-serial], 9-144
political science, 5-94, 10-3
politics [mailing list], 1-1101
politics and political systems, theory,
    2-2653
politics and politicians (clarinet),
    2-1257, 2-1258
politics, 1-1101, 2-472 to 2-495,
    2-2622, 2-2643 to 2-2653,
    5-98, 9-271
    british, 2-473
    bush, 2-474
    clinton, 2-475
    correct, 2-476
    discussion forum, 2-959
    economics, 2-478
    elections, 2-479
    equality, 2-480
    european community, 2-477
    for researchers and politicians,
        1-1106
    greens, 2-481
    homosexuality, 2-482
    indian, progressive, 2-483
    libertarian, 1-200, 2-484
    media, 2-485
    of sex, 2-491
    perot, 2-488
    political organizations, 2-486
    radical left, 2-489
    reform, 2-490
    republican party, 1-1173, 1-1174
    south america, 1-96
    turkey (in turkish), 1-1248
    u.s. states, 1-1316
    united nations, 2-487
    usa
        constitution, 2-492
        miscellaneous, 2-493
        republican, 2-494
    vietnamese, 2-495
pollen paleobiology, 5-4
pollination & palynology, 1-1102
polpal-l [mailing list], 1-1102
polyamory, 2-496
polymer physics, 1-1103
polymerp [mailing list], 1-1103

pons & fleischmann, cold fusion, 7-64
pool, 2-639
pop, see post office protocol
pop11 and the plug user group,
    2-1444
popmail, 5-77
population biology, 2-814, 5-52
por [mailing list], 1-1105
pork, complaints about, 2-80
portable *lisp simulator, 5-100
portugal, 2-2599
portuguese association for artificial
    intelligence, 7-40
poscim [mailing list], 1-1106
positron-emission tomography, 6-14
posix, ada binding, 1-1107
posix-ada [mailing list], 1-1107
posix-ada, 1-1107
post office protocol
    extended service offerings [rfc],
        15-371
    for pcs, 2-1934
    pop [mailing list], 1-1104
    pop2 & pop3, 1-1104
    version 2 [rfc], 15-477
postcard [mailing list], 1-1108
postcard collectors, 2-960
postcards, picture, 1-1108
postmodern culture, 9-192
postmodern jewish philosophy bitnet-
    work, 9-193
postmodernism, semiotics, decon-
    struction, etc., 2-497
postscript pdl, 2-1445
postscript, source code for programs,
    2-1623
potato researchers & specialists,
    1-1308
pound, ezra, 10-5
powderkeg, 9-194
powderworks [mailing list], 1-1109
power to the people mover, [e-serial],
    9-195
power-l [mailing list], 1-1110
power-l ibm rs/6000 power family,
    2-961
powerglove, 5-115
powerh-l [mailing list], 1-1111
powerhouse discussion list, 2-962
powerhouse, application development
    language, 1-1111
pp, 5-29
ppp, see point-to-point protocol
practical anarchy online, 9-196
practical christian life, 2-858
prague academical network, 6-42
prairie home companion, 2-2115
pratchett, terry, 2-249
pre-emption (updates ien 125) [rfc],

ABOUT THE AUTHOR

Eric Braun usually writes software for a living, but couldn't resist the opportunity to stay up until all hours of the night doing something other than programming. He is also the author of Snap Mail, an easy-to-use e-mail package for Macintosh networks that is published by Casady & Greene. He dials into the Internet from Brooklyn, New York, and plans to get at least eight hours of sleep every night until it's time to put together the next edition of this book.